CALIFORNIA

CODE OF CIVIL PROCEDURE

2026 EDITION

VOLUME 1

League Publishing Inc.

ISBN: 979-8-90113-562-4
www.californiacodeofcivilprocedure.com

EDITORIAL NOTE

This volume compiles the preliminary provisions and selected portions of the California Code of Civil Procedure. The statutory text is presented in its enacted form and organized for ease of reference. No commentary, analysis, or interpretation is intended.

This volume includes foundational provisions governing the operation of civil procedure in California, including definitions, computation of time, judicial remedies, civil actions, special proceedings, and the organization and jurisdiction of courts. It further covers provisions relating to judicial officers, court powers, judicial holidays, court access, small claims procedure, limited civil cases, jury selection, court reporters, attorneys, ministerial officers, and related court administration.

The volume also includes provisions governing the commencement of civil actions, statutes of limitation, claims involving real and personal property, professional negligence, survival of actions after death, wrongful death, parties to civil actions, joinder, minors and persons lacking legal capacity, and procedural rules affecting civil litigation.

The California Code of Civil Procedure is a work of the public domain. This publication does not claim authorship of the statutory text. The material has been compiled, arranged, and formatted solely for usability and reference purposes.

This compilation was prepared by Jeremy J. Salvador, who served exclusively in an editorial and organizational capacity. Responsibility for the substance and content of the law remains with the Legislature of the State of California. Users are advised to consult relevant case law, court rules, administrative regulations, and other legal authorities when applying the Code to specific situations.

The Code is organized in accordance with its official statutory structure, including the Preliminary Provisions and selected portions of Part 1: Of Courts of Justice [Section 35 - 286] and Part 2: Of Civil Actions [Section 307 – 709.030], together with their respective titles, chapters, articles, and sections as enacted.

CONTENTS

CODE OF CIVIL PROCEDURE - CCP

TITLE OF THE ACT

Enacted 1872

1. This act shall be known as the Code of Civil Procedure, and is divided into four parts, as follows:[57]

Part I.	Of Courts of Justice.
II.	Of Civil Actions.
III.	Of Special Proceedings of a Civil Nature.
IV.	Miscellaneous Provisions.

PRELIMINARY PROVISIONS

Enacted 1872

2. This Code takes effect at twelve o'clock noon, on the first day of January, eighteen hundred and seventy-three.[1]

3. No part of it is retroactive, unless expressly so declared.[1]

4. The rule of the common law, that statutes in derogation thereof are to be strictly construed, has no application to this Code. The Code establishes the law of this State respecting the subjects to which it relates, and its provisions and all proceedings under it are to be liberally construed, with a view to effect its objects and to promote justice.[1]

5. The provisions of this Code, so far as they are substantially the same as existing statutes, must be construed as continuations thereof, and not as new enactments.[1]

6. All persons who at the time this Code takes effect hold office under any of the Acts repealed, continue to hold the same according to the tenure thereof, except those offices which are not continued by one of the Codes adopted at this session of the Legislature.[1]

7. When any office is abolished by the repeal of any Act, and such Act is not in substance reënacted or continued in either of the Codes, such office ceases at the time the Codes take effect.[1]

8. No action or proceeding commenced before this Code takes effect, and no right accrued, is affected by its provisions, but the proceedings therein must conform to the requirements of this Code as far as applicable.[1]

9. When a limitation or period of time prescribed in any existing statute for acquiring a right or barring a remedy, or for any other purpose, has begun to run before this code goes into effect, and the same or any limitation is prescribed in this code, the time that has already run shall be deemed part of the time prescribed as such limitation by this code.[736]

10. Holidays within the meaning of this code are every Sunday and any other days that are specified or provided for as judicial holidays in Section 135.[462]

11. Wherever any notice or other communication is required by this code to be mailed by registered mail by or to any person or corporation, the mailing of such notice or other communication by certified mail shall be deemed to be a sufficient compliance with the requirements of law.[42]

12. The time in which any act provided

by law is to be done is computed by excluding the first day, and including the last, unless the last day is a holiday, and then it is also excluded.[1]

12a. (a) If the last day for the performance of any act provided or required by law to be performed within a specified period of time is a holiday, then that period is hereby extended to and including the next day that is not a holiday. For purposes of this section, "holiday" means all day on Saturdays, all holidays specified in Section 135 and, to the extent provided in Section 12b, all days that by terms of Section 12b are required to be considered as holidays.
(b) This section applies to Sections 659, 659a, and 921, and to all other provisions of law providing or requiring an act to be performed on a particular day or within a specified period of time, whether expressed in this or any other code or statute, ordinance, rule, or regulation.[598]

12b. If any city, county, state, or public office, other than a branch office, is closed for the whole of any day, insofar as the business of that office is concerned, that day shall be considered as a holiday for the purposes of computing time under Sections 12 and 12a.[28]

12c. (a) Where any law requires an act to be performed no later than a specified number of days before a hearing date, the last day to perform that act shall be determined by counting backward from the hearing date, excluding the day of the hearing as provided by Section 12.
(b) Any additional days added to the specified number of days because of a particular method of service shall be computed by counting backward from the day determined in accordance with subdivision (a).[615]

13. Whenever any act of a secular nature, other than a work of necessity or mercy, is appointed by law or contract to be performed upon a particular day, which day falls upon a holiday, such act may be performed upon the next business day with the same effect as if it had been performed upon the day appointed.[1]

13a. Any act required by law to be performed on a particular day or within a specified period of time may be performed (but is not hereby required to be performed) on a special holiday as that term is used in Section 6705 of the Government Code, with like effect as if performed on a day which is not a holiday.[43]

13b. Any act required by law to be performed on a particular day or within a specified period may be performed (but is not hereby required to be performed) on a Saturday, with like effect as if performed on a day which is not a holiday.[46]

14. When the seal of a Court, public officer, or person is required by law to be affixed to any paper, the word "seal" includes an impression of such seal upon the paper alone as well as upon wax or a wafer affixed thereto.[1]

15. Words giving a joint authority to three or more public officers or other persons are construed as giving such authority to a majority of them, unless it is otherwise expressed in the Act giving the authority.[1]

16. Words and phrases are construed according to the context and the ap-

proved usage of the language; but technical words and phrases, and such others as have acquired a peculiar and appropriate meaning in law, or are defined in the succeeding section, are to be construed according to such peculiar and appropriate meaning or definition.[1]

17. (a) Words used in this code in the present tense include the future as well as the present. Words used in the masculine gender include the feminine and neuter. The singular number includes the plural and the plural number includes the singular.

(b) As used in this code, the following words have the following meanings, unless otherwise apparent from the context:

(1) "Affinity" signifies the connection existing in consequence of marriage, between each of the married persons and the blood relatives of the other when applied to the marriage relation.

(2) "County" includes "city and county."

(3) "Electronic signature" means an electronic sound, symbol, or process attached to or logically associated with an electronic record and executed or adopted by a person with the intent to sign the electronic record.

(4) "Month" means a calendar month, unless otherwise expressed.

(5) "Oath" includes an affirmation or declaration.

(A) "Depose" includes any written statement made under oath or affirmation.

(B) "Testify" includes any mode of oral statement made under oath or affirmation.

(6) "Person" includes a corporation as well as a natural person.

(7) "Process" signifies a writ or summons issued in the course of a judicial proceeding.

(8) "Property" includes both personal and real property.

(A) "Personal property" includes money, goods, chattels, things in action, and evidences of debt.

(B) "Real property" is coextensive with lands, tenements, and hereditaments.

(9) "Section" refers to a section of this code, unless some other code or statute is expressly mentioned.

(10) "Sheriff" includes marshal.

(11) "Signature" or "subscription" includes a mark of a person's name, if the person cannot write, with his or her name being written near it by a person who writes his or her own name as a witness. In order that a mark may be acknowledged or serve as the signature to any sworn statement, it shall be witnessed by two persons who shall subscribe their own names as witnesses thereto.

(12) "Spouse" includes "registered domestic partner," as required by Section 297.5 of the Family Code.

(13) "State" includes the District of Columbia and the territories when applied to the different parts of the United States, and the words "United States" may include the district and territories.

(14) "Will" includes codicil.

(15) "Writ" means an order or precept in writing, issued in the name of the people, or of a court or judicial officer.

(16) "Writing" includes printing and typewriting.[724]

18. No statute, law, or rule is continued in force because it is consistent with the provisions of this Code on the same subject; but in all cases provided

for by this Code, all statutes, laws, and rules heretofore in force in this State, whether consistent or not with the provisions of this Code, unless expressly continued in force by it, are repealed and abrogated. This repeal or abrogation does not revive any former law heretofore repealed, nor does it affect any right already existing or accrued, or any action or proceeding already taken, except as in this Code provided; nor does it affect any private statute not expressly repealed.[1]

19. This Act, whenever cited, enumerated, referred to, or amended, may be designated simply as "The Code of Civil Procedure," adding, when necessary, the number of the section.[1]

20. Judicial remedies are such as are administered by the Courts of justice, or by judicial officers empowered for that purpose by the Constitution and statutes of this State.[1]

21. These remedies are divided into two classes:
1. Actions; and,
2. Special proceedings.[1]

22. An action is an ordinary proceeding in a court of justice by which one party prosecutes another for the declaration, enforcement, or protection of a right, the redress or prevention of a wrong, or the punishment of a public offense.[15]

23. Every other remedy is a special proceeding.[1]

24. Actions are of two kinds:
1. Civil; and,
2. Criminal.[1]

25. A civil action arises out of:
1. An obligation;
2. An injury.[1]

26. An obligation is a legal duty, by which one person is bound to do or not to do a certain thing, and arises from either of the following:
(a) Contract.
(b) Operation of law.[737]

27. An injury is of two kinds:
1. To the person; and,
2. To property.[1]

28. An injury to property consists in depriving its owner of the benefit of it, which is done by taking, withholding, deteriorating, or destroying it.[1]

29. Every other injury is an injury to the person.[1]

30. A civil action is prosecuted by one party against another for the declaration, enforcement or protection of a right, or the redress or prevention of a wrong.[15]

31. The Penal Code defines and provides for the prosecution of a criminal action.[1]

32. When the violation of a right admits of both a civil and criminal remedy, the right to prosecute the one is not merged in the other.[1]

32.5. The "jurisdictional classification" of a case means its classification as a limited civil case or an unlimited civil case.[487]

33. A prosecuting attorney, in his or her discretion, may assist in the civil resolution of a violation of an offense described in Title 13 (commencing with Section 450) of Part 1 of the Penal Code in lieu of filing a criminal complaint.[164]

34. An electronic signature, as defined in Section 17, by a court or judicial officer shall be as effective as an original

signature.[705]

PART 1:
OF COURTS OF JUSTICE

PART 1 REPEALED AND ADDED BY CODE AMENDMENTS 1880, CH. 35

SECTION 35 - 286

TITLE 1: ORGANIZATION AND JURISDICTION

Title 1 repealed and added by Code Amendments 1880, Ch. 35.

Chapter 1: Courts of Justice in General

Chapter 1 added by Code Amendments 1880, Ch. 35

35. (a) Proceedings in cases involving the registration or denial of registration of voters, the certification or denial of certification of candidates, the certification or denial of certification of ballot measures, election contests, actions under Section 20010 or 20012 of the Elections Code, actions under Chapter 7 (commencing with Section 20510) of Division 20 of the Elections Code, and actions under Chapter 2 (commencing with Section 21100) of Division 21 of the Elections Code shall be placed on the calendar in the order of their date of filing and shall be given precedence.
(b) This section shall remain in effect only until January 1, 2027, and as of that date is repealed, unless a later enacted statute, that is enacted before January 1, 2027, deletes or extends that date.[818]

35. (a) Proceedings in cases involving the registration or denial of registration of voters, the certification or denial of certification of candidates, the certification or denial of certification of ballot measures, election contests, actions under Section 20012 of the Elections Code, actions under Chapter 7 (commencing with Section 20510) of Division 20 of the Elections Code, and actions under Chapter 2 (commencing with Section 21100) of Division 21 of the Elections Code shall be placed on the calendar in the order of their date of filing and shall be given precedence.
(b) This section shall become operative January 1, 2027.[819]

36. (a) A party to a civil action who is over 70 years of age may petition the court for a preference, which the court shall grant if the court makes both of the following findings:
(1) The party has a substantial interest in the action as a whole.
(2) The health of the party is such that a preference is necessary to prevent prejudicing the party's interest in the litigation.
(b) A civil action to recover damages for wrongful death or personal injury shall be entitled to preference upon the motion of any party to the action who is under 14 years of age unless the court finds that the party does not have a substantial interest in the case as a whole. A civil action subject to subdivision (a) shall be given preference over a case subject to this subdivision.
(c) Unless the court otherwise orders:
(1) A party may file and serve a motion for preference supported by a declaration of the moving party that all essential parties have been served with process or have appeared.

(2) At any time during the pendency of the action, a party who reaches 70 years of age may file and serve a motion for preference.

(d) In its discretion, the court may also grant a motion for preference that is accompanied by clear and convincing medical documentation that concludes that one of the parties suffers from an illness or condition raising substantial medical doubt of survival of that party beyond six months, and that satisfies the court that the interests of justice will be served by granting the preference.

(e) Notwithstanding any other provision of law, the court may in its discretion grant a motion for preference that is supported by a showing that satisfies the court that the interests of justice will be served by granting this preference.

(f) Upon the granting of such a motion for preference, the court shall set the matter for trial not more than 120 days from that date and there shall be no continuance beyond 120 days from the granting of the motion for preference except for physical disability of a party or a party's attorney, or upon a showing of good cause stated in the record. Any continuance shall be for no more than 15 days and no more than one continuance for physical disability may be granted to any party.

(g) Upon the granting of a motion for preference pursuant to subdivision (b), a party in an action based upon a health provider's alleged professional negligence, as defined in Section 364, shall receive a trial date not sooner than six months and not later than nine months from the date that the motion is granted.[611]

36.5. An affidavit submitted in support of a motion for preference under subdivision (a) of Section 36 may be signed by the attorney for the party seeking preference based upon information and belief as to the medical diagnosis and prognosis of any party. The affidavit is not admissible for any purpose other than a motion for preference under subdivision (a) of Section 36.[271]

37. (a) A civil action shall be entitled to preference, if the action is one in which the plaintiff is seeking damages which were alleged to have been caused by the defendant during the commission of a felony offense for which the defendant has been criminally convicted.

(b) The court shall endeavor to try the action within 120 days of the grant of preference.[194]

38. Unless the provision or context otherwise requires, a reference in a statute to a judicial district means:

(a) As it relates to a court of appeal, the court of appeal district.

(b) As it relates to a superior court, the county.[741]

Chapter 3: Supreme Court

Chapter 3 added by Code Amendments 1880, Ch. 35.

41. The Supreme Court and the courts of appeal may transact business at any time.[64]

42. Adjournments from day to day, or from time to time, are to be construed as recesses in the sessions, and shall not prevent the Supreme Court or the courts of appeal from sitting at any time.[62]

43. The Supreme Court, and the courts

of appeal, may affirm, reverse, or modify any judgment or order appealed from, and may direct the proper judgment or order to be entered, or direct a new trial or further proceedings to be had. In giving its decision, if a new trial be granted, the court shall pass upon and determine all the questions of law involved in the case, presented upon such appeal, and necessary to the final determination of the case. Its judgment in appealed cases shall be remitted to the court from which the appeal was taken.[63]

44. Appeals in probate proceedings, in contested election cases, and in actions for libel or slander by a person who holds any elective public office or a candidate for any such office alleged to have occurred during the course of an election campaign shall be given preference in hearing in the courts of appeal, and in the Supreme Court when transferred thereto. All these cases shall be placed on the calendar in the order of their date of issue, next after cases in which the people of the state are parties.[174]

45. An appeal from a judgment freeing a minor who is a dependent child of the juvenile court from parental custody and control, or denying a recommendation to free a minor from parental custody or control, shall have precedence over all cases in the court to which an appeal in the matter is taken. In order to enable the child to be available for adoption as soon as possible and to minimize the anxiety to all parties, the appellate court shall grant an extension of time to a court reporter or to counsel only upon an exceptional showing of good cause.[382]

46. Appeals in actions brought under Section 1094.9 shall be given preference in scheduling for hearing in the courts of appeal, and in the Supreme Court.[880]

Chapter 4: Superior Courts

Chapter 4 added by Code Amendments 1880, Ch. 35.

71. The process of superior courts shall extend throughout the state.[60]

73c. Notwithstanding anything to the contrary contained in any other law of this state, the judges of the superior court of the county in which is located the principal office in this state of any savings and loan association of whose business, property and assets possession shall have been taken by the Commissioner of Financial Institutions, may, in their discretion, whenever those judges deem it necessary or advisable, hold hearings relating to the sale, exchange or other disposition of any parcel of real property or any item of personal property of the association, regardless of the location of the property, at the county seat of any county in this state or at the places in the county in which the principal office in this state of the association is located at which sessions of the superior court are held.[526]

73d. Whenever, under Section 73c, it becomes necessary for a judge, clerk, deputy clerk, court reporter or bailiff of or sitting in the superior court of the county in this state in which is located the principal office of any savings and loan association whose business, property and assets are in the possession of the Commissioner of Financial Institutions, to travel to another county, there temporarily to attend hearings relating to the sale, exchange or other disposition of real or personal property of the association, each judge, clerk, deputy clerk, court reporter or bailiff shall be allowed the necessary expenses in going to, returning from and attending upon the business of the court. The expenses shall, upon order of the court, be a charge against the funds of the association and paid out of those funds by the Commissioner of Financial Institutions.[526]

73e. Notwithstanding any other provisions of law, in each county wherein the juvenile hall is not located at the county seat of the county, a majority of the judges of the superior court in and for such county may by an order filed with the clerk of the court direct that a session or sessions of the superior court, while sitting for the purpose of hearing and determining cases and proceedings arising under Chapter 2 of Part 1 of Division 2 or Chapter 2 of Part 1 of Division 6 or Chapter 4 of Part 4 of Division 6 of the Welfare and Institutions Code, may be held or continued in any place in the county in which the juvenile hall is located and thereafter such session or sessions of the court may be held or continued in the location designated in such order. In a county having two superior court judges the presiding judge may make the order.[488]

74. Adjournments from day to day, or from time to time, are to be construed as recesses in the sessions, and shall not prevent the Court from sitting at any time.[6]

75. The superior court in any county may by rule provide that, whenever all judges are absent from the county, any noncontested matter in which no evidence is required, or which may be submitted upon affidavits, shall be deemed submitted upon the filing with the clerk of a statement of submission by the party or the party's attorney or upon the date set for the hearing.[489]

77. (a) In every county there is an appellate division of the superior court consisting of three judges or, when the Chief Justice finds it necessary, four judges.

The Chief Justice shall assign judges to the appellate division for specified terms pursuant to rules, not inconsistent with statute, adopted by the Judicial Council to promote the independence and quality of each appellate division. Each judge assigned to the appellate division of a superior court shall be a judge of that court, a judge of the superior court of another county, or a judge retired from the superior court or a court of higher jurisdiction in this state.

The Chief Justice shall designate one of the judges of each appellate division as the presiding judge of the division.

(b) In each appellate division, no more than three judges shall participate in a hearing or decision. The presiding judge of the division shall designate the three judges who shall participate.

(c) In addition to their other duties, the judges designated as members of the appellate division of the superior court shall serve for the period specified in the order of designation. Whenever a judge is designated to serve in the appellate division of the superior court of a county other than the county in which that judge was elected or appointed as a superior court judge, or if the judge is retired, in a county other than the county in which the judge resides, the judge shall receive expenses for travel, board, and lodging. If the judge is out of the judge's county overnight or longer, by reason of the designation, that judge shall be paid a per diem allowance in lieu of expenses for board and lodging in the same amounts as are payable for those purposes to justices of the Supreme Court under the rules of the Department of General Services. In addition, a retired judge shall receive for the time so served, amounts equal to that which the judge would have received if the judge had been assigned to the superior court of the county.

(d) The concurrence of two judges of the appellate division of the superior court shall be necessary to render the decision in every case in, and to transact any other business except business that may be done at chambers by the presiding judge of, the division. A judgment of the appellate division in an appeal shall contain a brief statement of the reasons for the judgment. A judgment stating only "affirmed" or "reversed" is insufficient. The presiding judge shall convene the appellate division when necessary. The presiding judge shall also supervise its business and transact any business that may be done at chambers.

(e) The appellate division of the superior court has jurisdiction on appeal in all cases in which an appeal may be taken to the superior court or the appellate division of the superior court as provided by law, except where the appeal is a retrial in the superior court.

(f) The powers of each appellate division shall be the same as are now or may hereafter be provided by law or rule of the Judicial Council relating to appeals to the appellate division of the superior courts.

(g) The Judicial Council shall promulgate rules, not inconsistent with law, to promote the independence of, and govern the practice and procedure and the disposition of the business of, the appellate division.

(h) Notwithstanding subdivisions (b) and (d), appeals from convictions of traffic infractions may be heard and decided by one judge of the appellate division of the superior court.[742]

Chapter 5.1: Limited Civil Cases

Chapter 5.1 added by Stats. 1998, Ch. 931, Sec. 28.

Article 1: Jurisdiction in Limited Civil Cases

Article 1 added by Stats. 1998, Ch. 931, Sec. 28.

85. Notwithstanding any law, including, but not limited to, a law that classified an action or special proceeding as a limited civil case, an action or special proceeding shall be treated as a limited civil case only if all of the following conditions are satisfied:

(a) The amount in controversy does not exceed thirty-five thousand dollars ($35,000). As used in this section, "amount in controversy" means the amount of the demand, or the recovery sought, or the value of the property, or the amount of the lien, that is in controversy in the action, exclusive of attorneys' fees, interest, and costs.

(b) The relief sought is a type that may be granted in a limited civil case.

(c) The relief sought, whether in the complaint, a cross-complaint, or otherwise, is exclusively of a type described in one or more laws that classify an action or special proceeding as a limited civil case or that provide that an action or special proceeding is within the original jurisdiction of the superior court, including, but not limited to, the following provisions:

(1) Section 798.61 or 798.88 of the Civil Code.

(2) Section 1719 of the Civil Code.

(3) Section 3342.5 of the Civil Code.

(4) Section 86.

(5) Section 86.1.

(6) Section 1710.20.

(7) Section 7581 of the Food and Agricultural Code.

(8) Section 12647 of the Food and Agricultural Code.

(9) Section 27601 of the Food and Agricultural Code.

(10) Section 31503 of the Food and Agricultural Code.

(11) Section 31621 of the Food and Agricultural Code.

(12) Section 52514 of the Food and Agricultural Code.

(13) Section 53564 of the Food and Agricultural Code.

(14) Section 53069.4 of the Government Code.

(15) Section 53075.6 of the Government Code.

(16) Section 53075.61 of the Government Code.

(17) Section 5411.5 of the Public Utilities Code.

(18) Section 9872.1 of the Vehicle Code.

(19) Section 10751 of the Vehicle Code.

(20) Section 14607.6 of the Vehicle Code.

(21) Section 40230 of the Vehicle Code.

(22) Section 40256 of the Vehicle Code.[832]

86. (a) The following civil cases and proceedings are limited civil cases:

(1) A case at law if the demand, exclusive of interest, or the value of the property in controversy amounts to thirty-five thousand dollars ($35,000) or less. This paragraph does not apply to a case that involves the legality of any tax, impost, assessment, toll, or municipal fine, except an action to enforce payment of delinquent unsecured personal property taxes if the legality of the tax is not contested by the defendant.

(2) An action for dissolution of partnership if the total assets of the partnership do not exceed thirty-five thousand dollars ($35,000) or an action of interpleader if the amount of money or the value of the property involved does not exceed thirty-five thousand dollars ($35,000).

(3) An action to cancel or rescind a contract if the relief is sought in connection with an action to recover money not exceeding thirty-five thousand dollars ($35,000) or property of a value not exceeding thirty-five thousand dollars ($35,000), paid or delivered under, or in consideration of, the contract; an action to revise a contract where the relief is sought in an action upon the contract if the action otherwise is a limited civil case.

(4) A proceeding in forcible entry or forcible or unlawful detainer if the whole amount of damages claimed is thirty-five thousand dollars ($35,000) or less.

(5) An action to enforce and foreclose a lien on personal property if the amount of the lien is thirty-five thousand dollars ($35,000) or less.

(6) An action to enforce and foreclose, or a petition to release, a lien arising under Chapter 4 (commencing

with Section 8400) of Title 2 of Part 6 of Division 4 of the Civil Code, or to enforce and foreclose an assessment lien on a common interest development as defined in Section 4100 or 6534 of the Civil Code, if the amount of the liens is thirty-five thousand dollars ($35,000) or less. However, if an action to enforce the lien affects property that is also affected by a similar pending action that is not a limited civil case, or if the total amount of liens sought to be foreclosed against the same property aggregates an amount in excess of thirty-five thousand dollars ($35,000), the action is not a limited civil case.

(7) An action for declaratory relief if brought pursuant to either of the following:

(A) By way of cross-complaint as to a right of indemnity with respect to the relief demanded in the complaint or a cross-complaint in an action or proceeding that is otherwise a limited civil case.

(B) To conduct a trial after a nonbinding fee arbitration between an attorney and client, pursuant to Article 13 (commencing with Section 6200) of Chapter 4 of Division 3 of the Business and Professions Code, if the amount in controversy is thirty-five thousand dollars ($35,000) or less.

(8) An action to issue a temporary restraining order or preliminary injunction; to take an account, if necessary to preserve the property or rights of any party to a limited civil case; to make any order or perform any act, pursuant to Title 9 (commencing with Section 680.010) of Part 2 (enforcement of judgments) in a limited civil case; to appoint a receiver pursuant to Section 564 in a limited civil case; or to determine title to personal property seized in a limited civil case.

(9) An action under Article 3 (commencing with Section 708.210) of Chapter 6 of Division 2 of Title 9 of Part 2 for the recovery of an interest in personal property or to enforce the liability of the debtor of a judgment debtor if the interest claimed adversely is of a value not exceeding thirty-five thousand dollars ($35,000) or the debt denied does not exceed thirty-five thousand dollars ($35,000).

(10) An arbitration-related petition filed pursuant to either of the following:

(A) Article 2 (commencing with Section 1292) of Chapter 5 of Title 9 of Part 3, except for uninsured motorist arbitration proceedings in accordance with Section 11580.2 of the Insurance Code, if the petition is filed before the arbitration award becomes final and the matter to be resolved by arbitration is a limited civil case under paragraphs (1) to (9), inclusive, of subdivision (a) or if the petition is filed after the arbitration award becomes final and the amount of the award and all other rulings, pronouncements, and decisions made in the award are within paragraphs (1) to (9), inclusive, of subdivision (a).

(B) To confirm, correct, or vacate a fee arbitration award between an attorney and client that is binding or has become binding, pursuant to Article 13 (commencing with Section 6200) of Chapter 4 of Division 3 of the Business and Professions Code, if the arbitration award is thirty-five thousand dollars ($35,000) or less.

(b) The following cases in equity are limited civil cases:

(1) A case to try title to personal property when the amount involved is not more than thirty-five thousand dollars ($35,000).

(2) A case when equity is pleaded as a defensive matter in any case that is otherwise a limited civil case.

(3) A case to vacate a judgment or order of the court obtained in a limited civil case through extrinsic fraud, mistake, inadvertence, or excusable neglect.[833]

86.1. An action brought pursuant to the Long-Term Care, Health, Safety, and Security Act of 1973 (Chapter 2.4 (commencing with Section 1417) of Division 2 of the Health and Safety Code) is a limited civil case if civil penalties are not sought or amount to thirty-five thousand dollars ($35,000) or less.[834]

87. (a) A limited civil case may be brought in the small claims division if the case is within the jurisdiction of the small claims division as otherwise provided by statute. Where a statute or rule applicable to a small claims case conflicts with a statute or rule applicable to a limited civil case, the statute or rule applicable to a small claims case governs the small claims case and the statute or rule applicable to a limited civil case does not.

(b) Nothing in this section affects the jurisdiction of the small claims division as otherwise provided by statute.[405]

88. A civil action or proceeding other than a limited civil case may be referred to as an unlimited civil case.[406]

89. (a) The existence of a statute relating to the authority of the court in a limited civil case does not, by itself, imply that the same authority does or does not exist in an unlimited civil case.

(b) The existence of a statute relating to the authority of the court in an unlimited civil case does not, by itself, imply that the same authority does or does not exist in a limited civil case.[458]

Article 2: Economic Litigation for Limited Civil Cases

Article 2 heading repealed (as part of Chapter 5) and added (to Chapter 5.1) by Stats. 1998, Ch. 931, Sec. 35.

90. Except where changed by the provisions of this article, all provisions of law applicable to civil actions generally apply to actions subject to this article.[527]

91. (a) Except as otherwise provided in this section, the provisions of this article apply to every limited civil case.

(b) The provisions of this article do not apply to any action under Chapter 5.5 (commencing with Section 116.110) or any proceeding under Chapter 4 (commencing with Section 1159) of Title 3 of Part 3.

(c) Any action may, upon noticed motion, be withdrawn from the provisions of this article, upon a showing that it is impractical to prosecute or defend the action within the limitations of these provisions.[389]

92. (a) The pleadings allowed are complaints, answers, cross-complaints, answers to cross-complaints and general demurrers.

(b) The answer need not be verified, even if the complaint or cross-complaint is verified.

(c) Special demurrers are not allowed.

(d) Motions to strike are allowed only on the ground that the damages or relief sought are not supported by the allegations of the complaint.
(e) Except as limited by this section, all other motions are permitted.[175]

93. (a) The plaintiff has the option to serve case questionnaires with the complaint, using forms approved by the Judicial Council. The questionnaires served shall include a completed copy of the plaintiff's completed case questionnaire, and a blank copy of the defendant's case questionnaire.
(b) Any defendant upon whom a case questionnaire is served shall serve a completed defendant's case questionnaire upon the requesting plaintiff with the answer.
(c) The case questionnaire shall be designed to elicit fundamental information about each party's case, including names and addresses of all witnesses with knowledge of any relevant facts, a list of all documents relevant to the case, a statement of the nature and amount of damages, and information covering insurance coverages, injuries and treating physicians. The Judicial Council shall design and develop forms for case questionnaires.
(d) Approved forms shall be made available by the clerk of the court.
(e) If a party on whom a case questionnaire has been served under subdivision (a) or (b) fails to serve a timely or a complete response to that questionnaire, the party serving the questionnaire may move for an order compelling a response or a further response and for a monetary sanction under Chapter 7 (commencing with Section 2023.010) of Title 4 of Part 4. If a party then fails to obey an order compelling a response or a further response, the court may make those orders that are just, including the imposition of an issue sanction, an evidence sanction, or a terminating sanction under Chapter 7 (commencing with Section 2023.010) of Title 4 of Part 4. In lieu of or in addition to that sanction, the court may impose a monetary sanction under Chapter 7 (commencing with Section 2023.010) of Title 4 of Part 4.[545]

94. Discovery is permitted only to the extent provided by this section and Section 95. This discovery shall comply with the notice and format requirements of the particular method of discovery, as provided in Title 4 (commencing with Section 2016.010) of Part 4. As to each adverse party, a party may use the following forms of discovery:
(a) Any combination of 35 of the following:
(1) Interrogatories (with no subparts) under Chapter 13 (commencing with Section 2030.010) of Title 4 of Part 4.
(2) Demands to produce documents or things under Chapter 14 (commencing with Section 2031.010) of Title 4 of Part 4.
(3) Requests for admission (with no subparts) under Chapter 16 (commencing with Section 2033.010) of Title 4 of Part 4.
(b) One oral or written deposition under Chapter 9 (commencing with Section 2025.010), Chapter 10 (commencing with Section 2026.010), or Chapter 11 (commencing with Section 2028.010) of Title 4 of Part 4. For purposes of this subdivision, a deposition of an organization shall be treated as a single deposition even though more than one person may be designated or

required to testify pursuant to Section 2025.230.

(c) Any party may serve on any person a deposition subpoena duces tecum requiring the person served to mail copies of documents, books, or records to the party's counsel at a specified address, along with an affidavit complying with Section 1561 of the Evidence Code.

The party who issued the deposition subpoena shall mail a copy of the response to any other party who tenders the reasonable cost of copying it.

(d) Physical and mental examinations under Chapter 15 (commencing with Section 2032.010) of Title 4 of Part 4.

(e) The identity of expert witnesses under Chapter 18 (commencing with Section 2034.010) of Title 4 of Part 4.[586]

95. (a) The court may, on noticed motion and subject to such terms and conditions as are just, authorize a party to conduct additional discovery, but only upon a showing that the moving party will be unable to prosecute or defend the action effectively without the additional discovery. In making a determination under this section, the court shall take into account whether the moving party has used all applicable discovery in good faith, and whether the party has attempted to secure the additional discovery by stipulation or by means other than formal discovery.

(b) The parties may stipulate to additional discovery.[172]

96. (a) Any party may serve on any other party a request in substantially the following form:

TO: ,
attorney for :

You are requested to serve on the undersigned, within 20 days, a statement of: the names and addresses of witnesses (OTHER THAN A PARTY WHO IS AN INDIVIDUAL) you intend to call at trial; a description of physical evidence you intend to offer; and a description and copies of documentary evidence you intend to offer or, if the documents are not available to you, a description of them. Witnesses and evidence that will be used only for impeachment need not be included. YOU WILL NOT BE PERMITTED TO CALL ANY WITNESS, OR INTRODUCE ANY EVIDENCE, NOT INCLUDED IN THE STATEMENT SERVED IN RESPONSE TO THIS REQUEST, EXCEPT AS OTHERWISE PROVIDED BY LAW.

(b) The request shall be served no more than 45 days or less than 30 days prior to the date first set for trial, unless otherwise ordered.

(c) A statement responding to the request shall be served within 20 days from the service of the request.

(d) No additional, amended or late statement is permitted except by written stipulation or unless ordered for good cause on noticed motion.

(e) No request or statement served under this section shall be filed, unless otherwise ordered.

(f) The clerk shall furnish forms for requests under this rule.

(g) The time for performing acts required under this section shall be computed as provided by law, including Section 1013.[172]

97. (a) Except as provided in this section, upon objection of a party who served a request in compliance with Section 96, no party required to serve a responding statement may call a witness or introduce evidence, except for purposes of impeachment, against the objecting party unless the witness or evidence was included in the statement served.
(b) The exceptions to subdivision (a) are:
(1) A person who, in his or her individual capacity, is a party to the litigation and who calls himself or herself as a witness.
(2) An adverse party.
(3) Witnesses and evidence used solely for purposes of impeachment.
(4) Documents obtained by discovery authorized by this chapter.
(5) The court may, upon such terms as may be just (including, but not limited to, continuing the trial for a reasonable period of time and awarding costs and litigation expenses), permit a party to call a witness or introduce evidence which is required to be, but is not included in such party's statement so long as the court finds that such party has made a good faith effort to comply with subdivision (c) of Section 96 or that the failure to comply was the result of his or her mistake, inadvertence, surprise or excusable neglect as provided in Section 473.
(c) Nothing in this article limits the introduction of evidence in any hearing pursuant to Section 585.[176]

98. A party may, in lieu of presenting direct testimony, offer the prepared testimony of relevant witnesses in the form of affidavits or declarations under penalty of perjury. The prepared testimony may include, but need not be limited to, the opinions of expert witnesses, and testimony which authenticates documentary evidence. To the extent the contents of the prepared testimony would have been admissible were the witness to testify orally thereto, the prepared testimony shall be received as evidence in the case, provided that either of the following applies:
(a) A copy has been served on the party against whom it is offered at least 30 days prior to the trial, together with a current address of the affiant that is within 150 miles of the place of trial, and the affiant is available for service of process at that place for a reasonable period of time, during the 20 days immediately prior to trial.
(b) The statement is in the form of all or part of a deposition in the case, and the party against whom it is offered had an opportunity to participate in the deposition.
The court shall determine whether the affidavit or declaration shall be read into the record in lieu of oral testimony or admitted as a documentary exhibit.[813]

99. A judgment or final order, in respect to the matter directly adjudged, is conclusive between the parties and their successors in interest but does not operate as collateral estoppel of a party or a successor in interest to a party in other litigation with a person who was not a party or a successor in interest to a party to the action in

which the judgment or order is rendered.[172]

100. Any party shall have the right to appeal any judgment or final order consistent with the law governing appeals.[172]

Chapter 5.5: Small Claims Court

Chapter 5.5 repealed (as Chapter 5A) and added by Stats. 1990, Ch. 1305, Sec. 3.

Article 1: General Provisions
Article 1 added by Stats. 1990, Ch. 1305, Sec. 3.

116.110. This chapter shall be known and may be cited as "The Small Claims Act."[272]

116.120. The Legislature hereby finds and declares as follows:
(a) Individual minor civil disputes are of special importance to the parties and of significant social and economic consequence collectively.
(b) In order to resolve minor civil disputes expeditiously, inexpensively, and fairly, it is essential to provide a judicial forum accessible to all parties directly involved in resolving these disputes.
(c) The small claims divisions have been established to provide a forum to resolve minor civil disputes, and for that reason constitute a fundamental element in the administration of justice and the protection of the rights and property of individuals.
(d) The small claims divisions, the provisions of this chapter, and the rules of the Judicial Council regarding small claims actions shall operate to ensure that the convenience of parties and witnesses who are individuals shall prevail, to the extent possible, over the convenience of any other parties or witnesses.[390]

116.130. In this chapter, unless the context indicates otherwise:
(a) "Plaintiff" means the party who has filed a small claims action. The term includes a defendant who has filed a claim against a plaintiff.
(b) "Defendant" means the party against whom the plaintiff has filed a small claims action. The term includes a plaintiff against whom a defendant has filed a claim.
(c) "Judgment creditor" means the party, whether plaintiff or defendant, in whose favor a money judgment has been rendered.
(d) "Judgment debtor" means the party, whether plaintiff or defendant, against whom a money judgment has been rendered.
(e) "Person" means an individual, corporation, partnership, limited liability partnership, limited liability company, firm, association, or other entity.
(f) "Individual" means a natural person.
(g) "Party" means a plaintiff or defendant.
(h) "Motion" means a party's written request to the court for an order or other action. The term includes an informal written request to the court, such as a letter.
(i) "Declaration" means a written statement signed by an individual which includes the date and place of signing, and a statement under penalty of perjury under the laws of this state that its contents are true and correct.
(j) "Good cause" means circumstances sufficient to justify the requested order or other action, as determined by the judge.
(k) "Mail" means first-class mail with postage fully prepaid, unless stated otherwise.[535]

116.140. The following do not apply in small claims actions:
(a) Subdivision (a) of Section 1013 and subdivision (b) of Section 1005, on the extension of the time for taking action when notice is given by mail.
(b) Title 6.5 (commencing with Section 481.010) of Part 2, on the issuance of prejudgment attachments.[277]

Article 2: Small Claims Court
Article 2 added by Stats. 1990, Ch. 1305, Sec. 3.

116.210. In each superior court there shall be a small claims division. The small claims division may be known as the small claims court.[490]

116.220. (a) The small claims court has jurisdiction in the following actions:
(1) Except as provided in subdivisions (c), (e), and (f), for recovery of money, if the amount of the demand does not exceed six thousand two hundred fifty dollars ($6,250).
(2) Except as provided in subdivisions (c), (e), and (f), to enforce payment of delinquent unsecured personal property taxes in an amount not to exceed six thousand two hundred fifty dollars ($6,250), if the legality of the tax is not contested by the defendant.
(3) To issue the writ of possession authorized by Sections 1861.5 and 1861.10 of the Civil Code if the amount of the demand does not exceed six thousand two hundred fifty dollars ($6,250).
(4) To confirm, correct, or vacate a fee arbitration award not exceeding six thousand two hundred fifty dollars ($6,250) between an attorney and client that is binding or has become binding, or to conduct a hearing de novo between an attorney and client after nonbinding arbitration of a fee dispute involving no more than six thousand two hundred fifty dollars ($6,250) in controversy, pursuant to Article 13 (commencing with Section 6200) of Chapter 4 of Division 3 of the Business and Professions Code.
(5) For an injunction or other equitable relief only when a statute expressly authorizes a small claims court to award that relief.
(b) In any action seeking relief authorized by paragraphs (1) to (4), inclusive, of subdivision (a), the court may grant equitable relief in the form of rescission, restitution, reformation, and specific performance, in lieu of, or in addition to, money damages. The court may issue a conditional judgment. The court shall retain jurisdiction until full payment and performance of any judgment or order.
(c) Notwithstanding subdivision (a), the small claims court has jurisdiction over a defendant guarantor as follows:
(1) For any action brought by a natural person against the Registrar of the Contractors State License Board as the defendant guarantor, the small claims jurisdictional limit stated in Section 116.221 shall apply.
(2) For any action against a defendant guarantor that does not charge a fee for its guarantor or surety services, if the amount of the demand does not exceed three thousand one hundred twenty-five dollars ($3,125).
(3) For any action brought by a natural person against a defendant guarantor that charges a fee for its guarantor or surety services, if the amount of the demand does not exceed eight thousand one hundred twenty-five dollars ($8,125).

(4) For any action brought by an entity other than a natural person against a defendant guarantor that charges a fee for its guarantor or surety services or against the Registrar of the Contractors State License Board as the defendant guarantor, if the amount of the demand does not exceed five thousand dollars ($5,000).
(d) In any case in which the lack of jurisdiction is due solely to an excess in the amount of the demand, the excess may be waived, but any waiver is not operative until judgment.
(e) Notwithstanding subdivision (a), in any action filed by a plaintiff incarcerated in a Department of Corrections and Rehabilitation facility, the small claims court has jurisdiction over a defendant only if the plaintiff has alleged in the complaint that the plaintiff has exhausted the plaintiff's administrative remedies against that department, including compliance with Sections 905.2 and 905.4 of the Government Code. The final administrative adjudication or determination of the plaintiff's administrative claim by the department may be attached to the complaint at the time of filing in lieu of that allegation.
(f) In any action governed by subdivision (e), if the plaintiff fails to provide proof of compliance with the requirements of subdivision (e) at the time of trial, the judicial officer shall, at the plaintiff's discretion, either dismiss the action or continue the action to give the plaintiff an opportunity to provide that proof.
(g) For purposes of this section, "department" includes an employee of a department against whom a claim has been filed under this chapter arising out of an employee's duties as an employee of that department.[835]

116.221. In addition to the jurisdiction conferred by Section 116.220, the small claims court has jurisdiction in an action brought by a natural person, if the amount of the demand does not exceed twelve thousand five hundred dollars ($12,500), except as otherwise prohibited by subdivision (c) of Section 116.220 or subdivision (a) of Section 116.231.[836]

116.222. If the action is to enforce the payment of a debt, the statement of calculation of liability shall separately state the original debt, each payment credited to the debt, each fee and charge added to the debt, each payment credited against those fees and charges, all other debits or charges to the account, and an explanation of the nature of those fees, charges, debits, and all other credits to the debt, by source and amount.[573]

116.225. An agreement entered into or renewed on or after January 1, 2003, establishing a forum outside of California for an action arising from an offer or provision of goods, services, property, or extensions of credit primarily for personal, family, or household purposes that is otherwise within the jurisdiction of a small claims court of this state is contrary to public policy and is void and unenforceable.[479]

116.230. (a) In a small claims case, the clerk of the court shall charge and collect only those fees authorized under this chapter.
(b) If the party filing a claim has filed 12 or fewer small claims in the state within the previous 12 months, the filing fee is the following:

(1) Thirty dollars ($30) if the amount of the demand is one thousand five hundred dollars ($1,500) or less.

(2) Fifty dollars ($50) if the amount of the demand is more than one thousand five hundred dollars ($1,500) but less than or equal to five thousand dollars ($5,000).

(3) Seventy-five dollars ($75) if the amount of the demand is more than five thousand dollars ($5,000).

(c) If the party has filed more than 12 other small claims in the state within the previous 12 months, the filing fee is one hundred dollars ($100).

(d) (1) If, after having filed a claim and paid the required fee under paragraph (1) of subdivision (b), a party files an amended claim or amendment to a claim that raises the amount of the demand so that the filing fee under paragraph (2) of subdivision (b) would be charged, the filing fee for the amended claim or amendment is twenty dollars ($20).

(2) If, after having filed a claim and paid the required fee under paragraph (2) of subdivision (b), a party files an amended claim or amendment to a claim that raises the amount of the demand so that the filing fee under paragraph (3) of subdivision (b) would be charged, the filing fee for the amended claim or amendment is twenty-five dollars ($25).

(3) If, after having filed a claim and paid the required fee under paragraph (1) of subdivision (b), a party files an amended claim or amendment to a claim that raises the amount of the demand so that the filing fee under paragraph (3) of subdivision (b) would be charged, the filing fee for the amended claim or amendment is forty-five dollars ($45).

(4) The additional fees paid under this subdivision are due upon filing. The court shall not reimburse a party if the party's claim is amended to demand a lower amount that falls within the range for a filing fee lower than that originally paid.

(e) Each party filing a claim shall file a declaration with the claim stating whether that party has filed more than 12 other small claims in the state within the last 12 months.

(f) The clerk of the court shall deposit fees collected under this section into a bank account established for this purpose by the Administrative Office of the Courts and maintained under rules adopted by or trial court financial policies and procedures authorized by the Judicial Council under subdivision (a) of Section 77206 of the Government Code. The deposits shall be made as required under Section 68085.1 of the Government Code and trial court financial policies and procedures authorized by the Judicial Council.

(g) (1) The Administrative Office of the Courts shall distribute six dollars ($6) of each thirty-dollar ($30) fee, eight dollars ($8) of each fifty-dollar ($50) fee, ten dollars ($10) of each seventy-five-dollar ($75) fee, and fourteen dollars ($14) of each one hundred-dollar ($100) fee collected under subdivision (b) or (c) to a special account in the county in which the court is located to be used for the small claims advisory services described in Section 116.940, or, if the small claims advisory services are administered by the court, to the court. The Administrative Office of the Courts shall also distribute two dollars ($2) of each seventy-five-dollar ($75) fee collected under subdivision (b) to the law library fund in the county in which the court is located.

(2) From the fees collected under subdivision (d), the Administrative Office of the Courts shall distribute two dollars ($2) to the law library fund in the county in which the court is located, and three dollars ($3) to the small claims advisory services described in Section 116.940, or, if the small claims advisory services are administered by the court, to the court.

(3) Records of these moneys shall be available from the Administrative Office of the Courts for inspection by the public on request.

(4) Nothing in this section precludes the court or county from contracting with a third party to provide small claims advisory services as described in Section 116.940.

(h) The remainder of the fees collected under subdivisions (b), (c), and (d) shall be transmitted monthly to the Controller for deposit in the Trial Court Trust Fund.

(i) All money distributed under this section to be used for small claims advisory services shall be used only for providing those services as described in Section 116.940. Nothing in this section shall preclude the county or the court from procuring other funding to comply with the requirements of Section 116.940.[605]

116.231. (a) Except as provided in subdivision (d), no person may file more than two small claims actions in which the amount demanded exceeds two thousand five hundred dollars ($2,500), anywhere in the state in any calendar year.

(b) Except as provided in subdivision (d), if the amount demanded in any small claims action exceeds two thousand five hundred dollars ($2,500), the party making the demand shall file a declaration under penalty of perjury attesting to the fact that not more than two small claims actions in which the amount of the demand exceeded two thousand five hundred dollars ($2,500) have been filed by that party in this state within the calendar year.

(c) The Legislature finds and declares that the pilot project conducted under the authority of Chapter 1196 of the Statutes of 1991 demonstrated the efficacy of the removal of the limitation on the number of actions public entities may file in the small claims courts on claims exceeding two thousand five hundred dollars ($2,500).

(d) The limitation on the number of filings exceeding two thousand five hundred dollars ($2,500) does not apply to filings where the claim does not exceed five thousand dollars ($5,000) that are filed by a city, county, city and county, school district, county office of education, community college district, local district, or any other local public entity. If any small claims action is filed by a city, county, city and county, school district, county office of education, community college district, local district, or any other local public entity pursuant to this section, and the defendant informs the court either in advance of the hearing by written notice or at the time of the hearing, that he or she is represented in the action by legal counsel, the action shall be transferred out of the small claims division. A city, county, city and county, school district, county office of education, community college district, local district, or any other local public entity may not file a claim within the small claims division if the amount of the demand exceeds five thousand dollars ($5,000).[391]

116.232. A fee of fifteen dollars ($15) shall be charged and collected from the plaintiff for each defendant to whom the court clerk mails a copy of the claim under Section 116.340. This fee shall be distributed to the court in which it was collected.[681]

116.240. (a) With the consent of the parties who appear at the hearing, the court may order a case to be heard by a temporary judge who is a member of the State Bar, and who has been sworn and empowered to act until final determination of the case.
(b) Prior to serving as a temporary judge in small claims court, on and after July 1, 2006, and at least every three years thereafter, each temporary judge shall take the course of study offered by the courts on ethics and substantive law under rules adopted by the Judicial Council. The course shall include, but not be limited to, state and federal consumer laws, landlord-tenant law along with any applicable county specific rent deposit law, the state and federal Fair Debt Collection Practices Acts, the federal Truth in Lending Act, the federal Fair Credit Billing Act, the federal Electronic Fund Transfer Act, tort law, and contract law, including defenses to contracts and defenses to debts. On substantive law, the courts may receive assistance from the Department of Consumer Affairs, to the extent that the department is fiscally able to provide that assistance.[574]

116.250. (a) Sessions of the small claims court may be scheduled at any time and on any day, including Saturdays, but excluding other judicial holidays.
(b) Each small claims division of a superior court with seven or more judicial officers shall conduct at least one night session or Saturday session each month for the purpose of hearing small claims cases other than small claims appeals. The term “session” includes, but is not limited to, a proceeding conducted by a member of the State Bar acting as a mediator or referee.[528]

116.260. In each county, individual assistance shall be made available to advise small claims litigants and potential litigants without charge as provided in Section 116.940 and by rules adopted by the Judicial Council.[272]

116.270. Any small claims division may use law clerks to assist the judge with legal research of small claims cases.[272]

Article 3: Actions
Article 3 added by Stats. 1990, Ch. 1305, Sec. 3.

116.310. (a) No formal pleading, other than the claim described in Section 116.320 or 116.360, is necessary to initiate a small claims action.
(b) The pretrial discovery procedures described in Section 2019.010 are not permitted in small claims actions.[547]

116.320. (a) A plaintiff may commence an action in the small claims court by filing a claim under oath with the clerk of the small claims court in person, by mail, by facsimile transmission if authorized pursuant to Section 1010.5, or by electronic means as authorized by Section 1010.6.
(b) The claim form shall be a simple nontechnical form approved or adopted by the Judicial Council. The

claim form shall set forth a place for (1) the name and address of the defendant, if known; (2) the amount and the basis of the claim; (3) that the plaintiff, where possible, has demanded payment and, in applicable cases, possession of the property; (4) that the defendant has failed or refused to pay, and, where applicable, has refused to surrender the property; and (5) that the plaintiff understands that the judgment on his or her claim will be conclusive and without a right of appeal.

(c) The form or accompanying instructions shall include information that the plaintiff (1) may not be represented by an attorney, (2) has no right of appeal, and (3) may ask the court to waive fees for filing and serving the claim on the ground that the plaintiff is unable to pay them, using the forms approved by the Judicial Council for that purpose.[606]

116.330. (a) When a claim is filed, the clerk shall schedule the case for hearing and shall issue an order directing the parties to appear at the time set for the hearing with witnesses and documents to prove their claim or defense. The case shall be scheduled for hearing no earlier than 20 days but not more than 70 days from the date of the order.

(b) In lieu of the method of setting the case for hearing described in subdivision (a), at the time a claim is filed the clerk may do all of the following:

(1) Cause a copy of the claim to be mailed to the defendant by any form of mail providing for a return receipt.

(2) On receipt of proof that the claim was served as provided in paragraph (1), issue an order scheduling the case for hearing in accordance with subdivision (a) and directing the parties to appear at the time set for the hearing with witnesses and documents to prove their claim or defense.

(3) Cause a copy of the order setting the case for hearing and directing the parties to appear, to be served upon the parties by any form of mail providing for a return receipt.[575]

116.340. (a) Service of the claim and order on the defendant may be made by any one of the following methods:

(1) The clerk may cause a copy of the claim and order to be mailed to the defendant by any form of mail providing for a return receipt.

(2) The plaintiff may cause a copy of the claim and order to be delivered to the defendant in person.

(3) The plaintiff may cause service of a copy of the claim and order to be made by substituted service as provided in subdivision (a) or (b) of Section 415.20 without the need to attempt personal service on the defendant. For these purposes, substituted service as provided in subdivision (b) of Section 415.20 may be made at the office of the sheriff or marshal who shall deliver a copy of the claim and order to any person authorized by the defendant to receive service, as provided in Section 416.90, who is at least 18 years of age, and thereafter mailing a copy of the claim and order to the defendant's usual mailing address.

(4) The clerk may cause a copy of the claim to be mailed, the order to be issued, and a copy of the order to be mailed as provided in subdivision (b) of Section 116.330.

(b) Service of the claim and order on the defendant shall be completed at least 15 days before the hearing date if

the defendant resides within the county in which the action is filed, or at least 20 days before the hearing date if the defendant resides outside the county in which the action is filed.
(c) Proof of service of the claim and order shall be filed with the small claims court at least five days before the hearing.
(d) Service by the methods described in subdivision (a) shall be deemed complete on the date that the defendant signs the mail return receipt, on the date of the personal service, as provided in Section 415.20, or as established by other competent evidence, whichever applies to the method of service used.
(e) Service shall be made within this state, except as provided in subdivisions (f) and (g).
(f) The owner of record of real property in California who resides in another state and who has no lawfully designated agent in California for service of process may be served by any of the methods described in this section if the claim relates to that property.
(g) A nonresident owner or operator of a motor vehicle involved in an accident within this state may be served pursuant to the provisions on constructive service in Sections 17450 to 17461, inclusive, of the Vehicle Code without regard to whether the defendant was a nonresident at the time of the accident or when the claim was filed. Service shall be made by serving both the Director of the California Department of Motor Vehicles and the defendant, and may be made by any of the methods authorized by this chapter or by registered mail as authorized by Section 17454 or 17455 of the Vehicle Code.
(h) If an action is filed against a principal and his or her guaranty or surety pursuant to a guarantor or suretyship agreement, a reasonable attempt shall be made to complete service on the principal. If service is not completed on the principal, the action shall be transferred to the court of appropriate jurisdiction.[576]

116.360. (a) The defendant may file a claim against the plaintiff in the same action in an amount not to exceed the jurisdictional limits stated in Sections 116.220, 116.221, and 116.231. The claim need not relate to the same subject or event as the plaintiff's claim.
(b) The defendant's claim shall be filed and served in the manner provided for filing and serving a claim of the plaintiff under Sections 116.330 and 116.340.
(c) The defendant shall cause a copy of the claim and order to be served on the plaintiff at least five days before the hearing date, unless the defendant was served 10 days or less before the hearing date, in which event the defendant shall cause a copy of the defendant's claim and order to be served on the plaintiff at least one day before the hearing date.[581]

116.370. (a) Venue and court location requirements in small claims actions shall be the same as in other civil actions. The court may prescribe by local rule the proper court locations for small claims actions.
(b) A defendant may challenge venue or court location by writing to the court and mailing a copy of the challenge to each of the other parties to the

action, without personally appearing at the hearing.

(c) In all cases, including those in which the defendant does not either challenge venue or court location or appear at the hearing, the court shall inquire into the facts sufficiently to determine whether venue and court location are proper, and shall make its determination accordingly.

(1) If the court determines that the action was not commenced in the proper venue, the court, on its own motion, shall dismiss the action without prejudice, unless all defendants are present and agree that the action may be heard. If the court determines that the action was not commenced in the proper court location, the court may transfer the action to a proper location pursuant to local rule.

(2) If the court determines that the action was commenced in the proper venue and court location, the court may hear the case if all parties are present. If the defendant challenged venue or court location and all parties are not present, the court shall postpone the hearing for at least 15 days and shall notify all parties by mail of the court's decision and the new hearing date, time, and place.[514]

116.390. (a) If a defendant has a claim against a plaintiff that exceeds the jurisdictional limits stated in Sections 116.220, 116.221, and 116.231, and the claim relates to the contract, transaction, matter, or event which is the subject of the plaintiff's claim, the defendant may commence an action against the plaintiff in a court of competent jurisdiction and request the small claims court to transfer the small claims action to that court.

(b) The defendant may make the request by filing with the small claims court in which the plaintiff commenced the action, at or before the time set for the hearing of that action, a declaration stating the facts concerning the defendant's action against the plaintiff with a true copy of the complaint so filed by the defendant against the plaintiff. The defendant shall cause a copy of the declaration and complaint to be personally delivered to the plaintiff at or before the time set for the hearing of the small claims action.

(c) In ruling on a motion to transfer, the small claims court may do any of the following: (1) render judgment on the small claims case prior to the transfer; (2) not render judgment and transfer the small claims case; (3) refuse to transfer the small claims case on the grounds that the ends of justice would not be served. If the small claims action is transferred prior to judgment, both actions shall be tried together in the transferee court.

(d) When the small claims court orders the action transferred, it shall transmit all files and papers to the transferee court.

(e) The plaintiff in the small claims action shall not be required to pay to the clerk of the transferee court any transmittal, appearance, or filing fee unless the plaintiff appears in the transferee court, in which event the plaintiff shall be required to pay the filing fee and any other fee required of a defendant in the transferee court. However, if the transferee court rules against the plaintiff in the action filed in that court, the court may award to the defendant in that action the costs incurred as a consequence of the transfer, including attorney's fees and filing fees.[583]

Article 4: Parties

Article 4 added by Stats. 1990, Ch. 1305, Sec. 3.

116.410. (a) Any person who is at least 18 years of age, or legally emancipated, and mentally competent may be a party to a small claims action.
(b) A minor or incompetent person may appear by a guardian ad litem appointed by a judge of the court in which the action is filed.[542]

116.420. (a) No claim shall be filed or maintained in small claims court by the assignee of the claim.
(b) This section does not prevent the filing or defense of an action in the small claims court by (1) a trustee in bankruptcy in the exercise of the trustee's duties as trustee, or (2) by the holder of a security agreement, retail installment contract, or lien contract subject to the Unruh Act (Chapter 1 (commencing with Section 1801) of Title 2 of Part 4 of Division 3 of the Civil Code) or the Automobile Sales Finance Act (Chapter 2b (commencing with Section 2981) of Title 14 of Part 4 of Division 3 of the Civil Code), purchased by the holder for the holder's portfolio of investments, provided that the holder is not an assignee for the purpose of collection.
(c) This section does not prevent the filing in small claims court by a local government which is self-insured for purposes of workers' compensation and is seeking subrogation pursuant to Section 3852 of the Labor Code.[334]

116.430. (a) If the plaintiff operates or does business under a fictitious business name and the claim relates to that business, the claim shall be accompanied by the filing of a declaration stating that the plaintiff has complied with the fictitious business name laws by executing, filing, and publishing a fictitious business name statement as required.
(b) A small claims action filed by a person who has not complied with the applicable fictitious business name laws by executing, filing, and publishing a fictitious business name statement as required shall be dismissed without prejudice.
(c) For purposes of this section, "fictitious business name" means the term as defined in Section 17900 of the Business and Professions Code, and "fictitious business name statement" means the statement described in Section 17913 of the Business and Professions Code.[278]

Article 5: Hearing

Article 5 added by Stats. 1990, Ch. 1305, Sec. 3.

116.510. The hearing and disposition of the small claims action shall be informal, the object being to dispense justice promptly, fairly, and inexpensively.[279]

116.520. (a) The parties have the right to offer evidence by witnesses at the hearing or, with the permission of the court, at another time.
(b) If the defendant fails to appear, the court shall still require the plaintiff to present evidence to prove his or her claim.
(c) The court may consult witnesses informally and otherwise investigate the controversy with or without notice to the parties.[273]

116.530. (a) Except as permitted by this section, no attorney may take part in the conduct or defense of a small claims action.

(b) Subdivision (a) does not apply if the attorney is appearing to maintain or defend an action in any of the following capacities:

(1) By or against himself or herself.

(2) By or against a partnership in which he or she is a general partner and in which all the partners are attorneys.

(3) By or against a professional corporation of which he or she is an officer or director and of which all other officers and directors are attorneys.

(c) Nothing in this section shall prevent an attorney from doing any of the following:

(1) Providing advice to a party to a small claims action, either before or after the commencement of the action.

(2) Testifying to facts of which he or she has personal knowledge and about which he or she is competent to testify.

(3) Representing a party in an appeal to the superior court.

(4) Representing a party in connection with the enforcement of a judgment.[536]

116.531. Nothing in this article shall prevent a representative of an insurer or other expert in the matter before the small claims court from rendering assistance to a party in the litigation except during the conduct of the hearing, either before or after the commencement of the action, unless otherwise prohibited by law; nor shall anything in this article prevent those individuals from testifying to facts of which they have personal knowledge and about which they are competent to testify.[276]

116.540. (a) Except as permitted by this section, no individual other than the plaintiff and the defendant may take part in the conduct or defense of a small claims action.

(b) Except as additionally provided in subdivision (i), a corporation may appear and participate in a small claims action only through a regular employee, or a duly appointed or elected officer or director, who is employed, appointed, or elected for purposes other than solely representing the corporation in small claims court.

(c) A party who is not a corporation or a natural person may appear and participate in a small claims action only through a regular employee, or a duly appointed or elected officer or director, or in the case of a partnership, a partner, engaged for purposes other than solely representing the party in small claims court.

(d) If a party is an individual doing business as a sole proprietorship, the party may appear and participate in a small claims action by a representative and without personally appearing if both of the following conditions are met:

(1) The claim can be proved or disputed by evidence of an account that constitutes a business record as defined in Section 1271 of the Evidence Code, and there is no other issue of fact in the case.

(2) The representative is a regular employee of the party for purposes other than solely representing the party in small claims actions and is qualified to testify to the identity and mode of preparation of the business record.

(e) A plaintiff who is a service member is not required to personally appear, and may submit declarations to serve as evidence supporting their claim, appear via video appearance, or allow another individual to appear and participate on their behalf, if the service member is assigned to a location more than 100 miles from the court where the action is proceeding, or is otherwise unable to personally appear due to the performance of military duty, the representative is serving without compensation, other than compensation from the United States or the State of California, and, except as to representatives who are employed by the United States or the State of California, the representative has appeared in small claims actions on behalf of others no more than four times during the calendar year. The defendant may file a claim in the same action in an amount not to exceed the jurisdictional limits stated in Sections 116.220, 116.221, and 116.231.

(f) A party incarcerated in a county jail, a Department of Corrections and Rehabilitation facility, or a Division of Juvenile Facilities facility is not required to personally appear, and may submit declarations to serve as evidence supporting their claim, or may authorize another individual to appear and participate on their behalf if that individual is serving without compensation and has appeared in small claims actions on behalf of others no more than four times during the calendar year.

(g) A defendant who is a nonresident owner of real property may defend against a claim relating to that property without personally appearing by (1) submitting written declarations to serve as evidence supporting their defense, (2) allowing another individual to appear and participate on their behalf if that individual is serving without compensation and has appeared in small claims actions on behalf of others no more than four times during the calendar year, or (3) taking the action described in both (1) and (2).

(h) A party who is an owner of rental real property may appear and participate in a small claims action through a property agent under contract with the owner to manage the rental of that property, if (1) the owner has retained the property agent principally to manage the rental of that property and not principally to represent the owner in small claims court, and (2) the claim relates to the rental property.

(i) A party that is an association created to manage a common interest development, as defined in Section 4100 or in Sections 6528 and 6534 of the Civil Code, may appear and participate in a small claims action through an agent, a management company representative, or bookkeeper who appears on behalf of that association.

(j) At the hearing of a small claims action, the court shall require any individual who is appearing as a representative of a party under subdivisions (b) to (i), inclusive, to file a declaration stating (1) that the individual is authorized to appear for the party, and (2) the basis for that authorization. If the representative is appearing under subdivision (b), (c), (d), (h), or (i), the declaration also shall state that the individual is not employed solely to represent the party in small claims court. If the representative is appearing under subdivision (e), (f), or (g), the declaration also shall state that the representative is serving without compensation, and has appeared in small claims actions on behalf of others no more than four times during the calendar year.

(k) A spouse who sues or who is sued with their spouse may appear and participate on behalf of their spouse if (1) the claim is a joint claim, (2) the represented spouse has given their consent, and (3) the court determines that the interests of justice would be served.

(l) If the court determines that a party cannot properly present their claim or defense and needs assistance, the court may in its discretion allow another individual to assist that party.

(m) Nothing in this section shall operate or be construed to authorize an attorney to participate in a small claims action except as expressly provided in Section 116.530.[486]

116.541. (a) Notwithstanding Section 116.540 or any other provision of law, the Department of Corrections or the Department of the Youth Authority may appear and participate in a small claims action through a regular employee, who is employed or appointed for purposes other than solely representing that department in small claims court.

(b) Where the Department of Corrections or the Department of the Youth Authority is named as a defendant in small claims court, the representative of the department is not required to personally appear to challenge the plaintiff's compliance with the pleading requirements and may submit pleadings or declarations to assert that challenge.

(c) At the hearing of a small claims action, the court shall require any individual who is appearing as a representative of the Department of Corrections or the Department of the Youth Authority under subdivision (a) to file a declaration stating (1) that the individual is authorized to appear for the party, (2) the basis for that authorization, and (3) that the individual is not employed solely to represent the party in small claims court.

(d) Nothing in this section shall operate or be construed to authorize an attorney to participate in a small claims action except as expressly provided in Section 116.530.

(e) For purposes of this section, all references to the Department of Corrections or the Department of the Youth Authority include an employee thereof, against whom a claim has been filed under this chapter arising out of his or her duties as an employee of that department.[344]

116.560. (a) Whenever a claim that is filed against a person operating or doing business under a fictitious business name relates to the defendant's business, the court shall inquire at the time of the hearing into the defendant's correct legal name and the name or names under which the defendant does business. If the correct legal name of the defendant, or the name actually used by the defendant, is other than the name stated on the claim, the court shall amend the claim to state the correct legal name of the defendant, and the name or names actually used by the defendant.

(b) The plaintiff may request the court at any time, whether before or after judgment, to amend the plaintiff's claim or judgment to include both the correct legal name and the name or names actually used by the defendant. Upon a showing of good cause, the court shall amend the claim or judgment to state the correct legal name of the defendant, and the name or names actually used by the defendant.

(c) For purposes of this section, "fictitious business name" means the term as defined in Section 17900 of the Business and Professions Code.[280]

116.570. (a) Any party may submit a written request to postpone a hearing date for good cause.

(1) The written request may be made either by letter or on a form adopted or approved by the Judicial Council.

(2) The request shall be filed at least 10 days before the hearing date, unless the court determines that the requesting party has good cause to file the request at a later date.

(3) On the date of making the written request, the requesting party shall mail or personally deliver a copy to each of the other parties to the action.

(4) (A) If the court finds that the interests of justice would be served by postponing the hearing, the court shall postpone the hearing, and shall notify all parties by mail of the new hearing date, time, and place.

(B) On one occasion, upon the written request of a defendant guarantor, the court shall postpone the hearing for at least 30 days, and the court shall take this action without a hearing. This subparagraph does not limit the discretion of the court to grant additional postponements under subparagraph (A).

(5) The court shall provide a prompt response by mail to any person making a written request for postponement of a hearing date under this subdivision.

(b) If service of the claim and order upon the defendant is not completed within the number of days before the hearing date required by subdivision (b) of Section 116.340, and the defendant has not personally appeared and has not requested a postponement, the court shall postpone the hearing for at least 15 days. If a postponement is ordered under this subdivision, the clerk shall promptly notify all parties by mail of the new hearing date, time, and place.

(c) This section does not limit the inherent power of the court to order postponements of hearings in appropriate circumstances.

(d) A fee of ten dollars ($10) shall be charged and collected for the filing of a request for postponement and rescheduling of a hearing date after timely service pursuant to subdivision (b) of Section 116.340 has been made upon the defendant.[515]

Article 6: Judgment
Article 6 added by Stats. 1990, Ch. 1305, Sec. 3.

116.610. (a) The small claims court shall give judgment for damages, or equitable relief, or both damages and equitable relief, within the jurisdictional limits stated in Sections 116.220, 116.221, and 116.231, and may make any orders as to time of payment or otherwise as the court deems just and equitable for the resolution of the dispute.

(b) The court may, at its discretion or on request of any party, continue the matter to a later date in order to permit and encourage the parties to attempt resolution by informal or alternative means.

(c) The judgment shall include a determination whether the judgment resulted from a motor vehicle accident on a California highway caused by the defendant's operation of a motor vehicle, or by the operation by some other individual, of a motor vehicle registered in the defendant's name.

(d) If the defendant has filed a claim against the plaintiff, or if the judgment is against two or more defendants, the judgment, and the statement of decision if one is rendered, shall specify the basis for and the character and amount of the liability of each of the parties, including, in the case of multiple judgment debtors, whether the liability of each is joint or several.

(e) If specific property is referred to in the judgment, whether it be personal or real, tangible or intangible, the property shall be identified with sufficient detail to permit efficient implementation or enforcement of the judgment.

(f) In an action against several defendants, the court may, in its discretion, render judgment against one or more of them, leaving the action to proceed against the others, whenever a several judgment is proper.

(g) (1) The prevailing party is entitled to the costs of the action, including the costs of serving the order for the appearance of the defendant.

(2) Notwithstanding paragraph (1) of this subdivision and subdivision (b) of Section 1032, the amount of the small claims court fee paid by a party pursuant to subdivision (c) of Section 116.230 that exceeds the amount that would have been paid if the party had paid the fee pursuant to subdivision (b) of Section 116.230 shall not be recoverable as costs.

(h) When the court renders judgment, the clerk shall promptly deliver or mail notice of entry of the judgment to the parties, and shall execute a certificate of personal delivery or mailing and place it in the file.

(i) The notice of entry of judgment shall be on a form approved or adopted by the Judicial Council.[582]

116.620. (a) The judgment debtor shall pay the amount of the judgment either immediately or at the time and upon the terms and conditions, including payment by installments, which the court may order.

(b) The court may at any time, for good cause, upon motion by a party and notice by the clerk to all affected parties at their last known address, amend the terms and conditions for payment of the judgment to provide for payment by installment. The determination shall be made without regard to the nature of the underlying debt and without regard to whether the moving party appeared before entry of the judgment.

(c) In determining the terms and conditions of payment, the court may consider any factors which would be relevant to a claim of exemption under Chapter 4 (commencing with Section 703.010) of Division 2 of Title 9 of Part 2.[272]

116.630. The court may, at any time after judgment, for good cause, upon motion by a party and notice by the clerk to all affected parties at their last known address, amend the name of any party to include both the correct legal name and the actually used name or names of that party.[272]

Article 7: Motion to Vacate, Appeal, and Related Matters

Heading of Article 7 amended by Stats. 2012, Ch. 470, Sec. 2.

116.710. (a) The plaintiff in a small claims action shall have no right to appeal the judgment on the plaintiff's claim, but a plaintiff who did not appear at the hearing may file a motion to vacate the judgment in accordance with Section 116.720.

(b) The defendant with respect to the plaintiff's claim, and a plaintiff with respect to a claim of the defendant, may appeal the judgment to the superior court in the county in which the action was heard.

(c) With respect to the plaintiff's claim, the insurer of the defendant may appeal the judgment to the superior court in the county in which the matter was heard if the judgment exceeds two thousand five hundred dollars ($2,500) and the insurer stipulates that its policy with the defendant covers the matter to which the judgment applies.

(d) A defendant who did not appear at the hearing has no right to appeal the judgment, but may file a motion to vacate the judgment in accordance with Section 116.730 or 116.740 and also may appeal the denial of that motion.[274]

116.720. (a) A plaintiff who did not appear at the hearing in the small claims court may file a motion to vacate the judgment with the clerk of the small claims court. The motion shall be filed within 30 days after the clerk has mailed notice of entry of the judgment to the parties.

(b) The clerk shall schedule the hearing on the motion to vacate for a date no earlier than 10 days after the clerk has mailed written notice of the date, time, and place of the hearing to the parties.

(c) Upon a showing of good cause, the small claims court may grant the motion. If the defendant is not present, the court shall hear the motion in the defendant's absence.

(d) If the motion is granted, and if all parties are present and agree, the court may hear the case without rescheduling it. If the defendant is not present, the judge or clerk shall reschedule the case and give notice in accordance with Section 116.330.[281]

116.725. (a) A motion to correct a clerical error in a judgment or to set aside and vacate a judgment on the ground of an incorrect or erroneous legal basis for the decision may be made as follows:

(1) By the court on its own motion at any time.

(2) By a party within 30 days after the clerk mails notice of entry of judgment to the parties.

(b) Each party may file only one motion to correct a clerical error or to set aside and vacate the judgment on the ground of an incorrect or erroneous legal basis for the decision.[580]

116.730. (a) A defendant who did not appear at the hearing in the small claims court may file a motion to vacate the judgment with the clerk of the small claims court. The motion shall be filed within 30 days after the clerk has mailed notice of entry of the judgment to the parties.

(b) The defendant shall appear at any hearing on the motion, or submit written justification for not appearing together with a declaration in support of the motion.

(c) Upon a showing of good cause, the court may grant the motion to vacate the judgment. If the plaintiff is not present, the court shall hear the motion in the plaintiff's absence.

(d) If the motion is granted, and if all parties are present and agree, the court may hear the case without rescheduling it. If the plaintiff is not present, the judge or clerk shall reschedule the case and give notice in accordance with Section 116.330.

(e) If the motion is denied, the defendant may appeal to the superior court only on the denial of the motion to vacate the judgment. The defendant shall file the notice of appeal with the clerk of the small claims court within 10 days after the small claims court has mailed or delivered notice of the court's denial of the motion to vacate the judgment.

(f) If the superior court determines that the defendant's motion to vacate the judgment should have been granted, the superior court may hear the claims of all parties without rescheduling the matter, provided that all parties are present and the defendant has previously complied with this article, or may order the case transferred to the small claims court for a hearing.[282]

116.740. (a) If the defendant was not properly served as required by Section 116.330 or 116.340 and did not appear at the hearing in the small claims court, the defendant may file a motion to vacate the judgment with the clerk of the small claims court. The motion shall be accompanied by a supporting declaration, and shall be filed within 180 days after the defendant discovers or should have discovered that judgment was entered against the defendant.

(b) The court may order that the enforcement of the judgment shall be suspended pending a hearing and determination of the motion to vacate the judgment.

(c) Upon a showing of good cause, the court may grant the motion to vacate the judgment. If the plaintiff is not present, the court shall hear the motion in the plaintiff's absence.

(d) Subdivisions (d), (e), and (f) of Section 116.730 apply to any motion to vacate a judgment.[283]

116.745. The clerk shall collect a fee of twenty dollars ($20) for the filing of a motion to vacate.[555]

116.750. (a) An appeal from a judgment in a small claims action is taken by filing a notice of appeal with the clerk of the small claims court.

(b) A notice of appeal shall be filed not later than 30 days after the clerk has delivered or mailed notice of entry of the judgment to the parties. A notice of appeal filed after the 30-day period is ineffective for any purpose.

(c) The time for filing a notice of appeal is not extended by the filing of a request to correct a mistake or by virtue of any subsequent proceedings on that request, except that a new period for filing notice of appeal shall begin on the delivery or mailing of notice of entry of any modified judgment.[284]

116.760. (a) The appealing party shall pay a fee of seventy-five dollars ($75) for filing a notice of appeal.

(b) A party who does not appeal shall not be charged any fee for filing any document relating to the appeal.

(c) The fee shall be distributed as follows:

(1) To the county law library fund, as provided in Section 6320 of the Business and Professions Code, the amount specified in Section 6321 and 6322.1 of the Business and Professions Code.

(2) To the Trial Court Trust Fund, the remainder of the fee.[556]

116.770. (a) The appeal to the superior court shall consist of a new hearing before a judicial officer other than the judicial officer who heard the action in the small claims division.
(b) The hearing on an appeal to the superior court shall be conducted informally. The pretrial discovery procedures described in Section 2019.010 are not permitted, no party has a right to a trial by jury, and no tentative decision or statement of decision is required.
(c) Article 5 (commencing with Section 116.510) on hearings in the small claims court applies in hearings on appeal in the superior court, except that attorneys may participate.
(d) The scope of the hearing shall include the claims of all parties who were parties to the small claims action at the time the notice of appeal was filed. The hearing shall include the claim of a defendant that was heard in the small claims court.
(e) The clerk of the superior court shall schedule the hearing for the earliest available time and shall mail written notice of the hearing to the parties at least 14 days prior to the time set for the hearing.
(f) The Judicial Council may prescribe by rule the practice and procedure on appeal and the time and manner in which the record on appeal shall be prepared and filed.[546]

116.780. (a) The judgment of the superior court after a hearing on appeal is final and not appealable.
(b) Article 6 (commencing with Section 116.610) on judgments of the small claims court applies to judgments of the superior court after a hearing on appeal, except as provided in subdivision (c).
(c) For good cause and where necessary to achieve substantial justice between the parties, the superior court may award a party to an appeal reimbursement of (1) attorney's fees actually and reasonably incurred in connection with the appeal, not exceeding one hundred fifty dollars ($150), and (2) actual loss of earnings and expenses of transportation and lodging actually and reasonably incurred in connection with the appeal, not exceeding one hundred fifty dollars ($150).[659]

116.790. If the superior court finds that the appeal was without substantial merit and not based on good faith, but was intended to harass or delay the other party, or to encourage the other party to abandon the claim, the court may award the other party (a) attorney's fees actually and reasonably incurred in connection with the appeal, not exceeding one thousand dollars ($1,000), and (b) any actual loss of earnings and any expenses of transportation and lodging actually and reasonably incurred in connection with the appeal, not exceeding one thousand dollars ($1,000), following a hearing on the matter.[285]

116.795. (a) The superior court may dismiss the appeal if the appealing party does not appear at the hearing or if the appeal is not heard within one year from the date of filing the notice of appeal with the clerk of the small claims court.
(b) Upon dismissal of an appeal by the superior court, the small claims court shall thereafter have the same jurisdiction as if no appeal had been filed.[272]

116.798. (a) (1) A petition that seeks a writ of review, a writ of mandate, or a writ of prohibition relating to an act of the small claims division, other than a postjudgment enforcement order, may be heard by a judge who is assigned to the appellate division of the superior court.

(2) A petition described by paragraph (1) may also be heard by the court of appeal or by the Supreme Court.

(3) Where a judge described in paragraph (1) grants a writ directed to the small claims division, the small claims division is an inferior tribunal for purposes of Title 1 (commencing with Section 1067) of Part 3.

(4) The fee for filing a writ petition in the superior court under paragraph (1) is the same as the fee for filing a notice of appeal under Section 116.760.

(5) The Judicial Council shall promulgate procedural rules for a writ proceeding under paragraph (1).

(6) An appeal shall not be taken from a judgment granting or denying a petition under paragraph (1) for issuance of a writ. An appellate court may, in its discretion, upon petition for extraordinary writ, review the judgment.

(b) A petition that seeks a writ of review, a writ of mandate, or a writ of prohibition relating to an act of a superior court in a small claims appeal may be heard by the court of appeal or by the Supreme Court.

(c) A petition that seeks a writ of review, a writ of mandate, or a writ of prohibition relating to a postjudgment enforcement order of the small claims division may be heard by the appellate division of the superior court, by the court of appeal, or by the Supreme Court.[679]

Article 8: Satisfaction and Enforcement of Judgment

Article 8 added by Stats. 1990, Ch. 1305, Sec. 3.

116.810. (a) Enforcement of the judgment of a small claims court, including the issuance or recording of any abstract of the judgment, is automatically suspended, without the filing of a bond by the defendant, until the expiration of the time for appeal.

(b) If an appeal is filed as provided in Article 7 (commencing with Section 116.710), enforcement of the judgment of the small claims court is suspended unless (1) the appeal is dismissed by the superior court pursuant to Section 116.795, or (2) the superior court determines that the small claims court properly denied the defendant's motion to vacate filed under Section 116.730 or 116.740. In either of those events, the judgment of the small claims court may be enforced.

(c) The scope of the suspension of enforcement under this section and, unless otherwise ordered, of any suspension of enforcement ordered by the court, shall include any enforcement procedure described in Title 9 (commencing with Section 680.010) of Part 2 and in Sections 674 and 1174.[286]

116.820. (a) The judgment of a small claims court, or the judgment of the superior court after a hearing on appeal, may be enforced by the small claims court as provided in Title 9 (commencing with Section 680.010) of Part 2 and in Sections 674 and 1174 on the enforcement of judgments of other courts.

(b) The clerk of the court shall charge and collect all fees associated with the enforcement of judgments under Title

9 (commencing with Section 680.010) of Part 2. The clerk shall immediately deposit all the fees collected under this section into a bank account established for this purpose by the Administrative Office of the Courts. The money shall be remitted to the State Treasury under rules adopted by, or trial court financial policies and procedures authorized by, the Judicial Council under subdivision (a) of Section 77206 of the Government Code. The Controller shall distribute the fees to the Trial Court Trust Fund as provided in Section 68085.1 of the Government Code.
(c) The prevailing party in any action subject to this chapter is entitled to the costs of enforcing the judgment and accrued interest.[660]

116.830. (a) At the time judgment is rendered, or notice of entry of the judgment is mailed to the parties, the clerk shall deliver or mail to the judgment debtor a form containing questions regarding the nature and location of any assets of the judgment debtor.
(b) Within 30 days after the clerk has mailed notice of entry of the judgment, unless the judgment has been satisfied, the judgment debtor shall complete the form and cause it to be delivered to the judgment creditor.
(c) In the event a motion is made to vacate the judgment or a notice of appeal is filed, a judgment debtor shall complete and deliver the form within 30 days after the clerk has delivered or mailed notice of denial of the motion to vacate, or notice of dismissal of or entry of judgment on the appeal, whichever is applicable.
(d) In case of the judgment debtor's willful failure to comply with subdivision (b) or (c), the judgment creditor may request the court to apply the sanctions, including arrest and attorney's fees, as provided in Section 708.170, on contempt of court.
(e) The Judicial Council shall approve or adopt the form to be used for the purpose of this section.[287]

116.840. (a) At the option of the judgment debtor, payment of the judgment may be made either (1) to the judgment creditor in accordance with Section 116.850, or (2) to the court in which the judgment was entered in accordance with Section 116.860.
(b) The small claims court may order entry of satisfaction of judgment in accordance with subdivisions (c) and (d) of Section 116.850, or subdivision (b) of Section 116.860.[272]

116.850. (a) If full payment of the judgment is made to the judgment creditor or to the judgment creditor's assignee of record, then immediately upon receipt of payment, the judgment creditor or assignee shall file with the clerk of the court an acknowledgment of satisfaction of the judgment.
(b) Any judgment creditor or assignee of record who, after receiving full payment of the judgment and written demand by the judgment debtor, fails without good cause to execute and file an acknowledgment of satisfaction of the judgment with the clerk of the court in which the judgment is entered within 14 days after receiving the request, is liable to the judgment debtor or the judgment debtor's grantees or heirs for all damages sustained by reason of the failure and, in addition, the sum of fifty dollars ($50).
(c) The clerk of the court shall enter a satisfaction of judgment at the request of the judgment debtor if the judgment

debtor either (1) establishes a rebuttable presumption of full payment under subdivision (d), or (2) establishes a rebuttable presumption of partial payment under subdivision (d) and complies with subdivision (c) of Section 116.860.

(d) A rebuttable presumption of full or partial payment of the judgment, whichever is applicable, is created if the judgment debtor files both of the following with the clerk of the court in which the judgment was entered:

(1) Either a canceled check or money order for the full or partial amount of the judgment written by the judgment debtor after judgment and made payable to and endorsed by the judgment creditor, or a cash receipt for the full or partial amount of the judgment written by the judgment debtor after judgment and signed by the judgment creditor.

(2) A declaration stating that (A) the judgment debtor has made full or partial payment of the judgment including accrued interest and costs; (B) the judgment creditor has been requested to file an acknowledgment of satisfaction of the judgment and refuses to do so, or refuses to accept subsequent payments, or the present address of the judgment creditor is unknown; and (C) the documents identified in and accompanying the declaration constitute evidence of the judgment creditor's receipt of full or partial payment.[288]

116.860. (a) A judgment debtor who desires to make payment to the court in which the judgment was entered may file a request to make payment, which shall be made on a form approved or adopted by the Judicial Council.

(b) Upon the filing of the request to make payment and the payment to the clerk of the amount of the judgment and any accrued interest and costs after judgment, plus any required fee authorized by this section, the clerk shall enter satisfaction of the judgment and shall remit payment to the judgment creditor as provided in this section.

(c) If partial payment of the judgment has been made to the judgment creditor, and the judgment debtor files the declaration and evidence of partial payment described in subdivision (d) of Section 116.850, the clerk shall enter satisfaction of the judgment upon receipt by the clerk of the balance owing on the judgment, including any accrued interest and costs after judgment, and the fee required by this section.

(d) If payment is made by means other than money order, certified or cashier's check, or cash, entry of satisfaction of the judgment shall be delayed for 30 days.

(e) The clerk shall notify the judgment creditor, at his or her last known address, that the judgment debtor has satisfied the judgment by making payment to the court. The notification shall explain the procedures which the judgment creditor has to follow to receive payment.

(f) For purposes of this section, "costs after judgment" consist of only those costs itemized in a memorandum of costs filed by the judgment creditor or otherwise authorized by the court.

(g) Payments that remain unclaimed for three years shall go to the superior court pursuant to Section 68084.1 of the Government Code.

(h) A fee of twenty dollars ($20) shall be paid by the judgment debtor for the costs of administering this section.[557]

116.870. (a) Sections 16250 to 16381, inclusive, of the Vehicle Code, regarding the suspension of the judgment debtor's privilege to operate a motor vehicle for failing to satisfy a judgment, apply if the judgment (1) was for damage to property in excess of one thousand dollars ($1,000) or for bodily injury to, or death of, a person in any amount, and (2) resulted from the operation of a motor vehicle upon a California highway by the defendant, or by any other person for whose conduct the defendant was liable, unless the liability resulted from the defendant's signing the application of a minor for a driver's license.
(b) This section shall become operative on January 1, 2017.[712]

116.880. (a) If the judgment (1) was for one thousand dollars ($1,000) or less, (2) resulted from a motor vehicle accident occurring on a California highway caused by the defendant's operation of a motor vehicle, and (3) has remained unsatisfied for more than 90 days after the judgment became final, the judgment creditor may file with the Department of Motor Vehicles a notice requesting a suspension of the judgment debtor's privilege to operate a motor vehicle.
(b) The notice shall state that the judgment has not been satisfied, and shall be accompanied by (1) a fee set by the department, (2) the judgment of the court determining that the judgment resulted from a motor vehicle accident occurring on a California highway caused by the judgment debtor's operation of a motor vehicle, and (3) a declaration that the judgment has not been satisfied. The fee shall be used by the department to finance the costs of administering this section and shall not exceed the department's actual costs.
(c) Upon receipt of a notice, the department shall attempt to notify the judgment debtor by telephone, if possible, otherwise by certified mail, that the judgment debtor's privilege to operate a motor vehicle will be suspended for a period of 90 days, beginning 20 days after receipt of notice by the department from the judgment creditor, unless satisfactory proof, as provided in subdivision (e), is provided to the department before that date.
(d) At the time the notice is filed, the department shall give the judgment creditor a copy of the notice that indicates the filing fee paid by the judgment creditor, and includes a space to be signed by the judgment creditor acknowledging payment of the judgment by the judgment debtor. The judgment creditor shall mail or deliver a signed copy of the acknowledgment to the judgment debtor once the judgment is satisfied.
(e) The department shall terminate the suspension, or the suspension proceedings, upon the occurrence of one or more of the following:
(1) Receipt of proof that the judgment has been satisfied, either (A) by a copy of the notice required by this section signed by the judgment creditor acknowledging satisfaction of the judgment, or (B) by a declaration of the judgment debtor stating that the judgment has been satisfied.
(2) Receipt of proof that the judgment debtor is complying with a court-ordered payment schedule.

(3) Proof that the judgment debtor had insurance covering the accident sufficient to satisfy the judgment.

(4) A deposit with the department of the amount of the unsatisfied judgment, if the judgment debtor presents proof, satisfactory to the department, of inability to locate the judgment creditor.

(5) At the end of 90 days.

(f) If the suspension has been terminated under subdivision (e), the action is final and shall not be reinstituted. If the suspension is terminated, Section 14904 of the Vehicle Code shall apply. Money deposited with the department under this section shall be handled in the same manner as money deposited under paragraph (4) of subdivision (a) of Section 16377 of the Vehicle Code.

(g) A public agency is not liable for an injury caused by the suspension, termination of suspension, or the failure to suspend a person's privilege to operate a motor vehicle as authorized by this section.

(h) This section shall become operative on January 1, 2017.[713]

Article 9: Administration

Article 9 added by Stats. 1990, Ch. 1305, Sec. 3.

116.920. (a) The Judicial Council shall provide by rule for the practice and procedure and for the forms and their use in small claims actions. The rules and forms so adopted shall be consistent with this chapter.

(b) The Judicial Council, in consultation with the Department of Consumer Affairs, shall adopt rules to ensure that litigants receive adequate notice of the availability of assistance from small claims advisors, to prescribe other qualifications and the conduct of advisors, to prescribe training standards for advisors and for temporary judges hearing small claims matters, to prescribe, where appropriate, uniform rules and procedures regarding small claims actions and judgments, and to address other matters that are deemed necessary and appropriate.[289]

116.930. (a) Each small claims division shall provide in each courtroom in which small claims actions are heard a current copy of a publication describing small claims court law and the procedures that are applicable in the small claims courts, including the law and procedures that apply to the enforcement of judgments. The Small Claims Court and Consumer Law California Judge's Bench Book developed by the California Center for Judicial Education and Research is illustrative of a publication that satisfies the requirement of this subdivision.

(b) Each small claims division may formulate and distribute to litigants and the public a manual on small claims court rules and procedures. The manual shall explain how to complete the necessary forms, how to determine the proper court in which small claims actions may be filed, how to present and defend against claims, how to appeal, how to enforce a judgment, how to protect property that is exempt from execution, and such other matters that the court deems necessary or desirable.

(c) If the Department of Consumer Affairs determines there are sufficient private or public funds available in addition to the funds available within the department's current budget, the department, in cooperation with the Judicial Council, shall prepare a manual or information booklet on small claims court rules and procedures. The department shall distribute copies to the general public and to each small claims division.

(d) If funding is available, the Judicial Council, in cooperation with the Department of Consumer Affairs, shall prepare and distribute to each judge who sits in a small claims court a bench book describing all state and federal consumer protection laws reasonably likely to apply in small claims actions.[272]

116.940. (a) Except as otherwise provided in this section or in rules adopted by the Judicial Council, which are consistent with the requirements of this section, the characteristics of the small claims advisory service required by Section 116.260 shall be determined by each county, or by the superior court in a county where the small claims advisory service is administered by the court, in accordance with local needs and conditions.

(b) Each advisory service shall provide the following services:

(1) Individual personal advisory services, in person or by telephone, and by any other means reasonably calculated to provide timely and appropriate assistance. The topics covered by individual personal advisory services shall include, but not be limited to, preparation of small claims court filings, procedures, including procedures related to the conduct of the hearing, and information on the collection of small claims court judgments.

(2) Recorded telephone messages may be used to supplement the individual personal advisory services, but shall not be the sole means of providing advice available in the county.

(3) Adjacent counties, superior courts in adjacent counties, or any combination thereof, may provide advisory services jointly.

(c) In a county in which the number of small claims actions filed annually is 1,000 or less as averaged over the immediately preceding two fiscal years, the county or the superior court may elect to exempt itself from the requirements set forth in subdivision (b). If the small claims advisory service is administered by the county, this exemption shall be formally noticed through the adoption of a resolution by the board of supervisors. If the small claims advisory service is administered by the superior court, this exemption shall be formally noticed through adoption of a local rule. If a county or court so exempts itself, the county or court shall nevertheless provide the following minimum advisory services in accordance with rules adopted by the Judicial Council:

(1) Recorded telephone messages providing general information relating to small claims actions filed in the county shall be provided during regular business hours.

(2) Small claims information booklets shall be provided in the court clerk's office of each superior court, appropriate county offices, and in any other location that is convenient to prospective small claims litigants in the county.

(d) The advisory service shall operate in conjunction and cooperation with the small claims division, and shall be administered so as to avoid the existence or appearance of a conflict of interest between the individuals providing the advisory services and any party to a particular small claims action or any judicial officer deciding small claims actions.

(e) Advisers may be volunteers, and shall be members of the State Bar, law students, paralegals, or persons experienced in resolving minor disputes, and shall be familiar with small claims court rules and procedures. Advisers may not appear in court as an advocate for any party.

(f) Advisers, including independent contractors, other employees, and volunteers, have the immunity conferred by Section 818.9 of the Government Code with respect to advice provided as a public service on behalf of a court or county to small claims litigants and potential litigants under this chapter.

(g) This section does not preclude a court or county from contracting with a third party to provide small claims advisory services as described in this section.[687]

116.950. (a) This section shall become operative only if the Department of Consumer Affairs determines that sufficient private or public funds are available in addition to the funds available in the department's current budget to cover the costs of implementing this section.

(b) There shall be established an advisory committee, constituted as set forth in this section, to study small claims practice and procedure, with particular attention given to the improvement of procedures for the enforcement of judgments.

(c) The members of the advisory committee shall serve without compensation, but shall be reimbursed for expenses actually and necessarily incurred by them in the performance of their duties.

(d) The advisory committee shall be composed as follows:

(1) The Attorney General or a representative.

(2) Two consumer representatives from consumer groups or agencies, appointed by the Secretary of the State and Consumer Services Agency.

(3) One representative appointed by the Speaker of the Assembly and one representative appointed by the President pro Tempore of the Senate.

(4) Two representatives appointed by the Board of Governors of the State Bar.

(5) Two representatives of the business community, appointed by the Secretary of Technology, Trade, and Commerce.

(6) Six judicial officers who have extensive experience presiding in small claims court, appointed by the Judicial Council. Judicial officers appointed under this subdivision may include judicial officers of the superior court, judges of the appellate courts, retired judicial officers, and temporary judges.

(7) One representative appointed by the Governor.

(8) Two clerks of the court appointed by the Judicial Council.

(e) Staff assistance to the advisory committee shall be provided by the Department of Consumer Affairs, with the assistance of the Judicial Council, as needed.[491]

Chapter 6: General Provisions Respecting Courts of Justice

Heading of Chapter 6 renumbered from Chapter 7 by Stats. 1951, Ch. 1737.

Article 1: Open Court Access

Article 1 repealed and added by Stats. 2021, Ch. 526, Sec. 2.

124. (a) Except as provided in Section 214 of the Family Code or any other law, the sittings of every court shall be public.

(b) (1) The court shall not exclude the public from physical access because remote access is available, unless it is necessary to restrict or limit physical access to protect the health or safety of the public or court personnel.

(2) When a courthouse is physically closed, to the extent permitted by law, the court shall provide, at a minimum, a public audio stream or telephonic means by which to listen to the proceedings. This paragraph does not apply to proceedings pursuant to Section 214 of the Family Code or other law that authorizes or requires a proceeding to be closed.

(3) For purposes of this subdivision, "remote access" shall include, but is not limited to, an audio stream that is available on an internet website or telephonic means to listen to a court proceeding.[792]

Article 2: Incidental Powers and Duties of Courts

Article 2 added by Code Amendments 1880, Ch. 35.

128. (a) Every court shall have the power to do all of the following:

(1) To preserve and enforce order in its immediate presence.

(2) To enforce order in the proceedings before it, or before a person or persons empowered to conduct a judicial investigation under its authority.

(3) To provide for the orderly conduct of proceedings before it, or its officers.

(4) To compel obedience to its judgments, orders, and process, and to the orders of a judge out of court, in an action or proceeding pending therein.

(5) To control in furtherance of justice, the conduct of its ministerial officers, and of all other persons in any manner connected with a judicial proceeding before it, in every matter pertaining thereto.

(6) To compel the attendance of persons to testify in an action or proceeding pending therein, in the cases and manner provided in this code.

(7) To administer oaths in an action or proceeding pending therein, and in all other cases where it may be necessary in the exercise of its powers and duties.

(8) To amend and control its process and orders so as to make them conform to law and justice. An appellate court shall not reverse or vacate a duly entered judgment upon an agreement or stipulation of the parties unless the court finds both of the following:

(A) There is no reasonable possibility that the interests of nonparties or the public will be adversely affected by the reversal.

(B) The reasons of the parties for requesting reversal outweigh the erosion of public trust that may result from the nullification of a judgment and the risk that the availability of stipulated reversal will reduce the incentive for pretrial settlement.

(b) Notwithstanding Section 1211 or any other law, if an order of contempt is made affecting an attorney, his or her agent, investigator, or any person acting under the attorney's direction, in the preparation and conduct of any action or proceeding, the execution of any sentence shall be stayed pending the filing within three judicial days of a petition for extraordinary relief testing the lawfulness of the court's order, the violation of which is the basis of the contempt except for the conduct as may be proscribed by subdivision (b) of Section 6068 of the Business and Professions Code, relating to an attorney's duty to maintain respect due to the courts and judicial officers.

(c) Notwithstanding Section 1211 or any other law, if an order of contempt is made affecting a public safety employee acting within the scope of employment for reason of the employee's failure to comply with a duly issued subpoena or subpoena duces tecum, the execution of any sentence shall be stayed pending the filing within three judicial days of a petition for extraordinary relief testing the lawfulness of the court's order, a violation of which is the basis for the contempt.

As used in this subdivision, "public safety employee" includes any peace officer, firefighter, paramedic, or any other employee of a public law enforcement agency whose duty is either to maintain official records or to analyze or present evidence for investigative or prosecutorial purposes.

(d) Notwithstanding Section 1211 or any other law, if an order of contempt is made affecting the victim of a sexual assault, where the contempt consists of refusing to testify concerning that sexual assault, the execution of any sentence shall be stayed pending the filing within three judicial days of a petition for extraordinary relief testing the lawfulness of the court's order, a violation of which is the basis for the contempt.

As used in this subdivision, "sexual assault" means any act made punishable by Section 261, 262, 264.1, 285, 286, 287, 288, or 289 of, or former Section 288a of, the Penal Code.

(e) Notwithstanding Section 1211 or any other law, if an order of contempt is made affecting the victim of domestic violence, where the contempt consists of refusing to testify concerning that domestic violence, the execution of any sentence shall be stayed pending the filing within three judicial days of a petition for extraordinary relief testing the lawfulness of the court's order, a violation of which is the basis for the contempt.

As used in this subdivision, the term "domestic violence" means "domestic violence" as defined in Section 6211 of the Family Code.

(f) Notwithstanding Section 1211 or any other provision of law, no order of contempt shall be made affecting a county government or any member of its governing body acting pursuant to its constitutional or statutory authority unless the court finds, based on a review of evidence presented at a hearing conducted for this purpose, that either of the following conditions exist:

(1) That the county has the resources necessary to comply with the order of the court.

(2) That the county has the authority, without recourse to voter approval or without incurring additional indebtedness, to generate the additional resources necessary to comply with the order of the court, that compliance

with the order of the court will not expose the county, any member of its governing body, or any other county officer to liability for failure to perform other constitutional or statutory duties, and that compliance with the order of the court will not deprive the county of resources necessary for its reasonable support and maintenance.[748]

128.5. (a) A trial court may order a party, the party's attorney, or both, to pay the reasonable expenses, including attorney's fees, incurred by another party as a result of actions or tactics, made in bad faith, that are frivolous or solely intended to cause unnecessary delay. This section also applies to judicial arbitration proceedings under Chapter 2.5 (commencing with Section 1141.10) of Title 3 of Part 3.

(b) For purposes of this section:

(1) "Actions or tactics" include, but are not limited to, the making or opposing of motions or the filing and service of a complaint, cross-complaint, answer, or other responsive pleading. The mere filing of a complaint without service thereof on an opposing party does not constitute "actions or tactics" for purposes of this section.

(2) "Frivolous" means totally and completely without merit or for the sole purpose of harassing an opposing party.

(c) Expenses pursuant to this section shall not be imposed except on notice contained in a party's moving or responding papers or, on the court's own motion, after notice and opportunity to be heard. An order imposing expenses shall be in writing and shall recite in detail the action or tactic or circumstances justifying the order.

(d) In addition to any award pursuant to this section for an action or tactic described in subdivision (a), the court may assess punitive damages against the plaintiff on a determination by the court that the plaintiff's action was an action maintained by a person convicted of a felony against the person's victim, or the victim's heirs, relatives, estate, or personal representative, for injuries arising from the acts for which the person was convicted of a felony, and that the plaintiff is guilty of fraud, oppression, or malice in maintaining the action.

(e) This section shall not apply to disclosures and discovery requests, responses, objections, and motions.

(f) Sanctions ordered pursuant to this section shall be ordered pursuant to the following conditions and procedures:

(1) If, after notice and a reasonable opportunity to respond, the court issues an order pursuant to subdivision (a), the court may, subject to the conditions stated below, impose an appropriate sanction upon the party, the party's attorneys, or both, for an action or tactic described in subdivision (a). In determining what sanctions, if any, should be ordered, the court shall consider whether a party seeking sanctions has exercised due diligence.

(A) A motion for sanctions under this section shall be made separately from other motions or requests and shall describe the specific alleged action or tactic, made in bad faith, that is frivolous or solely intended to cause unnecessary delay.

(B) If the alleged action or tactic is the making or opposing of a written motion or the filing and service of a complaint, cross-complaint, answer, or other responsive pleading that can be withdrawn or appropriately corrected, a notice of motion shall be served as provided in Section 1010, but shall not be filed with or presented to the court, unless 21 days after service of the motion or any other period as the court may prescribe, the challenged action or tactic is not withdrawn or appropriately corrected.

(C) If warranted, the court may award to the party prevailing on the motion the reasonable expenses and attorney's fees incurred in presenting or opposing the motion. Absent exceptional circumstances, a law firm shall be held jointly responsible for violations committed by its partners, associates, and employees.

(D) If the alleged action or tactic is the making or opposing of a written motion or the filing and service of a complaint, cross-complaint, answer, or other responsive pleading that can be withdrawn or appropriately corrected, the court on its own motion may enter an order describing the specific action or tactic, made in bad faith, that is frivolous or solely intended to cause unnecessary delay, and direct an attorney, law firm, or party to show cause why it has made an action or tactic as defined in subdivision (b), unless, within 21 days of service of the order to show cause, the challenged action or tactic is withdrawn or appropriately corrected.

(2) An order for sanctions pursuant to this section shall be limited to what is sufficient to deter repetition of the action or tactic or comparable action or tactic by others similarly situated. Subject to the limitations in subparagraphs (A) and (B), the sanction may consist of, or include, directives of a nonmonetary nature, an order to pay a penalty into court, or, if imposed on motion and warranted for effective deterrence, an order directing payment to the movant of some or all of the reasonable attorney's fees and other expenses incurred as a direct result of the action or tactic described in subdivision (a).

(A) Monetary sanctions may not be awarded against a represented party for a violation of presenting a claim, defense, and other legal contentions that are warranted by existing law or by a nonfrivolous argument for the extension, modification, or reversal of existing law or the establishment of new law.

(B) Monetary sanctions may not be awarded on the court's motion unless the court issues its order to show cause before a voluntary dismissal or settlement of the claims made by or against the party that is, or whose attorneys are, to be sanctioned.

(g) A motion for sanctions brought by a party or a party's attorney primarily for an improper purpose, such as to harass or to cause unnecessary delay or needless increase in the cost of litigation, shall itself be subject to a motion for sanctions. It is the intent of the Legislature that courts shall vigorously use its sanction authority to deter the improper actions or tactics or comparable actions or tactics of others similarly situated.

(h) The liability imposed by this section is in addition to any other liability imposed by law for acts or omissions within the purview of this section.

(i) This section applies to actions or tactics that were part of a civil case filed on or after January 1, 2015.[704]

128.7. (a) Every pleading, petition, written notice of motion, or other similar paper shall be signed by at least one attorney of record in the attorney's individual name, or, if the party is not represented by an attorney, shall be signed by the party. Each paper shall state the signer's address and telephone number, if any. Except when otherwise provided by law, pleadings need not be verified or accompanied by affidavit. An unsigned paper shall be stricken unless omission of the signature is corrected promptly after being called to the attention of the attorney or party.

(b) By presenting to the court, whether by signing, filing, submitting, or later advocating, a pleading, petition, written notice of motion, or other similar paper, an attorney or unrepresented party is certifying that to the best of the person's knowledge, information, and belief, formed after an inquiry reasonable under the circumstances, all of the following conditions are met:

(1) It is not being presented primarily for an improper purpose, such as to harass or to cause unnecessary delay or needless increase in the cost of litigation.

(2) The claims, defenses, and other legal contentions therein are warranted by existing law or by a nonfrivolous argument for the extension, modification, or reversal of existing law or the establishment of new law.

(3) The allegations and other factual contentions have evidentiary support or, if specifically so identified, are likely to have evidentiary support after a reasonable opportunity for further investigation or discovery.

(4) The denials of factual contentions are warranted on the evidence or, if specifically so identified, are reasonably based on a lack of information or belief.

(c) If, after notice and a reasonable opportunity to respond, the court determines that subdivision (b) has been violated, the court may, subject to the conditions stated below, impose an appropriate sanction upon the attorneys, law firms, or parties that have violated subdivision (b) or are responsible for the violation. In determining what sanctions, if any, should be ordered, the court shall consider whether a party seeking sanctions has exercised due diligence.

(1) A motion for sanctions under this section shall be made separately from other motions or requests and shall describe the specific conduct alleged to violate subdivision (b). Notice of motion shall be served as provided in Section 1010, but shall not be filed with or presented to the court unless, within 21 days after service of the motion, or any other period as the court may prescribe, the challenged paper, claim, defense, contention, allegation, or denial is not withdrawn or appropriately corrected. If warranted, the court may award to the party prevailing on the motion the reasonable expenses and attorney's fees incurred in presenting or opposing the motion. Absent exceptional circumstances, a law firm shall be held jointly responsible for violations committed by its partners, associates, and employees.

(2) On its own motion, the court may enter an order describing the specific

conduct that appears to violate subdivision (b) and directing an attorney, law firm, or party to show cause why it has not violated subdivision (b), unless, within 21 days of service of the order to show cause, the challenged paper, claim, defense, contention, allegation, or denial is withdrawn or appropriately corrected.

(d) A sanction imposed for violation of subdivision (b) shall be limited to what is sufficient to deter repetition of this conduct or comparable conduct by others similarly situated. Subject to the limitations in paragraphs (1) and (2), the sanction may consist of, or include, directives of a nonmonetary nature, an order to pay a penalty into court, or, if imposed on motion and warranted for effective deterrence, an order directing payment to the movant of some or all of the reasonable attorney's fees and other expenses incurred as a direct result of the violation.

(1) Monetary sanctions may not be awarded against a represented party for a violation of paragraph (2) of subdivision (b).

(2) Monetary sanctions may not be awarded on the court's motion unless the court issues its order to show cause before a voluntary dismissal or settlement of the claims made by or against the party that is, or whose attorneys are, to be sanctioned.

(e) When imposing sanctions, the court shall describe the conduct determined to constitute a violation of this section and explain the basis for the sanction imposed.

(f) In addition to any award pursuant to this section for conduct described in subdivision (b), the court may assess punitive damages against the plaintiff upon a determination by the court that the plaintiff's action was an action maintained by a person convicted of a felony against the person's victim, or the victim's heirs, relatives, estate, or personal representative, for injuries arising from the acts for which the person was convicted of a felony, and that the plaintiff is guilty of fraud, oppression, or malice in maintaining the action.

(g) This section shall not apply to disclosures and discovery requests, responses, objections, and motions.

(h) A motion for sanctions brought by a party or a party's attorney primarily for an improper purpose, such as to harass or to cause unnecessary delay or needless increase in the cost of litigation, shall itself be subject to a motion for sanctions. It is the intent of the Legislature that courts shall vigorously use its sanctions authority to deter that improper conduct or comparable conduct by others similarly situated.

(i) This section shall apply to a complaint or petition filed on or after January 1, 1995, and any other pleading, written notice of motion, or other similar paper filed in that matter.[577]

129. (a) Notwithstanding any other law, a copy, reproduction, or facsimile of any kind of a photograph, negative, or print, including instant photographs and video recordings, of the body, or any portion of the body, of a deceased person, taken by or for the coroner at the scene of death or in the course of a post mortem examination or autopsy, shall not be made or disseminated except as follows:

(1) For use in a criminal action or proceeding in this state that relates to the death of that person.

(2) As a court of this state permits, by order after good cause has been

shown and after written notification of the request for the court order has been served, at least five days before the order is made, upon the district attorney of the county in which the post mortem examination or autopsy has been made or caused to be made.

(3) For use or potential use in a civil action or proceeding in this state that relates to the death of that person, if either of the following applies:

(A) The coroner receives written authorization from a legal heir, representative, or family member of that person. The written authorization may be provided before the action is filed or while the action is pending. To verify the identity of the legal heir, representative, or family member, all of the following shall be provided to the coroner:

(i) A declaration under penalty of perjury that the individual is a legal heir, representative, or family member of the deceased person.

(ii) A valid form of identification.

(iii) A certified death certificate.

(B) A subpoena is issued by a party who is a legal heir or representative of the deceased person in a pending civil action.

(b) This section shall not apply to the making or dissemination of a copy, reproduction, or facsimile for use in the field of forensic pathology, in medical or scientific education or research, or by a coroner or any law enforcement agency in the United States for investigative purposes, including identification and identification confirmation.

(c) This section shall apply to a copy, reproduction, or facsimile, and to a photograph, negative, or print, regardless of when it was made.

(d) A coroner is not personally liable for monetary damages in a civil action for any act or omission in compliance with this section.

(e) For the purposes of this section, "family member" means a parent, sibling, or child of the deceased.[863]

130. (a) Subject to the provisions of this section, when a child who is under 18 years of age is killed as a result of a criminal act and a person has been convicted and sentenced for the commission of that criminal act, or a person has been found to have committed that offense by the juvenile court and adjudged a ward of the juvenile court, upon the request of a qualifying family member of the deceased child, the autopsy report and evidence associated with the examination of the victim in the possession of a public agency, as defined in Section 7920.525 of the Government Code, shall be sealed and not disclosed, except that an autopsy report and evidence associated with the examination of the victim that has been sealed pursuant to this section may be disclosed, as follows:

(1) To law enforcement, prosecutorial agencies and experts hired by those agencies, public social service agencies, child death review teams, or the hospital that treated the child immediately prior to death, to be used solely for investigative, prosecutorial, or review purposes, and may not be disseminated further.

(2) To the defendant and the defense team in the course of criminal proceedings or related habeas proceedings, to be used solely for investigative, criminal defense, and review purposes, including review for the purpose of initiating any criminal proceeding or related habeas proceeding,

and may not be disseminated further. The "defense team" includes, but is not limited to, all of the following: attorneys, investigators, experts, paralegals, support staff, interns, students, and state and privately funded legal assistance projects hired or consulted for the purposes of investigation, defense, appeal, or writ of habeas corpus on behalf of the person accused of killing the deceased child victim.

(3) To civil litigants in a cause of action related to the victim's death with a court order upon a showing of good cause and proper notice under Section 129, to be used solely to pursue the cause of action, and may not be disseminated further.

(b) Nothing in this section shall prohibit the use of autopsy reports and evidence in relation to court proceedings.

(c) Nothing in this section shall abrogate the rights of victims, their authorized representatives, or insurance carriers to request the release of information pursuant to Article 1 (commencing with Section 7923.600) of Chapter 1 of Part 5 of Division 10 of Title 1 of the Government Code. However, if a seal has been requested, an insurance carrier receiving items pursuant to a request under that article is prohibited from disclosing the requested items except as necessary in the normal course of business. An insurance carrier shall not, under any circumstances, disclose to the general public items received pursuant to Article 1 (commencing with Section 7923.600) of Chapter 1 of Part 5 of Division 10 of Title 1 of the Government Code.

(d) This section may not be invoked by a qualifying family member who has been charged with or convicted of any act in furtherance of the victim's death. Upon the filing of those charges against a qualifying family member, any seal maintained at the request of that qualifying family member under this section shall be removed.

(e) A coroner or medical examiner shall not be liable for damages in a civil action for any reasonable act or omission taken in good faith in compliance with this section.

(f) If sealing of the autopsy report has been requested by a qualifying family member and another qualifying family member opposes sealing, the opposing party may request a hearing in the superior court in the county with jurisdiction over the crime leading to the child's death for a determination of whether the sealing should be maintained. The opposing party shall notify all other qualifying family members, the medical examiner's office that conducted the autopsy, and the district attorney's office with jurisdiction over the crime at least 10 court days in advance of the hearing. At the hearing, the court shall consider the interests of all qualifying family members, the protection of the memory of the deceased child, any evidence that the qualifying family member requesting the seal was involved in the crime that resulted in the death of the child, the public interest in scrutiny of the autopsy report or the performance of the medical examiner, any impact that unsealing would have on pending investigations or pending litigation, and any other relevant factors. Official information in the possession of a public agency necessary to the determination of the hearing shall be received in camera upon a proper showing. In its discretion, the court may, to the extent allowable by law and with good cause shown, restrict the dissemination of an autopsy report or evidence associated with the examination of a victim. This section shall not apply if a public agency has independently determined that the autopsy report may not be disclosed pursuant to Article 1 (commencing with Section 7923.600) of Chapter 1 of Part 5 of Division 10 of Title 1 of the Government Code because it is an investigative file. In that instance, nothing in this section shall preclude the application of Part 5 (commencing with Section 7923.000) of Division 10 of Title 1 of the Government Code.

(g) If a seal has been maintained pursuant to this section, a qualifying family member, or a biological or adoptive aunt, uncle, sibling, first cousin, child, or grandparent of the deceased child may request that the seal be removed. The request to remove the seal shall be adjudicated pursuant to subdivision (f), with the party requesting the removal of the seal being the opposing party.

(h) Nothing in this section shall limit the public access to information contained in the death certificate including: name, age, gender, race, date, time and location of death, the name of a physician reporting a death in a hospital, the name of the certifying pathologist, date of certification, burial information, and cause of death.

(i) When a medical examiner declines a request to provide a copy of an autopsy report that has been sealed pursuant to this section, the examiner shall cite this section as the reason for declining to provide a copy of the report.

(j) For purposes of this section:

(1) A "child who is under 18 years of age" does not include any child who comes within either of the following descriptions:

(A) The child was a dependent child of the juvenile court pursuant to Section 300 of the Welfare and Institutions Code at the time of the child's death, or, pursuant to subdivision (b) of Section 10850.4 of the Welfare and Institutions Code, abuse or neglect is determined to have led to the child's death.

(B) The child was residing in a state or county juvenile facility, or a private facility under contract with the state or county for the placement of juveniles, as a ward of the juvenile court pursuant to Section 602 of the Welfare and Institutions Code at the time of the child's death.

(2) "Evidence associated with the examination of a victim" means any object, writing, diagram, recording, computer file, photograph, video, DVD, CD, film, digital device, or other item that was collected during, or serves to document, the autopsy of a deceased child.

(3) "Qualifying family member" means the biological or adoptive parent, spouse, or legal guardian.

(k) Nothing in this section shall limit the discovery provisions set forth in Chapter 10 (commencing with Section 1054) of Title 6 of the Penal Code.

(l) Nothing in this section shall be construed to limit the authority of the court to seal records or restrict the dissemination of an autopsy report or evidence associated with the examination of a victim under case law, other statutory law, or the rules of court.

(m) The provisions of this section are severable. If any provision of this section or its application is held invalid, that invalidity shall not affect other provisions or applications that can be given effect without the invalid provision or application.[793]

Article 3: Judicial Holidays
Article 3 repealed and added by Stats. 1985, Ch. 1450, Sec. 2.

133. Courts of justice may be held and judicial business transacted on any day, except as provided in this article.[237]

134. (a) Except as provided in subdivision (c), the courts shall be closed for the transaction of judicial business on judicial holidays for all but the following purposes:

(1) To give, upon their request, instructions to a jury when deliberating on their verdict.

(2) To receive a verdict or discharge a jury.

(3) For the conduct of arraignments and the exercise of the powers of a magistrate in a criminal action, or in a proceeding of a criminal nature.

(4) For the conduct of Saturday small claims court sessions pursuant to the Small Claims Act set forth in Chapter 5.5 (commencing with Section 116.110).

(b) Injunctions and writs of prohibition may be issued and served on any day.

(c) In any superior court, one or more departments of the court may remain open and in session for the transaction of any business that may come before the department in the exercise of the civil or criminal jurisdiction of the court, or both, on a judicial holiday or at any hours of the day or night, or both, as the judges of the court prescribe.

(d) The fact that a court is open on a judicial holiday shall not make that day a nonholiday for purposes of computing the time required for the conduct of any proceeding nor for the performance of any act. Any paper lodged with the court at a time when the court is open pursuant to subdivision (c), shall be filed by the court on the next day that is not a judicial holiday, if the document meets appropriate criteria for filing.[492]

135. Every full day designated as a holiday by Section 6700 of the Government Code, including that Thursday of November declared by the President to be Thanksgiving Day, is a judicial holiday, except the date corresponding with the second new moon following the winter solstice, or the third new moon following the winter solstice should an intercalary month intervene, known as "Lunar New Year," the 15th day of the month of Kartik in the Hindu lunar calendar of each year, known as "Diwali," April 24, known as "Genocide Remembrance Day," September 9, known as "Admission Day," the second Monday in October, known as "Columbus Day," and any other day appointed by the President, but not by the Governor, for a public fast, thanksgiving, or holiday. If a judicial holiday falls on a Saturday or a Sunday, the Judicial Council may designate an alternative day for observance of the holiday. Every Saturday and the day after Thanksgiving Day are judicial holidays. Officers and employees of the courts shall observe only the judicial holidays established pursuant to this section.[878]

136. If a day appointed for the holding or sitting of a court, or to which it is adjourned, falls on a judicial holiday, it shall be deemed appointed for or adjourned to the next day.[236]

Article 4: Proceedings in Case of Absence of Judge
Article 4 added by Code Amendments 1880, Ch. 35.

139. If no judge attends on the day appointed for the holding or sitting of a court, or on the day to which it may have been adjourned, within one hour after the time appointed, the sheriff, marshal, or clerk shall adjourn the same until the next day, at 10 o'clock a.m., and if no judge attend on that day, before noon, the sheriff, marshal, or clerk shall adjourn the same until the following day at the same hour; and so on, from day to day unless the judge, by written order, directs it to be adjourned to someday certain, fixed in said order, in which case it shall be so adjourned.[365]

Article 6: Seals of Courts
Article 6 added by Code Amendments 1880, Ch. 35.

153. Except as otherwise expressly provided by law, the seal of a court need not be affixed to any proceeding therein, or to any document, except to the following:
(a) A writ.
(b) A summons.
(c) A warrant of arrest.[258]

Article 7: Special Immigrant Juvenile Findings
Chapter 7 added by Stats. 2014, Ch. 685, Sec. 1.

155. (a) (1) A superior court has jurisdiction under California law to make judicial determinations regarding the dependency or custody, or both, and care of children within the meaning of the federal Immigration and Nationality Act (8 U.S.C. Sec. 1101 et seq. and 8 C.F.R. Sec. 204.11), which includes, but is not limited to, the juvenile, probate, and family court divisions of the superior court. These courts have jurisdiction to make the judicial determinations necessary to enable a child to petition the United States Citizenship and Immigration Services for classification as a special immigrant juvenile pursuant to Section 1101(a)(27)(J) of Title 8 of the United States Code.
(2) The judicial determinations set forth in paragraph (1) of subdivision (b) may be made for a child up to 21 years of age at any point in a proceeding regardless of the division of the superior court or type of proceeding if the prerequisites of that subdivision are met. A nunc pro tunc entry is permissible and shall not require proof of any clerical or other error, as long as the determinations could have been made as of the nunc pro tunc date.
(b) (1) If an order is requested from the superior court making the necessary determinations regarding special immigrant juvenile status pursuant to Section 1101(a)(27)(J) of Title 8 of the United States Code, and there is evidence to support those determinations, which may consist solely of, but is not limited to, a declaration by the child who is the subject of the petition, the court shall issue the order, which

shall include all of the following determinations, each of which shall be supported by reference to the relevant provisions of California law:

(A) The child was either of the following:

(i) Declared a dependent of the court.

(ii) Legally committed to, or placed under the custody of, a state agency or department, or an individual or entity appointed by the court. The court shall indicate the date on which the dependency, commitment, or custody was ordered and the factual basis for making the order.

(B) That reunification of the child with one or both of the child's parents was determined not to be viable because of abuse, neglect, abandonment, or a similar basis pursuant to California law. The court shall indicate the date on which reunification was determined not to be viable, and the factual basis for making the determination.

(C) That it is not in the best interest of the child to be returned to the child's, or the child's parent's, previous country of nationality or country of last habitual residence. The court shall indicate the factual basis for making the determination.

(2) The superior court may make additional determinations pursuant to this section that are supported by evidence only if requested by a party. The asserted, purported, or perceived motivation of the child seeking classification as a special immigrant juvenile shall not be admissible in making the findings under this section. The court shall not include nor reference the asserted, purported, or perceived motivation of the child seeking classification as a special immigrant juvenile in the court's findings under this section.

(3) If a court grants an order that includes the determinations described in paragraph (1), and the person who requested the determinations has submitted a request for expedited processing accompanied by a properly conformed proposed order, the court shall provide the person who requested the determinations with a certified copy of the order within three court days of the date of the hearing at which the determinations were made, or the date the proposed order was submitted, whichever is later.

(c) In any judicial proceedings in response to a request that the superior court make the determinations necessary to support a petition for classification as a special immigrant juvenile, information regarding the child's immigration status that is not otherwise protected by state confidentiality laws shall remain confidential and shall be available for inspection only by the court, the child who is the subject of the proceeding, the parties, the attorneys for the parties, the child's counsel, and the child's guardian.

(d) In any judicial proceedings in response to a request that the superior court make the findings necessary to support a petition for classification as a special immigrant juvenile, records of the proceedings that are not otherwise protected by state confidentiality laws may be sealed using the procedure set forth in California Rules of Court 2.550 and 2.551.

(e) This section shall be operative on January 1, 2025.[828]

TITLE 2: JUDICIAL OFFICERS

Title 2 repealed and added by Code Amendments 1880, Ch. 35.

Chapter 2: Powers of Judges at Chambers

Chapter 2 added by Code Amendments 1880, Ch. 35.

165. The justices of the Supreme Court and of the courts of appeal, or any of them, may, at chambers, grant all orders and writs which are usually granted in the first instance upon an ex parte application, except writs of mandamus, certiorari, and prohibition; and may, in their discretion, hear applications to discharge such orders and writs.[61]

166. (a) The judges of the superior courts may, in chambers:

(1) Grant all orders and writs that are usually granted in the first instance upon an ex parte application, and hear and dispose of those orders and writs, appoint referees, require and receive inventories and accounts to be filed, order notice of settlement of supplemental accounts, suspend the powers of personal representatives, guardians, or conservators in the cases allowed by law, appoint special administrators, grant letters of temporary guardianship or conservatorship, approve or reject claims, and direct the issuance from the court of all writs and process necessary in the exercise of their powers in matters of probate.

(2) Hear and determine all motions made pursuant to Section 657 or 663.

(3) Hear and determine all uncontested actions, proceedings, demurrers, motions, petitions, applications, and other matters pending before the court other than actions for dissolution of marriage, for legal separation, or for a judgment of nullity of the marriage, and except also applications for confirmation of sale of real property in probate proceedings.

(4) Hear and determine motions to tax costs of enforcing a judgment.

(5) Approve bonds and undertakings.

(b) A judge may, out of court, anywhere in the state, exercise all the powers and perform all the functions and duties conferred upon a judge as contradistinguished from the court, or that a judge may exercise or perform in chambers.[493]

166.1. Upon the written request of any party or his or her counsel, or at the judge's discretion, a judge may indicate in any interlocutory order a belief that there is a controlling question of law as to which there are substantial grounds for difference of opinion, appellate resolution of which may materially advance the conclusion of the litigation. Neither the denial of a request for, nor the objection of another party or counsel to, such a commentary in the interlocutory order, may be grounds for a writ or appeal.[485]

167. Any act required or permitted to be performed by the clerk of a court may be performed by a judge thereof.[268]

Chapter 3: Disqualifications of Judges

Chapter 3 added by Code Amendments 1880, Ch. 35.

170. A judge has a duty to decide any proceeding in which he or she is not disqualified.[227]

170.1. (a) A judge shall be disqualified

if any one or more of the following are true:

(1) (A) The judge has personal knowledge of disputed evidentiary facts concerning the proceeding.

(B) A judge shall be deemed to have personal knowledge within the meaning of this paragraph if the judge, or the spouse of the judge, or a person within the third degree of relationship to either of them, or the spouse of such a person is to the judge's knowledge likely to be a material witness in the proceeding.

(2) (A) The judge served as a lawyer in the proceeding, or in any other proceeding involving the same issues he or she served as a lawyer for a party in the present proceeding or gave advice to a party in the present proceeding upon a matter involved in the action or proceeding.

(B) A judge shall be deemed to have served as a lawyer in the proceeding if within the past two years:

(i) A party to the proceeding, or an officer, director, or trustee of a party, was a client of the judge when the judge was in the private practice of law or a client of a lawyer with whom the judge was associated in the private practice of law.

(ii) A lawyer in the proceeding was associated in the private practice of law with the judge.

(C) A judge who served as a lawyer for, or officer of, a public agency that is a party to the proceeding shall be deemed to have served as a lawyer in the proceeding if he or she personally advised or in any way represented the public agency concerning the factual or legal issues in the proceeding.

(3) (A) The judge has a financial interest in the subject matter in a proceeding or in a party to the proceeding.

(B) A judge shall be deemed to have a financial interest within the meaning of this paragraph if:

(i) A spouse or minor child living in the household has a financial interest.

(ii) The judge or the spouse of the judge is a fiduciary who has a financial interest.

(C) A judge has a duty to make reasonable efforts to inform himself or herself about his or her personal and fiduciary interests and those of his or her spouse and the personal financial interests of children living in the household.

(4) The judge, or the spouse of the judge, or a person within the third degree of relationship to either of them, or the spouse of such a person is a party to the proceeding or an officer, director, or trustee of a party.

(5) A lawyer or a spouse of a lawyer in the proceeding is the spouse, former spouse, child, sibling, or parent of the judge or the judge's spouse or if such a person is associated in the private practice of law with a lawyer in the proceeding.

(6) (A) For any reason:

(i) The judge believes his or her recusal would further the interests of justice.

(ii) The judge believes there is a substantial doubt as to his or her capacity to be impartial.

(iii) A person aware of the facts might reasonably entertain a doubt that the judge would be able to be impartial.

(B) Bias or prejudice toward a lawyer in the proceeding may be grounds for disqualification.

(7) By reason of permanent or temporary physical impairment, the judge is unable to properly perceive the evidence or is unable to properly conduct the proceeding.

(8) (A) The judge has a current arrangement concerning prospective employment or other compensated service as a dispute resolution neutral or is participating in, or, within the last two years has participated in, discussions regarding prospective employment or service as a dispute resolution neutral, or has been engaged in that employment or service, and any of the following applies:

(i) The arrangement is, or the prior employment or discussion was, with a party to the proceeding.

(ii) The matter before the judge includes issues relating to the enforcement of either an agreement to submit a dispute to an alternative dispute resolution process or an award or other final decision by a dispute resolution neutral.

(iii) The judge directs the parties to participate in an alternative dispute resolution process in which the dispute resolution neutral will be an individual or entity with whom the judge has the arrangement, has previously been employed or served, or is discussing or has discussed the employment or service.

(iv) The judge will select a dispute resolution neutral or entity to conduct an alternative dispute resolution process in the matter before the judge, and among those available for selection is an individual or entity with whom the judge has the arrangement, with whom the judge has previously been employed or served, or with whom the judge is discussing or has discussed the employment or service.

(B) For the purposes of this paragraph, all of the following apply:

(i) "Participating in discussions" or "has participated in discussion" means that the judge solicited or otherwise indicated an interest in accepting or negotiating possible employment or service as an alternative dispute resolution neutral, or responded to an unsolicited statement regarding, or an offer of, that employment or service by expressing an interest in that employment or service, making an inquiry regarding the employment or service, or encouraging the person making the statement or offer to provide additional information about that possible employment or service. If a judge's response to an unsolicited statement regarding, a question about, or offer of, prospective employment or other compensated service as a dispute resolution neutral is limited to responding negatively, declining the offer, or declining to discuss that employment or service, that response does not constitute participating in discussions.

(ii) "Party" includes the parent, subsidiary, or other legal affiliate of any entity that is a party and is involved in the transaction, contract, or facts that gave rise to the issues subject to the proceeding.

(iii) "Dispute resolution neutral" means an arbitrator, mediator, temporary judge appointed under Section 21 of Article VI of the California Constitution, referee appointed under Section 638 or 639, special master, neutral evaluator, settlement officer, or settlement facilitator.

(9) (A) The judge has received a contribution in excess of one thousand five hundred dollars ($1500) from a party or lawyer in the proceeding, and either of the following applies:

(i) The contribution was received in support of the judge's last election, if the last election was within the last six years.

(ii) The contribution was received in anticipation of an upcoming election.

(B) Notwithstanding subparagraph (A), the judge shall be disqualified based on a contribution of a lesser amount if subparagraph (A) of paragraph (6) applies.

(C) The judge shall disclose any contribution from a party or lawyer in a matter that is before the court that is required to be reported under subdivision (f) of Section 84211 of the Government Code, even if the amount would not require disqualification under this paragraph. The manner of disclosure shall be the same as that provided in Canon 3E of the Code of Judicial Ethics.

(D) Notwithstanding paragraph (1) of subdivision (b) of Section 170.3, the disqualification required under this paragraph may be waived by the party that did not make the contribution unless there are other circumstances that would prohibit a waiver pursuant to paragraph (2) of subdivision (b) of Section 170.3.

(b) A judge before whom a proceeding was tried or heard shall be disqualified from participating in any appellate review of that proceeding.

(c) At the request of a party or on its own motion an appellate court shall consider whether in the interests of justice it should direct that further proceedings be heard before a trial judge other than the judge whose judgment or order was reviewed by the appellate court.[636]

170.2. It shall not be grounds for disqualification that the judge:

(a) Is or is not a member of a racial, ethnic, religious, sexual or similar group and the proceeding involves the rights of such a group.

(b) Has in any capacity expressed a view on a legal or factual issue presented in the proceeding, except as provided in paragraph (2) of subdivision (a) of, or subdivision (b) or (c) of, Section 170.1.

(c) Has as a lawyer or public official participated in the drafting of laws or in the effort to pass or defeat laws, the meaning, effect or application of which is in issue in the proceeding unless the judge believes that his or her prior involvement was so well known as to raise a reasonable doubt in the public mind as to his or her capacity to be impartial.[229]

170.3. (a) (1) If a judge determines himself or herself to be disqualified, the judge shall notify the presiding judge of the court of his or her recusal and shall not further participate in the proceeding, except as provided in Section 170.4, unless his or her disqualification is waived by the parties as provided in subdivision (b).

(2) If the judge disqualifying himself or herself is the only judge or the presiding judge of the court, the notification shall be sent to the person having authority to assign another judge to replace the disqualified judge.

(b) (1) A judge who determines himself or herself to be disqualified after disclosing the basis for his or her disqualification on the record may ask the parties and their attorneys whether they wish to waive the disqualification, except where the basis for disqualification is as provided in paragraph (2). A waiver of disqualification shall recite the basis for the disqualification, and is effective only when signed by all parties and their attorneys and filed in the record.

(2) There shall be no waiver of disqualification if the basis therefor is either of the following:

(A) The judge has a personal bias or prejudice concerning a party.

(B) The judge served as an attorney in the matter in controversy, or the judge has been a material witness concerning that matter.

(3) The judge shall not seek to induce a waiver and shall avoid any effort to discover which lawyers or parties favored or opposed a waiver of disqualification.

(4) If grounds for disqualification are first learned of or arise after the judge has made one or more rulings in a proceeding, but before the judge has completed judicial action in a proceeding, the judge shall, unless the disqualification be waived, disqualify himself or herself, but in the absence of good cause the rulings he or she has made up to that time shall not be set aside by the judge who replaces the disqualified judge.

(c) (1) If a judge who should disqualify himself or herself refuses or fails to do so, any party may file with the clerk a written verified statement objecting to the hearing or trial before the judge and setting forth the facts constituting the grounds for disqualification of the judge. The statement shall be presented at the earliest practicable opportunity after discovery of the facts constituting the ground for disqualification. Copies of the statement shall be served on each party or his or her attorney who has appeared and shall be personally served on the judge alleged to be disqualified, or on his or her clerk, provided that the judge is present in the courthouse or in chambers.

(2) Without conceding his or her disqualification, a judge whose impartiality has been challenged by the filing of a written statement may request any other judge agreed upon by the parties to sit and act in his or her place.

(3) Within 10 days after the filing or service, whichever is later, the judge may file a consent to disqualification in which case the judge shall notify the presiding judge or the person authorized to appoint a replacement of his or her recusal as provided in subdivision (a), or the judge may file a written verified answer admitting or denying any or all of the allegations contained in the party's statement and setting forth any additional facts material or relevant to the question of disqualification. The clerk shall forthwith transmit a copy of the judge's answer to each party or his or her attorney who has appeared in the action.

(4) A judge who fails to file a consent or answer within the time allowed shall be deemed to have consented to his or her disqualification and the clerk shall notify the presiding judge or person authorized to appoint a replacement of the recusal as provided in subdivision (a).

(5) A judge who refuses to recuse

himself or herself shall not pass upon his or her own disqualification or upon the sufficiency in law, fact, or otherwise, of the statement of disqualification filed by a party. In that case, the question of disqualification shall be heard and determined by another judge agreed upon by all the parties who have appeared or, in the event they are unable to agree within five days of notification of the judge's answer, by a judge selected by the chairperson of the Judicial Council, or if the chairperson is unable to act, the vice chairperson. The clerk shall notify the executive officer of the Judicial Council of the need for a selection. The selection shall be made as expeditiously as possible. No challenge pursuant to this subdivision or Section 170.6 may be made against the judge selected to decide the question of disqualification.

(6) The judge deciding the question of disqualification may decide the question on the basis of the statement of disqualification and answer and any written arguments as the judge requests, or the judge may set the matter for hearing as promptly as practicable. If a hearing is ordered, the judge shall permit the parties and the judge alleged to be disqualified to argue the question of disqualification and shall for good cause shown hear evidence on any disputed issue of fact. If the judge deciding the question of disqualification determines that the judge is disqualified, the judge hearing the question shall notify the presiding judge or the person having authority to appoint a replacement of the disqualified judge as provided in subdivision (a).

(d) The determination of the question of the disqualification of a judge is not an appealable order and may be reviewed only by a writ of mandate from the appropriate court of appeal sought only by the parties to the proceeding. The petition for the writ shall be filed and served within 10 days after service of written notice of entry of the court's order determining the question of disqualification. If the notice of entry is served by mail, that time shall be extended as provided in subdivision (a) of Section 1013.[589]

170.4. (a) A disqualified judge, notwithstanding his or her disqualification may do any of the following:

(1) Take any action or issue any order necessary to maintain the jurisdiction of the court pending the assignment of a judge not disqualified.

(2) Request any other judge agreed upon by the parties to sit and act in his or her place.

(3) Hear and determine purely default matters.

(4) Issue an order for possession prior to judgment in eminent domain proceedings.

(5) Set proceedings for trial or hearing.

(6) Conduct settlement conferences.

(b) Notwithstanding paragraph (5) of subdivision (c) of Section 170.3, if a statement of disqualification is untimely filed or if on its face it discloses no legal grounds for disqualification, the trial judge against whom it was filed may order it stricken.

(c) (1) If a statement of disqualification is filed after a trial or hearing has commenced by the start of voir dire, by the swearing of the first witness or by the submission of a motion for decision, the judge whose impartiality has been questioned may order the trial or hearing to continue, notwithstanding the filing of the statement of disqualification. The issue of disqualification shall be referred to another judge for decision as provided in subdivision (a) of Section 170.3, and if it is determined that the judge is disqualified, all orders and rulings of the judge found to be disqualified made after the filing of the statement shall be vacated.

(2) For the purposes of this subdivision, if (A) a proceeding is filed in a single judge court or has been assigned to a single judge for comprehensive disposition, and (B) the proceeding has been set for trial or hearing 30 or more days in advance before a judge whose name was known at the time, the trial or hearing shall be deemed to have commenced 10 days prior to the date scheduled for trial or hearing as to any grounds for disqualification known before that time.

(3) A party may file no more than one statement of disqualification against a judge unless facts suggesting new grounds for disqualification are first learned of or arise after the first statement of disqualification was filed. Repetitive statements of disqualification not alleging facts suggesting new grounds for disqualification shall be stricken by the judge against whom they are filed.

(d) Except as provided in this section, a disqualified judge shall have no power to act in any proceeding after his or her disqualification or after the filing of a statement of disqualification until the question of his or her disqualification has been determined.[230]

170.5. For the purposes of Sections 170 to 170.5, inclusive, the following definitions apply:

(a) "Judge" means judges of the superior courts, and court commissioners and referees.

(b) "Financial interest" means ownership of more than a 1 percent legal or equitable interest in a party, or a legal or equitable interest in a party of a fair market value in excess of one thousand five hundred dollars ($1,500), or a relationship as director, advisor or other active participant in the affairs of a party, except as follows:

(1) Ownership in a mutual or common investment fund that holds securities is not a "financial interest" in those securities unless the judge participates in the management of the fund.

(2) An office in an educational, religious, charitable, fraternal, or civic organization is not a "financial interest" in securities held by the organization.

(3) The proprietary interest of a policyholder in a mutual insurance company, or a depositor in a mutual savings association, or a similar proprietary interest, is a "financial interest" in the organization only if the outcome of the proceeding could substantially affect the value of the interest.

(c) "Officer of a public agency" does not include a Member of the Legislature or a state or local agency official acting in a legislative capacity.

(d) The third degree of relationship shall be calculated according to the civil law system.

(e) "Private practice of law" includes a fee for service, retainer, or salaried representation of private clients or public agencies, but excludes lawyers as full-time employees of public agencies or lawyers working exclusively for legal aid offices, public defender offices, or

similar nonprofit entities whose clientele is by law restricted to the indigent.
(f) "Proceeding" means the action, case, cause, motion, or special proceeding to be tried or heard by the judge.
(g) "Fiduciary" includes any executor, trustee, guardian, or administrator.[494]

170.6. (a) (1) A judge, court commissioner, or referee of a superior court of the State of California shall not try a civil or criminal action or special proceeding of any kind or character nor hear any matter therein that involves a contested issue of law or fact when it is established as provided in this section that the judge or court commissioner is prejudiced against a party or attorney or the interest of a party or attorney appearing in the action or proceeding.
(2) A party to, or an attorney appearing in, an action or proceeding may establish this prejudice by an oral or written motion without prior notice supported by affidavit or declaration under penalty of perjury, or an oral statement under oath, that the judge, court commissioner, or referee before whom the action or proceeding is pending, or to whom it is assigned, is prejudiced against a party or attorney, or the interest of the party or attorney, so that the party or attorney cannot, or believes that he or she cannot, have a fair and impartial trial or hearing before the judge, court commissioner, or referee. If the judge, other than a judge assigned to the case for all purposes, court commissioner, or referee assigned to, or who is scheduled to try, the cause or hear the matter is known at least 10 days before the date set for trial or hearing, the motion shall be made at least 5 days before that date. If directed to the trial of a cause with a master calendar, the motion shall be made to the judge supervising the master calendar not later than the time the cause is assigned for trial. If directed to the trial of a criminal cause that has been assigned to a judge for all purposes, the motion shall be made to the assigned judge or to the presiding judge by a party within 10 days after notice of the all purpose assignment, or if the party has not yet appeared in the action, then within 10 days after the appearance. If directed to the trial of a civil cause that has been assigned to a judge for all purposes, the motion shall be made to the assigned judge or to the presiding judge by a party within 15 days after notice of the all purpose assignment, or if the party has not yet appeared in the action, then within 15 days after the appearance. If the court in which the action is pending is authorized to have no more than one judge, and the motion claims that the duly elected or appointed judge of that court is prejudiced, the motion shall be made before the expiration of 30 days from the date of the first appearance in the action of the party who is making the motion or whose attorney is making the motion. In no event shall a judge, court commissioner, or referee entertain the motion if it is made after the drawing of the name of the first juror, or if there is no jury, after the making of an opening statement by counsel for plaintiff, or if there is no opening statement by counsel for plaintiff, then after swearing in the first witness or the giving of any evidence or after trial of the cause has otherwise commenced. If the motion is directed to a

hearing, other than the trial of a cause, the motion shall be made not later than the commencement of the hearing. In the case of trials or hearings not specifically provided for in this paragraph, the procedure specified herein shall be followed as nearly as possible. The fact that a judge, court commissioner, or referee has presided at, or acted in connection with, a pretrial conference or other hearing, proceeding, or motion prior to trial, and not involving a determination of contested fact issues relating to the merits, shall not preclude the later making of the motion provided for in this paragraph at the time and in the manner herein provided.

A motion under this paragraph may be made following reversal on appeal of a trial court's decision, or following reversal on appeal of a trial court's final judgment, if the trial judge in the prior proceeding is assigned to conduct a new trial on the matter. Notwithstanding paragraph (4), the party who filed the appeal that resulted in the reversal of a final judgment of a trial court may make a motion under this section regardless of whether that party or side has previously done so. The motion shall be made within 60 days after the party or the party's attorney has been notified of the assignment.

(3) A party to a civil action making that motion under this section shall serve notice on all parties no later than five days after making the motion.

(4) If the motion is duly presented, and the affidavit or declaration under penalty of perjury is duly filed or an oral statement under oath is duly made, thereupon and without any further act or proof, the judge supervising the master calendar, if any, shall assign some other judge, court commissioner, or referee to try the cause or hear the matter. In other cases, the trial of the cause or the hearing of the matter shall be assigned or transferred to another judge, court commissioner, or referee of the court in which the trial or matter is pending or, if there is no other judge, court commissioner, or referee of the court in which the trial or matter is pending, the Chair of the Judicial Council shall assign some other judge, court commissioner, or referee to try the cause or hear the matter as promptly as possible. Except as provided in this section, no party or attorney shall be permitted to make more than one such motion in any one action or special proceeding pursuant to this section. In actions or special proceedings where there may be more than one plaintiff or similar party or more than one defendant or similar party appearing in the action or special proceeding, only one motion for each side may be made in any one action or special proceeding.

(5) Unless required for the convenience of the court or unless good cause is shown, a continuance of the trial or hearing shall not be granted by reason of the making of a motion under this section. If a continuance is granted, the cause or matter shall be continued from day to day or for other limited periods upon the trial or other calendar and shall be reassigned or transferred for trial or hearing as promptly as possible.

(6) Any affidavit filed pursuant to this section shall be in substantially the following form:

(Here set forth court and cause)

State of California, ss. PEREMPTORY CHALLENGE

County of

_____, being duly sworn, deposes and says: That he or she is a party (or attorney for a party) to the within action (or special proceeding). That _____ the judge, court commissioner, or referee before whom the trial of the (or a hearing in the) action (or special proceeding) is pending (or to whom it is assigned) is prejudiced against the party (or his or her attorney) or the interest of the party (or his or her attorney) so that affiant cannot or believes that he or she cannot have a fair and impartial trial or hearing before the judge, court commissioner, or referee.

Subscribed and sworn to before me this

_______ day of _______, 20___.

(Clerk or notary public or other

officer administering oath)

(7) Any oral statement under oath or declaration under penalty of perjury made pursuant to this section shall include substantially the same contents as the affidavit above.

(b) Nothing in this section shall affect or limit Section 170 or Title 4 (commencing with Section 392) of Part 2, and this section shall be construed as cumulative thereto.

(c) If any provision of this section or the application to any person or circumstance is held invalid, that invalidity shall not affect other provisions or applications of the section that can be given effect without the invalid provision or application and, to this end, the provisions of this section are declared to be severable.[633]

170.7. Section 170.6 does not apply to a judge designated or assigned to serve on the appellate division of a superior court in the judge's capacity as a judge of that division.[392]

170.8. When there is no judge of a court qualified to hear an action or proceeding, the clerk shall forthwith notify the Chairman of the Judicial Council of that fact. The judge assigned by the Chairman of the Judicial Council shall hear the action or proceeding at the time fixed therefor or, if no time has been fixed or good cause appears for changing the time theretofore fixed, the judge shall fix a time for hearing in accordance with law and rules and hear the action or proceeding at the time so fixed.[269]

170.9. (a) A judge shall not accept gifts from a single source in a calendar year with a total value of more than two hundred fifty dollars ($250). This section shall not be construed to authorize the receipt of gifts that would otherwise be prohibited by the Code of Judicial Ethics adopted by the California Supreme Court or any other law.

(b) This section shall not prohibit or limit the following:

(1) Payments, advances, or reimbursements for travel and related lodging and subsistence permitted by subdivision (e).

(2) Wedding gifts and gifts exchanged between individuals on birthdays, holidays, and other similar occasions, if the gifts exchanged are not substantially disproportionate in value.

(3) A gift, bequest, favor, or loan from a person whose preexisting relationship with a judge would prevent the judge from hearing a case involving that person, under the Code of Judicial Ethics adopted by the California Supreme Court.

(c) For purposes of this section, "judge" includes all of the following:

(1) Judges of the superior courts.

(2) Justices of the courts of appeal and the Supreme Court.

(3) Subordinate judicial officers, as defined in Section 71601 of the Government Code.

(d) The gift limitation amounts in this section shall be adjusted biennially by the Commission on Judicial Performance to reflect changes in the Consumer Price Index, rounded to the nearest ten dollars ($10).

(e) Payments, advances, or reimbursements for travel, including actual transportation and related lodging and subsistence that is reasonably related to a judicial or governmental purpose, or to an issue of state, national, or international public policy, are not prohibited or limited by this section if any of the following apply:

(1) The travel is in connection with a speech, practice demonstration, or group or panel discussion given or participated in by the judge, the lodging and subsistence expenses are limited to the day immediately preceding, the day of, and the day immediately following the speech, demonstration, or discussion, and the travel is within the United States.

(2) The travel is provided by a government, a governmental agency or authority, a foreign government, a foreign bar association, an international service organization, a bona fide public or private educational institution, as defined in Section 203 of the Revenue and Taxation Code, or a nonprofit charitable or religious organization that is exempt from taxation under Section 501(c)(3) of the Internal Revenue Code, or by a person domiciled outside the United States who substantially satisfies the requirements for tax-exempt status under Section 501(c)(3) of the Internal Revenue Code.

For purposes of this section, "foreign bar association" means an association of attorneys located outside the United States (A) that performs functions substantially equivalent to those performed by state or local bar associations in this state and (B) that permits membership by attorneys in that country representing various legal specialties and does not limit membership to attorneys generally representing one side or another in litigation. "International service organization" means a bona fide international service organization of which the judge is a member. A judge who accepts travel payments from an international service organization pursuant to this subdivision shall not preside over or participate in decisions affecting that organization, its state or local chapters, or its local members.

(3) The travel is provided by a state or local bar association or judges professional association in connection with testimony before a governmental body or attendance at any professional function hosted by the bar association or judges professional association, the lodging and subsistence expenses are limited to the day immediately preceding, the day of, and the day immediately following the professional function.

(f) Payments, advances, and reimbursements for travel not described in subdivision (e) are subject to the limit in subdivision (a).

(g) No judge shall accept any honorarium.

(h) "Honorarium" means a payment made in consideration for any speech given, article published, or attendance at a public or private conference, convention, meeting, social event, meal, or like gathering.

(i) "Honorarium" does not include earned income for personal services that are customarily provided in connection with the practice of a bona fide business, trade, or profession, such as teaching or writing for a publisher, and does not include fees or other things of value received pursuant to Section 94.5 of the Penal Code for performance of a marriage.

For purposes of this section, "teaching" shall include presentations to impart educational information to lawyers in events qualifying for credit under mandatory continuing legal education, to students in bona fide educational institutions, and to associations or groups of judges.

(j) Subdivisions (a) and (e) shall apply to all payments, advances, and reimbursements for travel and related lodging and subsistence.

(k) This section does not apply to any honorarium that is not used and, within 30 days after receipt, is either returned to the donor or delivered to the Controller for deposit in the General Fund without being claimed as a deduction from income for tax purposes.

(l) "Gift" means a payment to the extent that consideration of equal or greater value is not received and includes a rebate or discount in the price of anything of value unless the rebate or discount is made in the regular course of business to members of the public without regard to official status. A person, other than a defendant in a criminal action, who claims that a payment is not a gift by reason of receipt of consideration has the burden of proving that the consideration received is of equal or greater value. However, the term "gift" does not include any of the following:

(1) Informational material such as books, reports, pamphlets, calendars, periodicals, cassettes and discs, or free or reduced-price admission, tuition, or registration, for informational conferences or seminars. No payment for travel or reimbursement for any expenses shall be deemed "informational material."

(2) Gifts that are not used and, within 30 days after receipt, are returned to the donor or delivered to a charitable organization without being claimed as a charitable contribution for tax purposes.

(3) Gifts from a judge's spouse, child, parent, grandparent, grandchild, brother, sister, parent-in-law, brother-in-law, sister-in-law, nephew, niece, aunt, uncle, or first cousin or the spouse of any such person. However, a gift from any of those persons shall be considered a gift if the donor is acting as an agent or intermediary for a person not covered by this paragraph.

(4) Campaign contributions required to be reported under Chapter 4 (commencing with Section 84100) of Title 9 of the Government Code.

(5) Any devise or inheritance.

(6) Personalized plaques and trophies with an individual value of less than two hundred fifty dollars ($250).

(7) Admission to events hosted by state or local bar associations or judges professional associations, and provision of related food and beverages at those events, when attendance does not require "travel," as described in paragraph (3) of subdivision (e).

(m) The Commission on Judicial Performance shall enforce the prohibitions of this section with regard to judges of the superior courts and justices of the courts of appeal and the Supreme Court. With regard to subordinate judicial officers, consistent with Section 18.1 of Article VI of the California Constitution, the court employing the subordinate judicial officer shall exercise initial jurisdiction to enforce the prohibitions of this section, and the Commission on Judicial Performance shall exercise discretionary jurisdiction with respect to the enforcement of the prohibitions of this section.[655]

Chapter 4: Incidental Powers and Duties of Judicial Officers

Chapter 4 added by Code Amendments 1880, Ch. 35.

177. A judicial officer shall have power:
(a) To preserve and enforce order in the officer's immediate presence, and in proceedings before the officer, when the officer is engaged in the performance of official duty.
(b) To compel obedience to the officer's lawful orders as provided in this code.
(c) To compel the attendance of persons to testify in a proceeding before the officer, in the cases and manner provided in this code.
(d) To administer oaths to persons in a proceeding pending before the officer, and in all other cases where it may be necessary in the exercise of the officer's powers and duties.
(e) To prohibit activities that threaten access to state courthouses and court proceedings, and to prohibit interruption of judicial administration, including protecting the privilege from civil arrest at courthouses and court proceedings.[761]

177.5. A judicial officer shall have the power to impose reasonable money sanctions, not to exceed fifteen hundred dollars ($1,500), notwithstanding any other provision of law, payable to the court, for any violation of a lawful court order by a person, done without good cause or substantial justification. This power shall not apply to advocacy of counsel before the court. For the purposes of this section, the term "person" includes a witness, a party, a party's attorney, or both.
Sanctions pursuant to this section shall not be imposed except on notice contained in a party's moving or responding papers; or on the court's own motion, after notice and opportunity to be heard. An order imposing sanctions shall be in writing and shall recite in detail the conduct or circumstances justifying the order.[558]

178. For the effectual exercise of the powers conferred by the last section, a judicial officer may punish for contempt in the cases provided in this Code.[6]

179. Each of the justices of the Supreme Court and of any court of appeal and the judges of the superior courts, shall have power in any part of the state to take and certify:
(a) The proof and acknowledgment of a conveyance of real property, or of any other written instrument.
(b) The acknowledgment of satisfaction of a judgment of any court.
(c) An affidavit or deposition to be used in this state.[524]

Chapter 5: Miscellaneous Provisions Respecting Courts of Justice

Heading of Chapter 5 amended by Stats. 1933, Ch. 743.

182. The heading to this chapter shall not be deemed to govern or limit the scope or meaning of this chapter.[33]

184. No proceeding in any court of justice, in an action or special proceeding pending therein, shall be affected by a vacancy in the office of all or any of the judges or justices thereof.[16]

185. (a) Every written proceeding in a court of justice in this state shall be in

the English language, and judicial proceedings shall be conducted, preserved, and published in no other. Nothing in this section shall prohibit a court from providing an unofficial translation of a court order issued pursuant to Section 527.6 or 527.8 of the Code of Civil Procedure, or Part 1 (commencing with Section 6200) of Division 10 of the Family Code, or Section 136.2 of the Penal Code, in a language other than English.
(b) The Judicial Council shall, by July 1, 2001, make available to all courts, translations of domestic violence protective order forms in languages other than English, as the Judicial Council deems appropriate, for protective orders issued pursuant to Section 527.6 or 527.8 of the Code of Civil Procedure, or Part 1 (commencing with Section 6200) of Division 10 of the Family Code, or Section 136.2 of the Penal Code.[408]

186. Such abbreviations as are in common use may be used, and numbers may be expressed by figures or numerals in the customary manner.[6]

187. When jurisdiction is, by the Constitution or this Code, or by any other statute, conferred on a Court or judicial officer, all the means necessary to carry it into effect are also given; and in the exercise of this jurisdiction, if the course of proceeding be not specifically pointed out by this Code or the statute, any suitable process or mode of proceeding may be adopted which may appear most conformable to the spirit of this Code.[6]

TITLE 3: PERSONS SPECIALLY INVESTED WITH POWERS OF A JUDICIAL NATURE

Title 3 repealed and added by Code Amendments 1880, Ch. 35.

Chapter 1: Trial Jury Selection and Management Act

Chapter 1 repealed *and added by Stats. 1988, Ch. 1245, Sec. 2.*

190. This chapter shall be known and may be cited as the Trial Jury Selection and Management Act.[261]

191. The Legislature recognizes that trial by jury is a cherished constitutional right, and that jury service is an obligation of citizenship.
It is the policy of the State of California that all persons selected for jury service shall be selected at random from the population of the area served by the court; that all qualified persons have an equal opportunity, in accordance with this chapter, to be considered for jury service in the state and an obligation to serve as jurors when summoned for that purpose; and that it is the responsibility of jury commissioners to manage all jury systems in an efficient, equitable, and cost-effective manner, in accordance with this chapter.[261]

192. This chapter applies to the selection of jurors, and the formation of trial juries, for both civil and criminal cases, in all trial courts of the state.[261]

193. Juries are of three kinds:
(a) Grand juries established pursuant to Title 4 (commencing with Section 888) of Part 2 of the Penal Code.
(b) Trial juries.
(c) Juries of inquest.[261]

194. The following definitions govern

the construction of this chapter:
(a) "County" means any county or any coterminous city and county.
(b) "Court" means a superior court of this state, and includes, when the context requires, any judge of the court.
(c) "Deferred jurors" are those prospective jurors whose request to reschedule their service to a more convenient time is granted by the jury commissioner.
(d) "Excused jurors" are those prospective jurors who are excused from service by the jury commissioner for valid reasons based on statute, state or local court rules, and policies.
(e) "Juror pool" means the group of prospective qualified jurors appearing for assignment to trial jury panels.
(f) "Jury of inquest" is a body of persons summoned from the citizens before the sheriff, coroner, or other ministerial officers, to inquire of particular facts.
(g) "Master list" means a list of names randomly selected from the source lists.
(h) "Potential juror" means any person whose name appears on a source list.
(i) "Prospective juror" means a juror whose name appears on the master list.
(j) "Qualified juror" means a person who meets the statutory qualifications for jury service.
(k) "Qualified juror list" means a list of qualified jurors.
(l) "Random" means that which occurs by mere chance indicating an unplanned sequence of selection where each juror's name has substantially equal probability of being selected.
(m) "Source list" means a list used as a source of potential jurors.
(n) "Summons list" means a list of prospective or qualified jurors who are summoned to appear or to be available for jury service.
(o) "Trial jurors" are those jurors sworn to try and determine by verdict a question of fact.
(p) "Trial jury" means a body of persons selected from the citizens of the area served by the court and sworn to try and determine by verdict a question of fact.
(q) "Trial jury panel" means a group of prospective jurors assigned to a courtroom for the purpose of voir dire.[495]

195. (a) In each county, there shall be one jury commissioner who shall be appointed by, and serve at the pleasure of, a majority of the judges of the superior court. In any county where there is a superior court administrator or executive officer, that person shall serve as ex officio jury commissioner. In any court jurisdiction where any person other than a court administrator or clerk/administrator is serving as jury commissioner on the effective date of this section, that person shall continue to so serve at the pleasure of a majority of the judges of the appointing court.
(b) Any jury commissioner may, whenever the business of court requires, appoint deputy jury commissioners. Salaries and benefits of those deputies shall be fixed in the same manner as salaries and benefits of other court employees.
(c) The jury commissioner shall be primarily responsible for managing the jury system under the general supervision of the court in conformance with the purpose and scope of this act. He or she shall have authority to establish policies and procedures necessary to fulfill this responsibility.[496]

196. (a) The jury commissioner or the court shall inquire as to the qualifications of persons on the master list or source list who are or may be summoned for jury service. The commissioner or the court may require any person to answer, under oath, orally or in written form, all questions as may be addressed to that person, regarding the person's qualifications and ability to serve as a prospective trial juror. The commissioner and his or her assistants shall have power to administer oaths and shall be allowed actual traveling expenses incurred in the performance of their duties.
(b) Response to the jury commissioner or the court concerning an inquiry or summons may be made by any person having knowledge that the prospective juror is unable to respond to such inquiry or summons.
(c) Any person who fails to respond to jury commissioner or court inquiry as instructed, may be summoned to appear before the jury commissioner or the court to answer the inquiry, or may be deemed to be qualified for jury service in the absence of a response to the inquiry. Any information thus acquired by the court or jury commissioner shall be noted in jury commissioner or court records.[529]

197. (a) All persons selected for jury service shall be selected at random, from a source or sources inclusive of a representative cross section of the population of the area served by the court. Sources may include, in addition to other lists, customer mailing lists, telephone directories, or utility company lists.
(b) (1) The list of registered voters and the Department of Motor Vehicles' list of licensed drivers and identification cardholders resident within the area served by the court, are appropriate source lists for selection of jurors. Until January 1, 2022, only these two source lists, when substantially purged of duplicate names, shall be considered inclusive of a representative cross section of the population, within the meaning of subdivision (a).
(2) The list of resident state tax filers is an appropriate source list for selection of jurors. Beginning on January 1, 2022, the list of resident state tax filers, the list of registered voters, and the Department of Motor Vehicles' list of licensed drivers and identification cardholders resident within the area served by the court, when substantially purged of duplicate names, shall be considered inclusive of a representative cross section of the population, within the meaning of subdivision (a).
(c) The Department of Motor Vehicles shall furnish the jury commissioner of each county with the current list of the names, addresses, and other identifying information of persons residing in the county who are age 18 years or older and who are holders of a current driver's license or identification card issued pursuant to Article 3 (commencing with Section 12800) of, or Article 5 (commencing with Section 13000) of, Chapter 1 of Division 6 of the Vehicle Code. The conditions under which these lists shall be compiled semiannually shall be determined by the director, consistent with any rules which may be adopted by the Judicial Council. This service shall be provided by the Department of Motor Vehicles pursuant to Section 1812 of the Vehicle Code. The jury commissioner shall not disclose the information furnished

by the Department of Motor Vehicles pursuant to this section to any person, organization, or agency.

(d) (1) The Franchise Tax Board shall annually furnish the jury commissioner of each county with a list of resident state tax filers for their county in consultation with the Judicial Council.

(2) The list of resident state tax filers shall be submitted to the jury commissioner of each county by November 1, 2021, and each November 1 thereafter.

(3) (A) For purposes of this section, "list of resident state tax filers" means a list that includes the name, date of birth, principal residence address, and county of principal residence, of persons who are 18 years of age or older and have filed a California resident income tax return for the preceding taxable year.

(B) For purposes of this paragraph, "county of principal residence" means the county in which the taxpayer has their principal residence on the date that the taxpayer filed their California resident income tax return.

(C) For the purposes of this paragraph, "principal residence" is used in the same manner it is used in Section 121 of the Internal Revenue Code.[777]

198. (a) Random selection shall be utilized in creating master and qualified juror lists, commencing with selection from source lists, and continuing through selection of prospective jurors for voir dire.

(b) The jury commissioner shall, at least once in each 12-month period, randomly select names of prospective trial jurors from the source list or lists, to create a master list.

(c) The master jury list shall be used by the jury commissioner, as provided by statute and state and local court rules, for the purpose of (1) mailing juror questionnaires and subsequent creation of a qualified juror list, and (2) summoning prospective jurors to respond or appear for qualification and service.[261]

198.5. If sessions of the superior court are held in a location other than the county seat, the names for master jury lists and qualified jury lists to serve in a session may be selected from the area in which the session is held, pursuant to a local superior court rule that divides the county in a manner that provides all qualified persons in the county an equal opportunity to be considered for jury service. Nothing in this section precludes the court, in its discretion, from ordering a countywide venire in the interest of justice.[505]

201. In any superior court, a separate trial jury panel may be drawn, summoned, and impaneled for each judge, or any one panel may be drawn, summoned, and impaneled by any one of the judges, for use in the trial of cases before any of the judges, as occasion may require. In those courts, when a panel of jurors is in attendance for service before one or more of the judges, whether impaneled for common use or not, the whole or any number of the jurors from such panel may be required to attend and serve in the trial of cases, or to complete a panel, or jury, before any other of the judges.[497]

202. Mechanical, electric, or electronic equipment, which in the opinion of the jury commissioner is satisfactory therefor, may be used in the performance of any function specified by this

chapter for the selection and drawing of jurors.[260]

203. (a) All persons are eligible and qualified to be prospective trial jurors, except the following:

(1) Persons who are not citizens of the United States.

(2) Persons who are less than 18 years of age.

(3) Persons who are not domiciliaries of the State of California, as determined pursuant to Article 2 (commencing with Section 2020) of Chapter 1 of Division 2 of the Elections Code.

(4) Persons who are not residents of the jurisdiction wherein they are summoned to serve.

(5) Persons who have been convicted of malfeasance in office and whose civil rights have not been restored.

(6) Persons who are not possessed of sufficient knowledge of the English language, provided that no person shall be deemed incompetent solely because of the loss of sight or hearing in any degree or other disability which impedes the person's ability to communicate or which impairs or interferes with the person's mobility.

(7) Persons who are serving as grand or trial jurors in any court of this state.

(8) Persons who are the subject of conservatorship.

(9) Persons while they are incarcerated in any prison or jail.

(10) Persons who have been convicted of a felony and are currently on parole, postrelease community supervision, felony probation, or mandated supervision for the conviction of a felony.

(11) Persons who are currently required to register as a sex offender pursuant to Section 290 of the Penal Code based on a felony conviction.

(b) No person shall be excluded from eligibility for jury service in the State of California, for any reason other than those reasons provided by this section.

(c) The provisions of this section are severable. If any provision of this section or its application is held invalid, that invalidity shall not affect other provisions or applications that can be given effect without the invalid provision or application.[760]

204. (a) No eligible person shall be exempt from service as a trial juror by reason of occupation, economic status, or any characteristic listed or defined in Section 11135 of the Government Code, or for any other reason. No person shall be excused from service as a trial juror except as specified in subdivision (b).

(b) An eligible person may be excused from jury service only for undue hardship, upon themselves or upon the public, as defined by the Judicial Council.[603]

205. (a) If a jury commissioner requires a person to complete a questionnaire, the questionnaire shall ask only questions related to juror identification, qualification, and ability to serve as a prospective juror.

(b) Except as ordered by the court, the questionnaire referred to in subdivision (a) shall be used solely for qualifying prospective jurors, and for management of the jury system, and not for assisting in the courtroom voir dire process of selecting trial jurors for specific cases.

(c) The court may require a prospective juror to complete such additional questionnaires as may be deemed relevant and necessary for assisting in the voir dire process or to ascertain whether a fair cross section of the population is represented as required by law, if such procedures are established by local court rule.
(d) The trial judge may direct a prospective juror to complete additional questionnaires as proposed by counsel in a particular case to assist the voir dire process.
(e) The Judicial Council shall adopt a standard of judicial administration to ensure that juror identification and any juror questionnaire is inclusive, including allowing a juror the ability to express their gender identity or gender expression, if applicable.
(f) This section shall become operative on January 1, 2026.[870]

206. (a) Prior to discharging the jury from the case, the judge in a criminal action shall inform the jurors that they have an absolute right to discuss or not to discuss the deliberation or verdict with anyone. The judge shall also inform the jurors of the provisions set forth in subdivisions (b), (d), and (e).
(b) Following the discharge of the jury in a criminal case, the defendant, or his or her attorney or representative, or the prosecutor, or his or her representative, may discuss the jury deliberation or verdict with a member of the jury, provided that the juror consents to the discussion and that the discussion takes place at a reasonable time and place.
(c) If a discussion of the jury deliberation or verdict with a member of the jury pursuant to subdivision (b) occurs at any time more than 24 hours after the verdict, prior to discussing the jury deliberation or verdict with a member of a jury pursuant to subdivision (b), the defendant or his or her attorney or representative, or the prosecutor or his or her representative, shall inform the juror of the identity of the case, the party in that case which the person represents, the subject of the interview, the absolute right of the juror to discuss or not discuss the deliberations or verdict in the case with the person, and the juror's right to review and have a copy of any declaration filed with the court.
(d) Any unreasonable contact with a juror by the defendant, or his or her attorney or representative, or by the prosecutor, or his or her representative, without the juror's consent shall be immediately reported to the trial judge.
(e) Any violation of this section shall be considered a violation of a lawful court order and shall be subject to reasonable monetary sanctions in accordance with Section 177.5 of the Code of Civil Procedure.
(f) Nothing in the section shall prohibit a peace officer from investigating an allegation of criminal conduct.
(g) Pursuant to Section 237, a defendant or defendant's counsel may, following the recording of a jury's verdict in a criminal proceeding, petition the court for access to personal juror identifying information within the court's records necessary for the defendant to communicate with jurors for the purpose of developing a motion for new trial or any other lawful purpose. This information consists of jurors' names, addresses, and telephone numbers. The court shall consider all requests

for personal juror identifying information pursuant to Section 237.[469]

207. (a) The jury commissioner shall maintain records regarding selection, qualification, and assignment of prospective jurors.
(b) The jury commissioner shall maintain records providing a clear audit trail regarding a juror's attendance, jury fees, and mileage.
(c) All records and papers maintained or compiled by the jury commissioner in connection with the selection or service of a juror may be kept on an electronic or microfilm medium and such records shall be preserved for at least three years after the list used in their selection is prepared, or for any longer period ordered by the court or the jury commissioner.[260]

208. The jury commissioner shall estimate the number of prospective jurors that may be required to serve the needs of the court, and shall summon prospective jurors for service. Prospective jurors shall be summoned by mailing a summons by first-class mail or by personal service or, in urgency situations, as elsewhere provided by law. The summons, when served by mail, shall be mailed at least 10 days prior to the date of required appearance. Once a prospective juror has been summoned, the date, time, or place of appearance may be modified or further specified by the jury commissioner, by means of written, telegraphic, telephonic, or direct oral communication with the prospective juror.[530]

209. (a) Any prospective trial juror who has been summoned for service, and who fails to attend as directed or to respond to the court or jury commissioner and to be excused from attendance, may be attached and compelled to attend. Following an order to show cause hearing, the court may find the prospective juror in contempt of court, punishable by fine, incarceration, or both, as otherwise provided by law.
(b) In lieu of imposing sanctions for contempt as set forth in subdivision (a), the court may impose reasonable monetary sanctions, as provided in this subdivision, on a prospective juror who has not been excused pursuant to Section 204 after first providing the prospective juror with notice and an opportunity to be heard. If a juror fails to respond to the initial summons the court may issue a second summons indicating that the person failed to appear in response to a previous summons and ordering the person to appear for jury duty. The second summons may be issued no earlier than 90 days after the initial failure to appear. Upon the failure of the juror to appear in response to the second summons, the court may issue a failure to appear notice informing the person that failure to respond may result in the imposition of money sanctions. If the prospective juror does not attend the court within the time period as directed by the failure to appear notice, the court shall issue an order to show cause. Payment of monetary sanctions imposed pursuant to this subdivision does not relieve the person of his or her obligation to perform jury duty.
(c) (1) The court may give notice of its intent to impose sanctions by either of the following means:
(A) Verbally to a prospective juror appearing in person in open court.
(B) The issuance on its own motion

of an order to show cause requiring the prospective juror to demonstrate reasons for not imposing sanctions. The court may serve the order to show cause by certified or first-class mail.

(2) The monetary sanctions imposed pursuant to subdivision (b) may not exceed two hundred fifty dollars ($250) for the first violation, seven hundred fifty dollars ($750) for the second violation, and one thousand five hundred dollars ($1,500) for the third and any subsequent violation. Monetary sanctions may not be imposed on a prospective juror more than once during a single juror pool cycle. The prospective juror may be excused from paying sanctions pursuant to subdivision (b) of Section 204 or in the interests of justice. The full amount of any sanction paid shall be deposited in a bank account established for this purpose by the Administrative Office of the Courts and transmitted from that account monthly to the Controller for deposit in the Trial Court Trust Fund, as provided in Section 68085.1 of the Government Code. It is the intent of the Legislature that the funds derived from the monetary sanctions authorized in this section be allocated, to the extent feasible, to the family courts and the civil courts. The Judicial Council shall, by rule, provide for a procedure by which a prospective juror against whom a sanction has been imposed by default may move to set aside the default.[590]

Note: This amendment deleted the former Jan. 1, 2010, repeal date and extended this version's provisions indefinitely.

210. The summons shall contain the date, time, and place of appearance required of the prospective juror or, alternatively, instructions as to the procedure for calling the jury commissioner for telephonic instructions for appearance as well as such additional juror information as deemed appropriate by the jury commissioner.[260]

210.5. The Judicial Council shall adopt a standardized jury summons for use, with appropriate modifications, around the state, that is understandable and has consumer appeal. The standardized jury summons shall include a specific reference to the rules for breast-feeding mothers. The use of the standardized jury summons shall be voluntary, unless otherwise prescribed by the rules of court.[470]

211. When a court has no prospective jurors remaining available for voir dire from panels furnished by, or available from, the jury commissioner, and finds that not proceeding with voir dire will place a party's right to a trial by jury in jeopardy, the court may direct the sheriff or marshal to summon, serve, and immediately attach the person of a sufficient number of citizens having the qualifications of jurors, to complete the panel.[366]

213. Unless excused by reason of undue hardship, all or any portion of the summoned prospective jurors shall be available on one-hour notice by telephone to appear for service, when the jury commissioner determines that it will efficiently serve the operational requirements of the court.

Jurors available on one-hour telephone notice shall receive credit for each day of such availability towards their jury service obligation, but they shall not be paid unless they are actually required to make an appearance.[260]

214. The jury commissioner shall provide orientation for new jurors, which shall include necessary basic information concerning jury service. The jury commissioner shall notify each juror of paragraph (1) of subdivision (a) of Section 12945.8 of the Government Code.[869]

215. (a) Except as provided in subdivision (b), on and after July 1, 2000, the fee for jurors in the superior court, in civil and criminal cases, is fifteen dollars ($15) a day for each day's attendance as a juror after the first day.
(b) A juror who is employed by a federal, state, or local government entity, or by any other public entity as defined in Section 481.200, and who receives regular compensation and benefits while performing jury service, shall not be paid the fee described in subdivision (a).
(c) All jurors in the superior court, in civil and criminal cases, shall be reimbursed for mileage at the rate of thirty-four cents ($0.34) per mile for each mile actually traveled in attending and returning from court as a juror after the first day.
(d) All jurors and prospective jurors who have been summoned shall be provided with access to existing public transit services at no cost utilizing one of the following options:
(1) Courts may partner with public transit operators in their county to create new programs or continue existing public transit programs that provide no-cost service for jurors and prospective jurors who have been summoned.
(2) A method of reimbursement determined by the court up to a daily maximum of twelve dollars ($12).
(e) Subdivision (d) does not apply to a court in an area where a public transit operator does not provide existing service that is reasonably available to the court facility.
(f) In determining whether transit service is reasonably available to the court facility, the court shall consider factors that include, but are not limited to, all of the following:
(1) Proximity of transit service to the court location.
(2) Hours of operation of transit service in the vicinity of the court location.
(3) Frequency of operation of transit service in the vicinity of the court location.
(4) Availability of transit access to all areas of the court's jurisdiction from which a potential juror may reside.
(g) Prior to determining that transit service is not reasonably available to the court facility, the court shall contact the public transit operator to inquire whether new transit options may be implemented near the court.[799]

216. (a) At each court facility where jury cases are heard, the court shall provide a deliberation room or rooms for use of jurors when they have retired for deliberation. The deliberation rooms shall be designed to minimize unwarranted intrusions by other persons in the court facility, shall have suitable furnishings, equipment, and supplies, and shall also have restroom accommodations for male and female jurors.
(b) Unless authorized by the jury commissioner, jury assembly facilities shall

be restricted to use by jurors and jury commissioner staff.[767]

217. In criminal cases only, while the jury is kept together, either during the progress of the trial or after their retirement for deliberation, the court may direct the sheriff or marshal to provide the jury with suitable and sufficient food and lodging, or other reasonable necessities. The expenses incurred under this section shall be charged against the Trial Court Operations Fund of the county in which the court is held. All those expenses shall be paid on the order of the court.[498]

218. The jury commissioner shall hear the excuses of jurors summoned, in accordance with the standards prescribed by the Judicial Council. It shall be left to the discretion of the jury commissioner to accept an excuse under subdivision (b) of Section 204 without a personal appearance. All excuses shall be in writing setting forth the basis of the request and shall be signed by the juror.[260]

219. (a) Except as provided in subdivision (b), the jury commissioner shall randomly select jurors for jury panels to be sent to courtrooms for voir dire.
(b) (1) Notwithstanding subdivision (a), no peace officer, as defined in Section 830.1, subdivision (a) of Section 830.2, and subdivision (a) of Section 830.33, of the Penal Code, shall be selected for voir dire in civil or criminal matters.
(2) Notwithstanding subdivision (a), no peace officer, as defined in subdivisions (b) and (c) of Section 830.2 of the Penal Code, shall be selected for voir dire in criminal matters.[460]

219.5. The Judicial Council shall adopt a rule of court, on or before January 1, 2005, requiring the trial courts to establish procedures for jury service that gives peace officers, as defined by Section 830.5 of the Penal Code, scheduling accommodations when necessary.[533]

220. A trial jury shall consist of 12 persons, except that in civil actions and cases of misdemeanor, it may consist of 12 or any number less than 12, upon which the parties may agree.[260]

222. (a) Except as provided in subdivision (b), when an action is called for trial by jury, the clerk shall randomly select the names of the jurors for voir dire, until the jury is selected or the panel is exhausted.
(b) When the jury commissioner has provided the court with a listing of the trial jury panel in random order, the court shall seat prospective jurors for voir dire in the order provided by the panel list.[599]

222.5. (a) To select a fair and impartial jury in a civil jury trial, the trial judge shall conduct an initial examination of prospective jurors. At the final status conference or at the first practical opportunity prior to voir dire, whichever comes first, the trial judge shall consider and discuss with counsel the form and subject matter of voir dire questions. Before voir dire by the trial judge, the parties may submit questions to the trial judge. The trial judge may include additional questions requested by the parties as the trial judge deems proper.
(b) (1) Upon completion of the trial judge's initial examination, counsel for each party shall have the right to examine, by oral and direct questioning, any of the prospective jurors in order to

enable counsel to intelligently exercise both peremptory challenges and challenges for cause. The scope of the examination conducted by counsel shall be within reasonable limits prescribed by the trial judge in the judge's sound discretion subject to the provisions of this chapter. During any examination conducted by counsel for the parties, the trial judge shall permit liberal and probing examination calculated to discover bias or prejudice with regard to the circumstances of the particular case before the court. The fact that a topic has been included in the trial judge's examination shall not preclude appropriate followup questioning in the same area by counsel. The trial judge shall permit counsel to conduct voir dire examination without requiring prior submission of the questions unless a particular counsel engages in improper questioning.

(2) The trial judge shall not impose specific unreasonable or arbitrary time limits or establish an inflexible time limit policy for voir dire.

(3) For purposes of this section, an "improper question" is any question that, as its dominant purpose, attempts to precondition the prospective jurors to a particular result, indoctrinate the jury, or question the prospective jurors concerning the pleadings or the applicable law.

(c) (1) In exercising the judge's sound discretion, the trial judge shall give due consideration to all of the following:

(A) The amount of time requested by trial counsel.

(B) Any unique or complex elements, legal or factual, in the case.

(C) Length of the trial.

(D) Number of parties.

(E) Number of witnesses.

(F) Whether the case is designated as a complex or long cause.

(2) As voir dire proceeds, the judge shall permit supplemental time for questioning based on any of the following:

(A) Individual responses or conduct of jurors that may evince attitudes inconsistent with suitability to serve as a fair and impartial juror in the particular case.

(B) Composition of the jury panel.

(C) An unusual number of for cause challenges.

(d) Upon the request of a party, the trial judge shall allow a brief opening statement by counsel for each party prior to the commencement of the oral questioning phase of the voir dire process.

(e) In civil cases, the trial judge may, upon stipulation by counsel for all the parties appearing in the action, permit counsel to examine the prospective jurors outside a judge's presence.

(f) A trial judge shall not arbitrarily or unreasonably refuse to submit reasonable written questionnaires, the contents of which are determined by the court in its sound discretion, when requested by counsel. If a questionnaire is utilized, the parties shall be given reasonable time to evaluate the responses to the questionnaires before oral questioning commences.

(g) To help facilitate the jury selection process, at the earliest practical time, the judge in a civil trial shall provide the parties with both the alphabetical list and the list of prospective jurors in the order in which they will be called.[734]

223. (a) To select a fair and impartial jury in a criminal jury trial, the trial

judge shall conduct an initial examination of prospective jurors. At the first practical opportunity prior to voir dire, the trial judge shall consider the form and subject matter of voir dire questions. Before voir dire by the trial judge, the parties may submit questions to the trial judge. The trial judge may include additional questions requested by the parties as the trial judge deems proper.

(b) (1) Upon completion of the trial judge's initial examination, counsel for each party shall have the right to examine, by oral and direct questioning, any of the prospective jurors. The scope of the examination conducted by counsel shall be within reasonable limits prescribed by the trial judge in the judge's sound discretion subject to the provisions of this chapter. During any examination conducted by counsel for the parties, the trial judge shall permit liberal and probing examination calculated to discover bias or prejudice with regard to the circumstances of the particular case or the parties before the court. The fact that a topic has been included in the trial judge's examination shall not preclude appropriate followup questioning in the same area by counsel. The trial judge should permit counsel to conduct voir dire examination without requiring prior submission of the questions unless a particular counsel engages in improper questioning.

(2) The trial judge shall not impose specific unreasonable or arbitrary time limits or establish an inflexible time limit policy for voir dire. As voir dire proceeds, the trial judge shall permit supplemental time for questioning based on individual responses or conduct of jurors that may evince attitudes inconsistent with suitability to serve as a fair and impartial juror in the particular case.

(3) For purposes of this section, an "improper question" is any question that, as its dominant purpose, attempts to precondition the prospective jurors to a particular result or indoctrinate the jury.

(c) In exercising the judge's sound discretion, the trial judge shall consider all of the following:

(1) The amount of time requested by trial counsel.

(2) Any unique or complex legal or factual elements in the case.

(3) The length of the trial.

(4) The number of parties.

(5) The number of witnesses.

(d) Voir dire of any prospective jurors shall, where practicable, take place in the presence of the other jurors in all criminal cases, including death penalty cases. Examination of prospective jurors shall be conducted only in aid of the exercise of challenges for cause.

(e) The trial judge shall, in his or her sound discretion, consider reasonable written questionnaires when requested by counsel. If a questionnaire is utilized, the parties shall be given reasonable time to evaluate the responses to the questionnaires before oral questioning commences.

(f) To help facilitate the jury selection process, at the earliest practical time, the trial judge in a criminal trial shall provide the parties with the list of prospective jurors in the order in which they will be called.

(g) The trial judge's exercise of discretion in the manner in which voir dire is conducted, including any limitation on the time that will be allowed for direct questioning of prospective jurors by counsel and any determination that a question is not in aid of the exercise of challenges for cause, is not cause for a conviction to be reversed, unless the exercise of that discretion results in a miscarriage of justice, as specified in Section 13 of Article VI of the California Constitution.[732]

Note: This section was added on June 5, 1990, by initiative Prop. 115 (the Crime Victims Justice Reform Act)

224. (a) If a party does not cause the removal by challenge of an individual juror who is deaf, hard of hearing, blind, visually impaired, or speech impaired and who requires auxiliary services to facilitate communication, the party shall stipulate to the presence of a service provider in the jury room during jury deliberations, and prepare and deliver to the court proposed jury instructions to the service provider.

(b) As used in this section, "service provider" includes, but is not limited to, a person who is a sign language interpreter, oral interpreter, deaf-blind interpreter, reader, or speech interpreter. If auxiliary services are required during the course of jury deliberations, the court shall instruct the jury and the service provider that the service provider for the juror with a disability is not to participate in the jury's deliberations in any manner except to facilitate communication between the juror with a disability and other jurors.

(c) The court shall appoint a service provider whose services are needed by a juror with a disability to facilitate communication or participation. A sign language interpreter, oral interpreter, or deaf-blind interpreter appointed pursuant to this section shall be a qualified interpreter, as defined in subdivision (f) of Section 754 of the Evidence Code. Service providers appointed by the court under this subdivision shall be compensated in the same manner as provided in subdivision (i) of Section 754 of the Evidence Code.[723]

225. A challenge is an objection made to the trial jurors that may be taken by any party to the action, and is of the following classes and types:

(a) A challenge to the trial jury panel for cause.

(1) A challenge to the panel may only be taken before a trial jury is sworn. The challenge shall be reduced to writing, and shall plainly and distinctly state the facts constituting the ground of challenge.

(2) Reasonable notice of the challenge to the jury panel shall be given to all parties and to the jury commissioner, by service of a copy thereof.

(3) The jury commissioner shall be permitted the services of legal counsel in connection with challenges to the jury panel.

(b) A challenge to a prospective juror by either:

(1) A challenge for cause, for one of the following reasons:

(A) General disqualification-that the juror is disqualified from serving in the action on trial.

(B) Implied bias-as, when the existence of the facts as ascertained, in judgment of law disqualifies the juror.

(C) Actual bias-the existence of a state of mind on the part of the juror in reference to the case, or to any of the parties, which will prevent the juror from acting with entire impartiality, and without prejudice to the substantial rights of any party.

(2) A peremptory challenge to a prospective juror.[261]

226. (a) A challenge to an individual juror may only be made before the jury is sworn.
(b) A challenge to an individual juror may be taken orally or may be made in writing, but no reason need be given for a peremptory challenge, and the court shall exclude any juror challenged peremptorily.
(c) All challenges for cause shall be exercised before any peremptory challenges may be exercised.
(d) All challenges to an individual juror, except a peremptory challenge, shall be taken, first by the defendants, and then by the people or plaintiffs.[261]

227. The challenges of either party for cause need not all be taken at once, but they may be taken separately, in the following order, including in each challenge all the causes of challenge belonging to the same class and type:
(a) To the panel.
(b) To an individual juror, for a general disqualification.
(c) To an individual juror, for an implied bias.
(d) To an individual juror, for an actual bias.[261]

228. Challenges for general disqualification may be taken on one or both of the following grounds, and for no other:
(a) A want of any of the qualifications prescribed by this code to render a person competent as a juror.
(b) The existence of any incapacity which satisfies the court that the challenged person is incapable of performing the duties of a juror in the particular action without prejudice to the substantial rights of the challenging party.[522]

229. A challenge for implied bias may be taken for one or more of the following causes, and for no other:
(a) Consanguinity or affinity within the fourth degree to any party, to an officer of a corporation which is a party, or to any alleged witness or victim in the case at bar.
(b) Standing in the relation of, or being the parent, spouse, or child of one who stands in the relation of, guardian and ward, conservator and conservatee, master and servant, employer and clerk, landlord and tenant, principal and agent, or debtor and creditor, to either party or to an officer of a corporation which is a party, or being a member of the family of either party; or a partner in business with either party; or surety on any bond or obligation for either party, or being the holder of bonds or shares of capital stock of a corporation which is a party; or having stood within one year previous to the filing of the complaint in the action in the relation of attorney and client with either party or with the attorney for either party. A depositor of a bank or a holder of a savings account in a savings and loan association shall not be deemed a creditor of that bank or savings and loan association for the purpose of this paragraph solely by reason of his or her being a depositor or account holder.
(c) Having served as a trial or grand juror or on a jury of inquest in a civil or criminal action or been a witness on a previous or pending trial between the same parties, or involving the same specific offense or cause of action; or having served as a trial or grand juror

or on a jury within one year previously in any criminal or civil action or proceeding in which either party was the plaintiff or defendant or in a criminal action where either party was the defendant.

(d) Interest on the part of the juror in the event of the action, or in the main question involved in the action, except his or her interest as a member or citizen or taxpayer of a county, city and county, incorporated city or town, or other political subdivision of a county, or municipal water district.

(e) Having an unqualified opinion or belief as to the merits of the action founded upon knowledge of its material facts or of some of them.

(f) The existence of a state of mind in the juror evincing enmity against, or bias towards, either party.

(g) That the juror is party to an action pending in the court for which he or she is drawn and which action is set for trial before the panel of which the juror is a member.

(h) If the offense charged is punishable with death, the entertaining of such conscientious opinions as would preclude the juror finding the defendant guilty; in which case the juror may neither be permitted nor compelled to serve.[260]

230. Challenges for cause shall be tried by the court. The juror challenged and any other person may be examined as a witness in the trial of the challenge, and shall truthfully answer all questions propounded to them.[260]

231. (a) In criminal cases, if the offense charged is punishable with death, or with imprisonment in the state prison for life, the defendant is entitled to 20 and the people to 20 peremptory challenges. Except as provided in subdivision (b), in a trial for any other offense, the defendant is entitled to 10 and the state to 10 peremptory challenges. When two or more defendants are jointly tried, their challenges shall be exercised jointly, but each defendant shall also be entitled to five additional challenges which may be exercised separately, and the people shall also be entitled to additional challenges equal to the number of all the additional separate challenges allowed the defendants.

(b) If the offense charged is punishable with a maximum term of imprisonment of 90 days or less, the defendant is entitled to six and the state to six peremptory challenges. When two or more defendants are jointly tried, their challenges shall be exercised jointly, but each defendant shall also be entitled to four additional challenges which may be exercised separately, and the state shall also be entitled to additional challenges equal to the number of all the additional separate challenges allowed the defendants.

(c) In civil cases, each party shall be entitled to six peremptory challenges. If there are more than two parties, the court shall, for the purpose of allotting peremptory challenges, divide the parties into two or more sides according to their respective interests in the issues. Each side shall be entitled to eight peremptory challenges. If there are several parties on a side, the court shall divide the challenges among them as nearly equally as possible. If there are more than two sides, the court shall grant such additional peremptory challenges to a side as the interests of jus-

tice may require, provided that the peremptory challenges of one side shall not exceed the aggregate number of peremptory challenges of all other sides. If any party on a side does not use his or her full share of peremptory challenges, the unused challenges may be used by the other party or parties on the same side.
(d) Peremptory challenges shall be taken or passed by the sides alternately, commencing with the plaintiff or people, and each party shall be entitled to have the panel full before exercising any peremptory challenge. When each side passes consecutively, the jury shall then be sworn, unless the court, for good cause, shall otherwise order. The number of peremptory challenges remaining with a side shall not be diminished by any passing of a peremptory challenge.
(e) If all the parties on both sides pass consecutively, the jury shall then be sworn, unless the court, for good cause, shall otherwise order. The number of peremptory challenges remaining with a side shall not be diminished by any passing of a peremptory challenge.
(f) This section shall become operative on January 1, 2021.[720]

231.5. A party shall not use a peremptory challenge to remove a prospective juror on the basis of an assumption that the prospective juror is biased merely because of a characteristic listed or defined in Section 11135 of the Government Code, or similar grounds.[706]

231.7. (a) A party shall not use a peremptory challenge to remove a prospective juror on the basis of the prospective juror's race, ethnicity, gender, gender identity, sexual orientation, national origin, or religious affiliation, or the perceived membership of the prospective juror in any of those groups.
(b) A party, or the trial court on its own motion, may object to the improper use of a peremptory challenge under subdivision (a). After the objection is made, any further discussion shall be conducted outside the presence of the panel. The objection shall be made before the jury is impaneled, unless information becomes known that could not have reasonably been known before the jury was impaneled.
(c) Notwithstanding Section 226, upon objection to the exercise of a peremptory challenge pursuant to this section, the party exercising the peremptory challenge shall state the reasons the peremptory challenge has been exercised.
(d) (1) The court shall evaluate the reasons given to justify the peremptory challenge in light of the totality of the circumstances. The court shall consider only the reasons actually given and shall not speculate on, or assume the existence of, other possible justifications for the use of the peremptory challenge. If the court determines there is a substantial likelihood that an objectively reasonable person would view race, ethnicity, gender, gender identity, sexual orientation, national origin, or religious affiliation, or perceived membership in any of those groups, as a factor in the use of the peremptory challenge, then the objection shall be sustained. The court need not find purposeful discrimination to sustain the objection. The court shall explain the reasons for its ruling on the record. A motion brought under this

section shall also be deemed a sufficient presentation of claims asserting the discriminatory exclusion of jurors in violation of the United States and California Constitutions.

(2) (A) For purposes of this section, an objectively reasonable person is aware that unconscious bias, in addition to purposeful discrimination, have resulted in the unfair exclusion of potential jurors in the State of California.

(B) For purposes of this section, a "substantial likelihood" means more than a mere possibility but less than a standard of more likely than not.

(C) For purposes of this section, "unconscious bias" includes implicit and institutional biases.

(3) In making its determination, the circumstances the court may consider include, but are not limited to, any of the following:

(A) Whether any of the following circumstances exist:

(i) The objecting party is a member of the same perceived cognizable group as the challenged juror.

(ii) The alleged victim is not a member of that perceived cognizable group.

(iii) Witnesses or the parties are not members of that perceived cognizable group.

(B) Whether race, ethnicity, gender, gender identity, sexual orientation, national origin, or religious affiliation, or perceived membership in any of those groups, bear on the facts of the case to be tried.

(C) The number and types of questions posed to the prospective juror, including, but not limited to, any of the following:

(i) Consideration of whether the party exercising the peremptory challenge failed to question the prospective juror about the concerns later stated by the party as the reason for the peremptory challenge pursuant to subdivision (c).

(ii) Whether the party exercising the peremptory challenge engaged in cursory questioning of the challenged potential juror.

(iii) Whether the party exercising the peremptory challenge asked different questions of the potential juror against whom the peremptory challenge was used in contrast to questions asked of other jurors from different perceived cognizable groups about the same topic or whether the party phrased those questions differently.

(D) Whether other prospective jurors, who are not members of the same cognizable group as the challenged prospective juror, provided similar, but not necessarily identical, answers but were not the subject of a peremptory challenge by that party.

(E) Whether a reason might be disproportionately associated with a race, ethnicity, gender, gender identity, sexual orientation, national origin, or religious affiliation, or perceived membership in any of those groups.

(F) Whether the reason given by the party exercising the peremptory challenge was contrary to or unsupported by the record.

(G) Whether counsel or counsel's office, if it is a public entity, exercising the challenge has used peremptory challenges disproportionately against a given race, ethnicity, gender, gender identity, sexual orientation, national origin, or religious affiliation, or perceived membership in any of those groups, in the present case or in past cases, including whether the counsel or counsel's office, if it is a public entity, who made the challenge has a history of prior violations under Batson v. Kentucky (1986) 476 U.S. 79, People v. Wheeler (1978) 22 Cal.3d 258, Section 231.5, or this section.

(e) A peremptory challenge for any of the following reasons is presumed to be invalid unless the party exercising the peremptory challenge can show by clear and convincing evidence that an objectively reasonable person would view the rationale as unrelated to a prospective juror's race, ethnicity, gender, gender identity, sexual orientation, national origin, or religious affiliation, or perceived membership in any of those groups, and that the reasons articulated bear on the prospective juror's ability to be fair and impartial in the case:

(1) Expressing a distrust of or having a negative experience with law enforcement or the criminal legal system.

(2) Expressing a belief that law enforcement officers engage in racial profiling or that criminal laws have been enforced in a discriminatory manner.

(3) Having a close relationship with people who have been stopped, arrested, or convicted of a crime.

(4) A prospective juror's neighborhood.

(5) Having a child outside of marriage.

(6) Receiving state benefits.

(7) Not being a native English speaker.

(8) The ability to speak another language.

(9) Dress, attire, or personal appearance.

(10) Employment in a field that is disproportionately occupied by members listed in subdivision (a) or that serves a population disproportionately comprised of members of a group or groups listed in subdivision (a).

(11) Lack of employment or underemployment of the prospective juror or prospective juror's family member.

(12) A prospective juror's apparent friendliness with another prospective juror of the same group as listed in subdivision (a).

(13) Any justification that is similarly applicable to a questioned prospective juror or jurors, who are not members of the same cognizable group as the challenged prospective juror, but were not the subject of a peremptory challenge by that party. The unchallenged prospective juror or jurors need not share any other characteristics with the challenged prospective juror for peremptory challenge relying on this justification to be considered presumptively invalid.

(f) For purposes of subdivision (e), the term "clear and convincing" refers to the degree of certainty the factfinder must have in determining whether the reasons given for the exercise of a peremptory challenge are unrelated to the prospective juror's cognizable group membership, bearing in mind conscious and unconscious bias. To determine that a presumption of invalidity has been overcome, the factfinder shall determine that it is highly probable that the reasons given for the exercise of a peremptory challenge are unrelated to conscious or unconscious bias and are instead specific to the juror and bear on that juror's ability to be fair and impartial in the case.

(g) (1) The following reasons for peremptory challenges have historically been associated with improper discrimination in jury selection:

(A) The prospective juror was inattentive, or staring or failing to make eye contact.

(B) The prospective juror exhibited either a lack of rapport or problematic attitude, body language, or demeanor.

(C) The prospective juror provided unintelligent or confused answers.

(2) The reasons set forth in paragraph (1) are presumptively invalid unless the trial court is able to confirm that the asserted behavior occurred, based on the court's own observations or the observations of counsel for the objecting party. Even with that confirmation, the counsel offering the reason shall explain why the asserted demeanor, behavior, or manner in which the prospective juror answered questions matters to the case to be tried.

(h) Upon a court granting an objection to the improper exercise of a peremptory challenge, the court shall do one or more of the following:

(1) Quash the jury venire and start jury selection anew. This remedy shall be provided if requested by the objecting party.

(2) If the motion is granted after the jury has been impaneled, declare a mistrial and select a new jury if requested by the defendant.

(3) Seat the challenged juror.

(4) Provide the objecting party additional challenges.

(5) Provide another remedy as the court deems appropriate.

(i) This section applies in all jury trials in which jury selection begins on or after January 1, 2022.

(j) The denial of an objection made under this section shall be reviewed by the appellate court de novo, with the trial court's express factual findings reviewed for substantial evidence. The appellate court shall not impute to the trial court any findings, including findings of a prospective juror's demeanor, that the trial court did not expressly state on the record. The reviewing court shall consider only reasons actually given under subdivision (c) and shall not speculate as to or consider reasons that were not given to explain either the party's use of the peremptory challenge or the party's failure to challenge similarly situated jurors who are not members of the same cognizable group as the challenged juror, regardless of whether the moving party made a comparative analysis argument in the trial court. Should the appellate court determine that the objection was erroneously denied, that error shall be deemed prejudicial, the judgment shall be reversed, and the case remanded for a new trial.

(k) (1) Except as specified in paragraph (2), this section shall not apply to civil cases.

(2) This section shall apply in the following civil cases:

(A) Civil cases involving a civil rights violation, including the following:

(i) Actions alleging a violation against a protected class enumerated in subdivision (a).

(ii) Actions alleging a violation of the Tom Bane Civil Rights Act (Section 52.1 of the Civil Code) or the Unruh Civil Rights Act (Section 51 of the Civil Code).

(iii) Actions alleging a violation pursuant to Section 1983 of Title 42 of the United States Code.

(iv) Actions alleging a violation of Title VI of the federal Civil Rights Act of 1964 (42 U.S.C. Sec. 2000d, et seq.), the federal Voting Rights Act of 1965 (52 U.S.C. Sec. 10301 et seq.), or the federal Fair Housing Act (42 U.S.C. Sec. 3601 et seq.).

(v) Actions alleging a violation of the California Fair Employment and Housing Act (Part 2.8 (commencing with Section 12900) of Division 3 of Title 2 of the Government Code), including, but not limited to, actions alleging discrimination, harassment, or retaliation.

(B) Actions for the civil commitment of a person, including a person who is determined to be a sexually violent predator pursuant to Article 4 (commencing with Section 6600) of Chapter 2 of Part 2 of Division 6 of the Welfare and Institutions Code.

(C) Civil cases for damages arising from a hate crime.

(l) For civil cases governed under paragraph (2) of subdivision (k), the party bringing the claim described in paragraph (2) of subdivision (k) shall notify the court and the other party or parties, after the final status conference, or, if no final status conference is held, at least 15 calendar days before the date of the trial, that the procedures under this section apply.

(m) It is the intent of the Legislature that enactment of this section shall not, in purpose or effect, lower the standard for judging challenges for cause or expand use of challenges for cause.

(n) The provisions of this section are severable. If any provision of this section or its application is held invalid, that invalidity shall not affect other provisions or applications that can be given effect without the invalid provision or application.[778]

232. (a) Prior to the examination of prospective trial jurors in the panel assigned for voir dire, the following perjury acknowledgment and agreement shall be obtained from the panel, which shall be acknowledged by the prospective jurors with the statement "I do":

"Do you understand and agree, under penalty of perjury, that you will accurately and truthfully answer all questions about your qualifications and ability to serve as a juror in this case, and that failure to do so may result in criminal prosecution?"

(b) As soon as the selection of the trial jury is completed, the following acknowledgment and agreement shall be obtained from the trial jurors, which shall be acknowledged by the statement "I do":

"Do you understand and agree that you will carefully consider the case being heard in this court, and that you will reach a verdict based only on the evidence presented to you and the instructions on the law given by the court?"[872]

233. If, before the jury has returned its verdict to the court, a juror becomes sick or, upon other good cause shown to the court, is found to be unable to perform his or her duty, the court may order the juror to be discharged. If any alternate jurors have been selected as provided by law, one of them shall then be designated by the court to take

the place of the juror so discharged. If after all alternate jurors have been made regular jurors or if there is no alternate juror, a juror becomes sick or otherwise unable to perform the juror's duty and has been discharged by the court as provided in this section, the jury shall be discharged and a new jury then or afterwards impaneled, and the cause may again be tried. Alternatively, with the consent of all parties, the trial may proceed with only the remaining jurors, or another juror may be sworn and the trial begin anew.[260]

234. Whenever, in the opinion of a judge of a superior court about to try a civil or criminal action or proceeding, the trial is likely to be a protracted one, or upon stipulation of the parties, the court may cause an entry to that effect to be made in the minutes of the court and thereupon, immediately after the jury is impaneled and sworn, the court may direct the calling of one or more additional jurors, in its discretion, to be known as "alternate jurors."

These alternate jurors shall be drawn from the same source, and in the same manner, and have the same qualifications, as the jurors already sworn, and shall be subject to the same examination and challenges. However, each side, or each defendant, as provided in Section 231, shall be entitled to as many peremptory challenges to the alternate jurors as there are alternate jurors called.

The alternate jurors shall be seated so as to have equal power and facilities for seeing and hearing the proceedings in the case, and shall take the same oath as the jurors already selected, and shall, unless excused by the court, attend at all times upon the trial of the cause in company with the other jurors, but shall not participate in deliberation unless ordered by the court, and for a failure to do so are liable to be punished for contempt.

They shall obey the orders of and be bound by the admonition of the court, upon each adjournment of the court; but if the regular jurors are ordered to be kept in the custody of the sheriff or marshal during the trial of the cause, the alternate jurors shall also be kept in confinement with the other jurors; and upon final submission of the case to the jury, the alternate jurors shall be kept in the custody of the sheriff or marshal who shall not suffer any communication to be made to them except by order of the court, and shall not be discharged until the original jurors are discharged, except as provided in this section.

If at any time, whether before or after the final submission of the case to the jury, a juror dies or becomes ill, or upon other good cause shown to the court is found to be unable to perform his or her duty, or if a juror requests a discharge and good cause appears therefor, the court may order the juror to be discharged and draw the name of an alternate, who shall then take his or her place in the jury box, and be subject to the same rules and regulations as though he or she had been selected as one of the original jurors.

All laws relative to fees, expenses, and mileage or transportation of jurors shall be applicable to alternate jurors, except that in civil cases the sums for fees and mileage or transportation need not be deposited until the judge directs alternate jurors to be impaneled.[632]

235. At the request of the sheriff, coroner, or other ministerial officer, the jury commissioner shall provide such prospective jurors as may be required to form a jury of inquest. Prospective jurors so provided shall be selected, obligated, and compensated in the same manner as other jurors selected under the provisions of this chapter.[260]

236. When six or more prospective jurors of inquest attend, they shall be sworn by the coroner to inquire who the person was, and when, where, and by what means the person came to his or her death, to inquire into the circumstances attending the death, and to render a true verdict thereon, according to the evidence offered them or arising from the inspection of the body.[260]

237. (a) (1) The names of qualified jurors drawn from the qualified juror list for the superior court shall be made available to the public upon request unless the court determines that a compelling interest, as defined in subdivision (b), requires that this information should be kept confidential or its use limited in whole or in part.

(2) Upon the recording of a jury's verdict in a criminal jury proceeding, the court's record of personal juror identifying information of trial jurors, as defined in Section 194, consisting of names, addresses, and telephone numbers, shall be sealed until further order of the court as provided by this section.

(3) For purposes of this section, "sealed" or "sealing" means extracting or otherwise removing the personal juror identifying information from the court record.

(4) This subdivision applies only to cases in which a jury verdict was returned on or after January 1, 1996.

(b) Any person may petition the court for access to these records. The petition shall be supported by a declaration that includes facts sufficient to establish good cause for the release of the juror's personal identifying information. The court shall set the matter for hearing if the petition and supporting declaration establish a prima facie showing of good cause for the release of the personal juror identifying information, but shall not set the matter for hearing if there is a showing on the record of facts that establish a compelling interest against disclosure. A compelling interest includes, but is not limited to, protecting jurors from threats or danger of physical harm. If the court does not set the matter for hearing, the court shall by minute order set forth the reasons and make express findings either of a lack of a prima facie showing of good cause or the presence of a compelling interest against disclosure.

(c) If a hearing is set pursuant to subdivision (b), the petitioner shall provide notice of the petition and the time and place of the hearing at least 20 days prior to the date of the hearing to the parties in the criminal action. The court shall provide notice to each affected former juror by personal service or by first-class mail, addressed to the last known address of the former juror as shown in the records of the court. In a capital case, the petitioner shall also serve notice on the Attorney General. Any affected former juror may appear in person, in writing, by telephone, or by counsel to protest the granting of the petition. A former juror who wishes to appear at the hearing to oppose the unsealing of the personal juror identifying information may request the court to close the hearing in order to protect the former juror's anonymity.

(d) After the hearing, the records shall be made available as requested in the petition, unless a former juror's protest to the granting of the petition is sustained. The court shall sustain the protest of the former juror if, in the discretion of the court, the petitioner fails to show good cause, the record establishes the presence of a compelling interest against disclosure as defined in subdivision (b), or the juror is unwilling to be contacted by the petitioner. The court shall set forth reasons and make express findings to support the granting or denying of the petition to disclose. The court may require the person to whom disclosure is made, or his or her agent or employee, to agree not to divulge jurors' identities or identifying information to others; the court may otherwise limit disclosure in any manner it deems appropriate.

(e) Any court employee who has legal access to personal juror identifying information sealed under subdivision (a), who discloses the information, knowing it to be a violation of this section or a court order issued under this section, is guilty of a misdemeanor.

(f) Any person who intentionally solicits another to unlawfully access or disclose personal juror identifying information contained in records sealed under subdivision (a), knowing that the records have been sealed, or who, knowing that the information was unlawfully secured, intentionally discloses it to another person is guilty of a misdemeanor.[364]

242. (a) Following the receipt of a verdict and before discharging the jury in a criminal action or proceeding alleging a violent felony, the court shall provide written information to the trial jurors about mental health awareness, including information about stress relief and symptoms that may be experienced following exposure to trauma.

(b) Following the receipt of a verdict in a criminal action or proceeding alleging a violent felony, the court shall distribute, in a manner determined by the court, information to the alternate jurors who have been discharged from their duty about mental health awareness, including information about stress relief and symptoms that may be experienced following exposure to trauma.

(c) At the conclusion of a criminal action or proceeding alleging a violent felony in which evidence was presented, but a verdict was not rendered by the jury, the court shall provide written information about mental health awareness, including information about stress relief and symptoms that may be experienced following exposure to trauma, before discharging the jury and alternate jurors. The information shall only be provided after the jurors and alternate jurors are no longer responsible for rendering a verdict in the trial.

(d) The court may share this information with jurors and alternate jurors following the conclusion of a criminal action or proceeding alleging an offense that is not a violent felony.

(e) The Judicial Council shall develop the written educational information that the court shall print and distribute pursuant to this section. The information shall include, but shall not be limited to, the signs and symptoms of distress, healthy coping mechanisms, and how to seek help for exposure to trauma if needed.

(f) For the purposes of this section, "violent felony" has the same definition as in subdivision (c) of Section 667.5 of the Penal Code.[844]

Chapter 2: Court Commissioners

Chapter 2 added by Code Amendments 1880, Ch. 35.

259. Subject to the supervision of the court, every court commissioner shall have power to do all of the following:

(a) Hear and determine ex parte motions for orders and alternative writs and writs of habeas corpus in the superior court for which the court commissioner is appointed.

(b) Take proof and make and report findings thereon as to any matter of fact upon which information is required by the court. Any party to any contested proceeding may except to the report and the subsequent order of the court made thereon within five days after written notice of the court's action. A copy of the exceptions shall be filed and served upon opposing party or counsel within the five days. The party may argue any exceptions before the court on giving notice of motion for that purpose within 10 days from entry thereof. After a hearing before the court on the exceptions, the court may sustain, or set aside, or modify its order.

(c) Take and approve any bonds and undertakings in actions or proceedings, and determine objections to the bonds and undertakings.

(d) Act as temporary judge when otherwise qualified so to act and when appointed for that purpose, on stipulation of the parties litigant. While acting as temporary judge the commissioner shall receive no compensation therefor other than compensation as commissioner.

(e) Hear and report findings and conclusions to the court for approval, rejection, or change, all preliminary matters including motions or petitions for the custody and support of children, the allowance of temporary spousal support, costs and attorneys' fees, and issues of fact in contempt proceedings in proceedings for support, dissolution of marriage, nullity of marriage, or legal separation.

(f) Hear actions to establish paternity and to establish or enforce child and spousal support pursuant to subdivision (a) of Section 4251 of the Family Code.

(g) Hear, report on, and determine all uncontested actions and proceedings subject to the requirements of subdivision (d).[541]

TITLE 4: MINISTERIAL OFFICERS OF COURTS OF JUSTICE

Title 4 repealed and added by Code Amendments 1880, Ch. 35.

Chapter 1: Of Ministerial Officers Generally

Chapter 1 added by Code Amendments 1880, Ch. 35.

262. The direction or authority of a party or his or her attorney to a sheriff, in respect to the execution of process or return thereof, or to any related act or omission, is not available to discharge or excuse the sheriff from a liability for neglect or misconduct, unless it is contained in written instructions by the attorney of the party, including the signature and name of the attorney of the party, or by the party, if he or

she has no attorney. Subject to subdivision (c) of Section 263, the instructions may be transmitted electronically pursuant to Chapter 2 (commencing with Section 263).[637]

262.1. A sheriff or other ministerial officer is justified in the execution of, and shall execute, all process and orders regular on their face and issued by competent authority, whatever may be the defect in the proceedings upon which they were issued.[28]

262.2. Except as otherwise provided, the officer executing process shall, so long as he or she retains the original process, show it to any interested person, upon request. The officer shall show the process, with all papers, or electronic copies of all papers, attached, at his or her office whenever the office is open for business.[638]

262.3. When any process remains with the sheriff unexecuted, in whole or in part, at the time of his death, resignation of office, or at the expiration of his term of office, such process shall be executed by his successor or successors in office.[28]

262.4. If the sheriff sells real estate, under and by virtue of an execution or order of court, the sheriff, or his or her successors in office, shall execute and deliver to the purchaser or purchasers all deeds and conveyances required by law and necessary for the purpose, and those deeds and conveyances shall be valid in law as if they had been executed by the sheriff who made the sale. The deeds and conveyances may be recorded electronically pursuant to Chapter 2 (commencing with Section 263) if they comply with the Electronic Recording Delivery Act of 2004 (Article 6 (commencing with Section 27390) of Chapter 6 of Part 3 of Division 2 of Title 3 of the Government Code).[639]

262.5. Service of a paper, other than process, upon the sheriff may be made by delivering it to him or to one of his deputies, or to a person in charge of the office during office hours, or, if no such person is there, by leaving it in a conspicuous place in the office.[28]

262.6. When the sheriff is a party to an action or proceeding, the process and orders therein, which it would otherwise be the duty of the sheriff to execute, shall be executed by the coroner of the county.[28]

262.7. If an action is begun against a sheriff, all process and orders may be served by any person in the manner provided in this code.[703]

262.8. Process or orders in an action or proceeding may be executed by a person residing in the county, designated by the court, or the judge thereof, and denominated an elisor, in the following cases:

(a) When the sheriff and coroner are both parties.

(b) When either of these officers is a party, and the process is against the other.

(c) When either of these officers is a party, and there is a vacancy in the office of the other, or where it appears, by affidavit, to the satisfaction of the court in which the proceeding is pending, or the judge thereof, that both of these officers are disqualified, or by reason of any bias, prejudice, or other cause would not act promptly or impartially.[28]

262.9. When process is delivered to an elisor, he shall execute and return it in the same manner as the sheriff is required to execute similar process.[28]

262.10. Whenever process is executed, or any act performed by a coroner or elisor, he shall receive a reasonable compensation, to be fixed by the court, to be paid by the plaintiff in case of the summoning of jurors to complete the panel, and by the person or party requiring the service in all other cases in private action. If rendered at the instance of the people, it shall be audited and paid as a county charge.[28]

262.11. In all cases where new counties have been or may hereafter be created, and executions, orders of sale upon foreclosures of mortgages, or other process affecting specific real estate have been or may hereafter be adjudged by the final judgment or decree of a court of competent jurisdiction, to be executed by the sheriff of the county in which such real estate was originally situated, such process may be executed by the sheriff of the new county in which such real estate is found to be situated, with the like effect as if he were the sheriff of the county designated in the judgment, decree, or order of sale to execute the same.[33]

Chapter 2: Levying Officer Electronic Transactions Act

Chapter 2 added by Stats. 2010, Ch. 680, Sec. 4.

263. (a) This chapter may be cited as the Levying Officer Electronic Transactions Act.
(b) The Legislature finds and declares that modern technologies offer alternatives to paper-based systems and provide the means to create, store, retrieve, and transmit records and documents in electronic form resulting in increased efficiency, taxpayer savings, and improved public access to levying officers. It is the intent of the Legislature in enacting this act to accommodate current and future technologies based on industry standards.
(c) Nothing in this chapter shall be construed to require a court or levying officer to comply with any of its provisions unless the court and the levying officer have (1) jointly determined that both the court and the sheriff's department have the resources and the technological capacity to do so, and (2) have mutually agreed to electronically act upon documents as provided in this chapter.[640]

263.1. As used in this chapter, the following terms have the following definitions:
(a) "Electronic mail" or "e-mail" means an electronic message that is sent to an e-mail address and transmitted between two or more telecommunications devices, computers, or electronic devices capable of receiving electronic messages through a local, regional, or global computer network, whether or not the message is converted to hard copy format after receipt, viewed upon transmission, or stored for later retrieval.
(b) "Electronic record" means a document or record created, generated, sent, communicated, received, or stored by electronic means.
(c) "Electronic signature" means an electronic sound, symbol, or process attached to, or logically associated with, an electronic record and executed or adopted by a person with the intent to sign the electronic record.

(d) "Fax" is an abbreviation for "facsimile" and refers, as indicated by the context, to a facsimile transmission or to a document so transmitted.
(e) "Fax machine" means a machine that can send and receive a facsimile transmission using industry standards and includes a fax modem connected to a computer.
(f) "Fax transmission" means the electronic transmission and reconstruction of a document that prints a duplicate of the original document at the receiving end. "Fax transmission" includes, but is not limited to, the use of a facsimile machine or the process of integrating an electronic fax software application to automate the sending and receiving of a faxed document as an electronic record, in portable data format, by e-mail or similar electronic means.
(g) "Information processing system" means an electronic system for creating, generating, sending, receiving, storing, displaying, retrieving, or processing information, but does not include a fax machine.
(h) "Instructions" and "levying officer instructions" mean a written request to a levying officer to serve process, perform a levy, execute an arrest warrant, or perform some other act.
(i) "Legal entity" means the legal form of an artificial person and includes a corporation, defunct corporation, unincorporated association, partnership, public agency, limited liability company, joint stock company or association, and limited liability partnership.
(j) "Levying officer" means the sheriff or marshal acting as a ministerial officer pursuant to Section 26608 of the Government Code.
(k) "Record" means information that is inscribed on a tangible medium, or that is stored in an electronic or other medium and is retrievable in perceivable form.
(l) "Transmission record" means the electronic record or document printed by the sending fax machine, stating the telephone number of the receiving fax machine, the number of pages sent, the transmission time and date, and an indication of any errors in transmission.[640]

263.2. (a) A levying officer may utilize an information processing system to create, generate, send, receive, store, display, retrieve, or process information, electronic records, and documents when based on industry standards and only to the extent that the levying officer has the resources and technological capacity to do so.
(b) If a technical problem with the levying officer's system prevents the levying officer from receiving an electronic transmission during regular business hours on a particular court day, and the electronic sender demonstrates an attempt to electronically transmit the document on that day, the levying officer shall deem the document or record as filed on that day.[640]

263.3. Whenever the fax transmission of a document or record to a levying officer is authorized pursuant to this chapter, all of the following shall apply:
(a) A levying officer may act upon an electronic record or document transmitted by a facsimile machine in the same manner as the paper record or document upon which the electronic record or document is based.

(b) A facsimile cover sheet shall accompany the faxed record or document and include all of the following information:

(1) The name of the sender.

(2) The fax number of the sender.

(3) The name of the levying officer.

(4) The fax number of the levying officer.

(5) A description of the record or document, including its name, if any, and the number of pages.

(6) A statement directing the recipient of the faxed document or record to fax to the sender a confirmation, if true, that the fax was properly received.

(c) A person authorized to fax a record or document to the levying officer pursuant to this chapter shall do all of the following:

(1) Retain the paper version of the record or document.

(2) Print or otherwise retain a transmission record of the fax transmission.

(3) Deliver the paper version of the record, document, or transmission record to the levying officer within five days after a request to do so has been mailed to the sender by the levying officer.

(d) The levying officer shall retain the facsimile cover sheet together with the faxed record or document.

(e) The levying officer may electronically copy and store the printed cover sheet, record, or document as an electronic record.[640]

263.4. (a) A levying officer may create, store, print, or transmit an electronic record in the place of, and in the same manner as, the paper record or document upon which the electronic record is based.

(b) An electronic record transmitted to a levying officer shall be accompanied by all of the following information:

(1) The name of the sender.

(2) The electronic address of the sender.

(3) The name of the levying officer.

(4) The electronic address or fax number of the levying officer.

(c) The person transmitting the electronic record shall do both of the following:

(1) Retain the paper version of the record or document.

(2) Deliver the paper version of the record or document to the levying officer within five days after a request to do so has been mailed to the sender by the levying officer.

(d) For the purpose of this section, "transmission" of an electronic record includes sending the electronic record included in, or in conjunction with, an electronic mail message, as defined in Section 263.1.[640]

263.6. (a) In lieu of returning to court the paper version of an original writ of execution, the levying officer may retain the original writ or an electronic copy of the original writ and file only a return of the levying officer's actions.

(b) If the original writ is not returned to court as provided in subdivision (a), the levying officer shall retain, for not less than two years after the levying officer's return is filed with court, each of the following, as applicable:

(1) The original paper writ or digital image of the writ.

(2) The memorandum of garnishee.

(3) The employer's return.

(4) An inventory of the levied property.

(c) A creditor seeking the issuance of a writ directed to another county may direct the levying officer to file an accounting of the levying officer's actions with the court.

(1) The filing of the accounting described in this subdivision does not constitute a return of the writ.

(2) The accounting shall indicate that the levying officer is in possession of an active writ.[640]

263.7. (a) A levying officer shall exclude or redact the following identifiers from any record or document made available to the public:

(1) Social security number.

(2) Financial account number.

(b) If an identifier is redacted, only the last four digits of the number may be used.

(c) A levying officer also shall exclude or redact the identifiers listed in subdivision (a) from any writ return filed with the court.

(d) The term "public" does not include the creditor, debtor, garnishee, or third-party claimant.[640]

Chapter 3: Phonographic Reporters

Chapter 3 added by Code Amendments 1880, Ch. 35.

269. (a) An official reporter or official reporter pro tempore of the superior court shall take down in shorthand all testimony, objections made, rulings of the court, exceptions taken, arraignments, pleas, sentences, arguments of the attorneys to the jury, and statements and remarks made and oral instructions given by the judge or other judicial officer, in the following cases:

(1) In a civil case, on the order of the court or at the request of a party.

(2) In a felony case, on the order of the court or at the request of the prosecution, the defendant, or the attorney for the defendant.

(3) In a misdemeanor or infraction case, on the order of the court.

(b) If a transcript is ordered by the court or requested by a party, or if a nonparty requests a transcript that the nonparty is entitled to receive, regardless of whether the nonparty was permitted to attend the proceeding to be transcribed, the official reporter or official reporter pro tempore shall, within a reasonable time after the trial of the case that the court designates, write the transcripts out, or the specific portions thereof as may be requested, in plain and legible longhand, or by typewriter, or other printing machine, and certify that the transcripts were correctly reported and transcribed, and when directed by the court, file the transcripts with the clerk of the court.

(c) If a defendant is convicted of a felony, after a trial on the merits, the record on appeal shall be prepared immediately after the verdict or finding of guilt is announced unless the court determines that it is likely that no appeal from the decision will be made. The court's determination of a likelihood of appeal shall be based upon standards and rules adopted by the Judicial Council.[478]

271. (a) An official reporter or official reporter pro tempore shall deliver a transcript in electronic form, in compliance with the California Rules of Court, to any court, party, or person entitled to the transcript, unless any of the following apply:

(1) The party or person entitled to the transcript requests the reporter's transcript in paper form.

(2) Prior to January 1, 2023, the court

lacks the technical ability to use or store a transcript in electronic form pursuant to this section and provides advance notice of this fact to the official reporter or official reporter pro tempore.

(3) Prior to January 1, 2023, the official reporter or official reporter pro tempore lacks the technical ability to deliver a transcript in electronic form pursuant to this section and provides advance notice of this fact to the court, party, or person entitled to the transcript.

(b) If a paper transcript is delivered in lieu of an electronic transcript described in subdivision (a), within 120 days of the official reporter or official reporter pro tempore filing or delivering the paper transcript, the official reporter or official reporter pro tempore shall provide, upon request, a copy of the original transcript in full text-searchable portable document format (PDF) if the proceedings were produced with computer-aided transcription equipment. The copy of the original transcript in full text-searchable PDF format shall not be deemed to be an original transcript.

(c) Nothing in this section changes any requirement set forth in Section 69950 or 69954 of the Government Code, regardless of whether a transcript is delivered in electronic or paper form.

(d) Except as provided in subdivision (b), an electronic transcript delivered in accordance with this section shall be deemed to be an original transcript for all purposes, including any obligation of an attorney to maintain or deliver a file to a client.

(e) An electronic transcript shall comply with any format requirement imposed pursuant to subdivision (a). However, an official reporter or official reporter pro tempore shall not be required to use a specific vendor, technology, or software to comply with this section, unless the official reporter or official reporter pro tempore agrees with the court, party, or person entitled to the transcript to use a specific vendor, technology, or software. Absent that agreement, an official reporter or official reporter pro tempore may select the vendor, technology, and software to comply with this section and the California Rules of Court. In adopting transcript format requirements for the California Rules of Court, consideration shall be given on a technology-neutral basis to the availability of relevant vendors of transcript products, technologies, and software.

(f) After January 1, 2023, if new or updated rule of court format requirements for electronic transcripts necessitate a significant change in equipment or software owned by official reporters or official reporters pro tempore, the official reporters and official reporters pro tempore shall be given no less than one year to comply with the format requirements. If the change is necessary to address a security issue, then a reasonable time shall be given to comply with the new format requirements.[735]

273. (a) The report of the official reporter, or official reporter pro tempore, of any court, duly appointed and sworn, when transcribed and certified as being a correct transcript of the testimony and proceedings in the case, is prima facie evidence of that testimony and proceedings.

(b) The report of the official reporter, or official reporter pro tempore, of any court, duly appointed and sworn,

when prepared as a rough draft transcript, shall not be certified and cannot be used, cited, distributed, or transcribed as the official certified transcript of the proceedings. A rough draft transcript shall not be cited or used in any way or at any time to rebut or contradict the official certified transcript of the proceedings as provided by the official reporter or official reporter pro tempore. The production of a rough draft transcript shall not be required.
(c) This section shall become operative on January 1, 2022.[614]

274a. Any judge of the superior court may have any opinion given or rendered by the judge in the trial of a felony case or an unlimited civil case, pending in that court, or any necessary order, petition, citation, commitment or judgment in any probate proceeding, proceeding concerning new or additional bonds of county officials or juvenile court proceeding, or the testimony or judgment relating to the custody or support of minor children in any proceeding in which the custody or support of minor children is involved, taken down in shorthand and transcribed together with such copies as the court may deem necessary by the official reporter or an official reporter pro tempore of the court.[499]

TITLE 5: PERSONS SPECIALLY INVESTED WITH MINISTERIAL POWERS RELATING TO COURTS OF JUSTICE

Title 5 repealed and added by Code Amendments 1880, Ch. 35.

Chapter 1: Attorneys and Counselors at Law

Chapter 1 added by Code Amendments 1880, Ch. 35.

283. An attorney and counselor shall have authority:
1. To bind his client in any of the steps of an action or proceeding by his agreement filed with the Clerk, or entered upon the minutes of the Court, and not otherwise;
2. To receive money claimed by his client in an action or proceeding during the pendency thereof, or after judgment, unless a revocation of his authority is filed, and upon the payment thereof, and not otherwise, to discharge the claim or acknowledge satisfaction of the judgment.[6]

284. The attorney in an action or special proceeding may be changed at any time before or after judgment or final determination, as follows:
1. Upon the consent of both client and attorney, filed with the clerk, or entered upon the minutes;
2. Upon the order of the court, upon the application of either client or attorney, after notice from one to the other.[66]

285. When an attorney is changed, as provided in the last section, written notice of the change and of the substitution of a new attorney, or of the appearance of the party in person, must be given to the adverse party. Until

then he must recognize the former attorney.[6]

285.1. An attorney of record for any party in any civil action or proceeding for dissolution of marriage, legal separation, or for a declaration of void or voidable marriage, or for the support, maintenance or custody of minor children may withdraw at any time subsequent to the time when any judgment in such action or proceeding, other than an interlocutory judgment, becomes final, and prior to service upon him of pleadings or motion papers in any proceeding then pending in said cause, by filing a notice of withdrawal. Such notice shall state (a) date of entry of final decree or judgment, (b) the last known address of such party, (c) that such attorney withdraws as attorney for such party. A copy of such notice shall be mailed to such party at his last known address and shall be served upon the adverse party.[70]

285.2. If a reduction in public funding for legal service materially impairs a legal service agency attorney's ability to represent an indigent client, the court, on its own motion or on the motion of either the client or attorney, shall permit the withdrawal of such attorney upon a showing that all of the following apply:
(a) There are not adequate public funds to continue the effective representation of the indigent client.
(b) A good faith effort was made to find alternate representation for such client.
(c) All reasonable steps to reduce the legal prejudice to the client have been taken.
A showing of indigency of the client, in and of itself, will not be deemed sufficient cause to deny the application for withdrawal.[190]

285.3. The court, upon the granting of a motion for withdrawal pursuant to Section 285.2, may toll the running of any statute of limitations, filing requirement, statute providing for mandatory dismissal, notice of appeal, or discovery requirement, for a period not to exceed 90 days, on the court's own motion or on motion of any party or attorney, when the court finds that tolling is required to avoid legal prejudice caused by the withdrawal of the legal service agency attorney.[191]

285.4. The court, upon the granting of a motion for withdrawal pursuant to Section 285.2, may appoint any member of the bar or any law firm or professional law corporation to represent the indigent client without compensation, upon a showing of good cause. Nothing herein shall preclude the appointed attorney from recovering any attorneys' fees and costs to which the client may be entitled by law. In determining the existence of good cause, the court may consider, but is not limited to, the following factors:
(a) The probable merit of the client's claim.
(b) The client's financial ability to pay for legal services.
(c) The availability of alternative legal representation.
(d) The need for legal representation to avoid irreparable legal prejudice to the indigent client.
(e) The ability of appointed counsel to effectively represent the indigent client.

(f) Present and recent pro bono work of the appointed attorney, law firm or private law corporation.
(g) The ability of the indigent client to represent himself.
(h) The workload of the appointed attorney.[192]

286. When an attorney dies, or is removed or suspended, or ceases to act as such, a party to an action, for whom he was acting as attorney, must, before any further proceedings are had against him, be required by the adverse party, by written notice, to appoint another attorney, or to appear in person.[6]

PART 2:
OF CIVIL ACTIONS

PART 2 ENACTED 1872.
SECTION 307 – 709.030.

TITLE 1: OF THE FORM OF CIVIL ACTIONS

Title 1 enacted 1872.

307. There is in this State but one form of civil actions for the enforcement or protection of private rights and the redress or prevention of private wrongs.[1]

308. In such action the party complaining is known as the plaintiff, and the adverse party as the defendant.[1]

309. A question of fact not put in issue by the pleadings may be tried by a jury, upon an order for the trial, stating distinctly and plainly the question of fact to be tried; and such order is the only authority necessary for a trial.[1]

TITLE 2: OF THE TIME OF COMMENCING CIVIL ACTIONS

Title 2 enacted 1872.

Chapter 1: The Time of Commencing Actions in General

Chapter 1 enacted 1872.

312. Civil actions, without exception, can only be commenced within the periods prescribed in this title, after the cause of action shall have accrued, unless where, in special cases, a different limitation is prescribed by statute.[7]

313. The general procedure for the presentation of claims as a prerequisite to commencement of actions for money or damages against the State of California, counties, cities, cities and counties, districts, local authorities, and other political subdivisions of the State, and against the officers, employees, and servants thereof, is prescribed by Division 3.6 (commencing with Section 810) of Title 1 of the Government Code.[50]

Chapter 2: The Time of Commencing Actions for the Recovery of Real Property

Chapter 2 enacted 1872.

315. The people of this State will not sue any person for or in respect to any real property, or the issues or profits thereof, by reason of the right or title of the people to the same, unless:
1. Such right or title shall have accrued within ten years before any action or other proceeding for the same is commenced; or,
2. The people, or those from whom they claim, shall have received the rents and profits of such real property, or of some part thereof, within the space of ten years.[1]

316. No action can be brought for or in respect to real property by any person claiming under letters patent or grants from this State, unless the same might have been commenced by the people as herein specified, in case such patent had not been issued or grant made.[1]

[317.] Section Three Hundred and Seventeen. When letters patent or grants of real property issued or made by the people of this State, are declared void by the determination of a competent Court, an action for the recovery of the property so conveyed may be brought, either by the people of the State, or by any subsequent patentee or grantee of the property, his heirs or assigns, within five years after such determination, but not after that period.[2]

318. No action for the recovery of real property, or for the recovery of the possession thereof, can be maintained, unless it appear that the plaintiff, his ancestor, predecessor, or grantor, was seized or possessed of the property in question, within five years before the commencement of the action.[1]

319. No cause of action, or defense to an action, arising out of the title to real property, or to rents or profits out of the same, can be effectual, unless it appear that the person prosecuting the action, or making the defense, or under whose title the action is prosecuted, or the defense is made, or the ancestor, predecessor, or grantor of such person was seized or possessed of the premises in question within five years before the commencement of the Act in respect to which such action is prosecuted or defense made.[1]

320. No entry upon real estate is deemed sufficient or valid as a claim, unless an action be commenced thereupon within one year after making such entry, and within five years from the time when the right to make it descended or accrued.[1]

321. In every action for the recovery of real property, or the possession thereof, the person establishing a legal title to the property is presumed to have been possessed thereof within the time required by law, and the occupation of the property by any other person is deemed to have been under and in subordination to the legal title, unless it appear that the property has been held and possessed adversely to such legal title, for five years before the commencement of the action.[1]

322. When it appears that the occupant, or those under whom he claims, entered into the possession of the property under claim of title, exclusive of other right, founding such claim upon a written instrument, as being a conveyance of the property in question, or upon the decree or judgment of a competent Court, and that there has been a continued occupation and possession of the property included in such instrument, decree, or judgment, or of some part of the property, under such claim, for five years, the property so included is deemed to have been held adversely, except that when it consists of a tract divided into lots, the possession of one lot is not deemed a possession of any other lot of the same tract.[1]

323. For the purpose of constituting an adverse possession by any person claiming a title founded upon a written instrument, or a judgment or decree, land is deemed to have been possessed and occupied in the following cases:
1. Where it has been usually cultivated or improved;
2. Where it has been protected by a substantial inclosure;
3. Where, although not inclosed, it has been used for the supply of fuel, or of fencing timber for the purposes of husbandry, or for pasturage, or for the ordinary use of the occupant;
4. Where a known farm or single lot

has been partly improved, the portion of such farm or lot that may have been left not cleared, or not inclosed according to the usual course and custom of the adjoining country, shall be deemed to have been occupied for the same length of time as the part improved and cultivated.[1]

324. Where it appears that there has been an actual continued occupation of land, under a claim of title, exclusive of any other right, but not founded upon a written instrument, judgment, or decree, the land so actually occupied, and no other, is deemed to have been held adversely.[1]

325. (a) For the purpose of constituting an adverse possession by a person claiming title, not founded upon a written instrument, judgment, or decree, land is deemed to have been possessed and occupied in the following cases only:

(1) Where it has been protected by a substantial enclosure.

(2) Where it has been usually cultivated or improved.

(b) In no case shall adverse possession be considered established under the provision of any section of this code, unless it shall be shown that the land has been occupied and claimed for the period of five years continuously, and the party or persons, their predecessors and grantors, have timely paid all state, county, or municipal taxes that have been levied and assessed upon the land for the period of five years during which the land has been occupied and claimed. Payment of those taxes by the party or persons, their predecessors and grantors shall be established by certified records of the county tax collector.[628]

326. When the relation of landlord and tenant has existed between any persons, the possession of the tenant is deemed the possession of the landlord until the expiration of five years from the termination of the tenancy, or, where there has been no written lease, until the expiration of five years from the time of the last payment of rent, notwithstanding that such tenant may have acquired another title, or may have claimed to hold adversely to his landlord. But such presumptions cannot be made after the periods herein limited.[1]

327. The right of a person to the possession of real property is not impaired or affected by a descent cast in consequence of the death of a person in possession of such property.[1]

328. If a person entitled to commence an action for the recovery of real property, or for the recovery of the possession thereof, or to make an entry or defense founded on the title to real property, or to rents or services out of the property, is, at the time title first descends or accrues, either under the age of majority or lacking legal capacity to make decisions, the time, not exceeding 20 years, during which the disability continues is not deemed a portion of the time in this chapter limited for the commencement of the action, or the making of the entry or defense, but the action may be commenced, or entry or defense made, within the period of five years after the disability shall cease, or after the death of the person entitled, who shall die under the disability. The action shall not be commenced, or entry or defense made, after that period.[697]

328.5. If a person entitled to commence an action for the recovery of real property, or for the recovery of the possession thereof, or to make any entry or defense founded on the title to real property, or to rents or services out of the property, is, at the time the title first descends or accrues, imprisoned on a criminal charge, or in execution upon conviction of a criminal offense, for a term less than life, the time, not exceeding two years, during which imprisonment continues is not deemed any portion of the time in this chapter limited for the commencement of the action, or the making of the entry or defense, but the action may be commenced, or entry or defense made, within the period of five years after the imprisonment ceases, or after the death of the person entitled, who dies while imprisoned; but the action shall not be commenced, or entry or defense made, after that period.[339]

329. The time within which an action for the foreclosure of a lien securing an assessment against real property for street improvements, the proceedings for which are prescribed by legislation of any political unit other than the state, may be commenced, shall be two years from and after the date on which the assessment, or any bond secured thereby, or the last installment of the assessment or bond, shall be due, or, as to existing rights of action not heretofore barred, one year after the effective date hereof, whichever time is later. After that time, if the lien has not been otherwise removed, the lien ceases to exist and the assessment is conclusively presumed to be paid. The official having charge of the records of the assessment shall mark it "Conclusively presumed paid," if, at the expiration of the time within which such action might be brought he has received no written notice of the pendency of the action.[114]

329.5. The validity of an assessment or supplemental assessment against real property for public improvements, the proceedings for which are prescribed by the legislative body of any chartered city, shall not be contested in any action or proceeding unless the action or proceeding is commenced within 30 days after the assessment is levied, or such longer period as the legislative body may provide. Any appeal from a final judgment in such an action or proceeding shall be perfected within 30 days after the entry of judgment. (Added by Stats. 1959, Ch. 1007.)

330. In all cases in which there is now vested or there shall hereafter be vested in a treasurer, street superintendent, or other public official the power to sell at public auction, after demand upon him by the holder of any public improvement bond, any lot or parcel of land upon which exists or which shall hereafter exist a lien to secure the payment of a public improvement assessment represented by said bond, and the act or law establishing such power fails to prescribe the time within which such official may act, said official may sell at any time prior to the expiration of four years after the due date of said bond or of the last installment thereof or of the last principal coupon attached thereto, or prior to January 1, 1947, whichever is later, but not thereafter. This section is not intended to extend, enlarge or revive any power of sale which has heretofore been lost by reason of lapse of time or otherwise.[24]

Chapter 3: The Time of Commencing Actions Other Than for the Recovery of Real Property

Chapter 3 enacted 1872.

335. The periods prescribed for the commencement of actions other than for the recovery of real property, are as follows:[1]

335.1. Within two years: An action for assault, battery, or injury to, or for the death of, an individual caused by the wrongful act or neglect of another.[481]

336. Within five years:
(a) An action for mesne profits of real property.
(b) An action for violation of a restriction, as defined in Section 784 of the Civil Code. The period prescribed in this subdivision runs from the time the person seeking to enforce the restriction discovered or, through the exercise of reasonable diligence, should have discovered the violation. A failure to commence an action for violation of a restriction within the period prescribed in this subdivision does not waive the right to commence an action for any other violation of the restriction and does not, in itself, create an implication that the restriction is abandoned, obsolete, or otherwise unenforceable. This subdivision shall not bar commencement of an action for violation of a restriction before January 1, 2001, and until January 1, 2001, any other applicable statutory or common law limitation shall continue to apply to that action.[383]

336a. Within six years:
(a) An action upon any bonds, notes, or debentures issued by any corporation or pursuant to permit of the Commissioner of Financial Protection and Innovation, or upon any coupons issued with the bonds, notes, or debentures, if those bonds, notes, or debentures shall have been issued to or held by the public.
(b) An action upon any mortgage, trust deed, or other agreement pursuant to which the bonds, notes, or debentures were issued. This section does not apply to bonds or other evidences of indebtedness of a public district or corporation.[800]

337. Within four years:
(a) An action upon any contract, obligation or liability founded upon an instrument in writing, except as provided in Section 336a; provided, that the time within which any action for a money judgment for the balance due upon an obligation for the payment of which a deed of trust or mortgage with power of sale upon real property or any interest therein was given as security, following the exercise of the power of sale in such deed of trust or mortgage, may be brought shall not extend beyond three months after the time of sale under such deed of trust or mortgage.
(b) An action to recover (1) upon a book account whether consisting of one or more entries; (2) upon an account stated based upon an account in writing, but the acknowledgment of the account stated need not be in writing; (3) a balance due upon a mutual, open and current account, the items of which are in writing; provided, however, that if an account stated is based upon an account of one item, the time shall begin to run from the date of the item, and if an account stated is based upon an account of more than one item, the time shall begin to run from the date of the last item.

(c) An action based upon the rescission of a contract in writing. The time begins to run from the date upon which the facts that entitle the aggrieved party to rescind occurred. Where the ground for rescission is fraud or mistake, the time shall not begin to run until the discovery by the aggrieved party of the facts constituting the fraud or mistake. Where the ground for rescission is misrepresentation under Section 359 of the Insurance Code, the time shall not begin to run until the representation becomes false.
(d) When the period in which an action must be commenced under this section has run, a person shall not bring suit or initiate an arbitration or other legal proceeding to collect the debt. The period in which an action may be commenced under this section shall only be extended pursuant to Section 360.[743]

337a. (a) The term "book account" means a detailed statement which constitutes the principal record of one or more transactions between a debtor and a creditor arising out of a contract or some fiduciary relation, and shows the debits and credits in connection therewith, and against whom and in favor of whom entries are made, is entered in the regular course of business as conducted by such creditor or fiduciary, and is kept in a reasonably permanent form and manner and is (1) in a bound book, or (2) on a sheet or sheets fastened in a book or to backing but detachable therefrom, or (3) on a card or cards of a permanent character, or is kept in any other reasonably permanent form and manner. A "book account" does not include consumer debt.
(b) For purposes of this section, "consumer debt" means any obligation or alleged obligation, incurred on or after July 1, 2024, of a consumer to pay money arising out of a transaction in which the money, property, insurance, or services that are the subject of the transaction are primarily for personal, family, or household purposes and where the obligation to pay appears on the face of a note or in a written contract.[829]

337.1. (a) Except as otherwise provided in this section, no action shall be brought to recover damages from any person performing or furnishing the design, specifications, surveying, planning, supervision or observation of construction or construction of an improvement to real property more than four years after the substantial completion of such improvement for any of the following:
(1) Any patent deficiency in the design, specifications, surveying, planning, supervision or observation of construction or construction of an improvement to, or survey of, real property;
(2) Injury to property, real or personal, arising out of any such patent deficiency; or
(3) Injury to the person or for wrongful death arising out of any such patent deficiency.
(b) If, by reason of such patent deficiency, an injury to property or the person or an injury causing wrongful death occurs during the fourth year after such substantial completion, an action in tort to recover damages for such an injury or wrongful death may be brought within one year after the date on which such injury occurred, irrespective of the date of death, but in

no event may such an action be brought more than five years after the substantial completion of construction of such improvement.

(c) Nothing in this section shall be construed as extending the period prescribed by the laws of this state for the bringing of any action.

(d) The limitation prescribed by this section shall not be asserted by way of defense by any person in actual possession or the control, as owner, tenant or otherwise, of such an improvement at the time any deficiency in such an improvement constitutes the proximate cause of the injury or death for which it is proposed to bring an action.

(e) As used in this section, "patent deficiency" means a deficiency which is apparent by reasonable inspection.

(f) Subdivisions (a) and (b) shall not apply to any owner-occupied single-unit residence.[67]

337.15. (a) No action may be brought to recover damages from any person, or the surety of a person, who develops real property or performs or furnishes the design, specifications, surveying, planning, supervision, testing, or observation of construction or construction of an improvement to real property more than 10 years after the substantial completion of the development or improvement for any of the following:

(1) Any latent deficiency in the design, specification, surveying, planning, supervision, or observation of construction or construction of an improvement to, or survey of, real property.

(2) Injury to property, real or personal, arising out of any such latent deficiency.

(b) As used in this section, "latent deficiency" means a deficiency which is not apparent by reasonable inspection.

(c) As used in this section, "action" includes an action for indemnity brought against a person arising out of that person's performance or furnishing of services or materials referred to in this section, except that a cross-complaint for indemnity may be filed pursuant to subdivision (b) of Section 428.10 in an action which has been brought within the time period set forth in subdivision (a) of this section.

(d) Nothing in this section shall be construed as extending the period prescribed by the laws of this state for bringing any action.

(e) The limitation prescribed by this section shall not be asserted by way of defense by any person in actual possession or the control, as owner, tenant or otherwise, of such an improvement, at the time any deficiency in the improvement constitutes the proximate cause for which it is proposed to bring an action.

(f) This section shall not apply to actions based on willful misconduct or fraudulent concealment.

(g) The 10-year period specified in subdivision (a) shall commence upon substantial completion of the improvement, but not later than the date of one of the following, whichever first occurs:

(1) The date of final inspection by the applicable public agency.

(2) The date of recordation of a valid notice of completion.

(3) The date of use or occupation of the improvement.

(4) One year after termination or cessation of work on the improvement.

The date of substantial completion shall relate specifically to the performance or furnishing design, specifications, surveying, planning, supervision, testing, observation of construction or construction services by each profession or trade rendering services to the improvement.[113]

337.2. Where a lease of real property is in writing, no action shall be brought under Section 1951.2 of the Civil Code more than four years after the breach of the lease and abandonment of the property, or more than four years after the termination of the right of the lessee to possession of the property, whichever is the earlier time.[72]

337.5. Within 10 years:
(a) An action upon any general obligation bonds or coupons, not secured in whole or in part by a lien on real property, issued by any county, city and county, municipal corporation, district (including school districts), or other political subdivision of the State of California.
(b) An action upon a judgment or decree of any court of the United States or of any state within the United States.[648]

337.6. Notwithstanding the provisions of Section 337.5 of this code actions may be brought on bonds or coupons as set forth in subsection 2 of said section, against which the statute of limitations ran on or after August 27, 1937; provided, such actions are brought on or before June 30, 1959. Upon presentation for payment they shall be registered and payment shall not be made thereon until the next fiscal year following presentation unless available funds are sufficient to first pay obligations which are due or will become due from the same fund during the fiscal year of presentation and during the next succeeding six months. Interest shall not be paid on bonds or coupons registered for the purpose of this section.[37]

338. Within three years:
(a) An action upon a liability created by statute, other than a penalty or forfeiture.
(b) An action for trespass upon or injury to real property.
(c) (1) An action for taking, detaining, or injuring goods or chattels, including an action for the specific recovery of personal property.
(2) The cause of action in the case of theft, as described in Section 484 of the Penal Code, of an article of historical, interpretive, scientific, or artistic significance is not deemed to have accrued until the discovery of the whereabouts of the article by the aggrieved party, the aggrieved party's agent, or the law enforcement agency that originally investigated the theft.
(3) (A) Notwithstanding paragraphs (1) and (2), an action for the specific recovery of a work of fine art brought against a museum, gallery, auctioneer, or dealer, in the case of an unlawful taking or theft, as described in Section 484 of the Penal Code, of a work of fine art, including a taking or theft by means of fraud or duress, shall be commenced within six years of the actual discovery by the claimant or the claimant's agent, of both of the following:
(i) The identity and the whereabouts of the work of fine art. In the case where there is a possibility of misidentification of the object of fine art in question, the identity can be satisfied by the identification of facts sufficient to determine that the work of fine art is likely to be the

work of fine art that was unlawfully taken or stolen.

(ii) Information or facts that are sufficient to indicate that the claimant has a claim for a possessory interest in the work of fine art that was unlawfully taken or stolen.

(B) This paragraph shall apply to all pending and future actions commenced on or before December 31, 2017, including an action dismissed based on the expiration of statutes of limitations in effect prior to the date of enactment of this statute if the judgment in that action is not yet final or if the time for filing an appeal from a decision on that action has not expired, provided that the action concerns a work of fine art that was taken within 100 years prior to the date of enactment of this statute.

(C) For purposes of this paragraph:

(i) "Actual discovery," notwithstanding Section 19 of the Civil Code, does not include constructive knowledge imputed by law.

(ii) "Auctioneer" means an individual who is engaged in, or who by advertising or otherwise holds the individual out as being available to engage in, the calling for, the recognition of, and the acceptance of, offers for the purchase of goods at an auction as defined in subdivision (b) of Section 1812.601 of the Civil Code.

(iii) "Dealer" means a person who holds a valid seller's permit and who is actively and principally engaged in, or conducting the business of, selling works of fine art.

(iv) "Duress" means a threat of force, violence, danger, or retribution against an owner of the work of fine art in question, or the owner's family member, sufficient to coerce a reasonable person of ordinary susceptibilities to perform an act that otherwise would not have been performed or to acquiesce to an act to which the person would otherwise not have acquiesced.

(v) "Fine art" has the same meaning as defined in paragraph (1) of subdivision (d) of Section 982 of the Civil Code.

(vi) "Museum or gallery" shall include any public or private organization or foundation operating as a museum or gallery.

(4) Section 361 shall not apply to an action brought pursuant to paragraph (3).

(5) A party in an action to which paragraph (3) applies may raise all equitable and legal affirmative defenses and doctrines, including, without limitation, laches and unclean hands.

(6) Notwithstanding any other law or prior judicial decision, in any action brought by a California resident, or by an heir, trustee, assignee, or representative of the estate of a California resident, involving claims relating to title, ownership, or recovery of personal property as described in paragraph (2) or (3), or in the Holocaust Expropriated Art Recovery Act of 2016 (HEAR) (Pub. L. No. 114-308), including claims for money damages, California substantive law shall apply. This paragraph shall apply to all actions pending on the date this paragraph becomes operative or that are commenced thereafter, including any action in which the judgment is not yet final or the time for filing any appeal, including a petition for a writ of certiorari in the United States Supreme Court, has not expired, or, if filed, has

not been decided.

(d) An action for relief on the ground of fraud or mistake. The cause of action in that case is not deemed to have accrued until the discovery, by the aggrieved party, of the facts constituting the fraud or mistake.

(e) An action upon a bond of a public official except any cause of action based on fraud or embezzlement is not deemed to have accrued until the discovery, by the aggrieved party or the aggrieved party's agent, of the facts constituting the cause of action upon the bond.

(f) (1) An action against a notary public on the notary public's bond or in the notary public's official capacity except that a cause of action based on malfeasance or misfeasance is not deemed to have accrued until discovery, by the aggrieved party or the aggrieved party's agent, of the facts constituting the cause of action.

(2) Notwithstanding paragraph (1), an action based on malfeasance or misfeasance shall be commenced within one year from discovery, by the aggrieved party or the aggrieved party's agent, of the facts constituting the cause of action or within three years from the performance of the notarial act giving rise to the action, whichever is later.

(3) Notwithstanding paragraph (1), an action against a notary public on the notary public's bond or in the notary public's official capacity shall be commenced within six years.

(g) An action for slander of title to real property.

(h) An action commenced under Section 17536 of the Business and Professions Code. The cause of action in that case shall not be deemed to have accrued until the discovery by the aggrieved party, the Attorney General, the district attorney, the county counsel, the city prosecutor, or the city attorney of the facts constituting grounds for commencing the action.

(i) An action commenced under the Porter-Cologne Water Quality Control Act (Division 7 (commencing with Section 13000) of the Water Code). The cause of action in that case shall not be deemed to have accrued until the discovery by the State Water Resources Control Board or a regional water quality control board of the facts constituting grounds for commencing actions under their jurisdiction.

(j) An action to recover for physical damage to private property under Section 19 of Article I of the California Constitution.

(k) An action commenced under Division 26 (commencing with Section 39000) of the Health and Safety Code. These causes of action shall not be deemed to have accrued until the discovery by the State Air Resources Board or by a district, as defined in Section 39025 of the Health and Safety Code, of the facts constituting grounds for commencing the action under its jurisdiction.

(l) An action commenced under Section 1602, 1615, or 5650.1 of the Fish and Game Code. These causes of action shall not be deemed to have accrued until discovery by the agency bringing the action of the facts constituting the grounds for commencing the action.

(m) An action challenging the validity of the levy upon a parcel of a special tax levied by a local agency on a per parcel basis.

(n) An action commencing under Section 51.7 of the Civil Code.

(o) An action commenced under Section 4601.1 of the Public Resources Code, if the underlying violation is of Section 4571, 4581, or 4621 of the Public Resources Code, or of Section 1103.1 of Title 14 of the California Code of Regulations, and the underlying violation is related to the conversion of timberland to nonforestry-related agricultural uses. These causes of action shall not be deemed to have accrued until discovery by the Department of Forestry and Fire Protection.

(p) An action for civil penalties commenced under Section 26038 of the Business and Professions Code.[848]

338.1. An action for civil penalties or punitive damages authorized under Chapter 6.5 (commencing with Section 25100), Chapter 6.67 (commencing with Section 25270), Chapter 6.7 (commencing with Section 25280), or Chapter 6.95 (commencing with Section 25500) of Division 20 of, or Part 2 (commencing with Section 78000) of Division 45 of, the Health and Safety Code, or Chapter 1 (commencing with Section 3000) of Division 3 of the Public Resources Code, shall be commenced within five years after the discovery by the agency bringing the action of the facts constituting the grounds for commencing the action.[794]

338.2. (a) A California resident, or an heir, trustee, assignee, or representative of the estate of a California resident, may bring an action for damages, other financial recovery, title, recovery, or ownership, of artwork or other personal property that was taken or otherwise lost as a result of political persecution.

(b) Notwithstanding any other law, actions brought pursuant to this section shall be commenced within six years of the actual discovery by the claimant or the claimant's agent, of both of the following:

(1) The identity and the whereabouts of the artwork or other personal property. Where there is a possibility of misidentification of the object in question, the identity can be satisfied by the identification of facts sufficient to determine that the artwork or other personal property is likely to be the artwork or other personal property that was unlawfully taken or stolen.

(2) Information or facts that are sufficient to indicate that the claimant has a claim for a possessory interest in the artwork or other personal property that was unlawfully taken or stolen.

(c) If a claimant had actual knowledge of the facts described in subdivision (b) prior to the enactment of this section, any action brought pursuant to this section shall be commenced within of six years of actual discovery or two years from the enactment of this section, whichever is later.

(d) For purposes of this section the following definitions shall apply:

(1) "Artwork or other personal property" means any of the following:

(A) Pictures, paintings, and drawings.

(B) Statuary art and sculpture.

(C) Engravings, prints lithographs, and other works of graphic art.

(D) Applied art and original artistic assemblages and montages.

(E) Books, archives, musical instruments, musical objects, and manuscripts, including musical manuscripts and sheets, and sound, photographic, and cinematographic archives and mediums.

(F) Sacred and ceremonial objects.
(G) Objects of cultural significance.
(2) "Political persecution" means persecution of a specific group of individuals based on their membership in a protected class under the state's Unruh Civil Rights Act (Section 51 of the Civil Code).
(e) Notwithstanding any other provision of law or prior judicial decision, in any action brought pursuant to this section or in the Holocaust Expropriated Art Recovery Act of 2016 (HEAR) (Pub. L. No. 114-308), California substantive law shall apply.
(f) In an action brought pursuant to this section, where an item specified in subdivision (d) is taken or lost as a result of political persecution, clear title is not conveyed to any subsequent purchaser or owner. Defenses that the defendant acquired the title in good faith, by acquisitive prescription, or by adverse possession, and the defense of laches do not apply to cases brought under this section.
(g) An action may be brought by a claimant who, prior to the enactment of this section, brought a claim to recover personal property that was stolen or lost due to political persecution, and the case was dismissed by a court based on any of the defenses listed in subdivision (f), or based on any procedural basis such as standing, personal jurisdiction, or subject matter jurisdiction. Any such actions shall be commenced within two years of the effective date of this section or the entry of a final judgment and the termination of all appeals, including any petition for a writ of certiorari, whichever is later.
(h) A prevailing plaintiff shall be entitled to reasonable attorney's costs and fees.[849]

339. Within two years: 1. An action upon a contract, obligation or liability not founded upon an instrument of writing, except as provided in Section 2725 of the Commercial Code or subdivision 2 of Section 337 of this code; or an action founded upon a contract, obligation or liability, evidenced by a certificate, or abstract or guaranty of title of real property, or by a policy of title insurance; provided, that the cause of action upon a contract, obligation or liability evidenced by a certificate, or abstract or guaranty of title of real property or policy of title insurance shall not be deemed to have accrued until the discovery of the loss or damage suffered by the aggrieved party thereunder.
2. An action against a sheriff or coroner upon a liability incurred by the doing of an act in an official capacity and in virtue of office, or by the omission of an official duty including the nonpayment of money collected in the enforcement of a judgment.
3. An action based upon the rescission of a contract not in writing. The time begins to run from the date upon which the facts that entitle the aggrieved party to rescind occurred. Where the ground for rescission is fraud or mistake, the time does not begin to run until the discovery by the aggrieved party of the facts constituting the fraud or mistake.[367]

339.5. Where a lease of real property is not in writing, no action shall be brought under Section 1951.2 of the Civil Code more than two years after the breach of the lease and abandonment of the property, or more than two years after the termination of the right of the lessee to possession of the property, whichever is the earlier time.[72]

340. Within one year:
(a) An action upon a statute for a penalty or forfeiture, if the action is given to an individual, or to an individual and the state, except if the statute imposing it prescribes a different limitation.
(b) An action upon a statute for a forfeiture or penalty to the people of this state.
(c) An action for libel, slander, false imprisonment, seduction of a person below the age of legal consent, or by a depositor against a bank for the payment of a forged or raised check, or a check that bears a forged or unauthorized endorsement, or against any person who boards or feeds an animal or fowl or who engages in the practice of veterinary medicine as defined in Section 4826 of the Business and Professions Code, for that person's neglect resulting in injury or death to an animal or fowl in the course of boarding or feeding the animal or fowl or in the course of the practice of veterinary medicine on that animal or fowl.
(d) An action against an officer to recover damages for the seizure of any property for a statutory forfeiture to the state, or for the detention of, or injury to property so seized, or for damages done to any person in making that seizure.
(e) An action by a good faith improver for relief under Chapter 10 (commencing with Section 871.1) of Title 10 of Part 2. The time begins to run from the date upon which the good faith improver discovers that the good faith improver is not the owner of the land upon which the improvements have been made.[482]

340.1. (a) There is no time limit for the commencement of any of the following actions for recovery of damages suffered as a result of childhood sexual assault:
(1) An action against any person for committing an act of childhood sexual assault.
(2) An action for liability against any person or entity who owed a duty of care to the plaintiff, if a wrongful or negligent act by that person or entity was a legal cause of the childhood sexual assault that resulted in the injury to the plaintiff.
(3) An action for liability against any person or entity if an intentional act by that person or entity was a legal cause of the childhood sexual assault that resulted in the injury to the plaintiff.
(b) (1) In an action described in subdivision (a), a person who is sexually assaulted and proves it was as the result of a cover up may recover up to treble damages against a defendant who is found to have covered up the sexual assault of a minor, unless prohibited by another law.
(2) For purposes of this subdivision, a "cover up" is a concerted effort to hide evidence relating to childhood sexual assault.
(c) "Childhood sexual assault" as used in this section includes any act committed against the plaintiff that occurred when the plaintiff was under the age of 18 years and that would have been proscribed by Section 266j of the Penal Code; Section 285 of the Penal Code; paragraph (1) or (2) of subdivision (b), or of subdivision (c), of Section 286 of the Penal Code; subdivision (a) or (b) of Section 288 of the Pe-

nal Code; paragraph (1) or (2) of subdivision (b), or of subdivision (c), of Section 287 or of former Section 288a of the Penal Code; subdivision (h), (i), or (j) of Section 289 of the Penal Code; any sexual conduct as defined in paragraph (1) of subdivision (d) of Section 311.4 of the Penal Code; Section 647.6 of the Penal Code; or any prior laws of this state of similar effect at the time the act was committed. This subdivision does not limit the availability of causes of action permitted under subdivision (a), including causes of action against persons or entities other than the alleged perpetrator of the abuse.

(d) This section shall not be construed to alter the otherwise applicable burden of proof, as defined in Section 115 of the Evidence Code, that a plaintiff has in a civil action subject to this section.

(e) Every plaintiff 40 years of age or older at the time the action is filed shall file certificates of merit as specified in subdivision (f).

(f) Certificates of merit setting forth the facts that support the declaration shall be executed by the attorney for the plaintiff and by a licensed mental health practitioner selected by the plaintiff declaring, respectively, as follows:

(1) That the attorney has reviewed the facts of the case, consulted with at least one mental health practitioner who the attorney reasonably believes is knowledgeable of the relevant facts and issues involved in the particular action, and concluded on the basis of that review and consultation that there is reasonable and meritorious cause for the filing of the action.

(2) That the mental health practitioner consulted is licensed to practice and practices in this state and is not a party to the action, that the practitioner is not treating and has not treated the plaintiff, and that the practitioner has interviewed the plaintiff and is knowledgeable of the relevant facts and issues involved in the particular action, and has concluded, on the basis of the practitioner's knowledge of the facts and issues, that in the practitioner's professional opinion there is a reasonable basis to believe that the plaintiff had been subject to childhood sexual abuse.

(g) If certificates are required pursuant to subdivision (e), the attorney for the plaintiff shall execute a separate certificate of merit for each defendant named in the complaint.

(h) In any action subject to subdivision (e), a defendant shall not be served, and the duty to serve a defendant with process does not attach, until the court has reviewed the certificates of merit filed pursuant to subdivision (f) with respect to that defendant, and has found, in camera, based solely on those certificates of merit, that there is reasonable and meritorious cause for the filing of the action against that defendant. At that time, the duty to serve that defendant with process shall attach.

(i) A violation of this section may constitute unprofessional conduct and may be the grounds for discipline against the attorney.

(j) The failure to file certificates in accordance with this section shall be grounds for a demurrer pursuant to Section 430.10 or a motion to strike pursuant to Section 435.

(k) In any action subject to subdivision (e), a defendant shall be named by "Doe" designation in any pleadings or papers filed in the action until there has been a showing of corroborative fact as to the charging allegations against that defendant.

(l) At any time after the action is filed, the plaintiff may apply to the court for permission to amend the complaint to substitute the name of the defendant or defendants for the fictitious designation, as follows:

(1) The application shall be accompanied by a certificate of corroborative fact executed by the attorney for the plaintiff. The certificate shall declare that the attorney has discovered one or more facts corroborative of one or more of the charging allegations against a defendant or defendants, and shall set forth in clear and concise terms the nature and substance of the corroborative fact. If the corroborative fact is evidenced by the statement of a witness or the contents of a document, the certificate shall declare that the attorney has personal knowledge of the statement of the witness or of the contents of the document, and the identity and location of the witness or document shall be included in the certificate. For purposes of this section, a fact is corroborative of an allegation if it confirms or supports the allegation. The opinion of any mental health practitioner concerning the plaintiff shall not constitute a corroborative fact for purposes of this section.

(2) If the application to name a defendant is made before that defendant's appearance in the action, neither the application nor the certificate of corroborative fact by the attorney shall be served on the defendant or defendants, nor on any other party or their counsel of record.

(3) If the application to name a defendant is made after that defendant's appearance in the action, the application shall be served on all parties and proof of service provided to the court, but the certificate of corroborative fact by the attorney shall not be served on any party or their counsel of record.

(m) The court shall review the application and the certificate of corroborative fact in camera and, based solely on the certificate and any reasonable inferences to be drawn from the certificate, shall, if one or more facts corroborative of one or more of the charging allegations against a defendant has been shown, order that the complaint may be amended to substitute the name of the defendant or defendants.

(n) The court shall keep under seal and confidential from the public and all parties to the litigation, other than the plaintiff, any and all certificates of corroborative fact filed pursuant to subdivision (l).

(o) Upon the favorable conclusion of the litigation with respect to any defendant for whom a certificate of merit was filed or for whom a certificate of merit should have been filed pursuant to this section, the court may, upon the motion of a party or upon the court's own motion, verify compliance with this section by requiring the attorney for the plaintiff who was required by subdivision (f) to execute the certificate to reveal the name, address, and telephone number of the person or persons consulted with pursuant to subdivision (f) that were relied upon by the attorney in preparation of the certificate of merit. The name, address, and telephone number shall be disclosed to the trial judge in camera and in the absence of the moving party. If the court finds there has been a failure to comply with this section, the court may order a party, a party's attorney, or both, to pay any reasonable expenses, including attorney's fees, incurred by the defendant for whom a certificate of merit should have been filed.

(p) This section applies to any claim in which the childhood sexual assault occurred on and after January 1, 2024. Notwithstanding any other law, a claim for damages based on conduct described in paragraphs (1) through (3), inclusive, of subdivision (a), in which the childhood sexual assault occurred on or before December 31, 2023 may only be commenced pursuant to the applicable statute of limitations set forth in existing law as it read on December 31, 2023.

(q) Notwithstanding any other law, including Chapter 1 of Part 3 of Division 3.6 of Title 1 of the Government Code (commencing with Section 900) and Chapter 2 of Part 3 of Division 3.6 of Title 1 of the Government Code (commencing with Section 910), a claim for damages described in paragraphs (1) through (3), inclusive, of subdivision (a), is not required to be presented to any government entity prior to the commencement of an action.[827]

340.11. (a) (1) Notwithstanding Section 340.1, in an action for recovery of damages suffered as a result of childhood sexual assault that occurred before January 1, 2024, the time for commencement of the action shall be within 22 years of the date the plaintiff attains the age of majority or within five years of the date the plaintiff discovers or reasonably should have discovered that psychological injury or illness occurring after the age of majority was caused by the sexual assault, whichever period expires later, for any of the following actions:

(A) An action against any person for committing an act of childhood sexual assault.

(B) An action for liability against any person or entity who owed a duty of care to the plaintiff, if a wrongful or negligent act by that person or entity was a legal cause of the childhood sexual assault that resulted in the injury to the plaintiff.

(C) An action for liability against any person or entity if an intentional act by that person or entity was a legal cause of the childhood sexual assault that resulted in the injury to the plaintiff.

(2) Notwithstanding paragraph (1) or Section 340.1, in an action for recovery of damages suffered as a result of childhood sexual assault that occurred before January 1, 2024, involving an act that would have been proscribed by Sections 311.1 or 311.2 of the Penal Code, the time for commencement of the action shall be within 22 years of the date the plaintiff attains the age of majority or within 10 years of the date the plaintiff discovers or reasonably should have discovered, after the age of majority, the existence of obscene matter, for any of the actions identified in subparagraphs (A) to (C), inclusive, of paragraph (1).

(b) (1) In an action described in subdivision (a), a person who is sexually assaulted and proves it was as the result of a cover up may recover up to treble damages against a defendant who is found to have covered up the sexual assault of a minor, unless prohibited by another law.

(2) For purposes of this subdivision, a

"cover up" is a concerted effort to hide evidence relating to childhood sexual assault.

(c) An action described in subparagraph (B) or (C) of paragraph (1) of subdivision (a) shall not be commenced on or after the plaintiff's 40th birthday unless the person or entity knew or had reason to know, or was otherwise on notice, of any misconduct that creates a risk of childhood sexual assault by an employee, volunteer, representative, or agent, or the person or entity failed to take reasonable steps or to implement reasonable safeguards to avoid acts of childhood sexual assault. For purposes of this subdivision, providing or requiring counseling is not sufficient, in and of itself, to constitute a reasonable step or reasonable safeguard. Nothing in this subdivision shall be construed to constitute a substantive change in negligence law.

(d) "Childhood sexual assault" as used in this section includes any act committed against the plaintiff that occurred when the plaintiff was under the age of 18 years and that would have been proscribed by Section 266j of the Penal Code; Section 285 of the Penal Code; paragraph (1) or (2) of subdivision (b), or of subdivision (c), of Section 286 of the Penal Code; subdivision (a) or (b) of Section 288 of the Penal Code; paragraph (1) or (2) of subdivision (b), or of subdivision (c), of Section 287 or of former Section 288a of the Penal Code; subdivision (h), (i), or (j) of Section 289 of the Penal Code; subdivision (a) of Section 311.1 of the Penal Code; subdivisions (b) to (d), inclusive, of Section 311.2 of the Penal Code; any sexual conduct as defined in paragraph (1) of subdivision (d) of Section 311.4 of the Penal Code; Section 647.6 of the Penal Code; or any prior laws of this state of similar effect at the time the act was committed. This subdivision does not limit the availability of causes of action permitted under subdivision (a), including causes of action against persons or entities other than the alleged perpetrator of the abuse.

(e) This section shall not be construed to alter the otherwise applicable burden of proof, as defined in Section 115 of the Evidence Code, that a plaintiff has in a civil action subject to this section.

(f) Every plaintiff 40 years of age or older at the time the action is filed shall file certificates of merit as specified in subdivision (g).

(g) Certificates of merit shall be executed by the attorney for the plaintiff and by a licensed mental health practitioner selected by the plaintiff declaring, respectively, as follows:

(1) That the attorney has reviewed the facts of the case, consulted with at least one mental health practitioner who the attorney reasonably believes is knowledgeable of the relevant facts and issues involved in the particular action, and concluded on the basis of that review and consultation that there is reasonable and meritorious cause for the filing of the action.

(2) That the mental health practitioner consulted is licensed to practice and practices in this state and is not a party to the action, that the practitioner is not treating and has not treated the plaintiff, and that the practitioner has interviewed the plaintiff and is knowledgeable of the relevant facts and issues involved in the particular action,

and has concluded, on the basis of the practitioner's knowledge of the facts and issues, that in the practitioner's professional opinion there is a reasonable basis to believe that the plaintiff had been subject to childhood sexual abuse.

(3) That the attorney was unable to obtain the consultation required by paragraph (1) because a statute of limitations would impair the action and that the certificates required by paragraphs (1) and (2) could not be obtained before the impairment of the action. If a certificate is executed pursuant to this paragraph, the certificates required by paragraphs (1) and (2) shall be filed within 60 days after filing the complaint.

(h) If certificates are required pursuant to subdivision (f), the attorney for the plaintiff shall execute a separate certificate of merit for each defendant named in the complaint.

(i) In any action subject to subdivision (f), a defendant shall not be served, and the duty to serve a defendant with process does not attach, until the court has reviewed the certificates of merit filed pursuant to subdivision (g) with respect to that defendant, and has found, in camera, based solely on those certificates of merit, that there is reasonable and meritorious cause for the filing of the action against that defendant. At that time, the duty to serve that defendant with process shall attach.

(j) A violation of this section may constitute unprofessional conduct and may be the grounds for discipline against the attorney.

(k) The failure to file certificates in accordance with this section shall be grounds for a demurrer pursuant to Section 430.10 or a motion to strike pursuant to Section 435.

(l) In any action subject to subdivision (f), a defendant shall be named by "Doe" designation in any pleadings or papers filed in the action until there has been a showing of corroborative fact as to the charging allegations against that defendant.

(m) At any time after the action is filed, the plaintiff may apply to the court for permission to amend the complaint to substitute the name of the defendant or defendants for the fictitious designation, as follows:

(1) The application shall be accompanied by a certificate of corroborative fact executed by the attorney for the plaintiff. The certificate shall declare that the attorney has discovered one or more facts corroborative of one or more of the charging allegations against a defendant or defendants, and shall set forth in clear and concise terms the nature and substance of the corroborative fact. If the corroborative fact is evidenced by the statement of a witness or the contents of a document, the certificate shall declare that the attorney has personal knowledge of the statement of the witness or of the contents of the document, and the identity and location of the witness or document shall be included in the certificate. For purposes of this section, a fact is corroborative of an allegation if it confirms or supports the allegation. The opinion of any mental health practitioner concerning the plaintiff shall not constitute a corroborative fact for purposes of this section.

(2) If the application to name a defendant is made before that defendant's appearance in the action, neither the application nor the certificate of

corroborative fact by the attorney shall be served on the defendant or defendants, nor on any other party or their counsel of record.

(3) If the application to name a defendant is made after that defendant's appearance in the action, the application shall be served on all parties and proof of service provided to the court, but the certificate of corroborative fact by the attorney shall not be served on any party or their counsel of record.

(n) The court shall review the application and the certificate of corroborative fact in camera and, based solely on the certificate and any reasonable inferences to be drawn from the certificate, shall, if one or more facts corroborative of one or more of the charging allegations against a defendant has been shown, order that the complaint may be amended to substitute the name of the defendant or defendants.

(o) The court shall keep under seal and confidential from the public and all parties to the litigation, other than the plaintiff, any and all certificates of corroborative fact filed pursuant to subdivision (m).

(p) Upon the favorable conclusion of the litigation with respect to any defendant for whom a certificate of merit was filed or for whom a certificate of merit should have been filed pursuant to this section, the court may, upon the motion of a party or upon the court's own motion, verify compliance with this section by requiring the attorney for the plaintiff who was required by subdivision (g) to execute the certificate to reveal the name, address, and telephone number of the person or persons consulted with pursuant to subdivision (g) that were relied upon by the attorney in preparation of the certificate of merit. The name, address, and telephone number shall be disclosed to the trial judge in camera and in the absence of the moving party. If the court finds there has been a failure to comply with this section, the court may order a party, a party's attorney, or both, to pay any reasonable expenses, including attorney's fees, incurred by the defendant for whom a certificate of merit should have been filed.

(q) Notwithstanding any other law, a claim for damages described in subparagraphs (A) to (C), inclusive, of paragraph (1) of subdivision (a) that has not been litigated to finality and that would otherwise be barred as of January 1, 2020, because the applicable statute of limitations, claim presentation deadline, or any other time limit had expired, is revived, and these claims may be commenced within three years of January 1, 2020. A plaintiff shall have the later of the three-year time period under this subdivision or the time period under subdivision (a) as amended by the act that added this subdivision.

(r) The changes made to the time period under subdivision (a) of Section 340.1 by Chapter 861 of the Statutes of 2019 apply to and revive any action commenced on or after the date of enactment of that act, and to any action filed before the date of enactment, and still pending on that date, including any action or causes of action that would have been barred by the laws in effect before the date of enactment.

(s) Notwithstanding any other law, including Chapter 1 of Part 3 of Division 3.6 of Title 1 of the Government Code (commencing with Section 900) and Chapter 2 of Part 3 of Division 3.6 of

Title 1 of the Government Code (commencing with Section 910), a claim for damages described in paragraphs (1) to (3), inclusive, of subdivision (a), is not required to be presented to any government entity prior to the commencement of an action.[837]

340.15. (a) In any civil action for recovery of damages suffered as a result of domestic violence, the time for commencement of the action shall be the later of the following:

(1) Within three years from the date of the last act of domestic violence by the defendant against the plaintiff.

(2) Within three years from the date the plaintiff discovers or reasonably should have discovered that an injury or illness resulted from an act of domestic violence by the defendant against the plaintiff.

(b) As used in this section, "domestic violence" has the same meaning as defined in Section 6211 of the Family Code.[384]

340.16. (a) In any civil action for recovery of damages suffered as a result of sexual assault, where the assault occurred on or after the plaintiff's 18th birthday, the time for commencement of the action shall be the later of the following:

(1) Within 10 years from the date of the last act, attempted act, or assault with the intent to commit an act, of sexual assault against the plaintiff.

(2) Within three years from the date the plaintiff discovers or reasonably should have discovered that an injury or illness resulted from an act, attempted act, or assault with the intent to commit an act, of sexual assault against the plaintiff.

(b) (1) As used in this section, "sexual assault" means any of the crimes described in Section 243.4, 261, 264.1, 286, 287, or 289, or former Sections 262 and 288a, of the Penal Code, assault with the intent to commit any of those crimes, or an attempt to commit any of those crimes.

(2) For the purpose of this section, it is not necessary that a criminal prosecution or other proceeding have been brought as a result of the sexual assault or, if a criminal prosecution or other proceeding was brought, that the prosecution or proceeding resulted in a conviction or adjudication. This subdivision does not limit the availability of causes of action permitted under subdivision (a), including causes of action against persons or entities other than the alleged person who committed the crime.

(3) This section applies to any action described in subdivision (a) that is based upon conduct that occurred on or after January 1, 2009, and is commenced on or after January 1, 2019, that would have been barred solely because the applicable statute of limitations has or had expired. Such claims are hereby revived and may be commenced until December 31, 2026. This subdivision does not revive any of the following claims:

(A) A claim that has been litigated to finality in a court of competent jurisdiction before January 1, 2023.

(B) A claim that has been compromised by a written settlement agreement between the parties entered into before January 1, 2023.

(c) (1) Notwithstanding any other law, any claim seeking to recover more than two hundred fifty thousand dollars ($250,000) in damages arising out of a sexual assault or other inappropriate contact, communication, or activity of a sexual nature by a physician occurring at a student health center between January 1, 1988, and January 1, 2017, that would otherwise be barred before January 1, 2020, solely because the applicable statute of limitations has or had expired, is hereby revived and, a cause of action may proceed if already pending in court on October 2, 2019, or, if not filed by that date, may be commenced between January 1, 2020, and December 31, 2020.

(2) This subdivision does not revive any of the following claims:

(A) A claim that has been litigated to finality in a court of competent jurisdiction before January 1, 2020.

(B) A claim that has been compromised by a written settlement agreement between the parties entered into before January 1, 2020.

(C) A claim brought against a public entity.

(3) An attorney representing a claimant seeking to recover under this subdivision shall file a declaration with the court under penalty of perjury stating that the attorney has reviewed the facts of the case and consulted with a mental health practitioner, and that the attorney has concluded on the basis of this review and consultation that it is the attorney's good faith belief that the claim value is more than two hundred fifty thousand dollars ($250,000). The declaration shall be filed upon filing the complaint, or for those claims already pending, by December 1, 2019.

(d) (1) Notwithstanding any other law, any claim seeking to recover damages arising out of a sexual assault or other inappropriate contact, communication, or activity of a sexual nature by a physician while employed by a medical clinic owned and operated by the University of California, Los Angeles, or a physician who held active privileges at a hospital owned and operated by the University of California, Los Angeles, at the time that the sexual assault or other inappropriate contact, communication, or activity of a sexual nature occurred, between January 1, 1983, and January 1, 2019, that would otherwise be barred before January 1, 2021, solely because the applicable statute of limitations has or had expired, is hereby revived, and a cause of action may proceed if already pending in court on January 1, 2021, or, if not filed by that date, may be commenced between January 1, 2021, and December 31, 2021.

(2) This subdivision does not revive either of the following claims:

(A) A claim that has been litigated to finality in a court of competent jurisdiction before January 1, 2021.

(B) A claim that has been compromised by a written settlement agreement between the parties entered into before January 1, 2021.

(e) (1) Notwithstanding any other law, any claim seeking to recover damages suffered as a result of a sexual assault that occurred on or after the plaintiff's 18th birthday that would otherwise be barred before January 1, 2026, solely because the applicable statute of limitations has or had expired, is hereby revived, and a cause of action may proceed if already pending in court on January 1, 2026, or, if not filed by that date, may be commenced between January 1, 2026, and December 31, 2027.

(2) This subdivision revives claims against an entity brought by a plaintiff

who alleges that the plaintiff was sexually assaulted and both of the following:

(A) One or more entities or persons, including, but not limited to, the perpetrator of the sexual assault, are legally responsible for damages arising out of sexual assault by an alleged perpetrator against the plaintiff.

(B) An entity or entities, including, but not limited to, their officers, directors, representatives, employees, or agents, engaged in a cover up or attempted a cover up of a previous instance or allegations of sexual assault by an alleged perpetrator of such abuse.

(3) This subdivision revives claims against the perpetrator of the sexual assault brought by a plaintiff who alleges that the plaintiff was sexually assaulted and that one or more entities or persons, including, but not limited to, the perpetrator of the sexual assault, are legally responsible for damages arising out of the sexual assault against the plaintiff.

(4) Failure to allege a cover up as required by subparagraph (B) of paragraph (2) as to one entity does not affect revival of the plaintiff's claim or claims against any other entity or person, including the perpetrator of the sexual assault.

(5) For purposes of this subdivision:

(A) "Cover up" means a concerted effort to hide evidence relating to a sexual assault that incentivizes individuals to remain silent or prevents information relating to a sexual assault from becoming public or being disclosed to the plaintiff, including, but not limited to, the use of nondisclosure agreements or confidentiality agreements.

(B) "Entity" means a sole proprietorship, partnership, limited liability company, corporation, association, or other legal entity, other than a public entity.

(C) "Legally responsible" means that the person, entity, or entities are liable under any theory of liability established by statute or common law, including, but not limited to, negligence, intentional torts, and vicarious liability.

(6) This subdivision revives any related claims, including, but not limited to, wrongful termination and sexual harassment, arising out of the sexual assault that is the basis for a claim pursuant to this subdivision.

(7) This subdivision does not revive any of the following claims:

(A) A claim that has been litigated to finality in a court of competent jurisdiction before January 1, 2026.

(B) A claim that has been compromised by a written settlement agreement between the parties entered into before January 1, 2026.

(C) A claim, including a direct claim, derivative claim, and a vicarious liability claim, brought against a public entity. For any claim against the perpetrator or other persons, a public entity shall not have a duty to indemnify the perpetrator or other persons under Section 825 of the Government Code or any other law.

(8) This subdivision shall not be construed to alter the otherwise applicable burden of proof, as defined in Section 115 of the Evidence Code, that a plaintiff has in a civil action subject to this section.

(9) Nothing in this subdivision precludes a plaintiff from bringing an action for sexual assault pursuant to

subdivisions (a) and (b).[900]

340.2. (a) In any civil action for injury or illness based upon exposure to asbestos, the time for the commencement of the action shall be the later of the following:

(1) Within one year after the date the plaintiff first suffered disability.

(2) Within one year after the date the plaintiff either knew, or through the exercise of reasonable diligence should have known, that such disability was caused or contributed to by such exposure.

(b) "Disability" as used in subdivision (a) means the loss of time from work as a result of such exposure which precludes the performance of the employee's regular occupation.

(c) In an action for the wrongful death of any plaintiff's decedent, based upon exposure to asbestos, the time for commencement of an action shall be the later of the following:

(1) Within one year from the date of the death of the plaintiff's decedent.

(2) Within one year from the date the plaintiff first knew, or through the exercise of reasonable diligence should have known, that the death was caused or contributed to by such exposure.[111]

340.3. (a) Unless a longer period is prescribed for a specific action, in any action for damages against a defendant based upon the defendant's commission of a felony offense for which the defendant has been convicted, the time for commencement of the action shall be within one year after judgment is pronounced.

(b) (1) Notwithstanding subdivision (a), an action for damages against a defendant based upon the defendant's commission of a felony offense for which the defendant has been convicted may be commenced within 10 years of the date on which the defendant is discharged from parole if the conviction was for any offense specified in paragraph (1), except voluntary manslaughter, (2), (3), (4), (5), (6), (7), (9), (16), (17), (20), (22), (25), (34), or (35) of subdivision (c) of Section 1192.7 of the Penal Code.

(2) No civil action may be commenced pursuant to paragraph (1) if any of the following applies:

(A) The defendant has received either a certificate of rehabilitation as provided in Chapter 3.5 (commencing with Section 4852.01) of Title 6 of Part 3 of the Penal Code or a pardon as provided in Chapter 1 (commencing with Section 4800) or Chapter 3 (commencing with Section 4850) of Title 6 of Part 3 of the Penal Code.

(B) Following a conviction for murder or attempted murder, the defendant has been paroled based in whole or in part upon evidence presented to the Board of Prison Terms that the defendant committed the crime because he or she was the victim of intimate partner battering.

(C) The defendant was convicted of murder or attempted murder in the second degree in a trial at which substantial evidence was presented that the person committed the crime because he or she was a victim of intimate partner battering.

(D) The defendant was unlawfully imprisoned or restrained but has been released from prison after successfully prosecuting a writ of habeas corpus pursuant to Chapter 1 (commencing with Section 1473) of Title

12 of Part 2 of the Penal Code.

(c) If the sentence or judgment is stayed, the time for the commencement of the action shall be tolled until the stay is lifted. For purposes of this section, a judgment is not stayed if the judgment is appealed or the defendant is placed on probation.

(d) (1) Subdivision (b) shall apply to any action commenced before, on, or after the effective date of this section, including any action otherwise barred by a limitation of time in effect prior to the effective date of this section, thereby reviving those causes of action that had lapsed or expired under the law in effect prior to the effective date of this section.

(2) Paragraph (1) does not apply to either of the following:

(A) Any claim that has been litigated to finality on the merits in any court of competent jurisdiction prior to January 1, 2003. For purposes of this section, termination of a prior action on the basis of the statute of limitations does not constitute a claim that has been litigated to finality on the merits.

(B) Any written, compromised settlement agreement that has been entered into between a plaintiff and a defendant if the plaintiff was represented by an attorney who was admitted to practice law in this state at the time of the settlement, and the plaintiff signed the agreement.

(e) Any restitution paid by the defendant to the victim shall be credited against any judgment, award, or settlement obtained pursuant to this section. Any judgment, award, or settlement obtained pursuant to an action under this section shall be subject to the provisions of Section 13963 of the Government Code.[714]

340.35. (a) This section shall apply if both of the following conditions are met:

(1) A complaint, information, or indictment was filed in a criminal case initiated pursuant to subdivision (f), (g), or (h) of Section 803 of the Penal Code.

(2) The case was dismissed or overturned pursuant to the United States Supreme Court's decision in Stogner v. California (2003) 156 L.Ed.2d 544.

(b) Unless a longer period is prescribed for a specific action, any action for damages against an individual for committing an act of childhood sexual abuse shall be commenced before January 1, 2006.

(c) This section shall apply to any action commenced before, on, or after the effective date of this section, including any action otherwise barred by a limitation of time in effect prior to the effective date of this section, thereby reviving those causes of action that had lapsed or expired under the law in effect prior to the effective date of this section.

(d) This section shall not apply to any of the following:

(1) Any claim against a person or entity other than the individual against whom a complaint, information, or indictment was filed as described in paragraph (1) of subdivision (a).

(2) Any claim that has been litigated to finality on the merits in any court of competent jurisdiction prior to the effective date of this section. For purposes of this section, termination of a prior action on the basis of the statute of limitations does not constitute a claim that has been "litigated to finality on the merits."

(3) Any written, compromised settlement agreement that has been entered into between a plaintiff and a defendant, if the plaintiff was represented by an attorney who was admitted to practice law in this state at the time of the settlement, and the plaintiff signed the agreement.

(e) Any restitution paid by the defendant to the victim shall be credited against any judgment, award, or settlement obtained pursuant to this section. Any judgment, award, or settlement obtained pursuant to an action under this section shall be subject to Section 13966.01 of the Government Code.[554]

340.4. An action by or on behalf of a minor for personal injuries sustained before or in the course of his or her birth must be commenced within six years after the date of birth, and the time the minor is under any disability mentioned in Section 352 shall not be excluded in computing the time limited for the commencement of the action.[293]

340.5. In an action for injury or death against a health care provider based upon such person's alleged professional negligence, the time for the commencement of action shall be three years after the date of injury or one year after the plaintiff discovers, or through the use of reasonable diligence should have discovered, the injury, whichever occurs first. In no event shall the time for commencement of legal action exceed three years unless tolled for any of the following: (1) upon proof of fraud, (2) intentional concealment, or (3) the presence of a foreign body, which has no therapeutic or diagnostic purpose or effect, in the person of the injured person. Actions by a minor shall be commenced within three years from the date of the alleged wrongful act except that actions by a minor under the full age of six years shall be commenced within three years or prior to his eighth birthday whichever provides a longer period. Such time limitation shall be tolled for minors for any period during which parent or guardian and defendant's insurer or health care provider have committed fraud or collusion in the failure to bring an action on behalf of the injured minor for professional negligence.

For the purposes of this section:

(1) "Health care provider" means any person licensed or certified pursuant to Division 2 (commencing with Section 500) of the Business and Professions Code, or licensed pursuant to the Osteopathic Initiative Act, or the Chiropractic Initiative Act, or licensed pursuant to Chapter 2.5 (commencing with Section 1440) of Division 2 of the Health and Safety Code; and any clinic, health dispensary, or health facility, licensed pursuant to Division 2 (commencing with Section 1200) of the Health and Safety Code. "Health care provider" includes the legal representatives of a health care provider;

(2) "Professional negligence" means a negligent act or omission to act by a health care provider in the rendering of professional services, which act or omission is the proximate cause of a personal injury or wrongful death, provided that such services are within the scope of services for which the provider is licensed and which are not within any restriction imposed by the

licensing agency or licensed hospital.[91]

340.6. (a) An action against an attorney for a wrongful act or omission, other than for actual fraud, arising in the performance of professional services shall be commenced within one year after the plaintiff discovers, or through the use of reasonable diligence should have discovered, the facts constituting the wrongful act or omission, or four years from the date of the wrongful act or omission, whichever occurs first. If the plaintiff is required to establish the plaintiff's factual innocence for an underlying criminal charge as an element of the plaintiff's claim, the action shall be commenced within two years after the plaintiff achieves postconviction exoneration in the form of a final judicial disposition of the criminal case. Except for a claim for which the plaintiff is required to establish the plaintiff's factual innocence, the time for commencement of legal action shall not exceed four years except that the period shall be tolled during the time that any of the following exist:

(1) The plaintiff has not sustained actual injury.

(2) The attorney continues to represent the plaintiff regarding the specific subject matter in which the alleged wrongful act or omission occurred.

(3) The attorney willfully conceals the facts constituting the wrongful act or omission when those facts are known to the attorney, except that this subdivision shall toll only the four-year limitation.

(4) The plaintiff is under a legal or physical disability that restricts the plaintiff's ability to commence legal action.

(5) A dispute between the lawyer and client concerning fees, costs, or both is pending resolution under Article 13 (commencing with Section 6200) of Chapter 4 of Division 3 of the Business and Professions Code. As used in this paragraph, "pending" means from the date a request for arbitration is filed until 30 days after receipt of notice of the award of the arbitrators, or receipt of notice that the arbitration is otherwise terminated, whichever occurs first.

(b) In an action based upon an instrument in writing, the effective date of which depends upon some act or event of the future, the period of limitations provided for by this section shall commence to run upon the occurrence of that act or event.[752]

340.7. (a) Notwithstanding Section 335.1, a civil action brought by, or on behalf of, a Dalkon Shield victim against the Dalkon Shield Claimants' Trust, shall be brought in accordance with the procedures established by A.H. Robins Company, Inc. Plan of Reorganization, and shall be brought within 15 years of the date on which the victim's injury occurred, except that the statute shall be tolled from August 21, 1985, the date on which the A.H. Robins Company filed for Chapter 11 Reorganization in Richmond, Virginia.

(b) This section applies regardless of when the action or claim shall have accrued or been filed and regardless of whether it might have lapsed or otherwise be barred by time under California law. However, this section shall only apply to victims who, prior to January 1, 1990, filed a civil action, a timely claim, or a claim that is declared to be timely under the sixth Amended and Restated Disclosure Statement filed pursuant to Section 1125 of the Federal Bankruptcy Code in re: A.H. Robins Company, Inc., dated March 28, 1988, U.S. Bankruptcy Court, Eastern District of Virginia (case number 85-01307-R).[609]

340.8. (a) In any civil action for injury or illness based upon exposure to a hazardous material or toxic substance, the time for commencement of the action shall be no later than either two years from the date of injury, or two years after the plaintiff becomes aware of, or reasonably should have become aware of, (1) an injury, (2) the physical cause of the injury, and (3) sufficient facts to put a reasonable person on inquiry notice that the injury was caused or contributed to by the wrongful act of another, whichever occurs later.

(b) In an action for the wrongful death of any plaintiff's decedent, based upon exposure to a hazardous material or toxic substance, the time for commencement of an action shall be no later than either (1) two years from the date of the death of the plaintiff's decedent, or (2) two years from the first date on which the plaintiff is aware of, or reasonably should have become aware of, the physical cause of the death and sufficient facts to put a reasonable person on inquiry notice that the death was caused or contributed to by the wrongful act of another, whichever occurs later.

(c) For purposes of this section:

(1) A "civil action for injury or illness based upon exposure to a hazardous material or toxic substance" does not include an action subject to Section 340.2 or 340.5.

(2) Media reports regarding the hazardous material or toxic substance contamination do not, in and of themselves, constitute sufficient facts to put a reasonable person on inquiry notice that the injury or death was caused or contributed to by the wrongful act of another.

(d) Nothing in this section shall be construed to limit, abrogate, or change the law in effect on the effective date of this section with respect to actions not based upon exposure to a hazardous material or toxic substance.[540]

340.9. (a) Notwithstanding any other provision of law or contract, any insurance claim for damages arising out of the Northridge earthquake of 1994 which is barred as of the effective date of this section solely because the applicable statute of limitations has or had expired is hereby revived and a cause of action thereon may be commenced provided that the action is commenced within one year of the effective date of this section. This subdivision shall only apply to cases in which an insured contacted an insurer or an insurer's representative prior to January 1, 2000, regarding potential Northridge earthquake damage.

(b) Any action pursuant to this section commenced prior to, or within one year from, the effective date of this section shall not be barred based upon this limitations period.

(c) Nothing in this section shall be construed to alter the applicable limitations period of an action that is not time barred as of the effective date of this section.

(d) This section shall not apply to either of the following:

(1) Any claim that has been litigated to finality in any court of competent

jurisdiction prior to the effective date of this section.
(2) Any written compromised settlement agreement which has been made between an insurer and its insured where the insured was represented by counsel admitted to the practice of law in California at the time of the settlement, and who signed the agreement.[457]

340.10. (a) For purposes of this section, "terrorist victim" means any individual who died or was injured as a consequence of the terrorist-related aircraft crashes of September 11, 2001, including persons who were present at the World Trade Center in New York City, New York, the Pentagon in Arlington, Virginia, or at the site of the crash at Shanksville, Pennsylvania, or in the immediate aftermath of the terrorist-related aircraft crashes of September 11, 2001, including members of the flight crew and passengers on American Airlines Flight 11, American Airlines Flight 77, United Airlines Flight 175, and United Airlines Flight 93, and who suffered physical harm or death as a result of any of the crashes, as defined in Section 40101 of Title 49 of the United States Code and the related, applicable regulations, other than an individual identified by the Attorney General of the United States as a participant or conspirator in the terrorist-related aircraft crashes, or a representative or heir of such an individual.
(b) The statute of limitations for injury or death set forth in Section 335.1 shall apply to any action brought for injury to, or for the death of, any terrorist victim described in subdivision (a) and caused by the wrongful act or neglect of another, regardless of whether that action lapsed or was otherwise barred by time under California law predating the passage of this section and Section 335.1.[483]

341. Within six months:
An action against an officer, or officer de facto:
1. To recover any goods, wares, merchandise, or other property, seized by any such officer in his official capacity as tax collector, or to recover the price or value of any goods, wares, merchandise, or other personal property so seized, or for damages for the seizure, detention, sale of, or injury to any goods, wares, merchandise, or other personal property seized, or for damages done to any person or property in making any such seizure.
2. To recover stock sold for a delinquent assessment, as provided in section three hundred forty-seven of the Civil Code.
3. To set aside or invalidate any action taken or performed by a majority of the trustees of any corporation heretofore or hereafter dissolved by operation of law, including the revivor of any such corporation.[13]

341.5. Notwithstanding any other provision of law, any action or proceeding in which a county, city, city and county, school district, special district, or any other local agency is a plaintiff or petitioner, that is brought against the State of California challenging the constitutionality of any statute relating to state funding for counties, cities, cities and counties, school districts, special districts, or other local agencies, shall be commenced within 90 days of the effective date of the statute at issue in the action. For purposes of this section, "State of California" means the State of California itself, or any of its agencies, departments, commissions, boards, or public officials.[333]

341a. All civil actions for the recovery or conversion of personal property, wearing apparel, trunks, valises or baggage alleged to have been left at a hotel, hospital, rest home, sanitarium, boarding house, lodging house, furnished apartment house, or furnished bungalow court, shall be begun within 90 days from and after the date of the departure of the owner of said personal property, wearing apparel, trunks, valises or baggage from said hotel, hospital, rest home, sanitarium, boarding house, lodging house, furnished apartment house, or furnished bungalow court.[23]

342. An action against a public entity upon a cause of action for which a claim is required to be presented in accordance with Chapter 1 (commencing with Section 900) and Chapter 2 (commencing with Section 910) of Part 3 of Division 3.6 of Title 1 of the Government Code must be commenced within the time provided in Section 945.6 of the Government Code.[51]

343. An action for relief not hereinbefore provided for must be commenced within four years after the cause of action shall have accrued.[1]

344. In an action brought to recover a balance due upon a mutual, open, and current account, where there have been reciprocal demands between the parties, the cause of action is deemed to have accrued from the time of the last item proved in the account on either side.[1]

345. The limitations prescribed in this chapter apply to actions brought in the name of the state or county or for the benefit of the state or county, in the same manner as to actions by private parties. Accounts for the support of patients at state or county hospitals are book accounts as defined in Section 337a, and actions on them may be commenced at any time within four years after the last date of service or the last date of payment.[225]

346. An action to redeem a mortgage of real property, with or without an account of rents and profits, may be brought by the mortgagor or those claiming under him, against the mortgagee in possession, or those claiming under him, unless he or they have continuously maintained an adverse possession of the mortgaged premises for five years after breach of some condition of the mortgage.[1]

347. If there is more than one such mortgagor, or more than one person claiming under a mortgagor, some of whom are not entitled to maintain such an action under the provisions of this Chapter, any one of them who is entitled to maintain such an action may redeem therein a divided or undivided part of the mortgaged premises, according as his interest may appear and have an accounting, for a part of the rents and profits proportionate to his interest in the mortgaged premises, on payment of a part of the mortgage money, bearing the same proportion to the whole of such money as the value of his divided or undivided interest in the premises bears to the whole of such premises.[1]

348. To actions brought to recover money or other property deposited with any bank, banker, trust company,

building and loan association, or savings and loan society or evidenced by a certificate issued by an industrial loan company or credit union there is no limitation.

This section shall not apply to banks, bankers, trust companies, building and loan associations, industrial loan companies, credit unions, and savings and loan societies which have become insolvent and are in process of liquidation and in such cases the statute of limitations shall be deemed to have commenced to run from the beginning of the process of liquidation; provided, however, nothing herein contained shall be construed so as to relieve any stockholder of any banking corporation or trust company from stockholders' liability as shall at any time, be provided by law.[34]

348.5. An action upon any bonds or coupons issued by the State of California shall have no limitation.[649]

349.05. Within one hundred eighty days:

(a) An action to enjoin, abate, or for damages on account of, an underground trespass, use or occupancy, by means of a well drilled for oil or gas or both from a surface location on land other than real property in which the aggrieved party has some right, title or interest or in respect to which the aggrieved party has some right, title or interest.

(b) An action for conversion or for the taking or removing of oil, gas or other liquid, or fluids by means of any such well.

When any of said acts is by means of a new well the actual drilling of which is commenced after this section becomes effective, and such act was knowingly committed with actual intent to commit such act, the cause of action in such case shall not be deemed to have accrued until the discovery, by the aggrieved party, of the act or acts complained of; but in all other cases, and as to wells heretofore or hereafter drilled, the cause of action shall be deemed to have accrued ten days after the time when the well which is the subject of the cause of action was first placed on production.

Notwithstanding the continuing character of any such act, there shall be but one cause of action for any such act, and the cause of action shall accrue as aforesaid.

In all cases where oil or gas has been heretofore or is hereafter extracted from any existing or subsequently drilled well in this state, by a person without right but asserting a claim of right in good faith or acting under an honest mistake of law or fact, the measure of damages, if there be any right of recovery under existing law, shall be the value of the oil or gas at the time of extraction, without interest, after deducting all costs of development, operation and production, which costs shall include taxes and interest on all expenditures from the date thereof.

This section applies to causes of action existing when this section becomes effective. The time for commencement of existing causes of action which would be barred by this section within the first one hundred eighty days after this section becomes effective, shall be the said first one hundred eighty days.

Whenever the term "oil" is used in this section it shall be taken to include "petroleum," and the term "gas" shall mean natural gas coming from the earth.

The limitations prescribed by this section do not apply to rights of action or actions to be brought in the name of or for the benefit of the people of this State, or of any county, city and county, city or other political subdivision of this State.[770]

349.1. The validity of any acts or proceedings taken under color of law for the formation, organization, incorporation, dissolution, consolidation, change of organization or reorganization of, or for any change in the territorial boundaries of, any city, county, city and county, special district, public corporation or other public entity, or improvement district within any of the foregoing, shall not be contested in any action unless such action shall have been brought within six months from the date of completion of said acts or proceedings. Unless an action is commenced within said period all said acts or proceedings shall be held valid and in every respect legal and incontestable.

This section shall not amend or repeal any existing statute prescribing a shorter period of limitation than that specified herein.[59]

349.2. Where any acts or proceedings are taken under color of law by or on behalf of any city, county, city and county, special district, public corporation or other public entity for the authorization, sale or issuance of bonds:

(1) The validity of any such acts or proceedings for the authorization of bonds shall not be contested in any action unless such action shall have been brought within six months from the date of election authorizing said bonds, in cases where said bonds are required by law to be authorized at an election, or within six months from the date of adoption of a resolution or ordinance authorizing such bonds, in cases where bonds are not required by law to be authorized at an election;

(2) The validity of any such acts or proceedings for the sale of bonds (including all acts or proceedings taken prior thereto and providing for the issuance of such bonds) shall not be contested in any action unless such action shall have been brought within six months from the date of sale of said bonds;

(3) The validity of any such acts or proceedings for the issuance and delivery of, or payment for, bonds shall not be contested in any action unless such action shall have been brought within six months from the date of issuance and delivery of, or payment for, said bonds.

Unless an action is commenced within the applicable time hereinabove specified, said acts or proceedings for the authorization, sale or issuance of bonds shall be held valid and in every respect legal and incontestable.

This section shall not amend or repeal any existing statute prescribing a shorter period of limitation than that specified herein.

As used in this section, the term "bonds" means all instruments evidencing indebtedness incurred or to be incurred for any public purpose, all instruments evidencing the borrowing of money in anticipation of taxes, revenues or other income of a public body, all instruments payable from revenues or special funds, and all instruments funding or refunding any thereof or any indebtedness, but shall not include any special assessment bonds, special assessment refunding bonds, or bonds or other instruments issued to represent special assessments which are, directly or indirectly, secured by or payable from specific assessments levied against lands benefited, including bonds or other instruments issued under or pursuant to any statute, charter or ordinance providing for the improvement of streets, the opening and widening of streets, the provision for off-street parking, or the refunding of any of the same.[38]

349.4. All acts and proceedings heretofore or hereafter taken under color of law for the formation, organization or incorporation of, or for any change in the territorial boundaries of, any city, county, city and county, special district, public corporation or other public entity, or improvement district, annexed area or zone within any of the foregoing, and for the authorization, issuance, sale, or exchange of bonds of the entity or the territory thereof may be confirmed, validated, and declared legally effective in the manner provided in this section.

The legislative body of the entity may instruct its clerk or secretary to mail a notice to all owners of property within the entity, within the improvement district or zone, or within the annexed area, as the case may be, as their names and addresses appear on the last equalized county assessment roll, or as known to the clerk or secretary. Such notice shall include the name of the entity, the date the entity or the zone or improvement district therein was ordered formed or its territory changed by annexation or otherwise, as the case may be, the amount of bonds authorized, if any, and a statement that commencing with the date of mailing of said notice there shall be a 60-calendar-day period during which period any property owner may file an action contesting the validity of the formation of the entity, or of such improvement district or zone, or of such change of boundaries by annexation or otherwise, as the case may be, or the validity of the bond authorization, if any. The clerk or secretary shall make and file with the legislative body of the entity a certificate of mailing of the notices. The legislative body of the entity may order the clerk or secretary to include in such notice such other additional information that it deems pertinent.

If no action is filed during such 60-day period, the formation of the entity or of such improvement district or zone, or the change of boundaries by annexation or otherwise, as the case may be, and the bond authorization, if any, are valid and uncontestable.[103]

Chapter 4: General Provisions as to the Time of Commencing Actions

Chapter 4 enacted 1872.

350. An action is commenced, within the meaning of this Title, when the complaint is filed.[1]

351. If, when the cause of action accrues against a person, he is out of the State, the action may be commenced within the term herein limited, after his return to the State, and if, after the cause of action accrues, he departs from the State, the time of his absence is not part of the time limited for the commencement of the action.[1]

352. (a) If a person entitled to bring an action, mentioned in Chapter 3 (commencing with Section 335) is, at the time the cause of action accrued either under the age of majority or lacking the

legal capacity to make decisions, the time of the disability is not part of the time limited for the commencement of the action.
(b) This section shall not apply to an action against a public entity or public employee upon a cause of action for which a claim is required to be presented in accordance with Chapter 1 (commencing with Section 900) or Chapter 2 (commencing with Section 910) of Part 3, or Chapter 3 (commencing with Section 950) of Part 4, of Division 3.6 of Title 1 of the Government Code. This subdivision shall not apply to any claim presented to a public entity prior to January 1, 1971.[698]

352.1. (a) If a person entitled to bring an action, mentioned in Chapter 3 (commencing with Section 335), is, at the time the cause of action accrued, imprisoned on a criminal charge, or in execution under the sentence of a criminal court for a term less than for life, the time of that disability is not a part of the time limited for the commencement of the action, not to exceed two years.
(b) This section does not apply to an action against a public entity or public employee upon a cause of action for which a claim is required to be presented in accordance with Chapter 1 (commencing with Section 900) or Chapter 2 (commencing with Section 910) of Part 3, or Chapter 3 (commencing with Section 950) of Part 4, of Division 3.6 of Title 1 of the Government Code. This subdivision shall not apply to any claim presented to a public entity prior to January 1, 1971.
(c) This section does not apply to an action, other than an action to recover damages or that portion of an action that is for the recovery of damages, relating to the conditions of confinement, including an action brought by that person pursuant to Section 1983 of Title 42 of the United States Code.[340]

352.5. If, after a cause of action accrues against a person, that person comes under an order for restitution as a condition of probation with respect to the specific act or omission giving rise to such person's liability, the time during which the order is in effect is not a part of the time limited for the commencement of such an action based upon that act or omission.[99]

353.1. If a person entitled to bring an action or other proceeding, which action or other proceeding has not been filed or otherwise instituted, is represented by an attorney over whose practice a court of this state has assumed jurisdiction pursuant to Section 6180 or Section 6190 of the Business and Professions Code, and the application for the court to assume jurisdiction is filed prior to the expiration of the applicable statute of limitation or claim statute, the person shall have six months from the date of entry of the order assuming jurisdiction within which to file or otherwise institute the matter, if the applicable statute of limitation otherwise would have expired.[189]

354. When a person is, by reason of the existence of a state of war, under a disability to commence an action, the time of the continuance of such disability is not part of the period limited for the commencement of the action whether such cause of action shall have accrued prior to or during the period of such disability.[22]

354.3. (a) The following definitions govern the construction of this section:

(1) "Entity" means any museum or gallery that displays, exhibits, or sells any article of historical, interpretive, scientific, or artistic significance.

(2) "Holocaust-era artwork" means any article of artistic significance taken as a result of Nazi persecution during the period of 1929 to 1945, inclusive.

(b) Notwithstanding any other provision of law, any owner, or heir or beneficiary of an owner, of Holocaust-era artwork, may bring an action to recover Holocaust-era artwork from any entity described in paragraph (1) of subdivision (a). Subject to Section 410.10, that action may be brought in a superior court of this state, which court shall have jurisdiction over that action until its completion or resolution. Section 361 does not apply to this section.

(c) Any action brought under this section shall not be dismissed for failure to comply with the applicable statute of limitation, if the action is commenced on or before December 31, 2010.[480]

354.4. (a) The following definitions govern the construction of this section:

(1) "Armenian Genocide victim" means any person of Armenian or other ancestry living in the Ottoman Empire during the period of 1915 to 1923, inclusive, who died, was deported, or escaped to avoid persecution during that period.

(2) "Insurer" means an insurance provider doing business in the state, or whose contacts in the state satisfy the constitutional requirements for jurisdiction, that sold life, property, liability, health, annuities, dowry, educational, casualty, or any other insurance covering persons or property to persons in Europe or Asia at any time between 1875 and 1923.

(b) Notwithstanding any other provision of law, any Armenian Genocide victim, or heir or beneficiary of an Armenian Genocide victim, who resides in this state and has a claim arising out of an insurance policy or policies purchased or in effect in Europe or Asia between 1875 and 1923 from an insurer described in paragraph (2) of subdivision (a), may bring a legal action or may continue a pending legal action to recover on that claim in any court of competent jurisdiction in this state, which court shall be deemed the proper forum for that action until its completion or resolution.

(c) Any action, including any pending action brought by an Armenian Genocide victim or the heir or beneficiary of an Armenian Genocide victim, whether a resident or nonresident of this state, seeking benefits under the insurance policies issued or in effect between 1875 and 1923 shall not be dismissed for failure to comply with the applicable statute of limitation, provided the action is filed on or before December 31, 2016.

(d) The provisions of this section are severable. If any provision of this section or its application is held invalid, that invalidity shall not affect other provisions or applications that can be given effect without the invalid provision or application.[652]

354.45. (a) For purposes of this section, the following terms have the following meanings:

(1) "Armenian Genocide victim" means any person of Armenian or other ancestry living in the Ottoman Empire during the period of 1890 to 1923, inclusive, who died, was injured in person or property, was deported, or escaped to avoid persecution during that period.

(2) "Bank" means any banking or financial institution, including any institution that issued bonds, that conducted business in Ottoman Turkey at any time during the period of 1890 to 1923, inclusive.

(3) "Deposited assets" means any and all cash, securities, bonds, gold, jewels or jewelry, or any other tangible or intangible items of personal property, or any documents indicating ownership or possessory interests in real, personal, or intangible property, that were deposited with and held by a bank.

(4) "Looted assets" means any and all personal, commercial, real, and intangible property, including cash, securities, gold, jewelry, businesses, artwork, equipment, and intellectual property, that was taken from the ownership or control of an individual, organization, or entity, by theft, forced transfer, or exploitation, during the period of 1890 to 1923, inclusive, by any person, organization, or entity acting on behalf of, or in furtherance of the acts of, the Turkish Government, that were received by and deposited with a bank.

(b) Notwithstanding any other law, any Armenian Genocide victim, or heir or beneficiary of an Armenian Genocide victim, who resides in this state and has a claim arising out of a failure of a bank to pay or turn over deposited assets, or to turn over looted assets, may bring an action or may continue a pending action, to recover on that claim in any court of competent jurisdiction in this state, which court shall be deemed the proper forum for that action until its completion or resolution.

(c) Any action, including any pending action brought by an Armenian Genocide victim, or the heir or beneficiary of an Armenian Genocide victim, who resides in this state, seeking payment for, or the return of, deposited assets, or the return of looted assets, shall not be dismissed for failure to comply with the applicable statute of limitation, if the action is filed on or before December 31, 2016.

(d) The provisions of this section are severable. If any provision of this section or its application is held invalid, that invalidity shall not affect other provisions or applications that can be given effect without the invalid provision or application.[585]

354.5. (a) The following definitions govern the construction of this section:

(1) "Holocaust victim" means any person who was persecuted during the period of 1929 to 1945, inclusive, by Nazi Germany, its allies, or sympathizers.

(2) "Related company" means any parent, subsidiary, reinsurer, successor in interest, managing general agent, or affiliate company of the insurer.

(3) "Insurer" means an insurance provider doing business in the state, or whose contacts in the state satisfy the constitutional requirements for jurisdiction, that sold life, property, liability, health, annuities, dowry, educational, casualty, or any other insurance

covering persons or property to persons in Europe at any time before 1945, directly or through a related company, whether the sale of the insurance occurred before or after the insurer and the related company became related.

(b) Notwithstanding any other provision of law, any Holocaust victim, or heir or beneficiary of a Holocaust victim, who resides in this state and has a claim arising out of an insurance policy or policies purchased or in effect in Europe before 1945 from an insurer described in paragraph (3) of subdivision (a), may bring a legal action to recover on that claim in any superior court of the state for the county in which the plaintiff or one of the plaintiffs resides, which court shall be vested with jurisdiction over that action until its completion or resolution.

(c) Any action brought by a Holocaust victim or the heir or beneficiary of a Holocaust victim, whether a resident or nonresident of this state, seeking proceeds of the insurance policies issued or in effect before 1945 shall not be dismissed for failure to comply with the applicable statute of limitation, provided the action is commenced on or before December 31, 2010.[410]

354.6. (a) As used in this section:

(1) "Second World War slave labor victim" means any person taken from a concentration camp or ghetto or diverted from transportation to a concentration camp or from a ghetto to perform labor without pay for any period of time between 1929 and 1945, by the Nazi regime, its allies and sympathizers, or enterprises transacting business in any of the areas occupied by or under control of the Nazi regime or its allies and sympathizers.

(2) 'Second World War forced labor victim" means any person who was a member of the civilian population conquered by the Nazi regime, its allies or sympathizers, or prisoner-of-war of the Nazi regime, its allies or sympathizers, forced to perform labor without pay for any period of time between 1929 and 1945, by the Nazi regime, its allies and sympathizers, or enterprises transacting business in any of the areas occupied by or under control of the Nazi regime or its allies and sympathizers.

(3) "Compensation" means the present value of wages and benefits that individuals should have been paid and damages for injuries sustained in connection with the labor performed. Present value shall be calculated on the basis of the market value of the services at the time they were performed, plus interest from the time the services were performed, compounded annually to date of full payment without diminution for wartime or postwar currency devaluation.

(b) Any Second World War slave labor victim, or heir of a Second World War slave labor victim, Second World War forced labor victim, or heir of a Second World War forced labor victim, may bring an action to recover compensation for labor performed as a Second World War slave labor victim or Second World War forced labor victim from any entity or successor in interest thereof, for whom that labor was performed, either directly or through a subsidiary or affiliate. That action may be brought in a superior court of this state, which court shall have jurisdiction over that action until its completion or resolution.

(c) Any action brought under this section shall not be dismissed for failure to comply with the applicable statute of limitation, if the action is commenced on or before December 31, 2010.[403]

354.7. (a) The following definitions govern the construction of this section:

(1) "Bracero" means any person who participated in the labor importation program known as the Bracero program between January 1, 1942, and January 1, 1950, pursuant to agreements between the United States and Mexico.

(2) "Savings fund" means funds withheld from the wages of braceros as savings to be paid to braceros upon their return to Mexico.

(b) Notwithstanding any other provision of law, any bracero, or heir or beneficiary of a bracero, who has a claim arising out of a failure to pay or turn over savings fund amounts may bring a legal action or may continue a pending legal action to recover on that claim in any court of competent jurisdiction in this state, which court shall be deemed a proper forum for that action until its completion or resolution.

(c) Notwithstanding any other provision of law, any action brought by a bracero, or heir or beneficiary of a bracero, arising out of a failure to pay or turn over savings fund amounts shall not be dismissed for failure to comply with the otherwise applicable statute of limitations, provided the action is filed on or before December 31, 2005.

(d) The provisions of this section are severable. If any provision of this section or its application is held invalid, that invalidity shall not affect other provisions or applications that can be given effect without the invalid provision or application.[523]

354.8. (a) Notwithstanding any other law, including, but not limited to Section 335.1, the following actions shall be commenced within 10 years:

(1) An action for assault, battery, or both, where the conduct constituting the assault or battery would also constitute any of the following:

(A) An act of torture, as described in Section 206 of the Penal Code.

(B) An act of genocide, as described in Section 1091(a) of Title 18 of the United States Code.

(C) A war crime, as defined in Section 2441 of Title 18 of the United States Code.

(D) An attempted extrajudicial killing, as defined in Section 3(a) of Public Law 102-256.

(E) (i) Crimes against humanity.

(ii) For purposes of this paragraph, "crimes against humanity" means any of the following acts as part of a widespread or systematic attack directed against a civil population, with knowledge of the attack:

(I) Murder.

(II) Extermination.

(III) Enslavement.

(IV) Forcible transfer of population.

(V) Arbitrary detention.

(VI) Rape, sexual slavery, enforced prostitution, forced pregnancy, enforced sterilization, or any other form of sexual violence of comparable gravity.

(VII) Persecution on political, race, national, ethnic, cultural, religious, or gender grounds.

(VIII) Enforced disappearance of persons.

(IX) Other inhuman acts of similar character intentionally causing great suffering, serious bodily injury, or serious mental injury.

(2) An action for wrongful death, where the death arises out of conduct constituting any of the acts described in paragraph (1), or where the death would constitute an extrajudicial killing, as defined in Section 3(a) of Public Law 102-256.

(3) An action for the taking of property in violation of international law, in which either of the following apply:

(A) That property, or any property exchanged for such property, is present in the United States in connection with a commercial activity carried on in the United States by a foreign state.

(B) That property, or any property exchanged for such property, is owned or operated by an agency or instrumentality of a foreign state and that agency or instrumentality is engaged in a commercial activity in the United States.

(4) An action seeking benefits under an insurance policy where the insurance claim arises out of any of the conduct described in paragraphs (1) to (3), inclusive.

(b) An action brought under this section shall not be dismissed for failure to comply with any previously applicable statute of limitations.

(c) Section 361 shall not apply to an action brought pursuant to this section if all or part of the unlawful act or acts out of which the action arises occurred in this state.

(d) A prevailing plaintiff may be awarded reasonable attorney's fees and litigation costs including, but not limited to, expert witness fees and expenses as part of the costs.

(e) This section shall apply to all actions commenced concerning an act described in paragraphs (1) to (4), inclusive, of subdivision (a), that occurs on or after January 1, 2016.

(f) The provisions of this section are severable. If any provision of this section or its application is held invalid, that invalidity shall not affect other provisions or applications that can be given effect without the invalid provision or application.[715]

355. If an action is commenced within the time prescribed therefor, and a judgment therein for the plaintiff be reversed on appeal other than on the merits, a new action may be commenced within one year after the reversal.[305]

356. When the commencement of an action is stayed by injunction or statutory prohibition, the time of the continuance of the injunction or prohibition is not part of the time limited for the commencement of the action.[1]

357. No person can avail himself of a disability, unless it existed when his right of action accrued.[1]

358. When two or more disabilities coexist at the time the right of action accrues, the limitation does not attach until they are removed.[1]

359. This title does not affect actions against directors, shareholders, or members of a corporation, to recover a penalty or forfeiture imposed, or to enforce a liability created by law; but such actions must be brought within three years after the discovery by the aggrieved party of the facts upon

which the penalty or forfeiture attached, or the liability was created.[107]

359.5. If the obligations under a surety bond are conditioned upon performance of the principal, the expiration of the statute of limitations with respect to the obligations of the principal, other than the obligations of the principal under the bond, shall also bar an action against the principal or surety under the bond, unless the terms of the bond provide otherwise.[118]

360. No acknowledgment or promise is sufficient evidence of a new or continuing contract, by which to take the case out of the operation of this title, unless the same is contained in some writing, signed by the party to be charged thereby, provided that any payment on account of principal or interest due on a promissory note made by the party to be charged shall be deemed a sufficient acknowledgment or promise of a continuing contract to stop, from time to time as any such payment is made, the running of the time within which an action may be commenced upon the principal sum or upon any installment of principal or interest due on such note, and to start the running of a new period of time, but no such payment of itself shall revive a cause of action once barred.[35]

360.5. No waiver shall bar a defense to any action that the action was not commenced within the time limited by this title unless the waiver is in writing and signed by the person obligated. No waiver executed prior to the expiration of the time limited for the commencement of the action by this title shall be effective for a period exceeding four years from the date of expiration of the time limited for commencement of the action by this title and no waiver executed after the expiration of such time shall be effective for a period exceeding four years from the date thereof, but any such waiver may be renewed for a further period of not exceeding four years from the expiration of the immediately preceding waiver. Such waivers may be made successively. The provisions of this section shall not be applicable to any acknowledgment, promise or any form of waiver which is in writing and signed by the person obligated and given to any county to secure repayment of indigent aid or the repayment of moneys fraudulently or illegally obtained from the county.[32]

361. When a cause of action has arisen in another State, or in a foreign country, and by the laws thereof an action thereon cannot there be maintained against a person by reason of the lapse of time, an action thereon shall not be maintained against him in this State, except in favor of one who has been a citizen of this State, and who has held the cause of action from the time it accrued.[1]

362. This Title does not extend to actions already commenced, nor to cases where the time prescribed in any existing statute for acquiring a right or barring a remedy has fully run, but the laws now in force are applicable to such actions and cases, and are repealed subject to the provisions of this section.[1]

363. The word "action" as used in this Title is to be construed, whenever it is necessary so to do, as including a special proceeding of a civil nature.[1]

Chapter 5: The Commencement of Actions Based Upon Professional Negligence

Chapter 5 added by Stats. 1975, 2nd Ex. Sess., Ch. 1.

364. (a) No action based upon the health care provider's professional negligence may be commenced unless the defendant has been given at least 90 days' prior notice of the intention to commence the action.
(b) No particular form of notice is required, but it shall notify the defendant of the legal basis of the claim and the type of loss sustained, including with specificity the nature of the injuries suffered.
(c) The notice may be served in the manner prescribed in Chapter 5 (commencing with Section 1010) of Title 14 of Part 2.
(d) If the notice is served within 90 days of the expiration of the applicable statute of limitations, the time for the commencement of the action shall be extended 90 days from the service of the notice.
(e) The provisions of this section shall not be applicable with respect to any defendant whose name is unknown to the plaintiff at the time of filing the complaint and who is identified therein by a fictitious name, as provided in Section 474.
(f) For the purposes of this section:
(1) "Health care provider" means any person licensed or certified pursuant to Division 2 (commencing with Section 500) of the Business and Professions Code, or licensed pursuant to the Osteopathic Initiative Act, or the Chiropractic Initiative Act, or licensed pursuant to Chapter 2.5 (commencing with Section 1440) of Division 2 of the Health and Safety Code; and any clinic, health dispensary, or health facility, licensed pursuant to Division 2 (commencing with Section 1200) of the Health and Safety Code. "Health care provider" includes the legal representatives of a health care provider;
(2) "Professional negligence" means negligent act or omission to act by a health care provider in the rendering of professional services, which act or omission is the proximate cause of a personal injury or wrongful death, provided that such services are within the scope of services for which the provider is licensed and which are not within any restriction imposed by the licensing agency or licensed hospital.[91]

365. Failure to comply with this chapter shall not invalidate any proceedings of any court of this state, nor shall it affect the jurisdiction of the court to render a judgment therein. However, failure to comply with such provisions by any attorney at law shall be grounds for professional discipline and the State Bar of California shall investigate and take appropriate action in any such cases brought to its attention.[90]

Chapter 6: Time of Commencement of Action After Person's Death

Chapter 6 added by Stats. 1992, Ch. 178, Sec. 8.

366.1. If a person entitled to bring an action dies before the expiration of the applicable limitations period, and the cause of action survives, an action may be commenced before the expiration of the later of the following times:
(a) Six months after the person's death.
(b) The limitations period that would

have been applicable if the person had not died.[306]

366.2. (a) If a person against whom an action may be brought on a liability of the person, whether arising in contract, tort, or otherwise, and whether accrued or not accrued, dies before the expiration of the applicable limitations period, and the cause of action survives, an action may be commenced within one year after the date of death, and the limitations period that would have been applicable does not apply.
(b) The limitations period provided in this section for commencement of an action shall not be tolled or extended for any reason except as provided in any of the following, where applicable:
(1) Sections 12, 12a, and 12b of this code.
(2) Part 4 (commencing with Section 9000) of Division 7 of the Probate Code (creditor claims in administration of estates of decedents).
(3) Part 8 (commencing with Section 19000) of Division 9 of the Probate Code (payment of claims, debts, and expenses from revocable trust of deceased settlor).
(4) Former Part 3 (commencing with Section 21300) of Division 11 of the Probate Code (no contest clauses), as that part read prior to its repeal by Chapter 174 of the Statutes of 2008.
(c) This section applies to actions brought on liabilities of persons dying on or after January 1, 1993.[620]

366.3. (a) If a person has a claim that arises from a promise or agreement with a decedent to distribution from an estate or trust or under another instrument, whether the promise or agreement was made orally or in writing, an action to enforce the claim to distribution may be commenced within one year after the date of death, and the limitations period that would have been applicable does not apply.
(b) The limitations period provided in this section for commencement of an action shall not be tolled or extended for any reason except as provided in Sections 12, 12a, and 12b of this code, and former Part 3 (commencing with Section 21300) of Division 11 of the Probate Code, as that part read prior to its repeal by Chapter 174 of the Statutes of 2008.
(c) This section applies to actions brought on claims concerning persons dying on or after the effective date of this section.[621]

TITLE 3: OF THE PARTIES TO CIVIL ACTIONS

Title 3 enacted 1872.

Chapter 1: General Provisions

Heading of Chapter 1 added by Stats. 1992, Ch. 178, Sec. 9

367. Every action must be prosecuted in the name of the real party in interest, except as otherwise provided by statute.[307]

367.3. (a) For purposes of this section, the following definitions apply:
(1) "Identifying characteristics" means the name or any part thereof, address or any part thereof, city or unincorporated area of residence, age, marital status, relationship to other parties, and race or ethnic background, telephone number, email address, social media profiles, online identifiers, contact information, or any other information, including images of the protected person, from

which the protected person's identity can be discerned.

(2) "Online identifiers" means any personally identifying information or signifiers that would tie an individual to a particular electronic service, device, or internet application, website, or platform account, including, access names, access codes, account names, aliases, avatars, credentials, gamer tags, display names, handles, login names, member names, online identities, pseudonyms, screen names, user accounts, user identifications, usernames, Uniform Resource Locators (URLs), domain names, Internet Protocol (IP) addresses, and media access control (MAC) addresses.

(3) "Protected person" means a person who is an active participant in the address confidentiality program created pursuant to Chapter 3.1 (commencing with Section 6205) of Division 7 of Title 1 of the Government Code.

(b) (1) A protected person who is a party in a civil proceeding may proceed using a pseudonym, either John Doe, Jane Doe, or Doe, for the true name of the protected person and may exclude or redact from all pleadings and documents filed in the action other identifying characteristics of the protected person. A protected person who proceeds using a pseudonym as provided in this section shall file with the court and serve upon all other parties to the proceeding a confidential information form for this purpose that includes the protected person's name and other identifying characteristics being excluded or redacted. The court shall keep the confidential information form confidential.

(2) In cases where a protected person proceeds using a pseudonym under this section, the following provisions shall apply, subject to sanction for an intentional violation:

(A) Except as provided in subparagraph (B), all parties and their agents and attorneys shall use the pseudonym in all pleadings, discovery requests or discovery motion documents, and other documents filed or served in the action, and at hearings, trial, and other court proceedings that are open to the public.

(B) A party seeking discovery in which the true name of the protected person and identifying information must be divulged for the purposes of fair and reasonable discovery, may use the true name of the protected person and identifying information for purposes of that discovery. The discovery request and all information collected through the discovery process shall not be made public and, if filed in court, shall be subject to subparagraph (C).

(C) (i) A party filing a pleading, discovery document, or other document in the action shall exclude or redact any identifying characteristics of the protected person from the pleading, discovery document, or other document, except for a confidential information form filed pursuant to this subdivision.

(ii) A party excluding or redacting identifying characteristics shall file with the court and serve upon all other parties a confidential information form that includes the protected person's name and other identifying characteristics being excluded or redacted. The court shall keep the confidential information form confidential.

(D) Following final disposition of the proceedings a party in possession of any pleading, discovery document, or other document containing confidential information of the protected person obtained in the course of the action shall treat the documents as a nonpublic consumer record in accordance with Section 1798.81 of the Civil Code, subject to penalty for violations of that section.

(E) If the protected person is a minor dependent or minor ward of the state, the minor's parent, guardian, or attorney shall inform the minor's social worker or probation officer of the minor's participation in the action. The social worker or probation officer shall keep this information confidential.

(3) The responsibility to exclude or redact identifying characteristics of the protected person from documents filed with the court rests solely with the parties and their attorneys. This section does not require the court to review pleadings or other papers for compliance.

(4) The court, on motion of the protected person, may order a record or part of a record to be filed under seal in accordance with Rules 2.550 and 2.551 of the California Rules of Court, as those rules may be amended.

(c) In an action filed under this section, the plaintiff shall state in the caption of the complaint "ACTION BASED ON CODE OF CIVIL PROCEDURE SECTION 367.3."

(d) This section does not alter or negate any rights, obligations, or immunities of an interactive service provider under Section 230 of Title 47 of the United States Code. This section does not limit or preclude a plaintiff from securing or recovering any other available remedy.

(e) The Judicial Council shall coordinate with the Secretary of State to adopt or revise as appropriate rules and forms to implement this section, on or before January 1, 2021.

(f) The provisions of this section are severable. If any provision of this section or its application is held invalid, that invalidity shall not affect other provisions or applications that can be given effect without the invalid provision or application.[754]

367.75. (a) (1) Except as provided in subdivisions (b) and (d), in civil cases, when a party has provided notice to the court and all other parties that it intends to appear remotely, a party may appear remotely and the court may conduct conferences, hearings, and proceedings, in whole or in part, through the use of remote technology.

(2) This section does not apply to any of the following type of proceedings:

(A) Any proceeding in matters identified in paragraph (1) of subdivision (a) of Section 367.76.

(B) A juvenile justice proceeding covered by Section 679.5 of the Welfare and Institutions Code.

(b) Except as otherwise provided by law, the court may require a party or witness to appear in person at a conference, hearing, or proceeding described in subdivision (a), or under subdivisions (e) and (h), if any of the following conditions are present:

(1) The court with jurisdiction over the case does not have the technology necessary to conduct the conference, hearing, or proceeding remotely.

(2) Although the court has the requisite technology, the quality of the

technology or audibility at a conference, hearing, or proceeding prevents the effective management or resolution of the conference, hearing, or proceeding.

(3) The court determines on a hearing-by-hearing basis that an in-person appearance would materially assist in the determination of the conference, hearing, or proceeding or in the effective management or resolution of the particular case.

(4) The quality of the technology or audibility at a conference, hearing, or proceeding inhibits the court reporter's ability to accurately prepare a transcript of the conference, hearing, or proceeding.

(5) The quality of the technology or audibility at a conference, hearing, or proceeding prevents an attorney from being able to provide effective representation to the attorney's client.

(6) The quality of the technology or audibility at a conference, hearing, or proceeding inhibits a court interpreter's ability to provide language access to a court user or authorized individual.

(c) Notwithstanding paragraph (3) of subdivision (b), an expert witness may appear remotely absent good cause to compel in-person testimony.

(d) (1) Except as otherwise provided by law and subject to the limitations of subdivision (b), upon its own motion or the motion of any party, the court may conduct a trial or evidentiary hearing, in whole or in part, through the use of remote technology, absent a showing by the opposing party as to why a remote appearance or testimony should not be allowed.

(2) (A) Except as provided in Section 269 of the Code of Civil Procedure and Section 69957 of the Government Code, if the court conducts a trial, in whole or in part, through the use of remote technology, the official reporter or official reporter pro tempore shall be physically present in the courtroom.

(B) If the court conducts a trial, in whole or in part, through the use of remote technology, upon request, the court interpreter shall be physically present in the courtroom.

(e) (1) Before the court with jurisdiction over the case may proceed with a remote conference, hearing, proceeding, or trial, the court shall have a process for a party, witness, official reporter, official reporter pro tempore, court interpreter, or other court personnel to alert the judicial officer of technology or audibility issues that arise during the conference, hearing, proceeding, or trial.

(2) The court shall require that a remote appearance by a party or witness have the necessary privacy and security appropriate for the conference, hearing, proceeding, or trial.

(3) The court shall inform all parties, particularly parties without legal representation, about the potential technological or audibility issues that could arise when using remote technology, which may require a delay of or halt the conference, hearing, proceeding, or trial. The court shall make information available to self-represented parties regarding the options for appearing in person and through the use of remote technology.

(f) The court shall not require a party to appear through the use of remote technology. If the court permits an appearance through remote technology, the court must ensure that technology in the courtroom enables all parties, whether appearing remotely or in person, to fully participate in the conference, hearing, or proceeding.

(g) A self-represented party may appear remotely in a conference, hearing, or proceeding conducted through the use of remote technology only if they agree to do so.

(h) Any juvenile dependency proceeding may be conducted in whole or in part through the use of remote technology subject to the following:

(1) Any person authorized to be present may request to appear remotely.

(2) (A) Any party to the proceeding may request that the court compel the physical presence of a witness or party. A witness, including a party providing testimony, may appear through remote technology only with the consent of all parties, except as provided in subparagraph (B), and if the witness has access to the appropriate technology.

(B) A parent, child, nonminor dependent, or Indian tribe as defined in Section 224.1 of the Welfare and Institutions Code, may utilize remote technology for the appearance of an expert witness without the consent of all parties.

(3) A court shall not require a party to appear through the use of remote technology.

(4) The confidentiality requirements that apply to an in-person juvenile dependency proceeding shall apply to a juvenile dependency proceeding conducted through the use of remote technology.

(i) (1) Notwithstanding Section 8613.5 of the Family Code, in an adoption proceeding under Division 13 (commencing with Section 8500) of the Family Code, the court may conduct an adoption finalization hearing, in whole or in part, through the use of remote technology, without the court finding that it is impossible or impracticable for either prospective adoptive parent to make the appearance in person.

(2) A court shall not require a party to appear through the use of remote technology.

(3) The confidentiality and privacy requirements that apply to an in-person adoption finalization hearing, including, but not limited to, the requirements in Section 8611 of the Family Code, apply to an adoption finalization hearing conducted through the use of remote technology.

(j) For purposes of this section, a party includes a nonparty subject to Chapter 6 of Title 4 of Part 4 (commencing with Section 2020.010).

(k) Subject to the limitations in subdivision (b), this section is not intended to prohibit the use of appearances through the use of remote technology when stipulated by attorneys for represented parties.

(l) Consistent with its constitutional rulemaking authority, the Judicial Council shall adopt rules to implement the policies and provisions in this section to promote statewide consistency, including, but not limited to, the following procedures:

(1) A deadline by which a party must notify the court and the other parties of their request to appear remotely.

(2) Procedures and standards for a judicial officer to determine when a conference, hearing, or proceeding may be conducted through the use of remote technology. The procedures

and standards shall require that a judicial officer give consideration to the limited access to technology or transportation that a party or witness might have.

(m) This section shall remain in effect only until January 1, 2027, and as of that date is repealed.[868]

367.76. (a) (1) This section applies to proceedings in the following matters:

(A) Judicial commitments under Part 2 (commencing with Section 6250) of Division 6 of the Welfare and Institutions Code, except for delinquency proceedings.

(B) Involuntary treatment and conservatorships of gravely disabled persons under Chapter 1 (commencing with Section 5000), Chapter 2 (commencing with Section 5150), and Chapter 3 (commencing with Section 5350) of Part 1 of Division 5 of the Welfare and Institutions Code, including Murphy conservatorships.

(C) Contempt proceedings under Title 5 (commencing with Section 1209) of Part 3 of this code.

(D) Mentally disordered offender proceedings under Article 4 (commencing with Section 2960) of Chapter 7 of Title 1 of Part 3 of the Penal Code.

(E) Commitment proceedings under Section 1026, et seq. of the Penal Code.

(F) Competency proceedings under Chapter 6 (commencing with Section 1367) of Title 10 of Part 2 of the Penal Code.

(G) Placement and revocation proceedings pursuant to Section 1600 et seq. of the Penal Code.

(H) Involuntary medication and treatment hearings for individuals committed or awaiting admission to a State Department of State Hospitals facility as described in Section 4100 of the Welfare and Institutions Code.

(2) This section does not apply to proceedings in matters brought pursuant to Sections 601 and 602 of the Welfare and Institutions Code.

(b) For the purposes of this section, the following definitions apply:

(1) "Person" means the person subject to any proceeding in matters described in paragraph (1) of subdivision (a).

(2) "Proceeding" or "proceedings" includes, but is not limited to, all hearings, conferences, and trials in matters described in paragraph (1) of subdivision (a).

(3) "Remote technology" means technology that provides for the two-way transmission of video and audio signals except that audio signals alone may be permitted where specifically authorized by law. Remote technology shall include, but not be limited to, a computer, tablet, telephone, cellular telephone, or other electronic or communications device. Notwithstanding the foregoing and subject to subdivision (h), the person subject to the proceeding, in consultation with counsel if represented, may, at their request, participate through audio-only technology.

(c) Proceedings in matters arising under subdivision (a) may be conducted through the use of remote technology subject to the following:

(1) A person has the right to be physically present for all proceedings and shall not be required to appear through the use of remote technology.

(2) A person may waive their right to

be physically present and may elect to appear remotely.

(3) Except as provided in subdivisions (d), (e), and (h), a party, counsel for a party, or witness may appear through the use of remote technology.

(4) The confidentiality requirements that apply to inperson proceedings shall apply with equal force and effect when conducted through the use of remote technology.

(d) If the person is physically present in court the following shall apply:

(1) Absent exceptional circumstances and except as provided in paragraphs (3) and (4), counsel for the person, counsel for the other party or parties, the other party or parties, and the judicial officer shall be physically present in the courtroom.

(2) Except as provided in paragraphs (3) and (4) and paragraph (3) of subdivision (b) of Section 1370 of the Penal Code, absent a waiver by the person or a finding of good cause by the court, any witness the other party or parties calls shall be physically present in the courtroom. In determining whether good cause exists to excuse the physical presence of a witness, the court shall consider the distance the witness must travel, the nature of the testimony, and the nature of the proceeding.

(3) Notwithstanding paragraphs (1) and (2), counsel and witnesses for the State Department of Developmental Services shall not be required to be physically present in the courtroom absent a finding of good cause by the court.

(4) Notwithstanding paragraphs (1) and (2), counsel and witnesses for the State Department of State Hospitals shall not be required to be physically present in the courtroom in any nonjury trial matters or proceedings described in paragraph (1) of subdivision (a) absent a finding of good cause by the court.

(e) Notwithstanding any other law, unless good cause exists, a court shall not compel the physical presence of the person who is a patient in a State Department of State Hospitals or State Department of Developmental Services facility or other inpatient or outpatient treatment facility absent consent of the person in consultation with counsel. In determining whether good cause exists to compel the physical presence of a patient, the court shall consider the nature of the hearing and whether requiring the physical presence of the patient would interfere with the person's program of treatment or be detrimental to their mental or physical health.

(f) (1) Until July 1, 2024, when the court conducts proceedings that will be reported by an official reporter or official reporter pro tempore, the reporter shall be physically present in the same room as the judicial officer except where the court finds that, as the result of unusual circumstances, this requirement would place extreme or undue hardship on the court or the litigants. For purposes of this paragraph, "unusual circumstances" means a work stoppage, a circumstance described in subdivision (a) of Section 68115 of the Government Code, an unforeseen emergency, court proceedings conducted in a remote court location to which a judicial officer is not regularly assigned to sit, or when a judicial officer has to travel to a location outside of a courthouse to conduct the proceeding.

(2) Beginning July 1, 2024, when the court conducts proceedings that will be reported by an official reporter or official reporter pro tempore, the reporter shall be physically present in the same room as the judicial officer if the court cannot provide the technology standards described in subdivision (o).

(g) If the court conducts a trial, in whole or in part, through the use of remote technology, upon request, the court interpreter shall be physically present in the courtroom.

(h) (1) If any of the following conditions are present and cannot be resolved, the court shall not permit any party, counsel, or witness to appear or participate in proceedings through the use of remote technology, and shall continue any proceeding being conducted with the use of remote technology:

(A) The court does not have the technology necessary to conduct the proceeding remotely.

(B) Although the court has the requisite technology, the quality of the technology or audibility at a proceeding prevents the effective management or resolution of the proceeding.

(C) The quality of the technology or audibility at a proceeding inhibits the court reporter's ability to accurately prepare and certify a transcript of the proceeding.

(D) The court reporter is unable to capture the verbatim record and certify a transcript of any proceeding that is conducted remotely, in whole or in part, to the same extent and in the same manner as if it were not conducted remotely.

(E) The quality of the technology or audibility at a proceeding inhibits the ability of the person to understand or participate in the proceeding.

(F) The quality of the technology or audibility at a proceeding inhibits counsel from being able to provide effective representation to the person.

(G) The court does not have the technology necessary for secure, confidential communication between counsel and the person.

(H) The quality of the technology or audibility at a proceeding inhibits a court interpreter's ability to provide language access, including to communicate and interpret directly with the person and the court during the proceedings.

(2) Except as provided in subdivision (e) or otherwise provided by law, the court may require a party or witness to appear in person at a proceeding if the court determines on a hearing-by-hearing basis that an inperson appearance would materially assist in the determination of the proceeding or resolution of the case. The court's determination shall be based on the individual case before the court and shall be entered into the minutes or otherwise made on the record. In making its determination, the court shall consider the request of the person, the nature of the proceedings, and whether requiring the physical presence of the person would disrupt the person's program of treatment or be detrimental to their mental or physical health.

(3) The court shall not continue proceedings beyond statutory time limits pursuant to this section absent a waiver by the person in consultation with counsel.

(i) Subject to the limitations in subdivision (h), this section is not intended to prohibit the use of appearances through the use of remote technology when stipulated by attorneys for represented parties.

(j) Before the court may conduct proceedings through the use of remote technology, the court shall have a process for a party, witness, official reporter, official reporter pro tempore, court interpreter, or other court personnel to alert the judicial officer of technology or audibility issues that arise during the proceedings.

(k) The court shall inform all parties, particularly parties without legal representation, about the potential technological or audibility issues that could arise when using remote technology, which may require a delay of or halt the proceedings. The court shall make information available to self-represented parties regarding the options for appearing in person and through the use of remote technology.

(l) A self-represented party may appear remotely in a proceeding conducted through the use of remote technology only if they agree to do so.

(m) For purposes of this section, a party includes a nonparty subject to Chapter 6 (commencing with Section 2020.010) of Title 4 of Part 4.

(n) Consistent with its constitutional rulemaking authority, the Judicial Council shall adopt such other rules and standards as are necessary to implement the policies and provisions of this section and the intent of the Legislature.

(o) By April 1, 2024, the Judicial Council shall adopt, and trial courts shall implement by July 1, 2024, minimum standards for the courtroom technology necessary to permit remote participation in proceedings subject to this section. Those standards shall include, but not be limited to, hard-wired or other reliable high-speed internet connections in the courtroom for the judicial officer and court reporter, and monitors, dedicated cameras, speakers, and microphones so the judicial officer, court reporter, and court interpreter can appropriately see and hear remote participants, as well as to ensure that remote participants can appropriately see and hear the judicial officer and other courtroom participants.

(p) Consistent with federal and California labor law, a trial court shall not retaliate or threaten to retaliate against an official reporter or an official reporter pro tempore who notifies the judicial officer that technology or audibility issues are impeding the creation of the verbatim record of a proceeding that includes participation through remote technology. This subdivision shall only apply to an official reporter and an official reporter pro tempore when they meet the definition of "trial court employee" under subdivision (l) of Section 71601 of the Government Code.

(q) This section shall remain in effect only until January 1, 2027, and as of that date is repealed.[838]

367.8. (a) Each superior court shall report to the Judicial Council on or before October 1, 2023, and annually thereafter, and the Judicial Council shall report to the Legislature on or before December 31, 2023, and annually thereafter, to assess the impact of technology issues or problems affecting remote proceedings, as included under Sections 367.75 and 367.76 of this code, and Section 679.5 of the Welfare and Institutions Code, and all purchases and leases of technology or equipment to facilitate remote conferences, hearings, or proceedings. The report by each superior court and the Judicial Council shall specify all of the following for each annual reporting period:

(1) The number of proceedings conducted with the use of remote technology.

(2) Any superior court in which technology issues or problems occurred.

(3) The superior courts in which remote technology was used.

(4) The types of trial court conferences, hearings, or proceedings in which remote technology was used.

(5) The cost of purchasing, leasing, or upgrading remote technology.

(6) The type of technology and equipment purchased or leased.

(7) Any other information necessary to evaluate the use of remote proceedings by the courts.

(b) Each superior court shall report to the Judicial Council on or before October 1, 2025, and annually thereafter, and the Judicial Council shall report to the Legislature on or before December 31, 2025, and annually thereafter, the information identified in subdivision (a) to assess the impact of technology issues or problems affecting criminal remote proceedings, as included under Sections 977, 977.3, and 1043.5 of the Penal Code.

(c) (1) By October 1, 2025, and annually thereafter, the court executive officer of each superior court shall certify to the Judicial Council, in a form and manner determined by the Judicial Council, that each courtroom of the superior court in which the court is conducting a remote proceeding meets the minimum standards for courtroom technology required pursuant to subdivision (o) of Section 367.76 of this code, subdivision (j) of Section 977 of the Penal Code, or subdivision (n) of Section 679.5 of the Welfare and Institutions Code.

(2) By December 31, 2025, and annually thereafter, the Judicial Council shall report the information identified in paragraph (1) to the Legislature.

(d) A report to be submitted to the Legislature pursuant to this section shall be submitted in compliance with Section 9795 of the Government Code.

(e) This section shall remain in effect only until January 1, 2027, and as of that date is repealed.[839]

367.10. Consistent with its constitutional rulemaking authority, the Judicial Council shall adopt rules that include standards for when a judicial officer, in limited situations and in the interest of justice, may preside over a remote court proceeding from a location other than a courtroom.[812]

368. In the case of an assignment of a thing in action, the action by the assignee is without prejudice to any setoff, or other defense existing at the time of, or before, notice of the assignment; but this section does not apply to a negotiable promissory note or bill of exchange, transferred in good faith, and upon good consideration, before maturity.[1]

368.5. An action or proceeding does not abate by the transfer of an interest in the action or proceeding or by any other transfer of an interest. The action or proceeding may be continued in the name of the original party, or the court may allow the person to whom the transfer is made to be substituted in the action or proceeding.[308]

369. (a) The following persons may sue without joining as parties the persons for whose benefit the action is prosecuted:

(1) A personal representative, as defined in subdivision (a) of Section 58 of the Probate Code.

(2) A trustee of an express trust.

(3) Except for a person upon whom a power of sale has been conferred pursuant to a deed of trust or mortgage, a person with whom, or in whose name, a contract is made for the benefit of another.

(4) Any other person expressly authorized by statute.

(b) Notwithstanding subdivision (a), a trustee upon whom a power of sale has been conferred pursuant to a deed of trust or mortgage may sue to exercise the trustee's powers and duties pursuant to Chapter 2 (commencing with Section 2920) of Title 14 of Part 4 of Division 3 of the Civil Code.[309]

369.5. (a) A partnership or other unincorporated association, whether organized for profit or not, may sue and be sued in the name it has assumed or by which it is known.

(b) A member of the partnership or other unincorporated association may be joined as a party in an action against the unincorporated association. If service of process is made on the member as an individual, whether or not the member is also served as a person upon whom service is made on behalf of the unincorporated association, a judgment against the member based on the member's personal liability may be obtained in the action, whether the liability is joint, joint and several, or several.[310]

Chapter 2: Married Person

Heading of Chapter 2 added by Stats. 1992, Ch. 178, Sec. 14.

370. A married person may be sued without his or her spouse being joined as a party, and may sue without his or her spouse being joined as a party in all actions.[97]

371. If spouses are sued together, each may defend for his or her own right, but if one spouse neglects to defend, the other spouse may defend for that spouse's right also.[722]

Chapter 3: Disability of Party

Heading of Chapter 3 added by Stats. 1992, Ch. 178, Sec. 15.

372. (a) (1) When a minor, a person who lacks legal capacity to make decisions, or a person for whom a conservator has been appointed is a party, that person shall appear either by a guardian or conservator of the estate or by a guardian ad litem appointed by the court in which the action or proceeding is pending, or by a judge thereof, in each case.

(2) (A) A guardian ad litem may be appointed in any case when it is deemed by the court in which the action or proceeding is prosecuted, or by a judge thereof, expedient to appoint a guardian ad litem to represent the minor, person who lacks legal capacity to make decisions, or person for whom a conservator has been appointed, notwithstanding that the person may have a guardian or conservator of the estate and may have appeared by the guardian or conservator of the estate.

(B) If application is made for appointment of a guardian ad litem for a person described in paragraph (1), and that person has a guardian or conservator of the estate, the application may be granted only if all of the following occur:

(i) The applicant gives notice and a copy of the application to the guardian or conservator of the estate upon filing the application.

(ii) The application discloses the existence of a guardian or conservator of the estate.

(iii) The application sets forth the reasons why the guardian or conservator of the estate is inadequate to represent the interests of the proposed ward in the action

(C) The guardian or conservator of the estate shall have five court days from receiving notice of the application to file any opposition to the application.

(3) The guardian or conservator of the estate or guardian ad litem so appearing for any minor, person who lacks legal capacity to make decisions, or person for whom a conservator has been appointed shall have power, with the approval of the court in which the action or proceeding is pending, to compromise the same, to agree to the order or judgment to be entered therein for or against the ward or conservatee, and to satisfy any judgment or order in favor of the ward or conservatee or release or discharge any claim of the ward or conservatee pursuant to that compromise. Money or other property to be paid or delivered pursuant to the order or judgment for the benefit of a minor, person lacking legal capacity to make decisions, or person for whom a conservator has been appointed shall be paid and delivered as provided in Chapter 4 (commencing with Section 3600) of Part 8 of Division 4 of the Probate Code.

(4) Where reference is made in this chapter to "a person who lacks legal capacity to make decisions," the reference shall be deemed to include all of the following:

(A) A person who lacks capacity to understand the nature or consequences of the action or proceeding.

(B) A person who lacks capacity to assist the person's attorney in the preparation of the case.

(C) A person for whom a conservator may be appointed pursuant to Section 1801 of the Probate Code.

(5) Nothing in this section, or in any other provision of this code, the Civil Code, the Family Code, or the Probate Code is intended by the Legislature to prohibit a minor from exercising an intelligent and knowing waiver of the minor's constitutional rights in a proceeding under the Juvenile Court Law (Chapter 2 (commencing with Section 200) of Part 1 of Division 2 of the Welfare and Institutions Code).

(b) (1) Notwithstanding subdivision (a), a minor 12 years of age or older may appear in court without a guardian, counsel, or guardian ad litem, for the purpose of requesting or opposing a request for any of the following:

(A) An injunction or temporary restraining order or both to prohibit harassment pursuant to Section 527.6.

(B) An injunction or temporary restraining order or both against violence or a credible threat of violence in the workplace pursuant to Section 527.8.

(C) A protective order pursuant to

Division 10 (commencing with Section 6200) of the Family Code.

(D) A protective order pursuant to Sections 7710 and 7720 of the Family Code.

The court may, either upon motion or in its own discretion, and after considering reasonable objections by the minor to the appointment of specific individuals, appoint a guardian ad litem to assist the minor in obtaining or opposing the order, provided that the appointment of the guardian ad litem does not delay the issuance or denial of the order being sought. In making the determination concerning the appointment of a particular guardian ad litem, the court shall consider whether the minor and the guardian have divergent interests.

(2) For purposes of this subdivision only, upon the issuance of an order pursuant to paragraph (1), if the minor initially appeared in court seeking an order without a guardian or guardian ad litem, and if the minor is residing with a parent or guardian, the court shall send a copy of the order to at least one parent or guardian designated by the minor, unless, in the discretion of the court, notification of a parent or guardian would be contrary to the best interest of the minor. The court is not required to send the order to more than one parent or guardian.

(c) (1) Notwithstanding subdivision (a), a minor may appear in court without a guardian ad litem in the following proceedings if the minor is a parent of the child who is the subject of the proceedings:

(A) Family court proceedings pursuant to Part 3 (commencing with Section 7600) of Division 12 of the Family Code.

(B) Dependency proceedings pursuant to Chapter 2 (commencing with Section 200) of Part 1 of Division 2 of the Welfare and Institutions Code.

(C) Guardianship proceedings for a minor child pursuant to Part 2 (commencing with Section 1500) of Division 4 of the Probate Code.

(D) Any other proceedings concerning child custody, visitation, or support.

(2) If the court finds that the minor parent is unable to understand the nature of the proceedings or to assist counsel in preparing the case, the court shall, upon its own motion or upon a motion by the minor parent or the minor parent's counsel, appoint a guardian ad litem.

(d) Before a court appoints a guardian ad litem pursuant to this chapter, a proposed guardian ad litem shall disclose both of the following to the court and all parties to the action or proceeding:

(1) Any known actual or potential conflicts of interest that would or might arise from the appointment.

(2) Any familial or affiliate relationship the proposed guardian ad litem has with any of the parties.

(e) If a guardian ad litem becomes aware that a potential conflict of interest has become an actual conflict of interest or that a new potential or actual conflict of interest exists, the guardian ad litem shall promptly disclose the conflict of interest to the court.[806]

372.5. (a) The court may appoint a guardian ad litem under a pseudonym pursuant to the requirements of this section.

(b) A person who applies for appointment as a guardian ad litem under a pseudonym shall, at the same time that the application is filed, file an ex parte request for leave to appear under a pseudonym. The ex parte request shall allege facts and circumstances establishing the guardian ad litem's overriding interest in preserving his or her anonymity.

(c) To permit an applicant for appointment as a guardian ad litem to appear under pseudonym, the court shall make each of the following findings:

(1) That the applicant has an overriding interest in preserving anonymity that supports permitting the applicant to appear under a pseudonym.

(2) That there is a substantial probability that the applicant's interest in preserving anonymity will be prejudiced if the applicant is not permitted to appear under a pseudonym.

(3) That permitting the applicant to appear under a pseudonym is narrowly tailored to serve the applicant's interest in preserving anonymity without unduly prejudicing the public's right of access or the ability of the other parties to prosecute, defend, or resolve the action.

(4) That there are no less restrictive means of protecting the applicant's interest in preserving his or her anonymity.

(d) (1) The court may make any further orders necessary to preserve the applicant's anonymity or to allow the other parties or financial institutions to know the applicant's identity to the extent necessary to prosecute, defend, or resolve the action.

(2) In addition to any other orders, the court may require a guardian ad litem who is permitted to appear under a pseudonym and is not represented by counsel to designate a mailing or electronic address for service of process and to consent to accept service of process under the pseudonym at that address for purposes of the action.

(e) (1) If a guardian ad litem is permitted to appear under a pseudonym, all court decisions, orders, petitions, and any documents filed with the court shall be written in a manner that protects the name and personal identifying information of the guardian ad litem from public disclosure, except to the extent the information is necessary for the parties to prosecute, defend, or resolve the action.

(2) For purposes of this subdivision, "personal identifying information" includes the guardian ad litem's name or any part thereof, his or her address or any part thereof, and the city or unincorporated area of the guardian ad litem's residence.

(f) The responsibility for excluding the name and personal identifying information of the guardian ad litem from documents filed with the court rests solely with the parties and their attorneys. This section does not require the court to review pleadings or other papers for compliance with this subdivision.

(g) After granting permission for a guardian ad litem to appear under a pseudonym pursuant to this section, the court shall retain discretion to reconsider its decision.

(h) This section does not affect the right of a plaintiff or petitioner to pursue litigation under a pseudonym in appropriate circumstances.[750]

373. When a guardian ad litem is appointed, he or she shall be appointed as follows:

(a) If the minor is the plaintiff the appointment must be made before the summons is issued, upon the application of the minor, if the minor is 14 years of age or older, or, if under that age, upon the application of a relative or friend of the minor.

(b) If the minor is the defendant, upon the application of the minor, if the minor is 14 years of age or older, and the minor applies within 10 days after the service of the summons, or, if under that age or if the minor neglects to apply, then upon the application of a relative or friend of the minor, or of any other party to the action, or by the court on its own motion.

(c) If the person lacking legal competence to make decisions is a party to an action or proceeding, upon the application of a relative or friend of the person lacking legal competence to make decisions, or of any other party to the action or proceeding, or by the court on its own motion.[699]

373.5. If under the terms of a written instrument, or otherwise, a person or persons of a designated class who are not ascertained or who are not in being, or a person or persons who are unknown, may be or may become legally or equitably interested in any property, real or personal, the court in which any action, petition or proceeding of any kind relative to or affecting the property is pending, may, upon the representation of any party thereto, or of any person interested, appoint a suitable person to appear and act therein as guardian ad litem of the person or persons not ascertained, not in being, or who are unknown; and the judgment, order or decree in the proceedings, made after the appointment, shall be conclusive upon all persons for whom the guardian ad litem was appointed.

The guardian ad litem shall have power, with the approval of the court in which the action, petition or proceeding is pending, to compromise the same, to agree to the order or judgment to be entered therein for or against the persons for whom the guardian ad litem was appointed, and to satisfy any judgment or order in favor of the persons, or release, or discharge any claim of the persons pursuant to the compromise. The court shall have the same power with respect to the money or other property to be paid or delivered under such order or judgment as is provided in Section 372 of this code.

The reasonable expenses of the guardian ad litem, including compensation and counsel fees, shall be determined by the court and paid as it may order, either out of the property or by plaintiff or petitioner. If the expenses are to be paid by the plaintiff or petitioner, execution therefor may issue in the name of the guardian ad litem.[44]

374. (a) A minor under 12 years of age, accompanied by a duly appointed and acting guardian ad litem, shall be permitted to appear in court without counsel for the limited purpose of requesting or opposing a request for (1) an injunction or temporary restraining order or both to prohibit harassment pursuant to Section 527.6, (2) an injunction or temporary restraining order or both against violence or a credible threat of violence in the workplace pursuant to Section 527.8, (3) a protective order pursuant to Division 10 (commencing with Section 6200) of the Family Code, or (4) a protective order pursuant to Sections 7710 and 7720 of the Family Code.

(b) In making the determination concerning appointment of a particular guardian ad litem for purposes of this section, the court shall consider whether the minor and the guardian have divergent interests.

(c) The Judicial Council shall adopt forms by July 1, 1999, to implement this section. The forms shall be designed to facilitate the appointment of the guardian ad litem for purposes of this section.[386]

374.5. A proceeding initiated by or brought against a minor for any of the injunctions or orders described in paragraph (1) of subdivision (b) of Section 372 or subdivision (a) of Section 374 shall be heard in the court assigned to hear those matters; except that, if the minor bringing the action or against whom the action is brought has previously been adjudged a dependent child or a ward of the juvenile court, the matter shall be heard in the juvenile court having jurisdiction over the minor.[387]

375. An action or proceeding does not abate by the disability of a party. The court, on motion, shall allow the action or proceeding to be continued by or against the party's representative.[311]

376. (a) The parents of a legitimate unmarried minor child, acting jointly, may maintain an action for injury to the child caused by the wrongful act or neglect of another. If either parent fails on demand to join as plaintiff in the action or is dead or cannot be found, then the other parent may maintain the action. The parent, if living, who does not join as plaintiff shall be joined as a defendant and, before trial or hearing of any question of fact, shall be served with summons either in the manner provided by law for the service of a summons in a civil action or by sending a copy of the summons and complaint by registered mail with proper postage prepaid addressed to that parent's last known address with request for a return receipt. If service is made by registered mail, the production of a return receipt purporting to be signed by the addressee creates a rebuttable presumption that the summons and complaint have been duly served. The presumption established by this section is a presumption affecting the burden of producing evidence. The respective rights of the parents to any award shall be determined by the court.

(b) A parent may maintain an action for such an injury to his or her illegitimate unmarried minor child if a guardian has not been appointed. Where a parent who does not have care, custody, or control of the child brings the action, the parent who has care, custody, or control of the child shall be served with the summons either in the manner provided by law for the serving of a summons in a civil action or by sending a copy of the summons and complaint by registered mail, with proper postage prepaid, addressed to the last known address of that parent, with request for a return receipt. If service is made by registered mail, the production of a return receipt purporting to be signed by the addressee creates a rebuttable presumption that the summons and complaint have been duly served. The presumption established by this section is a presumption affecting the burden of producing evidence. The respective rights of the parents to any award shall be determined by the court.

(c) The father of an illegitimate child

who maintains an action under this section shall have acknowledged in writing prior to the child's injury, in the presence of a competent witness, that he is the father of the child, or, prior to the child's injury, have been judicially determined to be the father of the child.
(d) A parent of an illegitimate child who does not maintain an action under this section may be joined as a party thereto.
(e) A guardian may maintain an action for such an injury to his or her ward.
(f) An action under this section may be maintained against the person causing the injury. If any other person is responsible for the wrongful act or neglect, the action may also be maintained against the other person. The death of the child or ward does not abate the parents' or guardian's cause of action for the child's injury as to damages accruing before the child's death.
(g) In an action under this section, damages may be awarded that, under all of the circumstances of the case, may be just, except that:
(1) In an action maintained after the death of the child, the damages recoverable are as provided in Section 377.34.
(2) Where the person causing the injury is deceased, the damages recoverable in an action against the decedent's personal representative are as provided in Section 377.42.
(h) If an action arising out of the same wrongful act or neglect may be maintained pursuant to Section 377.60 for wrongful death of a child described in this section, the action authorized by this section may be consolidated therewith for trial as provided in Section 1048.[312]

Chapter 4: Effect of Death

Chapter 4 added by Stats. 1992, Ch. 178, Sec. 20.

Article 1: Definitions
Article 1 added by Stats. 1992, Ch. 178, Sec. 20.

377.10. For the purposes of this chapter, "beneficiary of the decedent's estate" means:
(a) If the decedent died leaving a will, the sole beneficiary or all of the beneficiaries who succeed to a cause of action, or to a particular item of property that is the subject of a cause of action, under the decedent's will.
(b) If the decedent died without leaving a will, the sole person or all of the persons who succeed to a cause of action, or to a particular item of property that is the subject of a cause of action, under Sections 6401 and 6402 of the Probate Code or, if the law of a sister state or foreign nation governs succession to the cause of action or particular item of property, under the law of the sister state or foreign nation.[313]

377.11. For the purposes of this chapter, "decedent's successor in interest" means the beneficiary of the decedent's estate or other successor in interest who succeeds to a cause of action or to a particular item of the property that is the subject of a cause of action.[313]

Article 2: Survival and Continuation
Article 2 added by Stats. 1992, Ch. 178, Sec. 20.

377.20. (a) Except as otherwise provided by statute, a cause of action for or against a person is not lost by reason of the person's death, but survives subject to the applicable limitations period.

(b) This section applies even though a loss or damage occurs simultaneously with or after the death of a person who would have been liable if the person's death had not preceded or occurred simultaneously with the loss or damage.[313]

377.21. A pending action or proceeding does not abate by the death of a party if the cause of action survives.[313]

377.22. Nothing in this chapter shall be construed as affecting the assignability of causes of action.[313]

Article 3: Decedent's Cause of Action
Article 3 added by Stats. 1992, Ch. 178, Sec. 20.

377.30. A cause of action that survives the death of the person entitled to commence an action or proceeding passes to the decedent's successor in interest, subject to Chapter 1 (commencing with Section 7000) of Part 1 of Division 7 of the Probate Code, and an action may be commenced by the decedent's personal representative or, if none, by the decedent's successor in interest.[313]

377.31. On motion after the death of a person who commenced an action or proceeding, the court shall allow a pending action or proceeding that does not abate to be continued by the decedent's personal representative or, if none, by the decedent's successor in interest.[313]

377.32. (a) The person who seeks to commence an action or proceeding or to continue a pending action or proceeding as the decedent's successor in interest under this article, shall execute and file an affidavit or a declaration under penalty of perjury under the laws of this state stating all of the following:

(1) The decedent's name.

(2) The date and place of the decedent's death.

(3) "No proceeding is now pending in California for administration of the decedent's estate."

(4) If the decedent's estate was administered, a copy of the final order showing the distribution of the decedent's cause of action to the successor in interest.

(5) Either of the following, as appropriate, with facts in support thereof:

(A) "The affiant or declarant is the decedent's successor in interest (as defined in Section 377.11 of the California Code of Civil Procedure) and succeeds to the decedent's interest in the action or proceeding."

(B) "The affiant or declarant is authorized to act on behalf of the decedent's successor in interest (as defined in Section 377.11 of the California Code of Civil Procedure) with respect to the decedent's interest in the action or proceeding."

(6) "No other person has a superior right to commence the action or proceeding or to be substituted for the decedent in the pending action or proceeding."

(7) "The affiant or declarant affirms or declares under penalty of perjury under the laws of the State of California that the foregoing is true and correct."

(b) Where more than one person executes the affidavit or declaration under this section, the statements required by

subdivision (a) shall be modified as appropriate to reflect that fact.
(c) A certified copy of the decedent's death certificate shall be attached to the affidavit or declaration.[313]

377.33. The court in which an action is commenced or continued under this article may make any order concerning parties that is appropriate to ensure proper administration of justice in the case, including appointment of the decedent's successor in interest as a special administrator or guardian ad litem.[313]

377.34. (a) In an action or proceeding by a decedent's personal representative or successor in interest on the decedent's cause of action, the damages recoverable are limited to the loss or damage that the decedent sustained or incurred before death, including any penalties or punitive or exemplary damages that the decedent would have been entitled to recover had the decedent lived, and do not include damages for pain, suffering, or disfigurement.
(b) Notwithstanding subdivision (a), in an action or proceeding by a decedent's personal representative or successor in interest on the decedent's cause of action, the damages recoverable may include damages for pain, suffering, or disfigurement if the action or proceeding was granted a preference pursuant to Section 36 before January 1, 2022, or was filed on or after January 1, 2022, and before January 1, 2026.
(c) A plaintiff who recovers damages pursuant to subdivision (b) between January 1, 2022, and January 1, 2025, inclusive, shall, within 60 days after obtaining a judgment, consent judgment, or court-approved settlement agreement entitling the plaintiff to the damages, submit to the Judicial Council a copy of the judgment, consent judgment, or court-approved settlement agreement, along with a cover sheet detailing all of the following information:
(1) The date the action was filed.
(2) The date of the final disposition of the action.
(3) The amount and type of damages awarded, including economic damages and damages for pain, suffering, or disfigurement.
(d) (1) On or before January 1, 2025, the Judicial Council shall transmit to the Legislature a report detailing the information received pursuant to subdivision (c) for all judgments, consent judgments, or court-approved settlement agreements rendered from January 1, 2022, to July 31, 2024, inclusive, in which damages were recovered pursuant to subdivision (b). The report shall comply with Section 9795 of the Government Code.
(2) This subdivision shall become inoperative on January 1, 2029, pursuant to Section 10231.5 of the Government Code.
(e) Nothing in this section alters Section 3333.2 of the Civil Code.
(f) Nothing in this section affects claims brought pursuant to Chapter 11 (commencing with Section 15600) of Part 3 of Division 9 of the Welfare and Institutions Code.[814]

377.35. On or after January 1, 1993, this article applies to the commencement of an action or proceeding the decedent was entitled to commence, and to the continuation of an action or proceeding commenced by the decedent, regardless of whether the decedent died before, on, or after January

1, 1993.[313]

Article 4: Cause of Action Against Decedent
Article 4 added by Stats. 1992, Ch. 178, Sec. 20.

377.40. Subject to Part 4 (commencing with Section 9000) of Division 7 of the Probate Code governing creditor claims, a cause of action against a decedent that survives may be asserted against the decedent's personal representative or, to the extent provided by statute, against the decedent's successor in interest.[313]

377.41. On motion, the court shall allow a pending action or proceeding against the decedent that does not abate to be continued against the decedent's personal representative or, to the extent provided by statute, against the decedent's successor in interest, except that the court may not permit an action or proceeding to be continued against the personal representative unless proof of compliance with Part 4 (commencing with Section 9000) of Division 7 of the Probate Code governing creditor claims is first made.[313]

377.42. In an action or proceeding against a decedent's personal representative or, to the extent provided by statute, against the decedent's successor in interest, on a cause of action against the decedent, all damages are recoverable that might have been recovered against the decedent had the decedent lived except damages recoverable under Section 3294 of the Civil Code or other punitive or exemplary damages.[313]

377.43. This article applies to the commencement on or after January 1, 1993, of an action or proceeding against the decedent's personal representative or successor in interest, or to the making of a motion on or after January 1, 1993, to continue a pending action or proceeding against the decedent's personal representative or successor in interest, regardless of whether the decedent died before, on, or after January 1, 1993.[313]

Article 5: Insured Claims
Article 5 added by Stats. 1992, Ch. 178, Sec. 20.

377.50. An action to establish the decedent's liability for which the decedent was protected by insurance may be commenced or continued against the decedent's estate as provided in Chapter 1 (commencing with Section 550) of Part 13 of Division 2 of the Probate Code.[313]

Article 6: Wrongful Death
Article 6 added by Stats. 1992, Ch. 178, Sec. 20.

377.60. A cause of action for the death of a person caused by the wrongful act or neglect of another may be asserted by any of the following persons or by the decedent's personal representative on their behalf:
(a) The decedent's surviving spouse, domestic partner, children, and issue of deceased children, or, if there is no surviving issue of the decedent, the persons, including the surviving spouse or domestic partner, who would be entitled to the property of the decedent by intestate succession. If the parents of the decedent would be entitled to bring an action under this subdivision, and the parents are deceased, then the legal guardians of the

decedent, if any, may bring an action under this subdivision as if they were the decedent's parents.
(b) (1) Whether or not qualified under subdivision (a), if they were dependent on the decedent, the putative spouse, children of the putative spouse, stepchildren, parents, or the legal guardians of the decedent if the parents are deceased.
(2) As used in this subdivision, "putative spouse" means the surviving spouse of a void or voidable marriage who is found by the court to have believed in good faith that the marriage to the decedent was valid.
(c) A minor, whether or not qualified under subdivision (a) or (b), if, at the time of the decedent's death, the minor resided for the previous 180 days in the decedent's household and was dependent on the decedent for one-half or more of the minor's support.
(d) This section applies to any cause of action arising on or after January 1, 1993.
(e) The addition of this section by Chapter 178 of the Statutes of 1992 was not intended to adversely affect the standing of any party having standing under prior law, and the standing of parties governed by that version of this section as added by Chapter 178 of the Statutes of 1992 shall be the same as specified herein as amended by Chapter 563 of the Statutes of 1996.
(f) (1) For the purpose of this section, "domestic partner" means a person who, at the time of the decedent's death, was the domestic partner of the decedent in a registered domestic partnership established in accordance with subdivision (b) of Section 297 of the Family Code.
(2) Notwithstanding paragraph (1), for a death occurring prior to January 1, 2002, a person may maintain a cause of action pursuant to this section as a domestic partner of the decedent by establishing the factors listed in paragraphs (1) to (6), inclusive, of subdivision (b) of Section 297 of the Family Code, as it read pursuant to Section 3 of Chapter 893 of the Statutes of 2001, prior to its becoming inoperative on January 1, 2005.
(3) The amendments made to this subdivision during the 2003–04 Regular Session of the Legislature are not intended to revive any cause of action that has been fully and finally adjudicated by the courts, or that has been settled, or as to which the applicable limitations period has run.[763]

377.61. In an action under this article, damages may be awarded that, under all the circumstances of the case, may be just, but may not include damages recoverable under Section 377.34. The court shall determine the respective rights in an award of the persons entitled to assert the cause of action.[313]

377.62. (a) An action under Section 377.30 may be joined with an action under Section 377.60 arising out of the same wrongful act or neglect.
(b) An action under Section 377.60 and an action under Section 377.31 arising out of the same wrongful act or neglect may be consolidated for trial as provided in Section 1048.[313]

Chapter 5: Permissive Joinder

Heading of Chapter 5 added by Stats. 1992, Ch. 178, Sec. 21.

378. (a) All persons may join in one action as plaintiffs if:
(1) They assert any right to relief jointly, severally, or in the alternative,

in respect of or arising out of the same transaction, occurrence, or series of transactions or occurrences and if any question of law or fact common to all these persons will arise in the action; or

(2) They have a claim, right, or interest adverse to the defendant in the property or controversy which is the subject of the action.

(b) It is not necessary that each plaintiff be interested as to every cause of action or as to all relief prayed for. Judgment may be given for one or more of the plaintiffs according to their respective right to relief.[74]

379. (a) All persons may be joined in one action as defendants if there is asserted against them:

(1) Any right to relief jointly, severally, or in the alternative, in respect of or arising out of the same transaction, occurrence, or series of transactions or occurrences and if any question of law or fact common to all these persons will arise in the action; or

(2) A claim, right, or interest adverse to them in the property or controversy which is the subject of the action.

(b) It is not necessary that each defendant be interested as to every cause of action or as to all relief prayed for. Judgment may be given against one or more defendants according to their respective liabilities.

(c) Where the plaintiff is in doubt as to the person from whom he or she is entitled to redress, he or she may join two or more defendants, with the intent that the question as to which, if any, of the defendants is liable, and to what extent, may be determined between the parties.[97]

379.5. When parties have been joined under Section 378 or 379, the court may make such orders as may appear just to prevent any party from being embarrassed, delayed, or put to undue expense, and may order separate trials or make such other order as the interests of justice may require.[73]

382. If the consent of any one who should have been joined as plaintiff cannot be obtained, he may be made a defendant, the reason thereof being stated in the complaint; and when the question is one of a common or general interest, of many persons, or when the parties are numerous, and it is impracticable to bring them all before the court, one or more may sue or defend for the benefit of all.[74]

382.4. If a proposed settlement in a class action established pursuant to Section 382, including a consent judgment, decree, or settlement agreement, provides for the distribution of money or any other thing of value to a person or entity that is not a party to the action, an attorney for a party to the action shall, in connection with the hearing for preliminary approval pursuant to subdivision (c) of Rule 3.769 of the California Rules of Court, notify the court if the attorney has a connection to or a relationship with a nonparty recipient of the distribution that could reasonably create the appearance of impropriety as between the selection of the recipient of the money or thing of value and the interests of the class.[739]

384. (a) It is the policy of the State of California to ensure that the unpaid cash residue and unclaimed or abandoned funds in class action litigation are distributed, to the fullest extent

possible, in a manner designed either to further the purposes of the underlying class action or causes of action, or to promote justice for all Californians. The Legislature finds that the use of funds for these purposes is in the public interest, is a proper use of the funds, and is consistent with essential public and governmental purposes.

(b) Except as provided in subdivision (c), before the entry of a judgment in a class action established pursuant to Section 382 that provides for the payment of money to members of the class, the court shall determine the total amount that will be payable to all class members if all class members are paid the amount to which they are entitled pursuant to the judgment. The court shall also set a date when the parties shall report to the court the total amount that was actually paid to the class members. After the report is received, the court shall amend the judgment to direct the defendant to pay the sum of the unpaid residue or unclaimed or abandoned class member funds, plus any interest that has accrued thereon, to nonprofit organizations or foundations to support projects that will benefit the class or similarly situated persons, or that promote the law consistent with the objectives and purposes of the underlying cause of action, to child advocacy programs, or to nonprofit organizations providing civil legal services to the indigent. The court shall ensure that the distribution of any unpaid residue or unclaimed or abandoned class member funds derived from multistate or national cases brought under California law shall provide substantial or commensurate benefit to California consumers. For purposes of this subdivision, "judgment" includes a consent judgment, decree, or settlement agreement that has been approved by the court.

(c) This section shall not apply to any class action brought against any public entity, as defined in Section 811.2 of the Government Code, or against any public employee, as defined in Section 811.4 of the Government Code. However, this section shall not be construed to abrogate any equitable cy pres remedy that may be available in any class action with regard to all or part of the cash residue or unclaimed or abandoned class member funds.[749]

384.5. If a judgment in a class action established pursuant to Section 382, including a consent judgment, decree, or settlement agreement that has been approved by a court, provides for a distribution of money or any other thing of value to a person or entity that is not a party to the action, the court shall transmit a copy of the order, judgment, or decree to the Judicial Council. The order, judgment, or decree shall contain, at a minimum, the information necessary for the California Research Bureau to complete the report required by Section 68520 of the Government Code.[740]

Chapter 6: Interpleader

Heading of Chapter 6 added by Stats. 1992, Ch. 178, Sec. 23.

386. (a) A defendant, against whom an action is pending upon a contract, or for specific personal property, may, at any time before answer, upon affidavit that a person not a party to the action makes against him, and without any collusion with him, a demand upon

such contract, or for such property, upon notice to such person and the adverse party, apply to the court for an order to substitute such person in his place, and discharge him from liability to either party, on his depositing in court the amount claimed on the contract, or delivering the property or its value to such person as the court may direct; and the court may, in its discretion, make the order; or such defendant may file a verified cross-complaint in interpleader, admitting that he has no interest in such amount or such property claimed, or in a portion of such amount or such property and alleging that all or such portion of the amount or property is demanded by parties to such action or cross-action and apply to the court upon notice to such parties for an order to deliver such property or portion thereof or its value to such person as the court shall direct. And whenever conflicting claims are or may be made upon a person for or relating to personal property, or the performance of an obligation, or any portion thereof, such person may bring an action against the conflicting claimants to compel them to interplead and litigate their several claims. The order of substitution may be made and the action of interpleader may be maintained, and the applicant or interpleading party be discharged from liability to all or any of the conflicting claimants, although their titles or claims have not a common origin, or are not identical but are adverse to and independent of one another.

(b) Any person, firm, corporation, association or other entity against whom double or multiple claims are made, or may be made, by two or more persons which are such that they may give rise to double or multiple liability, may bring an action against the claimants to compel them to interplead and litigate their several claims.

When the person, firm, corporation, association or other entity against whom such claims are made, or may be made, is a defendant in an action brought upon one or more of such claims, it may either file a verified cross-complaint in interpleader, admitting that it has no interest in the money or property claimed, or in only a portion thereof, and alleging that all or such portion is demanded by parties to such action, and apply to the court upon notice to such parties for an order to deliver such money or property or such portion thereof to such person as the court shall direct; or may bring a separate action against the claimants to compel them to interplead and litigate their several claims. The action of interpleader may be maintained although the claims have not a common origin, are not identical but are adverse to and independent of one another, or the claims are unliquidated and no liability on the part of the party bringing the action or filing the cross-complaint has arisen. The applicant or interpleading party may deny liability in whole or in part to any or all of the claimants. The applicant or interpleading party may join as a defendant in such action any other party against whom claims are made by one or more of the claimants or such other party may interplead by cross-complaint; provided, however, that such claims arise out of the same transaction or occurrence.

(c) Any amount which a plaintiff or cross-complainant admits to be payable may be deposited by him with the clerk of the court at the time of the filing of the complaint or cross-complaint in interpleader without first obtaining an order of the court therefor. Any interest on amounts deposited and any right to damages for detention of property so delivered, or its value, shall cease to accrue after the date of such deposit or delivery.

(d) A defendant named in a complaint to compel conflicting claimants to interplead and litigate their claims, or a defendant named in a cross-complaint in interpleader, may, in lieu of or in addition to any other pleading, file an answer to the complaint or cross-complaint which shall be served upon all other parties to the action and which shall contain allegations of fact as to his ownership of or other interest in the amount or property and any affirmative defenses and the relief requested. The allegations in such answer shall be deemed denied by all other parties to the action, unless otherwise admitted in the pleadings.

(e) Except in cases where by the law a right to a jury trial is now given, conflicting claims to funds or property or the value thereof so deposited or delivered shall be deemed issues triable by the court, and such issues may be first tried. In the event the amount deposited shall be less than the amount claimed to be due by one or more of the conflicting claimants thereto, or in the event the property or the value thereof delivered is less than all of the property or the value thereof claimed by one or more of such conflicting claimants, any issues of fact involved in determining whether there is a deficiency in such deposit or delivery shall be tried by the court or a jury as provided in Title 8 (commencing with Section 577) of Part 2 of this code.

(f) After any such complaint or cross-complaint in interpleader has been filed, the court in which it is filed may enter its order restraining all parties to the action from instituting or further prosecuting any other proceeding in any court in this state affecting the rights and obligations as between the parties to the interpleader until further order of the court.[93]

386.1. Where a deposit has been made pursuant to Section 386, the court shall, upon the application of any party to the action, order such deposit to be invested in an insured interest-bearing account. Interest on such amount shall be allocated to the parties in the same proportion as the original funds are allocated.[108]

386.5. Where the only relief sought against one of the defendants is the payment of a stated amount of money alleged to be wrongfully withheld, such defendant may, upon affidavit that he is a mere stakeholder with no interest in the amount or any portion thereof and that conflicting demands have been made upon him for the amount by parties to the action, upon notice to such parties, apply to the court for an order discharging him from liability and dismissing him from the action on his depositing with the clerk of the court the amount in dispute and the court may, in its discretion, make such order.[31]

386.6. (a) A party to an action who follows the procedure set forth in Section 386 or 386.5 may insert in his motion, petition, complaint, or cross complaint a request for allowance of his costs and reasonable attorney fees incurred in such action. In ordering the discharge of such party, the court may, in its discretion, award such party his costs and reasonable attorney fees from the amount in dispute which has been deposited with the court. At the time of final judgment in the action the court may make such further provision for assumption of such costs and attorney fees by one or more of the adverse claimants as may appear proper.

(b) A party shall not be denied the attorney fees authorized by subdivision (a) for the reason that he is himself an attorney, appeared in pro se, and performed his own legal services.[87]

Chapter 7: Intervention

Heading of Chapter 7 added by Stats. 1992, Ch. 178, Sec. 24.

387. (a) For purposes of this section:

(1) "Defendant" includes a cross-defendant.

(2) "Plaintiff" includes a cross-complainant.

(b) An intervention takes place when a nonparty, deemed an intervenor, becomes a party to an action or proceeding between other persons by doing any of the following:

(1) Joining a plaintiff in claiming what is sought by the complaint.

(2) Uniting with a defendant in resisting the claims of a plaintiff.

(3) Demanding anything adverse to both a plaintiff and a defendant.

(c) A nonparty shall petition the court for leave to intervene by noticed motion or ex parte application. The petition shall include a copy of the proposed complaint in intervention or answer in intervention and set forth the grounds upon which intervention rests.

(d) (1) The court shall, upon timely application, permit a nonparty to intervene in the action or proceeding if either of the following conditions is satisfied:

(A) A provision of law confers an unconditional right to intervene.

(B) The person seeking intervention claims an interest relating to the property or transaction that is the subject of the action and that person is so situated that the disposition of the action may impair or impede that person's ability to protect that interest, unless that person's interest is adequately represented by one or more of the existing parties.

(2) The court may, upon timely application, permit a nonparty to intervene in the action or proceeding if the person has an interest in the matter in litigation, or in the success of either of the parties, or an interest against both.

(e) If leave to intervene is granted by the court, the intervenor shall do both of the following:

(1) Separately file the complaint in intervention, answer in intervention, or both.

(2) Serve a copy of the order, or notice of the court's decision or order, granting leave to intervene and the pleadings in intervention as follows:

(A) A party to the action or proceeding who has not yet appeared shall be served in the same manner for service of summons pursuant to Article 3 (commencing with Section 415.10) of Chapter 4 of Title 5 of Part 2.

(B) A party who has appeared in the action or proceeding, whether represented by an attorney or not represented by an attorney, shall be served in the same manner for service of summons pursuant to Article 3 (commencing with Section 415.10) of Chapter 4 of Title 5 of Part 2, or in the manner provided by Chapter 5 (commencing with Section 1010) of Title 14 of Part 2.

(f) Within 30 days after service of a complaint in intervention or answer in intervention, a party may move, demur, or otherwise plead to the complaint in intervention or answer in intervention in the same manner as to an original complaint or answer.[730]

388. In an action brought by a party for relief of any nature other than solely for money damages where a pleading alleges facts or issues concerning alleged pollution or adverse environmental effects which could affect the public generally, the party filing the pleading shall furnish a copy to the Attorney General of the State of California. The copy shall be furnished by the party filing the pleading within 10 days after filing.[330]

Chapter 8: Compulsory Joinder

Heading of Chapter 8 added by Stats. 1992, Ch. 178, Sec. 27.

389. (a) A person who is subject to service of process and whose joinder will not deprive the court of jurisdiction over the subject matter of the action shall be joined as a party in the action if (1) in his absence complete relief cannot be accorded among those already parties or (2) he claims an interest relating to the subject of the action and is so situated that the disposition of the action in his absence may (i) as a practical matter impair or impede his ability to protect that interest or (ii) leave any of the persons already parties subject to a substantial risk of incurring double, multiple, or otherwise inconsistent obligations by reason of his claimed interest. If he has not been so joined, the court shall order that he be made a party.

(b) If a person as described in paragraph (1) or (2) of subdivision (a) cannot be made a party, the court shall determine whether in equity and good conscience the action should proceed among the parties before it, or should be dismissed without prejudice, the absent person being thus regarded as indispensable. The factors to be considered by the court include: (1) to what extent a judgment rendered in the person's absence might be prejudicial to him or those already parties; (2) the extent to which, by protective provisions in the judgment, by the shaping of relief, or other measures, the prejudice can be lessened or avoided; (3) whether a judgment rendered in the person's absence will be adequate; (4) whether the plaintiff or cross-complainant will have an adequate remedy if the action is dismissed for nonjoinder.

(c) A complaint or cross-complaint shall state the names, if known to the pleader, of any persons as described in paragraph (1) or (2) of subdivision (a) who are not joined, and the reasons why they are not joined.

(d) Nothing in this section affects the law applicable to class actions.[74]

389.5. When, in an action for the recovery of real or personal property, or to determine conflicting claims thereto, a person not a party to the action but having an interest in the subject thereof makes application to the court to be made a party, it may order him to be brought in by the proper amendment.[40]

TITLE 3A: VEXATIOUS LITIGANTS

Title 3A added by Stats. 1963, Ch. 1471.

391. As used in this title, the following terms have the following meanings:
(a) "Litigation" means any civil action or proceeding, commenced, maintained or pending in any state or federal court.
(b) "Vexatious litigant" means a person who does any of the following:
(1) In the immediately preceding seven-year period has commenced, prosecuted, or maintained in propria persona at least five litigations other than in a small claims court that have been (i) finally determined adversely to the person or (ii) unjustifiably permitted to remain pending at least two years without having been brought to trial or hearing.
(2) After a litigation has been finally determined against the person, repeatedly relitigates or attempts to relitigate, in propria persona, either (i) the validity of the determination against the same defendant or defendants as to whom the litigation was finally determined or (ii) the cause of action, claim, controversy, or any of the issues of fact or law, determined or concluded by the final determination against the same defendant or defendants as to whom the litigation was finally determined.
(3) In any litigation while acting in propria persona, repeatedly files unmeritorious motions, pleadings, or other papers, conducts unnecessary discovery, or engages in other tactics that are frivolous or solely intended to cause unnecessary delay.
(4) Has previously been declared to be a vexatious litigant by any state or federal court of record in any action or proceeding based upon the same or substantially similar facts, transaction, or occurrence.
(5) After being restrained pursuant to a restraining order issued after a hearing pursuant to Chapter 1 (commencing with Section 6300) of Part 4 of Division 10 of the Family Code, and while the restraining order is still in place, they commenced, prosecuted, or maintained one or more litigations against a person protected by the restraining order in this or any other court or jurisdiction that are determined to be meritless and caused the person protected by the order to be harassed or intimidated.
(c) "Security" means an undertaking to assure payment, to the party for whose benefit the undertaking is required to be furnished, of the party's reasonable expenses, including attorney's fees and not limited to taxable costs, incurred in or in connection with a litigation instituted, caused to be instituted, or maintained or caused to be maintained by a vexatious litigant.
(d) "Plaintiff" means the person who commences, institutes or maintains a litigation or causes it to be commenced, instituted or maintained, including an attorney at law acting in propria persona.
(e) "Defendant" means a person (including corporation, association, partnership and firm or governmental entity) against whom a litigation is brought or maintained or sought to be brought or maintained.[797]

391.1. (a) In any litigation pending in any court of this state, at any time until final judgment is entered, a defendant may move the court, upon notice and hearing, for an order requiring the

plaintiff to furnish security or for an order dismissing the litigation pursuant to subdivision (b) of Section 391.3. The motion for an order requiring the plaintiff to furnish security shall be based upon the ground, and supported by a showing, that the plaintiff is a vexatious litigant and that there is not a reasonable probability that they will prevail in the litigation against the moving defendant.
(b) A motion pursuant to subdivision (a) on the grounds that plaintiff is a vexatious litigant pursuant to paragraph (5) of subdivision (b) of Section 391 may be brought only by a person protected by the restraining order. A person filing a motion as described in this subdivision shall not be required to pay a filing fee.[798]

391.2. At the hearing upon the motion the court shall consider any evidence, written or oral, by witnesses or affidavit, as may be material to the ground of the motion. Except for an order dismissing the litigation pursuant to subdivision (b) of Section 391.3, no determination made by the court in determining or ruling upon the motion shall be or be deemed to be a determination of any issue in the litigation or of the merits thereof.[665]

391.3. (a) Except as provided in subdivision (b), if, after hearing the evidence upon the motion, the court determines that the plaintiff is a vexatious litigant and that there is no reasonable probability that the plaintiff will prevail in the litigation against the moving defendant, the court shall order the plaintiff to furnish, for the benefit of the moving defendant, security in such amount and within such time as the court shall fix.
(b) If, after hearing evidence on the motion, the court determines that the litigation has no merit and has been filed for the purposes of harassment or delay, the court shall order the litigation dismissed. This subdivision shall only apply to litigation filed in a court of this state by a vexatious litigant subject to a prefiling order pursuant to Section 391.7 who was represented by counsel at the time the litigation was filed and who became in propria persona after the withdrawal of his or her attorney.
(c) A defendant may make a motion for relief in the alternative under either subdivision (a) or (b) and shall combine all grounds for relief in one motion.[666]

391.4. When security that has been ordered furnished is not furnished as ordered, the litigation shall be dismissed as to the defendant for whose benefit it was ordered furnished.[49]

391.6. Except as provided in subdivision (b) of Section 391.3, when a motion pursuant to Section 391.1 is filed prior to trial the litigation is stayed, and the moving defendant need not plead, until 10 days after the motion shall have been denied, or if granted, until 10 days after the required security has been furnished and the moving defendant given written notice thereof. When a motion pursuant to Section 391.1 is made at any time thereafter, the litigation shall be stayed for such period after the denial of the motion or the furnishing of the required security as the court shall determine.[667]

391.7. (a) In addition to any other relief provided in this title, the court may, on its own motion or the motion of any party, enter a prefiling order which prohibits a vexatious litigant from filing any new litigation in the courts of this state in propria persona without first obtaining leave of the presiding justice or presiding judge of the court where the litigation is proposed to be filed. Disobedience of the order by a vexatious litigant may be punished as a contempt of court.

(b) The presiding justice or presiding judge shall permit the filing of that litigation only if it appears that the litigation has merit and has not been filed for the purposes of harassment or delay. The presiding justice or presiding judge may condition the filing of the litigation upon the furnishing of security for the benefit of the defendants as provided in Section 391.3.

(c) The clerk may not file any litigation presented by a vexatious litigant subject to a prefiling order unless the vexatious litigant first obtains an order from the presiding justice or presiding judge permitting the filing. If the clerk mistakenly files the litigation without the order, any party may file with the clerk and serve, or the presiding justice or presiding judge may direct the clerk to file and serve, on the plaintiff and other parties a notice stating that the plaintiff is a vexatious litigant subject to a prefiling order as set forth in subdivision (a). The filing of the notice shall automatically stay the litigation. The litigation shall be automatically dismissed unless the plaintiff within 10 days of the filing of that notice obtains an order from the presiding justice or presiding judge permitting the filing of the litigation as set forth in subdivision (b). If the presiding justice or presiding judge issues an order permitting the filing, the stay of the litigation shall remain in effect, and the defendants need not plead, until 10 days after the defendants are served with a copy of the order.

(d) For purposes of this section, "litigation" includes any petition, application, or motion other than a discovery motion, in a proceeding under the Family Code or Probate Code, for any order.

(e) The presiding justice or presiding judge of a court may designate a justice or judge of the same court to act on his or her behalf in exercising the authority and responsibilities provided under subdivisions (a) to (c), inclusive.

(f) The clerk of the court shall provide the Judicial Council a copy of any prefiling orders issued pursuant to subdivision (a). The Judicial Council shall maintain a record of vexatious litigants subject to those prefiling orders and shall annually disseminate a list of those persons to the clerks of the courts of this state.[650]

391.8. (a) A vexatious litigant subject to a prefiling order under Section 391.7 may file an application to vacate the prefiling order and remove his or her name from the Judicial Council's list of vexatious litigants subject to prefiling orders. The application shall be filed in the court that entered the prefiling order, either in the action in which the prefiling order was entered or in conjunction with a request to the presiding justice or presiding judge to file new litigation under Section 391.7. The application shall be made before the justice or judge who entered the order, if that justice or judge is available. If that justice or judge who entered the order is not available, the application shall be made before the presiding justice or presiding judge, or his or her designee.

(b) A vexatious litigant whose application under subdivision (a) was denied shall not be permitted to file another application on or before 12 months has elapsed after the date of the denial of the previous application.
(c) A court may vacate a prefiling order and order removal of a vexatious litigant's name from the Judicial Council's list of vexatious litigants subject to prefiling orders upon a showing of a material change in the facts upon which the order was granted and that the ends of justice would be served by vacating the order.[651]

TITLE 4: OF THE PLACE OF TRIAL, RECLASSIFICATION, AND COORDINATION OF CIVIL ACTIONS

Heading of Title 4 amended by Stats. 1999, Ch. 344, Sec. 6.

Chapter 1: Place of Trial

Heading of Chapter 1 amended by Stats. 1999, Ch. 344, Sec. 7.

392. (a) Subject to the power of the court to transfer actions and proceedings as provided in this title, the superior court in the county where the real property that is the subject of the action, or some part thereof, is situated, is the proper court for the trial of the following actions:
(1) For the recovery of real property, or of an estate or interest therein, or for the determination in any form, of that right or interest, and for injuries to real property.
(2) For the foreclosure of all liens and mortgages on real property.
(b) In the court designated as the proper court in subdivision (a), the proper court location for trial of a proceeding for an unlawful detainer, as defined in Section 1161, is the location where the court tries that type of proceeding that is nearest or most accessible to where the real property that is the subject of the action, or some part thereof, is situated. Otherwise any location of the superior court designated as the proper court in subdivision (a) is a proper court location for the trial. The court may specify by local rule the nearest or most accessible court location where the court tries that type of case.[516]

393. Subject to the power of the court to transfer actions and proceedings as provided in this title, the county in which the cause, or some part of the cause, arose, is the proper county for the trial of the following actions:
(a) For the recovery of a penalty or forfeiture imposed by statute, except, that when it is imposed for an offense committed on a lake, river, or other stream of water, situated in two or more counties, the action may be tried in any county bordering on the lake, river, or stream, and opposite to the place where the offense was committed.
(b) Against a public officer or person especially appointed to execute the duties of a public officer, for an act done by the officer or person in virtue of the office, or against a person who, by the officer's command or in the officer's aid, does anything touching the duties of the officer.[537]

394. (a) An action or proceeding against a county, or city and county, a city, or local agency, may be tried in the county, or city and county, or the county in which the city or local agency is situated, unless the action or proceeding is brought by a county, or city

and county, a city, or local agency, in which case it may be tried in any county, or city and county, not a party thereto and in which the city or local agency is not situated. Except for actions initiated by the local child support agency pursuant to Section 17400, 17402, 17404, or 17416 of the Family Code, any action or proceeding brought by a county, city and county, city, or local agency within a certain county, or city and county, against a resident of another county, city and county, or city, or a corporation doing business in the latter, shall be, on motion of either party, transferred for trial to a county, or city and county, other than the plaintiff, if the plaintiff is a county, or city and county, and other than that in which the plaintiff is situated, if the plaintiff is a city, or a local agency, and other than that in which the defendant resides, or is doing business, or is situated. Whenever an action or proceeding is brought against a county, city and county, city, or local agency, in any county, or city and county, other than the defendant, if the defendant is a county, or city and county, or, if the defendant is a city, or local agency, other than that in which the defendant is situated, the action or proceeding must be, on motion of that defendant, transferred for trial to a county, or city and county, other than that in which the plaintiff, or any of the plaintiffs, resides, or is doing business, or is situated, and other than the plaintiff county, or city and county, or county in which that plaintiff city or local agency is situated, and other than the defendant county, or city and county, or county in which the defendant city or local agency is situated; provided, however, that any action or proceeding against the city, county, city and county, or local agency for injury occurring within the city, county, or city and county, or within the county in which the local agency is situated, to person or property or person and property caused by the negligence or alleged negligence of the city, county, city and county, local agency, or its agents or employees, shall be tried in that county, or city and county, or if a city is a defendant, in the city or in the county in which the city is situated, or if a local agency is a defendant, in the county in which the local agency is situated. In that action or proceeding, the parties thereto may, by stipulation in writing, or made in open court, and entered in the minutes, agree upon any county, or city and county, for the place of trial thereof. When the action or proceeding is one in which a jury is not of right, or in case a jury is waived, then in lieu of transferring the cause, the court in the original county may request the chairperson of the Judicial Council to assign a disinterested judge from a neutral county to hear that cause and all proceedings in connection therewith. When the action or proceeding is transferred to another county for trial, a witness required to respond to a subpoena for a hearing within the original county shall be compelled to attend hearings in the county to which the cause is transferred. If the demand for transfer is made by one party and the opposing party does not consent thereto, the additional costs of the nonconsenting party occasioned by the transfer of the cause, including living and traveling expenses of the nonconsenting party and material witnesses, found by the court to be material, and called by the nonconsenting party, not to exceed five dollars ($5) per day each in excess of witness fees and mileage otherwise allowed by law, shall be assessed by the court hearing the cause against the party requesting the transfer. To the extent of that excess, those costs shall be awarded to the nonconsenting party regardless of the outcome of the trial. This section shall apply to actions or proceedings now pending or hereafter brought.

(b) For the purposes of this section, "local agency" shall mean any governmental district, board, or agency, or any other local governmental body or corporation, but shall not include the State of California or any of its agencies, departments, commissions, or boards.[520]

395. (a) Except as otherwise provided by law and subject to the power of the court to transfer actions or proceedings as provided in this title, the superior court in the county where the defendants or some of them reside at the commencement of the action is the proper court for the trial of the action. If the action is for injury to person or personal property or for death from wrongful act or negligence, the superior court in either the county where the injury occurs or the injury causing death occurs or the county where the defendants, or some of them reside at the commencement of the action, is a proper court for the trial of the action. In a proceeding for dissolution of marriage, the superior court in the county where either the petitioner or respondent has been a resident for three months next preceding the commencement of the proceeding is the proper court for the trial of the proceeding. In a proceeding for nullity of marriage or legal separation of the parties, the superior court in the county where either the petitioner or the respondent resides at the commencement of the proceeding is the proper court for the trial of the proceeding. In a proceeding to enforce an obligation of support under Section 3900 of the Family Code, the superior court in the county where the child resides is the proper court for the trial of the action. In a proceeding to establish and enforce a foreign judgment or court order for the support of a minor child, the superior court in the county where the child resides is the proper court for the trial of the action. Subject to subdivision (b), if a defendant has contracted to perform an obligation in a particular county, the superior court in the county where the obligation is to be performed, where the contract in fact was entered into, or where the defendant or any defendant resides at the commencement of the action is a proper court for the trial of an action founded on that obligation, and the county where the obligation is incurred is the county where it is to be performed, unless there is a special contract in writing to the contrary. If none of the defendants reside in the state or if they reside in the state and the county where they reside is unknown to the plaintiff, the action may be tried in the superior court in any county that the plaintiff may designate in his or her complaint, and, if the defendant is about to depart from the state, the action may be tried in the superior court in any county where either of the parties reside or service is made. If any

person is improperly joined as a defendant or has been made a defendant solely for the purpose of having the action tried in the superior court in the county where he or she resides, his or her residence shall not be considered in determining the proper place for the trial of the action.

(b) Subject to the power of the court to transfer actions or proceedings as provided in this title, in an action arising from an offer or provision of goods, services, loans or extensions of credit intended primarily for personal, family or household use, other than an obligation described in Section 1812.10 or Section 2984.4 of the Civil Code, or an action arising from a transaction consummated as a proximate result of either an unsolicited telephone call made by a seller engaged in the business of consummating transactions of that kind or a telephone call or electronic transmission made by the buyer or lessee in response to a solicitation by the seller, the superior court in the county where the buyer or lessee in fact signed the contract, where the buyer or lessee resided at the time the contract was entered into, or where the buyer or lessee resides at the commencement of the action is the proper court for the trial of the action. In the superior court designated in this subdivision as the proper court, the proper court location for trial of a case is the location where the court tries that type of case that is nearest or most accessible to where the buyer or lessee resides, where the buyer or lessee in fact signed the contract, where the buyer or lessee resided at the time the contract was entered into, or where the buyer or lessee resides at the commencement of the action. Otherwise, any location of the superior court designated as the proper court in this subdivision is a proper court location for the trial. The court may specify by local rule the nearest or most accessible court location where the court tries that type of case.

(c) Any provision of an obligation described in subdivision (b) waiving that subdivision is void and unenforceable.[517]

395.1. Except as otherwise provided in Section 17005 of the Probate Code pertaining to trustees, when a defendant is sued in an official or representative capacity as executor, administrator, guardian, conservator, or trustee on a claim for the payment of money or for the recovery of personal property, the county which has jurisdiction of the estate which the defendant represents shall be the proper county for the trial of the action.[248]

395.2. If an unincorporated association has filed a statement with the Secretary of State pursuant to statute, designating its principal office in this state, the proper county for the trial of an action against the unincorporated association is the same as it would be if the unincorporated association were a corporation and, for the purpose of determining the proper county, the principal place of business of the unincorporated association shall be deemed to be the principal office in this state listed in the statement.[543]

395.5. A corporation or association may be sued in the county where the contract is made or is to be performed, or where the obligation or liability arises, or the breach occurs; or in the county where the principal place of business of such corporation is situated, subject to the power of the court to change the place of trial as in other cases.[77]

396. (a) No appeal or petition filed in the superior court shall be dismissed solely because the appeal or petition was not filed in the proper state court.
(b) If the superior court lacks jurisdiction of an appeal or petition, and a court of appeal or the Supreme Court would have jurisdiction, the appeal or petition shall be transferred to the court having jurisdiction upon terms as to costs or otherwise as may be just, and proceeded with as if regularly filed in the court having jurisdiction.[608]

396a. In a case that is subject to Sections 1812.10 and 2984.4 of the Civil Code, or subdivision (b) of Section 395 of the Code of Civil Procedure, or in an action or proceeding for an unlawful detainer as defined in Section 1161 of the Code of Civil Procedure:
(a) The plaintiff shall state facts in the complaint, verified by the plaintiff's oath, or the oath of the plaintiff's attorney, or in an affidavit of the plaintiff or of the plaintiff's attorney filed with the complaint, showing that the action has been commenced in the proper superior court and the proper court location for the trial of the action or proceeding, and showing that the action is subject to the provisions of Sections 1812.10 and 2984.4 of the Civil Code or subdivision (b) of Section 395 of the Code of Civil Procedure, or is an action for an unlawful detainer. When the affidavit is filed with the complaint, a copy thereof shall be served with the summons. Except as provided in this section, if the complaint or affidavit is not filed pursuant to this subdivision, no further proceedings may occur in the action or proceeding, except to dismiss the action or proceeding without prejudice. However, the court may, on terms that are just, permit the affidavit to be filed after the filing of the complaint, and a copy of the affidavit shall be served on the defendant and the time to answer or otherwise plead shall date from that service.
(b) If it appears from the complaint or affidavit, or otherwise, that the superior court or court location where the action or proceeding is commenced is not the proper court or court location for the trial, the court where the action or proceeding is commenced, or a judge thereof, shall, whenever that fact appears, transfer it to the proper court or court location, on its own motion, or on motion of the defendant, unless the defendant consents in writing, or in open court (consent in open court being entered in the minutes of the court), to the keeping of the action or proceeding in the court or court location where commenced. If that consent is given, the action or proceeding may continue in the court or court location where commenced. Notwithstanding Section 1801.1 and subdivision (f) of Section 2983.7 of the Civil Code, that consent may be given by a defendant who is represented by counsel at the time the consent is given, and if an action or proceeding is subject to subdivision (b) of Section 395 or is for an unlawful detainer, that consent may only be given by a defendant who is represented by counsel at the time the consent is given.
(c) In any case where the transfer of the action or proceeding is ordered under subdivision (a) or (b), if summons

is served prior to the filing of the action or proceeding in the superior court or court location to which it is transferred, as to any defendant, so served, who has not appeared in the action or proceeding, the time to answer or otherwise plead shall date from service upon that defendant of written notice of the filing.

(d) If it appears from the complaint or affidavit of the plaintiff that the superior court and court location where the action or proceeding is commenced are a proper court and court location for the trial thereof, all proper proceedings may be had, and the action or proceeding may be tried in that court at that location.

(e) A motion for a transfer of the action or proceeding to a different superior court may be made as in other cases, within the time, upon the grounds, and in the manner provided in this title, and if upon that motion it appears that the action or proceeding is not pending in the proper court, or should for other cause be transferred, the action or proceeding shall be ordered transferred as provided in this title.

If any action or proceeding is ordered transferred to another court as provided in this section, proceedings shall be had, and the costs and fees shall be paid, as provided in Sections 398 and 399.

(f) If a motion is made for transfer of an action or proceeding to a different court location within the same superior court as provided in this section, proceedings shall be had as provided by local rules of the superior court.[600]

396b. (a) Except as otherwise provided in Section 396a, if an action or proceeding is commenced in a court having jurisdiction of the subject matter thereof, other than the court designated as the proper court for the trial thereof, under this title, the action may, notwithstanding, be tried in the court where commenced, unless the defendant, at the time he or she answers, demurs, or moves to strike, or, at his or her option, without answering, demurring, or moving to strike and within the time otherwise allowed to respond to the complaint, files with the clerk, a notice of motion for an order transferring the action or proceeding to the proper court, together with proof of service, upon the adverse party, of a copy of those papers. Upon the hearing of the motion the court shall, if it appears that the action or proceeding was not commenced in the proper court, order the action or proceeding transferred to the proper court.

(b) In its discretion, the court may order the payment to the prevailing party of reasonable expenses and attorney's fees incurred in making or resisting the motion to transfer whether or not that party is otherwise entitled to recover his or her costs of action. In determining whether that order for expenses and fees shall be made, the court shall take into consideration (1) whether an offer to stipulate to change of venue was reasonably made and rejected, and (2) whether the motion or selection of venue was made in good faith given the facts and law the party making the motion or selecting the venue knew or should have known. As between the party and his or her attorney, those expenses and fees shall be the personal liability of the attorney not chargeable to the party. Sanctions shall not be imposed pursuant to this subdivision except on notice contained in a party's papers, or on the court's own noticed motion, and after opportunity to be heard.

(c) The court in a proceeding for dissolution of marriage or legal separation or under the Uniform Parentage Act (Part 3 (commencing with Section 7600) of Division 12 of the Family Code) may, prior to the determination of the motion to transfer, consider and determine motions for allowance of temporary spousal support, support of children, and counsel fees and costs, and motions to determine custody of and visitation with children, and may make all necessary and proper orders in connection therewith.

(d) In any case, if an answer is filed, the court may consider opposition to the motion to transfer, if any, and may retain the action in the county where commenced if it appears that the convenience of the witnesses or the ends of justice will thereby be promoted.

(e) If the motion to transfer is denied, the court shall allow the defendant time to move to strike, demur, or otherwise plead if the defendant has not previously filed a response.[578]

397. The court may, on motion, change the place of trial in the following cases:

(a) When the court designated in the complaint is not the proper court.

(b) When there is reason to believe that an impartial trial cannot be had therein.

(c) When the convenience of witnesses and the ends of justice would be promoted by the change.

(d) When from any cause there is no judge of the court qualified to act.

(e) When a proceeding for dissolution of marriage has been filed in the county in which the petitioner has been a resident for three months next preceding the commencement of the proceeding, and the respondent at the time of the commencement of the proceeding is a resident of another county in this state, to the county of the respondent's residence when the ends of justice would be promoted by the change. If a motion to change the place of trial is made pursuant to this paragraph, the court may, prior to the determination of such motion, consider and determine motions for allowance of temporary spousal support, support of children, temporary restraining orders, attorneys' fees, and costs, and make all necessary and proper orders in connection therewith.[294]

397.5. In any proceeding under the Family Code where it appears that both petitioner and respondent have moved from the county rendering the order, the court may, when the ends of justice and the convenience of the parties would be promoted by the change, order that the proceedings be transferred to the county of residence of either party. In any proceeding in which there is a concurrent action or proceeding under Division 17 (commencing with Section 17000) of the Family Code involving the local child support agency, the court may transfer venue under this section for any action or proceeding not subject to Division 17 (commencing with Section 17000) of the Family Code, but shall redirect any motion pursuant to this section to the court of competent jurisdiction under Section 4251 of the Family Code for change of venue in those actions and proceedings subject to Division 17 (commencing with Section 17000) of the Family Code. The decision on any motion redirected pursuant to the preceding sentence shall apply only to the action or proceeding under Division 17 (commencing with Section 17000) of the Family Code and shall be at the sole discretion of the court of competent jurisdiction hearing the action or proceeding pursuant to Section 4251 of the Family Code.[864]

398. (a) If a court orders the transfer of an action or proceeding for a cause specified in subdivisions (b), (c), and (d) of Section 397, the action or proceeding shall be transferred to a court having jurisdiction of the subject matter of the action upon agreement of the parties by stipulation in writing, or in open court and entered in the minutes or docket. If the parties do not so agree, the action or proceeding shall be transferred to the nearest or most accessible court where the like objection or cause for making the order does not exist.

(b) If an action or proceeding is commenced in a court other than one designated as a proper court for the trial thereof by the provisions of this title, and the same is ordered transferred for that reason, the action or proceeding shall be transferred to a proper court upon agreement of the parties by stipulation in writing, or in open court and entered in the minutes or docket. If the parties do not so agree, the action or proceeding shall be transferred to a proper court in the county in which the action or proceeding was commenced which the defendant may designate or, if there is no proper court in that county, to a proper court, in a proper county, designated by the defendant. If the defendant does not designate the court as herein provided, or if the court orders the transfer of an action on its own motion as provided in this title, the action or proceeding shall be transferred to the proper court as determined by the court in which the action or proceeding is pending.

(c) The designation of the court by the defendant as provided for in subdivision (b), may be made in the notice of motion for change of venue or in open court and entered in the minutes or docket at the time the order for transfer is made.[707]

399. (a) If an order is made transferring an action or proceeding under any provision of this title, the clerk shall, after expiration of the time within which a petition for writ of mandate could have been filed pursuant to Section 400, or if a writ petition is filed after judgment denying the writ becomes final, and upon payment of the costs and fees, transmit the pleadings and papers of the action or proceeding, or, if the pleadings are oral, a transcript of the pleadings, to the clerk of the court to which the action or proceeding is transferred. If the transfer is sought on any ground specified in subdivision (b), (c), (d), or (e) of Section 397 or in Section 397.5, the costs and fees of the transfer, and of filing the papers in the court to which the transfer is ordered, shall be paid at the time the notice of motion is filed by the party making the motion for the transfer. If the transfer is sought solely, or is ordered, because the action or proceeding was commenced in a court other than that designated as proper by this title, those costs and fees, including any expenses

and attorney's fees awarded to the defendant pursuant to Section 396b, shall be paid by the plaintiff before the transfer is made. If the defendant has paid those costs and fees at the time of filing a notice of motion, those costs and fees shall be repaid to the defendant, upon the making of the transfer order. If those costs and fees have not been paid by the plaintiff within five days after service of notice of the transfer order, any other party interested in the action or proceeding, whether named in the complaint as a party or not, may pay those costs and fees, and the clerk shall transmit the papers and pleadings of the action or proceeding as if those costs and fees had been originally paid by the plaintiff, and those costs and fees shall be a proper item of costs of the party paying them, recoverable by that party if that party prevails in the action. Otherwise, those costs and fees shall be offset against and deducted from the amount, if any, awarded to the plaintiff if the plaintiff prevails against that party in the action. The cause of action shall not be further prosecuted in any court until those costs and fees are paid. If those costs and fees are not paid within 30 days after service of notice of the transfer order, if a copy of a petition for writ of mandate pursuant to Section 400 is filed in the trial court, or if an appeal is taken pursuant to Section 904.2, then, within 30 days after notice of finality of the order of transfer, the court on a duly noticed motion by any party may dismiss the action without prejudice to the cause on the condition that no other action on the cause may be commenced in another court before satisfaction of the court's order for costs and fees. If a petition for writ of mandate or appeal does not result in a stay of proceedings, the time for payment of those costs and fees shall be 60 days after service of the notice of the order.

(b) At the time of transmittal of the papers and pleadings, the clerk shall mail notice to all parties who have appeared in the action or special proceeding, stating the date on which the transmittal occurred. Promptly upon receipt of the papers and pleadings, the clerk of the court to which the action or proceeding is transferred shall mail notice to all parties who have appeared in the action or special proceeding, stating the date of the filing of the case and number assigned to the case in the court.

(c) The court to which an action or proceeding is transferred under this title shall have and exercise over the action or proceeding the like jurisdiction as if it had been originally commenced in that court, all prior proceedings being saved, and the court may require amendment of the pleadings, the filing and service of amended, additional, or supplemental pleadings, and the giving of notice, as may be necessary for the proper presentation and determination of the action or proceeding in the court.

(d) Notwithstanding subdivision (c), the court transferring jurisdiction of a family law action or proceeding pursuant to Section 397, 397.5, or 398 shall, if another court has not assumed jurisdiction over the action or proceeding, retain jurisdiction to make orders designed to prevent:

(1) Immediate danger or irreparable harm to a party or to the children involved in the matter.

(2) Immediate loss or damage to

property subject to disposition in the matter.

(e) By January 1, 2019, the Judicial Council shall, by rule of court, establish:

(1) The timeframe for a court to transfer jurisdiction over a family law action or proceeding.

(2) The timeframe for a court to assume jurisdiction over a family law action or proceeding.[865]

400. When an order is made by the superior court granting or denying a motion to change the place of trial, the party aggrieved by the order may, within 20 days after service of a written notice of the order, petition the court of appeal for the district in which the court granting or denying the motion is situated for a writ of mandate requiring trial of the case in the proper court. The superior court may, for good cause, and prior to the expiration of the initial 20-day period, extend the time for one additional period not to exceed 10 days. The petitioner shall file a copy of the petition in the trial court immediately after the petition is filed in the court of appeal. The court of appeal may stay all proceedings in the case, pending judgment on the petition becoming final. The clerk of the court of appeal shall file with the clerk of the trial court, a copy of any final order or final judgment immediately after the order or judgment becomes final.[407]

401.

(1) Whenever it is provided by any law of this State that an action or proceeding against the State or a department, institution, board, commission, bureau, officer or other agency thereof shall or may be commenced in, tried in, or removed to the County of Sacramento, the same may be commenced and tried in any city or city and county of this State in which the Attorney General has an office.

(2) Whenever it is provided by any law of this State that the State or a department, institution, board, commission, bureau, officer or other agency thereof shall or may commence an action or proceeding in the County of Sacramento, the same, on motion of the defendants or some of them, shall be removed for trial to the county or city and county in which the Attorney General has an office nearest to the county in which the defendants or some of them reside or have their principal office in this State.[25]

402. (a) Except as otherwise provided by law:

(1) A superior court may specify by local rule the locations where certain types of actions or proceedings are to be filed.

(2) A superior court may specify by local rule the locations where certain types of actions or proceedings are to be heard or tried.

(3) A superior court may not dismiss a case, and the clerk may not reject a case for filing, because it is filed, or a person seeks to file it, in a court location other than the location specified by local rule. However, the court may transfer the case on its own motion to the proper court location.

(b) A superior court may transfer an action or proceeding filed in one location to another location of the superior court. This section does not affect the authority of the presiding judge to apportion the business of the court as provided by the California Rules of Court.[518]

403. A judge may, on motion, transfer an action or actions from another court to that judge's court for coordination with an action involving a common question of fact or law within the meaning of Section 404. The motion shall be supported by a declaration stating facts showing that the actions meet the standards specified in Section 404.1, are not complex as defined by the Judicial Council and that the moving party has made a good faith effort to obtain agreement to the transfer from all parties to each action. Notice of the motion shall be served on all parties to each action and on each court in which an action is pending. Any party to that action may file papers opposing the motion within the time permitted by rule of the Judicial Council. The court to which a case is transferred may order the cases consolidated for trial pursuant to Section 1048 without any further motion or hearing.
The Judicial Council may adopt rules to implement this section, including rules prescribing procedures for preventing duplicative or conflicting transfer orders issued by different courts.[500]

Chapter 2: Reclassification of Civil Actions and Proceedings

Chapter 2 added by Stats. 1999, Ch. 344, Sec. 11.

403.010. Nothing in this chapter expands or limits the law on whether a plaintiff, cross-complainant, or petitioner may file an amended complaint or other amended initial pleading. Nothing in this chapter expands or limits the law on whether, and to what extent, an amendment relates back to the date of filing the original complaint or other initial pleading.
(Amended by Stats. 2002, Ch. 784, Sec. 56. Effective January 1, 2003.)

403.020. (a) If a plaintiff, cross-complainant, or petitioner files an amended complaint or other amended initial pleading that changes the jurisdictional classification from limited to unlimited, the party at the time of filing the pleading shall pay the reclassification fee provided in Section 403.060, and the clerk shall promptly reclassify the case. If the amendment changes the jurisdictional classification from unlimited to limited, no reclassification fee is required, and the clerk shall promptly reclassify the case.
(b) For purposes of this chapter, an amendment to an initial pleading shall be treated in the same manner as an amended initial pleading.[465]

403.030. If a party in a limited civil case files a cross-complaint that causes the action or proceeding to exceed the maximum amount in controversy for a limited civil case or otherwise fail to satisfy the requirements for a limited civil case as prescribed by Section 85, the caption of the cross-complaint shall state that the action or proceeding is a limited civil case to be reclassified by cross-complaint, or words to that effect. The party at the time of filing the cross-complaint shall pay the reclassification fees provided in Section 403.060, and the clerk shall promptly reclassify the case.[466]

403.040. (a) The plaintiff, cross-complainant, or petitioner may file a motion for reclassification within the time allowed for that party to amend the initial pleading. The defendant or cross-defendant may file a motion for reclassification within the time allowed for that party to respond to the initial pleading. The court, on its own motion, may reclassify a case at any time. A motion for reclassification does not extend the moving party's time to amend or answer or otherwise respond. The court shall grant the motion and enter an order for reclassification, regardless of any fault or lack of fault, if the case has been classified in an incorrect jurisdictional classification.

(b) If a party files a motion for reclassification after the time for that party to amend that party's initial pleading or to respond to a complaint, cross-complaint, or other initial pleading, the court shall grant the motion and enter an order for reclassification only if both of the following conditions are satisfied:

(1) The case is incorrectly classified.

(2) The moving party shows good cause for not seeking reclassification earlier.

(c) If the court grants a motion for reclassification, the payment of the reclassification fee shall be determined, unless the court orders otherwise, as follows:

(1) If a case is reclassified as an unlimited civil case, the party whose pleading causes the action or proceeding to exceed the maximum amount in controversy for a limited civil case or otherwise fails to satisfy the requirements of a limited civil case under Section 85 shall pay the reclassification fee provided in Section 403.060.

(2) If a case is reclassified as a limited civil case, no reclassification fee is required.

(d) If the court grants an order for reclassification of an action or proceeding pursuant to this section, the reclassification shall proceed as follows:

(1) If the required reclassification fee is paid pursuant to Section 403.060 or no reclassification fee is required, the clerk shall promptly reclassify the case.

(2) An action that has been reclassified pursuant to this section shall not be further prosecuted in any court until the required reclassification fee is paid. If the required reclassification fee has not been paid within five days after service of notice of the order for reclassification, any party interested in the case, regardless of whether that party is named in the complaint, may pay the fee, and the clerk shall promptly reclassify the case as if the fee had been paid as provided in Section 403.060. The fee shall then be a proper item of costs of the party paying it, recoverable if that party prevails in the action or proceeding. Otherwise, the fee shall be offset against and deducted from the amount, if any, awarded to the party responsible for the fee, if that party prevails in the action or proceeding.

(3) If the fee is not paid within 30 days after service of notice of an order of reclassification, the court on its own motion or the motion of any party may order the case to proceed as a limited civil case, dismiss the action or cross-action without prejudice on the condition that no other action or proceeding on the same matters may be commenced in any other court until the reclassification fee is paid, or take such other action as the court may deem appropriate.

(e) Nothing in this section shall be construed to require the superior court to reclassify an action or proceeding because the judgment to be rendered, as determined at the trial or hearing, is one that might have been rendered in a limited civil case.

(f) In any case where the misclassification is due solely to an excess in the amount of the demand, the excess may be remitted and the action may continue as a limited civil case.[467]

403.050. (a) The parties to the action or proceeding may stipulate to reclassification of the case within the time allowed to respond to the initial pleading.

(b) If the stipulation for reclassification changes the jurisdictional classification of the case from limited to unlimited, the reclassification fee provided in Section 403.060 shall be paid at the time the stipulation is filed.

(c) Upon filing of the stipulation and, if required under subdivision (b), the payment of the reclassification fee provided in Section 403.060, the clerk shall promptly reclassify the case.[468]

403.060. (a) For reclassification of a case from a limited civil case to an unlimited civil case, a fee shall be charged as provided in Section 70619 of the Government Code. This reclassification fee shall be in addition to any other fee due for that appearance or filing in a limited civil case. No additional amounts shall be charged for appearance or filing fees paid prior to reclassification. After reclassification, the fees ordinarily charged in an unlimited case shall be charged.

(b) If a reclassification fee is required and is not paid at the time an amended complaint or other initial pleading, a cross-complaint, or a stipulation for reclassification is filed under Section 403.020, 403.030, or 403.050, the clerk shall not reclassify the case and the case shall remain and proceed as a limited civil case.

(c) No fee shall be charged for reclassification of a case from an unlimited civil case to a limited civil case. The fees ordinarily required for filing or appearing in a limited civil case shall be charged at the time of filing a pleading that reclassifies the case. Parties are not entitled to a refund of the difference between any fees previously paid for appearance or filing in an unlimited civil case and the fees due in a limited civil case. After reclassification, the fees ordinarily charged in a limited civil case shall be charged.[559]

403.070. (a) An action or proceeding that is reclassified shall be deemed to have been commenced at the time the complaint or petition was initially filed, not at the time of reclassification.

(b) The court shall have and exercise over the reclassified action or proceeding the same authority as if the action or proceeding had been originally commenced as reclassified, all prior proceedings being saved. The court may allow or require whatever amendment of the pleadings, filing and service of amended, additional, or supplemental pleadings, or giving of notice, or other appropriate action, as may be necessary for the proper presentation and determination of the action or proceeding as reclassified.[404]

403.080. When an order is made by the superior court granting or denying a motion to reclassify an action or proceeding pursuant to Section 403.040, the party aggrieved by the order may, within 20 days after service of a written notice of the order, petition the court of appeal for the district in which the court granting or denying the motion is situated for a writ of mandate requiring proper classification of the action or proceeding pursuant to Section 403.040. The superior court may, for good cause, and prior to the expiration of the initial 20-day period, extend the time for one additional period not to exceed 10 days. The petitioner shall file a copy of the petition in the superior court immediately after the petition is filed in the court of appeal. The court of appeal may stay all proceedings in the case, pending judgment on the petition becoming final. The clerk of the court of appeal shall file with the clerk of the superior court, a copy of any final order or final judgment immediately after the order or judgment becomes final.[404]

403.090. The Judicial Council may prescribe rules, not inconsistent with statute, governing the procedure for reclassification of civil actions and proceedings.[404]

Chapter 3: Coordination

Heading of Chapter 3 renumbered from Chapter 2 by Stats. 1999, Ch. 344, Sec. 12.

404. When civil actions sharing a common question of fact or law are pending in different courts, a petition for coordination may be submitted to the Chairperson of the Judicial Council, by the presiding judge of any such court, or by any party to one of the actions after obtaining permission from the presiding judge, or by all of the parties plaintiff or defendant in any such action. A petition for coordination, or a motion for permission to submit a petition, shall be supported by a declaration stating facts showing that the actions are complex, as defined by the Judicial Council and that the actions meet the standards specified in Section 404.1. On receipt of a petition for coordination, the Chairperson of the Judicial Council may assign a judge to determine whether the actions are complex, and if so, whether coordination of the actions is appropriate, or the Chairperson of the Judicial Council may authorize the presiding judge of a court to assign the matter to judicial officers of the court to make the determination in the same manner as assignments are made in other civil cases.[501]

404.1. Coordination of civil actions sharing a common question of fact or law is appropriate if one judge hearing all of the actions for all purposes in a selected site or sites will promote the ends of justice taking into account whether the common question of fact or law is predominating and significant to the litigation; the convenience of parties, witnesses, and counsel; the relative development of the actions and the work product of counsel; the efficient utilization of judicial facilities and manpower; the calendar of the courts; the disadvantages of duplicative and inconsistent rulings, orders, or judgments; and, the likelihood of settlement of the actions without further litigation should coordination be denied.[82]

404.2. A judge assigned pursuant to Section 404 who determines that coordination is appropriate shall select the reviewing court having appellate jurisdiction if the actions to be coordinated are within the jurisdiction of more than one reviewing court. The assigned judge shall select the reviewing court which will promote the ends of justice as determined under the standards specified in Section 404.1.[361]

404.3. A judge assigned pursuant to Section 404 who determines that coordination is appropriate shall order the actions coordinated, report that fact to the Chairperson of the Judicial Council, and the Chairperson of the Judicial Council shall either assign a judge to hear and determine the actions in the site or sites the assigned judge finds appropriate or authorize the presiding judge of a court to assign the matter to judicial officers of the court in the same manner as assignments are made in other civil cases.[502]

404.4. The presiding judge of any court in which there is pending an action sharing a common question of fact or law with actions coordinated pursuant to Section 404, on the court's own motion or the motion of any party supported by an affidavit stating facts showing that the action meets the standards specified in Section 404.1, or all the parties plaintiff or defendant in any such action, supported by an affidavit stating facts showing that the action meets the standards specified in Section 404.1, may request the judge assigned to hear the coordinated actions for an order coordinating the action. Coordination of the action shall be determined under the standards specified in Section 404.1.[362]

404.5. Pending any determination of whether coordination is appropriate, the judge making that determination may stay any action being considered for, or affecting an action being considered for, coordination.[82]

404.6. Within 20 days after service upon him or her of a written notice of entry of an order of the court under this chapter, any party may petition the appropriate reviewing court for a writ of mandate to require the court to make such order as the reviewing court finds appropriate. The superior court may, for good cause, and prior to the expiration of the initial 20-day period, extend the time for one additional period not to exceed 10 days.[265]

404.7. Notwithstanding any other provision of law, the Judicial Council shall provide by rule the practice and procedure for coordination of civil actions in convenient courts, including provision for giving notice and presenting evidence.[82]

404.8. Expenses of the assigned judge, other necessary judicial officers and employees, and facilities for cases coordinated under Section 404 shall be paid or reimbursed by the state from funds appropriated to the Judicial Council.[363]

404.9. Any duties of the presiding judge specified in this chapter may be delegated by the presiding judge to another judge of the court.[503]

TITLE 4.5: RECORDING NOTICE OF CERTAIN ACTIONS

Title 4.5 repealed and added by Stats. 1992, Ch. 883, Sec. 2.

Chapter 1: Definitions and General Provisions

Chapter 1 added by Stats. 1992, Ch. 883, Sec. 2.

405. The definitions in this chapter govern the construction of this title.[319]

405.1. "Claimant" means a party to an action who asserts a real property claim and records a notice of the pendency of the action.[319]

405.2. "Notice of pendency of action" or "notice" means a notice of the pendency of an action in which a real property claim is alleged.[319]

405.3. "Probable validity," with respect to a real property claim, means that it is more likely than not that the claimant will obtain a judgment against the defendant on the claim.[319]

405.4. "Real property claim" means the cause or causes of action in a pleading which would, if meritorious, affect (a) title to, or the right to possession of, specific real property or (b) the use of an easement identified in the pleading, other than an easement obtained pursuant to statute by any regulated public utility.[319]

405.5. This title applies to an action pending in any United States District Court in the same manner that it applies to an action pending in the courts of this state.[319]

405.6. In an action by a public agency in eminent domain pursuant to Title 7 (commencing with Section 1230.010) of Part 3, the issuance, service, and recordation of a notice of pendency of action shall be governed by Section 1250.150 and shall not be subject to Chapter 2 (commencing with Section 405.20).[319]

405.7. Whenever an action is commenced to declare a building uninhabitable, the plaintiff public agency, at the time of filing the complaint, shall record in the office of the recorder of the county in which the building is situated, a notice of the pendency of the action, containing the names of the parties and a description of the real property upon which the building affected by the action is situated.[319]

405.8. Nothing in this title precludes any party from seeking an attachment, injunction, or other relief in connection with a real property claim or the expungement of a notice of pending action.[319]

Chapter 2: Recordation Service and Filing

Chapter 2 added by Stats. 1992, Ch. 883, Sec. 2.

405.20. A party to an action who asserts a real property claim may record a notice of pendency of action in which that real property claim is alleged. The notice may be recorded in the office of the recorder of each county in which all or part of the real property is situated. The notice shall contain the names of all parties to the action and a description of the property affected by the action.[551]

405.21. An attorney of record in an action may sign a notice of pendency of action. Alternatively, a judge of the court in which an action that includes a real property claim is pending may, upon request of a party thereto, approve a notice of pendency of action. A notice of pendency of action shall not be recorded unless (a) it has been signed by the attorney of record, (b) it is signed by a party acting in propria persona and approved by a judge as provided in this section, or (c) the action is subject to Section 405.6.[332]

405.22. Except in actions subject to Section 405.6, the claimant shall, prior to recordation of the notice, cause a copy of the notice to be mailed, by registered or certified mail, return receipt requested, to all known addresses of the parties to whom the real property claim is adverse and to all owners of record of the real property affected by the real property claim as shown by the latest county assessment roll. If there is no known address for service on an adverse party or owner, then as to that party or owner a declaration under penalty of perjury to that effect may be recorded instead of the proof of service required above, and the service on that party or owner shall not be required. Immediately following recordation, a copy of the notice shall also be filed with the court in which the action is pending. Service shall also be made immediately and in the same manner upon each adverse party later joined in the action.[552]

405.23. Any notice of pendency of action shall be void and invalid as to any adverse party or owner of record unless the requirements of Section 405.22 are met for that party or owner and a proof of service in the form and content specified in Section 1013a has been recorded with the notice of pendency of action.[319]

405.24. From the time of recording the notice of pendency of action, a purchaser, encumbrancer, or other transferee of the real property described in the notice shall be deemed to have constructive notice of the pendency of the noticed action as it relates to the real property and only of its pendency against parties not fictitiously named. The rights and interest of the claimant in the property, as ultimately determined in the pending noticed action, shall relate back to the date of the recording of the notice.[319]

Chapter 3: Expungement and Other Relief

Heading of Chapter 3 redesignated from Article 3 by Stats. 1994, Ch. 146, Sec. 21.

405.30. At any time after notice of pendency of action has been recorded, any party, or any nonparty with an interest in the real property affected thereby, may apply to the court in which the action is pending to expunge the notice. However, a person who is not a party to the action shall obtain leave to intervene from the court at or before the time the party brings the motion to expunge the notice. Evidence or declarations may be filed with the motion to expunge the notice. The court may permit evidence to be received in the form of oral testimony, and may make any orders it deems just to provide for discovery by any party affected by a motion to expunge the notice. The claimant shall have the burden of proof under Sections 405.31 and 405.32.[319]

405.31. In proceedings under this chapter, the court shall order the notice expunged if the court finds that the pleading on which the notice is based does not contain a real property claim. The court shall not order an undertaking to be given as a condition of expunging the notice where the court finds the pleading does not contain a real property claim.[319]

405.32. In proceedings under this chapter, the court shall order that the notice be expunged if the court finds that the claimant has not established by a preponderance of the evidence the probable validity of the real property claim. The court shall not order an undertaking to be given as a condition of expunging the notice if the court finds the claimant has not established the probable validity of the real property claim.[319]

405.33. In proceedings under this chapter, the court shall order that the notice be expunged if the court finds that the real property claim has probable validity, but adequate relief can be secured to the claimant by the giving of an undertaking. The expungement order shall be conditioned upon the giving of the undertaking of such nature and in such amount as will indemnify the claimant for all damages proximately resulting from the expungement which the claimant may incur if the claimant prevails upon the real property claim. In its order conditionally expunging the notice, the court shall set a return date for the moving party to show fulfillment of the condition, and if the moving party fails to show fulfillment of the condition on the return day, the court shall deny the motion to expunge without further notice or hearing. Recovery may be had on the undertaking pursuant to Section 996.440.

For purposes only of determining under this section whether the giving of an undertaking will secure adequate relief to the claimant, the presumption of Section 3387 of the Civil Code that real property is unique shall not apply, except in the case of real property improved with a single-family dwelling which the claimant intends to occupy.[319]

405.34. Subject to the provisions of Sections 405.31 and 405.32, at any time after a notice of pendency of action has been recorded, and regardless of whether a motion to expunge has been filed, the court may, upon motion by any person with an interest in the property, require the claimant to give the moving party an undertaking as a condition of maintaining the notice in the record title. However, a person who is not a party to the action shall obtain leave to intervene from the court at or before the time the person moves to require an undertaking. The court may permit evidence to be received in the form of oral testimony and may make any orders it deems just to provide for discovery by any affected party. An undertaking required pursuant to this section shall be of such nature and in such amount as the court may determine to be just. In its order requiring an undertaking, the court shall set a return date for the claimant to show compliance and if the claimant fails to show compliance on the return date, the court shall order the notice of pendency of action expunged without further notice or hearing.

Recovery on an undertaking required pursuant to this section may be had in an amount not to exceed the undertaking, pursuant to Section 996.440, upon a showing (a) that the claimant did not prevail on the real property claim and (b) that the person seeking recovery suffered damages as a result of the maintenance of the notice. In assessing these damages, the court shall not consider the claimant's intent or the presence or absence of probable cause.[319]

405.35. No order expunging a notice of pendency of action shall be effective, nor shall it be recorded in the office of any county recorder, until the time within which a petition for writ of mandate may be filed pursuant to Section 405.39 has expired. No order expunging a notice of pendency of action shall be effective, nor shall it be recorded in the office of any county recorder, after a petition for writ of mandate has been timely filed pursuant to Section 405.39, until the proceeding commenced by the petition is finally adjudicated. This section imposes no duty on the county recorder to determine whether the requirements of this section or of any order expunging a notice of pendency of action have been met.[319]

405.36. Once a notice of pending action has been expunged, the claimant may not record another notice of pending action as to the affected property without leave of the court in which the action is pending.[319]

405.37. After notice and hearing, for good cause and upon such terms as are just, the court may exonerate or modify any undertaking required by an order issued pursuant to Section 405.33 or 405.34 or pursuant to a stipulation made in lieu of such an order. An order of the court under this section may be made conditional upon the giving of a new undertaking under Section 405.33 or 405.34.[319]

405.38. The court shall direct that the party prevailing on any motion under this chapter be awarded the reasonable attorney's fees and costs of making or opposing the motion unless the court finds that the other party acted with substantial justification or that other circumstances make the imposition of attorney's fees and costs unjust.[319]

405.39. No order or other action of the court under this chapter shall be appealable. Any party aggrieved by an order made on a motion under this chapter may petition the proper reviewing court to review the order by writ of mandate. The petition for writ of mandate shall be filed and served within 20 days of service of written notice of the order by the court or any party. The court which issued the order may, within the initial 20-day period, extend the initial 20-day period for one additional period not to exceed 10 days. A copy of the petition for writ of mandate shall be delivered to the clerk of the court which issued the order with a request that it be placed in the court file.[319]

Chapter 4: Withdrawal

Heading of Chapter 4 redesignated from Article 4 by Stats. 1994, Ch. 146, Sec. 22.

405.50. At any time after notice of pendency of an action has been recorded pursuant to this title or other law, the notice may be withdrawn by recording in the office of the recorder in which the notice of pendency was recorded a notice of withdrawal executed by the party who recorded the notice of pendency of action or by the party's successor in interest. The notice of withdrawal shall be acknowledged.[319]

Chapter 5: Effect of Withdrawal or Expungement of Notice

Heading of Chapter 5 redesignated from Article 5 by Stats. 1994, Ch. 146, Sec. 23.

405.60. Upon the withdrawal of a notice of pendency of action pursuant to Section 405.50 or upon recordation of a certified copy of an order expunging a notice of pendency of action pursuant to this title, neither the notice nor any information derived from it, prior to the recording of a certified copy of the judgment or decree issued in the action, shall constitute actual or constructive notice of any of the matters contained, claimed, alleged, or contended therein, or of any of the matters related to the action, or create a duty of inquiry in any person thereafter dealing with the affected property.[319]

405.61. Upon the withdrawal of a notice of pendency of action pursuant to Section 405.50 or upon recordation of a certified copy of an order expunging a notice of pendency of action pursuant to this title, no person except a nonfictitious party to the action at the time of recording of the notice of withdrawal or order, who thereafter becomes, by conveyance recorded prior to the recording of a certified copy of the judgment or decree issued in the action, a purchaser, transferee, mortgagee, or other encumbrancer for a valuable consideration of any interest in the real property subject to the action, shall be deemed to have actual knowledge of the action or any of the matters contained, claimed, or alleged therein, or of any of the matters related to the action, irrespective of whether that person possessed actual knowledge of the action or matter and irrespective of when or how the knowledge was obtained.
It is the intent of the Legislature that this section shall provide for the absolute and complete free transferability of real property after the expungement or withdrawal of a notice of pendency of action.[319]

TITLE 5: JURISDICTION AND SERVICE OF PROCESS

Title 5 added by Stats. 1969, Ch. 1610.

Chapter 1: Jurisdiction and Forum

Heading of Chapter 1 amended by Stats. 1992, Ch. 615, Sec. 3.

Article 1: Jurisdiction

Article 1 added by Stats. 1969, Ch. 1610.

410.10. A court of this state may exercise jurisdiction on any basis not inconsistent with the Constitution of this state or of the United States.[71]

Article 2: Forum

Heading of Article 2 amended by Stats. 1992, Ch. 615, Sec. 4.

410.30. (a) When a court upon motion of a party or its own motion finds that in the interest of substantial justice an action should be heard in a forum outside this state, the court shall stay or dismiss the action in whole or in part on any conditions that may be just.
(b) The provisions of Section 418.10 do not apply to a motion to stay or dismiss the action by a defendant who has made a general appearance.[81]
Note: This version was suspended from Sept. 22, 1986, until Jan. 1, 1992, during operation of the temporary amendment by Stats. 1986, Ch. 968.

410.40. Any person may maintain an action or proceeding in a court of this state against a foreign corporation or nonresident person where the action or proceeding arises out of or relates to any contract, agreement, or undertaking for which a choice of California law has been made in whole or in part by the parties thereto and which (a) is a contract, agreement, or undertaking, contingent or otherwise, relating to a transaction involving in the aggregate not less than one million dollars ($1,000,000), and (b) contains a provision or provisions under which the foreign corporation or nonresident agrees to submit to the jurisdiction of the courts of this state.

This section applies to contracts, agreements, and undertakings entered into before, on, or after its effective date; it shall be fully retroactive. Contracts, agreements, and undertakings selecting California law entered into before the effective date of this section shall be valid, enforceable, and effective as if this section had been in effect on the date they were entered into; and actions and proceedings commencing in a court of this state before the effective date of this section may be maintained as if this section were in effect on the date they were commenced.[318]

410.42. (a) The following provisions of a contract between the contractor and a subcontractor with principal offices in this state, for the construction of a public or private work of improvement in this state, shall be void and unenforceable:

(1) A provision which purports to require any dispute between the parties to be litigated, arbitrated, or otherwise determined outside this state.

(2) A provision which purports to preclude a party from commencing such a proceeding or obtaining a judgment or other resolution in this state or the courts of this state.

(b) For purposes of this section, "construction" means any work or services performed on, or materials provided for, a work of improvement, as defined in Section 8050 of the Civil Code, and for which a lien may be claimed pursuant to Section 8400 of the Civil Code (whether or not a lien is in fact claimed) or for which such a lien could be claimed but for Section 8160 of the Civil Code.[646]

Article 3: Jurisdiction in Action
Article 3 added by Stats. 1969, Ch. 1610.

410.50. (a) Except as otherwise provided by statute, the court in which an action is pending has jurisdiction over a party from the time summons is served on him as provided by Chapter 4 (commencing with Section 413.10). A general appearance by a party is equivalent to personal service of summons on such party.

(b) Jurisdiction of the court over the parties and the subject matter of an action continues throughout subsequent proceedings in the action.[71]

410.60. In an action against a corporation which has forfeited its charter or right to do business, or has dissolved, the court in which the action is pending has jurisdiction over all the trustees of such corporation and of its stockholders or members from the time summons is served on one of the trustees as provided by Chapter 4 (commencing with Section 413.10).[71]

410.70. In an action against two or more persons who are jointly, jointly and severally, or severally liable on a contract, the court in which the action is pending has jurisdiction to proceed against such of the defendants as are served as if they were the only defendants.[71]

Chapter 2: Commencing Civil Actions

Chapter 2 added by Stats. 1969, Ch. 1610.

411.10. A civil action is commenced by filing a complaint with the court.[71]

411.20. (a) If the clerk accepts for filing a complaint or other first paper, or any subsequent filing, and payment is made by check which is later returned without payment, the clerk shall, by mail, notify the party who tendered the check that (1) the check has been returned without payment, (2) the administrative charge specified in subdivision (g) has been imposed to reimburse the court for the costs of processing the returned check and providing the notice specified in this subdivision, and (3) the party has 20 days from the date of mailing of the notice within which to pay the filing fee and the administrative charge, except as provided in subdivision (e). The notice also shall state that the administrative charge and the filing fee shall be paid in cash, by certified check, or by other means specified by the court, but not by traveler's check or personal check. If the person who tendered the check is not a party to the action or proposed action, but only is acting on behalf of a party, the clerk shall notify not only the person who tendered the check, but also the party or that party's attorney if the party is represented. The clerk's certificate as to the mailing of notice pursuant to this section establishes a rebuttable presumption that the fees were not paid. This presumption is a presumption affecting the burden of producing evidence.

(b) The clerk shall void the filing if the party who tendered a returned check or on whose behalf a returned check was tendered has not paid the full amount of the fee and the administrative charge by a means specified in subdivision (a) within 20 days of the date on which the notice required by subdivision (a) was mailed. Any filing voided by this section can be disposed of immediately after the 20 days have elapsed without preserving a copy in the court records, notwithstanding Section 68152 of the Government Code.

(c) If an adverse party files a response to a complaint, paper or filing referred to in subdivision (a), together with a filing fee, and the original filing is voided pursuant to subdivision (b), the responsive filing is not required and shall be voided. The court shall, by mail, provide notice to the parties or their attorneys that the initial paper and the response have been voided. The responding party's filing fee shall be refunded upon request, provided that the request for a refund is made within 20 days from the date on which the notice was mailed. Upon receipt of the request, the court shall refund the responding party's filing fee without imposing any administrative charge. A refund under this subdivision is available if the adverse party has filed only a responsive pleading, but not if the party has also filed a cross-complaint or other first paper seeking affirmative relief for which there is a filing fee.

(d) If an adverse party, or a person acting on behalf of the adverse party, tenders a check for a required filing fee that is later returned without payment, the procedures in subdivisions (a) and (b) shall apply.

(e) If any trial or other hearing is scheduled to be heard prior to the expiration of the 20-day period provided for in subdivision (a), the fee shall be paid prior to the trial or hearing. Failure of the party to pay the fee prior to the trial or hearing date shall cause the court to void the filing and proceed as if it had not been filed.

(f) If the clerk performs a service or issues any document for which a fee is required and payment is made by check which is later returned without payment, the court may order further proceedings suspended as to the party for whom the check was tendered. If the court so orders, the clerk shall, by mail, notify the party who tendered the check that proceedings have been suspended until the receipt of payment of the required fee and the administrative charge specified in subdivision (g), by cash cashier's check, or other means specified by the court, but not by personal check or traveler's check. If the person who tendered the check is not a party to the action or proposed action, but only is acting on behalf of a party, the clerk shall notify not only the person who tendered the check, but also the party or that party's attorney if the party is represented. The clerk's certificate as to the mailing of notice pursuant to this section establishes a rebuttable presumption that the fees were not paid. This presumption is a presumption affecting the burden of producing evidence.

(g) The clerk shall impose an administrative charge for providing notice that a check submitted for a filing fee has been returned without payment and for all related administrative, clerical, and other costs incurred under this section. The administrative charge shall, in each instance, be either twenty-five dollars ($25) or a reasonable amount that does not exceed the actual cost incurred by the court, as determined by the court. The notices provided by the court under subdivisions (a) and (f) shall state the specific amount of the administrative charge that shall be paid to the court. Each administrative charge collected shall be distributed to the court that incurred the charge as described in Section 68085.1 of the Government Code.[560]

411.20.5. If an electronic filing is made to the clerk by an electronic filing service provider acting as the agent of the court for purposes of collecting and remitting filing fees, and fees owed to the electronic filing service provider remain unpaid for a period of five days after notice to the attorney of record, and the filing was made by the attorney of record and not a self-represented party, the electronic filing service provider may notify the clerk that fees remain unpaid despite notice to the attorney of record. The clerk may then notify the attorney of record that the attorney of record may be sanctioned by the court for nonpayment of fees. The court may sanction the attorney of record if the fees to the electronic filing service provider remain unsatisfied 20 days after notice by the clerk.[744]

411.21. (a) If a complaint or other first paper is accompanied by payment by check in an amount less than the required fee, the clerk shall accept the paper for filing, but shall not issue a summons until the court receives full payment of the required fee. The clerk shall, by mail, notify the party tendering the check that (1) the check was made out for an amount less than the required filing fee, (2) the administrative charge specified in subdivision (g) has been imposed to reimburse the court for the costs of processing the partial payment and providing the notice specified in this subdivision, and (3) the party has 20 days from the date of mailing of the notice within which to pay the remainder of the required fee and the administrative charge, except as provided in subdivision (f). If the person who tendered the check is not a party to the action or proposed action, but only is acting on behalf of a party, the clerk shall notify not only the person who tendered the check, and also the party or that party's attorney, if the party is represented. The clerk's certificate as to the mailing of notice pursuant to this section establishes a rebuttable presumption that the fees were not paid. This presumption is a presumption affecting the burden of producing evidence. This subdivision does not apply to an unlawful detainer action.

(b) The clerk shall void the filing if the party who tendered a check in an amount less than the required filing fee or on whose behalf a check in an amount less than the required filing fee was tendered has not paid the full amount of the fee and the administrative charge by a means specified in subdivision (a) within 20 days of the date on which the notice required by subdivision (a) was mailed. Any filing voided by this section may be disposed of immediately after the 20 days have elapsed without preserving a copy in the court records notwithstanding Section 68152 of the Government Code.

(c) If a check for less than the required fee was tendered, the remainder of the required fee and the administrative charge were not paid within the period specified in subdivision (a), and a refund of the partial payment has not been requested in a writing mailed or presented by the party or person who tendered the check within 20 days from the date on which the remainder of the required fee was due, the partial payment shall be remitted to the State Treasurer to be deposited in the Trial Court Trust Fund, except for the amount of the administrative charge described in subdivision (g), that shall be deducted from the partial payment and shall be distributed as described in subdivision (g) to the court which incurred the charge. If the party or person who tendered the check for partial payment requests a refund of the partial payment, in writing, within the time specified in this subdivision, the clerk shall refund the amount of the partial payment less the amount of the administrative charge imposed by that court. All partial payments that the court received before January 1, 2006, and that remain on deposit for filings that the clerk voided pursuant to this section, once three years have passed from the date that the filing was voided, shall be remitted to the State Treasurer for deposit into the Trial Court Trust Fund.

(d) If an adverse party files a response to a complaint or other first paper referred to in subdivision (a), together with a filing fee, and the original filing is voided pursuant to subdivision (b), the responsive filing is not required and shall be voided. The court shall, by mail, provide notice to the parties that the initial paper and the response have been voided. The responding party's filing fee shall be refunded upon request, provided that the request for a refund is made in writing within 20 days from the date on which the notice was mailed. Upon receipt of the request, the court shall reimburse the responding party's filing fee without imposing any administrative charge. A refund under this subdivision is available if the adverse party has filed only a responsive pleading, but not if the party has also filed a cross-complaint or other first paper seeking affirmative relief for which there is a filing fee.

(e) If an adverse party, or a person acting on behalf of the adverse party, tenders a check for a required filing fee in an amount less than the required fee, the procedures in subdivisions (a), (b), and (c) shall apply.

(f) If any trial or other hearing is scheduled to be heard prior to the expiration of the 20-day period provided for in subdivision (a), the fee shall be paid prior to the trial or hearing. Failure of the party to pay the fee prior to the trial or hearing date shall cause the court to void the filing and proceed as if it had not been filed.

(g) The clerk shall impose an administrative charge for providing notice that a check submitted for a filing fee is in an amount less than the required fee and for all related administrative, clerical, and other costs incurred under this section. The administrative charge shall, in each instance, be either twenty-five dollars ($25) or a reasonable amount that does not exceed the actual cost incurred by the court, as determined by the court. The notices provided by the court under subdivision (a) shall state the specific amount of the administrative charge that shall be paid to the court. Each administrative charge collected shall be distributed to the court that incurred the charge as described in Section 68085.1 of the Government Code. When a partial payment is to be remitted to the State Treasurer under subdivision (c), the court shall notify the Administrative Office of the Courts of the amount of (1) the partial payment collected, and (2) the administrative charge to be deducted from the payment and to be distributed to the court.[607]

411.35. (a) In every action, including a cross-complaint for damages or indemnity, arising out of the professional negligence of a person holding a valid architect's certificate issued pursuant to Chapter 3 (commencing with Section 5500) of Division 3 of the Business and Professions Code, or of a person holding a valid registration as a professional engineer issued pursuant to Chapter 7 (commencing with Section 6700) of Division 3 of the Business and Professions Code, or a person holding a valid land surveyor's license issued pursuant to Chapter 15 (commencing with Section 8700) of Division 3 of the Business and Professions Code on or before the date of service of the complaint or cross-complaint on any defendant or cross-defendant, the attorney for the plaintiff or cross-complainant shall file and serve the certificate specified by subdivision (b).

(b) A certificate shall be executed by the attorney for the plaintiff or cross-complainant declaring one of the following:

(1) That the attorney has reviewed the facts of the case, that the attorney has consulted with and received an opinion from at least one architect, professional engineer, or land surveyor who is licensed to practice and practices in this state or any other state, or who

teaches at an accredited college or university and is licensed to practice in this state or any other state, in the same discipline as the defendant or cross-defendant and who the attorney reasonably believes is knowledgeable in the relevant issues involved in the particular action, and that the attorney has concluded on the basis of this review and consultation that there is reasonable and meritorious cause for the filing of this action. The person consulted may not be a party to the litigation. The person consulted shall render his or her opinion that the named defendant or cross-defendant was negligent or was not negligent in the performance of the applicable professional services.

(2) That the attorney was unable to obtain the consultation required by paragraph (1) because a statute of limitations would impair the action and that the certificate required by paragraph (1) could not be obtained before the impairment of the action. If a certificate is executed pursuant to this paragraph, the certificate required by paragraph (1) shall be filed within 60 days after filing the complaint.

(3) That the attorney was unable to obtain the consultation required by paragraph (1) because the attorney had made three separate good faith attempts with three separate architects, professional engineers, or land surveyors to obtain this consultation and none of those contacted would agree to the consultation.

(c) Where a certificate is required pursuant to this section, only one certificate shall be filed, notwithstanding that multiple defendants have been named in the complaint or may be named at a later time.

(d) Where the attorney intends to rely solely on the doctrine of "res ipsa loquitur," as defined in Section 646 of the Evidence Code, or exclusively on a failure to inform of the consequences of a procedure, or both, this section shall be inapplicable. The attorney shall certify upon filing of the complaint that the attorney is solely relying on the doctrines of "res ipsa loquitur" or failure to inform of the consequences of a procedure or both, and for that reason is not filing a certificate required by this section.

(e) For purposes of this section, and subject to Section 912 of the Evidence Code, an attorney who submits a certificate as required by paragraph (1) or (2) of subdivision (b) has a privilege to refuse to disclose the identity of the architect, professional engineer, or land surveyor consulted and the contents of the consultation. The privilege shall also be held by the architect, professional engineer, or land surveyor so consulted. If, however, the attorney makes a claim under paragraph (3) of subdivision (b) that he or she was unable to obtain the required consultation with the architect, professional engineer, or land surveyor, the court may require the attorney to divulge the names of architects, professional engineers, or land surveyors refusing the consultation.

(f) A violation of this section may constitute unprofessional conduct and be grounds for discipline against the attorney, except that the failure to file the certificate required by paragraph (1) of subdivision (b), within 60 days after filing the complaint and certificate provided for by paragraph (2) of subdivision (b), shall not be grounds for discipline against the attorney.

(g) The failure to file a certificate in accordance with this section shall be grounds for a demurrer pursuant to Section 430.10 or a motion to strike pursuant to Section 435.

(h) Upon the favorable conclusion of the litigation with respect to any party for whom a certificate of merit was filed or for whom a certificate of merit should have been filed pursuant to this section, the trial court may, upon the motion of a party or upon the court's own motion, verify compliance with this section, by requiring the attorney for the plaintiff or cross-complainant who was required by subdivision (b) to execute the certificate to reveal the name, address, and telephone number of the person or persons consulted with pursuant to subdivision (b) that were relied upon by the attorney in preparation of the certificate of merit. The name, address, and telephone number shall be disclosed to the trial judge in an in-camera proceeding at which the moving party shall not be present. If the trial judge finds there has been a failure to comply with this section, the court may order a party, a party's attorney, or both, to pay any reasonable expenses, including attorney's fees, incurred by another party as a result of the failure to comply with this section.

(i) For purposes of this section, "action" includes a complaint or cross-complaint for equitable indemnity arising out of the rendition of professional services whether or not the complaint or cross-complaint specifically asserts or utilizes the terms "professional negligence" or "negligence."[402]

Chapter 3: Summons

Chapter 3 added by Stats. 1969, Ch. 1610.

412.10. After payment of all applicable fees, the plaintiff may have the clerk issue one or more summons for any defendant. The clerk shall keep each original summons in the court records and provide a copy of each summons issued to the plaintiff who requested issuance of the summons.[567]

412.20. (a) Except as otherwise required by statute, a summons shall be directed to the defendant, signed by the clerk and issued under the seal of the court in which the action is pending, and it shall contain:

(1) The title of the court in which the action is pending.

(2) The names of the parties to the action.

(3) A direction that the defendant file with the court a written pleading in response to the complaint within 30 days after summons is served on the defendant.

(4) A notice that, unless the defendant so responds, their default will be entered upon application by the plaintiff, and the plaintiff may apply to the court for the relief demanded in the complaint, which could result in garnishment of wages, taking of money or property, or other relief.

(5) The following statement in boldface type: "You may seek the advice of an attorney in any matter connected with the complaint or this summons. Such attorney should be consulted promptly so that your pleading may be filed or entered within the time required by this summons."

(6) The following introductory legend at the top of the summons above all

other matter, in boldface type, in English and Spanish:

"Notice! You have been sued. The court may decide against you without your being heard unless you respond within 30 days. Read information below."

(b) Each county may, by ordinance, require that the legend contained in paragraph (6) of subdivision (a) be set forth in every summons issued out of the courts of that county in any additional foreign language, if the legend in the additional foreign language is set forth in the summons in the same manner as required in that paragraph.

(c) A summons in a form approved by the Judicial Council is deemed to comply with this section.

(d) For actions regarding residential property brought pursuant to Section 1161, the Judicial Council shall, by January 1, 2027, create for mandatory use a single summons form that includes the information described in paragraphs (3) to (6), inclusive, of subdivision (a) in English, Spanish, Chinese, Tagalog, Vietnamese, and Korean. The Judicial Council shall publish this form on its internet website.[569]

412.30. In an action against a corporation or an unincorporated association (including a partnership), the copy of the summons that is served shall contain a notice stating in substance: "To the person served: You are hereby served in the within action (or special proceeding) on behalf of (here state the name of the corporation or the unincorporated association) as a person upon whom a copy of the summons and of the complaint may be delivered to effect service on said party under the provisions of (here state appropriate provisions of Chapter 4 (commencing with Section 413.10) of the Code of Civil Procedure)." If service is also made on such person as an individual, the notice shall also indicate that service is being made on such person as an individual as well as on behalf of the corporation or the unincorporated association.

If such notice does not appear on the copy of the summons served, no default may be taken against such corporation or unincorporated association or against such person individually, as the case may be.[71]

Chapter 4: Service of Summons

Chapter 4 added by Stats. 1969, Ch. 1610.

Article 1: General

Article 1 added by Stats. 1969, Ch. 1610.

413.10. Except as otherwise provided by statute, a summons shall be served on a person:

(a) Within this state, as provided in this chapter.

(b) Outside this state but within the United States, as provided in this chapter or as prescribed by the law of the place where the person is served.

(c) Outside the United States, as provided in this chapter or as directed by the court in which the action is pending, or, if the court before or after service finds that the service is reasonably calculated to give actual notice, as prescribed by the law of the place where the person is served or as directed by the foreign authority in response to a letter rogatory. These rules are subject to the provisions of the Convention on the "Service Abroad of Judicial and Extrajudicial Documents" in Civil or Commercial Matters (Hague Service Convention).[202]

413.20. If a summons is served by mail pursuant to this chapter, the provisions of Section 1013 that extend the time for exercising a right or doing an act shall not extend any time specified in this title.[71]

413.30. (a) (1) If no provision is made in this chapter or other law for the service of summons, or if a plaintiff, despite exercising reasonable diligence, has been unable to effect service of the summons by any of the methods authorized under this chapter, the court in which the action is pending may, upon motion, direct that summons be served in a manner that is reasonably calculated to give actual notice to the party to be served, including by electronic mail or other electronic technology, and that proof of such service be made as prescribed by the court.

(2) A plaintiff seeking to establish reasonable diligence under this section shall set forth facts detailing all attempts to serve the defendant by each of the methods prescribed by statute, including facts demonstrating why each method was unsuccessful at every address or location where the defendant is likely to be found.

(b) This section does not apply in an action against a governmental entity or an agent or employee of the governmental entity who has been sued in an official or individual capacity.[879]

413.40. Any service of summons which complies with the provisions of this chapter shall not be rendered invalid or ineffective because it was made by a person in violation of Chapter 16 (commencing with Section 22350) of Division 8 of the Business and Professions Code.[75]

Article 2: Persons Who May Serve Summons

Article 2 added by Stats. 1969, Ch. 1610.

414.10. A summons may be served by any person who is at least 18 years of age and not a party to the action.[71]

Article 3: Manner of Service of Summons

Article 3 added by Stats. 1969, Ch. 1610.

415.10. A summons may be served by personal delivery of a copy of the summons and of the complaint to the person to be served. Service of a summons in this manner is deemed complete at the time of such delivery.

The date upon which personal delivery is made shall be entered on or affixed to the face of the copy of the summons at the time of its delivery. However, service of a summons without such date shall be valid and effective.[102]

415.20. (a) In lieu of personal delivery of a copy of the summons and complaint to the person to be served as specified in Section 416.10, 416.20, 416.30, 416.40, or 416.50, a summons may be served by leaving a copy of the summons and complaint during usual office hours in the person's office or, if no physical address is known, at the person's usual mailing address, other than a United States Postal Service post office box, with the person who is apparently in charge thereof, and by thereafter mailing a copy of the summons and complaint by first-class mail, postage prepaid to the person to be served at the place where a copy of the summons and complaint were left. When service is effected by leaving a copy of the summons and complaint at a mailing address, it shall be left with a person at least 18 years of age, who shall be informed of the contents thereof. Service of a summons in this manner is deemed complete on the 10th day after the mailing.

(b) If a copy of the summons and complaint cannot with reasonable diligence be personally delivered to the person to be served, as specified in Section 416.60, 416.70, 416.80, or 416.90, a summons may be served by leaving a copy of the summons and complaint at the person's dwelling house, usual place of abode, usual place of business, or usual mailing address other than a United States Postal Service post office box, in the presence of a competent member of the household or a person apparently in charge of their office, place of business, or usual mailing address other than a United States Postal Service post office box, at least 18 years of age, who shall be informed of the contents thereof, and by thereafter mailing a copy of the summons and of the complaint by first-class mail, postage prepaid to the person to be served at the place where a copy of the summons and complaint were left. Service of a summons in this manner is deemed complete on the 10th day after the mailing.

(c) Notwithstanding subdivision (b), if the only address reasonably known for the person to be served is a private mailbox obtained through a commercial mail receiving agency, service of process may be effected on the first delivery attempt by leaving a copy of the summons and complaint with the commercial mail receiving agency in the manner described in subdivision (d) of Section 17538.5 of the Business and Professions Code.

(d) This section shall remain in effect only until January 1, 2027, and as of that date is repealed.[881]

415.20. (a) In lieu of personal delivery of a copy of the summons and complaint to the person to be served as specified in Section 416.10, 416.20, 416.30, 416.40, or 416.50, a summons may be served by leaving a copy of the summons and complaint during usual office hours in the person's office or, if no physical address is known, at the person's usual mailing address, other than a United States Postal Service post office box, with the person who is apparently in charge thereof, and by thereafter mailing a copy of the summons and complaint by United States Postal Service first-class mail, Priority Mail with tracking, or Certified Mail with return receipt requested, with postage prepaid, to the person to be served at the place where a copy of the summons and complaint were left. When service is effected by leaving a copy of the summons and complaint at a mailing address, it shall be left with a person at least 18 years of age, who shall be informed of the contents thereof. Service of a summons in this manner is deemed complete on the 10th day after the mailing.

(b) (1) If a copy of the summons and complaint cannot with reasonable diligence be personally delivered to the person to be served, as specified in Section 416.60, 416.70, 416.80, or 416.90, a summons may be served by leaving a copy of the summons and complaint at the person's dwelling house, usual place of abode, usual place of business, or usual mailing address other than a United States Postal Service post office box, in the presence of a competent member of the household or a person apparently in charge of their office, place of business, or usual mailing address other than a

United States Postal Service post office box, at least 18 years of age, who shall be informed of the contents thereof, and by thereafter mailing a copy of the summons and of the complaint by United States Postal Service first-class mail, Priority Mail with tracking, or Certified Mail with return receipt requested, with postage prepaid, to the person to be served at the place where a copy of the summons and complaint were left. Service of a summons in this manner is deemed complete on the 10th day after the mailing.

(2) For purposes of this subdivision, a party shows reasonable diligence by attempting personal delivery of the summons and complaint, in good faith, on at least three occasions on three different days at three different times.

(3) In an action to collect "consumer debt," as defined in Section 1788.2 of the Civil Code, at least one of the service attempts shall be made at the dwelling place or usual place of abode of the person to be served, provided that the dwelling place or usual place of abode is known or could be determined with reasonable effort.

(c) Notwithstanding subdivision (b), if the only address reasonably known for the person to be served is a private mailbox obtained through a commercial mail receiving agency, service of process may be effected on the first delivery attempt by leaving a copy of the summons and complaint with the commercial mail receiving agency in the manner described in subdivision (d) of Section 17538.5 of the Business and Professions Code.

(d) This section does not affect the provisions of Section 6206 of the Government Code.

(e) This section shall become operative on January 1, 2027.[882]

415.21. (a) Notwithstanding any other law, any person shall be granted access to a gated community or a covered multifamily dwelling for a reasonable period of time for the sole purpose of performing lawful service of process or service of a subpoena upon displaying a current driver's license or other identification, and one of the following:

(1) A badge or other confirmation that the individual is acting in the individual's capacity as a representative of a county sheriff or marshal, or as an investigator employed by an office of the Attorney General, a county counsel, a city attorney, a district attorney, or a public defender.

(2) Evidence of current registration as a process server pursuant to Chapter 16 (commencing with Section 22350) of Division 8 of the Business and Professions Code or of licensure as a private investigator pursuant to Chapter 11.3 (commencing with Section 7512) of Division 3 of the Business and Professions Code.

(b) This section shall only apply to a gated community or a covered multifamily dwelling that is staffed at the time service of process is attempted by a guard or other security personnel assigned to control access to the community or dwelling.

(c) For purposes of this section, "covered multifamily dwelling" means either of the following:

(1) An apartment building, including a timeshare apartment building not considered a place of public accommodation or transient lodging, with

three or more dwelling units.
(2) A condominium, including a timeshare condominium not considered a place of public accommodation or transient lodging, with four or more dwelling units.[751]

415.30. (a) A summons may be served by mail as provided in this section. A copy of the summons and of the complaint shall be mailed (by first-class mail or airmail, postage prepaid) to the person to be served, together with two copies of the notice and acknowledgment provided for in subdivision (b) and a return envelope, postage prepaid, addressed to the sender.
(b) The notice specified in subdivision (a) shall be in substantially the following form:
(Title of court and cause, with action number, to be inserted by the sender prior to mailing)

NOTICE
To: (Here state the name of the person to be served.)
This summons is served pursuant to Section 415.30 of the California Code of Civil Procedure. Failure to complete this form and return it to the sender within 20 days may subject you (or the party on whose behalf you are being served) to liability for the payment of any expenses incurred in serving a summons upon you in any other manner permitted by law. If you are served on behalf of a corporation, unincorporated association (including a partnership), or other entity, this form must be signed in the name of such entity by you or by a person authorized to receive service of process on behalf of such entity. In all other cases, this form must be signed by you personally or by a person authorized by you to acknowledge receipt of summons. Section 415.30 provides that this summons is deemed served on the date of execution of an acknowledgment of receipt of summons.

Signature of sender

ACKNOWLEDGMENT OF RECEIPT OF SUMMONS

This acknowledges receipt on (insert date) of a copy of the summons and of the complaint at (insert address).

Date: (Date this acknowledgement is executed) Signature of person acknowledging receipt, with title if acknowledgment is made on behalf of another person

(c) Service of a summons pursuant to this section is deemed complete on the date a written acknowledgement of receipt of summons is executed, if such acknowledgement thereafter is returned to the sender.
(d) If the person to whom a copy of the summons and of the complaint are mailed pursuant to this section fails to complete and return the acknowledgement form set forth in subdivision (b) within 20 days from the date of such mailing, the party to whom the summons was mailed shall be liable for reasonable expenses thereafter incurred in serving or attempting to serve the party by another method permitted by this chapter, and, except for good cause shown, the court in which the action is pending, upon motion, with or without notice, shall award the party

such expenses whether or not he is otherwise entitled to recover his costs in the action.

(e) A notice or acknowledgment of receipt in form approved by the Judicial Council is deemed to comply with this section.[71]

415.40. A summons may be served on a person outside this state in any manner provided by this article or by sending a copy of the summons and of the complaint to the person to be served by first-class mail, postage prepaid, requiring a return receipt. Service of a summons by this form of mail is deemed complete on the 10th day after such mailing.[121]

415.45. (a) A summons in an action for unlawful detainer of real property may be served by posting if upon affidavit it appears to the satisfaction of the court in which the action is pending that the party to be served cannot with reasonable diligence be served in any manner specified in this article other than publication and that:

(1) A cause of action exists against the party upon whom service is to be made or they are a necessary or proper party to the action; or

(2) The party to be served has or claims an interest in real property in this state that is subject to the jurisdiction of the court or the relief demanded in the action consists wholly or in part in excluding such party from any interest in such property.

(b) The court shall order the summons to be posted on the premises in a manner most likely to give actual notice to the party to be served and direct that a copy of the summons and of the complaint be forthwith mailed by certified mail to such party at the party's last known address.

(c) Service of summons in this manner is deemed complete on the 10th day after posting and mailing.

(d) Notwithstanding an order for posting of the summons, a summons may be served in any other manner authorized by this article, except publication, in which event such service shall supersede any posted summons.

(e) This section shall remain in effect only until January 1, 2027, and as of that date is repealed.[883]

415.45. (a) A summons in an action for unlawful detainer of real property may be served by posting if upon affidavit it appears to the satisfaction of the court in which the action is pending that the party to be served cannot with reasonable diligence be served in any manner specified in this article other than publication and if either of the following conditions exists:

(1) A cause of action exists against the party upon whom service is to be made or they are a necessary or proper party to the action.

(2) The party to be served has or claims an interest in real property in this state that is subject to the jurisdiction of the court or the relief demanded in the action consists wholly or in part in excluding such party from any interest in such property.

(b) The court shall order the summons to be posted on the premises in a manner most likely to give actual notice to the party to be served and direct that a copy of the summons and of the complaint be forthwith mailed by certified mail to such party at the party's last known address.

(c) Service of summons in this manner is deemed complete on the 10th day after posting and mailing.

(d) (1) For purposes of this section, a party shows reasonable diligence by attempting personal delivery of the summons and complaint, in good faith, on at least three occasions on three different days at three different times.

(2) Except with respect to actions for unlawful detainer of "commercial real property," as defined under subdivision (d) of Section 1161.1 or "program participants," as defined under paragraph (9) of subdivision (a) of Section 6205.5 of the Government Code, at least one of the attempts shall be made at the dwelling place or usual place of abode of the person to be served, provided that the dwelling place or usual place of abode is known or could be determined with reasonable effort.

(e) Notwithstanding an order for posting of the summons, a summons may be served in any other manner authorized by this article, except publication, in which event such service shall supersede any posted summons.

(f) This section shall become operative on January 1, 2027.[884]

415.46. (a) In addition to the service of a summons and complaint in an action for unlawful detainer upon a tenant and subtenant, if any, as prescribed by this article, a prejudgment claim of right to possession may also be served on any person who appears to be or who may claim to have occupied the premises at the time of the filing of the action. Service upon occupants shall be made pursuant to subdivision (c) by serving a copy of a prejudgment claim of right to possession, as specified in subdivision (f), attached to a copy of the summons and complaint at the same time service is made upon the tenant and subtenant, if any.

(b) Service of the prejudgment claim of right to possession in this manner shall be effected by a marshal, sheriff, or registered process server.

(c) (1) When serving the summons and complaint upon a tenant and subtenant, if any, the marshal, sheriff, or registered process server shall make a reasonably diligent effort to ascertain whether there are other adult occupants of the premises who are not named in the summons and complaint by inquiring of the person or persons who are being personally served, or any person of suitable age and discretion who appears to reside upon the premises, whether there are other occupants of the premises.

(2) If the identity of such an occupant is disclosed to the officer or process server and the occupant is present at the premises, the officer or process server shall serve that occupant with a copy of the prejudgment claim of right to possession attached to a copy of the summons and complaint. If personal service cannot be made upon that occupant at that time, service may be effected by leaving a copy of a prejudgment claim of right to possession attached to a copy of the summons and complaint addressed to that occupant with a person of suitable age and discretion at the premises, affixing the same so that it is not readily removable in a conspicuous place on the premises in a manner most likely to give actual notice to that occupant, and sending the same addressed to that occupant by first-class mail.

(3) In addition to the service on an identified occupant, or if no occupant is disclosed to the officer or process server, or if substituted service is

made upon the tenant and subtenant, if any, the officer or process server shall serve a prejudgment claim of right to possession for all other persons who may claim to occupy the premises at the time of the filing of the action by leaving a copy of a prejudgment claim of right to possession attached to a copy of the summons and complaint at the premises at the same time service is made upon the tenant and subtenant, if any, affixing the same so that it is not readily removable in a conspicuous place on the premises so that it is likely to give actual notice to an occupant, and sending the same addressed to "all occupants in care of the named tenant" to the premises by first-class mail.

(4) The person serving process shall state the date of service on the prejudgment claim of right to possession form. However, the absence of the date of service on the prejudgment claim of right to possession does not invalidate the claim.

(d) Proof of service under this section shall be filed with the court and shall include a statement that service was made pursuant to this section. Service on occupants in accordance with this section shall not alter or affect service upon the tenant or subtenant, if any.

(e) (1) If an owner or his or her agent has directed and obtained service of a prejudgment claim of right to possession in accordance with this section, no occupant of the premises, whether or not that occupant is named in the judgment for possession, may object to the enforcement of that judgment as prescribed in Section 1174.3.

(2) In any action for unlawful detainer resulting from a foreclosure sale of a rental housing unit pursuant to Section 1161a, paragraph (1) shall not limit the right of any tenant or subtenant of the property to file a prejudgment claim of right of possession pursuant to subdivision (a) of Section 1174.25 at any time before judgment, or to object to enforcement of a judgment for possession as prescribed in Section 1174.3, regardless of whether the tenant or subtenant was served with a prejudgment claim of right to possession.

(f) The prejudgment claim of right to possession shall be made on the following form:

* *

NOTICE OF INCOMPLETE TEXT: The Prejudgment Claim of Right to Possession form appears in the published chaptered bill. See Sec. 7, Chapter 913 (pp. 73–76), Statutes of 2014.[702]

* *

Note: See published chaptered bill for complete section text. The Prejudgment Claim of Right to Possession form appears on pages 73 to 76 of Ch. 913.

415.47 (a) Where the lessee has given the lessor written notice of the lessee's intent not to abandon leased real property as provided in Section 1951.3 of the Civil Code, the summons in an action for unlawful detainer of the real property may be served on the lessee by certified mail, postage prepaid, addressed to the lessee at the address stated in the lessee's notice of intent not to abandon if such summons is deposited in the mail within 60 days from the date the lessee's notice of intent not to abandon is received by the lessor. Service in this manner is deemed completed on the 10th day after such mailing.

(b) Where the lessee has given the lessor written notice of the lessee's intent not to abandon leased real property as provided in Section 1951.3 of the Civil Code, but failed to include in such notice an address at which the lessee may be served by certified mail in any action for unlawful detainer of the real property, the summons in an action for unlawful detainer of the real property may be served on the lessee by certified mail, postage prepaid, addressed to the lessee at (1) the same address or addresses to which the lessor's notice of belief of abandonment was addressed if that notice was given by mail or (2) the address of the real property if the lessor's notice of belief of abandonment was personally served on the lessee. Service may not be made pursuant to this subdivision unless the summons is deposited in the mail within 60 days from the date the lessee's notice of intent not to abandon is received by the lessor. Service in the manner authorized by this subdivision is deemed completed on the 10th day after such mailing.

(c) This section provides an alternative method of service on the lessee and does not preclude service in any other manner authorized by this chapter.[88]

415.50. (a) A summons may be served by publication if upon affidavit it appears to the satisfaction of the court in which the action is pending that the party to be served cannot with reasonable diligence be served in another manner specified in this article and that either:

(1) A cause of action exists against the party upon whom service is to be made or he or she is a necessary or proper party to the action.

(2) The party to be served has or claims an interest in real or personal property in this state that is subject to the jurisdiction of the court or the relief demanded in the action consists wholly or in part in excluding the party from any interest in the property.

(b) The court shall order the summons to be published in a named newspaper, published in this state, that is most likely to give actual notice to the party to be served. If the party to be served resides or is located out of this state, the court may also order the summons to be published in a named newspaper outside this state that is most likely to give actual notice to that party. The order shall direct that a copy of the summons, the complaint, and the order for publication be forthwith mailed to the party if his or her address is ascertained before expiration of the time prescribed for publication of the summons. Except as otherwise provided by statute, the publication shall be made as provided by Section 6064 of the Government Code unless the court, in its discretion, orders publication for a longer period.

(c) Service of a summons in this manner is deemed complete as provided in Section 6064 of the Government Code.

(d) Notwithstanding an order for publication of the summons, a summons may be served in another manner authorized by this chapter, in which event the service shall supersede any published summons.

(e) As a condition of establishing that the party to be served cannot with reasonable diligence be served in another manner specified in this article, the court may not require that a search be conducted of public databases where access by a registered process server to residential addresses is prohibited by law or by published policy of the agency providing the database, including, but not limited to, voter registration rolls and records of the Department of Motor Vehicles.[538]

415.95. (a) A summons may be served on a business organization, form unknown, by leaving a copy of the summons and complaint during usual office hours with the person who is apparently in charge of the office of that business organization, and by thereafter mailing a copy of the summons and complaint by first-class mail, postage prepaid, to the person to be served at the place where a copy of the summons and complaint was left. Service of a summons in this manner is deemed complete on the 10th day after the mailing.

(b) Service of a summons pursuant to this section is not valid for a corporation with a registered agent for service of process listed with the Secretary of State.[525]

Article 4: Persons Upon Whom Summons May Be Served
Article 4 added by Stats. 1969, Ch. 1610.

416.10. A summons may be served on a corporation by delivering a copy of the summons and the complaint by any of the following methods:

(a) To the person designated as agent for service of process as provided by any provision in Section 202, 1502, 2105, or 2107 of the Corporations Code (or Sections 3301 to 3303, inclusive, or Sections 6500 to 6504, inclusive, of the Corporations Code, as in effect on December 31, 1976, with respect to corporations to which they remain applicable).

(b) To the president, chief executive officer, or other head of the corporation, a vice president, a secretary or assistant secretary, a treasurer or assistant treasurer, a controller or chief financial officer, a general manager, or a person authorized by the corporation to receive service of process.

(c) If the corporation is a bank, to a cashier or assistant cashier or to a person specified in subdivision (a) or (b).

(d) If authorized by any provision in Section 1701, 1702, 2110, or 2111 of the Corporations Code (or Sections 3301 to 3303, inclusive, or Sections 6500 to 6504, inclusive, of the Corporations Code, as in effect on December 31, 1976, with respect to corporations to which they remain applicable), as provided by that provision.[597]

416.20. A summons may be served on a corporation that has forfeited its charter or right to do business, or has dissolved, by delivering a copy of the summons and of the complaint:

(a) To a person who is a trustee of the corporation and of its stockholders or members; or

(b) When authorized by any provision in Sections 2011 or 2114 of the Corporations Code (or Sections 3301 to 3303, inclusive, or Sections 6500 to 6504, inclusive, of the Corporations Code as in effect on December 31,

1976, with respect to corporations to which they remain applicable), as provided by such provision.[105]

416.30. A summons may be served on a joint stock company or association by delivering a copy of the summons and of the complaint as provided by Section 416.10 or 416.20.[71]

416.40. A summons may be served on an unincorporated association (including a partnership) by delivering a copy of the summons and of the complaint:
(a) If the association is a general or limited partnership, to the person designated as agent for service of process in a statement filed with the Secretary of State or to a general partner or the general manager of the partnership;
(b) If the association is not a general or limited partnership, to the person designated as agent for service of process in a statement filed with the Secretary of State or to the president or other head of the association, a vice president, a secretary or assistant secretary, a treasurer or assistant treasurer, a general manager, or a person authorized by the association to receive service of process;
(c) When authorized by Section 18220 of the Corporations Code, as provided by that section.[544]

416.50. (a) A summons may be served on a public entity by delivering a copy of the summons and of the complaint to the clerk, secretary, president, presiding officer, or other head of its governing body.
(b) As used in this section, "public entity" includes the state and any office, department, division, bureau, board, commission, or agency of the state, the Regents of the University of California, a county, city, district, public authority, public agency, and any other political subdivision or public corporation in this state.[71]

416.60. A summons may be served on a minor by delivering a copy of the summons and of the complaint to his parent, guardian, conservator, or similar fiduciary, or, if no such person can be found with reasonable diligence, to any person having the care or control of such minor or with whom he resides or by whom he is employed, and to the minor if he is at least 12 years of age.[78]

416.70. A summons may be served on a person (other than a minor) for whom a guardian, conservator, or similar fiduciary has been appointed by delivering a copy of the summons and of the complaint to his guardian, conservator, or similar fiduciary and to such person, but, for good cause shown, the court in which the action is pending may dispense with delivery to such person.[78]

416.80. When authorized by Section 12 of the Elections Code, a summons may be served as provided by that section.[616]

416.90. A summons may be served on a person not otherwise specified in this article by delivering a copy of the summons and of the complaint to such person or to a person authorized by him to receive service of process.[71]

Article 5: Proof of Service
Article 5 added by Stats. 1969, Ch. 1610.

417.10. Proof that a summons was served on a person within this state shall be made:
(a) If served under Section 415.10,

415.20, or 415.30, by the affidavit of the person making the service showing the time, place, and manner of service and facts showing that the service was made in accordance with this chapter. The affidavit shall recite or in other manner show the name of the person to whom a copy of the summons and of the complaint were delivered, and, if appropriate, the person's title or the capacity in which the person is served, and that the notice required by Section 412.30 appeared on the copy of the summons served, if in fact it did appear.

If service is made by mail pursuant to Section 415.30, proof of service shall include the acknowledgment of receipt of summons in the form provided by that section or other written acknowledgment of receipt of summons satisfactory to the court.

(b) If served by publication pursuant to Section 415.50, by the affidavit of the publisher or printer, or the publisher's or the printer's foreperson or principal clerk, showing the time and place of publication, and an affidavit showing the time and place a copy of the summons and of the complaint were mailed to the party to be served, if in fact mailed.

(c) If served pursuant to another law of this state, in the manner prescribed by that law or, if no manner is prescribed, in the manner prescribed by this section for proof of a similar manner of service.

(d) By the written admission of the party.

(e) If served by posting pursuant to Section 415.45, by the affidavit of the person who posted the premises, showing the time and place of posting, and an affidavit showing the time and place copies of the summons and of the complaint were mailed to the party to be served, if in fact mailed.

(f) All proof of personal service shall be made on a form adopted by the Judicial Council.

(g) This section shall remain in effect only until January 1, 2027, and as of that date is repealed.[885]

417.10. Proof that a summons was served on a person within this state shall be made:

(a) If served under Section 415.10, 415.20, 415.30, or 415.45, by the affidavit of the person making the service showing the time, place, and manner of service and facts showing that the service was made in accordance with this chapter. The affidavit shall recite or in other manner show the name of any person to whom a copy of the summons and complaint were delivered, and, if appropriate, the person's title or the capacity in which the person is served, and that the notice required by Section 412.30 appeared on the copy of the summons served, if in fact it did appear.

(1) If served under Section 415.10, 415.20, or 415.45, the proof of service shall include one or more photographs of the site of each effected or attempted service of the summons and complaint.

(A) Each photograph shall contain a readable stamp that establishes and automatically records the date, time, and global positioning system (GPS) or equivalent coordinates of the effected or attempted service.

(B) If no GPS, cellular, or equivalent signal is available at the time and place of an effected or attempted service, the process server shall provide a detailed statement on or with the proof of service explaining the reason for the lack of a readable GPS or equivalent stamp on the photograph.

(2) (A) If the site of the effected or attempted service is a dwelling place or abode, for each effected or attempted service of the summons and complaint, at least one of the photographs required by paragraph (1) shall show the door, or, if the door is not reasonably accessible, the entrance of the house, apartment, or other dwelling place of the person to be served.

(B) If the site of the effected or attempted service is a place of business, for each effected or attempted service of the summons and complaint, at least one of the photographs required by paragraph (1) shall show the door, or, if the door is not reasonably accessible, the entrance of the specific office or other place of business of the person being served.

(C) For purposes of subparagraphs (A) and (B), if the door is not reasonably accessible and the process server takes a photograph of the entrance instead, the process server shall explain with specificity on or with the proof of service why the door was not accessible.

(3) If service is made by mail pursuant to Section 415.30, proof of service shall include the acknowledgment of receipt of summons in the form provided by that section or other written acknowledgment of receipt of summons satisfactory to the court.

(4) Notwithstanding paragraph (1), a photograph is not required if, in the reasonable judgment of the process server, taking a photograph would compromise the process server's safety. In such circumstances, the process server shall document the effected or attempted service on the proof of service and provide a detailed statement explaining why taking a photograph would have compromised their safety.

(5) The photograph required by paragraph (1) shall be taken by the process server as closely as practicable to the time of effecting or attempting service.

(b) If served by publication pursuant to Section 415.50, by the affidavit of the publisher or printer, or the publisher's or printer's foreperson or principal clerk, showing the time and place of publication, and an affidavit showing the time and place a copy of the summons and of the complaint were mailed to the party to be served, if in fact mailed.

(c) If served pursuant to another law of this state, in the manner prescribed by that law or, if no manner is prescribed, in the manner prescribed by this section for proof of a similar manner of service.

(d) By the written admission of the party.

(e) If served by posting pursuant to Section 415.45, by the affidavit of the person who posted the premises, showing the time and place of posting, and an affidavit showing the time and place copies of the summons and of the complaint were mailed to the party to be served, if in fact mailed.

(f) All proof of personal service shall be made on a form adopted by the Judicial Council.

(g) This section shall become operative on January 1, 2027.[886]

417.20. Proof that a summons was served on a person outside this state shall be made:

(a) If served in a manner specified in a statute of this state, as prescribed by Section 417.10, and if service is made by mail pursuant to Section 415.40, proof of service shall include evidence satisfactory to the court establishing actual delivery to the person to be served, by a signed return receipt or other evidence;
(b) In the manner prescribed by the court order pursuant to which the service is made;
(c) Subject to any additional requirements that may be imposed by the court in which the action is pending, in the manner prescribed by the law of the place where the person is served for proof of service in an action in its courts of general jurisdiction; or
(d) By the written admission of the party.
(e) If served by posting pursuant to Section 415.45, by the affidavit of the person who posted the premises, showing the time and place of posting, and an affidavit showing the time and place copies of the summons and of the complaint were mailed to the party to be served, if in fact mailed.[83]

417.30. After a summons has been served on a person, proof of service of the summons as provided in Section 417.10 or 417.20 shall be filed, unless the defendant has previously made a general appearance.[877]

417.40. (a) Any proof of service which is signed by a person registered under Chapter 16 (commencing with Section 22350) of Division 8 of the Business and Professions Code or the person's employee or independent contractor shall indicate the county in which the person is registered and the number assigned to the person pursuant to Section 22355 of the Business and Professions Code.
(b) This section shall remain in effect only until January 1, 2027, and as of that date is repealed.[887]

417.40. (a) A proof of service that is signed by a person who is required to be registered under Chapter 16 (commencing with Section 22350) of Division 8 of the Business and Professions Code or the person's employee or independent contractor shall indicate the number assigned to the person by the county clerk pursuant to Section 22355 of the Business and Professions Code.
(b) This section shall become operative on January 1, 2027.[895]

Chapter 5: Objection to Jurisdiction

Chapter 5 added by Stats. 1969, Ch. 1610.

418.10. (a) A defendant, on or before the last day of his or her time to plead or within any further time that the court may for good cause allow, may serve and file a notice of motion for one or more of the following purposes:
(1) To quash service of summons on the ground of lack of jurisdiction of the court over him or her.
(2) To stay or dismiss the action on the ground of inconvenient forum.
(3) To dismiss the action pursuant to the applicable provisions of Chapter 1.5 (commencing with Section 583.110) of Title 8.
(b) The notice shall designate, as the time for making the motion, a date not more than 30 days after filing of the notice. The notice shall be served in the same manner, and at the same times, prescribed by subdivision (b) of Section 1005. The service and filing of

the notice shall extend the defendant's time to plead until 15 days after service upon him or her of a written notice of entry of an order denying his or her motion, except that for good cause shown the court may extend the defendant's time to plead for an additional period not exceeding 20 days.

(c) If the motion is denied by the trial court, the defendant, within 10 days after service upon him or her of a written notice of entry of an order of the court denying his or her motion, or within any further time not exceeding 20 days that the trial court may for good cause allow, and before pleading, may petition an appropriate reviewing court for a writ of mandate to require the trial court to enter its order quashing the service of summons or staying or dismissing the action. The defendant shall file or enter his or her responsive pleading in the trial court within the time prescribed by subdivision (b) unless, on or before the last day of the defendant's time to plead, he or she serves upon the adverse party and files with the trial court a notice that he or she has petitioned for a writ of mandate. The service and filing of the notice shall extend the defendant's time to plead until 10 days after service upon him or her of a written notice of the final judgment in the mandate proceeding. The time to plead may for good cause shown be extended by the trial court for an additional period not exceeding 20 days.

(d) No default may be entered against the defendant before expiration of his or her time to plead, and no motion under this section, or under Section 473 or 473.5 when joined with a motion under this section, or application to the court or stipulation of the parties for an extension of the time to plead, shall be deemed a general appearance by the defendant.

(e) A defendant or cross-defendant may make a motion under this section and simultaneously answer, demur, or move to strike the complaint or cross-complaint.

(1) Notwithstanding Section 1014, no act by a party who makes a motion under this section, including filing an answer, demurrer, or motion to strike constitutes an appearance, unless the court denies the motion made under this section. If the court denies the motion made under this section, the defendant or cross-defendant is not deemed to have generally appeared until entry of the order denying the motion.

(2) If the motion made under this section is denied and the defendant or cross-defendant petitions for a writ of mandate pursuant to subdivision (c), the defendant or cross-defendant is not deemed to have generally appeared until the proceedings on the writ petition have finally concluded.

(3) Failure to make a motion under this section at the time of filing a demurrer or motion to strike constitutes a waiver of the issues of lack of personal jurisdiction, inadequacy of process, inadequacy of service of process, inconvenient forum, and delay in prosecution.[477]

418.11. An appearance at a hearing at which ex parte relief is sought, or an appearance at a hearing for which an ex parte application for a provisional remedy is made, is not a general appearance and does not constitute a waiver of the right to make a motion under Section 418.10.[252]

TITLE 6: OF THE PLEADINGS IN CIVIL ACTIONS

Title 6 enacted 1872

Chapter 1: The Pleadings in General

Chapter 1 enacted 1872.

420. The pleadings are the formal allegations by the parties of their respective claims and defenses, for the judgment of the Court.[1]

421. The forms of pleading in civil actions, and the rules by which the sufficiency of the pleadings is to be determined, are those prescribed in this Code.[1]

422.10. The pleadings allowed in civil actions are complaints, demurrers, answers, and cross-complaints.[73]

422.30. (a) Every pleading shall contain a caption setting forth:

(1) The name of the court and county in which the action is brought.

(2) The title of the action.

(b) In a limited civil case, the caption shall state that the case is a limited civil case, and the clerk shall classify the case accordingly.[504]

422.40. In the complaint, the title of the action shall include the names of all the parties; but, except as otherwise provided by statute or rule of the Judicial Council, in other pleadings it is sufficient to state the name of the first party on each side with an appropriate indication of other parties.[73]

Chapter 2: Pleadings Demanding Relief

Chapter 2 repealed and added by Stats. 1971, Ch. 244.

Article 1: General Provisions

Article 1 added by Stats. 1971, Ch. 244.

425.10. (a) A complaint or cross-complaint shall contain both of the following:

(1) A statement of the facts constituting the cause of action, in ordinary and concise language.

(2) A demand for judgment for the relief to which the pleader claims to be entitled. If the recovery of money or damages is demanded, the amount demanded shall be stated.

(b) Notwithstanding subdivision (a), where an action is brought to recover actual or punitive damages for personal injury or wrongful death, the amount demanded shall not be stated, but the complaint shall comply with Section 422.30 and, in a limited civil case, with subdivision (b) of Section 70613 of the Government Code.[561]

425.11. (a) As used in this section:

(1) "Complaint" includes a cross-complaint.

(2) "Plaintiff" includes a cross-complainant.

(3) "Defendant" includes a cross-defendant.

(b) When a complaint is filed in an action to recover damages for personal injury or wrongful death, the defendant may at any time request a statement setting forth the nature and amount of damages being sought. The request shall be served upon the plaintiff, who shall serve a responsive statement as to the damages within 15 days. In the event that a response is not served, the defendant, on notice to the plaintiff, may petition the court in which the action is pending to order the plaintiff to serve a responsive statement.

(c) If no request is made for the statement referred to in subdivision (b), the plaintiff shall serve the statement on the defendant before a default may be taken.

(d) The statement referred to in subdivision (b) shall be served in the following manner:

(1) If a party has not appeared in the action, the statement shall be served in the same manner as a summons.

(2) If a party has appeared in the action, the statement shall be served upon the party's attorney, or upon the party if the party has appeared without an attorney, in the manner provided for service of a summons or in the manner provided by Chapter 5 (commencing with Section 1010) of Title 14 of Part 2

(e) The statement referred to in subdivision (b) may be combined with the statement described in Section 425.115.[587]

425.115. (a) As used in this section:

(1) "Complaint" includes a cross-complaint.

(2) "Plaintiff" includes a cross-complainant.

(3) "Defendant" includes a cross-defendant.

(b) The plaintiff preserves the right to seek punitive damages pursuant to Section 3294 of the Civil Code on a default judgment by serving upon the defendant the following statement, or its substantial equivalent:

NOTICE TO:

(Insert name of defendant or cross-defendant)

reserves the right to seek

(Insert name of plaintiff or cross-complainant)

$ in punitive damages

(Insert dollar amount)

when seeks a judgment in the

(Insert name of plaintiff or cross-complainant)

suit filed against you.

(Insert name of attorney or party appearing in propria persona) (Date)

(c) If the plaintiff seeks punitive damages pursuant to Section 3294 of the Civil Code, and if the defendant appears in the action, the plaintiff shall not be limited to the amount set forth in the statement served on the defendant pursuant to this section.

(d) A plaintiff who serves a statement on the defendant pursuant to this section shall be deemed to have complied with Sections 425.10 and 580 of this code and Section 3295 of the Civil Code.

(e) The plaintiff may serve a statement upon the defendant pursuant to this section, and may serve the statement as part of the statement required by Section 425.11.

(f) The plaintiff shall serve the statement upon the defendant pursuant to this section before a default may be taken, if the motion for default judgment includes a request for punitive damages.

(g) The statement referred to in subdivision (b) shall be served by one of the following methods:

(1) If the party has not appeared in the action, the statement shall be served in the same manner as a summons pursuant to Article 3 (commencing with Section 415.10) of Chapter 4 of Title 5 of Part 2 of the Code of Civil Procedure.

(2) If the party has appeared in the action, the statement shall be served upon his or her attorney, or upon the party if he or she has appeared without an attorney, either in the same manner as a summons pursuant to Article 3 (commencing with Section 415.10) of Chapter 4 or in the manner provided by Chapter 5 (commencing with Section 1010) of Title 14.[579]

425.12. (a) The Judicial Council shall develop and approve official forms for use in trial courts of this state for any complaint, cross-complaint or answer in any action based upon personal injury, property damage, wrongful death, unlawful detainer, breach of contract or fraud.

(b) The Judicial Council shall develop and approve an official form for use as a statement of damages pursuant to Sections 425.11 and 425.115.

(c) In developing the forms required by this section, the Judicial Council shall consult with a representative advisory committee which shall include, but not be limited to, representatives of the plaintiff's bar, the defense bar, the public interest bar, court administrators and the public. The forms shall be drafted in nontechnical language and shall be made available through the office of the clerk of the appropriate trial court.[351]

425.13. (a) In any action for damages arising out of the professional negligence of a health care provider, no claim for punitive damages shall be included in a complaint or other pleading unless the court enters an order allowing an amended pleading that includes a claim for punitive damages to be filed. The court may allow the filing of an amended pleading claiming punitive damages on a motion by the party seeking the amended pleading and on the basis of the supporting and opposing affidavits presented that the plaintiff has established that there is a substantial probability that the plaintiff will prevail on the claim pursuant to Section 3294 of the Civil Code. The court shall not grant a motion allowing the filing of an amended pleading that includes a claim for punitive damages if the motion for such an order is not filed within two years after the complaint or initial pleading is filed or not less than nine months before the date the matter is first set for trial, whichever is earlier.

(b) For the purposes of this section, "health care provider" means any person licensed or certified pursuant to Division 2 (commencing with Section 500) of the Business and Professions Code, or licensed pursuant to the Osteopathic Initiative Act, or the Chiropractic Initiative Act, or licensed pursuant to Chapter 2.5 (commencing with Section 1440) of Division 2 of the Health and Safety Code; and any clinic, health dispensary, or health facility, licensed pursuant to Division 2 (commencing with Section 1200) of the Health and Safety Code. "Health care provider" includes the legal representatives of a health care provider.[257]

425.14. No claim for punitive or exemplary damages against a religious corporation or religious corporation sole shall be included in a complaint or other pleading unless the court enters an order allowing an amended pleading that includes a claim for punitive or exemplary damages to be filed. The court may allow the filing of an amended pleading claiming punitive or exemplary damages on a motion by the party seeking the amended pleading and upon a finding, on the basis of the supporting and opposing affidavits presented, that the plaintiff has established evidence which substantiates that plaintiff will meet the clear and convincing standard of proof under Section 3294 of the Civil Code.
Nothing in this section is intended to affect the plaintiff's right to discover evidence on the issue of punitive or exemplary damages.[262]

425.15. (a) No cause of action against a person serving without compensation as a director or officer of a nonprofit corporation described in this section, on account of any negligent act or omission by that person within the scope of that person's duties as a director acting in the capacity of a board member, or as an officer acting in the capacity of, and within the scope of the duties of, an officer, shall be included in a complaint or other pleading unless the court enters an order allowing the pleading that includes that claim to be filed after the court determines that the party seeking to file the pleading has established evidence that substantiates the claim. The court may allow the filing of a pleading that includes that claim following the filing of a verified petition therefor accompanied by the proposed pleading and supporting affidavits stating the facts upon which the liability is based. The court shall order service of the petition upon the party against whom the action is proposed to be filed and permit that party to submit opposing affidavits prior to making its determination. The filing of the petition, proposed pleading, and accompanying affidavits shall toll the running of any applicable statute of limitations until the final determination of the matter, which ruling, if favorable to the petitioning party, shall permit the proposed pleading to be filed.
(b) Nothing in this section shall affect the right of the plaintiff to discover evidence on the issue of damages.
(c) Nothing in this section shall be construed to affect any action against a nonprofit corporation for any negligent action or omission of a volunteer director or officer occurring within the scope of the person's duties.
(d) For the purposes of this section, "compensation" means remuneration whether by way of salary, fee, or other consideration for services rendered. However, the payment of per diem, mileage, or other reimbursement expenses to a director or officer shall not constitute compensation.
(e) (1) This section applies only to officers and directors of nonprofit corporations that are subject to Part 2 (commencing with Section 5110), Part 3 (commencing with Section 7110), or

Part 4 (commencing with Section 9110) of Division 2 of Title 1 of the Corporations Code that are organized to provide charitable, educational, scientific, social, or other forms of public service and that are exempt from federal income taxation under Section 501(c)(1), except any credit union, or Section 501(c)(4), 501(c)(5), 501(c)(7), or 501(c)(19) of the Internal Revenue Code.

(2) This section does not apply to any corporation that unlawfully restricts membership, services, or benefits conferred on the basis of political affiliation, age, or any characteristic listed or defined in subdivision (b) or (e) of Section 51 of the Civil Code.[604]

425.16. (a) The Legislature finds and declares that there has been a disturbing increase in lawsuits brought primarily to chill the valid exercise of the constitutional rights of freedom of speech and petition for the redress of grievances. The Legislature finds and declares that it is in the public interest to encourage continued participation in matters of public significance, and that this participation should not be chilled through abuse of the judicial process. To this end, this section shall be construed broadly.

(b) (1) A cause of action against a person arising from any act of that person in furtherance of the person's right of petition or free speech under the United States Constitution or the California Constitution in connection with a public issue shall be subject to a special motion to strike, unless the court determines that the plaintiff has established that there is a probability that the plaintiff will prevail on the claim.

(2) In making its determination, the court shall consider the pleadings, and supporting and opposing affidavits stating the facts upon which the liability or defense is based.

(3) If the court determines that the plaintiff has established a probability that the plaintiff will prevail on the claim, neither that determination nor the fact of that determination shall be admissible in evidence at any later stage of the case, or in any subsequent action, and no burden of proof or degree of proof otherwise applicable shall be affected by that determination in any later stage of the case or in any subsequent proceeding.

(c) (1) Except as provided in paragraph (2), in any action subject to subdivision (b), a prevailing defendant on a special motion to strike shall be entitled to recover that defendant's attorney's fees and costs. If the court finds that a special motion to strike is frivolous or is solely intended to cause unnecessary delay, the court shall award costs and reasonable attorney's fees to a plaintiff prevailing on the motion, pursuant to Section 128.5.

(2) A defendant who prevails on a special motion to strike in an action subject to paragraph (1) shall not be entitled to attorney's fees and costs if that cause of action is brought pursuant to Section 11130, 11130.3, 54960, or 54960.1 of the Government Code, or pursuant to Chapter 2 (commencing with Section 7923.100) of Part 4 of Division 10 of Title 1 of the Government Code. Nothing in this paragraph shall be construed to prevent a prevailing defendant from recovering attorney's fees and costs pursuant to Section 7923.115, 11130.5, or 54960.5 of the Government Code.

(d) This section shall not apply to any enforcement action brought in the name of the people of the State of California by the Attorney General, Insurance Commissioner, district attorney, or city attorney, acting as a public prosecutor.

(e) As used in this section, "act in furtherance of a person's right of petition or free speech under the United States or California Constitution in connection with a public issue" includes: (1) any written or oral statement or writing made before a legislative, executive, or judicial proceeding, or any other official proceeding authorized by law, (2) any written or oral statement or writing made in connection with an issue under consideration or review by a legislative, executive, or judicial body, or any other official proceeding authorized by law, (3) any written or oral statement or writing made in a place open to the public or a public forum in connection with an issue of public interest, or (4) any other conduct in furtherance of the exercise of the constitutional right of petition or the constitutional right of free speech in connection with a public issue or an issue of public interest.

(f) The special motion may be filed within 60 days of the service of the complaint or, in the court's discretion, at any later time upon terms it deems proper. The motion shall be scheduled by the clerk of the court for a hearing not more than 30 days after the service of the motion unless the docket conditions of the court require a later hearing.

(g) All discovery proceedings in the action shall be stayed upon the filing of a notice of motion made pursuant to this section. The stay of discovery shall remain in effect until notice of entry of the order ruling on the motion. The court, on noticed motion and for good cause shown, may order that specified discovery be conducted notwithstanding this subdivision.

(h) For purposes of this section, "complaint" includes "cross-complaint" and "petition," "plaintiff" includes "cross-complainant" and "petitioner," and "defendant" includes "cross-defendant" and "respondent."

(i) An order granting or denying a special motion to strike shall be appealable under Section 904.1.

(j) (1) Any party who files a special motion to strike pursuant to this section, and any party who files an opposition to a special motion to strike, shall, promptly upon so filing, transmit to the Judicial Council, by email or facsimile, a copy of the endorsed, filed caption page of the motion or opposition, a copy of any related notice of appeal or petition for a writ, and a conformed copy of any order issued pursuant to this section, including any order granting or denying a special motion to strike, discovery, or fees.

(2) The Judicial Council shall maintain a public record of information transmitted pursuant to this subdivision for at least three years, and may store the information on microfilm or other appropriate electronic media.[851]

425.17. (a) The Legislature finds and declares that there has been a disturbing abuse of Section 425.16, the California Anti-SLAPP Law, which has undermined the exercise of the constitutional rights of freedom of speech and petition for the redress of grievances, contrary to the purpose and intent of Section 425.16. The Legislature finds and declares that it is in the public interest to encourage continued participation in matters of public significance, and that this participation should not be chilled through abuse of the judicial process or Section 425.16.

(b) Section 425.16 does not apply to any action brought solely in the public interest or on behalf of the general public if all of the following conditions exist:

(1) The plaintiff does not seek any relief greater than or different from the relief sought for the general public or a class of which the plaintiff is a member. A claim for attorney's fees, costs, or penalties does not constitute greater or different relief for purposes of this subdivision.

(2) The action, if successful, would enforce an important right affecting the public interest, and would confer a significant benefit, whether pecuniary or nonpecuniary, on the general public or a large class of persons.

(3) Private enforcement is necessary and places a disproportionate financial burden on the plaintiff in relation to the plaintiff's stake in the matter.

(c) Section 425.16 does not apply to any cause of action brought against a person primarily engaged in the business of selling or leasing goods or services, including, but not limited to, insurance, securities, or financial instruments, arising from any statement or conduct by that person if both of the following conditions exist:

(1) The statement or conduct consists of representations of fact about that person's or a business competitor's business operations, goods, or services, that is made for the purpose of obtaining approval for, promoting, or securing sales or leases of, or commercial transactions in, the person's goods or services, or the statement or conduct was made in the course of delivering the person's goods or services.

(2) The intended audience is an actual or potential buyer or customer, or a person likely to repeat the statement to, or otherwise influence, an actual or potential buyer or customer, or the statement or conduct arose out of or within the context of a regulatory approval process, proceeding, or investigation, except where the statement or conduct was made by a telephone corporation in the course of a proceeding before the California Public Utilities Commission and is the subject of a lawsuit brought by a competitor, notwithstanding that the conduct or statement concerns an important public issue.

(d) Subdivisions (b) and (c) do not apply to any of the following:

(1) Any person enumerated in subdivision (b) of Section 2 of Article I of the California Constitution or Section 1070 of the Evidence Code, or any person engaged in the dissemination of ideas or expression in any book or academic journal, while engaged in the gathering, receiving, or processing of information for communication to the public.

(2) Any action against any person or entity based upon the creation, dissemination, exhibition, advertisement, or other similar promotion of any dramatic, literary, musical, political, or artistic work, including, but not limited to, a motion picture or television program, or an article published in a newspaper or magazine of general circulation.

(3) Any nonprofit organization that receives more than 50 percent of its annual revenues from federal, state,

or local government grants, awards, programs, or reimbursements for services rendered.

(e) If any trial court denies a special motion to strike on the grounds that the action or cause of action is exempt pursuant to this section, the appeal provisions in subdivision (i) of Section 425.16 and paragraph (13) of subdivision (a) of Section 904.1 do not apply to that action or cause of action.[657]

425.18. (a) The Legislature finds and declares that a SLAPPback is distinguishable in character and origin from the ordinary malicious prosecution action. The Legislature further finds and declares that a SLAPPback cause of action should be treated differently, as provided in this section, from an ordinary malicious prosecution action because a SLAPPback is consistent with the Legislature's intent to protect the valid exercise of the constitutional rights of free speech and petition by its deterrent effect on SLAPP (strategic lawsuit against public participation) litigation and by its restoration of public confidence in participatory democracy.

(b) For purposes of this section, the following terms have the following meanings:

(1) "SLAPPback" means any cause of action for malicious prosecution or abuse of process arising from the filing or maintenance of a prior cause of action that has been dismissed pursuant to a special motion to strike under Section 425.16.

(2) "Special motion to strike" means a motion made pursuant to Section 425.16.

(c) The provisions of subdivisions (c), (f), (g), and (i) of Section 425.16, and paragraph (13) of subdivision (a) of Section 904.1, shall not apply to a special motion to strike a SLAPPback.

(d) (1) A special motion to strike a SLAPPback shall be filed within any one of the following periods of time, as follows:

(A) Within 120 days of the service of the complaint.

(B) At the court's discretion, within six months of the service of the complaint.

(C) At the court's discretion, at any later time in extraordinary cases due to no fault of the defendant and upon written findings of the court stating the extraordinary case and circumstance.

(2) The motion shall be scheduled by the clerk of the court for a hearing not more than 30 days after the service of the motion unless the docket conditions of the court require a later hearing.

(e) A party opposing a special motion to strike a SLAPPback may file an ex parte application for a continuance to obtain necessary discovery. If it appears that facts essential to justify opposition to that motion may exist, but cannot then be presented, the court shall grant a reasonable continuance to permit the party to obtain affidavits or conduct discovery or may make any other order as may be just.

(f) If the court finds that a special motion to strike a SLAPPback is frivolous or solely intended to cause unnecessary delay, the court shall award costs and reasonable attorney's fees to a plaintiff prevailing on the motion, pursuant to Section 128.5.

(g) Upon entry of an order denying a special motion to strike a SLAPPback claim, or granting the special motion to strike as to some but less than all causes of action alleged in a complaint containing a SLAPPback claim, an aggrieved party may, within 20 days after service of a written notice of the entry of the order, petition an appropriate reviewing court for a peremptory writ.

(h) A special motion to strike may not be filed against a SLAPPback by a party whose filing or maintenance of the prior cause of action from which the SLAPPback arises was illegal as a matter of law.

(i) This section does not apply to a SLAPPback filed by a public entity.[570]

425.19. (a) The Legislature finds and declares all of the following:

(1) The lack of affordable housing is a critical problem that threatens the economic, environmental, and social quality of life in California.

(2) It is in the public interest to encourage priority housing development projects in which 100 percent of the units, exclusive of any manager's unit or units, are reserved for lower income households, as defined in Section 50079.5 of the Health and Safety Code, and ensure such developments are not unnecessarily delayed or caused to fail through abuse of the judicial process. To this end, this section shall be construed broadly.

(b) (1) (A) In all civil actions brought by any plaintiff to challenge the approval or permitting of a priority housing development project, including, but not limited to, actions brought pursuant to Section 21167 of the Public Resources Code, a defendant may bring a special motion to strike the whole or any part of a pleading. The court shall deny the motion to strike if it determines that the plaintiff has established that there is a probability that the plaintiff will prevail on the claim.

(B) The court shall make its determination on the special motion to strike based on the pleadings, and supporting and opposing affidavits stating the facts upon which the liability or defense is based. Affidavits submitted with the pleadings may include a request for judicial notice of facts and documents relevant to the court's determination.

(C) (i) If the court is unable to determine whether the plaintiff has established a probability that the plaintiff will prevail on the claim without reviewing the administrative record in an action where the administrative record is required, the court shall make its determination on the special motion to strike based on the documents specified in subparagraph (B) and the administrative record, once prepared.

(ii) If the court determines that an administrative record is required for its decision, the moving party may, notwithstanding the 60-day filing requirement pursuant to paragraph (4) and without appealing an order denying a special motion to strike pursuant to paragraph (7), file the special motion to strike within 60 days of the service of the administrative record or, in the court's discretion, at any later time it deems proper.

(D) If the court determines that the plaintiff has established a probability that the plaintiff will prevail on the claim, neither that determination nor the fact of that determination shall be admissible in evidence at any later stage of the case, or in any subsequent action, and no burden of proof or degree of proof otherwise applicable shall be affected by that determination in any later stage of the case or in any subsequent proceeding.

(2) In any action subject to paragraph (1), a prevailing defendant on a special motion to strike shall be entitled to recover that defendant's attorney's fees and costs. If the court finds that a special motion to strike is frivolous or is solely intended to cause unnecessary delay, the court shall award costs and reasonable attorney's fees to a plaintiff prevailing on the motion, pursuant to Section 128.5.

(3) This subdivision does not apply to any enforcement action brought in the name of the people of the State of California by the Attorney General, district attorney, or city attorney, acting as a public prosecutor.

(4) The special motion may be filed within 60 days of the service of the complaint or, in the court's discretion, at any later time upon terms it deems proper. The motion shall be scheduled by the clerk of the court for a hearing not more than 30 days after the service of the motion unless the docket conditions of the court require a later hearing.

(5) All discovery proceedings in the action shall be stayed upon the filing of a notice of motion made pursuant to this section. The stay of discovery shall remain in effect until notice of entry of the order ruling on the motion. The court, on noticed motion and for good cause shown, may order that specified discovery be conducted notwithstanding this subdivision.

(6) For purposes of this section, "complaint" includes "cross-complaint" and "petition," "plaintiff" includes "cross-complainant" and "petitioner," and "defendant" includes "cross-defendant" and "respondent."

(7) An order granting or denying a special motion to strike is appealable under Section 904.1.

(c) "Priority housing development" means a development in which 100 percent of the units, exclusive of any manager's unit or units, will be reserved for lower income households, as defined in Section 50079.5 of the Health and Safety Code, for at least 55 years.[831]

425.30. (a) In an action for collection of consumer debt, common counts may not be used. For purposes of this section, a "common count" includes, but is not limited to, a claim for recovery of any of the following:

(1) An open book account for money due.

(2) An account stated in writing by and between plaintiff and defendant in which it was agreed that defendant was indebted to plaintiff.

(3) Money had and received by defendant for the use and benefit of plaintiff.

(4) Work, labor, services, and materials rendered at the special instance and request of defendant and for which defendant promised to pay plaintiff.

(5) Goods, wares, and merchandise sold and delivered to defendant and for which defendant promised to pay plaintiff.

(6) Money lent by plaintiff to defendant at defendant's request.

(7) Money paid out, laid out, and expended to or for defendant at defendant's special instance and request.

(b) For purposes of this section, "consumer debt" means any obligation or alleged obligation, incurred on or after July 1, 2024, of a consumer to pay money arising out of a transaction in which the money, property, insurance, or services that are the subject of the transaction are primarily for personal, family, or household purposes and where the obligation to pay appears on the face of a note or in a written contract.

(c) In an action under this section for the collection of consumer debt brought by a debt buyer, as defined in Section 1788.50 of the Civil Code, the debt buyer shall also comply with Section 1788.58 of the Civil Code and the remaining provisions of Title 1.6C.5 (commencing with Section 1788.50) of Part 4 of Division 3 of the Civil Code.[830]

425.50. (a) An allegation of a construction-related accessibility claim in a complaint, as defined in subdivision (a) of Section 55.52 of the Civil Code, shall state facts sufficient to allow a reasonable person to identify the basis of the violation or violations supporting the claim, including all of the following:

(1) A plain language explanation of the specific access barrier or barriers the individual encountered, or by which the individual alleges he or she was deterred, with sufficient information about the location of the alleged barrier to enable a reasonable person to identify the access barrier.

(2) The way in which the barrier denied the individual full and equal use or access, or in which it deterred the individual, on each particular occasion.

(3) The date or dates of each particular occasion on which the claimant encountered the specific access barrier, or on which he or she was deterred.

(4) (A) Except in complaints that allege physical injury or damage to property, a complaint filed by or on behalf of a high-frequency litigant shall also state all of the following:

(i) Whether the complaint is filed by, or on behalf of, a high-frequency litigant.

(ii) In the case of a high-frequency litigant who is a plaintiff, the number of complaints alleging a construction-related accessibility claim that the high-frequency litigant has filed during the 12 months prior to filing the complaint.

(iii) In the case of a high-frequency litigant who is a plaintiff, the reason the individual was in the geographic area of the defendant's business.

(iv) In the case of a high-frequency litigant who is a plaintiff, the reason why the individual desired to access the defendant's business, including the specific commercial, business, personal, social, leisure, recreational, or other purpose.

(B) As used in this section "high-frequency litigant" has the same meaning as set forth in subdivision (b) of Section 425.55.

(b) (1) A complaint alleging a construction-related accessibility claim, as those terms are defined in subdivision (a) of Section 55.3 of the Civil Code, shall be verified by the plaintiff. A complaint filed without verification shall be subject to a motion to strike.

(2) A complaint alleging a construction-related accessibility claim filed by, or on behalf of, a high-frequency litigant shall state in the caption "ACTION SUBJECT TO THE SUPPLEMENTAL FEE IN GOVERNMENT CODE SECTION 70616.5."

(c) A complaint alleging a construction-related accessibility claim shall be signed by at least one attorney of record in the attorney's individual name, or, if the party is not represented by an attorney, shall be signed by the party. By signing the complaint, the attorney or unrepresented party is certifying that, to the best of the person's knowledge, information, and belief, formed after an inquiry reasonable under the circumstances, all of the following conditions are met:

(1) It is not being presented primarily for an improper purpose, such as to harass or to cause unnecessary delay or needless increase in the cost of litigation.

(2) The claims, defenses, and other legal contentions therein are warranted by existing law or by a nonfrivolous argument for the extension, modification, or reversal of existing law or the establishment of new law.

(3) The allegations and other factual contentions have evidentiary support or, if specifically so identified, are likely to have evidentiary support after a reasonable opportunity for further investigation or discovery.

(4) The denials of factual contentions are warranted on the evidence or, if specifically so identified, are reasonably based on a lack of information or belief.

(d) A court may, after notice and a reasonable opportunity to respond, determine whether subdivision (c) has been violated and, if so, impose sanctions as provided in Section 128.7 for violations of subdivision (b) of Section 128.7.

(e) Nothing in this section shall limit the right of a plaintiff to amend a complaint under Section 472, or with leave of the court under Section 473. However, an amended pleading alleging a construction-related accessibility claim shall be pled as required by subdivision (a).

(f) The determination whether an attorney is a high-frequency litigant shall be made solely on the basis of the verified complaint and any other publicly available documents. Notwithstanding any other law, no party to the proceeding may conduct discovery with respect to whether an attorney is a high-frequency litigant.

(g) This section shall become operative on January 1, 2013.[718]

425.55. (a) The Legislature finds and declares all of the following:

(1) Protection of the civil rights of persons with disabilities is of the utmost importance to this state, and private enforcement is the essential means of achieving that goal, as the law has been designed.

(2) According to information from the California Commission on Disability Access, more than one-half, or 54 percent, of all construction-related accessibility complaints filed between 2012 and 2014 were filed by two law firms. Forty-six percent of all complaints were filed by a total of 14 parties. Therefore, a very small number of plaintiffs have filed a disproportionately large number of the construction-related accessibility claims in the state, from 70 to 300 lawsuits each year. Moreover, these lawsuits are frequently filed against small businesses on the basis of boilerplate complaints, apparently seeking quick cash settlements rather than correction of the accessibility violation. This practice unfairly taints the reputation of other innocent disabled consumers

who are merely trying to go about their daily lives accessing public accommodations as they are entitled to have full and equal access under the state's Unruh Civil Rights Act (Section 51 of the Civil Code) and the federal Americans with Disability Act of 1990 (Public Law 101-336).

(3) Therefore, given these special and unique circumstances, the provisions of this section are warranted for this limited group of plaintiffs.

(b) For the purposes of this article, "high-frequency litigant" means a person, except as specified in paragraph (3), who utilizes court resources in actions arising from alleged construction-related access violations at such a high level that it is appropriate that additional safeguards apply so as to ensure that the claims are warranted. A "high-frequency litigant" means one or more of the following:

(1) A plaintiff who has filed 10 or more complaints alleging a construction-related accessibility violation within the 12-month period immediately preceding the filing of the current complaint alleging a construction-related accessibility violation.

(2) An attorney who has represented as attorney of record 10 or more high-frequency litigant plaintiffs in actions that were resolved within the 12-month period immediately preceding the filing of the current complaint alleging a construction-related accessibility violation, excluding all of the following actions:

(A) An action in which an early evaluation conference was held pursuant to Section 55.54 of the Civil Code.

(B) An action in which judgment was entered in favor of the plaintiff.

(C) An action in which the construction-related accessibility violations alleged in the complaint were remedied in whole or in part, or a favorable result was achieved, after the plaintiff filed a complaint or provided a demand letter, as defined in Section 55.3 of the Civil Code.

(3) This section does not apply to an attorney employed or retained by a qualified legal services project or a qualified support center, as defined in Section 6213 of the Business and Professions Code, when acting within the scope of employment to represent a client in asserting a construction-related accessibility claim, or the client in such a case.[719]

Article 2: Compulsory Cross-Complaints
Article 2 added by Stats. 1971, Ch. 244.

426.10. As used in this article:

(a) "Complaint" means a complaint or cross-complaint.

(b) "Plaintiff" means a person who files a complaint or cross-complaint.

(c) "Related cause of action" means a cause of action which arises out of the same transaction, occurrence, or series of transactions or occurrences as the cause of action which the plaintiff alleges in his complaint.[73]

426.30. (a) Except as otherwise provided by statute, if a party against whom a complaint has been filed and served fails to allege in a cross-complaint any related cause of action which (at the time of serving his answer to the complaint) he has against the plaintiff, such party may not thereafter in any other action assert against the plaintiff the related cause of action not pleaded.

(b) This section does not apply if either of the following are established:

(1) The court in which the action is pending does not have jurisdiction to render a personal judgment against the person who failed to plead the related cause of action.

(2) The person who failed to plead the related cause of action did not file an answer to the complaint against him.[73]

426.40. This article does not apply if any of the following are established:

(a) The cause of action not pleaded requires for its adjudication the presence of additional parties over whom the court cannot acquire jurisdiction.

(b) Both the court in which the action is pending and any other court to which the action is transferrable pursuant to Section 396 are prohibited by the federal or state constitution or by a statute from entertaining the cause of action not pleaded.

(c) At the time the action was commenced, the cause of action not pleaded was the subject of another pending action.[73]

426.50. A party who fails to plead a cause of action subject to the requirements of this article, whether through oversight, inadvertence, mistake, neglect, or other cause, may apply to the court for leave to amend his pleading, or to file a cross-complaint, to assert such cause at any time during the course of the action. The court, after notice to the adverse party, shall grant, upon such terms as may be just to the parties, leave to amend the pleading, or to file the cross-complaint, to assert such cause if the party who failed to plead the cause acted in good faith. This subdivision shall be liberally construed to avoid forfeiture of causes of action.[73]

426.60. (a) This article applies only to civil actions and does not apply to special proceedings.

(b) This article does not apply to actions in the small claims court.

(c) This article does not apply where the only relief sought is a declaration of the rights and duties of the respective parties in an action for declaratory relief under Chapter 8 (commencing with Section 1060) of Title 14 of this part.[73]

426.70. (a) Notwithstanding subdivision (a) of Section 426.60, this article applies to eminent domain proceedings.

(b) The related cause of action may be asserted by cross-complaint in an eminent domain proceeding whether or not the party asserting such cause of action has presented a claim in compliance with Part 3 (commencing with Section 900) of Division 3.6 of Title 1 of the Government Code to the plaintiff in the original eminent domain proceeding.[95]

Article 3: Permissive Joinder of Causes of Action

Article 3 added by Stats. 1971, Ch. 244.

427.10. (a) A plaintiff who in a complaint, alone or with coplaintiffs, alleges a cause of action against one or more defendants may unite with such cause any other causes which he has either alone or with any coplaintiffs against any of such defendants.

(b) Causes of action may be joined in a cross-complaint in accordance with Sections 428.10 and 428.30.[73]

Article 4: Cross-Complaints
Article 4 added by Stats. 1971, Ch. 244.

428.10. A party against whom a cause of action has been asserted in a complaint or cross-complaint may file a cross-complaint setting forth either or both of the following:
(a) Any cause of action he has against any of the parties who filed the complaint or cross-complaint against him. Nothing in this subdivision authorizes the filing of a cross-complaint against the plaintiff in an action commenced under Title 7 (commencing with Section 1230.010) of Part 3.
(b) Any cause of action he has against a person alleged to be liable thereon, whether or not such person is already a party to the action, if the cause of action asserted in his cross-complaint (1) arises out of the same transaction, occurrence, or series of transactions or occurrences as the cause brought against him or (2) asserts a claim, right, or interest in the property or controversy which is the subject of the cause brought against him.[96]

428.20. When a person files a cross-complaint as authorized by Section 428.10, he may join any person as a cross-complainant or cross-defendant, whether or not such person is already a party to the action, if, had the cross-complaint been filed as an independent action, the joinder of that party would have been permitted by the statutes governing joinder of parties.[73]

428.30. Where a person files a cross-complaint as authorized by Section 428.10, he may unite with the cause of action asserted in the cross-complaint any other causes of action he has against any of the cross-defendants, other than the plaintiff in an eminent domain proceeding, whether or not such cross-defendant is already a party to the action.[73]

428.40. The cross-complaint shall be a separate document.[73]

428.50. (a) A party shall file a cross-complaint against any of the parties who filed the complaint or cross-complaint against him or her before or at the same time as the answer to the complaint or cross-complaint.
(b) Any other cross-complaint may be filed at any time before the court has set a date for trial.
(c) A party shall obtain leave of court to file any cross-complaint except one filed within the time specified in subdivision (a) or (b). Leave may be granted in the interest of justice at any time during the course of the action.[187]

428.60. A cross-complaint shall be served on each of the parties in an action in the following manner:
(1) If a party has not appeared in the action, a summons upon the cross-complaint shall be issued and served upon him in the same manner as upon commencement of an original action.
(2) If a party has appeared in the action, the cross-complaint shall be served upon his attorney, or upon the party if he has appeared without an attorney, in the manner provided for service of summons or in the manner provided by Chapter 5 (commencing with Section 1010) of Title 14 of Part 2 of this code.[86]

428.70. (a) As used in this section:
(1) "Third-party plaintiff" means a person against whom a cause of action has been asserted in a complaint or cross-complaint, who claims the right to recover all or part of any

amounts for which he may be held liable on such cause of action from a third person, and who files a cross-complaint stating such claim as a cause of action against the third person.

(2) "Third-party defendant" means the person who is alleged in a cross-complaint filed by a third-party plaintiff to be liable to the third-party plaintiff if the third-party plaintiff is held liable on the claim against him.

(b) In addition to the other rights and duties a third-party defendant has under this article, he may, at the time he files his answer to the cross-complaint, file as a separate document a special answer alleging against the person who asserted the cause of action against the third-party plaintiff any defenses which the third-party plaintiff has to such cause of action. The special answer shall be served on the third-party plaintiff and on the person who asserted the cause of action against the third-party plaintiff.[73]

428.80. The counterclaim is abolished. Any cause of action that formerly was asserted by a counterclaim shall be asserted by a cross-complaint. Where any statute refers to asserting a cause of action as a counterclaim, such cause shall be asserted as a cross-complaint. The erroneous designation of a pleading as a counterclaim shall not affect its validity, but such pleading shall be deemed to be a cross-complaint.[73]

Article 5: Contents of Documents in Particular Actions or Proceedings
Article 5 added by Stats. 1971, Ch. 244.

429.30. (a) As used in this section:

(1) "Complaint" includes a cross-complaint.

(2) "Plaintiff" includes the person filing a cross-complaint.

(b) If the complaint contains a demand for relief on account of the alleged infringement of the plaintiff's rights in and to a literary, artistic, or intellectual production, there shall be attached to the complaint a copy of the production as to which the infringement is claimed and a copy of the alleged infringing production. If, by reason of bulk or the nature of the production, it is not practicable to attach a copy to the complaint, that fact and the reasons why it is impracticable to attach a copy of the production to the complaint shall be alleged; and the court, in connection with any demurrer, motion, or other proceedings in the cause in which a knowledge of the contents of such production may be necessary or desirable, shall make such order for a view of the production not attached as will suit the convenience of the court to the end that the contents of such production may be deemed to be a part of the complaint to the same extent and with the same force as though such production had been capable of being and had been attached to the complaint. The attachment of any such production in accordance with the provisions of this section shall not be deemed a making public of the production within the meaning of Section 983 of the Civil Code.[73]

Chapter 3: Objections to Pleadings; Denials and Defenses

Chapter 3 added by Stats. 1971, Ch. 244.

Article 1: Objections to Pleadings
Article 1 added by Stats. 1971, Ch. 244.

430.10. The party against whom a complaint or cross-complaint has been

filed may object, by demurrer or answer as provided in Section 430.30, to the pleading on any one or more of the following grounds:
(a) The court has no jurisdiction of the subject of the cause of action alleged in the pleading.
(b) The person who filed the pleading does not have the legal capacity to sue.
(c) There is another action pending between the same parties on the same cause of action.
(d) There is a defect or misjoinder of parties.
(e) The pleading does not state facts sufficient to constitute a cause of action.
(f) The pleading is uncertain. As used in this subdivision, "uncertain" includes ambiguous and unintelligible.
(g) In an action founded upon a contract, it cannot be ascertained from the pleading whether the contract is written, is oral, or is implied by conduct.
(h) No certificate was filed as required by Section 411.35.[779]

430.20. A party against whom an answer has been filed may object, by demurrer as provided in Section 430.30, to the answer upon any one or more of the following grounds:
(a) The answer does not state facts sufficient to constitute a defense.
(b) The answer is uncertain. As used in this subdivision, "uncertain" includes ambiguous and unintelligible.
(c) Where the answer pleads a contract, it cannot be ascertained from the answer whether the contract is written or oral.[73]

430.30 (a) When any ground for objection to a complaint, cross-complaint, or answer appears on the face thereof, or from any matter of which the court is required to or may take judicial notice, the objection on that ground may be taken by a demurrer to the pleading.
(b) When any ground for objection to a complaint or cross-complaint does not appear on the face of the pleading, the objection may be taken by answer.
(c) A party objecting to a complaint or cross-complaint may demur and answer at the same time.[73]

430.40. (a) A person against whom a complaint or cross-complaint has been filed may, within 30 days after service of the complaint or cross-complaint, demur to the complaint or cross-complaint.
(b) A party who has filed a complaint or cross-complaint may, within 10 days after service of the answer to his pleading, demur to the answer.[73]

430.41. (a) Before filing a demurrer pursuant to this chapter, the demurring party shall meet and confer in person, by telephone, or by video conference with the party who filed the pleading that is subject to demurrer for the purpose of determining whether an agreement can be reached that would resolve the objections to be raised in the demurrer. If an amended complaint, cross-complaint, or answer is filed, the responding party shall meet and confer again with the party who filed the amended pleading before filing a demurrer to the amended pleading.
(1) As part of the meet and confer process, the demurring party shall identify all of the specific causes of action that it believes are subject to demurrer and identify with legal support the basis of the deficiencies. The party who filed the complaint, cross-complaint, or answer shall provide legal

support for its position that the pleading is legally sufficient or, in the alternative, how the complaint, cross-complaint, or answer could be amended to cure any legal insufficiency.

(2) The parties shall meet and confer at least 5 days before the date the responsive pleading is due. If the parties are not able to meet and confer at least 5 days before the date the responsive pleading is due, the demurring party shall be granted an automatic 30-day extension of time within which to file a responsive pleading, by filing and serving, on or before the date on which a demurrer would be due, a declaration stating under penalty of perjury that a good faith attempt to meet and confer was made and explaining the reasons why the parties could not meet and confer. The 30-day extension shall commence from the date the responsive pleading was previously due, and the demurring party shall not be subject to default during the period of the extension. Any further extensions shall be obtained by court order upon a showing of good cause.

(3) The demurring party shall file and serve with the demurrer a declaration stating either of the following:

(A) The means by which the demurring party met and conferred with the party who filed the pleading subject to demurrer, and that the parties did not reach an agreement resolving the objections raised in the demurrer.

(B) That the party who filed the pleading subject to demurrer failed to respond to the meet and confer request of the demurring party or otherwise failed to meet and confer in good faith.

(4) A determination by the court that the meet and confer process was insufficient shall not be grounds to overrule or sustain a demurrer.

(b) A party demurring to a pleading that has been amended after a demurrer to an earlier version of the pleading was sustained shall not demur to any portion of the amended complaint, cross-complaint, or answer on grounds that could have been raised by demurrer to the earlier version of the complaint, cross-complaint, or answer.

(c) If a court sustains a demurrer to one or more causes of action and grants leave to amend, the court may order a conference of the parties before an amended complaint or cross-complaint or a demurrer to an amended complaint or cross-complaint, may be filed. If a conference is held, the court shall not preclude a party from filing a demurrer and the time to file a demurrer shall not begin until after the conference has concluded. This section does not prohibit the court from ordering a conference on its own motion at any time or prevent a party from requesting that the court order a conference to be held.

(d) This section does not apply to the following civil actions:

(1) An action in which a party not represented by counsel is incarcerated in a local, state, or federal correctional institution.

(2) A proceeding in forcible entry, forcible detainer, or unlawful detainer.

(e) (1) In response to a demurrer and prior to the case being at issue, a complaint or cross-complaint shall not be amended more than three times, absent an offer to the trial court as to such additional facts to be pleaded that there is a reasonable possibility the defect can be cured to state a cause of action. The three-amendment limit shall not include an amendment made without leave of the court pursuant to Section 472, provided the amendment is made before a demurrer to the original complaint or cross-complaint is filed.

(2) Nothing in this section affects the rights of a party to amend its pleading or respond to an amended pleading after the case is at issue.

(f) Nothing in this section affects appellate review or the rights of a party pursuant to Section 430.80.

(g) If a demurrer is overruled as to a cause of action and that cause of action is not further amended, the demurring party preserves its right to appeal after final judgment without filing a further demurrer.[820]

430.50. (a) A demurrer to a complaint or cross-complaint may be taken to the whole complaint or cross-complaint or to any of the causes of action stated therein.

(b) A demurrer to an answer may be taken to the whole answer or to any one or more of the several defenses set up in the answer.[73]

430.60. A demurrer shall distinctly specify the grounds upon which any of the objections to the complaint, cross-complaint, or answer are taken. Unless it does so, it may be disregarded.[73]

430.70. When the ground of demurrer is based on a matter of which the court may take judicial notice pursuant to Section 452 or 453 of the Evidence Code, such matter shall be specified in the demurrer, or in the supporting points and authorities for the purpose of invoking such notice, except as the court may otherwise permit.[73]

430.80. (a) If the party against whom a complaint or cross-complaint has been filed fails to object to the pleading, either by demurrer or answer, that party is deemed to have waived the objection unless it is an objection that the court has no jurisdiction of the subject of the cause of action alleged in the pleading or an objection that the pleading does not state facts sufficient to constitute a cause of action.

(b) If the party against whom an answer has been filed fails to demur thereto, that party is deemed to have waived the objection unless it is an objection that the answer does not state facts sufficient to constitute a defense.[197]

430.90. (a) Where the defendant has removed a civil action to federal court without filing a response in the original court and the case is later remanded for improper removal, the time to respond shall be as follows:

(1) If the defendant has not generally appeared in either the original or federal court, then 30 days from the day the original court receives the case on remand to move to dismiss the action pursuant to Section 583.250 or to move to quash service of summons or to stay or dismiss the action pursuant to Section 418.10, if the court has not ruled on a similar motion filed by the defendant prior to the removal of the action to federal court.

(2) If the defendant has not filed an answer in the original court, then 30 days from the day the original court receives the case on remand to do any of the following:

(A) Answer the complaint.

(B) Demur or move to strike all or a portion of the complaint if: (i) an answer was not filed in the federal court, and (ii) a demurrer or motion to strike raising the same or similar issues was not filed and ruled upon by the original court prior to the removal of the action to federal court or was not filed and ruled upon in federal court prior to the remand. If the demurrer or motion to strike is denied by the court, the defendant shall have 30 days to answer the complaint unless an answer was filed with the demurrer or motion to strike.

(b) For the purposes of this section, time shall be calculated from the date of the original court's receipt of the order of remand.[352]

Article 2: Denials and Defenses
Article 2 added by Stats. 1971, Ch. 244.

431.10. (a) A material allegation in a pleading is one essential to the claim or defense and which could not be stricken from the pleading without leaving it insufficient as to that claim or defense.

(b) An immaterial allegation in a pleading is any of the following:

(1) An allegation that is not essential to the statement of a claim or defense.

(2) An allegation that is neither pertinent to nor supported by an otherwise sufficient claim or defense.

(3) A demand for judgment requesting relief not supported by the allegations of the complaint or cross-complaint.

(c) An "immaterial allegation" means "irrelevant matter" as that term is used in Section 436.[239]

431.20. (a) Every material allegation of the complaint or cross-complaint, not controverted by the answer, shall, for the purposes of the action, be taken as true.

(b) The statement of any new matter in the answer, in avoidance or constituting a defense, shall, on the trial, be deemed controverted by the opposite party.[73]

431.30. (a) As used in this section:

(1) "Complaint" includes a cross-complaint.

(2) "Defendant" includes a person filing an answer to a cross-complaint.

(b) The answer to a complaint shall contain:

(1) The general or specific denial of the material allegations of the complaint controverted by the defendant.

(2) A statement of any new matter constituting a defense.

(c) Affirmative relief may not be claimed in the answer.

(d) If the complaint is subject to Article 2 (commencing with Section 90) of Chapter 5.1 of Title 1 of Part 1 or is not verified, a general denial is sufficient but only puts in issue the material allegations of the complaint. If the complaint is verified, unless the complaint is subject to Article 2 (commencing with Section 90) of Chapter 5.1 of Title 1 of Part 1, the denial of the allegations shall be made positively or according to the information and belief of the defendant. However, if the cause of action is a claim assigned to a third party for collection and the complaint is verified, the denial of the allegations shall be made positively or according to the information and belief of the defendant, even if the complaint is subject to Article 2 (commencing with Section 90) of Chapter 5.1 of Title 1 of Part 1.

(e) If the defendant has no information or belief upon the subject sufficient to enable him or her to answer an allegation of the complaint, he or she may so state in his or her answer and place his or her denial on that ground.

(f) The denials of the allegations controverted may be stated by reference to specific paragraphs or parts of the complaint; or by express admission of certain allegations of the complaint with a general denial of all of the allegations not so admitted; or by denial of certain allegations upon information and belief, or for lack of sufficient information or belief, with a general denial of all allegations not so denied or expressly admitted.

(g) The defenses shall be separately stated, and the several defenses shall refer to the causes of action which they are intended to answer, in a manner by which they may be intelligibly distinguished.[531]

431.40. (a) Any provision of law to the contrary notwithstanding, in any action in which the demand, exclusive of interest, or the value of the property in controversy does not exceed one thousand dollars ($1000), the defendant at his option, in lieu of demurrer or other answer, may file a general written denial and a brief statement of any new matter constituting a defense.

(b) Nothing in this section excuses the defendant from complying with the provisions of law applicable to a cross-complaint, and any cross-complaint of the defendant shall be subject to the requirements applicable in any other action.

(c) The general written denial described in subdivision (a) shall be on a blank available at the place of filing and shall be in a form prescribed by the Judicial Council. This form need not be verified.[104]

431.50. In an action to recover upon a contract of insurance wherein the defendant claims exemption from liability upon the ground that, although the proximate cause of the loss was a peril insured against, the loss was remotely caused by or would not have occurred but for a peril excepted in the contract of insurance, the defendant shall in his answer set forth and specify the peril which was the proximate cause of the loss, in what manner the peril excepted contributed to the loss or itself caused the peril insured against, and if he claims that the peril excepted caused the peril insured against, he shall in his answer set forth and specify upon what premises or at what place the peril excepted caused the peril insured against.[73]

431.70. Where cross-demands for money have existed between persons at any point in time when neither demand was barred by the statute of limitations, and an action is thereafter commenced by one such person, the other person may assert in the answer the defense of payment in that the two demands are compensated so far as they equal each other, notwithstanding that an independent action asserting the person's claim would at the time of filing the answer be barred by the statute of limitations. If the cross-demand would otherwise be barred by the statute of limitations, the relief accorded under this section shall not exceed the value of the relief granted to the other party. The defense provided by this section is not available if the cross-demand is barred for failure to assert it in a prior action under Section 426.30. Neither person can be deprived of the benefits of this section by the assignment or death of the other. For the purposes of this section, a money judgment is a "demand for money" and, as applied to a money judgment, the demand is barred by the statute of limitations when enforcement of the judgment is barred under Chapter 3 (commencing with Section 683.010) of Division 1 of Title 9.[122]

Article 3: Time to Respond to Cross-Complaint
Article 3 added by Stats. 1971, Ch. 244.

432.10. A party served with a cross-complaint may within 30 days after service move, demur, or otherwise plead to the cross-complaint in the same manner as to an original complaint.[73]

Chapter 4: Motion to Strike
Heading of Chapter 4 added by Stats. 1971, Ch. 244.

435. (a) As used in this section:
(1) The term "complaint" includes a cross-complaint.
(2) The term "pleading" means a demurrer, answer, complaint, or cross-complaint.
(b) (1) Any party, within the time allowed to respond to a pleading may serve and file a notice of motion to strike the whole or any part thereof, but this time limitation shall not apply to motions specified in subdivision (e).
(2) A notice of motion to strike the answer or the complaint, or a portion thereof, shall specify a hearing date set in accordance with Section 1005.
(3) A notice of motion to strike a demurrer, or a portion thereof, shall set the hearing thereon concurrently with the hearing on the demurrer.
(c) If a party serves and files a notice of motion to strike without demurring to the complaint, the time to answer is extended and no default may be entered against that defendant, except as provided in Sections 585 and 586.
(d) The filing of a notice of motion to strike an answer or complaint, or portion thereof, shall not extend the time within which to demur.
(e) A motion to strike, as specified in this section, may be made as part of a motion pursuant to subparagraph (A) of paragraph (1) of subdivision (i) of Section 438.[323]

435.5. (a) Before filing a motion to strike pursuant to this chapter, the moving party shall meet and confer in person, by telephone, or by video conference with the party who filed the pleading that is subject to the motion to strike for the purpose of determining if an agreement can be reached that resolves the objections to be raised in the motion to strike. If an amended pleading is filed, the responding party shall meet and confer again with the party who filed the amended pleading before filing a motion to strike the amended pleading.
(1) As part of the meet and confer process, the moving party shall identify all of the specific allegations that it believes are subject to being stricken and identify with legal support the basis of the deficiencies. The party who filed the pleading shall provide legal support for its position that the pleading is legally sufficient, or, in the alternative, how the pleading could be amended to cure any legal insufficiency.
(2) The parties shall meet and confer at least 5 days before the date a motion to strike must be filed. If the parties are unable to meet and confer at

least 5 days before the date the motion to strike must be filed, the moving party shall be granted an automatic 30-day extension of time within which to file a motion to strike, by filing and serving, on or before the date a motion to strike must be filed, a declaration stating under penalty of perjury that a good faith attempt to meet and confer was made and explaining the reasons why the parties could not meet and confer. The 30-day extension shall commence from the date the motion to strike was previously due, and the moving party shall not be subject to default during the period of the extension. Any further extensions shall be obtained by court order upon a showing of good cause.

(3) The moving party shall file and serve with the motion to strike a declaration stating either of the following:

(A) The means by which the moving party met and conferred with the party who filed the pleading subject to the motion to strike, and that the parties did not reach an agreement resolving the objections raised by the motion to strike.

(B) That the party who filed the pleading subject to the motion to strike failed to respond to the meet and confer request of the moving party or otherwise failed to meet and confer in good faith.

(4) A determination by the court that the meet and confer process was insufficient shall not be grounds to grant or deny the motion to strike.

(b) A party moving to strike a pleading that has been amended after a motion to strike an earlier version of the pleading was granted shall not move to strike any portion of the pleadings on grounds that could have been raised by a motion to strike as to the earlier version of the pleading.

(c) (1) If a court grants a motion to strike and grants leave to amend, the court may order a conference of the parties before an amended pleading, or a motion to strike an amended pleading, may be filed. If the conference is held, the court shall not preclude a party from filing a motion to strike and the time to file a motion to strike shall not begin until after the conference has concluded.

(2) This section does not prohibit the court from ordering a conference on its own motion at any time or prevent a party from requesting that the court order that a conference be held.

(d) This section does not apply to any of the following:

(1) An action in which a party not represented by counsel is incarcerated in a local, state, or federal correctional institution.

(2) A proceeding in forcible entry, forcible detainer, or unlawful detainer.

(3) A special motion brought pursuant to Section 425.16.

(4) A motion brought less than 30 days before trial.

(e) (1) In response to a motion to strike and before the case is at issue, a pleading shall not be amended more than three times, absent an offer to the trial court of additional facts to be pleaded that, if pleaded, would result in a reasonable possibility that the defect can be cured. The three-amendment limit does not include an amendment made without leave of the court pursuant to Section 472, if the amendment is made before a motion to strike as to the original pleading is filed.

(2) This section does not affect the rights of a party to amend its pleading or respond to an amended pleading after the case is at issue.

(f) This section does not affect appellate review or the rights of a party pursuant to Section 430.80.

(g) If a motion to strike is denied and the pleading is not further amended, the moving party preserves its right to appeal after final judgment without filing a further motion to strike.[821]

436. The court may, upon a motion made pursuant to Section 435, or at any time in its discretion, and upon terms it deems proper:

(a) Strike out any irrelevant, false, or improper matter inserted in any pleading.

(b) Strike out all or any part of any pleading not drawn or filed in conformity with the laws of this state, a court rule, or an order of the court.[198]

437. (a) The grounds for a motion to strike shall appear on the face of the challenged pleading or from any matter of which the court is required to take judicial notice.

(b) Where the motion to strike is based on matter of which the court may take judicial notice pursuant to Section 452 or 453 of the Evidence Code, such matter shall be specified in the notice of motion, or in the supporting points and authorities, except as the court may otherwise permit.[133]

Chapter 5: Summary Judgments and Motions for Judgment on the Pleadings

Heading of Chapter 5 amended by Stats. 1993, Ch. 456, Sec. 4.

437c. (a) (1) A party may move for summary judgment in an action or proceeding if it is contended that the action has no merit or that there is no defense to the action or proceeding. The motion may be made at any time after 60 days have elapsed since the general appearance in the action or proceeding of each party against whom the motion is directed or at any earlier time after the general appearance that the court, with or without notice and upon good cause shown, may direct.

(2) Notice of the motion and supporting papers shall be served on all other parties to the action at least 81 days before the time appointed for hearing. If the notice is served by mail, the required 81-day period of notice shall be increased by 5 days if the place of address is within the State of California, 10 days if the place of address is outside the State of California but within the United States, and 20 days if the place of address is outside the United States. If the notice is served by facsimile transmission, express mail, or another method of delivery providing for overnight delivery, the required 81-day period of notice shall be increased by two court days.

(3) The motion shall be heard no later than 30 days before the date of trial, unless the court for good cause orders otherwise. The filing of the motion shall not extend the time within which a party must otherwise file a responsive pleading.

(4) A party shall not bring more than one motion for summary judgment against an adverse party to the action or proceeding. This limitation does not apply to motions for summary adjudication.

(5) Notwithstanding any other provi-

sion of this section, on motion or application of any party and a showing of good cause, the court may grant leave for the moving party to bring an additional motion for summary judgment. The moving party shall serve the notice and supporting papers for any such additional motion in accordance with paragraph (2) of subdivision (a).

(b) (1) The motion shall be supported by affidavits, declarations, admissions, answers to interrogatories, depositions, and matters of which judicial notice shall or may be taken. The supporting papers shall include a separate statement setting forth plainly and concisely all material facts that the moving party contends are undisputed. Each of the material facts stated shall be followed by a reference to the supporting evidence. The failure to comply with this requirement of a separate statement may in the court's discretion constitute a sufficient ground for denying the motion.

(2) An opposition to the motion shall be served and filed not less than 20 days preceding the noticed or continued date of hearing, unless the court for good cause orders otherwise. The opposition, where appropriate, shall consist of affidavits, declarations, admissions, answers to interrogatories, depositions, and matters of which judicial notice shall or may be taken.

(3) The opposition papers shall include a separate statement that responds to each of the material facts contended by the moving party to be undisputed, indicating if the opposing party agrees or disagrees that those facts are undisputed. The statement also shall set forth plainly and concisely any other material facts the opposing party contends are disputed. Each material fact contended by the opposing party to be disputed shall be followed by a reference to the supporting evidence. Failure to comply with this requirement of a separate statement may constitute a sufficient ground, in the court's discretion, for granting the motion.

(4) A reply to the opposition shall be served and filed by the moving party not less than 11 days preceding the noticed or continued date of hearing, unless the court for good cause orders otherwise. The reply shall not include any new evidentiary matter, additional material facts, or separate statement submitted with the reply and not presented in the moving papers or opposing papers.

(5) Evidentiary objections not made at the hearing shall be deemed waived.

(6) Except for subdivision (c) of Section 1005 relating to the method of service of opposition and reply papers, Sections 1005 and 1013, extending the time within which a right may be exercised or an act may be done, do not apply to this section.

(7) An incorporation by reference of a matter in the court's file shall set forth with specificity the exact matter to which reference is being made and shall not incorporate the entire file.

(c) The motion for summary judgment shall be granted if all the papers submitted show that there is no triable issue as to any material fact and that the moving party is entitled to a judgment as a matter of law. In determining if the papers show that there is no triable issue as to any material fact, the court shall consider all of the evidence set forth in the papers, except the evidence to which objections have been made and sustained by the court, and all inferences reasonably deducible from the evidence, except summary judgment shall not be granted by the court based on inferences reasonably deducible from the evidence if contradicted by other inferences or evidence that raise a triable issue as to any material fact.

(d) Supporting and opposing affidavits or declarations shall be made by a person on personal knowledge, shall set forth admissible evidence, and shall show affirmatively that the affiant is competent to testify to the matters stated in the affidavits or declarations. An objection based on the failure to comply with the requirements of this subdivision, if not made at the hearing, shall be deemed waived.

(e) If a party is otherwise entitled to summary judgment pursuant to this section, summary judgment shall not be denied on grounds of credibility or for want of cross-examination of witnesses furnishing affidavits or declarations in support of the summary judgment, except that summary judgment may be denied in the discretion of the court if the only proof of a material fact offered in support of the summary judgment is an affidavit or declaration made by an individual who was the sole witness to that fact; or if a material fact is an individual's state of mind, or lack thereof, and that fact is sought to be established solely by the individual's affirmation thereof.

(f) (1) A party may move for summary adjudication as to one or more causes of action within an action, one or more affirmative defenses, one or more claims for damages, or one or more issues of duty, if the party contends that the cause of action has no merit, that there is no affirmative defense to the cause of action, that there is no merit to an affirmative defense as to any cause of action, that there is no merit to a claim for damages, as specified in Section 3294 of the Civil Code, or that one or more defendants either owed or did not owe a duty to the plaintiff or plaintiffs. A motion for summary adjudication shall be granted only if it completely disposes of a cause of action, an affirmative defense, a claim for damages, or an issue of duty.

(2) A motion for summary adjudication may be made by itself or as an alternative to a motion for summary judgment and shall proceed in all procedural respects as a motion for summary judgment. A party shall not move for summary judgment based on issues asserted in a prior motion for summary adjudication and denied by the court unless that party establishes, to the satisfaction of the court, newly discovered facts or circumstances or a change of law supporting the issues reasserted in the summary judgment motion.

(g) Upon the denial of a motion for summary judgment on the ground that there is a triable issue as to one or more material facts, the court shall, by written or oral order, specify one or more material facts raised by the motion that the court has determined there exists a triable controversy. This determination shall specifically refer to the evidence proffered in support of and in opposition to the motion that indicates that a triable controversy exists. Upon the grant of a motion for summary judgment on the ground that there is no triable issue of material fact, the court shall, by written or oral order, specify the reasons for its determination. The order shall specifically refer to the evidence proffered in support of and, if applicable, in opposition to the motion that indicates no triable issue exists. The court shall also state its reasons for any other determination. The court shall record its determination by court reporter or written order.

(h) If it appears from the affidavits submitted in opposition to a motion for summary judgment or summary adjudication, or both, that facts essential to justify opposition may exist but cannot, for reasons stated, be presented, the court shall deny the motion, order a continuance to permit affidavits to be obtained or discovery to be had, or make any other order as may be just. The application to continue the motion to obtain necessary discovery may also be made by ex parte motion at any time on or before the date the opposition response to the motion is due.

(i) If, after granting a continuance to allow specified additional discovery, the court determines that the party seeking summary judgment has unreasonably failed to allow the discovery to be conducted, the court shall grant a continuance to permit the discovery to go forward or deny the motion for summary judgment or summary adjudication. This section does not affect or limit the ability of a party to compel discovery under the Civil Discovery Act (Title 4 (commencing with Section 2016.010) of Part 4).

(j) If the court determines at any time that an affidavit was presented in bad faith or solely for the purpose of delay, the court shall order the party who presented the affidavit to pay the other party the amount of the reasonable expenses the filing of the affidavit caused the other party to incur. Sanctions shall not be imposed pursuant to this subdivision except on notice contained in a party's papers or on the court's own noticed motion, and after an opportunity to be heard.

(k) Unless a separate judgment may properly be awarded in the action, a final judgment shall not be entered on a motion for summary judgment before the termination of the action, but the final judgment shall, in addition to any matters determined in the action, award judgment as established by the summary proceeding provided for in this section.

(l) In an action arising out of an injury to the person or to property, if a motion for summary judgment is granted on the basis that the defendant was without fault, no other defendant during trial, over plaintiff's objection, may attempt to attribute fault to, or comment on, the absence or involvement of the defendant who was granted the motion.

(m) (1) A summary judgment entered under this section is an appealable judgment as in other cases. Upon entry of an order pursuant to this section, except the entry of summary judgment, a party may, within 20 days after service upon the party of a written notice of entry of the order, petition an appropriate reviewing court for a peremptory writ. If the notice is served by mail, the initial period within which to file the petition shall be increased by five days if the place of address is within the State of California, 10 days if the place of address is outside the State of California but within the

United States, and 20 days if the place of address is outside the United States. If the notice is served by facsimile transmission, express mail, or another method of delivery providing for overnight delivery, the initial period within which to file the petition shall be increased by two court days. The superior court may, for good cause, and before the expiration of the initial period, extend the time for one additional period not to exceed 10 days.

(2) Before a reviewing court affirms an order granting summary judgment or summary adjudication on a ground not relied upon by the trial court, the reviewing court shall afford the parties an opportunity to present their views on the issue by submitting supplemental briefs. The supplemental briefs may include an argument that additional evidence relating to that ground exists, but the party has not had an adequate opportunity to present the evidence or to conduct discovery on the issue. The court may reverse or remand based upon the supplemental briefs to allow the parties to present additional evidence or to conduct discovery on the issue. If the court fails to allow supplemental briefs, a rehearing shall be ordered upon timely petition of a party.

(n) (1) If a motion for summary adjudication is granted, at the trial of the action, the cause or causes of action within the action, affirmative defense or defenses, claim for damages, or issue or issues of duty as to the motion that has been granted shall be deemed to be established and the action shall proceed as to the cause or causes of action, affirmative defense or defenses, claim for damages, or issue or issues of duty remaining.

(2) In the trial of the action, the fact that a motion for summary adjudication is granted as to one or more causes of action, affirmative defenses, claims for damages, or issues of duty within the action shall not bar any cause of action, affirmative defense, claim for damages, or issue of duty as to which summary adjudication was either not sought or denied.

(3) In the trial of an action, neither a party, a witness, nor the court shall comment to a jury upon the grant or denial of a motion for summary adjudication.

(o) A cause of action has no merit if either of the following exists:

(1) One or more of the elements of the cause of action cannot be separately established, even if that element is separately pleaded.

(2) A defendant establishes an affirmative defense to that cause of action.

(p) For purposes of motions for summary judgment and summary adjudication:

(1) A plaintiff or cross-complainant has met that party's burden of showing that there is no defense to a cause of action if that party has proved each element of the cause of action entitling the party to judgment on the cause of action. Once the plaintiff or cross-complainant has met that burden, the burden shifts to the defendant or cross-defendant to show that a triable issue of one or more material facts exists as to the cause of action or a defense thereto. The defendant or cross-defendant shall not rely upon the allegations or denials of its pleadings to show that a triable issue of material fact exists but, instead, shall set forth the specific facts showing that a triable issue of material fact exists as

to the cause of action or a defense thereto.

(2) A defendant or cross-defendant has met that party's burden of showing that a cause of action has no merit if the party has shown that one or more elements of the cause of action, even if not separately pleaded, cannot be established, or that there is a complete defense to the cause of action. Once the defendant or cross-defendant has met that burden, the burden shifts to the plaintiff or cross-complainant to show that a triable issue of one or more material facts exists as to the cause of action or a defense thereto. The plaintiff or cross-complainant shall not rely upon the allegations or denials of its pleadings to show that a triable issue of material fact exists but, instead, shall set forth the specific facts showing that a triable issue of material fact exists as to the cause of action or a defense thereto.

(q) In granting or denying a motion for summary judgment or summary adjudication, the court need rule only on those objections to evidence that it deems material to its disposition of the motion. Objections to evidence that are not ruled on for purposes of the motion shall be preserved for appellate review.

(r) This section does not extend the period for trial provided by Section 1170.5.

(s) Subdivisions (a) and (b) do not apply to actions brought pursuant to Chapter 4 (commencing with Section 1159) of Title 3 of Part 3.

(t) Notwithstanding subdivision (f), a party may move for summary adjudication of a legal issue or a claim for damages other than punitive damages that does not completely dispose of a cause of action, affirmative defense, or issue of duty pursuant to this subdivision.

(1) (A) Before filing a motion pursuant to this subdivision, the parties whose claims or defenses are put at issue by the motion shall submit to the court both of the following:

(i) A joint stipulation stating the issue or issues to be adjudicated.

(ii) A declaration from each stipulating party that the motion will further the interest of judicial economy by decreasing trial time or significantly increasing the likelihood of settlement.

(B) The joint stipulation shall be served on any party to the civil action who is not also a party to the motion.

(2) Within 15 days of receipt of the stipulation and declarations, unless the court has good cause for extending the time, the court shall notify the stipulating parties if the motion may be filed. In making this determination, the court may consider objections by a nonstipulating party made within 10 days of the submission of the stipulation and declarations.

(3) If the court elects not to allow the filing of the motion, the stipulating parties may request, and upon request the court shall conduct, an informal conference with the stipulating parties to permit further evaluation of the proposed stipulation. The stipulating parties shall not file additional papers in support of the motion.

(4) (A) A motion for summary adjudication made pursuant to this subdivision shall contain a statement in the notice of motion that reads substantially similar to the following: "This

motion is made pursuant to subdivision (t) of Section 437c of the Code of Civil Procedure. The parties to this motion stipulate that the court shall hear this motion and that the resolution of this motion will further the interest of judicial economy by decreasing trial time or significantly increasing the likelihood of settlement."

(B) The notice of motion shall be signed by counsel for all parties, and by those parties in propria persona, to the motion.

(5) A motion filed pursuant to this subdivision may be made by itself or as an alternative to a motion for summary judgment and shall proceed in all procedural respects as a motion for summary judgment.

(u) For purposes of this section, a change in law does not include a later enacted statute without retroactive application.[842]

438. (a) As used in this section:

(1) "Complaint" includes a cross-complaint.

(2) "Plaintiff" includes a cross-complainant.

(3) "Defendant" includes a cross-defendant.

(b) (1) A party may move for judgment on the pleadings.

(2) The court may upon its own motion grant a motion for judgment on the pleadings.

(c) (1) The motion provided for in this section may only be made on one of the following grounds:

(A) If the moving party is a plaintiff, that the complaint states facts sufficient to constitute a cause or causes of action against the defendant and the answer does not state facts sufficient to constitute a defense to the complaint.

(B) If the moving party is a defendant, that either of the following conditions exist:

(i) The court has no jurisdiction of the subject of the cause of action alleged in the complaint.

(ii) The complaint does not state facts sufficient to constitute a cause of action against that defendant.

(2) The motion provided for in this section may be made as to either of the following:

(A) The entire complaint or cross-complaint or as to any of the causes of action stated therein.

(B) The entire answer or one or more of the affirmative defenses set forth in the answer.

(3) If the court on its own motion grants the motion for judgment on the pleadings, it shall be on one of the following bases:

(A) If the motion is granted in favor of the plaintiff, it shall be based on the grounds that the complaint states facts sufficient to constitute a cause or causes of action against the defendant and the answer does not state facts sufficient to constitute a defense to the complaint.

(B) If the motion is granted in favor of the defendant, that either of the following conditions exist:

(i) The court has no jurisdiction of the subject of the cause of action alleged in the complaint.

(ii) The complaint does not state facts sufficient to constitute a cause of action against that defendant.

(d) The grounds for motion provided for in this section shall appear on the face of the challenged pleading or from any matter of which the court is required to take judicial notice. Where the motion is based on a matter of which the court may take judicial notice pursuant to Section 452 or 453 of the Evidence Code, the matter shall be specified in the notice of motion, or in the supporting points and authorities, except as the court may otherwise permit.

(e) No motion may be made pursuant to this section if a pretrial conference order has been entered pursuant to Section 575, or within 30 days of the date the action is initially set for trial, whichever is later, unless the court otherwise permits.

(f) The motion provided for in this section may be made only after one of the following conditions has occurred:

(1) If the moving party is a plaintiff, and the defendant has already filed his or her answer to the complaint and the time for the plaintiff to demur to the answer has expired.

(2) If the moving party is a defendant, and the defendant has already filed his or her answer to the complaint and the time for the defendant to demur to the complaint has expired.

(g) The motion provided for in this section may be made even though either of the following conditions exist:

(1) The moving party has already demurred to the complaint or answer, as the case may be, on the same grounds as is the basis for the motion provided for in this section and the demurrer has been overruled, provided that there has been a material change in applicable case law or statute since the ruling on the demurrer.

(2) The moving party did not demur to the complaint or answer, as the case may be, on the same grounds as is the basis for the motion provided for in this section.

(h) (1) The motion provided for in this section may be granted with or without leave to file an amended complaint or answer, as the case may be.

(2) Where a motion is granted pursuant to this section with leave to file an amended complaint or answer, as the case may be, then the court shall grant 30 days to the party against whom the motion was granted to file an amended complaint or answer, as the case may be.

(3) If the motion is granted with respect to the entire complaint or answer without leave to file an amended complaint or answer, as the case may be, then judgment shall be entered forthwith in accordance with the motion granting judgment to the moving party.

(4) If the motion is granted with leave to file an amended complaint or answer, as the case may be, then the following procedures shall be followed:

(A) If an amended complaint is filed after the time to file an amended complaint has expired, then the court may strike the complaint pursuant to Section 436 and enter judgment in favor of that defendant against that plaintiff or a plaintiff.

(B) If an amended answer is filed after the time to file an amended answer has expired, then the court may strike the answer pursuant to Section 436 and proceed to enter judgment in favor of that plaintiff and against that defendant or a defendant.

(C) Except where subparagraphs (A) and (B) apply, if the motion is granted with respect to the entire complaint or answer with leave to file an amended complaint or answer, as the case may be, but an amended complaint or answer is not filed, then after the time to file an amended complaint or answer, as the case may be, has expired, judgment shall be entered forthwith in favor of the moving party.

(i) (1) Where a motion for judgment on the pleadings is granted with leave to amend, the court shall not enter a judgment in favor of a party until the following proceedings are had:

(A) If an amended pleading is filed and the moving party contends that pleading is filed after the time to file an amended pleading has expired or that the pleading is in violation of the court's prior ruling on the motion, then that party shall move to strike the pleading and enter judgment in its favor.

(B) If no amended pleading is filed, then the party shall move for entry of judgment in its favor.

(2) All motions made pursuant to this subdivision shall be made pursuant to Section 1010.

(3) At the hearing on the motion provided for in this subdivision, the court shall determine whether to enter judgment in favor of a particular party.[335]

439. (a) Before filing a motion for judgment on the pleadings pursuant to this chapter, the moving party shall meet and confer in person, by telephone, or by video conference with the party who filed the pleading that is subject to the motion for judgment on the pleadings for the purpose of determining if an agreement can be reached that resolves the claims to be raised in the motion for judgment on the pleadings. If an amended pleading is filed, the responding party shall meet and confer again with the party who filed the amended pleading before filing a motion for judgment on the pleadings against the amended pleading.

(1) As part of the meet and confer process, the moving party shall identify all of the specific allegations that it believes are subject to judgment and identify with legal support the basis of the claims. The party who filed the pleading shall provide legal support for its position that the pleading is not subject to judgment, or, in the alternative, how the pleading could be amended to cure any claims it is subject to judgment.

(2) The parties shall meet and confer at least 5 days before the date a motion for judgment on the pleadings is filed. If the parties are unable to meet and confer by that time, the moving party shall be granted an automatic 30-day extension of time within which to file a motion for judgment on the pleadings, by filing and serving, on or before the date a motion for judgment on the pleadings must be filed, a declaration stating under penalty of perjury that a good faith attempt to meet and confer was made and explaining the reasons why the parties could not meet and confer. The 30-day extension shall commence from the date the motion for judgment on the pleadings was previously filed, and the moving party shall not be subject to default during the period of the extension. Any further extensions shall be obtained by court order upon a showing of good cause.

(3) The moving party shall file and serve with the motion for judgment on the pleadings a declaration stating either of the following:

(A) The means by which the moving party met and conferred with the party who filed the pleading subject to the motion for judgment on the pleadings, and that the parties did not reach an agreement resolving the claims raised by the motion for judgment on the pleadings.

(B) That the party who filed the pleading subject to the motion for judgment on the pleadings failed to respond to the meet and confer request of the moving party or otherwise failed to meet and confer in good faith.

(4) A determination by the court that the meet and confer process was insufficient shall not be grounds to grant or deny the motion for judgment on the pleadings.

(b) A party moving for judgment on a pleading that has been amended after a motion for judgment on the pleadings on an earlier version of the pleading was granted shall not move for judgment on any portion of the pleadings on grounds that could have been raised by a motion for judgment on the pleadings as to the earlier version of the pleading.

(c) (1) If a court grants a motion for judgment on the pleadings and grants leave to amend, the court may order a conference of the parties before an amended pleading, or a motion for judgment on an amended pleading, may be filed. If the conference is held, the court shall not preclude a party from filing a motion for judgment on the pleadings and the time to file a motion for judgment on the pleadings shall not begin until after the conference has concluded.

(2) This section does not prohibit the court from ordering a conference on its own motion at any time or prevent a party from requesting that the court order that a conference be held.

(d) This section does not apply to any of the following:

(1) An action in which a party not represented by counsel is incarcerated in a local, state, or federal correctional institution.

(2) A proceeding in forcible entry, forcible detainer, or unlawful detainer.

(3) A special motion brought pursuant to Section 425.16.

(4) A motion brought less than 30 days before trial.

(e) (1) In response to a motion for judgment on the pleadings and before the case is at issue, a pleading shall not be amended more than three times, absent an offer to the trial court of additional facts to be pleaded that, if pleaded, would result in a reasonable possibility that the defect can be cured. The three-amendment limit does not include an amendment made without leave of the court pursuant to Section 472, if the amendment is made before a motion for judgments on the pleadings as to the original pleading is filed.

(2) This section does not affect the rights of a party to amend its pleading or respond to an amended pleading after the case is at issue.

(f) This section does not affect appellate review or the rights of a party pursuant to Section 430.80.

(g) If a motion for judgment on the pleadings is denied and the pleading is not further amended, the moving party preserves its right to appeal after final judgment without filing a further motion for judgment on the pleadings.[822]

Chapter 6: Verification of Pleadings

Chapter 6 enacted 1872.

446. (a) Every pleading shall be sub-

scribed by the party or his or her attorney. When the state, any county thereof, city, school district, district, public agency, or public corporation, or any officer of the state, or of any county thereof, city, school district, district, public agency, or public corporation, in his or her official capacity, is plaintiff, the answer shall be verified, unless an admission of the truth of the complaint might subject the party to a criminal prosecution, or, unless a county thereof, city, school district, district, public agency, or public corporation, or an officer of the state, or of any county, city, school district, district, public agency, or public corporation, in his or her official capacity, is defendant. When the complaint is verified, the answer shall be verified. In all cases of a verification of a pleading, the affidavit of the party shall state that the same is true of his own knowledge, except as to the matters which are therein stated on his or her information or belief, and as to those matters that he or she believes it to be true; and where a pleading is verified, it shall be by the affidavit of a party, unless the parties are absent from the county where the attorney has his or her office, or from some cause unable to verify it, or the facts are within the knowledge of his or her attorney or other person verifying the same. When the pleading is verified by the attorney, or any other person except one of the parties, he or she shall set forth in the affidavit the reasons why it is not made by one of the parties.

When a corporation is a party, the verification may be made by any officer thereof. When the state, any county thereof, city, school district, district, public agency, or public corporation, or an officer of the state, or of any county thereof, city, school district, district, public agency, or public corporation, in his or her official capacity is plaintiff, the complaint need not be verified; and if the state, any county thereof, city, school district, district, public agency, or public corporation, or an officer of such state, county, city, school district, district, public agency, or public corporation, in his or her official capacity is defendant, its or his or her answer need not be verified.

When the verification is made by the attorney for the reason that the parties are absent from the county where he or she has his or her office, or from some other cause are unable to verify it, or when the verification is made on behalf of a corporation or public agency by any officer thereof, the attorney's or officer's affidavit shall state that he or she has read the pleading and that he or she is informed and believes the matters therein to be true and on that ground alleges that the matters stated therein are true. However, in those cases the pleadings shall not otherwise be considered as an affidavit or declaration establishing the facts therein alleged.

A person verifying a pleading need not swear to the truth or his or her belief in the truth of the matters stated therein but may, instead, assert the truth or his or her belief in the truth of those matters "under penalty of perjury."

(b) This section shall become operative on January 1, 1999, unless a statute that becomes effective on or before this date extends or deletes the repeal date of Section 446, as amended by Assembly Bill 3594 of the 1993–94 Regular Session.[354]

Chapter 7: General Rules of Pleading

Chapter 7 enacted 1872.

452. In the construction of a pleading, for the purpose of determining its effect, its allegations must be liberally construed, with a view to substantial justice between the parties.[1]

454. It is not necessary for a party to set forth in a pleading the items of an account therein alleged, but he must deliver to the adverse party, within ten days after a demand thereof in writing, a copy of the account, or be precluded from giving evidence thereof. The court or judge thereof may order a further account when the one delivered is too general, or is defective in any particular.
If the pleading is verified the account must be verified by the affidavit of the party to the effect that he believes it to be true; or if the facts are within the personal knowledge of the agent or attorney for the party, or the party is not within the county where the attorney has his office or from some cause unable to make the affidavit, by the affidavit of the agent or attorney.[19]

455. In an action for the recovery of real property, it must be described in the complaint with such certainty as to enable an officer, upon execution, to identify it.[1]

456. In pleading a judgment or other determination of a court, officer, or board, it is not necessary to state the facts conferring jurisdiction, but such judgment or determination may be stated to have been duly given or made and to have become final. If such allegation be controverted, the party pleading must establish on the trial the facts conferring jurisdiction and creating finality.[39]

457. In pleading the performance of conditions precedent in a contract, it is not necessary to state the facts showing such performance, but it may be stated generally that the party duly performed all the conditions on his part, and if such allegation be controverted, the party pleading must establish, on the trial, the facts showing such performance.[1]

458. In pleading the Statute of Limitations it is not necessary to state the facts showing the defense, but it may be stated generally that the cause of action is barred by the provisions of Section ____ (giving the number of the section and subdivision thereof, if it is so divided, relied upon) of The Code of Civil Procedure; and if such allegation be controverted, the party pleading must establish, on the trial, the facts showing that the cause of action is so barred.[1]

459. In pleading a private statute, or an ordinance of a county or municipal corporation, or a right derived therefrom, it is sufficient to refer to such statute or ordinance by its title and the day of its passage. In pleading the performance of conditions precedent under a statute or an ordinance of a county or municipal corporation, or of a right derived therefrom, it is not necessary to state the facts showing such performance, but it may be stated generally that the party duly performed all the conditions on his part required thereby; if such allegations be controverted the party pleading must establish on the trial the facts showing such performance.[10]

460. In an action for libel or slander it is not necessary to state in the complaint any extrinsic facts for the purpose of showing the application to the plaintiff of the defamatory matter out of which the cause of action arose; but it is sufficient to state, generally, that the same was published or spoken concerning the plaintiff; and if such allegation be controverted, the plaintiff must establish on the trial that it was so published or spoken.[1]

460.5. (a) In any action for libel or slander, for good cause shown upon ex parte written application, the court may order that the time to respond to the complaint is 20 days after the service of summons on the defendant. The application shall be supported by an affidavit stating facts showing, among other things, that the alleged defamatory matter has been continuously published and that there is a reasonable likelihood that the publication will continue. The order shall direct the clerk to endorse the summons to show that the time to respond has been shortened pursuant to this section. A copy of the application, affidavit, and order shall be served with the summons.

(b) In any such action, unless otherwise ordered by the court for good cause shown, the time allowed the defendant to respond to the complaint or amend the answer under Section 586 shall not exceed 10 days.

(c) The court shall give any such action precedence over all other civil actions, except actions to which special precedence is given by law, in the matter of the setting the case for hearing or trial, and in hearing the case, to the end that all such actions shall be quickly heard and determined. Except for good cause shown, the court shall not grant a continuance in excess of 10 days without the consent of the adverse party.

(d) For purposes of this section, "continuously published" means three or more publications within 15 days.[79]

460.7. (a) In any action by a candidate or former candidate for elective public office against a holder of elective public office or an opposing candidate for libel or slander that is alleged to have occurred during the course of an election campaign, the court shall order that the time to respond to the complaint is 20 days after the service of summons on the defendant. The order shall direct the clerk to endorse the summons to show that the time to respond has been shortened pursuant to this section. A copy of the affidavit and order shall be served with the summons.

(b) In any action described in subdivision (a), unless otherwise ordered by the court for good cause shown, the time allowed the defendant to respond to the complaint or amend the answer under Section 586 shall not exceed 10 days.

(c) The court shall give any action described in subdivision (a) precedence over all other civil actions, except actions to which special precedence is given by law, in the matter of the setting of the case of hearing or trial, and in hearing the case, to the end that all actions described in subdivision (a) shall be quickly heard and determined. Except for good cause shown, the court shall not grant a continuance in excess of 10 days without the consent of the adverse party.[588]

461. In any action within Section 460

or 460.5, the defendant may, in his answer, allege both the truth of the matter charged as defamatory, and any mitigating circumstances, to reduce the amount of damages. Whether he proves the justification or not, he may give in evidence the mitigating circumstances.[80]

464. (a) The plaintiff and defendant, respectively, may be allowed, on motion, to make a supplemental complaint or answer, alleging facts material to the case occurring after the former complaint or answer.
(b) The plaintiff and defendant, or petitioner and respondent, may, in any action in which the support of children is an issue, file a supplemental complaint seeking a judgment or order of paternity or support for a child of the mother and father of the child whose paternity and support are already in issue before the court. A supplemental complaint for paternity or child support may be filed without leave of court either before or after final judgment in the underlying action.
(c) Upon the filing of a supplemental complaint, the court clerk shall issue an amended or supplemental summons pursuant to Section 412.10. Service of the supplemental summons and complaint shall be made in the manner provided for the initial service of a summons by this code.[341]

465. Except with leave of the court, all pleadings subsequent to the complaint, together with proof of service unless a summons need be issued, shall be filed with the clerk or judge, and copies thereof served upon the adverse party or his or her attorney.[247]

Chapter 8: Variance—Mistakes in Pleadings and Amendments

Chapter 8 enacted 1872.

469. Variance between the allegation in a pleading and the proof shall not be deemed material, unless it has actually misled the adverse party to his or her prejudice in maintaining his or her action or defense upon the merits. If it appears that a party has been so misled, the court may order the pleading to be amended, upon such terms as may be just.[738]

470. Where the variance is not material, as provided in Section 469 the court may direct the fact to be found according to the evidence, or may order an immediate amendment, without costs.[240]

471. Where, however, the allegation of the claim or defense to which the proof is directed, is unproved, not in some particular or particulars only, but in its general scope and meaning, it is not to be deemed a case of variance, within the meaning of Sections 469 and 470, but a failure of proof.[241]

471.5. (a) If the complaint is amended, a copy of the amendments shall be filed, or the court may, in its discretion, require the complaint as amended to be filed, and a copy of the amendments or amended complaint must be served upon the defendants affected thereby. The defendant shall answer the amendments, or the complaint as amended, within 30 days after service thereof, or such other time as the court may direct, and judgment by default may be entered upon failure to answer, as in other cases. For the purposes of this subdivision, "complaint" includes

a cross-complaint, and "defendant" includes a person against whom a cross-complaint is filed.
(b) If the answer is amended, the adverse party has 10 days after service thereof, or such other time as the court may direct, in which to demur to the amended answer.[76]

472. (a) A party may amend its pleading once without leave of the court at any time before the answer, demurrer, or motion to strike is filed, or after a demurrer or motion to strike is filed but before the demurrer or motion to strike is heard if the amended pleading is filed and served no later than the date for filing an opposition to the demurrer or motion to strike. A party may amend the pleading after the date for filing an opposition to the demurrer or motion to strike, upon stipulation by the parties. The time for responding to an amended pleading shall be computed from the date of service of the amended pleading.
(b) This section shall not apply to a special motion brought pursuant to Section 425.16.[731]

472a. (a) A demurrer is not waived by an answer filed at the same time.
(b) Except as otherwise provided by rule adopted by the Judicial Council, if a demurrer to a complaint or to a cross-complaint is overruled and there is no answer filed, the court shall allow an answer to be filed upon such terms as may be just. If a demurrer to the answer is overruled, the action shall proceed as if no demurrer had been interposed, and the facts alleged in the answer shall be considered as denied to the extent mentioned in Section 431.20.
(c) Subject to the limitations imposed by subdivision (e) of Section 430.41, if a demurrer is sustained, the court may grant leave to amend the pleading upon any terms as may be just and shall fix the time within which the amendment or amended pleading shall be filed. If a demurrer is stricken pursuant to Section 436 and there is no answer filed, the court shall allow an answer to be filed on terms that are just.
(d) If a motion to strike is granted pursuant to Section 436, the court may order that an amendment or amended pleading be filed upon terms it deems proper. If a motion to strike a complaint or cross-complaint, or portion thereof, is denied, the court shall allow the party filing the motion to strike to file an answer.
(e) If a motion to dismiss an action pursuant to Article 2 (commencing with Section 583.210) of Chapter 1.5 of Title 8 is denied, the court shall allow a pleading to be filed.[771]

472b. When a demurrer to any pleading is sustained or overruled, and time to amend or answer is given, the time so given runs from the service of notice of the decision or order, unless the notice is waived in open court, and the waiver entered in the minutes. When an order sustaining a demurrer without leave to amend is reversed or otherwise remanded by any order issued by a reviewing court, any amended complaint shall be filed within 30 days after the clerk of the reviewing court mails notice of the issuance of the remittitur.[459]

472c. (a) When any court makes an order sustaining a demurrer without leave to amend the question as to whether or not such court abused its discretion in making such an order is open on appeal even though no request to amend such pleading was made.

(b) The following orders shall be deemed open on appeal where an amended pleading is filed after the court's order:

(1) An order sustaining a demurrer to a cause of action within a complaint or cross-complaint where the order did not sustain the demurrer as to the entire complaint or cross-complaint.

(2) An order sustaining a demurrer to an affirmative defense within an answer where the order sustaining the demurrer did not sustain the demurrer as to the entire answer.

(3) An order granting a motion to strike a portion of a pleading where the order granting the motion to strike did not strike the entire pleading.

(c) As used in this section, "open on appeal" means that a party aggrieved by an order listed in subdivision (b) may claim the order as error in an appeal from the final judgment in the action.[324]

472d. Whenever a demurrer in any action or proceeding is sustained, the court shall include in its decision or order a statement of the specific ground or grounds upon which the decision or order is based which may be by reference to appropriate pages and paragraphs of the demurrer.

The party against whom a demurrer has been sustained may waive these requirements.[45]

473. (a) (1) The court may, in furtherance of justice, and on any terms as may be proper, allow a party to amend any pleading or proceeding by adding or striking out the name of any party, or by correcting a mistake in the name of a party, or a mistake in any other respect; and may, upon like terms, enlarge the time for answer or demurrer. The court may likewise, in its discretion, after notice to the adverse party, allow, upon any terms as may be just, an amendment to any pleading or proceeding in other particulars; and may upon like terms allow an answer to be made after the time limited by this code.

(2) When it appears to the satisfaction of the court that the amendment renders it necessary, the court may postpone the trial, and may, when the postponement will by the amendment be rendered necessary, require, as a condition to the amendment, the payment to the adverse party of any costs as may be just.

(b) The court may, upon any terms as may be just, relieve a party or the party's legal representative from a judgment, dismissal, order, or other proceeding taken against the party through the party's mistake, inadvertence, surprise, or excusable neglect. Application for this relief shall be accompanied by a copy of the answer or other pleading proposed to be filed therein, otherwise the application shall not be granted, and shall be made within a reasonable time, in no case exceeding six months, after the judgment, dismissal, order, or proceeding was taken. However, in the case of a judgment, dismissal, order, or other proceeding determining the ownership or right to possession of real or personal property, without extending the six-month period, when a notice in writing is personally served within the

State of California both upon the party against whom the judgment, dismissal, order, or other proceeding has been taken, and upon the party's attorney of record, if any, notifying that party and the party's attorney of record, if any, that the order, judgment, dismissal, or other proceeding was taken against the party and that any rights the party has to apply for relief under the provisions of Section 473 of the Code of Civil Procedure shall expire 90 days after service of the notice, then the application shall be made within 90 days after service of the notice upon the defaulting party or the party's attorney of record, if any, whichever service shall be later. No affidavit or declaration of merits shall be required of the moving party. Notwithstanding any other requirements of this section, the court shall, whenever an application for relief is made no more than six months after entry of judgment, is in proper form, and is accompanied by an attorney's sworn affidavit attesting to the attorney's mistake, inadvertence, surprise, or neglect, vacate any (1) resulting default entered by the clerk against the attorney's client, and which will result in entry of a default judgment, or (2) resulting default judgment or dismissal entered against the attorney's client, unless the court finds that the default or dismissal was not in fact caused by the attorney's mistake, inadvertence, surprise, or neglect. The court shall, whenever relief is granted based on an attorney's affidavit of fault, direct the attorney to pay reasonable compensatory legal fees and costs to opposing counsel or parties. However, this section shall not lengthen the time within which an action shall be brought to trial pursuant to Section 583.310.

(c) (1) Whenever the court grants relief from a default, default judgment, or dismissal based on any of the provisions of this section, the court may do any of the following:

(A) Impose a penalty of no greater than one thousand dollars ($1,000) upon an offending attorney or party.

(B) Direct that an offending attorney pay an amount no greater than one thousand dollars ($1,000) to the State Bar Client Security Fund.

(C) Grant other relief as is appropriate.

(2) However, where the court grants relief from a default or default judgment pursuant to this section based upon the affidavit of the defaulting party's attorney attesting to the attorney's mistake, inadvertence, surprise, or neglect, the relief shall not be made conditional upon the attorney's payment of compensatory legal fees or costs or monetary penalties imposed by the court or upon compliance with other sanctions ordered by the court.

(d) The court may, upon motion of the injured party, or its own motion, correct clerical mistakes in its judgment or orders as entered, so as to conform to the judgment or order directed, and may, on motion of either party after notice to the other party, set aside any void judgment or order.

(e) This section shall remain in effect only until January 1, 2027, and as of that date is repealed.[888]

473. (a) (1) The court may, in furtherance of justice, and on any terms as may be proper, allow a party to amend any pleading or proceeding by adding or striking out the name of any party, or by correcting a mistake in the name

of a party, or a mistake in any other respect; and may, upon like terms, enlarge the time for answer or demurrer. The court may likewise, in its discretion, after notice to the adverse party, allow, upon any terms as may be just, an amendment to any pleading or proceeding in other particulars; and may upon like terms allow an answer to be made after the time limited by this code.

(2) When it appears to the satisfaction of the court that the amendment renders it necessary, the court may postpone the trial, and may, when the postponement will by the amendment be rendered necessary, require, as a condition to the amendment, the payment to the adverse party of any costs as may be just.

(b) The court may, upon any terms as may be just, relieve a party or the party's legal representative from a judgment, dismissal, order, or other proceeding taken against the party through the party's mistake, inadvertence, surprise, or excusable neglect. Application for this relief shall be accompanied by a copy of the answer or other pleading proposed to be filed therein, otherwise the application shall not be granted, and shall be made within a reasonable time, in no case exceeding six months, after the judgment, dismissal, order, or proceeding was taken. However, in the case of a judgment, dismissal, order, or other proceeding determining the ownership or right to possession of real or personal property, without extending the six-month period, when a notice in writing is personally served within the State of California both upon the party against whom the judgment, dismissal, order, or other proceeding has been taken, and upon the party's attorney of record, if any, notifying that party and the party's attorney of record, if any, that the order, judgment, dismissal, or other proceeding was taken against the party and that any rights the party has to apply for relief under the provisions of Section 473 of the Code of Civil Procedure shall expire 90 days after service of the notice, then the application shall be made within 90 days after service of the notice upon the defaulting party or the party's attorney of record, if any, whichever service shall be later. No affidavit or declaration of merits shall be required of the moving party. Notwithstanding any other requirements of this section, the court shall, whenever an application for relief is made no more than six months after entry of judgment, is in proper form, and is accompanied by an attorney's sworn affidavit attesting to the attorney's mistake, inadvertence, surprise, or neglect, vacate any (1) resulting default entered by the clerk against the attorney's client, and which will result in entry of a default judgment, or (2) resulting default judgment or dismissal entered against the attorney's client, unless the court finds that the default or dismissal was not in fact caused by the attorney's mistake, inadvertence, surprise, or neglect. The court shall, whenever relief is granted based on an attorney's affidavit of fault, direct the attorney to pay reasonable compensatory legal fees and costs to opposing counsel or parties. However, this section shall not lengthen the time within which an action shall be brought to trial pursuant to Section 583.310.

(c) (1) Whenever the court grants relief from a default, default judgment, or dismissal based on any of the provisions of this section, the court may do any of the following:

(A) Impose a penalty of no greater than one thousand dollars ($1,000) upon an offending attorney or party.

(B) Direct that an offending attorney pay an amount no greater than one thousand dollars ($1,000) to the State Bar Client Security Fund.

(C) Grant other relief as is appropriate.

(2) However, where the court grants relief from a default or default judgment pursuant to this section based upon the affidavit of the defaulting party's attorney attesting to the attorney's mistake, inadvertence, surprise, or neglect, the relief shall not be made conditional upon the attorney's payment of compensatory legal fees or costs or monetary penalties imposed by the court or upon compliance with other sanctions ordered by the court.

(d) The court may, upon motion of the injured party, or its own motion, correct clerical mistakes in its judgment or orders as entered, so as to conform to the judgment or order directed, and may, on motion of either party after notice to the other party, set aside any void judgment or order.

(e) Notwithstanding any other requirements of this section, a party to an action may bring a motion to vacate a default judgment that is void for lack of proper service at any time after entry of the judgment.

(f) This section shall become operative on January 1, 2027.[894]

473.1. The court may, upon such terms as may be just, relieve a party from a judgment, order, or other proceeding taken against him or her, including dismissal of an action pursuant to Section 581 or Chapter 1.5 (commencing with Section 583.110) of Title 8, where a court of this state has assumed jurisdiction, pursuant to Section 6180 or 6190 of the Business and Professions Code, over the law practice of the attorney for the party and the judgment, order or other proceeding was taken against the party after the application for the court to assume jurisdiction over the practice was filed. Application for this relief shall be made within a reasonable period of time, in no case exceeding six months, after the court takes jurisdiction over the practice. However, in the case of a judgment, order, or other proceeding determining the ownership or right to possession of real or personal property, without extending the six-month period, when a notice in writing is personally served within the state both upon the party against whom the judgment, order, or other proceeding has been taken, and upon the attorney appointed pursuant to Section 6180.5 of the Business and Professions Code to act under the court's direction, notifying the party and the appointed attorney that the order, judgment, or other proceeding was taken against him or her and that any rights the party has to apply for relief under the provisions of the section shall expire 90 days after service of notice, then application for relief must be made within 90 days after service of the notice upon the defaulting party or the attorney appointed to act under the court's direction pursuant to Section 6180.5 of the Business and Professions Code, whichever service is later. No affidavit or declaration of merits shall be required of the moving party.[326]

473.2. (a) A party that was not served with a summons and complaint in accordance with this chapter may file and serve a motion to set aside or vacate the default or default judgment and for leave to defend the action or to move for dismissal.

(b) (1) A party moving to set aside or vacate a default or a default judgment pursuant to subdivision (a) shall proffer evidence, through a sworn affidavit or otherwise, that service was not lawfully effected. Proffering evidence that service was not lawfully effected rebuts a presumption of the facts stated in the process server's return.

(2) If a process server files their return before the operative date of this section, the absence of the photograph required by Section 417.10 shall not by itself render the proof of service unlawful or insufficient.

(c) In responding to a motion that is filed pursuant to this section and that complies with subdivision (b), the party seeking a default or default judgment has the burden of proving by a preponderance of the evidence that service of the summons and complaint was lawful.

(d) In deciding a motion filed pursuant to subdivision (a), the court shall take evidence as to the lawfulness of the service of process and shall not deny a reasonable request by either party to conduct a hearing and permit oral testimony.

(e) This section does not limit any other remedies available under law.

(f) This section shall become operative on January 1, 2027.[889]

473.5. (a) When service of a summons has not resulted in actual notice to a party in time to defend the action and a default or default judgment has been entered against the party in the action, the party may serve and file a notice of motion to set aside the default or default judgment and for leave to defend the action. The notice of motion shall be served and filed within a reasonable time, but in no event exceeding the earlier of: (i) two years after entry of a default judgment against the party; or (ii) 180 days after service on the party of a written notice that the default or default judgment has been entered.

(b) A notice of motion to set aside a default or default judgment and for leave to defend the action shall designate as the time for making the motion a date prescribed by subdivision (b) of Section 1005, and it shall be accompanied by an affidavit showing under oath that the party's lack of actual notice in time to defend the action was not caused by the party's avoidance of service or inexcusable neglect. The party shall serve and file with the notice a copy of the answer, motion, or other pleading proposed to be filed in the action.

(c) Upon a finding by the court that the motion was made within the period permitted by subdivision (a) and that the party's lack of actual notice in time to defend the action was not caused by the party's avoidance of service or inexcusable neglect, it may set aside the default or default judgment on whatever terms as may be just and allow the party to defend the action.

(d) This section shall remain in effect only until January 1, 2027, and as of that date is repealed.[890]

473.5. (a) When service of a summons

was lawfully effected but has not resulted in actual notice to a party in time to defend the action and a default or default judgment has been entered against the party in the action, the party may serve and file a notice of motion to set aside the default or default judgment and for leave to defend the action. The notice of motion shall be served and filed within a reasonable time, but in no event exceeding the earlier of: (i) two years after entry of a default judgment against the party; or (ii) 180 days after service on the party of a written notice that the default or default judgment has been entered.

(b) A notice of motion to set aside a default or default judgment and for leave to defend the action shall designate as the time for making the motion a date prescribed by subdivision (b) of Section 1005, and it shall be accompanied by an affidavit showing under oath that the party's lack of actual notice in time to defend the action was not caused by the party's avoidance of service or inexcusable neglect. The party shall serve and file with the notice a copy of the answer, motion, or other pleading proposed to be filed in the action.

(c) Upon a finding by the court that the motion was made within the period permitted by subdivision (a) and that the party's lack of actual notice in time to defend the action was not caused by the party's avoidance of service or inexcusable neglect, it may set aside the default or default judgment on whatever terms as may be just and allow the party to defend the action.

(d) This section shall become operative on January 1, 2027.[891]

474. When the plaintiff is ignorant of the name of a defendant, he must state that fact in the complaint, or the affidavit if the action is commenced by affidavit, and such defendant may be designated in any pleading or proceeding by any name, and when his true name is discovered, the pleading or proceeding must be amended accordingly; provided, that no default or default judgment shall be entered against a defendant so designated, unless it appears that the copy of the summons or other process, or, if there be no summons or process, the copy of the first pleading or notice served upon such defendant bore on the face thereof a notice stating in substance: "To the person served: You are hereby served in the within action (or proceedings) as (or on behalf of) the person sued under the fictitious name of (designating it)." The certificate or affidavit of service must state the fictitious name under which such defendant was served and the fact that notice of identity was given by endorsement upon the document served as required by this section. The foregoing requirements for entry of a default or default judgment shall be applicable only as to fictitious names designated pursuant to this section and not in the event the plaintiff has sued the defendant by an erroneous name and shall not be applicable to entry of a default or default judgment based upon service, in the manner otherwise provided by law, of an amended pleading, process or notice designating defendant by his true name.[36]

475. The court must, in every stage of an action, disregard any error, improper ruling, instruction, or defect, in the pleadings or proceedings which, in the opinion of said court, does not af-

fect the substantial rights of the parties. No judgment, decision, or decree shall be reversed or affected by reason of any error, ruling, instruction, or defect, unless it shall appear from the record that such error, ruling, instruction, or defect was prejudicial, and also that by reason of such error, ruling, instruction, or defect, the said party complaining or appealing sustained and suffered substantial injury, and that a different result would have been probable if such error, ruling, instruction, or defect had not occurred or existed. There shall be no presumption that error is prejudicial, or that injury was done if error is shown.[8]

TITLE 6.5: ATTACHMENT

Title 6.5 added by Stats. 1974, Ch. 1516.

Chapter 1: Words and Phrases Defined

Chapter 1 added by Stats. 1974, Ch. 1516.

481.010. Unless the provision or context otherwise requires, the definitions in this chapter govern the construction of this title.[89]

481.020. "Account debtor" means "account debtor" as defined in paragraph (3) of subdivision (a) of Section 9102 of the Commercial Code.[411]

481.030. "Account receivable" means "account" as defined in paragraph (2) of subdivision (a) of Section 9102 of the Commercial Code.[412]

481.040. "Chattel paper" means "chattel paper" as defined in paragraph (11) of subdivision (a) of Section 9102 of the Commercial Code.[413]

481.055. "Costs" means costs and disbursements, including, but not limited to, statutory fees, charges, commissions, and expenses.[135]

481.060. "Complaint" includes a cross-complaint.[89]

481.070. "Defendant" includes a cross-defendant.[89]

481.080. "Deposit account" means "deposit account" as defined in paragraph (29) of subdivision (a) of Section 9102 of the Commercial Code.[414]

481.090. "Document of title" means "document" as defined in paragraph (30) of subdivision (a) of Section 9102 of the Commercial Code. A document of title is negotiable if it is negotiable within the meaning of Section 7104 of the Commercial Code.[415]

481.100. "Equipment" means tangible personal property in the possession of the defendant and used or bought for use primarily in the defendant's trade, business, or profession if it is not included in the definitions of inventory or farm products.[89]

481.110. "Farm products" means crops or livestock or supplies used or produced in farming operations or products of crops or livestock in their unmanufactured states (such as ginned cotton, wool clip, maple syrup, milk, and eggs), while in the possession of a defendant engaged in raising, fattening, grazing, or other farming operations. If tangible personal property is a farm product, it is neither equipment nor inventory.[136]

481.113. "Financial institution" means a state or national bank, state or federal savings and loan association or credit union, or like organization, and includes a corporation engaged in a safe deposit business.[137]

481.115. "General intangibles" means "general intangibles," as defined in paragraph (42) of subdivision (a) of Section 9102 of the Commercial Code, consisting of rights to payment.[416]

481.117. "Instrument" means "instrument" as defined in paragraph (47) of subdivision (a) of Section 9102 of the Commercial Code.[417]

481.120. "Inventory" means tangible personal property in the possession of a defendant that (a) is held by the defendant for sale or lease or to be furnished under contracts of service or (b) is raw materials, work in process, or materials used or consumed in his trade, business, or profession. Inventory of a person is not to be classified as his equipment.[89]

481.140. "Levying officer" means the sheriff or marshal who is directed to execute a writ or order issued under this title.[368]

481.170. "Person" includes a natural person, a corporation, a partnership or other unincorporated association, a limited liability company, and a public entity.[336]

481.175. "Personal property" includes both tangible and intangible personal property.[138]

481.180. "Plaintiff" means a person who files a complaint or cross-complaint.[89]

481.190. A claim has "probable validity" where it is more likely than not that the plaintiff will obtain a judgment against the defendant on that claim.[89]

481.195. "Property" includes real and personal property and any interest therein.[139]

481.200. "Public entity" includes the state, the Regents of the University of California, a county, a city, district, public authority, public agency, and any other political subdivision or public corporation in the state.[89]

481.203. "Real property" includes any right in real property, including, but not limited to, a leasehold interest in real property.[140]

481.205. "Registered process server" means a person registered as a process server pursuant to Chapter 16 (commencing with Section 22350) of Division 8 of the Business and Professions Code.[141]

481.207. "Secured party" means "secured party" as defined in paragraph (73) of subdivision (a) of Section 9102 of the Commercial Code.[691]

481.210. "Security" means a "security" as defined by Section 8102 of the Commercial Code.[89]

481.220. "Security agreement" means a "security agreement" as defined by paragraph (74) of subdivision (a) of Section 9102 of the Commercial Code.[692]

481.223. "Security interest" means "security interest" as defined in Section 1201 of the Commercial Code.[142]

481.225. "Tangible personal property" includes chattel paper, documents of title, instruments, securities, and money.[143]

Chapter 2: General Provisions

Chapter 2 added by Stats. 1974, Ch. 1516.

482.010. This title shall be known and may be cited as "The Attachment Law."[89]

482.020. Nothing in this title precludes the granting of relief pursuant to Chapter 3 (commencing with Section 525) of Title 7.[89]

482.030. (a) The Judicial Council may provide by rule for the practice and procedure in proceedings under this title.
(b) The Judicial Council shall prescribe the form of the applications, notices, orders, and other documents required by this title.[89]

482.040. The facts stated in each affidavit filed pursuant to this title shall be set forth with particularity. Except where matters are specifically permitted by this title to be shown by information and belief, each affidavit shall show affirmatively that the affiant, if sworn as a witness, can testify competently to the facts stated therein. As to matters shown by information and belief, the affidavit shall state the facts on which the affiant's belief is based, showing the nature of his information and the reliability of his informant. The affiant may be any person, whether or not a party to the action, who has knowledge of the facts. A verified complaint that satisfies the requirements of this section may be used in lieu of or in addition to an affidavit.[89]

482.050. (a) If the plaintiff so requests in writing at the time he files his complaint, the clerk of the court with whom the complaint is filed shall not make available to the public the records and documents in such action before either (1) 30 days after the filing of the complaint or (2) the filing pursuant to this title of the return of service of the notice of hearing and any temporary protective order, or of the writ of attachment if issued without notice, whichever event occurs first.
(b) Notwithstanding subdivision (a), the clerk of the court shall make the entire file in the action available for inspection at any time to any party named in the complaint or to his attorney.
(c) The request by plaintiff that the fact of filing of a complaint or application for relief not be made public may take the form of a notation to that effect, made by rubber stamp or other suitable means, at the top of the first page of the complaint filed with the clerk.[89]

482.060. (a) Except as otherwise provided in subdivision (b), the judicial duties to be performed under this title are subordinate judicial duties within the meaning of Section 22 of Article VI of the California Constitution and may be performed by appointed officers such as court commissioners.
(b) The judicial duties to be performed in the determination of the following matters are not subordinate judicial duties:
(1) A contested claim of exemption.
(2) A contested motion for determination of the liability and damages for wrongful attachment.
(3) A contested third-party claim.
(4) A contested proceeding to enforce a third person's liability.
(c) Nothing in subdivision (b) limits the power of a court to appoint a temporary judge pursuant to Section 21 of Article VI of the California Constitution.[144]

482.070. (a) (1) Except as otherwise provided in this title, legal process required or permitted to be served under this title may be served personally or by mail.

(2) For purposes of this title, the term "legal process" shall refer to each and all of the writs, notices, orders, or other papers required or permitted to be served pursuant to this title.

(b) Except as otherwise provided in this section, service of legal process under this title is governed by Article 1 (commencing with Section 684.010) and Article 2 (commencing with Section 684.110) of Chapter 4 of Division 1 of Title 9, including the provisions of Section 684.120 extending time when service is made by mail.

(c) For the purpose of subdivision (b), in Article 1 (commencing with Section 684.010) and Article 2 (commencing with Section 684.110) of Chapter 4 of Division 1 of Title 9:

(1) References to the "judgment debtor" shall be deemed references to the defendant.

(2) References to the "judgment creditor" shall be deemed references to the plaintiff.

(3) References to a "writ" shall be deemed references to a writ of attachment.

(4) References to a "notice of levy" shall be deemed references to a notice of attachment.

(d) If the defendant has not appeared in the action and legal process is required to be personally served on the defendant under this title, service shall be made in the same manner as a summons is served under Chapter 4 (commencing with Section 413.10) of Title 5.

(e) Except for service of a subpoena or other process to require the attendance of the defendant or service of a paper to bring the defendant into contempt, if the defendant has an attorney of record in the action, service shall be made on the attorney rather than on the defendant.

(f) Proof of service under this title is governed by Article 3 (commencing with Section 684.210) of Chapter 4 of Division 1 of Title 9.[671]

482.080. (a) If a writ of attachment is issued, the court may also issue an order directing the defendant to transfer to the levying officer either or both of the following:

(1) Possession of the property to be attached if the property is sought to be attached by taking it into custody.

(2) Possession of documentary evidence of title to property of or a debt owed to the defendant that is sought to be attached. An order pursuant to this paragraph may be served when the property or debt is levied upon or thereafter.

(b) The order shall be personally served on the defendant and shall contain a notice to the defendant that failure to comply with the order may subject the defendant to arrest and punishment for contempt of court.[145]

482.090. (a) Several writs in the same form may be issued simultaneously or from time to time upon the same undertaking, whether or not any writ previously issued has been returned.

(b) After the return of the writ of attachment, or upon the filing by the plaintiff of an affidavit setting forth the loss of the writ of attachment, the clerk, upon demand of the plaintiff at any time before judgment, may issue an alias writ which shall be in the same form as the original without requirement of a new undertaking.

(c) The date of issuance of a writ of attachment shall be deemed to be the date the writ is first issued.[89]

482.100. (a) The defendant may claim an exemption provided in Section 487.020 for property levied upon pursuant to a writ issued under this title if the right to the exemption is the result of a change in circumstances occurring after (1) the denial of a claim of exemption for the property earlier in the action or (2) the expiration of the time for claiming the exemption earlier in the action.
(b) A claim of exemption under this section shall follow the procedure provided in Article 2 (commencing with Section 703.510) of Chapter 4 of Division 2 of Title 9 except that, subject to subdivision (a), the defendant may claim the exemption at any time. For this purpose, references in Article 2 (commencing with Section 703.510) of Chapter 4 of Division 2 of Title 9 to the "judgment debtor" shall be deemed references to the defendant, and references to the "judgment creditor" shall be deemed references to the plaintiff.
(c) The exemption provided by subdivision (b) of Section 487.020 may be claimed at the defendant's option either pursuant to subdivision (b) of this section or by following the procedure provided in this subdivision. The claim shall be made by filing with the court and serving on the plaintiff a notice of motion. Service on the plaintiff shall be made not less than three days prior to the date set for the hearing. The hearing shall be held not more than five days after the filing of the notice of motion unless, for good cause shown, the court orders otherwise. The notice of motion shall state the relief requested and shall be accompanied by an affidavit supporting any factual issues raised and points and authorities supporting any legal issues raised. At the hearing on the motion, the defendant has the burden of showing that the property is exempt pursuant to subdivision (b) of Section 487.020. Upon this showing and the showing required by subdivision (a), the court shall order the release of the property.[146]

482.110. (a) The plaintiff's application for a right to attach order and a writ of attachment pursuant to this title may include an estimate of the costs and allowable attorney's fees.
(b) In the discretion of the court, the amount to be secured by the attachment may include an estimated amount for costs and allowable attorney's fees.[100]

482.120. If the court determines at the hearing on issuance of a writ of attachment under this title that the value of the defendant's interest in the property described in the plaintiff's application clearly exceeds the amount necessary to satisfy the amount to be secured by the attachment, the court may direct the order of levy on the property described in the writ or restrict the amount of the property to be levied upon.[100]

Chapter 3: Actions in Which Attachment Authorized

Chapter 3 added by Stats. 1974, Ch. 1516.

483.010. (a) Except as otherwise provided by statute, an attachment may be issued only in an action on a claim or claims for money, each of which is based upon a contract, express or implied, where the total amount of the claim or claims is a fixed or readily ascertainable amount not less than five hundred dollars ($500) exclusive of costs, interest, and attorney's fees.

(b) An attachment may not be issued on a claim which is secured by any interest in real property arising from agreement, statute, or other rule of law (including any mortgage or deed of trust of realty and any statutory, common law, or equitable lien on real property, but excluding any security interest in fixtures subject to Division 9 (commencing with Section 9101) of the Commercial Code). However, an attachment may be issued where the claim was originally so secured but, without any act of the plaintiff or the person to whom the security was given, the security has become valueless or has decreased in value to less than the amount then owing on the claim, in which event the amount to be secured by the attachment shall not exceed the lesser of the amount of the decrease or the difference between the value of the security and the amount then owing on the claim.

(c) If the action is against a defendant who is a natural person, an attachment may be issued only on a claim which arises out of the conduct by the defendant of a trade, business, or profession. An attachment may not be issued on a claim against a defendant who is a natural person if the claim is based on the sale or lease of property, a license to use property, the furnishing of services, or the loan of money where the property sold or leased, or licensed for use, the services furnished, or the money loaned was used by the defendant primarily for personal, family, or household purposes.

(d) An attachment may be issued pursuant to this section whether or not other forms of relief are demanded.[349]

483.012. Subject to the restrictions of Sections 580b and 580d, in an action to foreclose a mortgage or deed of trust on real property or an estate for years therein, pursuit of any remedy provided by this title shall not constitute an action for the recovery of a debt for purposes of subdivision (a) of Section 726 or a failure to comply with any other statutory or judicial requirement to proceed first against security.[376]

483.013. Notwithstanding Section 483.010, federal disability benefits awarded to veterans for service-connected disabilities pursuant to Chapter 11 of Title 38 of the United States Code shall be exempt from the claim of creditors, and shall not be liable to attachment, levy, or seizure by or under any legal or equitable process whatsoever, as provided by federal law. This section does not apply to that portion of service-connected disability benefits that are subject to child and spousal support enforcement under Section 659(h)(1)(A)(ii)(V) of Title 42 of the United States Code.[619]

483.015. (a) Subject to subdivision (b) and to Section 483.020, the amount to be secured by an attachment is the sum of the following:

(1) The amount of the defendant's indebtedness claimed by the plaintiff.

(2) Any additional amount included by the court under Section 482.110.

(b) The amount described in subdivision (a) shall be reduced by the sum of the following:

(1) The amount of any money judgment in favor of the defendant and against the plaintiff that remains unsatisfied and is enforceable.

(2) The amount of any indebtedness

of the plaintiff that the defendant has claimed in a cross-complaint filed in the action if the defendant's claim is one upon which an attachment could be issued.

(3) The amount of any claim of the defendant asserted as a defense in the answer pursuant to Section 431.70 if the defendant's claim is one upon which an attachment could be issued had an action been brought on the claim when it was not barred by the statute of limitations.

(4) The value of any security interest in the property of the defendant held by the plaintiff to secure the defendant's indebtedness claimed by the plaintiff, together with the amount by which the value of the security interest has decreased due to the act of the plaintiff or a prior holder of the security interest.[350]

483.020. (a) Subject to subdivisions (d) and (e), the amount to be secured by the attachment in an unlawful detainer proceeding is the sum of the following:

(1) The amount of the rent due and unpaid as of the date of filing the complaint in the unlawful detainer proceeding.

(2) Any additional amount included by the court under subdivision (c).

(3) Any additional amount included by the court under Section 482.110.

(b) In an unlawful detainer proceeding, the plaintiff's application for a right to attach order and a writ of attachment pursuant to this title may include (in addition to the rent due and unpaid as of the date of the filing of the complaint and any additional estimated amount authorized by Section 482.110) an amount equal to the rent for the period from the date the complaint is filed until the estimated date of judgment or such earlier estimated date as possession has been or is likely to be delivered to the plaintiff, such amount to be computed at the rate provided in the lease.

(c) The amount to be secured by the attachment in the unlawful detainer proceeding may, in the discretion of the court, include an additional amount equal to the amount of rent for the period from the date the complaint is filed until the estimated date of judgment or such earlier estimated date as possession has been or is likely to be delivered to the plaintiff, such amount to be computed at the rate provided in the lease.

(d) Except as provided in subdivision (e), the amount to be secured by the attachment as otherwise determined under this section shall be reduced by the amounts described in subdivision (b) of Section 483.015.

(e) Where the plaintiff has received a payment or holds a deposit to secure (1) the payment of rent and the performance of other obligations under the lease or (2) only the performance of other obligations under the lease, the amount of the payment or deposit shall not be subtracted in determining the amount to be secured by the attachment.[377]

Chapter 4: Noticed Hearing Procedure for Obtaining Writ of Attachment

Chapter 4 added by Stats. 1974, Ch. 1516.

Article 1: Right to Attach Order; Issuance of Writ of Attachment

Article 1 added by Stats. 1974, Ch. 1516.

484.010. Upon the filing of the complaint or at any time thereafter, the plaintiff may apply pursuant to this article for a right to attach order and a writ of attachment by filing an application for the order and writ with the court in which the action is brought.[89]

484.020. The application shall be executed under oath and shall include all of the following:
(a) A statement showing that the attachment is sought to secure the recovery on a claim upon which an attachment may be issued.
(b) A statement of the amount to be secured by the attachment.
(c) A statement that the attachment is not sought for a purpose other than the recovery on the claim upon which the attachment is based.
(d) A statement that the applicant has no information or belief that the claim is discharged in a proceeding under Title 11 of the United States Code (Bankruptcy) or that the prosecution of the action is stayed in a proceeding under Title 11 of the United States Code (Bankruptcy).
(e) A description of the property to be attached under the writ of attachment and a statement that the plaintiff is informed and believes that such property is subject to attachment. Where the defendant is a corporation, a reference to "all corporate property which is subject to attachment pursuant to subdivision (a) of Code of Civil Procedure Section 487.010" satisfies the requirements of this subdivision. Where the defendant is a partnership or other unincorporated association, a reference to "all property of the partnership or other unincorporated association which is subject to attachment pursuant to subdivision (b) of Code of Civil Procedure Section 487.010" satisfies the requirements of this subdivision. Where the defendant is a natural person, the description of the property shall be reasonably adequate to permit the defendant to identify the specific property sought to be attached.[147]

484.030. The application shall be supported by an affidavit showing that the plaintiff on the facts presented would be entitled to a judgment on the claim upon which the attachment is based.[89]

484.040. No order or writ shall be issued under this article except after a hearing. At the times prescribed by subdivision (b) of Section 1005, the defendant shall be served with all of the following:
(a) A copy of the summons and complaint.
(b) A notice of application and hearing.
(c) A copy of the application and of any affidavit in support of the application.[264]

484.050. The notice of application and hearing shall inform the defendant of all of the following:
(a) A hearing will be held at a place and at a time, to be specified in the notice, on plaintiff's application for a right to attach order and a writ of attachment.
(b) The order will be issued if the court finds that the plaintiff's claim is probably valid and the other requirements for issuing the order are established. The hearing is not for the purpose of determining whether the claim is actually valid. The determination of the actual validity of the claim will be made in subsequent proceedings in the action and will not be affected by the decisions at the hearing on the application for the order.
(c) The amount to be secured by the attachment is determined pursuant to Sections 482.110, 483.010, 483.015,

and 483.020, which statutes shall be summarized in the notice.

(d) If the right to attach order is issued, a writ of attachment will be issued to attach the property described in the plaintiff's application unless the court determines that such property is exempt from attachment or that its value clearly exceeds the amount necessary to satisfy the amount to be secured by the attachment. However, additional writs of attachment may be issued to attach other nonexempt property of the defendant on the basis of the right to attach order.

(e) If the defendant desires to oppose the issuance of the order, the defendant shall file with the court and serve on the plaintiff a notice of opposition and supporting affidavit as required by Section 484.060 not later than five court days prior to the date set for hearing.

(f) If the defendant claims that the personal property described in the application, or a portion thereof, is exempt from attachment, the defendant shall include that claim in the notice of opposition filed and served pursuant to Section 484.060 or file and serve a separate claim of exemption with respect to the property as provided in Section 484.070. If the defendant does not do so, the claim of exemption will be barred in the absence of a showing of a change in circumstances occurring after the expiration of the time for claiming exemptions.

(g) The defendant may obtain a determination at the hearing whether real or personal property not described in the application or real property described in the application is exempt from attachment by including the claim in the notice of opposition filed and served pursuant to Section 484.060 or by filing and serving a separate claim of exemption with respect to the property as provided in Section 484.070, but the failure to so claim that the property is exempt from attachment will not preclude the defendant from making a claim of exemption with respect to the property at a later time.

(h) Either the defendant or the defendant's attorney or both of them may be present at the hearing.

(i) The notice shall contain the following statement: "You may seek the advice of an attorney as to any matter connected with the plaintiff's application. The attorney should be consulted promptly so that the attorney may assist you before the time set for hearing."[378]

484.060. (a) If the defendant desires to oppose the issuance of the right to attach order sought by plaintiff or objects to the amount sought to be secured by the attachment, the defendant shall file and serve upon the plaintiff no later than five court days prior to the date set for the hearing a notice of opposition. The notice shall state the grounds on which the defendant opposes the issuance of the order or objects to the amount sought to be secured by the attachment and shall be accompanied by an affidavit supporting any factual issues raised and points and authorities supporting any legal issues raised. If the defendant fails to file a notice of opposition within the time prescribed, the defendant shall not be permitted to oppose the issuance of the order.

(b) If a defendant filing a notice of opposition desires to make any claim of exemption as provided in Section 484.070, the defendant may include that claim in the notice of opposition filed pursuant to this section.

(c) The plaintiff may file and serve upon the opposing party a reply two court days prior to the date set for the hearing.[275]

484.070. (a) If the defendant claims that the personal property described in the plaintiff's application, or a portion of such property, is exempt from attachment, the defendant shall claim the exemption as provided in this section. If the defendant fails to make the claim or makes the claim but fails to prove that the personal property is exempt, the defendant may not later claim the exemption except as provided in Section 482.100.

(b) If the defendant desires to claim at the hearing that real or personal property not described in the plaintiff's application or real property described in the plaintiff's application is exempt from attachment, in whole or in part, the defendant shall claim the exemption as provided in this section. Failure to make the claim does not preclude the defendant from later claiming the exemption. If the claim is made as provided in this section but the defendant fails to prove that the property is exempt from attachment, the defendant may not later claim that the property, or a portion thereof, is exempt except as provided in Section 482.100.

(c) The claim of exemption shall:

(1) Describe the property claimed to be exempt.

(2) Specify the statute section supporting the claim.

(d) The claim of exemption shall be accompanied by an affidavit supporting any factual issues raised by the claim and points and authorities supporting any legal issues raised.

(e) The claim of exemption, together with any supporting affidavit and points and authorities, shall be filed and served on the plaintiff not less than five court days before the date set for the hearing.

(f) If the plaintiff desires to oppose the claim of exemption, the plaintiff shall file and serve on the defendant, not less than two days before the date set for the hearing, a notice of opposition to the claim of exemption, accompanied by an affidavit supporting any factual issues raised and points and authorities supporting any legal issues raised. If the plaintiff does not file and serve a notice of opposition as provided in this subdivision, no writ of attachment shall be issued as to the property claimed to be exempt. If all of the property described in the plaintiff's application is claimed to be exempt and the plaintiff does not file and serve a notice of opposition as provided in this subdivision, no hearing shall be held and no right to attach order or writ of attachment shall be issued and any temporary protective order issued pursuant to Chapter 6 (commencing with Section 486.010) immediately expires.

(g) If the plaintiff files and serves a notice of opposition to the claim as provided in this section, the defendant has the burden of proving that the property is exempt from attachment.[399]

484.080. (a) At the time set for the hearing, the plaintiff shall be ready to proceed. If the plaintiff is not ready, or if he has failed to comply with Section 484.040, the court may either deny the application for the order or, for good cause shown, grant the plaintiff a continuance for a reasonable period. If such a continuance is granted, the effective period of any protective order issued pursuant to Chapter 6 (commencing with Section 486.010) may be extended by the court for a period ending not more than 10 days after the new hearing date if the plaintiff shows a continuing need for such protective order.

(b) The court may, in its discretion and for good cause shown, grant the defendant a continuance for a reasonable period to enable him to oppose the issuance of the right to attach order. If such a continuance is granted, the court shall extend the effective period of any protective order issued pursuant to Chapter 6 (commencing with Section 486.010) for a period ending not more than 10 days after the new hearing date unless the defendant shows pursuant to Section 486.100 that the protective order should be modified or vacated.[89]

484.090. (a) At the hearing, the court shall consider the showing made by the parties appearing and shall issue a right to attach order, which shall state the amount to be secured by the attachment determined by the court in accordance with Section 483.015 or 483.020, if it finds all of the following:

(1) The claim upon which the attachment is based is one upon which an attachment may be issued.

(2) The plaintiff has established the probable validity of the claim upon which the attachment is based.

(3) The attachment is not sought for a purpose other than the recovery on the claim upon which the attachment is based.

(4) The amount to be secured by the attachment is greater than zero.

(b) If, in addition to the findings required by subdivision (a), the court finds that the defendant has failed to prove that all the property sought to be attached is exempt from attachment, it shall order a writ of attachment to be issued upon the filing of an undertaking as provided by Sections 489.210 and 489.220.

(c) If the court determines that property of the defendant is exempt from attachment, in whole or in part, the right to attach order shall describe the exempt property and prohibit attachment of the property.

(d) The court's determinations shall be made upon the basis of the pleadings and other papers in the record; but, upon good cause shown, the court may receive and consider at the hearing additional evidence, oral or documentary, and additional points and authorities, or it may continue the hearing for the production of the additional evidence or points and authorities.[379]

484.100. The court's determinations under this chapter shall have no effect on the determination of any issues in the action other than issues relevant to proceedings under this chapter nor shall they affect the rights of the plaintiff or defendant in any other action arising out of the same claim of the plaintiff or defendant. The court's determinations under this chapter shall not be given in evidence nor referred to at the trial of any such action.[148]

484.110. (a) Neither the failure of the defendant to oppose the issuance of a right to attach order under this chapter nor the defendant's failure to rebut any evidence produced by the plaintiff in connection with proceedings under this chapter shall constitute a waiver of any defense to the plaintiff's claim in the action or any other action or have any effect on the right of the defendant to produce or exclude evidence at the trial of any such action.

(b) Neither the failure of the plaintiff to oppose the issuance of an order reducing the amount to be secured by the attachment under this chapter nor the plaintiff's failure to rebut any evidence produced by the defendant in connection with proceedings under this chapter shall constitute a waiver of any defense to the defendant's claim in the action or any other action or have any effect on the right of the plaintiff to produce or exclude evidence at the trial of any such action.[149]

Article 2: Noticed Hearing Procedure for Obtaining Additional Writs
Article 2 added by Stats. 1974, Ch. 1516.

484.310. At any time after a right to attach order has been issued under Article 1 (commencing with Section 484.010) or after the court has found pursuant to Section 485.240 that the plaintiff is entitled to a right to attach order, the plaintiff may apply for a writ of attachment under this article by filing an application with the court in which the action is brought.[89]

484.320. The application shall be executed under oath and shall include all of the following:
(a) A statement that the plaintiff has been issued a right to attach order under Article 1 (commencing with Section 484.010) or that the court has found pursuant to Section 485.240 that the plaintiff is entitled to a right to attach order.
(b) A statement of the amount to be secured by the attachment.
(c) A description of the property to be attached under the writ of attachment and a statement that the plaintiff is informed and believes that the property is subject to attachment. The description shall satisfy the requirements of Section 484.020.
(d) A statement that the applicant has no information or belief that the claim is discharged in a proceeding under Title 11 of the United States Code (Bankruptcy) or that the prosecution of the action is stayed in a proceeding under Title 11 of the United States Code (Bankruptcy).[150]

484.330. No writ of attachment shall be issued under this article except after a hearing. At least 15 days prior to the hearing, the defendant shall be served with both of the following:
(a) A notice of application and hearing.
(b) A copy of the application.[291]

484.340. The notice of application and hearing shall inform the defendant of all of the following:
(a) The plaintiff has applied for a writ of attachment to attach the property described in the application/
(b) A hearing will be held at a place and at a time, to be specified in the notice, to determine whether the plaintiff is entitled to the writ.
(c) A writ of attachment will be issued to attach the property described in the plaintiff's application unless the court determines that the property is exempt from attachment or that its value clearly exceeds the amount necessary to satisfy the amount to be secured by the attachment.
(d) If the defendant claims that the property described in the application,

or a portion thereof, is exempt from attachment, the defendant may file with the court and serve on the plaintiff a claim of exemption with respect to the property as provided in Section 484.350 not later than five days prior to the date set for hearing. If the defendant fails to make such a claim with respect to personal property, the defendant may not later claim the exemption in the absence of a showing of a change in circumstances occurring after the expiration of the time for claiming exemptions.

(e) Either the defendant or the defendant's attorney or both of them may be present at the hearing.

(f) The notice shall contain the following statement: "You may seek the advice of an attorney as to any matter connected with the plaintiff's application. The attorney should be consulted promptly so that the attorney may assist you before the time set for hearing."[151]

484.350. (a) If the defendant claims that the property described in the plaintiff's application, or a portion of such property, is exempt from attachment, the defendant may claim the exemption as provided in this section. If the defendant fails to make a claim with respect to personal property, or makes a claim with respect to real or personal property but fails to prove that the property is exempt, the defendant may not later claim the exemption except as provided in Section 482.100.

(b) The claim of exemption shall:

(1) Describe the property claimed to be exempt.

(2) Specify the statute section supporting the claim.

(c) The claim of exemption shall be accompanied by an affidavit supporting any factual issues raised by the claim and points and authorities supporting any legal issues raised.

(d) The claim of exemption, together with any supporting affidavit and points and authorities, shall be filed and served on the plaintiff not less than five court days before the date set for the hearing.[400]

484.360. (a) If the defendant files and serves a claim of exemption and the plaintiff desires to oppose the claim, he shall file and serve on the defendant, not less than two days before the date set for the hearing, a notice of opposition to the claim of exemption, accompanied by an affidavit supporting any factual issues raised and points and authorities supporting any legal issues raised.

(b) If the defendant files and serves a claim of exemption and supporting affidavit as provided in Section 484.350 and the plaintiff does not file and serve a notice of opposition as provided in this section, no writ of attachment shall be issued as to the property claimed to be exempt. If all of the property described in the plaintiff's application is claimed to be exempt and the plaintiff does not file and serve a notice of opposition as provided in this section, no hearing shall be held and no writ of attachment shall be issued.

(c) If the plaintiff files and serves a notice of opposition to the claim as provided in this section, the defendant has the burden of proving that the property is exempt from attachment.[89]

484.370. The hearing shall be conducted in the manner prescribed in

Section 484.090 and the court shall order a writ of attachment to be issued upon the filing of an undertaking as provided by Sections 489.210 and 489.220, if it finds both of the following:
(a) A right to attach order has been issued in the action pursuant to Article 1 (commencing with Section 484.010) or the court has found pursuant to Section 485.240 that the plaintiff is entitled to a right to attach order.
(b) The defendant has failed to prove that the property sought to be attached, or the portion thereof to be described in the writ, is exempt from attachment.[101]

Article 3: Ex Parte Procedure for Obtaining Additional Writs
Article 3 added by Stats. 1974, Ch. 1516.

484.510. (a) At any time after a right to attach order has been issued under Article 1 (commencing with Section 484.010) or after the court has found pursuant to Section 485.240 that the plaintiff is entitled to a right to attach order, the plaintiff may apply for a writ of attachment under this article by filing an application which meets the requirements of Section 484.320 with the court in which the action is brought.
(b) The application shall be accompanied by an affidavit showing that the property sought to be attached is not exempt from attachment. Such affidavit may be based on the affiant's information and belief.[89]

484.520. The court shall examine the application and supporting affidavit and shall order a writ of attachment to be issued upon the filing of an undertaking as provided by Sections 489.210 and 489.220, if it finds both of the following:
(a) A right to attach order has been issued in the action pursuant to Article 1 (commencing with Section 484.010) or the court has found pursuant to Section 485.240 that the plaintiff is entitled to a right to attach order.
(b) The affidavit accompanying the application shows that the property sought to be attached, or the portion thereof to be described in the writ, is not exempt from attachment.[101]

484.530. (a) The defendant may claim an exemption as to real or personal property levied upon pursuant to a writ issued under this article by following the procedure set forth in Article 2 (commencing with Section 703.510) of Chapter 4 of Division 2 of Title 9, except that the defendant shall claim the exemption as to personal property not later than 30 days after the levying officer serves the defendant with the notice of attachment describing such property. For this purpose, references in Article 2 (commencing with Section 703.510) of Chapter 4 of Division 2 of Title 9 to the "judgment debtor" shall be deemed references to the defendant, and references to the "judgment creditor" shall be deemed references to the plaintiff.
(b) The defendant may claim the exemption provided by subdivision (b) of Section 487.020 within the time provided by subdivision (a) of this section either (1) by following the procedure set forth in Article 2 (commencing with Section 703. 510) of Chapter 4 of Division 2 of Title 9 or (2) by following the procedure set forth in subdivision (c) of Section 482.100 except that the requirement of showing

changed circumstances under subdivision (a) of Section 482.100 does not apply.
(c) Notwithstanding subdivisions (a) and (b), a claim of exemption shall be denied if the claim has been denied earlier in the action and there is no change in circumstances affecting the claim.[152]

Chapter 5: Ex Parte Hearing Procedure for Obtaining Writ of Attachment

Chapter 5 added by Stats. 1974, Ch. 1516.

Article 1: Great or Irreparable Injury Requirement

Article 1 added by Stats. 1974, Ch. 1516.

485.010. (a) Except as otherwise provided by statute, no right to attach order or writ of attachment may be issued pursuant to this chapter unless it appears from facts shown by affidavit that great or irreparable injury would result to the plaintiff if issuance of the order were delayed until the matter could be heard on notice.
(b) The requirement of subdivision (a) is satisfied if any of the following are shown:
(1) Under the circumstances of the case, it may be inferred that there is a danger that the property sought to be attached would be concealed, substantially impaired in value, or otherwise made unavailable to levy if issuance of the order were delayed until the matter could be heard on notice.
(2) Under the circumstances of the case, it may be inferred that the defendant has failed to pay the debt underlying the requested attachment and the defendant is insolvent in the sense that the defendant is generally not paying his or her debts as those debts become due, unless the debts are subject to a bona fide dispute. Plaintiff's affidavit filed in support of the ex parte attachment shall state, in addition to the requirements of Section 485.530, the known undisputed debts of the defendant, that the debts are not subject to bona fide dispute, and the basis for plaintiff's determination that the defendant's debts are undisputed.
(3) A bulk sales notice has been recorded and published pursuant to Division 6 (commencing with Section 6101) of the Commercial Code with respect to a bulk transfer by the defendant.
(4) An escrow has been opened pursuant to the provisions of Section 24074 of the Business and Professions Code with respect to the sale by the defendant of a liquor license.
(5) Any other circumstance showing that great or irreparable injury would result to the plaintiff if issuance of the order were delayed until the matter could be heard on notice.
(c) Upon a writ being issued solely on a showing under paragraph (2) of subdivision (b), if the defendant requests the court to review the issuance of the writ, the court shall conduct a hearing within five court days after the plaintiff is served with notice of the defendant's request. A writ issued solely on a showing under paragraph (3) of subdivision (b) shall be limited to the property covered by the bulk sales notice or the proceeds of the sale of such property. In addition to any other service required by this title, such writ shall be served by the levying officer on the transferee or auctioneer identified by the bulk sales notice not more than five days after the levy of such writ. A

writ issued solely on a showing under paragraph (4) of subdivision (b) shall be limited to the plaintiff's pro rata share of the proceeds of the sale in escrow.[256]

Article 2: Order Determining Right to Attach; Issuance of Writ of Attachment
Article 2 added by Stats. 1974, Ch. 1516.

485.210. (a) Upon the filing of the complaint or at any time thereafter, the plaintiff may apply pursuant to this article for a right to attach order and a writ of attachment by filing an application for the order and writ with the court in which the action is brought.
(b) The application shall satisfy the requirements of Section 484.020 and, in addition, shall include a statement showing that the requirement of Section 485.010 is satisfied.
(c) The application shall be supported by an affidavit showing all of the following:
(1) The plaintiff on the facts presented would be entitled to a judgment on the claim upon which the attachment is based.
(2) The plaintiff would suffer great or irreparable injury (within the meaning of Section 485.010) if issuance of the order were delayed until the matter could be heard on notice.
(3) The property sought to be attached is not exempt from attachment.
(d) An affidavit in support of the showing required by paragraph (3) of subdivision (c) may be based on the affiant's information and belief.[89]

485.220. (a) The court shall examine the application and supporting affidavit and, except as provided in Section 486.030, shall issue a right to attach order, which shall state the amount to be secured by the attachment, and order a writ of attachment to be issued upon the filing of an undertaking as provided by Sections 489.210 and 489.220, if it finds all of the following:
(1) The claim upon which the attachment is based is one upon which an attachment may be issued.
(2) The plaintiff has established the probable validity of the claim upon which the attachment is based
(3) The attachment is not sought for a purpose other than the recovery upon the claim upon which the attachment is based.
(4) The affidavit accompanying the application shows that the property sought to be attached, or the portion thereof to be specified in the writ, is not exempt from attachment.
(5) The plaintiff will suffer great or irreparable injury (within the meaning of Section 485.010) if issuance of the order is delayed until the matter can be heard on notice.
(6) The amount to be secured by the attachment is greater than zero
(b) If the court finds that the application and the supporting affidavit do not satisfy the requirements of Section 485.010, it shall so state and deny the order. If denial is solely on the ground that Section 485.010 is not satisfied, the court shall so state and such denial does not preclude the plaintiff from applying for a right to attach order and writ of attachment under Chapter 4 (commencing with Section 484.010) with the same affidavits and supporting papers.[380]

485.230. Where a right to attach order has been issued by the court, a plaintiff may discover, through any means provided for by, and subject to the protections included in, Title 4 (commencing with Section 2016.010) of Part 4, the identity, location, and value of property in which the defendant has an interest.[548]

485.240. (a) Any defendant whose property has been attached pursuant to a writ issued under this chapter may apply for an order (1) that the right to attach order be set aside, the writ of attachment quashed, and any property levied upon pursuant to the writ be released, or (2) that the amount to be secured by the attachment be reduced as provided in Section 483.015. Such application shall be made by filing with the court and serving on the plaintiff a notice of motion.
(b) The notice of motion shall state the grounds on which the motion is based and shall be accompanied by an affidavit supporting any factual issues raised and points and authorities supporting any legal issues raised. It shall not be grounds to set aside an order that the plaintiff would not have suffered great or irreparable injury (within the meaning of Section 485.010) if issuance of the order had been delayed until the matter could have been heard on notice.
(c) At the hearing on the motion, the court shall determine whether the plaintiff is entitled to the right to attach order or whether the amount to be secured by the attachment should be reduced. If the court finds that the plaintiff is not entitled to the right to attach order, it shall order the right to attach order set aside, the writ of attachment quashed, and any property levied on pursuant to the writ released. If the court finds that the plaintiff is entitled to the right to attach order, thereafter the plaintiff may apply for additional writs pursuant to Article 2 (commencing with Section 484.310) or Article 3 (commencing with Section 484.510) of Chapter 4.
(d) The court's determinations shall be made upon the basis of the pleadings and other papers in the record; but, upon good cause shown, the court may receive and consider at the hearing additional evidence, oral or documentary, and additional points and authorities, or it may continue the hearing for the production of such additional evidence or points and authorities.
(e) The hearing provided for in this section shall take precedence over all other civil matters on the calendar of that day except older matters of the same character.[177]

Article 3: Procedure for Obtaining Additional Writs
Article 3 added by Stats. 1974, Ch. 1516.

485.510. At any time after a right to attach order and writ of attachment have been issued under Article 2 (commencing with Section 485.210), the plaintiff may apply for an additional writ of attachment under this article by filing an application with the court in which the action is brought.[89]

485.520. The application shall be executed under oath and shall include all of the following:
(a) A statement that the plaintiff has been issued a right to attach order and writ of attachment pursuant to Article 2 (commencing with Section 485.210) in the action.

(b) A statement of the amount to be secured by the attachment under the right to attach order.
(c) A description of the property to be attached under the writ of attachment and a statement that the plaintiff is informed and believes that the property is not exempt from attachment. The description shall satisfy the requirements of Section 484.020.
(d) A statement showing that the requirement of Section 485.010 has been satisfied.[153]

485.530. (a) The application shall be supported by an affidavit showing both of the following:
(1) The plaintiff would suffer great or irreparable injury (within the meaning of Section 485.010) if the issuance of the writ of attachment were delayed until the matter could be heard on notice.
(2) The property sought to be attached is not exempt from attachment.
(b) The affidavit in support of the showing required by paragraph (2) of subdivision (a) may be based on the affiant's information and belief.[101]

485.540. The court shall examine the application and supporting affidavit and shall order a writ of attachment to be issued upon the filing of an undertaking as provided by Sections 489.210 and 489.220, if it finds all of the following:
(a) A right to attach order has been issued in the action pursuant to Article 2 (commencing with Section 485.210).
(b) The affidavit accompanying the application shows that the property sought to be attached, or the portion thereof to be specified in the writ, is not exempt from attachment.
(c) The plaintiff will suffer great or irreparable injury (within the meaning of Section 485.010) if issuance of the writ of attachment is delayed until the matter can be heard on notice.[101]

Article 4: Claim of Exemption
Article 4 added by Stats. 1976, Ch. 437.

485.610. (a) The defendant may claim an exemption as to real or personal property levied upon pursuant to a writ of attachment issued under this chapter by following the procedure set forth in Article 2 (commencing with Section 703.510) of Chapter 4 of Division 2 of Title 9, except that the defendant shall claim the exemption as to personal property not later than 30 days after the levying officer serves the defendant with the notice of attachment describing such property and may claim an exemption for real property within the time provided in Section 487.030. For this purpose, references in Article 2 (commencing with Section 703.510) of Chapter 4 of Division 2 of Title 9 to the "judgment debtor" shall be deemed references to the defendant, and references to the "judgment creditor" shall be deemed references to the plaintiff.
(b) The defendant may claim the exemption provided by subdivision (b) of Section 487.020 within the time provided by subdivision (a) of this section either (1) by following the procedure set forth in Article 2 (commencing with Section 703. 510) of Chapter 4 of Division 2 of Title 9 or (2) by following the procedure set forth in subdivision (c) of Section 482.100 except that the requirement of showing changed circumstances under subdivision (a) of Section 482.100 does not apply.[204]

Chapter 6: Temporary Protective Order

Chapter 6 added by Stats. 1974, Ch. 1516.

486.010. (a) At the time of applying for a right to attach order under Chapter 4 (commencing with Section 484.010), the plaintiff may apply pursuant to this chapter for a temporary protective order by filing an application for the order with the court in which the action is brought.
(b) The application shall state what relief is requested and shall be supported by an affidavit, which may be based on information and belief, showing that the plaintiff would suffer great or irreparable injury (within the meaning of Section 485.010) if the temporary protective order were not issued.[89]

486.020. The court shall examine the application, supporting affidavit, and other papers on record and shall issue a temporary protective order, which shall state the amount sought to be secured by the attachment under the application for the right to attach order, upon the filing of an undertaking as provided by Sections 489.210 and 489.220, if it finds all of the following:
(a) The claim upon which the application for attachment is based is one upon which an attachment may be issued.
(b) The plaintiff has established the probable validity of the claim upon which the application for the attachment is based.
(c) The order is not sought for a purpose other than the recovery upon the claim upon which the application for the attachment is based.
(d) The plaintiff will suffer great or irreparable injury (within the meaning of Section 485.010) if the temporary protective order is not issued.[154]

486.030. (a) In any case where the plaintiff has applied for a right to attach order and writ of attachment under Chapter 5 (commencing with Section 485.010), the court may in its discretion deny the application for the order and writ and issue instead a temporary protective order under this chapter if it determines that the requirements of Section 485.220 are satisfied but that the issuance of the temporary protective order instead of the right to attach order and writ would be in the interest of justice and equity to the parties, taking into account the effect on the defendant of issuing a writ of attachment ex parte, the effect on the plaintiff of issuing the temporary protective order instead of the writ, and other factors that bear on equity and justice under the circumstances of the particular case.
(b) If the court issues a temporary protective order under this section, the plaintiff's application for a right to attach order and writ shall be treated as an application for a right to attach order and writ under Article 1 (commencing with Section 484.010) of Chapter 4 and the plaintiff shall comply with the requirements of service provided in Section 484.040.[89]

486.040. The temporary protective order issued under this chapter shall contain such provisions as the court determines would be in the interest of justice and equity to the parties, taking into account the effects on both the defendant and the plaintiff under the circumstances of the particular case.[89]

486.050. (a) Except as otherwise provided in Section 486.040, the temporary protective order may prohibit a transfer by the defendant of any of the defendant's property in this state subject to the levy of the writ of attachment. The temporary protective order shall describe the property in a manner adequate to permit the defendant to identify the property subject to the temporary protective order.

(b) Notwithstanding subdivision (a), if the property is farm products held for sale or is inventory, the temporary protective order shall not prohibit the defendant from transferring the property in the ordinary course of business, but the temporary protective order may impose appropriate restrictions on the disposition of the proceeds from that type of transfer.[610]

486.060. (a) Notwithstanding any terms of the temporary protective order, the defendant may issue any number of checks against any of the defendant's accounts in a financial institution in this state to the extent permitted by this section.

(b) The defendant may issue any number of checks in any amount for the following purposes:

(1) Payment of any payroll expense (including fringe benefits and taxes and premiums for workers' compensation and unemployment insurance) falling due in the ordinary course of business prior to the levy of a writ of attachment.

(2) Payment for goods thereafter delivered to the defendant C.O.D. for use in the defendant's trade, business, or profession.

(3) Payment of taxes if payment is necessary to avoid penalties which will accrue if there is any further delay in payment.

(4) Payment of reasonable legal fees and reasonable costs and expenses required for the representation of the defendant in the action.

(c) In addition to the checks permitted to be issued by subdivision (b), the defendant may issue any number of checks for any purpose so long as the total amount of the checks does not exceed the greater of the following:

(1) The amount by which the total amount on deposit exceeds the sum of the amount sought to be secured by the attachment and the amounts permitted to be paid pursuant to subdivision (b).

(2) One thousand dollars ($1,000).[155]

486.070. Except as otherwise provided by Section 486.110, a temporary protective order issued under this chapter binds only the defendant, whether or not any other person knows of or is served with a copy of the temporary protective order.[101]

486.080. The temporary protective order shall be personally served on the defendant together with the documents referred to in Section 484.040.[156]

486.090. Except as otherwise provided in this title, the temporary protective order shall expire at the earliest of the following times:

(a) Forty days after the issuance of the order or, if an earlier date is prescribed by the court in the order, on such earlier date.

(b) As to specific property described in the order, when a levy of attachment upon that property is made by the plaintiff.[101]

486.100. Upon ex parte application of the defendant or, if the court so orders, after a noticed hearing, the court may modify or vacate the temporary protective order if it determines that such action would be in the interest of justice and equity to the parties, taking into account the effect on the defendant of the continuance of the original order, the effect on the plaintiff of modifying or vacating the order, and any other factors.[89]

486.110. (a) The service upon the defendant of a temporary protective order pursuant to Section 486.080 creates a lien upon any property, or the proceeds thereof, which is described in the order, is owned by the defendant at the time of such service, and is subject to attachment pursuant to this title. The lien continues on property subject to the lien, notwithstanding the transfer or encumbrance of the property subject to the lien, unless the person receiving the property, whether real or personal, is a person listed in Section 697.740.
(b) The lien terminates upon the date of expiration of the temporary protective order except with respect to property levied upon while the temporary protective order is in effect under a writ of attachment issued upon application of the plaintiff.[205]

Chapter 7: Property Subject to Attachment

Chapter 7 added by Stats. 1974, Ch. 1516.

487.010. The following property of the defendant is subject to attachment:
(a) Where the defendant is a corporation, all corporate property for which a method of levy is provided by Article 2 (commencing with Section 488.300) of Chapter 8.
(b) Where the defendant is a partnership or other unincorporated association, all partnership or association property for which a method of levy is provided by Article 2 (commencing with Section 488.300) of Chapter 8.
(c) Where the defendant is a natural person, all of the following property:
(1) Interests in real property except leasehold estates with unexpired terms of less than one year.
(2) Accounts receivable, chattel paper, and general intangibles arising out of the conduct by the defendant of a trade, business, or profession, except any such individual claim with a principal balance of less than one hundred fifty dollars ($150).
(3) Equipment.
(4) Farm products.
(5) Inventory.
(6) Final money judgments arising out of the conduct by the defendant of a trade, business, or profession.
(7) Money on the premises where a trade, business, or profession is conducted by the defendant and, except for the first one thousand dollars ($1,000), money located elsewhere than on such premises and deposit accounts, but, if the defendant has more than one deposit account or has at least one deposit account and money located elsewhere than on the premises where a trade, business, or profession is conducted by the defendant, the court, upon application of the plaintiff, may order that the writ of attachment be levied so that an aggregate amount of one thousand dollars ($1,000) in the form of such money and in such accounts remains free of levy.
(8) Negotiable documents of title.
(9) Instruments.

(10) Securities.

(11) Minerals or the like (including oil and gas) to be extracted.

(d) In the case of a defendant described in subdivision (c), community property of a type described in subdivision (c) is subject to attachment if the community property would be subject to enforcement of the judgment obtained in the action in which the attachment is sought. Unless the provision or context otherwise requires, if community property that is subject to attachment is sought to be attached:

(1) Any provision of this title that applies to the property of the defendant or to obligations owed to the defendant also applies to the community property interest of the spouse of the defendant and to obligations owed to either spouse that are community property.

(2) Any provision of this title that applies to property in the possession or under the control of the defendant also applies to community property in the possession or under the control of the spouse of the defendant.[157]

487.020. Except as provided in paragraph (2) of subdivision (a) of Section 3439.07 of the Civil Code, the following property is exempt from attachment:

(a) All property exempt from enforcement of a money judgment.

(b) Property which is necessary for the support of a defendant who is a natural person or the family of such defendant supported in whole or in part by the defendant.

(c) "Earnings" as defined by Section 706.011.

(d) All property not subject to attachment pursuant to Section 487.010.[238]

487.025. (a) The recording of a homestead declaration (as defined in Section 704.910) does not limit or affect the right of a plaintiff to attach the declared homestead described in the homestead declaration, whether the homestead declaration is recorded before or after the declared homestead is attached.

(b) An attachment lien attaches to a homestead (as defined in Section 704.710) in the amount of any surplus over the total of the following:

(1) All liens and encumbrances on the homestead at the time the attachment lien is created.

(2) The homestead exemption set forth in Section 704.730.

(c) Nothing in subdivision (a) or (b) limits the right of the defendant to an exemption under subdivision (b) of Section 487.020.

(d) Notwithstanding subdivision (b), a homestead (as defined in Section 704.710) is exempt from sale to the extent provided in Section 704.800 when it is sought to be sold to enforce the judgment obtained in the action in which the attachment was obtained.

(Added by Stats. 1982, Ch. 1198, Sec. 47.5. Operative July 1, 1983, by Sec. 70 of Ch. 1198.)

487.030. (a) At any time prior to the entry of judgment in the action, the defendant may claim any exemption provided by subdivision (a) of Section 487.020 with respect to real property by following the procedure set forth in Article 2 (commencing with Section 703.510) of Chapter 4 of Division 2 of Title 9. A claim of exemption under this subdivision shall be denied if the claim has been denied earlier in the action.

(b) At any time prior to the entry of judgment in the action, the defendant may claim the exemption provided by subdivision (b) of Section 487.020 with respect to real property either (1) by following the procedure set forth in Article 2 (commencing with Section 703.510) of Chapter 4 of Division 2 of Title 9 or (2) by following the procedure set forth in subdivision (c) of Section 482.100 except that the requirement of showing changed circumstances under subdivision (a) of Section 482.100 does not apply. A claim of exemption under this subdivision shall be denied if the claim has been denied earlier in the action and there is no change in circumstances affecting the claim.
(c) For the purposes of this section, references in Article 2 (commencing with Section 703.510) of Chapter 4 of Division 2 of Title 9 to the "judgment debtor" shall be deemed references to the defendant, and references to the "judgment creditor" shall be deemed references to the plaintiff.
(d) Nothing in this section limits the right to claim after the entry of judgment a homestead exemption for real property under Article 4 (commencing with Section 704.710) of Chapter 4 of Division 2 of Title 9 unless prior to entry of judgment the defendant has claimed the exemption provided by subdivision (a) of Section 487.020 with respect to such property and the claim has been denied.[158]

Chapter 8: Levy Procedures; Lien of Attachment; Management and Disposition of Attached Property

Chapter 8 repealed and added by Stats. 1982, Ch. 1198, Sec. 50.

Article 1: General Provisions

Article 1 added by Stats. 1982, Ch. 1198, Sec. 50.

488.010. The writ of attachment shall include the following information:
(a) The date of issuance of the writ.
(b) The title of the court that issued the writ and the cause and number of the action.
(c) The name and address of the plaintiff and the name and last known address of the defendant.
(d) The amount to be secured by the attachment.
(e) A description of the property to be levied upon to satisfy the attachment.[160]

488.020. (a) A writ of attachment shall be directed to a levying officer in the county in which property of the defendant described in the writ may be located and to any registered process server.
(b) Upon the receipt of written instructions from the plaintiff's attorney of record or, if the plaintiff has no attorney of record, from the plaintiff, the levying officer to whom the writ is directed and delivered shall levy the writ without delay in the manner provided in this chapter on the property described in the writ or so much thereof as is clearly sufficient to satisfy the amount to be secured by the attachment. The levying officer is not liable for a determination made in good faith under this subdivision.

(c) If a copy of the summons and complaint has not previously been served on the defendant, the instructions to the levying officer shall instruct the levying officer to make the service at the same time the levying officer serves the defendant with a copy of the writ of attachment.[160]

488.030. (a) The plaintiff shall give the levying officer instructions in writing. The instructions shall be signed by the plaintiff's attorney of record or, if the plaintiff does not have an attorney of record, by the plaintiff. The instructions shall contain the information needed or requested by the levying officer to comply with the provisions of this title, including but not limited to:

(1) An adequate description of any property to be levied upon.

(2) A statement whether the property is a dwelling.

(3) If the property is a dwelling, whether it is real or personal property.

(b) Subject to subdivision (c), the levying officer shall act in accordance with the written instructions to the extent the actions are taken in conformance with the provisions of this title.

(c) Except to the extent the levying officer has actual knowledge that the information is incorrect, the levying officer may rely on any information contained in the written instructions.[160]

488.040. (a) If the levying officer is required by any provision of this title to serve any writ, order, notice, or other paper on any person, the plaintiff shall include in the instructions to the levying officer the correct name and address of the person. The plaintiff shall use reasonable diligence to ascertain the correct name and address of the person.

(b) Unless the levying officer has actual knowledge that the name or address included in the instructions is incorrect, the levying officer shall rely on the instructions in serving the writ, order, notice, or other paper on the person.[160]

488.050. (a) Except as otherwise provided by law:

(1) As a prerequisite to the performance by the levying officer of a duty under this title, the plaintiff shall deposit a sum of money with the levying officer sufficient to pay the costs of performing the duty.

(2) As a prerequisite to the taking of property into custody by the levying officer under this chapter, whether by keeper or otherwise, the plaintiff shall deposit with the levying officer a sum of money sufficient to pay the costs of taking the property and keeping it safely for a period not to exceed 15 days. If continuation of the custody of the property is required, the levying officer shall, from time to time, demand orally or in writing that the plaintiff deposit additional amounts to cover estimated costs for periods not to exceed 30 days each. A written demand may be mailed or delivered to the plaintiff. The plaintiff has not less than three business days after receipt of the demand within which to comply with the demand. If the amount demanded is not paid within the time specified in the oral or written demand, the levying officer shall release the property.

(b) The levying officer is not liable for failure to take or hold property unless the plaintiff has complied with the provisions of this section.[160]

488.060. The notice of attachment

shall inform the person notified of all of the following:
(a) The capacity in which the person is notified.
(b) The specific property which is sought to be attached.
(c) The person's rights under the attachment, including the right to make a third-party claim pursuant to Division 4 (commencing with Section 720.010) of Title 9.
(d) The person's duties under the attachment.[160]

488.065. A copy of the original notice of attachment which has been served upon a third party holding the property sought to be attached, if served upon the defendant or any other party, shall suffice as the notice of attachment to that person.[224]

488.070. If a writ of attachment has been issued and personal property sought to be attached under the writ is located in a private place of the defendant:
(a) The levying officer shall comply with the provisions of Section 699.030.
(b) The plaintiff may obtain the relief provided under Section 699.030 in the manner and subject to the requirements of that section.[160]

488.080. (a) A registered process server may levy under a writ of attachment on the following types of property:
(1) Real property, pursuant to Section 488.315.
(2) Growing crops, timber to be cut, or minerals or the like, including oil and gas, to be extracted or accounts receivable resulting from the sale thereof at the wellhead or minehead, pursuant to Section 488.325.
(3) Personal property in the custody of a levying officer, pursuant to Section 488.355.
(4) Equipment of a going business, pursuant to Section 488.375.
(5) Motor vehicles, vessels, mobilehomes, or commercial coaches used as equipment of a going business, pursuant to Section 488.385.
(6) Farm products or inventory of a going business, pursuant to Section 488.405.
(7) Personal property used as a dwelling, pursuant to subdivision (a) of Section 700.080.
(8) Deposit accounts, pursuant to Section 488.455.
(9) Property in a safe-deposit box, pursuant to Section 488.460.
(10) Accounts receivable or general intangibles, pursuant to Section 488.470.
(11) Final money judgments, pursuant to Section 488.480.
(12) Interest of a defendant in personal property in the estate of a decedent, pursuant to Section 488.485.
(b) Before levying under the writ of attachment, the registered process server shall cause to be deposited with the levying officer a copy of the writ and the fee, as provided by Section 26721 of the Government Code.
(c) If a registered process server levies on property pursuant to subdivision (a), the registered process server shall do both of the following:
(1) Comply with the applicable levy, posting, and service provisions of Article 2 (commencing with Section 488.300).
(2) Request any third person served to give a garnishee's memorandum to the levying officer in compliance with Section 488.610 on a form provided by the registered process server.

(d) Within five court days after levy under this section, all of the following shall be filed with the levying officer:

(1) The writ of attachment.

(2) A proof of service by the registered process server stating the manner of levy performed.

(3) Proof of service of the copy of the writ and notice of attachment on other persons, as required by Article 2 (commencing with Section 488.300).

(4) Instructions in writing, as required by the provisions of Section 488.030.

(e) If the fee provided by Section 26721 of the Government Code has been paid, the levying officer shall perform all other duties under the writ as if the levying officer had levied under the writ and shall return the writ to the court. If the registered process server does not comply with subdivisions (b) and (d), the levy is ineffective and the levying officer shall not be required to perform any duties under the writ, and may issue a release for any property sought to be attached. The levying officer is not liable for actions taken in conformance with the provisions of this title in reliance on information provided to the levying officer under subdivision (d), except to the extent that the levying officer has actual knowledge that the information is incorrect. Nothing in this subdivision limits any liability the plaintiff or registered process server may have if the levying officer acts on the basis of incorrect information provided under subdivision (d).

(f) The fee for services of a registered process server under this section is a recoverable cost pursuant to Section 1033.5.[726]

488.090. Except as otherwise provided by statute, where the method of levy upon property requires that property be taken into custody or where the levying officer is otherwise directed to take property into custody, the levying officer may do so by any of the following methods:

(a) Removing the property to a place of safekeeping.

(b) Installing a keeper.

(c) Otherwise obtaining possession or control of the property.[160]

488.100. The levying officer has a special lien, dependent upon possession, on personal property levied upon in the amount of the levying officer's costs for which an advance has not been made.[159]

488.110. A third person shall claim an interest in property attached in the manner provided for third-party claims under Division 4 (commencing with Section 720.010) of Title 9.[159]

488.120. In any case where property has been levied upon and, pursuant to a levy, a copy of the writ of attachment and a notice of attachment are required by statute to be posted or to be served on or mailed to the defendant or other person, failure to post, serve, or mail the copy of the writ and the notice does not affect the attachment lien created by the levy.[159]

488.130. (a) The levying officer to whom the writ of attachment is delivered shall return the writ to the court from which the writ issued, together with a report of the levying officer's actions. The return shall be made promptly in accordance with the plaintiff's instructions given to the levying officer but in no event later than 60 days after the levying officer receives the writ.

(b) The levying officer shall make a full inventory of property attached and return the inventory with the writ.[159]

488.140. (a) The levying officer or registered process server is not liable for actions taken in conformance with the provisions of this title, including actions taken in conformance with the provisions of this title in reliance on information contained in the written instructions of the plaintiff except to the extent the levying officer or registered process server has actual knowledge that the information is incorrect. Nothing in this subdivision limits any liability the plaintiff may have if the levying officer or registered process server acts on the basis of incorrect information given in the written instructions.

(b) Unless the levying officer is negligent in the care or handling of the property, the levying officer is not liable to either the plaintiff or the defendant for loss by fire, theft, injury, or damage of any kind to personal property while (1) in the possession of the levying officer either in a warehouse or other storage place or in the custody of a keeper or (2) in transit to or from a warehouse or other storage place.[178]

Article 2: Methods of Levy
Article 2 added by Stats. 1982, Ch. 1198, Sec. 50.

488.300. If the method of levy under a writ of execution is incorporated by this article, for the purposes of this article references in Article 4 (commencing with Section 700.010) of Chapter 3 of Division 2 of Title 9 to:

(a) "Judgment creditor" shall be deemed references to the plaintiff.

(b) "Judgment debtor" shall be deemed references to the defendant.

(c) "Notice of levy" shall be deemed references to a notice of attachment.

(d) "Writ" shall be deemed references to a writ of attachment.[159]

488.305. At the time of levy pursuant to this article or promptly thereafter, the levying officer shall serve a copy of the writ of attachment and a notice of attachment on the defendant.[159]

488.315. To attach real property, the levying officer shall comply with Section 700.015 and the recorder shall index the copy of the writ of attachment and a notice of attachment as provided in that section.[159]

488.325. To attach (1) growing crops, (2) timber to be cut, or (3) minerals or the like (including oil and gas) to be extracted or accounts receivable resulting from the sale thereof at the wellhead or minehead, the levying officer shall comply with Section 700.020 and the recorder shall index the copy of the writ of attachment and a notice of attachment as provided in that section.[159]

488.335. Unless another method of attachment is provided by this article, to attach tangible personal property in the possession or under the control of the defendant, the levying officer shall take the property into custody.[159]

488.345. Unless another method of attachment is provided by this article, to attach tangible personal property in the possession or under the control of a third person, the levying officer shall comply with Section 700.040.[159]

488.355. (a) To attach personal property in the custody of a levying officer, the plaintiff or levying officer shall comply with subdivision (a) of Section 700.050.

(b) The levying officer having custody of the property shall comply with the writs in the order they are received and is not subject to the provisions of Article 4 (commencing with Section 488.600).[159]

488.365. To attach goods in the possession of a bailee (as defined in Section 7102 of the Commercial Code) other than one who has issued a negotiable document of title therefor, the levying officer shall comply with Section 700.060.[159]

488.375. (a) Except as provided by Section 488.385, to attach equipment of a going business in the possession or under the control of the defendant, the levying officer shall file with the office of the Secretary of State a notice of attachment, in the form prescribed by the Secretary of State, which shall contain all of the following:

(1) The name and mailing address of the plaintiff.

(2) The name and last known mailing address of the defendant.

(3) The title of the court where the action is pending and the cause and number of the action.

(4) A description of the specific property attached.

(5) A statement that the plaintiff has acquired an attachment lien on the specified property of the defendant.

(b) Upon presentation of a notice of attachment under this section for filing, and tender of the filing fee to the office of the Secretary of State, the notice of attachment shall be filed, marked, and indexed in the same manner as a financing statement. The fee for filing in the office of the Secretary of State is the same as the fee for filing a financing statement in the standard form.

(c) Upon the request of any person, the Secretary of State shall issue a certificate showing whether there is on file in that office on the date and hour stated therein any notice of attachment filed against the equipment of a particular person named in the request. If a notice of attachment is on file, the certificate shall state the date and hour of filing of each such notice and any notice affecting any such notice of attachment and the name and address of the plaintiff. Upon request, the Secretary of State shall furnish a copy of any notice of attachment or notice affecting a notice of attachment. The certificate shall be issued as part of a combined certificate pursuant to Section 9528 of the Commercial Code, and the fee for the certificate and copies shall be in accordance with that section.

(d) The fee for filing, indexing, and furnishing filing data for a notice of extension of attachment is the same as the fee for a continuation statement under Section 9525 of the Commercial Code. The fee for filing, indexing, and furnishing filing data for a notice of release of attachment is the same as the fee for a statement of release under Section 9525 of the Commercial Code.

(e) If property subject to an attachment lien under this section becomes a fixture (as defined in paragraph (41) of subdivision (a) of Section 9102 of the Commercial Code), the attachment lien under this section is extinguished.[786]

488.385. (a) To attach a vehicle or vessel for which a certificate of ownership has been issued by the Department of

Motor Vehicles, or a mobilehome or commercial coach for which a certificate of title has been issued by the Department of Housing and Community Development, which is equipment of a going business in the possession or under the control of the defendant, the levying officer shall file with the appropriate department a notice of attachment, in the form prescribed by the appropriate department, which shall contain all of the following:

(1) The name and mailing address of the plaintiff.

(2) The name and last known mailing address of the defendant.

(3) The title of the court where the action is pending and the cause and number of the action.

(4) A description of the specific property attached.

(5) A statement that the plaintiff has acquired an attachment lien on the specific property of the defendant.

(b) Upon presentation of a notice of attachment, notice of extension, or notice of release under this section for filing and tender of the filing fee to the appropriate department, the notice shall be filed and indexed. The fee for filing and indexing the notice is fifteen dollars ($15).

(c) Upon the request of any person, the department shall issue its certificate showing whether there is on file in that department on the date and hour stated therein any notice of attachment filed against the property of a particular person named in the request. If a notice of attachment is on file, the certificate shall state the date and hour of filing of each such notice of attachment and any notice affecting any such notice of attachment and the name and address of the plaintiff. The fee for the certificate issued pursuant to this subdivision is fifteen dollars ($15). Upon request, the department shall furnish a copy of any notice of attachment or notice affecting a notice of attachment for a fee of one dollar ($1) per page.

(d) If property subject to an attachment lien under this section becomes a fixture (as defined in paragraph (41) of subdivision (a) of Section 9102 of the Commercial Code), the attachment lien under this section is extinguished.[539]

488.395. Except as specified in subdivision (e) and as provided by Sections 488.325 and 488.405:

(a) To attach farm products or inventory of a going business in the possession or under the control of the defendant, the levying officer shall place a keeper in charge of the property for the period prescribed by subdivisions (b) and (c). During the keeper period, the business may continue to operate in the ordinary course of business provided that all sales are final and are for cash or its equivalent. For the purpose of this subdivision, a check is the equivalent of cash. The levying officer is not liable for accepting payment in the form of a cash equivalent. The keeper shall take custody of the proceeds from all sales unless otherwise directed by the plaintiff.

(b) Subject to subdivision (c), the period during which the business may continue to operate under the keeper is:

(1) Ten days, if the defendant is a natural person and the writ of attachment has been issued ex parte pursuant to Article 3 (commencing with Section 484.510) of Chapter 4 or pursuant to Chapter 5 (commencing with Section 485.010).

(2) Two days, in cases not described in paragraph (1).

(c) Unless some other disposition is agreed upon by the plaintiff and the defendant, the levying officer shall take the farm products or inventory into exclusive custody at the earlier of the following times:

(1) At any time the defendant objects to placement of a keeper in charge of the business.

(2) At the conclusion of the applicable period prescribed by subdivision (b).

(d) A defendant described in paragraph (1) of subdivision (b) may claim an exemption pursuant to subdivision (b) of Section 487.020 by following the procedure set forth in subdivision (c) of Section 482.100 except that the requirement of showing changed circumstances under subdivision (a) of Section 482.100 does not apply. Upon a showing that the property is exempt pursuant to subdivision (b) of Section 487.020, the court shall order the release of the exempt property and may make such further order as the court deems appropriate to protect against frustration of the collection of the plaintiff's claim. The order may permit the plaintiff to attach farm products or inventory of the going business and proceeds or after-acquired property, or both, by filing pursuant to Section 488.405 and may provide reasonable restrictions on the disposition of the property previously attached.

(e) This section does not apply to the placement of a keeper in a business for the purpose of attaching tangible personal property consisting solely of money or equivalent proceeds of sales, which shall be conducted in the same manner as provided in Section 700.070.[374]

488.405. (a) This section provides an alternative method of attaching farm products or inventory of a going business in the possession or under the control of the defendant, but this section does not apply to property described in Section 488.325. This section applies if the plaintiff instructs the levying officer to attach the farm products or inventory under this section.

(b) To attach under this section farm products or inventory of a going business in the possession or under the control of the defendant, the levying officer shall file a notice of attachment with the Secretary of State.

(c) Except as provided in subdivisions (d) and (e), the filing of the notice of attachment gives the plaintiff an attachment lien on all of the following:

(1) The farm products or inventory described in the notice.

(2) Identifiable cash proceeds (as that term is used in Section 9315 of the Commercial Code).

(3) If permitted by the writ of attachment or court order, after-acquired property.

(d) The attachment lien created by the filing of the notice of attachment under this section does not extend to either of the following:

(1) A vehicle or vessel required to be registered with the Department of Motor Vehicles or a mobilehome or commercial coach required to be registered pursuant to the Health and Safety Code.

(2) The inventory of a retail merchant held for sale except to the extent that the inventory of the retail merchant consists of durable goods having a unit retail value of at least five hundred dollars ($500). For the purposes of this paragraph, "retail merchant"

does not include (A) a person whose sales for resale exceeded 75 percent in dollar volume of the person's total sales of all goods during the 12 months preceding the filing of the notice of attachment or (B) a cooperative association organized pursuant to Chapter 1 (commencing with Section 54001) of Division 20 of the Food and Agricultural Code (agricultural cooperative associations) or Part 3 (commencing with Section 13200) of Division 3 of Title 1 of the Corporations Code (Fish Marketing Act).

(e) If property subject to an attachment lien under this section becomes a fixture (as defined in paragraph (41) of subdivision (a) of Section 9102 of the Commercial Code), the attachment lien under this section is extinguished.

(f) The notice of attachment shall be in the form prescribed by the Secretary of State and shall contain all of the following:

(1) The name and mailing address of the plaintiff.

(2) The name and last known mailing address of the defendant.

(3) The title of the court where the action is pending and the cause and number of the action.

(4) A description of the farm products and inventory attached.

(5) A statement that the plaintiff has acquired an attachment lien on the described property and on identifiable cash proceeds (as that term is used in Section 9315 of the Commercial Code) and, if permitted by the writ of attachment or court order, on after-acquired property.

(g) Upon presentation of a notice of attachment under this section for filing and tender of the filing fee to the office of the Secretary of State, the notice of attachment shall be filed, marked, and indexed in the same manner as a financing statement. The fee for filing in the office of the Secretary of State is the same as the fee for filing a financing statement in the standard form.

(h) Upon the request of any person, the Secretary of State shall issue a certificate showing whether there is on file in that office on the date and hour stated therein any notice of attachment filed against the farm products or inventory of a particular person named in the request. If a notice of attachment is on file, the certificate shall state the date and hour of filing of each such notice of attachment and any notice affecting any such notice of attachment and the name and address of the plaintiff. Upon request, the Secretary of State shall furnish a copy of any notice of attachment or notice affecting a notice of attachment. The certificate shall be issued as part of a combined certificate pursuant to Section 9528 of the Commercial Code, and the fee for the certificate and copies shall be in accordance with that section.

(i) The fee for filing, indexing, and furnishing filing data for a notice of extension of attachment is the same as the fee for a continuation statement under Section 9525 of the Commercial Code. The fee for filing, indexing, and furnishing filing data for a notice of release of attachment is the same as the fee for a statement of release under Section 9525 of the Commercial Code.[787]

488.415. To attach personal property used as a dwelling, the levying officer shall comply with Section 700.080.[159]

488.425. If a vehicle or vessel is attached and a certificate of ownership has been issued by the Department of Motor Vehicles for the vehicle or vessel and the certificate of ownership is still in effect, or if a mobilehome or commercial coach is attached and a certificate of title has been issued by the Department of Housing and Community Development for the mobilehome or commercial coach and the certificate of title is still in effect, the levying officer shall comply with Section 700.090.[159]

488.435. (a) To attach chattel paper, the levying officer shall comply with Section 700.100.
(b) In addition to any other rights created by a levy on chattel paper, the levy creates a lien on the defendant's rights in specific goods subject to the chattel paper.[159]

488.440. To attach an instrument, the levying officer shall comply with Section 700.110.[159]

488.445. To attach a negotiable document of title, the levying officer shall comply with Section 700.120.[159]

488.450. To attach a security, the levying officer shall comply with Section 8112 of the Commercial Code. The legal process referred to in Section 8112 of the Commercial Code means the legal process required by the state in which the chief executive office of the issuer of the security is located and, where that state is California, means personal service by the levying officer of a copy of the writ of attachment and notice of attachment on the person who is to be served.[359]

488.455. (a) Subject to Sections 488.465 and 684.115, to attach a deposit account, the levying officer shall personally serve a copy of the writ of attachment and a notice of attachment on the financial institution with which the deposit account is maintained.
(b) The attachment lien that arises upon service of a writ of attachment and notice of attachment reaches only amounts in a deposit account at the time of service on the financial institution, including the amount of any deposit not yet finally collected, unless the deposit is returned unpaid to the financial institution.
(c) The levying officer shall serve a copy of the writ of attachment and a notice of attachment on any third person in whose name any deposit account described therein stands. That service shall be made personally or by mail as follows:
(1) At the time of levy or promptly thereafter, if the party seeking the levy informs the levying officer of that person and his, her, or its residence or business address.
(2) Promptly following the levying officer's receipt of a garnishee's memorandum if service was not accomplished pursuant to paragraph (1), if the garnishee's memorandum identifies that person and his, her, or its residence or business address.
(d) The financial institution shall not honor a withdrawal request or a check or other order for the payment of money from the deposit account if presentation of that withdrawal request or item to the financial institution occurs during the time the attachment lien is in effect unless, following that withdrawal or payment, sufficient funds are available to cover the levy. For these purposes, a withdrawal from the deposit account to cover the financial institution's standard fee or charge for processing the levy shall not be

considered a payment of money from the account in violation of this subdivision.

(e) During the time the attachment lien is in effect, the financial institution is not liable to any person for any of the following:

(1) Performance of the duties of a garnishee under the levy.

(2) Nonpayment of a check or other order for the payment or transfer of money drawn or presented against the deposit account if the nonpayment is pursuant to the requirements of subdivision (d).

(3) Refusal to pay a withdrawal from the deposit account if the refusal is pursuant to the requirements of subdivision (d).

(f) For the purposes of this section, none of the following is a third person in whose name the deposit account stands:

(1) A person who is only a person named as the beneficiary of a Totten trust account.

(2) A person who is only a payee designated in a pay-on-death provision in an account pursuant to Section 18318.5 of the Financial Code or Section 5140 of the Probate Code, or other similar provision.

(3) A person who is only acting in a representative or custodial capacity with respect to benefits paid or payable by the United States government. Rather, accounts maintained by the representative or custodian shall be deemed to stand in that beneficiary's name, and the amounts therein shall be covered by a levy against that beneficiary.

(g) For purposes of this section, final payment of a deposit shall be deemed to have occurred in accordance with Section 4215 or 11210 of the Commercial Code or with automated clearinghouse or Federal Reserve System rule, regulation, operating circular, or similar governing document, as applicable to the deposit. If, for any reason, a deposit is returned by the financial institution upon which it is drawn, that deposit shall not be deemed finally collected for purposes of this subdivision regardless of any later payment by the financial institution upon which the deposit is drawn.

(h) When a deposit account has been attached, as an alternative to paying the amount of the deposit account that is attached to the levying officer as required by Section 488.600, the financial institution may continue to hold the deposit account until the deposit account is levied upon after judgment in the action or is earlier released, the deposit account to be held in one of the following manners:

(1) If the entire deposit account is attached, the financial institution may hold the deposit account on the terms applicable before the attachment, subject to the requirements of subdivision (d).

(2) If less than the entire deposit account is attached:

(A) With the consent of the defendant, and any third person in whose name the deposit account stands, the financial institution may hold in the deposit account on the same terms an amount larger than the attached amount as necessary to avoid a penalty or a reduction of the rate of interest.

(B) If the defendant, and any third person in whose name the deposit account stands, do not consent as provided in subparagraph (A), the financial institution may hold the attached amount on the same terms affecting the deposit account before the attachment, subject to the requirements of subdivision (d).

(3) The financial institution may hold the attached deposit account in any other manner agreed upon by the plaintiff, the defendant, and any third person in whose name the deposit account stands.

(i) Subdivision (h) does not prevent a financial institution that is holding an attached deposit account as provided in subdivision (h) from paying the attached amount to the levying officer before the time the financial institution otherwise is required to pay the amount under subdivision (h).[672]

488.460. (a) Subject to Sections 488.465 and 684.115, to attach property in a safe-deposit box, the levying officer shall personally serve a copy of the writ of attachment and a notice of attachment on the financial institution with which the safe-deposit box is maintained.

(b) At the time of levy or promptly thereafter, the levying officer shall serve a copy of the writ of attachment and a notice of attachment on any third person in whose name the safe-deposit box stands.

(c) During the time the attachment lien is in effect, the financial institution may not permit the removal of any of the contents of the safe-deposit box except as directed by the levying officer.

(d) Upon receipt of a garnishee's memorandum from the financial institution, as required by Section 488.610, indicating a safe-deposit box is under levy, the levying officer shall promptly mail a written notice to the judgment creditor demanding an additional fee as required by Section 26723 of the Government Code, plus the costs to open the safe-deposit box and seize and store the contents. The levying officer shall release the levy on the safe-deposit box if the plaintiff does not pay the required fee, plus costs, within three business days plus the extended time period specified in subdivision (a) of Section 1013 for service by mail by the levying officer.

(e) The levying officer may first give the person in whose name the safe-deposit box stands an opportunity to open the safe-deposit box to permit the removal pursuant to the attachment of the attached property. The financial institution may refuse to permit the forcible opening of the safe-deposit box to permit the removal of the attached property unless the plaintiff or levying officer pays in advance the cost of forcibly opening the safe-deposit box and of repairing any damage caused thereby.

(f) During the time the attachment lien is in effect, the financial institution is not liable to any person for any of the following:

(1) Performance of the duties of a garnishee under the attachment.

(2) Refusal to permit access to the safe-deposit box by the person in whose name it stands.

(3) Removal of any of the contents of the safe-deposit box pursuant to the attachment.

(g) If the levying officer removes any property from the safe-deposit box to satisfy the levy, but allows other property to remain in the safe-deposit box, the attachment lien is released automatically with respect to any property that remains in the safe-deposit box.[673]

488.465. (a) Except as provided in subdivision (b), a deposit account or safe-deposit box standing in the name of a person other than the defendant, either alone or together with other third persons, is not subject to levy under Section 488.455 or 488.460 unless the levy is authorized by court order. The levying officer shall serve a copy of the court order on the third person at the time the copy of the writ of attachment and the notice of attachment are served on the third person.
(b) A court order is not required as a prerequisite to levy on a deposit account or safe-deposit box standing in the name of any of the following:
(1) The defendant, whether alone or together with third persons.
(2) The defendant's spouse, whether alone or together with other third persons. An affidavit showing that the person in whose name the account stands is the defendant's spouse shall be delivered to the financial institution at the time of levy.
(3) A fictitious business name if an unexpired fictitious business name statement filed pursuant to Chapter 5 (commencing with Section 17900) of Part 3 of Division 7 of the Business and Professions Code lists as the persons doing business under the fictitious business name either (A) the defendant or (B) the defendant's spouse or (C) the defendant and the defendant's spouse, but does not list any other person. A copy of a fictitious business name statement, certified as provided in Section 17926 of the Business and Professions Code, that satisfies these requirements shall be delivered to the financial institution at the time of levy and, if a person other than the defendant is listed in the statement, an affidavit showing that the other person is the defendant's spouse shall also be delivered to the financial institution at the time of levy.
(c) In any case where a deposit account in the name of a person other than the defendant, whether alone or together with the defendant, is levied upon, the financial institution shall not pay to the levying officer the amount levied upon until being notified to do so by the levying officer. The levying officer may not require the financial institution to pay the amount levied upon until the expiration of 15 days after service of notice of attachment on the third person.[207]

488.470. (a) Unless another method of attachment is provided by this article, to attach an account receivable or general intangible, the levying officer shall personally serve a copy of the writ of attachment and a notice of attachment on the account debtor.
(b) If an attachment is made under subdivision (a) and payments on the account receivable or general intangible are made to a person other than the defendant (whether pursuant to a security agreement, assignment for collection, or otherwise), the levying officer shall, if so instructed by the plaintiff, personally serve a copy of the writ of attachment and a notice of attachment on such third person. Service of the copy of the writ and notice of attachment on the third person is an attachment of any amounts owed to the defendant by the third person.[159]

488.475. (a) The following property

may be attached pursuant to this article notwithstanding that the property levied upon is the subject of a pending action or special proceeding:

(1) Real property.

(2) Growing crops, timber to be cut, or minerals or the like (including oil and gas) to be extracted or accounts receivable resulting from the sale thereof at the wellhead or minehead.

(3) Tangible personal property in the possession or under the control of the defendant or in the custody of a levying officer.

(4) The interest of a defendant in personal property in the estate of a decedent, whether the interest arises by testate or intestate succession.

(b) Except as provided in subdivision (a), attachment of property that is the subject of an action or special proceeding pending at the time of the attachment is not effective.

(c) If attachment is attempted but is ineffective under subdivision (b) and the levying officer has requested a garnishee's memorandum under Section 488.610 in connection with the ineffective attachment, the garnishee's memorandum shall include the following information in addition to that required by Section 488.610:

(1) A statement that the attachment of the property is not effective because the property is the subject of a pending action or special proceeding.

(2) The title of the court and the cause and number of the pending action or proceeding.

(d) For the purpose of this section, an action or proceeding is pending from the time the action or proceeding is commenced until judgment has been entered and the time for appeal has expired or, if an appeal is filed, until the appeal has been finally determined.

(e) Nothing in this section affects or limits the right of the plaintiff to obtain a lien pursuant to Article 3 (commencing with Section 491.410) of Chapter 11.[159]

488.480. (a) As used in this section, "final money judgment" means a money judgment after the time for appeal from the judgment has expired or, if an appeal is filed, after the appeal has been finally determined.

(b) To attach a final money judgment, the levying officer shall file a copy of the writ of attachment and a notice of attachment with the clerk of the court that entered the final money judgment. The court clerk shall endorse upon the judgment a statement of the existence of the attachment lien and the time it was created. If an abstract of the judgment is issued, it shall include a statement of the attachment lien in favor of the plaintiff.

(c) At the time of levy or promptly thereafter, the levying officer shall serve a copy of the writ of attachment and a notice of attachment on the judgment debtor obligated to pay the final money judgment attached.[206]

488.485. (a) To attach the interest of the defendant in personal property in the estate of a decedent, whether the interest arises by testate or intestate succession, the levying officer shall personally serve a copy of the writ of attachment and a notice of attachment on the personal representative of the decedent. The attachment does not impair the powers of the representative over the property for the purposes of administration.

(b) The personal representative shall report the attachment to the court in which the estate is being administered when any petition for distribution is filed. If a decree orders distribution to the defendant, the court making the decree shall order the attached property to be delivered to the levying officer. The property may not be delivered to the levying officer until the decree distributing the property has become final. To the extent the property delivered to the levying officer is not necessary to satisfy the attachment, it shall be released to the defendant.

(c) Promptly after the property is delivered to the levying officer pursuant to subdivision (b), the levying officer shall serve a notice describing the property on the defendant. Notwithstanding Sections 484.070, 484.350, 484.530, and 485.610, a claim of exemption for the property described in the notice may be made within 10 days after the notice was served on the defendant.[159]

Article 3: Lien of Attachment

Article 3 added by Stats. 1982, Ch. 1198, Sec. 50.

488.500. (a) A levy on property under a writ of attachment creates an attachment lien on the property from the time of levy until the expiration of the time provided by Section 488.510.

(b) Except as provided in subdivisions (c) and (d), if property subject to an attachment lien is transferred or encumbered, the property transferred or encumbered remains subject to the lien after the transfer or encumbrance to the same extent that the property would remain subject to an execution lien pursuant to Sections 697.720 to 697.750, inclusive.

(c) Except as otherwise provided in this title, if equipment is attached pursuant to Section 488.375 or farm products or inventory is attached pursuant to Section 488.405, the attachment lien on the property covered by the attachment lien has the same force and effect as a judgment lien on personal property created at the same time would have pursuant to Sections 697.590 to 697.620, inclusive.

(d) If equipment consisting of a vehicle, vessel, mobilehome, or commercial coach is attached pursuant to Section 488.385, the attachment lien on the specified property does not affect the rights of a person who is a bona fide purchaser or encumbrancer and obtains possession of both the property and its certificate of ownership issued by the Department of Motor Vehicles or its certificate of title or registration card issued by the Department of Housing and Community Development. If the levying officer obtains possession of the certificate of ownership or certificate of title or registration card, the attachment lien has the priority of the lien of a lien creditor under Sections 9317 and 9323 of the Commercial Code as of the time possession is obtained by the levying officer. If the levying officer does not obtain possession of the certificate of ownership or certificate of title or registration card, the attachment lien has the same force and effect as an unperfected security interest that attached at the same time as the notice of attachment was filed.

(e) If an attachment lien is created on property that is subject to the lien of a temporary protective order or a lien under Article 1 (commencing with Section 491.110) of Chapter 11, the priority of the attachment lien relates back to the date the earlier lien was created. Nothing in this subdivision affects priorities or rights of third persons established while the lien of the temporary protective order or the lien under Article 1 (commencing with Section 491.110) of Chapter 11 was in effect as determined under the law governing the effect of such lien.[418]

488.510. (a) Unless sooner released or discharged, any attachment shall cease to be of any force or effect, and the property levied upon shall be released from the operation of the attachment, at the expiration of three years from the date of issuance of the writ of attachment under which the levy was made.

(b) Notwithstanding subdivision (a), upon motion of the plaintiff, made not less than 10 or more than 60 days before the expiration of the three-year period and upon notice of not less than five days to the defendant whose property is attached, the court in which the action is pending may, by order filed prior to the expiration of the period and for good cause, extend the time of the attachment for a period not exceeding one year from the date on which the attachment would otherwise expire.

(c) The levying officer shall serve notice of the order upon any person holding property pursuant to an attachment and shall record or file the notice in any office where the writ and notice of attachment are recorded or filed prior to the expiration of the period described in subdivision (a) or any extension thereof. Where the attached property is real property, the plaintiff or the plaintiff's attorney, instead of the levying officer, may record the required notice.

(d) Any attachment may be extended from time to time in the manner prescribed in this section, but the maximum period of the attachment, including the extensions, shall not exceed eight years from the date of issuance of the writ of attachment under which the levy of attachment was made.

(e) The death of the defendant whose property is attached does not terminate the attachment.[160]

Article 4: Duties and Liabilities of Third Persons After Levy

Article 4 added by Stats. 1982, Ch. 1198, Sec. 50.

488.600. (a) Sections 701.010, 701.020, 701.040, 701.050, 701.060, and 701.070 prescribe duties and liabilities of a third person under a levy made under this title.

(b) For the purposes of this section, references in Sections 701.010, 701.020, 701.040, 701.050, and 701.060 to:

(1) "Amount required to satisfy the judgment" shall be deemed references to the amount required to satisfy the amount to be secured by the attachment.

(2) "Execution lien" or "lien" shall be deemed references to the attachment lien.

(3) "Judgment creditor" shall be deemed references to the plaintiff.

(4) "Judgment debtor" shall be deemed references to the defendant.

(5) "Levy" shall be deemed references to levy of attachment.

(6) "Notice of levy" shall be deemed references to notice of attachment.

(7) "Release" of property shall be

deemed references to release of property pursuant to this title.

(8) "Satisfaction or discharge of the judgment" shall be deemed references to the satisfaction or termination of the attachment.

(9) "Writ" or "writ of execution" shall be deemed references to a writ of attachment.

(c) For the purposes of this section, references in Section 701.070 to:

(1) "Levy" shall be deemed references to levy of attachment.

(2) "Notice of the levy" shall be deemed references to notice of attachment.[674]

488.610. (a) At the time of service of a copy of the writ of attachment and a notice of attachment on a third person, the levying officer shall request the third person to give the levying officer a garnishee's memorandum containing the information required by this section. Within 10 days after the request is made, the third person shall mail or deliver the garnishee's memorandum to the levying officer whether or not the levy is effective.

(b) The garnishee's memorandum shall be executed under oath and shall contain the following information:

(1) A description of any property of the defendant sought to be attached that is not delivered to the levying officer and the reason for not delivering the property.

(2) A statement of the amount and terms of any obligation to the defendant sought to be attached that is due and payable and is not paid to the levying officer and the reason for not paying the obligation.

(3) A statement of the amount and terms of any obligation to the defendant sought to be attached that is not due and payable at the time of levy.

(4) A description of claims and rights of other persons to the attached property or obligation that are known to the third person and the names and addresses of those other persons.

(5) A statement that the garnishee holds neither any property nor any obligations in favor of the judgment debtor.

(c) If a garnishee's memorandum is received from the third person, the levying officer shall promptly mail or deliver a copy of the memorandum to the plaintiff and attach the original to the writ when it is returned to the court. If a garnishee's memorandum is not received from the third person, the levying officer shall so state in the return.

(d) Except as provided in subdivisions (e) and (f), if a third person does not give the levying officer a garnishee's memorandum within the time provided in subdivision (a) or does not provide complete information, the third person may, in the court's discretion, be required to pay the costs and reasonable attorney's fees incurred in any proceedings to obtain the information required in the garnishee's memorandum.

(e) Notwithstanding subdivision (a), where a deposit account or property in a safe-deposit box is attached, the financial institution need not give a garnishee's memorandum to the levying officer if the financial institution fully complies with the levy and, if a garnishee's memorandum is required, the garnishee's memorandum need provide information with respect only to property which is carried on the records available at the office or branch where the levy is made, unless the levy has been served at a central location designated by a financial institution in accordance with Section 684.115, in which case the garnishee's memorandum shall apply to all offices and branches of the financial institution except to the extent acceptance of the levy at that central location is limited pursuant to paragraph (3) of subdivision (b) of Section 684.115.

(f) Notwithstanding subdivision (a), the third person need not give a garnishee's memorandum to the levying officer if both of the following conditions are satisfied:

(1) The third person has delivered to the levying officer all of the property sought to be attached.

(2) The third person has paid to the levying officer the amount due at the time of levy on any obligation to the defendant that was attached and there is no additional amount that thereafter will become payable on the obligation levied upon.[845]

488.620. A third person who gives a garnishee's memorandum pursuant to this title is not liable to any person for the disclosure in the garnishee's memorandum of any information contained in the garnishee's memorandum.[179]

Article 5: Management and Disposition of Attached Property
Article 5 added by Stats. 1982, Ch. 1198, Sec. 50.

488.700. (a) If property has been or is sought to be attached, the court may appoint a receiver or order the levying officer to take any action the court orders that is necessary to preserve the value of the property, including but not limited to selling the property, if the court determines that the property is perishable or will greatly deteriorate or greatly depreciate in value or that for some other reason the interests of the parties will be best served by the order. An order may be made under this subdivision upon application of the plaintiff, the defendant, or a person who has filed a third-party claim pursuant to Division 4 (commencing with Section 720.010) of Title 9. The application shall be made on noticed motion if the court so directs or a court rule so requires. Otherwise, the application may be made ex parte.

(b) If the levying officer determines that property is extremely perishable or will greatly deteriorate or greatly depreciate in value before a court order pursuant to subdivision (a) could be obtained, the levying officer may take any action necessary to preserve the value of the property or may sell the property. The levying officer is not liable for a determination made in good faith under this subdivision.

(c) Except as otherwise provided by order of the court, a sale of the property pursuant to this section shall be made in the manner provided by Article 6 (commencing with Section 701.510) of Chapter 3 of Division 2 of Title 9 and the proceeds shall be deposited in the court to abide the judgment in the action. Notwithstanding subdivisions (b) and (d) of Section 701.530, notice of sale shall be posted and served at a reasonable time before sale, considering the character and condition of the property.

(d) If a receiver is appointed, the court shall fix the daily fee of the receiver and may order the plaintiff to pay the fees and expenses of the receiver in advance or may direct that the whole or any part of the fees and expenses be paid from the proceeds of any sale of the property. Except as otherwise provided in this section, the provisions of Chapter 5 (commencing with Section 564) and Chapter 5a (commencing with Section 571) of Title 7 govern the appointment, qualifications, powers, rights, and duties of a receiver appointed under this section.[159]

488.710. (a) As used in this section, "instrument" means a check, draft, money order, or other order for the withdrawal of money from a financial institution, the United States, any state, or any public entity within any state.
(b) If an instrument is payable to the defendant on demand and comes into the possession of a levying officer pursuant to this title, the levying officer shall promptly endorse and present the instrument for payment.
(c) The levying officer shall endorse the instrument by writing on the instrument (1) the name of the defendant, (2) the name and official title of the levying officer, and (3) the title of the court and the cause in which the writ was issued. The endorsement is as valid as if the instrument were endorsed by the defendant. No financial institution or public entity on which the instrument is drawn is liable to any person for payment of the instrument to the levying officer rather than to the defendant by reason of the endorsement. No levying officer is liable by reason of endorsing, presenting, and obtaining payment of the instrument. The funds or credit resulting from the payment of the instrument shall be held by the levying officer subject to the lien of attachment.
(d) If it appears from the face of the instrument that it has been tendered to the defendant in satisfaction of a claim or demand and that endorsement of the instrument is considered a release and satisfaction by the defendant of the claim or demand, the levying officer shall not endorse the instrument unless the defendant has first endorsed it to the levying officer. If the defendant does not endorse the instrument to the levying officer, the levying officer shall hold the instrument for 30 days and is not liable to the defendant or to any other person for delay in presenting it for payment. At the end of the 30-day holding period, the levying officer shall return the instrument to the maker.[159]

488.720. (a) The defendant may apply by noticed motion to the court in which the action is pending or in which the judgment in the action was entered for an order releasing the attachment of property to the extent that the value of the defendant's interest in the property clearly exceeds the amount necessary to satisfy the amount to be secured by the attachment.
(b) The notice of motion shall state the grounds on which the motion is based and shall be accompanied by an affidavit supporting any factual issues raised and points and authorities supporting any legal issues raised.
(c) At the hearing on the motion, the court shall determine the value of the defendant's interest in the property and order the release of the attachment of the property to the extent that the value of the defendant's interest in the property attached clearly exceeds the amount necessary to satisfy the amount to be secured by the attachment. After entry of judgment in the action in which the property was attached, the court shall also take into

consideration in determining whether the attachment is clearly excessive the value of any property not attached in the action that (1) has been levied upon pursuant to a writ of execution issued to satisfy the judgment in the action or (2) otherwise has been sought to be applied to the satisfaction of the judgment in the action.

(d) The court's determinations shall be made upon the basis of the pleadings and other papers in the record; but, upon good cause shown, the court may receive and consider at the hearing additional evidence, oral or documentary, and additional points and authorities, or it may continue the hearing for the production of the additional evidence or points and authorities.[159]

488.730. (a) The levying officer shall release attached property when the levying officer receives a written direction to release the property from the plaintiff's attorney of record or, if the plaintiff does not have an attorney of record, from the plaintiff or when the levying officer receives a certified copy of a court order for release or when otherwise required to release the property. The release extinguishes any attachment lien in favor of the plaintiff on the property released.

(b) If the property to be released has been taken into custody under the levy, it shall be released to the person from whom it was taken unless otherwise ordered by the court. If the person does not claim the property to be released, the levying officer shall retain custody of the property and shall serve on the person a notice of where possession of the property may be obtained. If the person does not claim the property within 30 days after the notice is served, the levying officer shall sell the property (other than cash which does not have a value exceeding its face value) in the manner provided by Article 6 (commencing with Section 701.510) of Chapter 3 of Division 2 of Title 9. The levying officer shall deposit the proceeds of sale and cash, after first deducting the levying officer's costs, with the county treasurer of the county where the property is located payable to the order of the person. If the amount deposited is not claimed by the person or the legal representative of the person within five years after the deposit is made, by making application to the treasurer or other official designated by the county, it shall be paid into the general fund of the county.

(c) If the property to be released has not been taken into custody under the levy, the levying officer shall release the attachment by issuing a written notice of release and serving it on the person who was served with a copy of the writ and a notice of attachment to create the lien.

(d) If the property to be released was levied upon by recording or filing a copy of the writ and a notice of attachment, the levying officer shall record or file a written notice of release in the same office. If the notice of attachment had been filed with the Secretary of State, any release shall have the effect prescribed in Section 697.650.

(e) The levying officer is not liable for releasing an attachment in accordance with this section and no other person is liable for acting in conformity with the release.[263]

488.740. If the defendant recovers judgment against the plaintiff and no timely motion for vacation of judgment or for judgment notwithstanding the verdict or for a new trial is filed and served and is pending and no appeal is perfected and undertaking executed and filed as provided in Section 921, any undertaking received from the defendant in the action, all the proceeds of sales and money collected by the levying officer, and all the property attached remaining in the levying officer's hands shall be delivered to the person from whom it was collected or taken, unless otherwise ordered by the court; and the court shall order the discharge of any attachment made in the action and the release of any property held thereunder.[159]

Chapter 9: Undertakings

Chapter 9 added by Stats. 1974, Ch. 1516.

Article 1: General Provisions

Article 1 added by Stats. 1974, Ch. 1516.

489.010. The Bond and Undertaking Law (Chapter 2 (commencing with Section 995. 010) of Title 14) applies to a bond given pursuant to this title, except to the extent this title prescribes a different rule or is inconsistent.[233]

489.060. (a) Except as provided in subdivision (b), all undertakings given pursuant to this title shall be presented to a proper court for approval and upon approval shall be filed with the court in which the action is pending.
(b) If the surety on the undertaking is an admitted surety insurer, the undertaking is not required to be approved by the court.[125]

489.130. Where the court orders the amount of the undertaking increased pursuant to Section 489.220 or 489.410, the plaintiff's failure to increase the amount of the undertaking is not a wrongful attachment within the meaning of Section 490.010.[100]

Article 2: Undertakings to Obtain Writ of Attachment or Protective Order

Article 2 added by Stats. 1974, Ch. 1516.

489.210. Before issuance of a writ of attachment, a temporary protective order, or an order under subdivision (b) of Section 491.415, the plaintiff shall file an undertaking to pay the defendant any amount the defendant may recover for any wrongful attachment by the plaintiff in the action.[208]

489.220. (a) Except as provided in subdivision (b), the amount of an undertaking filed pursuant to this article shall be ten thousand dollars ($10,000).
(b) If, upon objection to the undertaking, the court determines that the probable recovery for wrongful attachment exceeds the amount of the undertaking, it shall order the amount of the undertaking increased to the amount it determines to be the probable recovery for wrongful attachment if it is ultimately determined that the attachment was wrongful.[463]

489.230. (a) The notice of attachment shall include a statement, in a form adopted by the Judicial Council, advising the defendant that the undertaking has been filed and informing the defendant of the right to object to the undertaking.
(b) The form for the temporary protective order shall include a statement comparable to the one required by subdivision (a).[127]

Article 3: Undertaking to Obtain Release of Attachment or Protective Order
Article 3 added by Stats. 1974, Ch. 1516.

489.310. (a) Whenever a writ is issued, a defendant who has appeared in the action may apply by noticed motion to the court in which the action is pending for an order permitting the defendant to substitute an undertaking for any of his property in the state which has been or is subject to being attached.
(b) In a case (1) where the defendant applies for an order to release a portion of property which has been attached or (2) where the defendant applies for an order preventing the attachment of property and the amount of the undertaking to be given is less than the amount to be secured by the attachment, the application shall include a statement, executed under oath, describing the property to be so released or so protected from attachment.
(c) The defendant shall file an undertaking to pay the plaintiff the value of the property released not exceeding the amount of any judgment which may be recovered by the plaintiff in the action against the defendant. The amount of the undertaking filed pursuant to this section shall be equal to the lesser of (1) the value of the property attached or prevented from being attached or (2) the amount specified by the writ to be secured by the attachment. The court shall issue such order upon the condition that a sufficient undertaking be filed.
(d) Where an action is against more than one defendant, any defendant may make such application. The filing of an undertaking by such defendant shall not subject him to any demand against any other defendant; however, the levying officer shall not be prevented thereby from attaching, or be obliged to release from attachment, any property of any other defendant. Where all the defendants do not join in the application, the application shall include a statement, executed under oath, describing the character of the defendant's title to the property and the manner in which the defendant acquired such title and stating whether any other defendant who has not joined in the application has an interest in the property. Where two or more defendants have an interest in the same property, a joint application and undertaking shall be filed to secure the release of such property.[101]

489.320. (a) A defendant who has been served with a temporary protective order and who has appeared in the action may apply by noticed motion to the court in which the action is pending for an order terminating the temporary protective order with respect to that defendant.
(b) The defendant shall file an undertaking to pay the plaintiff the amount of any judgment recovered by the plaintiff in the action against the defendant. The amount of the undertaking filed pursuant to this section shall be equal to the amount sought to be secured by the attachment. The court shall issue the order terminating the temporary protective order with respect to the defendant upon the condition that a sufficient undertaking be filed.[161]

Article 4: Undertaking on Appeal
Article 4 added by Stats. 1974, Ch. 1516.

489.410. (a) At any time after entry of

judgment in favor of the defendant and before perfection of an appeal under Section 921, upon motion of the defendant, the trial court may order an increase in the amount of the original undertaking on attachment in such amount, if any, as is justified by the detriment reasonably to be anticipated by continuing the attachment. Unless such undertaking is filed within 10 days after such order, the attachment shall be set aside and the property released therefrom.

(b) If an order increasing the undertaking is made, the amount of the undertaking on appeal required by Section 921 shall be the same as the amount fixed by the trial court in such order.

(c) Neither the pendency nor granting of a motion timely filed and served by the plaintiff for vacation of judgment or for judgment notwithstanding the verdict or for new trial shall continue an attachment in force unless an undertaking is given by the plaintiff to pay all costs and damages sustained by continuing the attachment. The undertaking may be included in the undertaking specified in Section 921. If not so included, the same procedure shall apply as in case of an undertaking pursuant to Section 921.[89]

489.420. If a defendant appeals and the enforcement of the judgment against the defendant is stayed by the filing of a sufficient undertaking on appeal as provided by this code, all property of the defendant which has been attached in the action shall be released from the attachment upon the failure of the respondent to object to the undertaking within the time prescribed by statute or, if an objection is made, upon a determination that the undertaking is sufficient.[128]

Chapter 10: Liability for Wrongful Attachment

Chapter 10 added by Stats. 1974, Ch. 1516.

490.010. A wrongful attachment consists of any of the following:

(a) The levy under a writ of attachment or the service of a temporary protective order in an action in which attachment is not authorized, except that it is not a wrongful attachment if both of the following are established:

(1) The levy was not authorized solely because of the prohibition of subdivision (c) of Section 483.010.

(2) The person who sold or leased, or licensed for use, the property, furnished the services, or loaned the money reasonably believed that it would not be used primarily for personal, family, or household purposes.

(b) The levy under a writ of attachment or the service of a temporary protective order in an action in which the plaintiff does not recover judgment.

(c) The levy under writ of attachment obtained pursuant to Article 3 (commencing with Section 484.510) of Chapter 4 or Chapter 5 (commencing with Section 485.010) on property exempt from attachment except where the plaintiff shows that the plaintiff reasonably believed that the property attached was not exempt from attachment.[162]

490.020. (a) The liability of a plaintiff for causing a wrongful attachment under Section 490.010 includes both of the following:

(1) All damages proximately caused to the defendant by the wrongful attachment.

(2) All costs and expenses, including attorney's fees, reasonably expended

in defeating the attachment.

(b) The liability of a plaintiff for wrongful attachment pursuant to Section 490.010 is limited by the amount of the undertaking.[165]

490.040. The amount of any recovery for wrongful attachment shall be offset insofar as possible against any unsatisfied amounts owed to the plaintiff by the defendant on the judgment in the action for which wrongful attachment damages are awarded.[89]

490.060. Nothing in this chapter limits the right to recover for damages caused by an attachment or protective order on any common law theory of recovery.[89]

Chapter 11: Attaching Plaintiff's Miscellaneous Remedies

Chapter 11 repealed and added by Stats. 1982, Ch. 1198, Sec. 57.

Article 1: Examination of Third Person

Article 1 added by Stats. 1982, Ch. 1198, Sec. 57.

491.110. (a) Upon ex parte application by the plaintiff and proof by the plaintiff by affidavit or otherwise to the satisfaction of the proper court that the plaintiff has a right to attach order and that a third person has possession or control of property in which the defendant has an interest or is indebted to the defendant in an amount exceeding two hundred fifty dollars ($250), the court shall make an order directing the third person to appear before the court, or before a referee appointed by the court, at a time and place specified in the order, to answer concerning the property or debt. The affidavit in support of the plaintiff's application may be based on the affiant's information and belief.

(b) Not less than 10 days prior to the date set for the examination, a copy of the order shall be:

(1) Served personally on the third person.

(2) Served personally or by mail on the defendant.

(c) If the property or the debt is described in the affidavit or application for an order under subdivision (a) in a manner reasonably adequate to permit it to be identified, service of the order on the third person creates a lien on the defendant's interest in the property in the third person's possession or control or on the debt owed by the third person to the defendant. The lien continues for a period of one year from the date of the order unless extended or sooner terminated by the court.

(d) The order shall contain the following statement in 14-point boldface type if printed or in capital letters if typed: "NOTICE TO PERSON SERVED. If you fail to appear at the time and place specified in this order, you may be subject to arrest and punishment for contempt of court and the court may make an order requiring you to pay the reasonable attorney's fees incurred by the plaintiff in this proceeding."

(e) The order is not effective unless, at the time it is served on the third person, the person serving the order tenders to the third person fees for the mileage necessary to be traveled from the third person's residence to the place of examination. The fees shall be in the same amount generally provided for witnesses when legally required to attend civil proceedings in the court where the examination proceeding is to be conducted.[166]

491.120. In any proceeding for the examination of a third person under this article, witnesses, including the defendant, may be required to appear and testify before the court or referee in the same manner as upon the trial of an issue.[166]

491.130. (a) The examination proceedings authorized by this article may be conducted by a referee appointed by the court. The referee may issue, modify, or vacate an order authorized by Section 491.190, may make a protective order authorized by Section 491.180, and may issue a warrant authorized by Section 491.160, and has the same power as the court to grant adjournments, to preserve order, and to subpoena witnesses to attend the examination, but only the court that ordered the reference has power to do any of the following:

(1) Punish for contempt for disobeying an order of the referee.

(2) Make an award of attorney's fees pursuant to Section 491.160.

(3) Determine a third-party claim under Section 491.170.

(b) Only a member of the State Bar of California is eligible for appointment as a referee pursuant to this article.

(c) Nothing in subdivision (a) limits the power of a court to appoint a temporary judge pursuant to Section 21 of Article VI of the California Constitution.[166]

491.140. (a) If a corporation, partnership, association, trust, or other organization is served with an order to appear for an examination, it shall designate to appear and be examined one or more officers, directors, managing agents, or other persons who are familiar with its property and debts.

(b) If the order to appear for an examination requires the appearance of a specified individual, the specified individual shall appear for the examination and may be accompanied by one or more officers, directors, managing agents, or other persons familiar with the property and debts of the corporation, partnership, association, trust, or other organization.

(c) If the order to appear for the examination does not require the appearance of a specified individual, the order shall advise the corporation, partnership, association, trust, or other organization of its duty to make a designation under subdivision (a).

(d) A corporation, partnership, association, trust, or other organization, whether or not a party, may appear at an examination through any authorized officer, director, or employee, whether or not the person is an attorney.[209]

491.150. (a) Except as otherwise provided in this section, the proper court for examination of a person under this article is the court that issued the writ of attachment.

(b) A person sought to be examined may not be required to attend an examination before a court located outside the county in which the person resides or has a place of business unless the distance from the person's place of residence or place of business to the place of examination is less than 150 miles.

(c) If a person sought to be examined does not reside or have a place of business in the county where the court that issued the writ is located, the superior court in the county where the person resides or has a place of business is a proper court for examination of the person.

(d) If the plaintiff seeks an examination of a person before a court other than the court that issued the writ, the plaintiff shall file an application that shall include all of the following:

(1) A certified copy of the complaint in the pending action.

(2) An affidavit in support of the application stating the place of residence or place of business of the person sought to be examined.

(3) Any necessary affidavit or showing for the examination as required by Section 491.110.

(4) The filing fee for a motion as provided in subdivision (a) of Section 70617 of the Government Code.[562]

491.160. (a) If an order requiring a person to appear for an examination was served by a sheriff, marshal, a person specially appointed by the court in the order, or a registered process server, and the person fails to appear:

(1) The court may do either of the following:

(A) Pursuant to a warrant, have the person brought before the court to answer for the failure to appear and may punish the person for contempt.

(B) Issue a warrant for the arrest of the person who failed to appear as required by the court order, pursuant to Section 1993.

(2) If the person's failure to appear is without good cause, the plaintiff shall be awarded reasonable attorney's fees incurred in the examination proceeding.

(b) A person who willfully makes an improper service of an order for an examination which subsequently results in the arrest pursuant to subdivision (a) of the person who fails to appear is guilty of a misdemeanor.[584]

491.170. (a) Subject to subdivision (b), if a third person examined pursuant to this article claims an interest in the property adverse to the defendant or denies the debt, the court may, if the plaintiff so requests, determine the interests in the property or the existence of the debt. Such a determination is conclusive as to the plaintiff, the defendant, and the third person, but an appeal may be taken from the determination in the manner provided for appeals from the court in which the proceeding takes place. The court may grant a continuance for a reasonable time for discovery proceedings, the production of evidence, or other preparation for the hearing.

(b) The court may not make the determination provided in subdivision (a) if the third person's claim is made in good faith and any of the following conditions is satisfied:

(1) The court would not be a proper court for the trial of an independent civil action (including a creditor's suit) for the determination of the interests in the property or the existence of the debt, and the third person objects to the determination of the matter under subdivision (a).

(2) At the time an order for examination pursuant to this article is served on the third person a civil action (including a creditor's suit) is pending with respect to the interests in the property or the existence of the debt.

(3) The court determines that the interests in the property or the existence of the debt should be determined in a creditor's suit.

(c) Upon application of the plaintiff made ex parte, the court may make an order forbidding transfer of the property to the defendant or payment of the debt to the defendant until the interests in the property or the existence of the debt is determined pursuant to subdivision (a) or until a creditor's suit may be commenced and an order obtained pursuant to Section 491.340. An undertaking may be required in the discretion of the court. The court may modify or vacate the order at any time with or without a hearing on such terms as are just.

(d) Upon application of the plaintiff upon noticed motion, the court, if it determines that the defendant probably owns an interest in the property or that the debt probably is owed to the defendant, may make an order forbidding the transfer or other disposition of the property to any person or forbidding payment of the debt until the interests in the property or the existence of the debt is determined pursuant to subdivision (a) or until a creditor's suit may be commenced and an order obtained pursuant to Section 491.340. The court shall require the plaintiff to furnish an undertaking as provided in Section 529. The court may modify or vacate the order at any time after notice and hearing on such terms as are just.[166]

491.180. In any proceeding under this article, the court may, on motion of the person to be examined or on its own motion, make such protective orders as justice may require.[166]

491.190. (a) Except as provided in subdivision (b), at the conclusion of a proceeding pursuant to this article:

(1) The court may order the defendant's interest in the property in the possession or under the control of the third person or a debt owed by the third person to the defendant to be attached in the manner and under the conditions provided by this title or to be delivered or paid to the levying officer if the levying officer has a writ of attachment permitting the attachment of the property or debt. After the property or debt has been attached, the order may be enforced as provided in Section 491.360. The order creates a lien on the property or debt. The lien continues for a period of one year from the date of the order unless the court extends or reduces the period of the existence of the lien.

(2) If the property or debt has previously been attached, the court may make an order determining the third person's liability, and the order may be enforced as provided in Section 491.360.

(b) If a third person examined pursuant to this article claims an interest in the property adverse to the defendant or denies the debt and the court does not determine the matter as provided in subdivision (a) of Section 491.170, the court may not make an order under subdivision (a) of this section, but may make an order pursuant to subdivision (c) or (d) of Section 491.170 forbidding transfer or payment to the extent authorized by that section.[166]

491.200. A lien created under this article continues on property subject to the lien notwithstanding the transfer or encumbrance of the property subject to the lien unless the transfer or encumbrance is made to a person listed in Section 697.740.[166]

Article 2: Creditor's Suit

Article 2 added by Stats. 1982, Ch. 1198, Sec. 57.

491.310. If a third person has possession or control of property in which the defendant has an interest or is indebted to the defendant and the property or debt has been subjected to an attachment lien, the plaintiff may bring an action against the third person to enforce the third person's liability under this title.[166]

491.320. The defendant shall be joined in an action brought pursuant to this article but is not an indispensable party. The residence of the defendant may not be considered in the determination of proper venue unless otherwise provided by contract between the defendant and the third person.[166]

491.330. (a) Except as provided in subdivision (b), an action shall be commenced pursuant to this article before the expiration of the later of the following times:

(1) The time when the defendant may bring an action against the third person concerning the property or debt.

(2) One year after creation of an attachment lien on the property or debt pursuant to this title if the lien is created at the time when the defendant may bring an action against the third person concerning the property or debt.

(b) An action may not be commenced pursuant to this article if the attachment lien is not in effect.

(c) If an action is commenced pursuant to this article within the time permitted in this section, the action may be prosecuted to judgment so long as the attachment lien or a lien of the plaintiff on the same property pursuant to Title 9 (commencing with Section 680.010) is in effect.[166]

491.340. The plaintiff may apply to the court in which an action under this article is pending for either or both of the following:

(a) An order restraining the third person from transferring the attached property to the defendant or from paying the attached debt to the defendant. The order shall be made on noticed motion if the court so directs or a court rule so requires. Otherwise, the order may be made on ex parte application. The order shall remain in effect until judgment is entered in the action or until such earlier time as the court may provide in the order. An undertaking may be required in the discretion of the court. The court may modify or vacate the order at any time with or without a hearing on such terms as are just.

(b) A temporary restraining order or a preliminary injunction or both, restraining the third person from transferring to any person or otherwise disposing of the attached property, pursuant to Chapter 3 (commencing with Section 525) of Title 7, and the court may make, dissolve, and modify such orders as provided therein.[166]

491.350. There is no right to a jury trial in an action under this article.[166]

491.360. If the plaintiff establishes the liability of the third person, the court shall render judgment accordingly. The judgment may be enforced in the same manner as it could be enforced if it had been obtained by the defendant against the third party; but, prior to entry of judgment in favor of the plaintiff against the defendant, any money or property obtained in enforcing the judgment against the third party shall be paid or delivered into court to abide the judgment in the action of the plaintiff against the defendant or shall be held by a levying officer, or otherwise held, as ordered by the court.[166]

491.370. Costs incurred by or taxed against the plaintiff in an action under this article may not be recovered from the defendant.[166]

Article 3: Lien in Pending Action or Proceeding
Article 3 added by Stats. 1982, Ch. 1198, Sec. 57.

491.410. (a) If the defendant is a party to a pending action or special proceeding, the plaintiff may obtain a lien under this article, to the extent required to secure the amount to be secured by the attachment, on both of the following:
(1) Any cause of action of the defendant for money or property that is the subject of the other action or proceeding, if the money or property would be subject to attachment if the defendant prevails in the action or proceedings.
(2) The rights of the defendant to money or property under any judgment subsequently procured in the other action or proceeding, if the money or property would be subject to attachment.
(b) To obtain a lien under this article, the plaintiff shall file all of the following in the other pending action or special proceeding:
(1) A notice of lien.
(2) A copy of the right to attach order.
(3) A copy of an order permitting creation of a lien under this article made by the court that issued the right to attach order.
(c) At the time of the filing under subdivision (b) or promptly thereafter, the plaintiff shall serve on all parties who, prior thereto, have made an appearance in the other action or special proceeding a copy of the notice of lien and a statement of the date when the notice of lien was filed in the other action or special proceeding. Failure to serve all parties as required by this subdivision does not affect the lien created by the filing under subdivision (b), but the rights of a party are not affected by the lien until the party has notice of the lien.
(d) For the purpose of this article, an action or special proceeding is pending until the time for appeal from the judgment has expired or, if an appeal is filed, until the appeal has been finally determined.[210]

491.415. (a) For the purpose of applying for a right to attach order, the defendant's cause of action that is the subject of the pending action or proceeding and the defendant's rights to money or property under a judgment procured in the action or proceeding shall be treated as property subject to attachment.
(b) At the time the plaintiff applies for a right to attach order, the plaintiff may apply for an order permitting creation of a lien under this article. If the plaintiff has already obtained a right to attach order, an application for an order permitting creation of a lien under this article may be applied for in the same manner as a writ of attachment. As a prerequisite to obtaining an order under this subdivision, the plaintiff shall file an undertaking as provided by Sections 489.210 and 489.220.

(c) The defendant may, but is not required to, claim an exemption in a proceeding initiated by the plaintiff for an order permitting creation of a lien under this article. An exemption may be claimed if the money or property sought by the defendant would be exempt from attachment should the defendant prevail in the other action or proceeding. The exemption shall be claimed and determined pursuant to this subdivision in the same manner as an exemption is claimed and determined upon application for a writ of attachment.[211]

491.420. The notice of lien under Section 491.410 shall contain all of the following:

(a) A statement that a lien has been created under this article and the title of the court and the cause and number of the pending action or proceeding in which the notice of lien is filed.

(b) The name and last known address of the defendant.

(c) The name and address of the plaintiff.

(d) The title of the court where the plaintiff's action against the defendant is pending and the cause and number of the action.

(e) The amount required to secure the amount to be secured by the attachment at the time the notice of lien is filed in the action or proceeding.

(f) A statement that the lien attaches to any cause of action of the defendant that is the subject of such action or proceeding and to the defendant's rights to money or property under any judgment subsequently procured in the action or proceeding.

(g) A statement that no compromise, dismissal, settlement, or satisfaction of the pending action or proceeding or any of the defendant's rights to money or property under any judgment procured therein may be entered into by or on behalf of the defendant, and that the defendant may not enforce the defendant's rights to money or property under any judgment procured in the pending action or proceeding by a writ or otherwise, unless one of the following requirements is satisfied:

(1) The prior approval by order of the court in which the action or proceeding is pending has been obtained.

(2) The written consent of the plaintiff has been obtained or the plaintiff has released the lien.[166]

491.430. (a) The court in which the action or special proceeding subject to the lien under this article is pending may permit the plaintiff who has obtained the lien to intervene in the action or proceeding pursuant to Section 387.

(b) For the purposes of subdivision (a) of Section 491.460 and Section 491.470, a plaintiff shall be deemed to be a party to the action or special proceeding even though the plaintiff has not become a party to the action or proceeding under subdivision (a).[212]

491.440. (a) Except as provided in subdivision (c) of Section 491.410, unless the lien is released, the judgment recovered in the action or special proceeding in favor of the defendant may not be enforced by a writ or otherwise, and no compromise, dismissal, settlement, or satisfaction of the pending action or special proceeding or the judgment procured therein may be entered into by or on behalf of the defendant, without the written consent of the plaintiff or authorization by order of the court obtained under subdivision (b).

(b) Upon application by the defendant, the court in which the action or special proceeding subject to the lien under this article is pending or the judgment procured therein is entered may, in its discretion, after a hearing, make an order described in subdivision (a) that may include such terms and conditions as the court deems necessary. The application for an order under this subdivision shall be made on noticed motion. The notice of motion shall be served on the plaintiff.[166]

491.450. (a) If a lien is created pursuant to this article, the court clerk shall endorse upon the judgment recovered in the action or special proceeding a statement of the existence of the lien and the time it was created.

(b) Any abstract issued upon the judgment shall include a statement of the lien in favor of the plaintiff.[166]

491.460. (a) If the defendant is entitled to money or property under the judgment in the action or special proceeding and a lien created under this article exists, upon application of any party to the action or special proceeding, the court may order that the defendant's rights to money or property under the judgment be attached or otherwise applied to the satisfaction of the lien created under this article as ordered by the court. Application for an order under this section shall be on noticed motion. The notice of motion shall be served on all other parties.

(b) If the judgment determines that the defendant has an interest in property, the court may order the party having custody or control of the property not to transfer the property until it can be attached or otherwise applied to the satisfaction of the lien created under this article.

(c) If the court determines that a party (other than the defendant) having notice of the lien created under this article has transferred property that was subject to the lien, or has paid an amount to the defendant that was subject to the lien, the court shall render judgment against the party in an amount equal to the lesser of the following:

(1) The value of the defendant's interest in the property or the amount paid to the defendant.

(2) The amount of the plaintiff's lien created under this article.

(d) A judgment or order under this section may be enforced in the same manner as it could be enforced if it had been obtained by the defendant against the third party; but, prior to entry of judgment in favor of the plaintiff against the defendant, any money or property obtained in enforcing the judgment or order against the third party shall be paid or delivered into court to abide the judgment in the action of the plaintiff against the defendant or shall be held by a levying officer, or otherwise held, as ordered by the court.[166]

491.470. (a) If a lien is created under this article, the defendant may claim that all or any portion of the money or property that the defendant may recover in the action or special proceeding is exempt from attachment. The claim shall be made by application on noticed motion to the court in which the action or special proceeding is pending, filed, and served on the plaintiff not later than 30 days after the defendant has notice of the creation of lien. The defendant shall execute an affidavit in support of the application that includes the matters set forth in subdivision (c) of Section 484.070. No notice of opposition to the claim of exemption is required. The failure of the defendant to make a claim of exemption under this section constitutes a waiver of the exemption.

(b) The court may determine the exemption claim at any time prior to the entry of judgment in the action or special proceeding or may consolidate the exemption hearing with the hearing on a motion pursuant to Section 491.460.

(c) If the defendant establishes to the satisfaction of the court that the money or property that the defendant may recover in the action or special proceeding is all or partially exempt from attachment, the court shall order the termination of the lien created under this article on the exempt portion of the money or property.[213]

Chapter 12: Nonresident Attachment

Chapter 12 added by Stats. 1974, Ch. 1516.

492.010. Notwithstanding subdivision (a) of Section 483.010, an attachment may be issued in any action for the recovery of money brought against any of the following:

(a) A natural person who does not reside in this state.

(b) A foreign corporation not qualified to do business in this state under the provisions of Chapter 21 (commencing with Section 2100) of Division 1 of Title 1 of the Corporations Code.

(c) A foreign partnership which has not filed a designation pursuant to Section 15800 of the Corporations Code.[789]

492.020. (a) Upon the filing of the complaint or at any time thereafter, the plaintiff may apply pursuant to this chapter for a right to attach order and a writ of attachment by filing an application for the order and writ with the court in which the action is brought.

(b) The application shall satisfy the requirements of Section 484.020 and shall be supported by an affidavit showing all of the following:

(1) The action is one described in Section 492.010 and is brought against a defendant described in Section 492.010.

(2) The plaintiff on the facts presented would be entitled to a judgment on the claim upon which the attachment is based.

(3) The property sought to be attached is subject to attachment pursuant to Section 492.040.

(c) The affidavit in support of the showing required by paragraph (3) of subdivision (b) may be based on the affiant's information and belief.[89]

492.030. (a) The court shall examine the application and supporting affidavit and shall issue a right to attach order, which shall state the amount to be secured by the attachment, and order a writ of attachment to be issued upon the filing of an undertaking as provided by Sections 489.210 and 489.220, if it finds all of the following:

(1) The claim upon which the attachment is based is one upon which an attachment may be issued.

(2) The plaintiff has established the probable validity of the claim upon which the attachment is based.

(3) The defendant is one described in Section 492.010.

(4) The attachment is not sought for a purpose other than the recovery on

the claim upon which the attachment is based.

(5) The affidavit accompanying the application shows that the property sought to be attached, or the portion thereof to be specified in the writ, is subject to attachment pursuant to Section 492.040.

(6) The amount to be secured by the attachment is greater than zero.

(b) If the court finds that the application and supporting affidavit do not satisfy the requirements of this chapter, it shall so state and deny the order. If denial is solely on the ground that the defendant is not one described in Section 492.010, the judicial officer shall so state and such denial does not preclude the plaintiff from applying for a right to attach order and writ of attachment under Chapter 4 (commencing with Section 484.010) with the same affidavits and supporting papers.[381]

492.040. Notwithstanding Sections 487.010 and 487.020, a writ of attachment issued under this chapter may be levied upon any property of a defendant for which a method of levy is provided by Article 2 (commencing with Section 488.300) of Chapter 8. However, after the defendant has filed a general appearance in the action, only nonexempt property of the defendant may be levied upon and property previously levied upon which is exempt under Section 487.020 shall be released upon order of the court.[167]

492.050. (a) Any defendant whose property has been attached pursuant to a writ issued under this chapter may apply for an order that the right to attach order be set aside, the writ of attachment quashed, and any property levied upon pursuant to the writ released. Such application shall be made by filing with the court and serving on the plaintiff a notice of motion.

(b) The notice of motion shall state the grounds on which the motion is based and shall be accompanied by an affidavit supporting any factual issues raised and points and authorities supporting any legal issues raised.

(c) If the defendant has filed a general appearance in the action, the right to attach order shall be set aside unless the plaintiff shows that his right to attach is authorized by a provision other than Section 492.010.

(d) At the hearing on the motion, the court shall determine whether the plaintiff is entitled to a right to attach order. If the court finds that the plaintiff is not entitled to a right to attach order, it shall order the right to attach order set aside, the writ of attachment quashed, and any property levied upon pursuant to the writ released. If the court finds that the plaintiff is entitled to a right to attach order, the attachment shall continue in effect except as provided in Section 492.040 and, thereafter, the plaintiff may apply for additional writs pursuant to Article 2 (commencing with Section 484.310) or Article 3 (commencing with Section 484.510) of Chapter 4.

(e) The court's determination shall be made upon the basis of the pleadings and other papers in the record; but, upon good cause shown, the court may receive and consider at the hearing additional evidence, oral or documentary, and additional points and authorities, or it may continue the hearing for the production of such additional evidence or points and authorities.

(f) The hearing provided for in this section shall take precedence over all other civil matters on the calendar of that day except older matters of the same character.[89]

492.060. At any time after a right to attach order and writ of attachment have been issued under this chapter and before the hearing provided by Section 492.050, the plaintiff may apply for an additional writ of attachment under this chapter as provided in Sections 492.060 to 492.090, inclusive. The application shall be filed with the court in which the action is brought.[89]

492.070. The application shall be executed under oath and shall include all of the following:
(a) A statement that the plaintiff has been issued a right to attach order and writ of attachment pursuant to Section 492.030.
(b) A statement of the amount to be secured by the attachment.
(c) A description of the property to be attached under the writ of attachment and a statement that the plaintiff is informed and believes that such property is subject to attachment pursuant to Section 492.040. The description shall satisfy the requirements of Section 484.020.[163]

492.090. The court shall examine the application and supporting affidavit and shall order a writ of attachment to be issued upon the filing of an undertaking as provided by Sections 489.210 and 489.220, if it finds both of the following:
(a) A right to attach order has been issued in the action pursuant to Section 492.030.
(b) The affidavit accompanying the application shows that the property sought to be attached, or the portion thereof to be specified in the writ, is subject to attachment pursuant to Section 492.040.[101]

Chapter 13: Effect of Bankruptcy Proceedings and General Assignments for the Benefit of Creditors

Chapter 13 added by Stats. 1977, Ch. 499.

493.010. As used in this chapter, "general assignment for the benefit of creditors" means an assignment which satisfies all of the following requirements:
(a) The assignment is an assignment of all the defendant's assets that are transferable and not exempt from enforcement of a money judgment.
(b) The assignment is for the benefit of all the defendant's creditors.
(c) The assignment does not itself create a preference of one creditor or class of creditors over any other creditor or class of creditors, but the assignment may recognize the existence of preferences to which creditors are otherwise entitled.[168]

493.020. Notwithstanding any other provision of this title, the defendant may make a general assignment for the benefit of creditors.[106]

493.030. (a) The making of a general assignment for the benefit of creditors terminates a lien of a temporary protective order or of attachment if the lien was created within 90 days prior to the making of the general assignment.
(b) The filing of a petition commencing a voluntary or involuntary case under Title 11 of the United States Code (Bankruptcy) terminates a lien of a temporary protective order or of attachment if the lien was created within 90 days prior to the filing of the petition.

(c) Subdivisions (a) and (b) do not apply unless all liens of attachment on the defendant's property in other states that were created within 90 days prior to the making of a general assignment for the benefit of creditors or the filing of a petition commencing a case under Title 11 of the United States Code (Bankruptcy) have terminated.[109]

493.040. (a) Where a lien of attachment terminates pursuant to Section 493.030, the assignee under a general assignment for the benefit of creditors or, in the case of a bankruptcy, the trustee, interim trustee, or the debtor in possession if there is no trustee or interim trustee, may secure the release of the attached property by filing with the levying officer a request for release of attachment stating the grounds for release and describing the property to be released, executed under oath, together with a copy thereof.

(b) In the case of an assignee, the request shall include two copies of the general assignment for the benefit of creditors.

(c) In the case of a trustee, interim trustee, or debtor in possession, the request shall include a certified copy of the petition in bankruptcy, together with a copy thereof.

(d) If immediate release of the attachment is sought, the request shall be accompanied by an undertaking to pay the plaintiff any damages resulting from an improper release of the attachment, in the amount to be secured by the attachment, executed by an admitted surety insurer.

(e) Within five days after the filing of the request for release of attachment, the levying officer shall mail to the plaintiff:

(1) A copy of the request for release of the attachment, including the copy of the document filed pursuant to subdivision (b) or (c).

(2) If an undertaking has not been given, a notice that the attachment will be released pursuant to the request for release of attachment unless otherwise ordered by a court within 10 days after the date of mailing the notice.

(3) If an undertaking has been given, a notice that the attachment has been released.

(f) Unless otherwise ordered by a court, if an undertaking has not been given, the levying officer shall release the attachment pursuant to the request for release of attachment after the expiration of 10 days from the date of mailing the papers referred to in subdivision (e) to the plaintiff. If an undertaking has been given, the levying officer shall immediately release the attachment pursuant to the request for release of attachment.

(g) Where the attached property has been taken into custody, it shall be released to the person making the request for release of attachment or some other person designated in the request. Where the attached property has not been taken into custody, it shall be released as provided in subdivision (c) or (d) of Section 488.730.

(h) The levying officer is not liable for releasing an attachment in accordance with this section nor is any other person liable for acting in conformity with the release.[169]

493.050. (a) The lien of a temporary protective order or of attachment, which has terminated pursuant to Section 493.030, is reinstated with the same effect as if it had not been terminated in the following cases:

(1) Where the termination is the result of the making of a general assignment for the benefit of creditors and the general assignment for the benefit of creditors is set aside otherwise than by the filing of a petition commencing a case under Title 11 of the United States Code (Bankruptcy).
(2) Where the termination is the result of the filing of a petition commencing a case under Title 11 of the United States Code (Bankruptcy) and the petition is dismissed.
(3) Where the termination is the result of the filing of a petition commencing a case under Title 11 of the United States Code (Bankruptcy) and the trustee abandons property which had been subject to the lien of the temporary protective order or of attachment.
(b) The period from the making of a general assignment for the benefit of creditors until reinstatement of the lien of the temporary protective order or of attachment is not counted in determining the duration of the temporary protective order or the lien of attachment.[109]

493.060. (a) Upon the making of a general assignment for the benefit of creditors that terminates a lien under this chapter, the assignee is subrogated to the rights of the plaintiff under the temporary protective order or attachment.
(b) Upon the filing of a petition commencing a case under Title 11 of the United States Code (Bankruptcy), a lien terminated pursuant to this chapter is preserved for the benefit of the estate.[109]

TITLE 7: OTHER PROVISIONAL REMEDIES IN CIVIL ACTIONS

Heading of Title 7 added by Stats. 1974, Ch. 1516.

Chapter 1: General Provisions

Chapter 1 added by Stats. 1974, Ch. 1516.

501. A person may not be imprisoned in a civil action for debt or tort, whether before or after judgment. Nothing in this section affects any power a court may have to imprison a person who violates a court order.[89]

Chapter 2: Claim and Delivery of Personal Property

Chapter 2 added by Stats. 1973, Ch. 526.

Article 1: Words and Phrases Defined

Article 1 added by Stats. 1973, Ch. 526.

511.010. Unless the provision or context otherwise requires, the definitions in this article govern the construction of this chapter.[85]

511.020. "Complaint" includes a cross-complaint.[85]

511.030. "Defendant" includes a cross-defendant.[85]

511.040. "Farm products" means crops or livestock or supplies used or produced in farming operations or products of crops or livestock in their unmanufactured states (such as ginned cotton, wool clip, maple syrup, honey, milk, and eggs) while in the possession of a defendant engaged in raising, fattening, grazing, or other farming operations. If tangible personal property is a farm product, it is not inventory.[85]

511.050. "Inventory" means tangible personal property in the possession of a defendant who holds it for sale or lease or to be furnished under contracts of service.[85]

511.060. "Levying officer" means the sheriff or marshal who is directed to execute a writ of possession issued under this chapter. [369]

511.070. "Person" includes an individual, a corporation, a partnership or other unincorporated association, a limited liability company, and a public entity.[337]

511.080. "Plaintiff" means a person who files a complaint or cross-complaint.[85]

511.090. A claim has "probable validity" where it is more likely than not that the plaintiff will obtain a judgment against the defendant on that claim.[85]

511.100. "Public entity" includes the state, the Regents of the University of California, a county, city, district, public authority, public agency, and any other political subdivision or public corporation in the state.[85]

Article 2: Writ of Possession
Article 2 added by Stats. 1973, Ch. 526.

512.010. (a) Upon the filing of the complaint or at any time thereafter, the plaintiff may apply pursuant to this chapter for a writ of possession by filing a written application for the writ with the court in which the action is brought.
(b) The application shall be executed under oath and shall include all of the following:
(1) A showing of the basis of the plaintiff's claim and that the plaintiff is entitled to possession of the property claimed. If the basis of the plaintiff's claim is a written instrument, a copy of the instrument shall be attached.
(2) A showing that the property is wrongfully detained by the defendant, of the manner in which the defendant came into possession of the property, and, according to the best knowledge, information, and belief of the plaintiff, of the reason for the detention.
(3) A particular description of the property and a statement of its value.
(4) A statement, according to the best knowledge, information, and belief of the plaintiff, of the location of the property and, if the property, or some part of it, is within a private place which may have to be entered to take possession, a showing that there is probable cause to believe that such property is located there.
(5) A statement that the property has not been taken for a tax, assessment, or fine, pursuant to a statute; or seized under an execution against the property of the plaintiff; or, if so seized, that it is by statute exempt from such seizure.
(c) The requirements of subdivision (b) may be satisfied by one or more affidavits filed with the application.[85]

512.020. (a) Except as otherwise provided in this section, no writ shall be issued under this chapter except after a hearing on a noticed motion.
(b) A writ of possession may be issued ex parte pursuant to this subdivision if probable cause appears that any of the following conditions exists:
(1) The defendant gained possession of the property by feloniously taking the property from the plaintiff. This subdivision shall not apply where the

defendant has fraudulently appropriated property entrusted to him or obtained possession by false or fraudulent representation or pretense or by embezzlement.

(2) The property is a credit card.

(3) The defendant acquired possession of the property in the ordinary course of his trade or business for commercial purposes and:

(i) The property is not necessary for the support of the defendant or his family; and

(ii) There is an immediate danger that the property will become unavailable to levy by reason of being transferred, concealed, or removed from the state or will become substantially impaired in value by acts of destruction or by failure to take care of the property in a reasonable manner; and

(iii) The ex parte issuance of a writ of possession is necessary to protect the property.

The plaintiff's application for the writ shall satisfy the requirements of Section 512.010 and, in addition, shall include a showing that the conditions required by this subdivision exist. A writ of possession may issue if the court finds that the conditions required by this subdivision exist and the requirements of Section 512.060 are met. Where a writ of possession has been issued pursuant to this subdivision, a copy of the summons and complaint, a copy of the application and any affidavit in support thereof, and a notice which satisfies the requirements of subdivisions (c) and (d) of Section 512.040 and informs the defendant of his rights under this subdivision shall be served upon the defendant and any other person required by Section 514.020 to be served with a writ of possession. Any defendant whose property has been taken pursuant to a writ of possession issued under this subdivision may apply for an order that the writ be quashed and any property levied on pursuant to the writ be released. Such application shall be made by noticed motion, and the provisions of Section 512.050 shall apply. Pending the hearing on the defendant's application, the court may order that delivery pursuant to Section 514.030 of any property previously levied upon be stayed. If the court determines that the plaintiff is not entitled to a writ of possession, the court shall quash the writ of possession and order the release and redelivery of any property previously levied upon, and shall award the defendant any damages sustained by him which were proximately caused by the levy of the writ of possession and the loss of possession of the property pursuant to such levy.[85]

512.030. (a) Prior to the hearing required by subdivision (a) of Section 512.020, the defendant shall be served with all of the following:

(1) A copy of the summons and complaint.

(2) A Notice of Application and Hearing.

(3) A copy of the application and any affidavit in support thereof.

(b) If the defendant has not appeared in the action, and a writ, notice, order, or other paper is required to be personally served on the defendant under this title, service shall be made in the same manner as a summons is served under Chapter 4 (commencing with Section 413.10) of Title 5.[591]

512.040. The "Notice of Application

and Hearing" shall inform the defendant of all of the following:

(a) A hearing will be held at a place and at a time, to be specified in the notice, on plaintiff's application for a writ of possession.

(b) The writ will be issued if the court finds that the plaintiff's claim is probably valid and the other requirements for issuing the writ are established. The hearing is not for the purpose of determining whether the claim is actually valid. The determination of the actual validity of the claim will be made in subsequent proceedings in the action and will not be affected by the decision at the hearing on the application for the writ.

(c) If the defendant desires to oppose the issuance of the writ, he shall file with the court either an affidavit providing evidence sufficient to defeat the plaintiff's right to issuance of the writ or an undertaking to stay the delivery of the property in accordance with Section 515.020.

(d) The notice shall contain the following statement: "If you believe the plaintiff may not be entitled to possession of the property claimed, you may wish to seek the advice of an attorney. Such attorney should be consulted promptly so that he may assist you before the time set for the hearing."[85]

512.050. Each party shall file with the court and serve upon the other party within the time prescribed by rule any affidavits and points and authorities intended to be relied upon at the hearing. At the hearing, the court shall make its determinations upon the basis of the pleadings and other papers in the record; but, upon good cause shown, the court may receive and consider additional evidence and authority produced at the hearing or may continue the hearing for the production of such additional evidence, oral or documentary, or the filing of other affidavits or points and authorities.[85]

512.060. (a) At the hearing, a writ of possession shall issue if both of the following are found:

(1) The plaintiff has established the probable validity of the plaintiff's claim to possession of the property.

(2) The undertaking requirements of Section 515.010 are satisfied.

(b) No writ directing the levying officer to enter a private place to take possession of any property shall be issued unless the plaintiff has established that there is probable cause to believe that the property is located there.[473]

512.070. If a writ of possession is issued, the court may also issue an order directing the defendant to transfer possession of the property to the plaintiff. Such order shall contain a notice to the defendant that failure to turn over possession of such property to plaintiff may subject the defendant to being held in contempt of court.[98]

512.080. The writ of possession shall meet all of the following requirements:

(a) Be directed to the levying officer within whose jurisdiction the property is located.

(b) Describe the specific property to be seized.

(c) Specify any private place that may be entered to take possession of the property or some part of it.

(d) Direct the levying officer to levy on the property pursuant to Section 514.010 if found and to retain it in custody until released or sold pursuant to Section 514.030.

(e) Inform the defendant of the right to object to the plaintiff's undertaking, a copy of which shall be attached to the writ, or to obtain redelivery of the property by filing an undertaking as prescribed by Section 515.020.[119]

512.090. (a) The plaintiff may apply ex parte in writing to the court in which the action was brought for an endorsement on the writ directing the levying officer to seize the property at a private place not specified in the writ.
(b) The court shall make the endorsement if the plaintiff establishes by affidavit that there is probable cause to believe that the property or some part of it may be found at that place.[85]

512.100. Neither the failure of the defendant to oppose the issuance of a writ of possession under this chapter nor his failure to rebut any evidence produced by the plaintiff in connection with proceedings under this chapter shall constitute a waiver of any defense to plaintiff's claim in the action or any other action or have any effect on the right of the defendant to produce or exclude evidence at the trial of any such action.[85]

512.110. The determinations of the court under this chapter shall have no effect on the determination of any issues in the action other than the issues relevant to proceedings under this chapter, nor shall they affect the rights of any party in any other action arising out of the same claim. The determinations of the court under this chapter shall not be given in evidence nor referred to in the trial of any such action.[85]

512.120. If the plaintiff fails to recover judgment in the action, he shall redeliver the property to the defendant and be liable for all damages sustained by the defendant which are proximately caused by operation of the temporary restraining order and preliminary injunction, if any, the levy of the writ of possession, and the loss of possession of the property pursuant to levy of the writ of possession or in compliance with an order issued under Section 512.070.[85]

Article 3: Temporary Restraining Order
Article 3 added by Stats. 1973, Ch. 526.

513.010. (a) Except as otherwise provided by this chapter, the provisions of Chapter 3 (commencing with Section 525) of this title relating to the issuance of a temporary restraining order apply. At or after the time he files his application for writ of possession, the plaintiff may apply for a temporary restraining order by setting forth in the application a statement of grounds justifying the issuance of such order.
(b) A temporary restraining order may issue ex parte if all of the following are found:
(1) The plaintiff has established the probable validity of his claim to possession of the property.
(2) The plaintiff has provided an undertaking as required by Section 515.010.
(3) The plaintiff has established the probability that there is an immediate danger that the property claimed may become unavailable to levy by reason of being transferred, concealed, or removed or may become substantially impaired in value.
(c) If at the hearing on issuance of the writ of possession the court determines that the plaintiff is not entitled

to a writ of possession, the court shall dissolve any temporary restraining order; otherwise, the court may issue a preliminary injunction to remain in effect until the property claimed is seized pursuant to the writ of possession.[85]

513.020. In the discretion of the court, the temporary restraining order may prohibit the defendant from doing any or all of the following:
(a) Transferring any interest in the property by sale, pledge, or grant of security interest, or otherwise disposing of, or encumbering, the property. If the property is farm products held for sale or lease or is inventory, the order may not prohibit the defendant from transferring the property in the ordinary course of business, but the order may impose appropriate restrictions on the disposition of the proceeds from such transfer.
(b) Concealing or otherwise removing the property in such a manner as to make it less available to seizure by the levying officer.
(c) Impairing the value of the property either by acts of destruction or by failure to care for the property in a reasonable manner.[85]

Article 4: Levy and Custody
Article 4 added by Stats. 1973, Ch. 526.

514.010. (a) Except as otherwise provided in this section, upon receipt of the writ of possession the levying officer shall search for and take custody of the specified property, if it be in the possession of the defendant or his agent, either by removing the property to a place of safekeeping or by installing a keeper.
(b) If the specified property is used as a dwelling, such as a mobilehome or boat, levy shall be made by placing a keeper in charge of the property for two days, at the plaintiff's expense, after which period the levying officer shall remove the occupants and any contents not specified in the writ and shall take exclusive possession of the property.
(c) If the specified property or any part of it is in a private place, the levying officer shall at the time he demands possession of the property announce his identity, purpose, and authority. If the property is not voluntarily delivered, the levying officer may cause any building or enclosure where the property may be located to be broken open in such a manner as he reasonably believes will cause the least damage and may call upon the power of the county to aid and protect him, but, if he reasonably believes that entry and seizure of the property will involve a substantial risk of death or serious bodily harm to any person, he shall refrain from seizing the property and shall promptly make a return to the court from which the writ issued setting forth the reasons for his belief that the risk exists. In such case, the court shall make such orders as may be appropriate.
(d) Nothing in this section authorizes the levying officer to enter or search any private place not specified in the writ of possession or other order of the court.[85]

514.020. (a) At the time of levy, the levying officer shall deliver to the person in possession of the property a copy of the writ of possession, a copy of the plaintiff's undertaking, if any, and a copy of the order for issuance of the writ.
(b) If no one is in possession of the property at the time of levy, the levying

officer shall subsequently serve the writ and attached undertaking on the defendant. If the defendant has appeared in the action, service shall be accomplished in the manner provided by Chapter 5 (commencing with Section 1010) of Title 14. If the defendant has not appeared in the action, service shall be accomplished in the manner provided for the service of summons and complaint by Article 3 (commencing with Section 415.10) of Chapter 4 of Title 5.[474]

514.030. (a) After the levying officer takes possession pursuant to a writ of possession, the levying officer shall keep the property in a secure place. Except as otherwise provided by Sections 512.020 and 514.050:

(1) If notice of the filing of an undertaking for redelivery or notice of objection to the plaintiff's undertaking is not received by the levying officer within 10 days after levy of the writ of possession, the levying officer shall deliver the property to plaintiff, upon receiving the fees for taking and necessary expenses for keeping the property.

(2) If notice of the filing of an undertaking for redelivery is received by the levying officer within 10 days after levy of the writ of possession and defendant's undertaking is not objected to, the levying officer shall redeliver the property to defendant upon expiration of the time to so object, upon receiving the fees for taking and necessary expenses for keeping the property not already paid or advanced by the plaintiff.

(3) If notice of objection to the plaintiff's undertaking or notice of the filing of an undertaking for redelivery is received within 10 days after levy of the writ of possession and defendant's undertaking is objected to, the levying officer shall not deliver or redeliver the property until the time provided in Section 515.030.

(b) Notwithstanding subdivision (a), where not otherwise provided by contract and where an undertaking for redelivery has not been filed, upon a showing that the property is perishable or will greatly deteriorate or depreciate in value or for some other reason that the interests of the parties will be best served thereby, the court may order that the property be sold and the proceeds deposited in the court to abide the judgment in the action.[129]

514.040. The levying officer shall return the writ of possession, with his proceedings thereon, to the court in which the action is pending within 30 days after levy but in no event more than 60 days after the writ is issued.[85]

514.050. Where the property taken is claimed by a third person, the rules and proceedings applicable in cases of third-party claims under Division 4 (commencing with Section 720.010) of Title 9 apply.[123]

Article 5: Undertakings
Article 5 added by Stats. 1973, Ch. 526.

515.010. (a) Except as provided in subdivision (b), the court shall not issue a temporary restraining order or a writ of possession until the plaintiff has filed an undertaking with the court. The undertaking shall provide that the sureties are bound to the defendant for the return of the property to the defendant, if return of the property is ordered, and for the payment to the defendant of any sum recovered against the plaintiff. The undertaking shall be in an amount not less than twice the value of the defendant's interest in the property or in a greater amount. The value of the defendant's interest in the property is determined by the market value of the property less the amount due and owing on any conditional sales contract or security agreement and all liens and encumbrances on the property, and any other factors necessary to determine the defendant's interest in the property.

(b) If the court finds that the defendant has no interest in the property, the court shall waive the requirement of the plaintiff's undertaking and shall include in the order for issuance of the writ the amount of the defendant's undertaking sufficient to satisfy the requirements of subdivision (b) of Section 515.020.[475]

515.020. (a) The defendant may prevent the plaintiff from taking possession of property pursuant to a writ of possession or regain possession of property so taken by filing with the court in which the action was brought an undertaking in an amount equal to the amount of the plaintiff's undertaking pursuant to subdivision (a) of Section 515.010 or in the amount determined by the court pursuant to subdivision (b) of Section 515.010.

(b) The undertaking shall state that, if the plaintiff recovers judgment on the action, the defendant shall pay all costs awarded to the plaintiff and all damages that the plaintiff may sustain by reason of the loss of possession of the property. The damages recoverable by the plaintiff pursuant to this section shall include all damages proximately caused by the plaintiff's failure to gain or retain possession.

(c) The defendant's undertaking may be filed at any time before or after levy of the writ of possession. A copy of the undertaking shall be mailed to the levying officer.

(d) If an undertaking for redelivery is filed and the defendant's undertaking is not objected to, the levying officer shall deliver the property to the defendant, or, if the plaintiff has previously been given possession of the property, the plaintiff shall deliver the property to the defendant. If an undertaking for redelivery is filed and the defendant's undertaking is objected to, the provisions of Section 515.030 apply.[476]

515.030. (a) The defendant may object to the plaintiff's undertaking not later than 10 days after levy of the writ of possession. The defendant shall mail notice of objection to the levying officer.

(b) The plaintiff may object to the defendant's undertaking not later than 10 days after the defendant's undertaking is filed. The plaintiff shall mail notice of objection to the levying officer.

(c) If the court determines that the plaintiff's undertaking is insufficient and a sufficient undertaking is not filed within the time required by statute, the court shall vacate the temporary restraining order or preliminary injunction, if any, and the writ of possession and, if levy has occurred, order the levying officer or the plaintiff to return the property to the defendant. If the court determines that the plaintiff's undertaking is sufficient, the court shall order the levying officer to deliver the property to the plaintiff.

(d) If the court determines that the defendant's undertaking is insufficient and a sufficient undertaking is not filed within the time required by statute, the court shall order the levying officer to deliver the property to the plaintiff, or, if the plaintiff has previously been given possession of the property, the plaintiff shall retain possession. If the court determines that the defendant's undertaking is sufficient, the court shall order the levying officer or the plaintiff to deliver the property to the defendant.[214]

Article 6: Miscellaneous Provisions
Article 6 added by Stats. 1973, Ch. 526.

516.010. The Judicial Council may provide by rule for the practice and procedure in proceedings under this chapter.[85]

516.020. The Judicial Council shall prescribe the form of the applications, notices, orders, and other documents required by this chapter.[85]

516.030. The facts stated in each affidavit filed pursuant to this chapter shall be set forth with particularity. Except where matters are specifically permitted by this chapter to be shown by information and belief, each affidavit shall show affirmatively that the affiant, if sworn as a witness, can testify competently to the facts stated therein. The affiant may be any person, whether or not a party to the action, who has knowledge of the facts. A verified complaint that satisfies the requirements of this section may be used in lieu of or in addition to an ordinary affidavit.[85]

516.040. The judicial duties to be performed under this chapter are "subordinate judicial duties" within the meaning of Section 22 of Article VI of the California Constitution and may be performed by appointed officers such as court commissioners.[85]

516.050. Nothing in this chapter shall preclude the granting of relief pursuant to Chapter 3 (commencing with Section 525) of this title.[85]

Chapter 3: Injunction

Chapter 3 enacted 1872.

525. An injunction is a writ or order requiring a person to refrain from a particular act. It may be granted by the court in which the action is brought, or by a judge thereof; and when granted by a judge, it may be enforced as an order of the court.[9]

526. (a) An injunction may be granted in the following cases:

(1) When it appears by the complaint that the plaintiff is entitled to the relief demanded, and the relief, or any part thereof, consists in restraining the commission or continuance of the act complained of, either for a limited period or perpetually.

(2) When it appears by the complaint or affidavits that the commission or continuance of some act during the litigation would produce waste, or great or irreparable injury, to a party to the action.

(3) When it appears, during the litigation, that a party to the action is doing, or threatens, or is about to do, or is procuring or suffering to be done, some act in violation of the rights of another party to the action respecting the subject of the action, and tending to render the judgment ineffectual.

(4) When pecuniary compensation would not afford adequate relief.

(5) Where it would be extremely difficult to ascertain the amount of com-

pensation which would afford adequate relief.

(6) Where the restraint is necessary to prevent a multiplicity of judicial proceedings.

(7) Where the obligation arises from a trust.

(b) An injunction cannot be granted in the following cases:

(1) To stay a judicial proceeding pending at the commencement of the action in which the injunction is demanded, unless the restraint is necessary to prevent a multiplicity of proceedings.

(2) To stay proceedings in a court of the United States.

(3) To stay proceedings in another state upon a judgment of a court of that state.

(4) To prevent the execution of a public statute by officers of the law for the public benefit.

(5) To prevent the breach of a contract the performance of which would not be specifically enforced, other than a contract in writing for the rendition of personal services from one to another where the promised service is of a special, unique, unusual, extraordinary, or intellectual character, which gives it peculiar value, the loss of which cannot be reasonably or adequately compensated in damages in an action at law, and where the compensation for the personal services is as follows:

(A) As to contracts entered into on or before December 31, 1993, the minimum compensation provided in the contract for the personal services shall be at the rate of six thousand dollars ($6,000) per annum.

(B) As to contracts entered into on or after January 1, 1994, the criteria of clause (i) or (ii), as follows, are satisfied:

(i) The compensation is as follows:

(I) The minimum compensation provided in the contract shall be at the rate of nine thousand dollars ($9,000) per annum for the first year of the contract, twelve thousand dollars ($12,000) per annum for the second year of the contract, and fifteen thousand dollars ($15,000) per annum for the third to seventh years, inclusive, of the contract.

(II) In addition, after the third year of the contract, there shall actually have been paid for the services through and including the contract year during which the injunctive relief is sought, over and above the minimum contractual compensation specified in subclause (I), the amount of fifteen thousand dollars ($15,000) per annum during the fourth and fifth years of the contract, and thirty thousand dollars ($30,000) per annum during the sixth and seventh years of the contract. As a condition to petitioning for an injunction, amounts payable under this clause may be paid at any time prior to seeking injunctive relief.

(ii) The aggregate compensation actually received for the services provided under a contract that does not meet the criteria of subparagraph (A), is at least 10 times the applicable aggregate minimum amount specified in subclauses (I) and (II) of clause (i) through and including the contract year during which the injunctive relief is sought. As a condition to petitioning for an injunction, amounts payable under this subparagraph may be paid at any time prior to seeking injunctive relief.

(C) Compensation paid in any contract year in excess of the minimums specified in clauses (i) and (ii) of subparagraph (B) shall apply to reduce the compensation otherwise required to be paid under those provisions in any subsequent contract years. However, an injunction may be granted to prevent the breach of a contract entered into between any nonprofit cooperative corporation or association and a member or stockholder thereof, in respect to any provision regarding the sale or delivery to the corporation or association of the products produced or acquired by the member or stockholder.

(6) To prevent the exercise of a public or private office, in a lawful manner, by the person in possession.

(7) To prevent a legislative act by a municipal corporation.[328]

526a. (a) An action to obtain a judgment, restraining and preventing any illegal expenditure of, waste of, or injury to, the estate, funds, or other property of a local agency, may be maintained against any officer thereof, or any agent, or other person, acting in its behalf, either by a resident therein, or by a corporation, who is assessed for and is liable to pay, or, within one year before the commencement of the action, has paid, a tax that funds the defendant local agency, including, but not limited to, the following:

(1) An income tax.

(2) A sales and use tax or transaction and use tax initially paid by a consumer to a retailer.

(3) A property tax, including a property tax paid by a tenant or lessee to a landlord or lessor pursuant to the terms of a written lease.

(4) A business license tax.

(b) This section does not affect any right of action in favor of a local agency, or any public officer; provided, that no injunction shall be granted restraining the offering for sale, sale, or issuance of any municipal bonds for public improvements or public utilities.

(c) An action brought pursuant to this section to enjoin a public improvement project shall take special precedence over all civil matters on the calendar of the court except those matters to which equal precedence on the calendar is granted by law.

(d) For purposes of this section, the following definitions apply:

(1) "Local agency" means a city, town, county, or city and county, or a district, public authority, or any other political subdivision in the state.

(2) "Resident" means a person who lives, works, owns property, or attends school in the jurisdiction of the defendant local agency.[746]

526b. Every person or corporation bringing, instigating, exciting or abetting, any suit to obtain an injunction, restraining or enjoining the issuance, sale, offering for sale, or delivery, of bonds, or other securities, or the expenditure of the proceeds of the sale of such bonds or other securities, of any city, city and county, town, county, or other district organized under the laws of this state, or any other political subdivision of this state, proposed to be issued, sold, offered for sale or delivered by such city, city and county, town, county, district or other political subdivision, for the purpose of acquiring, constructing, completing, improving or extending water works, electric works, gas works or other public utility works or property, shall, if the injunction sought is finally denied, and if such person or corporation owns, controls, or is operating or interested in, a public utility business of the same nature as that for which such bonds or other securities are proposed to be issued, sold, offered for sale, or delivered, be liable to the defendant for all costs, damages and necessary expenses resulting to such defendant by reason of the filing of such suit.[14]

527. (a) A preliminary injunction may be granted at any time before judgment upon a verified complaint, or upon affidavits if the complaint in the one case, or the affidavits in the other, show satisfactorily that sufficient grounds exist therefor. No preliminary injunction shall be granted without notice to the opposing party.

(b) A temporary restraining order or a preliminary injunction, or both, may be granted in a class action, in which one or more of the parties sues or defends for the benefit of numerous parties upon the same grounds as in other actions, whether or not the class has been certified.

(c) No temporary restraining order shall be granted without notice to the opposing party, unless both of the following requirements are satisfied:

(1) It appears from facts shown by affidavit or by the verified complaint that great or irreparable injury will result to the applicant before the matter can be heard on notice.

(2) The applicant or the applicant's attorney certifies one of the following to the court under oath:

(A) That within a reasonable time prior to the application the applicant informed the opposing party or the opposing party's attorney at what time and where the application would be made.

(B) That the applicant in good faith attempted but was unable to inform the opposing party and the opposing party's attorney, specifying the efforts made to contact them.

(C) That for reasons specified the applicant should not be required to so inform the opposing party or the opposing party's attorney.

(d) In case a temporary restraining order is granted without notice in the contingency specified in subdivision (c):

(1) The matter shall be made returnable on an order requiring cause to be shown why a preliminary injunction should not be granted, on the earliest day that the business of the court will admit of, but not later than 15 days or, if good cause appears to the court, 22 days from the date the temporary restraining order is issued.

(2) The party who obtained the temporary restraining order shall, within five days from the date the temporary restraining order is issued or two days prior to the hearing, whichever is earlier, serve on the opposing party a copy of the complaint if not previously served, the order to show cause stating the date, time, and place of the hearing, any affidavits to be used in the application, and a copy of the points and authorities in support of the application. The court may for good cause, on motion of the applicant or on its own motion, shorten the time required by this paragraph for service on the opposing party.

(3) When the matter first comes up

for hearing, if the party who obtained the temporary restraining order is not ready to proceed, or if the party has failed to effect service as required by paragraph (2), the court shall dissolve the temporary restraining order.

(4) The opposing party is entitled to one continuance for a reasonable period of not less than 15 days or any shorter period requested by the opposing party, to enable the opposing party to meet the application for a preliminary injunction. If the opposing party obtains a continuance under this paragraph, the temporary restraining order shall remain in effect until the date of the continued hearing.

(5) Upon the filing of an affidavit by the applicant that the opposing party could not be served within the time required by paragraph (2), the court may reissue any temporary restraining order previously issued. The reissued order shall be made returnable as provided by paragraph (1), with the time for hearing measured from the date of reissuance. No fee shall be charged for reissuing the order.

(e) The opposing party may, in response to an order to show cause, present affidavits relating to the granting of the preliminary injunction, and if the affidavits are served on the applicant at least two days prior to the hearing, the applicant shall not be entitled to any continuance on account thereof. On the day the order is made returnable, the hearing shall take precedence over all other matters on the calendar of the day, except older matters of the same character, and matters to which special precedence may be given by law. When the cause is at issue it shall be set for trial at the earliest possible date and shall take precedence over all other cases, except older matters of the same character, and matters to which special precedence may be given by law.

(f) Notwithstanding failure to satisfy the time requirements of this section, the court may nonetheless hear the order to show cause why a preliminary injunction should not be granted if the moving and supporting papers are served within the time required by Section 1005 and one of the following conditions is satisfied:

(1) The order to show cause is issued without a temporary restraining order.

(2) The order to show cause is issued with a temporary restraining order, but is either not set for hearing within the time required by paragraph (1) of subdivision (d), or the party who obtained the temporary restraining order fails to effect service within the time required by paragraph (2) of subdivision (d).

(g) This section does not apply to an order issued under the Family Code.

(h) As used in this section:

(1) "Complaint" means a complaint or a cross-complaint.

(2) "Court" means the court in which the action is pending.[444] **Error! Bookmark not defined.**

527.3. (a) In order to promote the rights of workers to engage in concerted activities for the purpose of collective bargaining, picketing or other mutual aid or protection, and to prevent the evils which frequently occur when courts interfere with the normal processes of dispute resolution between employers and recognized employee organizations, the equity jurisdiction of the courts in cases involving or growing out of a labor dispute shall be no broader than as set forth in subdivision (b) of this section, and the provisions of subdivision (b) of this section shall be strictly construed in accordance with existing law governing labor disputes with the purpose of avoiding any unnecessary judicial interference in labor disputes.

(b) The acts enumerated in this subdivision, whether performed singly or in concert, shall be legal, and no court nor any judge nor judges thereof, shall have jurisdiction to issue any restraining order or preliminary or permanent injunction which, in specific or general terms, prohibits any person or persons, whether singly or in concert, from doing any of the following:

(1) Giving publicity to, and obtaining or communicating information regarding the existence of, or the facts involved in, any labor dispute, whether by advertising, speaking, patrolling any public street or any place where any person or persons may lawfully be, or by any other method not involving fraud, violence or breach of the peace.

(2) Peaceful picketing or patrolling involving any labor dispute, whether engaged in singly or in numbers.

(3) Assembling peaceably to do any of the acts specified in paragraphs (1) and (2) or to promote lawful interests.

(4) Except as provided in subparagraph (iv), for purposes of this section, "labor dispute" is defined as follows:

(i) A case shall be held to involve or to grow out of a labor dispute when the case involves persons who are engaged in the same industry, trade, craft, or occupation; or have direct or indirect interests therein; or who are employees of the same employer; or who are members of the same or an affiliated organization of employers or employees; whether such dispute is (a) between one or more employers or associations of employers and one or more employees or associations of employees; (b) between one or more employers or associations of employers and one or more employers or associations of employers; or (c) between one or more employees or associations of employees and one or more employees or associations of employees; or when the case involves any conflicting or competing interests in a "labor dispute" of "persons participating or interested" therein (as defined in subparagraph (ii)).

(ii) A person or association shall be held to be a person participating or interested in a labor dispute if relief is sought against him or it, and if he or it is engaged in the same industry, trade, craft, or occupation in which such dispute occurs, or has a direct or indirect interest therein, or is a member, officer, or agent of any association composed in whole or in part of employers or employees engaged in such industry, trade, craft, or occupation.

(iii) The term "labor dispute" includes any controversy concerning terms or conditions of employment, or concerning the association or representation of persons in negotiating, fixing, maintaining, changing, or seeking to arrange terms or conditions of employment regardless of whether or not the disputants stand in the proximate relation of employer and employee.

(iv) The term "labor dispute" does

not include a jurisdictional strike as defined in Section 1118 of the Labor Code.

(c) Nothing contained in this section shall be construed to alter or supersede the provisions of Chapter 1 of the 1975–76 Third Extraordinary Session, and to the extent of any conflict between the provisions of this act and that chapter, the provisions of the latter shall prevail.

(d) Nothing contained in this section shall be construed to alter the legal rights of public employees or their employers, nor shall this section alter the rights of parties to collective-bargaining agreements under the provisions of Section 1126 of the Labor Code.

(e) It is not the intent of this section to permit conduct that is unlawful including breach of the peace, disorderly conduct, the unlawful blocking of access or egress to premises where a labor dispute exists, or other similar unlawful activity.[94]

527.6. (a) (1) A person who has suffered harassment as defined in subdivision (b) may seek a temporary restraining order and an order after hearing prohibiting harassment as provided in this section.

(2) An individual need not be a resident of the state to file a petition for an order under this section. A petition for an order as specified in paragraph (1) may be filed in any superior court in this state, consistent with Section 410.10 of the Code of Civil Procedure, which may include, but is not limited to:

(A) The county in which the petitioner resides or is temporarily located.

(B) The county in which the defendant resides.

(C) The county in which the offense occurred.

(D) Any other court that may have jurisdiction over the parties or the subject matter of the case.

(3) A minor, under 12 years of age, accompanied by a duly appointed and acting guardian ad litem, shall be permitted to appear in court without counsel for the limited purpose of requesting or opposing a request for a temporary restraining order or order after hearing, or both, under this section as provided in Section 374.

(b) For purposes of this section, the following terms have the following meanings:

(1) "Course of conduct" is a pattern of conduct composed of a series of acts over a period of time, however short, evidencing a continuity of purpose, including following or stalking an individual, making harassing telephone calls to an individual, or sending harassing correspondence to an individual by any means, including, but not limited to, the use of public or private mails, interoffice mail, facsimile, or email. Constitutionally protected activity is not included within the meaning of "course of conduct."

(2) "Credible threat of violence" is a knowing and willful statement or course of conduct that would place a reasonable person in fear for the person's safety or the safety of the person's immediate family, and that serves no legitimate purpose.

(3) "Harassment" is unlawful violence, a credible threat of violence, or a knowing and willful course of conduct directed at a specific person that seriously alarms, annoys, or harasses the person, and that serves no legitimate purpose. The course of conduct

must be that which would cause a reasonable person to suffer substantial emotional distress, and must actually cause substantial emotional distress to the petitioner.

(4) "Petitioner" means the person to be protected by the temporary restraining order and order after hearing and, if the court grants the petition, the protected person.

(5) "Respondent" means the person against whom the temporary restraining order and order after hearing are sought and, if the petition is granted, the restrained person.

(6) "Temporary restraining order" and "order after hearing" mean orders that include any of the following restraining orders, whether issued ex parte or after notice and hearing:

(A) An order enjoining a party from harassing, intimidating, molesting, attacking, striking, stalking, threatening, sexually assaulting, battering, abusing, telephoning, including, but not limited to, making annoying telephone calls, as described in Section 653m of the Penal Code, destroying personal property, contacting, either directly or indirectly, by mail or otherwise, or coming within a specified distance of, or disturbing the peace of, the petitioner. On a showing of good cause, in an order issued pursuant to this subparagraph in connection with an animal owned, possessed, leased, kept, or held by the petitioner, or residing in the residence or household of the petitioner, the court may do either or both of the following:

(i) Grant the petitioner exclusive care, possession, or control of the animal.

(ii) Order the respondent to stay away from the animal and refrain from taking, transferring, encumbering, concealing, molesting, attacking, striking, threatening, harming, or otherwise disposing of the animal.

(B) An order enjoining a party from specified behavior that the court determines is necessary to effectuate orders described in subparagraph (A).

(7) "Unlawful violence" is any assault or battery, or stalking as prohibited in Section 646.9 of the Penal Code, but does not include lawful acts of self-defense or defense of others.

(c) In the discretion of the court, on a showing of good cause, a temporary restraining order or order after hearing issued under this section may include other named family or household members.

(d) Upon filing a petition for orders under this section, the petitioner may obtain a temporary restraining order in accordance with Section 527, except to the extent this section provides an inconsistent rule. The temporary restraining order may include any of the restraining orders described in paragraph (6) of subdivision (b). A temporary restraining order may be issued with or without notice, based on a declaration that, to the satisfaction of the court, shows reasonable proof of harassment of the petitioner by the respondent, and that great or irreparable harm would result to the petitioner.

(e) A request for the issuance of a temporary restraining order without notice under this section shall be granted or denied on the same day that the petition is submitted to the court. If the petition is filed too late in the day to permit effective review, the order shall be granted or denied on the next day of judicial business in sufficient time for the order to be filed that day with the clerk of the court.

(f) A temporary restraining order issued under this section shall remain in effect, at the court's discretion, for a period not to exceed 21 days, or, if the court extends the time for hearing under subdivision (g), not to exceed 25 days, unless otherwise modified or terminated by the court.

(g) Within 21 days, or, if good cause appears to the court, 25 days from the date that a petition for a temporary order is granted or denied, a hearing shall be held on the petition. If a request for a temporary order is not made, the hearing shall be held within 21 days, or, if good cause appears to the court, 25 days, from the date that the petition is filed.

(h) The respondent may file a response that explains, excuses, justifies, or denies the alleged harassment, or may file a cross-petition under this section.

(i) (1) At the hearing, the judge shall receive any testimony that is relevant, and may make an independent inquiry. If the judge finds by clear and convincing evidence that unlawful harassment exists, an order shall issue prohibiting the harassment.

(2) Commencing January 1, 2027, a party or witness may appear remotely at the hearing on a petition for an order under this section. The superior court of each county shall not charge a fee for a party to appear remotely at the hearing and shall develop local rules and instructions for remote appearances permitted under this paragraph, which shall be posted on its internet website.

(j) (1) In the discretion of the court, an order issued after notice and hearing under this section may have a duration of no more than five years, subject to termination or modification by further order of the court either on written stipulation filed with the court or on the motion of a party. The order may be renewed, upon the request of a party, for a duration of no more than five additional years, without a showing of any further harassment since the issuance of the original order, subject to termination or modification by further order of the court either on written stipulation filed with the court or on the motion of a party. A request for renewal may be brought any time within the three months before the order expires.

(2) The failure to state the expiration date on the face of the form creates an order with a duration of three years from the date of issuance.

(3) If an action is filed for the purpose of terminating or modifying a protective order before the expiration date specified in the order by a party other than the protected party, the party who is protected by the order shall be given notice, pursuant to subdivision (b) of Section 1005, of the proceeding by personal service or, if the protected party has satisfied the requirements of Chapter 3.1 (commencing with Section 6205) of Division 7 of Title 1 of the Government Code, by service on the Secretary of State. If the party who is protected by the order cannot be notified before the hearing for modification or termination of the protective order, the court shall deny the motion to modify or terminate the order without prejudice or continue

the hearing until the party who is protected can be properly noticed and may, upon a showing of good cause, specify another method for service of process that is reasonably designed to afford actual notice to the protected party. The protected party may waive the protected party's right to notice if the protected party is physically present in court and does not challenge the sufficiency of the notice.

(k) This section does not preclude either party from representation by private counsel or from appearing on the party's own behalf.

(l) In a proceeding under this section, if there are allegations of unlawful violence or credible threats of violence, a support person may accompany a party in court and, if the party is not represented by an attorney, may sit with the party at the table that is generally reserved for the party and the party's attorney. The support person is present to provide moral and emotional support for a person who alleges they are a victim of violence. The support person is not present as a legal adviser and may not provide legal advice. The support person may assist the person who alleges they are a victim of violence in feeling more confident that they will not be injured or threatened by the other party during the proceedings if the person who alleges the person is a victim of violence and the other party are required to be present in close proximity. This subdivision does not preclude the court from exercising its discretion to remove the support person from the courtroom if the court believes the support person is prompting, swaying, or influencing the party assisted by the support person.

(m) (1) Except as provided in paragraph (2), upon the filing of a petition under this section, the respondent shall be personally served with a copy of the petition, temporary restraining order, if any, and notice of hearing of the petition. Service shall be made at least five days before the hearing. The court may for good cause, on motion of the petitioner or on its own motion, shorten the time for service on the respondent.

(2) If the court determines at the hearing that, after a diligent effort, the petitioner has been unable to accomplish personal service, and that there is reason to believe that the respondent is evading service or cannot be located, then the court may specify another method of service that is reasonably calculated to give actual notice to the respondent and may prescribe the manner in which proof of service shall be made.

(n) A notice of hearing under this section shall notify the respondent that if the respondent does not attend the hearing, the court may make orders against the respondent that could last up to five years.

(o) The respondent shall be entitled, as a matter of course, to one continuance, for a reasonable period, to respond to the petition.

(p) (1) Either party may request a continuance of the hearing, which the court shall grant on a showing of good cause. The request may be made in writing before or at the hearing, or orally at the hearing. The court may also grant a continuance on its own motion.

(2) If the court grants a continuance, any temporary restraining order that has been granted shall remain in effect

until the end of the continued hearing, unless otherwise ordered by the court. In granting a continuance, the court may modify or terminate a temporary restraining order.

(q) (1) If a respondent named in a restraining order issued after a hearing has not been served personally with the order but has received actual notice of the existence and substance of the order through personal appearance in court to hear the terms of the order from the court, additional proof of service is not required for enforcement of the order.

(2) If the respondent named in a temporary restraining order is personally served with the order and notice of hearing with respect to a restraining order or protective order based on the temporary restraining order, but the respondent does not appear at the hearing, either personally or by an attorney, and the terms and conditions of the restraining order or protective order issued at the hearing are identical to the temporary restraining order, except for the duration of the order, the restraining order or protective order issued at the hearing may be served on the respondent by first-class mail sent to the respondent at the most current address for the respondent available to the court.

(3) The Judicial Council form for temporary orders issued pursuant to this subdivision shall contain a statement in substantially the following form:

"If you have been personally served with this temporary restraining order and notice of hearing, but you do not appear at the hearing either in person or by a lawyer, and a restraining order that is the same as this temporary restraining order except for the expiration date is issued at the hearing, a copy of the restraining order will be served on you by mail at the following address: ____.

If that address is not correct or you wish to verify that the temporary restraining order was converted to a restraining order at the hearing without substantive change and to find out the duration of that order, contact the clerk of the court."

(4) If information about a minor has been made confidential pursuant to subdivision (v), the notice shall identify the information, specifically, that has been made confidential and shall include a statement that disclosure or misuse of that information is punishable as a contempt of court.

(r) (1) Information on a temporary restraining order or order after hearing relating to civil harassment issued by a court pursuant to this section shall be transmitted to the Department of Justice in accordance with either paragraph (2) or (3).

(2) The court shall order the petitioner or the attorney for the petitioner to deliver a copy of an order issued under this section, or reissuance, extension, modification, or termination of the order, and any subsequent proof of service, by the close of the business day on which the order, reissuance, extension, modification, or termination was made, to a law enforcement agency having jurisdiction over the residence of the petitioner and to any additional law enforcement agencies within the court's discretion as are requested by the petitioner.

(3) Alternatively, the court or its de-

signee shall transmit, within one business day, to law enforcement personnel all information required under subdivision (b) of Section 6380 of the Family Code regarding any order issued under this section, or a reissuance, extension, modification, or termination of the order, and any subsequent proof of service, by either one of the following methods:

(A) Transmitting a physical copy of the order or proof of service to a local law enforcement agency authorized by the Department of Justice to enter orders into the California Law Enforcement Telecommunications System (CLETS).

(B) With the approval of the Department of Justice, entering the order or proof of service into CLETS directly.

(4) Each appropriate law enforcement agency shall make available information as to the existence and current status of orders issued under this section to law enforcement officers responding to the scene of reported harassment.

(5) An order issued under this section shall, on request of the petitioner, be served on the respondent, whether or not the respondent has been taken into custody, by any law enforcement officer who is present at the scene of reported harassment involving the parties to the proceeding. The petitioner shall provide the officer with an endorsed copy of the order and a proof of service that the officer shall complete and send to the issuing court.

(6) Upon receiving information at the scene of an incident of harassment that a protective order has been issued under this section, or that a person who has been taken into custody is the subject of an order, if the protected person cannot produce a certified copy of the order, a law enforcement officer shall immediately attempt to verify the existence of the order.

(7) If the law enforcement officer determines that a protective order has been issued but not served, the officer shall immediately notify the respondent of the terms of the order and shall at that time also enforce the order. Verbal notice of the terms of the order shall constitute service of the order and is sufficient notice for purposes of this section and for purposes of Section 29825 of the Penal Code. Verbal notice shall include the information required pursuant to paragraph (4) of subdivision (q).

(s) The prevailing party in an action brought pursuant to this section may be awarded court costs and attorney's fees, if any.

(t) Willful disobedience of a temporary restraining order or order after hearing granted pursuant to this section is punishable pursuant to Section 273.6 of the Penal Code.

(u) (1) A person subject to a protective order issued pursuant to this section shall not own, possess, purchase, receive, or attempt to purchase or receive a firearm or ammunition while the protective order is in effect.

(2) The court shall order a person subject to a protective order issued pursuant to this section to relinquish any firearms the person owns or possesses pursuant to Section 527.9.

(3) A person who owns, possesses, purchases, or receives, or attempts to purchase or receive, a firearm or ammunition while the protective order is in effect is punishable pursuant to

Section 29825 of the Penal Code.

(v) (1) A minor or the minor's legal guardian may petition the court to have information regarding the minor that was obtained in connection with a request for a protective order pursuant to this section, including, but not limited to, the minor's name, address, and the circumstances surrounding the request for a protective order with respect to that minor, be kept confidential.

(2) The court may order the information specified in paragraph (1) be kept confidential if the court expressly finds all of the following:

(A) The minor's right to privacy overcomes the right of public access to the information.

(B) There is a substantial probability that the minor's interest will be prejudiced if the information is not kept confidential.

(C) The order to keep the information confidential is narrowly tailored.

(D) No less restrictive means exist to protect the minor's privacy.

(3) (A) If the request is granted, except as provided in paragraph (4), information regarding the minor shall be maintained in a confidential case file and shall not become part of the public file in the proceeding or any other civil proceeding involving the parties. Except as provided in subparagraph (B), if the court determines that disclosure of confidential information has been made without a court order, the court may impose a sanction of up to one thousand dollars ($1,000). A minor who has alleged harassment, as defined in subdivision (b), shall not be sanctioned for disclosure of the confidential information. If the court imposes a sanction, the court shall first determine whether the person has or is reasonably likely to have the ability to pay.

(B) Confidential information may be disclosed without a court order only in the following circumstances:

(i) By the minor's legal guardian who petitioned to keep the information confidential pursuant to this subdivision or the protected party in an order pursuant to this division, provided that the disclosure is necessary to prevent harassment or is in the minor's best interest. A legal guardian or a protected party who makes a disclosure under this clause is subject to the sanction in subparagraph (A) only if the disclosure was malicious.

(ii) By a person to whom confidential information is disclosed, provided that the disclosure is necessary to prevent harassment or is in the best interest of the minor, no more information than necessary is disclosed, and a delay would be caused by first obtaining a court order to authorize the disclosure of the information. A person who makes a disclosure pursuant to this clause is subject to the sanction in subparagraph (A) if the person discloses the information in a manner that recklessly or maliciously disregards these requirements.

(4) (A) Confidential information shall be made available to both of the following:

(i) Law enforcement pursuant to subdivision (r), to the extent necessary and only for the purpose of enforcing the order.

(ii) The respondent to allow the respondent to comply with the order for confidentiality and to allow the respondent to comply with and respond to the protective order. A notice shall be provided to the respondent that identifies the specific information that has been made confidential and shall include a statement that disclosure is punishable by a monetary fine.

(B) At any time, the court on its own may authorize a disclosure of any portion of the confidential information to certain individuals or entities as necessary to prevent harassment, as defined under subdivision (b), including implementation of the protective order, or if it is in the best interest of the minor.

(C) The court may authorize a disclosure of any portion of the confidential information to any person that files a petition if necessary to prevent harassment, as defined under subdivision (b), or if it is in the best interest of the minor. The party who petitioned the court to keep the information confidential pursuant to this subdivision shall be served personally or by first-class mail with a copy of the petition and afforded an opportunity to object to the disclosure.

(w) This section does not apply to any action or proceeding covered by Title 1.6C (commencing with Section 1788) of Part 4 of Division 3 of the Civil Code or by Division 10 (commencing with Section 6200) of the Family Code. This section does not preclude a petitioner from using other existing civil remedies.

(x) (1) The Judicial Council shall develop forms, instructions, and rules relating to matters governed by this section. The petition and response forms shall be simple and concise, and their use by parties in actions brought pursuant to this section is mandatory.

(2) A temporary restraining order or order after hearing relating to civil harassment issued by a court pursuant to this section shall be issued on forms adopted by the Judicial Council and that have been approved by the Department of Justice pursuant to subdivision (i) of Section 6380 of the Family Code. However, the fact that an order issued by a court pursuant to this section was not issued on forms adopted by the Judicial Council and approved by the Department of Justice shall not, in and of itself, make the order unenforceable.

(y) (1) (A) Commencing January 1, 2027, a court that receives petitions for protective orders under this section shall permit those petitions and any filings related to those petitions to be submitted electronically. The court shall, based on the time of the receipt, act on those filings consistent with subdivision (e).

(B) The request, notice of the court date, copies of the request to serve on the respondent, and the temporary restraining order, if granted, shall be provided to a petitioner who filed the petition electronically, unless the petitioner notes, at the time of electronic filing, that these documents will be picked up from the court.

(2) (A) There is no filing fee for a petition that alleges that a person has inflicted or threatened violence against the petitioner, stalked the petitioner, or acted or spoken in any other manner that has placed the petitioner in reasonable fear of violence, and that seeks a protective or restraining order restraining stalking, future violence,

or threats of violence, in an action brought pursuant to this section.

(B) A fee shall not be paid for a subpoena filed in connection with a petition alleging these acts.

(C) A fee shall not be paid for filing a response to a petition alleging these acts.

(z) (1) Subject to paragraph (4) of subdivision (b) of Section 6103.2 of the Government Code, there shall not be a fee for the service of process by a sheriff or marshal of a protective or restraining order to be issued, if either of the following conditions apply:

(A) The protective or restraining order issued pursuant to this section is based upon stalking, as prohibited by Section 646.9 of the Penal Code.

(B) The protective or restraining order issued pursuant to this section is based upon unlawful violence or a credible threat of violence.

(2) The Judicial Council shall prepare and develop forms for persons who wish to avail themselves of the services described in this subdivision.[876]

527.7. (a) It shall be unlawful for any group, association, organization, society, or other assemblage of two or more persons to meet and to advocate, and to take substantial action in furtherance of, the commission of an unlawful act of violence or force directed to and likely to produce the imminent and unlawful infliction of serious bodily injury or death of another person within this state.

(b) Whenever it reasonably appears that any group, association, society, or other assemblage of two or more persons has met and taken substantial action in furtherance of the commission of an act of violence made unlawful by subdivision (a) and will engage in those acts in the future, any aggrieved individual may bring a civil action in the superior court to enjoin the advocacy of the commission of any act of violence made unlawful by subdivision (a) at any future meeting or meetings. Upon a proper showing by clear and convincing evidence, a permanent or preliminary injunction, restraining order, or writ of mandate shall be granted.

(c) Whenever it appears that an action brought under this section was groundless and brought in bad faith for the purpose of harassment, the trial court or any appellate court may award to the defendant attorney's fees and court costs incurred for the purpose of defending the action.[173]

527.8. (a) Any employer or collective bargaining representative of an employee who has suffered harassment, unlawful violence, or a credible threat of violence from any individual, that can reasonably be construed to be carried out or to have been carried out at the workplace, may seek a temporary restraining order and an order after hearing on behalf of the employee and, at the discretion of the court, any number of other employees at the workplace, and, if appropriate, other employees at other workplaces of the employer. For purposes of this section only, a person may bring a petition for a temporary restraining order and an order after hearing on behalf of an employee as their collective bargaining representative only if the person serves as a collective bargaining representative for that employee in employment or labor matters at the employee's workplace.

(b) For purposes of this section:

(1) "Course of conduct" is a pattern

of conduct composed of a series of acts over a period of time, however short, evidencing a continuity of purpose, including following or stalking an employee to or from the place of work; entering the workplace; following an employee during hours of employment; making telephone calls to an employee; or sending correspondence to an employee by any means, including, but not limited to, the use of the public or private mails, interoffice mail, facsimile, or computer email.

(2) "Credible threat of violence" is a knowing and willful statement or course of conduct that would place a reasonable person in fear for their safety, or the safety of their immediate family, and that serves no legitimate purpose.

(3) "Employer" and "employee" mean persons defined in Section 350 of the Labor Code. "Employer" also includes a federal agency, the state, a state agency, a city, county, or district, a joint powers authority, or a public transit operator, whether operated directly by a public entity or through a contract or subcontract, and a private, public, or quasi-public corporation, or any public agency thereof or therein. "Employee" also includes the members of boards of directors of private, public, and quasi-public corporations and elected and appointed public officers. For purposes of this section only, "employee" also includes a volunteer or independent contractor who performs services for the employer at the employer's worksite. The changes made to this paragraph during the 2025–26 Regular Session are declaratory of existing law.

(4) "Harassment" is a knowing and willful course of conduct directed at a specific person that seriously alarms, annoys, or harasses the person, and that serves no legitimate purpose. The course of conduct must be that which would cause a reasonable person to suffer substantial emotional distress, and must actually cause substantial emotional distress.

(5) "Petitioner" means the employer or collective bargaining representative that petitions under subdivision (a) for a temporary restraining order and order after hearing.

(6) "Respondent" means the person against whom the temporary restraining order and order after hearing are sought and, if the petition is granted, the restrained person.

(7) "Temporary restraining order" and "order after hearing" mean orders that include any of the following restraining orders, whether issued ex parte or after notice and hearing:

(A) An order enjoining a party from harassing, intimidating, molesting, attacking, striking, stalking, threatening, sexually assaulting, battering, abusing, telephoning, including, but not limited to, making annoying telephone calls as described in Section 653m of the Penal Code, destroying personal property, contacting, either directly or indirectly, by mail or otherwise, or coming within a specified distance of, or disturbing the peace of, the employee.

(B) An order enjoining a party from specified behavior that the court determines is necessary to effectuate orders described in subparagraph (A).

(8) "Unlawful violence" is any assault or battery, or stalking as prohibited in Section 646.9 of the Penal Code, or any violation of Section 243.3 of the

Penal Code, but shall not include lawful acts of self-defense or defense of others. The changes made to this paragraph during the 2025–26 Regular Session are declaratory of existing law.

(c) This section does not permit a court to issue a temporary restraining order or order after hearing prohibiting speech or other activities that are constitutionally protected, protected by the National Labor Relations Act (29 U.S.C. Sec. 151 et seq.), protected by Chapter 11.5 (commencing with Section 3555) of Division 4 of Title 1 of the Government Code, or otherwise protected by Section 527.3 or any other provision of law.

(d) In the discretion of the court, on a showing of good cause, a temporary restraining order or order after hearing issued under this section may include other named family or household members, or other persons employed at the employee's workplace or workplaces.

(e) Before filing a petition under this section, an employer or collective bargaining representative of an employee shall provide the employee who has suffered harassment, unlawful violence, or a credible threat of violence from any individual, an opportunity to decline to be named in the temporary restraining order. An employee's request to not be named in the temporary restraining order shall not prohibit an employer or collective bargaining representative from seeking a temporary restraining order on behalf of other employees at the workplace, and, if appropriate, other employees at other workplaces of the employer.

(f) (1) Upon filing a petition under this section, the petitioner may obtain a temporary restraining order in accordance with subdivision (a) of Section 527, if the petitioner also files a declaration that, to the satisfaction of the court, shows one of the following:

(A) Reasonable proof that an employee has suffered unlawful violence or a credible threat of violence by the respondent, and that great or irreparable harm would result to an employee.

(B) Clear and convincing evidence of all of the following:

(i) That an employee has suffered harassment by the respondent.

(ii) That great or irreparable harm would result to an employee.

(iii) That the course of conduct at issue served no legitimate purpose.

(iv) That the issuance of the order is not prohibited by subdivision (c).

(2) The temporary restraining order may include any of the protective orders described in paragraph (7) of subdivision (b).

(g) A request for the issuance of a temporary restraining order without notice under this section shall be granted or denied on the same day that the petition is submitted to the court, unless the petition is filed too late in the day to permit effective review, in which case the order shall be granted or denied on the next day of judicial business in sufficient time for the order to be filed that day with the clerk of the court.

(h) A temporary restraining order granted under this section shall remain in effect, at the court's discretion, for a period not to exceed 21 days, or if the court extends the time for hearing under subdivision (i), not to exceed 25 days, unless otherwise modified or terminated by the court.

(i) Within 21 days, or if good cause appears to the court, 25 days from the date that a petition for a temporary order is granted or denied, a hearing shall be held on the petition. If no request for temporary orders is made, the hearing shall be held within 21 days, or, if good cause appears to the court, 25 days, from the date that the petition is filed.

(j) The respondent may file a response that explains, excuses, justifies, or denies the alleged harassment, unlawful violence, or credible threats of violence.

(k) At the hearing, the judge shall receive any testimony that is relevant and may make an independent inquiry. Moreover, if the respondent is currently employed by the employer of the employee, as described in subdivision (a), the judge shall receive evidence concerning the employer's decision to retain, terminate, or otherwise discipline the respondent. If the judge finds by clear and convincing evidence that the respondent engaged in harassment, engaged in unlawful violence, or made a credible threat of violence, an order shall issue prohibiting further harassment, unlawful violence, or threats of violence.

(l) (1) In the discretion of the court, an order issued after notice and hearing under this section may have a duration of not more than three years, subject to termination or modification by further order of the court either on written stipulation filed with the court or on the motion of a party. These orders may be renewed, upon the request of a party, for a duration of not more than three years, without a showing of any further harassment, unlawful violence, or credible threats of violence since the issuance of the original order, subject to termination or modification by further order of the court either on written stipulation filed with the court or on the motion of a party. The request for renewal may be brought at any time within the three months before the expiration of the order.

(2) The failure to state the expiration date on the face of the form creates an order with a duration of three years from the date of issuance.

(3) If an action is filed for the purpose of terminating or modifying a protective order prior to the expiration date specified in the order by a party other than the protected party, the party who is protected by the order shall be given notice, pursuant to subdivision (b) of Section 1005, of the proceeding by personal service or, if the protected party has satisfied the requirements of Chapter 3.1 (commencing with Section 6205) of Division 7 of Title 1 of the Government Code, by service on the Secretary of State. If the party who is protected by the order cannot be notified prior to the hearing for modification or termination of the protective order, the court shall deny the motion to modify or terminate the order without prejudice or continue the hearing until the party who is protected can be properly noticed and may, upon a showing of good cause, specify another method for service of process that is reasonably designed to afford actual notice to the protected party. The protected party may waive their right to notice if they are physically present in court and does not challenge the sufficiency of the notice.

(m) This section does not preclude any party from representation by private counsel or from appearing on the party's own behalf.

(n) Upon filing of a petition under this section, the respondent shall be personally served with a copy of the petition, temporary restraining order, if any, and notice of hearing of the petition. Service shall be made at least five days before the hearing. The court may, for good cause, on motion of the petitioner or on its own motion, shorten the time for service on the respondent.

(o) A notice of hearing under this section shall notify the respondent that, if they do not attend the hearing, the court may make orders against them that could last up to three years.

(p) The respondent shall be entitled, as a matter of course, to one continuance, for a reasonable period, to respond to the petition.

(q) (1) Any party may request a continuance of the hearing, which the court shall grant on a showing of good cause. The request may be made in writing before or at the hearing or orally at the hearing. The court may also grant a continuance on its own motion.

(2) If the court grants a continuance, any temporary restraining order that has been granted shall remain in effect until the end of the continued hearing, unless otherwise ordered by the court. In granting a continuance, the court may modify or terminate a temporary restraining order.

(r) (1) If a respondent, named in a restraining order issued under this section after a hearing, has not been served personally with the order but has received actual notice of the existence and substance of the order through personal appearance in court to hear the terms of the order from the court, no additional proof of service is required for enforcement of the order.

(2) If the respondent named in a temporary restraining order is personally served with the order and notice of hearing with respect to a restraining order or protective order based on the temporary restraining order, but the person does not appear at the hearing, either personally or by an attorney, and the terms and conditions of the restraining order or protective order issued at the hearing are identical to the temporary restraining order, except for the duration of the order, then the restraining order or protective order issued at the hearing may be served on the person by first-class mail sent to that person at the most current address for the person available to the court.

(3) The Judicial Council form for temporary orders issued pursuant to this subdivision shall contain a statement in substantially the following form:

"If you have been personally served with this temporary restraining order and notice of hearing, but you do not appear at the hearing either in person or by a lawyer, and a restraining order that is the same as this restraining order except for the expiration date is issued at the hearing, a copy of the order will be served on you by mail at the following address: ____.

If that address is not correct or you wish to verify that the temporary restraining order was converted to a restraining order at the hearing without substantive change and to find out the duration of that order, contact the clerk of the court."

(s) (1) Information on a temporary restraining order or order after hearing relating to workplace violence issued by a court pursuant to this section shall be transmitted to the Department of Justice in accordance with either paragraph (2) or (3).

(2) The court shall order the petitioner or the attorney for the petitioner to deliver a copy of any order issued under this section, or a reissuance, extension, modification, or termination of the order, and any subsequent proof of service, by the close of the business day on which the order, reissuance, extension, modification, or termination was made, to each law enforcement agency having jurisdiction over the residence of the petitioner and to any additional law enforcement agencies within the court's discretion as are requested by the petitioner.

(3) Alternatively, the court or its designee shall transmit, within one business day, to law enforcement personnel all information required under subdivision (b) of Section 6380 of the Family Code regarding any order issued under this section, or a reissuance, extension, modification, or termination of the order, and any subsequent proof of service, by either one of the following methods:

(A) Transmitting a physical copy of the order or proof of service to a local law enforcement agency authorized by the Department of Justice to enter orders into the California Law Enforcement Telecommunications System (CLETS).

(B) With the approval of the Department of Justice, entering the order or proof of service into CLETS directly.

(4) Each appropriate law enforcement agency shall make available information as to the existence and current status of these orders to law enforcement officers responding to the scene of reported harassment, unlawful violence, or a credible threat of violence.

(5) At the request of the petitioner, an order issued under this section shall be served on the respondent, regardless of whether the respondent has been taken into custody, by any law enforcement officer who is present at the scene of reported harassment, unlawful violence, or a credible threat of violence involving the parties to the proceedings. The petitioner shall provide the officer with an endorsed copy of the order and proof of service that the officer shall complete and send to the issuing court.

(6) Upon receiving information at the scene of an incident of harassment, unlawful violence, or a credible threat of violence that a protective order has been issued under this section, or that a person who has been taken into custody is the subject of an order, if the petitioner or the protected person cannot produce an endorsed copy of the order, a law enforcement officer shall immediately attempt to verify the existence of the order.

(7) If the law enforcement officer determines that a protective order has been issued but not served, the officer shall immediately notify the respondent of the terms of the order and obtain the respondent's address. The law enforcement officer shall at that time also enforce the order, but may not arrest or take the respondent into custody for acts in violation of the order that were committed prior to the verbal notice of the terms and conditions of the order. The law enforcement officer's verbal notice of the terms of the

order shall constitute service of the order and constitutes sufficient notice for the purposes of this section and for the purposes of Section 29825 of the Penal Code. The petitioner shall mail an endorsed copy of the order to the respondent's mailing address provided to the law enforcement officer within one business day of the reported incident of harassment, unlawful violence, or a credible threat of violence at which a verbal notice of the terms of the order was provided by a law enforcement officer.

(t) (1) A person subject to a protective order issued under this section shall not own, possess, purchase, receive, or attempt to purchase or receive a firearm or ammunition while the protective order is in effect.

(2) The court shall order a person subject to a protective order issued under this section to relinquish any firearms they own or possess pursuant to Section 527.9.

(3) Every person who owns, possesses, purchases or receives, or attempts to purchase or receive a firearm or ammunition while the protective order is in effect is punishable pursuant to Section 29825 of the Penal Code.

(u) Any intentional disobedience of any temporary restraining order or order after hearing granted under this section is punishable pursuant to Section 273.6 of the Penal Code.

(v) This section shall not be construed as expanding, diminishing, altering, or modifying the duty, if any, of an employer to provide a safe workplace for employees and other persons.

(w) (1) The Judicial Council shall develop forms, instructions, and rules for relating to matters governed by this section. The forms for the petition and response shall be simple and concise, and their use by parties in actions brought pursuant to this section shall be mandatory.

(2) A temporary restraining order or order after hearing relating to harassment, unlawful violence, or a credible threat of violence issued by a court pursuant to this section shall be issued on forms adopted by the Judicial Council and that have been approved by the Department of Justice pursuant to subdivision (i) of Section 6380 of the Family Code. However, the fact that an order issued by a court pursuant to this section was not issued on forms adopted by the Judicial Council and approved by the Department of Justice shall not, in and of itself, make the order unenforceable.

(x) There is no filing fee for a petition that alleges that a person has inflicted or threatened violence against an employee employed or represented by the petitioner, or stalked the employee, or acted or spoken in any other manner that has placed the employee in reasonable fear of violence, and that seeks a protective or restraining order restraining stalking or future violence or threats of violence, in any action brought pursuant to this section. A fee shall not be paid for a subpoena filed in connection with a petition alleging these acts. A fee shall not be paid for filing a response to a petition alleging these acts.

(y) (1) Subject to paragraph (4) of subdivision (b) of Section 6103.2 of the Government Code, there shall be no fee for the service of process by a sheriff or marshal of a temporary restraining order or order after hearing to be issued pursuant to this section if either of the following conditions applies:

(A) The temporary restraining order or order after hearing issued pursuant to this section is based upon stalking, as prohibited by Section 646.9 of the Penal Code.

(B) The temporary restraining order or order after hearing issued pursuant to this section is based on unlawful violence or a credible threat of violence.

(2) The Judicial Council shall prepare and develop forms for persons who wish to avail themselves of the services described in this subdivision.

(z) This section shall become operative on January 1, 2025.[874]

527.85. (a) A chief administrative officer of a postsecondary educational institution, or an officer or employee designated by the chief administrative officer to maintain order on the school campus or facility, a student of which has suffered unlawful violence or a credible threat of violence may, with the written consent of the student, seek a temporary restraining order and an order after hearing on behalf of the student and, at the discretion of the court, any number of other students at the campus or facility who are similarly situated.

(b) For purposes of this section, the following definitions apply:

(1) "Chief administrative officer" means the principal, president, or highest ranking official of the postsecondary educational institution.

(2) "Course of conduct" means a pattern of conduct composed of a series of acts over a period of time, however short, evidencing a continuity of purpose, including any of the following:

(A) Following or stalking a student to or from school.

(B) Entering the school campus or facility.

(C) Following a student during school hours.

(D) Making telephone calls to a student.

(E) Sending correspondence to a student by any means, including, but not limited to, the use of the public or private mails, interoffice mail, facsimile, or computer email.

(3) "Credible threat of violence" means a knowing and willful statement or course of conduct that would place a reasonable person in fear for their safety, or the safety of their immediate family, and that serves no legitimate purpose.

(4) "Petitioner" means the chief administrative officer, or their designee, who petitions under subdivision (a) for a temporary restraining order and order after hearing.

(5) "Postsecondary educational institution" means an institution of vocational, professional, or postsecondary education.

(6) "Respondent" means the person against whom the temporary restraining order and order after hearing are sought and, if the petition is granted, the restrained person.

(7) "Student" means an adult currently enrolled in or applying for admission to a postsecondary educational institution.

(8) "Temporary restraining order" and "order after hearing" mean orders that include any of the following restraining orders, whether issued ex parte, or after notice and hearing:

(A) An order enjoining a party from harassing, intimidating, molesting, attacking, striking, stalking, threatening, sexually assaulting, battering, abusing, telephoning, including, but not limited to, making annoying telephone calls as described in Section 653m of the Penal Code, destroying personal property, contacting, either directly or indirectly, by mail or otherwise, or coming within a specified distance of, or disturbing the peace of, the student.

(B) An order enjoining a party from specified behavior that the court determines is necessary to effectuate orders described in subparagraph (A).

(9) "Unlawful violence" means any assault or battery, or stalking as prohibited in Section 646.9 of the Penal Code, but shall not include lawful acts of self-defense or defense of others.

(c) This section does not permit a court to issue a temporary restraining order or order after hearing prohibiting speech or other activities that are constitutionally protected, or otherwise protected by Section 527.3 or any other law.

(d) In the discretion of the court, on a showing of good cause, a temporary restraining order or order after hearing issued under this section may include other named family or household members of the student, or other students at the campus or facility.

(e) Upon filing a petition under this section, the petitioner may obtain a temporary restraining order in accordance with subdivision (a) of Section 527, if the petitioner also files a declaration that, to the satisfaction of the court, shows reasonable proof that a student has suffered unlawful violence or a credible threat of violence by the respondent, and that great or irreparable harm would result to the student. The temporary restraining order may include any of the protective orders described in paragraph (8) of subdivision (b).

(f) A request for the issuance of a temporary restraining order without notice under this section shall be granted or denied on the same day that the petition is submitted to the court, unless the petition is filed too late in the day to permit effective review, in which case the order shall be granted or denied on the next day of judicial business in sufficient time for the order to be filed that day with the clerk of the court.

(g) A temporary restraining order granted under this section shall remain in effect, at the court's discretion, for a period not to exceed 21 days, or if the court extends the time for hearing under subdivision (h), not to exceed 25 days, unless otherwise modified or terminated by the court.

(h) Within 21 days, or if good cause appears to the court, within 25 days, from the date that a petition for a temporary order is granted or denied, a hearing shall be held on the petition. If no request for temporary orders is made, the hearing shall be held within 21 days, or if good cause appears to the court, 25 days, from the date the petition is filed.

(i) The respondent may file a response that explains, excuses, justifies, or denies the alleged unlawful violence or credible threats of violence.

(j) At the hearing, the judge shall receive any testimony that is relevant and may make an independent inquiry. Moreover, if the respondent is a current student of the entity requesting the order, the judge shall receive evidence concerning the decision of the postsecondary educational institution decision to retain, terminate, or otherwise discipline the respondent. If the judge finds by clear and convincing evidence that the respondent engaged in unlawful violence or made a credible threat of violence, an order shall be issued prohibiting further unlawful violence or threats of violence.

(k) (1) In the discretion of the court, an order issued after notice and hearing under this section may have a duration of not more than three years, subject to termination or modification by further order of the court either on written stipulation filed with the court or on the motion of a party. These orders may be renewed, upon the request of a party, for a duration of not more than three years, without a showing of any further violence or threats of violence since the issuance of the original order, subject to termination or modification by further order of the court either on written stipulation filed with the court or on the motion of a party. The request for renewal may be brought at any time within the three months before the expiration of the order.

(2) The failure to state the expiration date on the face of the form creates an order with a duration of three years from the date of issuance.

(3) If an action is filed for the purpose of terminating or modifying a protective order prior to the expiration date specified in the order by a party other than the protected party, the party who is protected by the order shall be given notice, pursuant to subdivision (b) of Section 1005, of the proceeding by personal service or, if the protected party has satisfied the requirements of Chapter 3.1 (commencing with Section 6205) of Division 7 of Title 1 of the Government Code, by service on the Secretary of State. If the party who is protected by the order cannot be notified prior to the hearing for modification or termination of the protective order, the court shall deny the motion to modify or terminate the order without prejudice or continue the hearing until the party who is protected can be properly noticed and may, upon a showing of good cause, specify another method for service of process that is reasonably designed to afford actual notice to the protected party. The protected party may waive their right to notice if they are physically present in court and does not challenge the sufficiency of the notice.

(l) This section does not preclude either party from representation by private counsel or from appearing on their own behalf.

(m) Upon filing of a petition under this section, the respondent shall be personally served with a copy of the petition, temporary restraining order, if any, and notice of hearing of the petition. Service shall be made at least five days before the hearing. The court may, for good cause, on motion of the petitioner or on its own motion, shorten the time for service on the respondent.

(n) A notice of hearing under this section shall notify the respondent that if the respondent does not attend the hearing, the court may make orders against the respondent that could last up to three years.

(o) The respondent shall be entitled, as a matter of course, to one continuance, for a reasonable period, to respond to the petition.

(p) (1) Either party may request a continuance of the hearing, which the court shall grant on a showing of good cause. The request may be made in writing before or at the hearing or orally at the hearing. The court may also grant a continuance on its own motion.

(2) If the court grants a continuance, any temporary restraining order that has been granted shall remain in effect until the end of the continued hearing, unless otherwise ordered by the court. In granting a continuance, the court may modify or terminate a temporary restraining order.

(q) (1) If a respondent, named in an order issued under this section after a hearing, has not been served personally with the order but has received actual notice of the existence and substance of the order through personal appearance in court to hear the terms of the order from the court, no additional proof of service is required for enforcement of the order.

(2) If the respondent named in a temporary restraining order is personally served with the order and notice of hearing with respect to a restraining order or protective order based on the temporary restraining order, but the respondent does not appear at the hearing, either personally or by an attorney, and the terms and conditions of the restraining order or protective order issued at the hearing are identical to the temporary restraining order, except for the duration of the order, then the restraining order or protective order issued at the hearing may be served on the respondent by first-class mail sent to that person at the most current address for the respondent available to the court.

(3) The Judicial Council form for temporary orders issued pursuant to this subdivision shall contain a statement in substantially the following form:

"If you have been personally served with a temporary restraining order and notice of hearing, but you do not appear at the hearing either in person or by a lawyer, and a restraining order that is the same as this temporary restraining order except for the expiration date is issued at the hearing, a copy of the order will be served on you by mail at the following address:____.

If that address is not correct or you wish to verify that the temporary restraining order was converted to a restraining order at the hearing without substantive change and to find out the duration of that order, contact the clerk of the court."

(r) (1) Information on a temporary restraining order or order after hearing issued by a court pursuant to this section shall be transmitted to the Department of Justice in accordance with either paragraph (2) or (3).

(2) The court shall order the petitioner or the attorney for the petitioner to deliver a copy of any order issued under this section, or a reissuance, extension, modification, or termination of the order, and any subsequent proof of service, by the close of the business day on which the order, reissuance, or termination of the order, and any proof of service, was made, to each law enforcement agency having jurisdiction over the residence of the petition and to any additional law enforcement agencies within the court's discretion as are requested by the petitioner.

(3) Alternatively, the court or its designee shall transmit, within one business day, to law enforcement personnel all information required under subdivision (b) of Section 6380 of the Family Code regarding any order issued under this section, or a reissuance, extension, modification, or termination of the order, and any subsequent proof of service, by either one of the following methods:

(A) Transmitting a physical copy of the order or proof of service to a local law enforcement agency authorized by the Department of Justice to enter orders into the California Law Enforcement Telecommunications System (CLETS).

(B) With the approval of the Department of Justice, entering the order of proof of service into CLETS directly.

(4) Each appropriate law enforcement agency shall make available information as to the existence and current status of these orders to law enforcement officers responding to the scene of reported unlawful violence or a credible threat of violence.

(5) At the request of the petitioner, an order issued under this section shall be served on the respondent, regardless of whether the respondent has been taken into custody, by any law enforcement officer who is present at the scene of reported unlawful violence or a credible threat of violence involving the parties to the proceedings. The petitioner shall provide the officer with an endorsed copy of the order and proof of service that the officer shall complete and send to the issuing court.

(6) Upon receiving information at the scene of an incident of unlawful violence or a credible threat of violence that a protective order has been issued under this section, or that a person who has been taken into custody is the subject of an order, if the petitioner or the protected person cannot produce an endorsed copy of the order, a law enforcement officer shall immediately attempt to verify the existence of the order.

(7) If the law enforcement officer determines that a protective order has been issued but not served, the officer shall immediately notify the respondent of the terms of the order and obtain the respondent's address. The law enforcement officer shall at that time also enforce the order, but may not arrest or take the respondent into custody for acts in violation of the order that were committed prior to the verbal notice of the terms and conditions of the order. The law enforcement officer's verbal notice of the terms of the order shall constitute service of the order and constitutes sufficient notice for the purposes of this section, and Section 29825 of the Penal Code. The petitioner shall mail an endorsed copy of the order to the respondent's mailing address provided to the law enforcement officer within one business day of the reported incident of unlawful violence or a credible threat of violence at which a verbal notice of the terms of the order was provided by a law enforcement officer.

(s) (1) A person subject to a protective order issued under this section shall not own, possess, purchase, receive, or attempt to purchase or receive a firearm or ammunition while the protective order is in effect.

(2) The court shall order a person subject to a protective order issued

under this section to relinquish any firearms the person owns or possesses pursuant to Section 527.9.

(3) Every person who owns, possesses, purchases, or receives, or attempts to purchase or receive, a firearm or ammunition while the protective order is in effect is punishable pursuant to Section 29825 of the Penal Code.

(t) Any intentional disobedience of any temporary restraining order or order after hearing granted under this section is punishable pursuant to Section 273.6 of the Penal Code.

(u) This section shall not be construed as expanding, diminishing, altering, or modifying the duty, if any, of a postsecondary educational institution to provide a safe environment for students and other persons.

(v) (1) The Judicial Council shall develop forms, instructions, and rules relating to matters governed by this section. The forms for the petition and response shall be simple and concise, and their use by parties in actions brought pursuant to this section shall be mandatory.

(2) A temporary restraining order or order after hearing relating to unlawful violence or a credible threat of violence issued by a court pursuant to this section shall be issued on forms adopted by the Judicial Council that have been approved by the Department of Justice pursuant to subdivision (i) of Section 6380 of the Family Code. However, the fact that an order issued by a court pursuant to this section was not issued on forms adopted by the Judicial Council and approved by the Department of Justice shall not, in and of itself, make the order unenforceable.

(w) There is no filing fee for a petition that alleges that a person has inflicted unlawful violence, including stalking, or made a credible threat against a student of the petitioner, and that seeks a protective or restraining order restraining stalking or other future unlawful violence or threats of violence, in any action brought pursuant to this section. No fee shall be paid for a subpoena filed in connection with a petition alleging these acts. No fee shall be paid for filing a response to a petition alleging these acts.

(x) (1) Subject to paragraph (4) of subdivision (b) of Section 6103.2 of the Government Code, there shall be no fee for the service of process by a sheriff or marshal of a temporary restraining order or order after hearing to be issued pursuant to this section if either of the following conditions applies:

(A) The temporary restraining order or order after hearing issued pursuant to this section is based upon unlawful violence, including stalking, as prohibited by Section 646.9 of the Penal Code.

(B) The temporary restraining order or order after hearing issued pursuant to this section is based upon a credible threat of violence.

(2) The Judicial Council shall prepare and develop forms for persons who wish to avail themselves of the services described in this subdivision.

(y) This section shall become operative on January 1, 2026.[867]

527.9. (a) A person subject to a temporary restraining order or injunction issued pursuant to Section 527.6, 527.8, or 527.85 or subject to a restraining order issued pursuant to Section 136.2 of the Penal Code, or Section 15657.03 of the Welfare and Institutions Code, shall relinquish the firearm and ammunition pursuant to this section.

(b) Upon the issuance of a protective order against a person pursuant to subdivision (a), the court shall order that person to relinquish any firearm and ammunition in that person's immediate possession or control, or subject to that person's immediate possession or control, within 24 hours of being served with the order, either by surrendering the firearm and ammunition to the control of local law enforcement officials, or by selling the firearm to a licensed gun dealer, as specified in Article 1 (commencing with Section 26700) and Article 2 (commencing with Section 26800) of Chapter 2 of Division 6 of Title 4 of Part 6 of the Penal Code. The court shall provide the person with information on how any firearms or ammunition still in the restrained party's possession are to be relinquished, according to local procedures, and the process for submitting a receipt to the court showing proof of relinquishment. A person ordered to relinquish any firearm and ammunition pursuant to this subdivision shall file with the court a receipt showing the firearm and ammunition were surrendered to the local law enforcement agency or sold to a licensed gun dealer within 48 hours after receiving the order. A court holding a hearing on this matter shall review the file to determine whether the receipt has been filed and inquire of the respondent whether they have complied with the requirement. Violations of the firearms prohibition of any restraining order under this section shall be reported to the prosecuting attorney in the jurisdiction where the order has been issued within two business days of the court hearing unless the restrained party provides a receipt showing compliance at a subsequent hearing or by direct filing with the clerk of the court. If the person does not file a receipt with the court within 48 hours after receiving the order for a firearm in their possession, the court shall order the clerk of the court to immediately notify, by the most effective means available, appropriate law enforcement officials of the issuance and contents of a protective order, information about the firearm or ammunition, and of any other information the court deems appropriate. In the event that it is necessary to continue the date of any hearing due to a request for a relinquishment order pursuant to this section, the court shall ensure that all applicable protective orders described in Section 6218 of the Family Code remain in effect or bifurcate the issues and grant the permanent restraining order pending the date of the hearing.

(c) A local law enforcement agency may charge the person subject to the order or injunction a fee for the storage of any firearm or ammunition relinquished pursuant to this section. The fee shall not exceed the actual cost incurred by the local law enforcement agency for the storage of the firearm or ammunition. For purposes of this subdivision, "actual cost" means expenses directly related to taking possession of a firearm and ammunition, storing the firearm and ammunition, and surrendering possession of the firearm and ammunition to a licensed dealer as defined in Section 26700 of the Penal

Code or to the person relinquishing the firearm.

(d) The restraining order requiring a person to relinquish a firearm and ammunition pursuant to subdivision (b) shall state on its face that the respondent is prohibited from owning, possessing, purchasing, or receiving a firearm or ammunition while the protective order is in effect and that the firearm shall be relinquished to the local law enforcement agency for that jurisdiction or sold to a licensed gun dealer, and that proof of surrender or sale shall be filed with the court within a specified period of receipt of the order. The order shall also state on its face the expiration date for relinquishment. Nothing in this section shall limit a respondent's right under existing law to petition the court at a later date for modification of the order.

(e) The restraining order requiring a person to relinquish a firearm or ammunition pursuant to subdivision (b) shall prohibit the person from possessing or controlling any firearm for the duration of the order. At the expiration of the order, the local law enforcement agency shall return possession of any surrendered firearm and ammunition to the respondent, within five days after the expiration of the relinquishment order, unless the local law enforcement agency determines that (1) the firearm has been stolen, (2) the respondent is prohibited from possessing a firearm because the respondent is in any prohibited class for the possession of firearms, as defined in Chapter 2 (commencing with Section 29800) and Chapter 3 (commencing with Section 29900) of Division 9 of Title 4 of Part 6 of the Penal Code and Sections 8100 and 8103 of the Welfare and Institutions Code, or (3) another successive restraining order is issued against the respondent under this section. If the local law enforcement agency determines that the respondent is the legal owner of any firearm or ammunition deposited with the local law enforcement agency and is prohibited from possessing any firearm, the respondent shall be entitled to sell or transfer the firearm or ammunition to a licensed dealer as defined in Section 26700 of the Penal Code. If the firearm has been stolen, the firearm shall be restored to the lawful owner upon their identification of the firearm and proof of ownership.

(f) The court may, as part of the relinquishment order, grant an exemption from the relinquishment requirements of this section for a particular firearm or ammunition if the respondent is not otherwise prohibited from owning, possessing, controlling, or purchasing a firearm and ammunition under state or federal law and one of the following applies:

(1) (A) The respondent is currently employed as a sworn peace officer who is required, as a condition of continued employment, to carry a firearm, ammunition, or firearm and ammunition and the current employer is unable to reassign the peace officer to another position where use of a specified firearm or ammunition is unnecessary. In such a case, a court may allow the peace officer to continue to carry a specified firearm, ammunition, or firearm and ammunition, either on duty or off duty, if the court finds by a preponderance of the evidence, in writing or on the record, both of the following:

(i) The peace officer's personal

safety depends on the ability to carry that specific firearm, ammunition, or firearm and ammunition outside of scheduled work hours.

(ii) The peace officer does not pose an additional threat of harm to a protected party or the public by having access to that specific firearm, ammunition, or firearm and ammunition, including whether the peace officer might use the firearm for a purpose other than as permitted under this paragraph.

(B) Prior to making the finding in subparagraph (A), the court shall require a mandatory psychological evaluation of the peace officer by a licensed mental health professional with domestic violence expertise. The court shall consider the results of an evaluation and may require the peace officer to enter into counseling or another remedial treatment program to deal with a propensity for domestic violence.

(2) (A) The respondent is not a peace officer but is required to carry a specific firearm, ammunition, or firearm and ammunition during scheduled work hours as a condition of continued employment, and the current employer is unable to reassign the respondent to another position where the firearm, ammunition, or firearm and ammunition is unnecessary. In this case, a court may grant an exemption to allow the respondent to possess a specific firearm, ammunition, or firearm and ammunition only during scheduled work hours if the court finds by a preponderance of the evidence, in writing or on the record, that the respondent does not pose an additional threat of harm to a protected party or the public by having access to the specific firearm, ammunition, or firearm and ammunition only during scheduled work hours, including whether the respondent might utilize the firearm, ammunition, or firearm and ammunition for a purpose other than as permitted under this paragraph.

(B) To assist the court in making the determination pursuant to subparagraph (A), the court may order a psychological evaluation of the respondent by a licensed mental health professional with domestic violence expertise.

(C) If the court grants an exemption pursuant to this paragraph, the order shall provide that the specific firearm, ammunition, or firearm and ammunition shall be in the physical possession of the respondent only during scheduled work hours and that the exemption does not authorize the respondent to possess any other firearm or ammunition, or to possess the specific firearm, ammunition, or firearm and ammunition outside of scheduled work hours.

(g) (1) If an exemption is granted pursuant to subdivision (f) during the pendency of a temporary restraining order and the court subsequently issues a restraining order after hearing on the same application, the court shall review and make a finding, in writing or on the record, as to whether the exemption remains appropriate, based upon the criteria set forth in paragraph (1) or (2) of subdivision (f), as applicable, in light of the issuance of the order after hearing. This review and finding shall occur at the time the restraining order after hearing is issued.

(2) If an exemption is granted and the

court subsequently renews the restraining order pursuant to Section 6345 of the Family Code at the request of a party, the court shall review and make a finding, in writing or on the record, as to whether the exemption remains appropriate, based upon the criteria set forth in paragraph (1) or (2) of subdivision (f), as applicable, in light of the renewal. This finding shall be made at the time the restraining order after hearing is renewed.

(3) The court may terminate or modify an exemption granted pursuant to this subdivision at any time if the respondent demonstrates a need to modify the specific firearm, ammunition, or firearm and ammunition authorized by the court pursuant to subdivision (f), if the respondent no longer meets the requirements in this section, or if the respondent otherwise violates the restraining order.

(h) During the period of the relinquishment order, a respondent is entitled to make one sale of all firearms that are in the possession of a local law enforcement agency pursuant to this section. A licensed gun dealer, who presents a local law enforcement agency with a bill of sale indicating that all firearms owned by the respondent that are in the possession of the local law enforcement agency have been sold by the respondent to the licensed gun dealer, shall be given possession of those firearms, at the location where a respondent's firearms are stored, within five days of presenting the local law enforcement agency with a bill of sale.

(i) If the respondent declines to relinquish possession of a firearm or ammunition based on the assertion of the right against self-incrimination, as provided by the Fifth Amendment to the United States Constitution and Section 15 of Article I of the California Constitution, the court may grant use immunity for the act of relinquishing the firearm or ammunition required under this section.

(j) (1) The relinquishment or surrender of a firearm to a law enforcement agency pursuant to this section or the return of a firearm to a person pursuant to this section shall not be subject to the requirements of Section 27545 of the Penal Code.

(2) Returns of firearms or ammunition pursuant to this section shall be governed by the applicable provisions of Chapter 2 (commencing with Section 33850) of Division 11 of Title 4 of Part 6 of the Penal Code.

(k) This section shall become operative on January 1, 2026.[859]

527.10. (a) The court shall order that any party enjoined pursuant to Section 527.6, 527.8, or 527.85 be prohibited from taking any action to obtain the address or location of any protected person, unless there is good cause not to make that order.

(b) The Judicial Council shall develop forms necessary to effectuate this section.[634]

527.11. (a) When relevant information is presented to the court at any noticed hearing that a restrained person has a firearm, the court shall consider that information to determine, by a preponderance of the evidence, whether the person subject to an order defined in Section 527.6, 527.8, or 527.85 or Section 15657.03 of the Welfare and Institutions Code, has a firearm in or subject to their immediate possession or control in violation of the order.

(b) (1) In making a determination under this section, the court may consider whether the restrained person filed a firearm relinquishment, storage, or sales receipt or if an exemption from the firearm prohibition was granted.

(2) The court may make the determination at any noticed hearing where a restraining order is issued, at a subsequent review hearing, or at any subsequent hearing while the order remains in effect.

(3) If the court makes a determination that the restrained person has a firearm in violation of the order, the court must make a written record of the determination and provide a copy to any party who is present at the hearing and, upon request, to any party not present at the hearing.

(c) (1) When presented with information under subdivision (a), the court may set a review hearing to determine whether a violation of the order has taken place.

(2) The review hearing should be held within 10 court days after the noticed hearing at which the information was presented. If the restrained person is not present when the court sets the review hearing, the protected person must provide notice of the review hearing to the restrained person at least two court days before the review hearing, in accordance with Section 414.10, by personal service or by mail to the restrained person's last known address.

(3) The court may for good cause extend the date of the review hearing for a reasonable period or remove it from the calendar.

(4) The court shall order the restrained person to appear at the review hearing.

(5) The court may conduct the review hearing in the absence of the protected person.

(6) This section does not prohibit the court from permitting a party or witness to appear through technology that enables remote appearances, as determined by the court.

(d) The determination made pursuant to this section may be considered by the court in issuing an order to show cause for contempt pursuant to paragraph (5) of subdivision (a) of Section 1209 or an order for monetary sanctions pursuant to Section 177.5.

(e) This section shall become operative on January 1, 2026.[860]

527.12. (a) A peace officer shall, upon the request of a petitioner, serve any temporary restraining order, order after hearing, or protective order issued pursuant to Sections 527.6, 527.8, and 527.85, Section 136.2 of the Penal Code, or Section 15657.03 of the Welfare and Institutions Code, on the respondent, whether or not the respondent has been taken into custody.

(b) (1) The petitioner shall provide the peace officer with an endorsed copy of the order and the officer shall complete and transmit the proof of service to the issuing court. It is a rebuttable presumption that the proof of service was signed on the date of service.

(2) If the protected person cannot produce an endorsed copy of the order, the peace officer shall immediately verify the existence of the order in the California Restraining and Protective Order System.

(3) If the peace officer determines that an order subject to this section

has been issued but not served, the officer shall immediately notify the respondent of the terms of the order and advise the respondent to obtain a copy of the full order from the issuing court. Upon notice, the officer shall immediately enforce the order. The officer's verbal notice of the terms of the order shall constitute service of the order and is sufficient notice for the purposes of this section and for the purposes of Sections 273.6 and 29825 of the Penal Code.

(4) If an order served pursuant to this section is subject to the reporting requirements of Section 13730 of the Penal Code, the report shall include the name and assignment of the peace officer who served the order and the case number of the order. If a report is not required, the information specified in this paragraph shall be included in the daily incident log of the officer's employing law enforcement agency.

(c) Notwithstanding any law, a fee shall not be charged to the petitioner for service of an order pursuant to this section.

(d) (1) There shall be no civil liability on the part of, and no cause of action for false arrest or false imprisonment against, a peace officer who makes an arrest pursuant to a protective or restraining order that is regular upon its face, if the peace officer, in making the arrest, acts in good faith and has reasonable cause to believe that the person against whom the order is issued has notice of the order and has committed an act in violation of the order.

(2) If there is more than one order issued and one of the orders is an emergency protective order that has precedence in enforcement pursuant to paragraph (1) of subdivision (c) of Section 136.2 of the Penal Code, the peace officer shall enforce the emergency protective order. If there is more than one order issued, none of the orders issued is an emergency protective order that has precedence in enforcement, and one of the orders issued is a no-contact order, the peace officer shall enforce the no-contact order. If there is more than one civil order regarding the same parties and neither an emergency protective order that has precedence in enforcement nor a no-contact order has been issued, the peace officer shall enforce the order that was issued last. If there are both civil and criminal orders regarding the same parties and neither an emergency protective order that has precedence in enforcement nor a no-contact order has been issued, the peace officer shall enforce the criminal order issued last, subject to the provisions of subdivisions (h) and (i) of Section 136.2 of the Penal Code. This section does not exonerate a peace officer from liability for the unreasonable use of force in the enforcement of the order. The immunities afforded by this section shall not affect the availability of any other immunity that may apply, including, but not limited to, Sections 820.2 and 820.4 of the Government Code.

(e) For purposes of this section, "peace officer" has the same meaning as that term is defined in Section 830 of the Penal Code.

(f) This section shall become operative on January 1, 2026.[861]

528. An injunction cannot be allowed after the defendant has answered, unless upon notice, or upon an order to

show cause; but in such case the defendant may be restrained until the decision of the Court or Judge granting or refusing the injunction.[1]

529. (a) On granting an injunction, the court or judge must require an undertaking on the part of the applicant to the effect that the applicant will pay to the party enjoined any damages, not exceeding an amount to be specified, the party may sustain by reason of the injunction, if the court finally decides that the applicant was not entitled to the injunction. Within five days after the service of the injunction, the person enjoined may object to the undertaking. If the court determines that the applicant's undertaking is insufficient and a sufficient undertaking is not filed within the time required by statute, the order granting the injunction must be dissolved.
(b) This section does not apply to any of the following persons:
(1) Either spouse against the other in a proceeding for legal separation or dissolution of marriage.
(2) The applicant for an order described in Division 10 (commencing with Section 6200) of the Family Code.
(3) A public entity or officer described in Section 995.220.
(4) An applicant requesting an injunction under subdivision (d) of Section 1708.85 of the Civil Code.
(5) An applicant requesting an injunction under subdivision (d) of Section 1708.89 of the Civil Code.[862]

529.1. (a) In all actions in which the court has granted an injunction sought by any plaintiff to enjoin a construction project which has received all legally required licenses and permits, the defendant may apply to the court by noticed motion for an order requiring the plaintiff to furnish an undertaking as security for costs and any damages that may be incurred by the defendant by the conclusion of the action or proceeding as the result of a delay in the construction of the project. The motion shall be made on the grounds that there is no reasonable possibility that the plaintiff will obtain a judgment against the moving defendant and that the plaintiff will not suffer undue economic hardship by filing the undertaking.
(b) If the court, after hearing, determines that the grounds for the motion have been established, the court shall order that the plaintiff file the undertaking in an amount specified in the court's order as security for costs and damages of the defendant. The liability of the plaintiff pursuant to this section for the costs and damages of the defendant shall not exceed five hundred thousand dollars ($500,000).
(c) As used in this section, a construction project includes, but is not restricted to, the construction, surveying, design, specifications, alteration, repair, improvement, maintenance, removal, or demolition of any building, highway, road, parking facility, bridge, railroad, airport, pier or dock, excavation or other structure, development or other improvement to real or personal property.[843]

529.2. (a) In all civil actions, including, but not limited to, actions brought pursuant to Section 21167 of the Public Resources Code, brought by any plaintiff to challenge a housing project which is a development project, as defined by Section 65928 of the Government Code, and which meets or exceeds the requirements for low- or moderate-income housing as set forth in Section 65915 of the Government Code, a defendant may, if the bringing of the action or the seeking by the plaintiff of particular relief including, but not limited to, injunctions, has the effect of preventing or delaying the project from being carried out, apply to the court by noticed motion for an order requiring the plaintiff to furnish an undertaking as security for costs and any damages that may be incurred by the defendant by the conclusion of the action or proceeding as the result of a delay in carrying out the development project. The motion shall be made on the grounds that the action is without merit and that the action was brought in bad faith, vexatiously, for the purpose of delay, or to thwart the low- or moderate-income nature of the housing development project.

(b) In responding to a motion for undertaking, the plaintiff may seek to limit the amount of the undertaking by presenting admissible evidence that filing an undertaking will cause it, and in cases where the plaintiff is an unincorporated association, its members, to suffer undue economic hardship. If the court, after hearing, determines that the grounds for the motion have been established, the court shall order that the plaintiff file the undertaking in an amount specified in the court's order, taking into consideration any admitted evidence of plaintiff's economic hardship and avoiding causing the plaintiff to suffer undue economic hardship, as security for costs and damages of the defendant. The liability of the plaintiff pursuant to this section for the costs and damages of the defendant shall not exceed five hundred thousand dollars ($500,000). If the court concludes, based on all of the admissible evidence presented, that a bond in any amount would cause the plaintiff undue economic hardship, the court is authorized in its discretion to decline to impose a bond.

(c) If at any time after the plaintiff has filed an undertaking the housing development plan is changed by the developer in bad faith so that it fails to meet or exceed the requirements for low- or moderate-income housing as set forth in Section 65915 of the Government Code, the developer shall be liable to the plaintiff for the cost of obtaining the undertaking.[850]

530. In all actions which may be hereafter brought when an injunction or restraining order may be applied for to prevent the diversion, diminution or increase of the flow of water in its natural channels, to the ordinary flow of which the plaintiff claims to be entitled, the court shall first require due notice of the application to be served upon the defendant, unless it shall appear from the verified complaint or affidavits upon which the application therefor is made, that, within ten days prior to the time of such application, the plaintiff has been in the peaceable possession of the flow of such water, and that, within such time, said plaintiff has been deprived of the flow thereof by the wrongful diversion of such flow by the defendant, or that the plaintiff, at the time of such application, is, and for ten days prior thereto, has been, in possession of the flow of said water, and that the defendant threatens to divert the flow of such wa-

ter; and if such notice of such application be given and upon the hearing thereof, it be made to appear to the court that plaintiff is entitled to the injunction, but that the issuance thereof pending the litigation will entail great damage upon defendant, and that plaintiff will not be greatly damaged by the acts complained of pending the litigation, and can be fully compensated for such damage as he may suffer, the court may refuse the injunction upon the defendant giving a bond such as is provided for in section five hundred and thirty-two; and upon the trial the same proceedings shall be had, and with the same effect as in said section provided.[12]

531. An injunction to suspend the general and ordinary business of a corporation can not be granted without due notice of the application therefor to the proper officers or managing agent of the corporation, except when the people of this state are a party to the proceeding.[9]

532. (a) If an injunction is granted without notice to the person enjoined, the person may apply, upon reasonable notice to the judge who granted the injunction, or to the court in which the action was brought, to dissolve or modify the injunction. The application may be made upon the complaint or the affidavit on which the injunction was granted, or upon affidavit on the part of the person enjoined, with or without the answer. If the application is made upon affidavits on the part of the person enjoined, but not otherwise, the person against whom the application is made may oppose the application by affidavits or other evidence in addition to that on which the injunction was granted.

(b) In all actions in which an injunction or restraining order has been or may be granted or applied for, to prevent the diversion, pending the litigation, of water used, or to be used, for irrigation or domestic purposes only, if it is made to appear to the court that great damage will be suffered by the person enjoined, in case the injunction is continued, and that the person in whose behalf it issued can be fully compensated for any damages suffered by reason of the continuance of the acts enjoined during the pendency of the litigation, the court in its discretion, may dissolve or modify the injunction. The dissolution or modification shall be subject to the person enjoined giving a bond in such amount as may be fixed by the court or judge, conditioned that the enjoined person will pay all damages which the person in whose behalf the injunction issued may suffer by reason of the continuance, during the litigation, of the acts complained of. Upon the trial the amount of the damages must be ascertained, and in case judgment is rendered for the person in whose behalf the injunction was granted, the amount fixed as damages must be included in the judgment, together with reasonable attorney's fees. In any proceedings to enforce the liability on the bond, the amount of the damages as fixed in the judgment is conclusive.[120]

533. In any action, the court may on notice modify or dissolve an injunction or temporary restraining order upon a showing that there has been a material change in the facts upon which the injunction or temporary restraining order was granted, that the law upon

which the injunction or temporary restraining order was granted has changed, or that the ends of justice would be served by the modification or dissolution of the injunction or temporary restraining order.[353]

534. In any action brought by a riparian owner to enjoin the diversion of water appropriated or proposed to be appropriated, or the use thereof, against any person or persons appropriating or proposing to appropriate such waters, the defendant may set up in his answer that the water diverted or proposed to be diverted is for the irrigation of land or other public use, and, in such case, he shall also in such answer set forth the quantity of water desired to be taken and necessary to such irrigation of land or the public use, the nature of such use, the place where the same is used or proposed to be used, the duration and extent of the diversion or the proposed diversion, including the stages of the flow of the stream at and during the time in which the water is to be diverted, and that the same may be diverted without interfering with the actual and necessary beneficial uses of the plaintiff, and that such defendant so answering desires that the court shall ascertain and fix the damages, if any, that will result to the plaintiff or to his riparian lands from the appropriation of the water so appropriated or intended to be appropriated by defendant.

The plaintiff may serve and file a reply to the defendant's answer stating plaintiff's rights to the water and the damage plaintiff will suffer by the defendant's taking of the water, and plaintiff may implead as parties to the action all persons necessary to a full determination of the rights of plaintiff to the water and the damages plaintiff will suffer by the proposed taking by defendant, and the court shall have jurisdiction to hear and determine all the rights to water of the plaintiff and other parties to the action, and said parties shall have a right to state and prove their rights, and shall be bound by the judgment rendered the same as though made parties plaintiff at the commencement of the action.

Upon the trial of the case the court shall receive and hear evidence on behalf of the respective parties, and if the court finds that the allegations of such answer are true as to the aforesaid matters, and that the appropriation and diversion of such waters is for irrigation of land or other public use and that, after allowing sufficient water for the actual and necessary beneficial uses of the plaintiff and other parties, there is water available to be beneficially appropriated by such defendant so answering, the court shall fix the time and manner and extent of such appropriation and the actual damages, if any, resulting to the plaintiff or other parties on account of the same, and in fixing such damages the court shall be guided by Article 5 (commencing with Section 1263.410) of Chapter 9 of Title 7 of Part 3, and if, upon the ascertainment and fixing of such damages the defendant, within the time allowed in Section 1268.010 for the payment of damages in proceedings in eminent domain, shall pay into court the amount of damages fixed and the costs adjudged to be paid by such defendant, or give a good and sufficient bond to pay the same upon the final settlement of the case, the injunction prayed for by the plaintiff shall be denied to the extent of the amount the defendant is permitted to appropriate, as aforesaid, and the temporary injunction, if any has been granted, shall be vacated to the extent aforesaid; provided, that any of the parties may appeal from such judgment as in other cases; and provided, further, that if such judgment is in favor of the defendant and if he upon and pending such appeal shall keep on deposit with the clerk of said court the amount of such damages and costs, or the bond, if it be given, so awarded to be paid to the plaintiff or other parties in the event such judgment shall be affirmed, no injunction against the appropriation of the amount the defendant is permitted to appropriate as aforesaid shall be granted or enforced pending such appeal, and, upon the acceptance by the plaintiff or other parties of such amount so awarded or upon the affirmation of such decision on appeal so that such judgment shall become final, the defendant shall have the right to divert and appropriate from such stream, against such plaintiff or other parties and his successors in interest, the quantity of water therein adjudged and allowed. Upon the filing of such answer as is herein provided for, the parties plaintiff or other parties and defendant shall be entitled to a jury trial upon the issues as to damages so raised, as provided in Title 7 (commencing with Section 1230.010) of Part 3, applying to proceedings in eminent domain.[96]

Chapter 5: Receivers

Chapter 5 enacted 1872.

564. (a) A receiver may be appointed, in the manner provided in this chapter, by the court in which an action or proceeding is pending in any case in which the court is empowered by law to appoint a receiver.

(b) A receiver may be appointed by the court in which an action or proceeding is pending, or by a judge of that court, in the following cases:

(1) In an action by a vendor to vacate a fraudulent purchase of property, or by a creditor to subject any property or fund to the creditor's claim, or between partners or others jointly owning or interested in any property or fund, on the application of the plaintiff, or of any party whose right to or interest in the property or fund, or the proceeds of the property or fund, is probable, and where it is shown that the property or fund is in danger of being lost, removed, or materially injured.

(2) In an action by a secured lender for the foreclosure of a deed of trust or mortgage and sale of property upon which there is a lien under a deed of trust or mortgage, where it appears that the property is in danger of being lost, removed, or materially injured, or that the condition of the deed of trust or mortgage has not been performed, and that the property is probably insufficient to discharge the deed of trust or mortgage debt.

(3) After judgment, to carry the judgment into effect.

(4) After judgment, to dispose of the property according to the judgment, or to preserve it during the pendency of an appeal, or pursuant to the Enforcement of Judgments Law (Title 9 (commencing with Section 680.010)), or after sale of real property pursuant to a decree of foreclosure, during the redemption period, to collect, expend, and disburse rents as directed

by the court or otherwise provided by law.

(5) Where a corporation has been dissolved, as provided in Section 565.

(6) Where a corporation is insolvent, or in imminent danger of insolvency, or has forfeited its corporate rights.

(7) In an action of unlawful detainer.

(8) At the request of the Public Utilities Commission pursuant to Section 1825 or 1826 of the Public Utilities Code.

(9) In all other cases where necessary to preserve the property or rights of any party.

(10) At the request of the Office of Statewide Health Planning and Development, or the Attorney General, pursuant to Section 129173 of the Health and Safety Code.

(11) In an action by a secured lender for specific performance of an assignment of rents provision in a deed of trust, mortgage, or separate assignment document. The appointment may be continued after entry of a judgment for specific performance if appropriate to protect, operate, or maintain real property encumbered by a deed of trust or mortgage or to collect rents therefrom while a pending nonjudicial foreclosure under power of sale in a deed of trust or mortgage is being completed.

(12) In a case brought by an assignee under an assignment of leases, rents, issues, or profits pursuant to subdivision (g) of Section 2938 of the Civil Code.

(c) A receiver may be appointed, in the manner provided in this chapter, including, but not limited to, Section 566, by the superior court in an action brought by a secured lender to enforce the rights provided in Section 2929.5 of the Civil Code, to enable the secured lender to enter and inspect the real property security for the purpose of determining the existence, location, nature, and magnitude of any past or present release or threatened release of any hazardous substance into, onto, beneath, or from the real property security. The secured lender shall not abuse the right of entry and inspection or use it to harass the borrower or tenant of the property. Except in case of an emergency, when the borrower or tenant of the property has abandoned the premises, or if it is impracticable to do so, the secured lender shall give the borrower or tenant of the property reasonable notice of the secured lender's intent to enter and shall enter only during the borrower's or tenant's normal business hours. Twenty-four hours' notice shall be presumed to be reasonable notice in the absence of evidence to the contrary.

(d) Any action by a secured lender to appoint a receiver pursuant to this section shall not constitute an action within the meaning of subdivision (a) of Section 726.

(e) For purposes of this section:

(1) "Borrower" means the trustor under a deed of trust, or a mortgagor under a mortgage, where the deed of trust or mortgage encumbers real property security and secures the performance of the trustor or mortgagor under a loan, extension of credit, guaranty, or other obligation. The term includes any successor in interest of the trustor or mortgagor to the real property security before the deed of trust or mortgage has been discharged, reconveyed, or foreclosed upon.

(2) "Hazardous substance" means any

of the following:

(A) Any "hazardous substance" as defined in subdivision (h) of Section 25281 of the Health and Safety Code.

(B) Any "waste" as defined in subdivision (d) of Section 13050 of the Water Code.

(C) Petroleum including crude oil or any fraction thereof, natural gas, natural gas liquids, liquefied natural gas, or synthetic gas usable for fuel, or any mixture thereof.

(3) "Real property security" means any real property and improvements, other than a separate interest and any related interest in the common area of a residential common interest development, as the terms "separate interest," "common area," and "common interest development" are defined in Sections 4095, 4100, and 4185 of the Civil Code, or real property consisting of one acre or less that contains 1 to 15 dwelling units.

(4) "Release" means any spilling, leaking, pumping, pouring, emitting, emptying, discharging, injecting, escaping, leaching, dumping, or disposing into the environment, including continuing migration, of hazardous substances into, onto, or through soil, surface water, or groundwater.

(5) "Secured lender" means the beneficiary under a deed of trust against the real property security, or the mortgagee under a mortgage against the real property security, and any successor in interest of the beneficiary or mortgagee to the deed of trust or mortgage.[768]

565. Upon the dissolution of any corporation, the Superior Court of the county in which the corporation carries on its business or has its principal place of business, on application of any creditor of the corporation, or of any stockholder or member thereof, may appoint one or more persons to be receivers or trustees of the corporation, to take charge of the estate and effects thereof, and to collect the debts and property due and belonging to the corporation, and to pay the outstanding debts thereof, and to divide the moneys and other property that shall remain over among the stockholders or members.[4]

566. (a) No party, or attorney of a party, or person interested in an action, or related to any judge of the court by consanguinity or affinity within the third degree, can be appointed receiver therein without the written consent of the parties, filed with the clerk.

(b) If a receiver is appointed upon an ex parte application, the court, before making the order, must require from the applicant an undertaking in an amount to be fixed by the court, to the effect that the applicant will pay to the defendant all damages the defendant may sustain by reason of the appointment of the receiver and the entry by the receiver upon the duties, in case the applicant shall have procured the appointment wrongfully, maliciously, or without sufficient cause.[130]

567. Before entering upon the duties of a receiver:

(a) The receiver must be sworn to perform the duties faithfully.

(b) The receiver shall give an undertaking to the State of California, in such sum as the court or judge may direct, to the effect that the receiver will faithfully discharge the duties of receiver in the action and obey the orders of the court therein. The receiver shall be allowed the cost of the undertaking.[131]

568. The receiver has, under the control of the Court, power to bring and defend actions in his own name, as receiver; to take and keep possession of the property, to receive rents, collect debts, to compound for and compromise the same, to make transfers, and generally to do such acts respecting the property as the Court may authorize.[1]

568.1. Any securities in the hands of a receiver may, under the control of the court, be deposited by the receiver in a securities depository, as defined in Section 30004 of the Financial Code, which is licensed under Section 30200 of the Financial Code or exempted from licensing thereunder by Section 30005 or 30006 of the Financial Code, and such securities may be held by such securities depository in the manner authorized by Section 775 of the Financial Code.[84]

568.2. (a) A receiver of real property containing rental housing shall notify the court of the existence of any order or notice to correct any substandard or unsafe condition, as defined in Section 17920.3 or 17920.10 of the Health and Safety Code, with which the receiver cannot comply within the time provided by the order or notice.

(b) The notice shall be filed within 30 days after the receiver's appointment or, if the substandard condition occurs subsequently, within 15 days of its occurrence.

(c) The notice shall inform the court of all of the following:

(1) The substandard conditions that exist.

(2) The threat or danger that the substandard conditions pose to any occupant of the property or the public.

(3) The approximate cost and time involved in abating the conditions. If more time is needed to approximate the cost, then the notice shall provide the date on which the approximate cost will be filed with the court and that date shall be within 10 days of the filing.

(4) Whether the receivership estate is likely to contain sufficient funds to abate the conditions.

(d) If the receivership estate does not contain sufficient funds to abate the conditions, the receiver shall request further instructions or orders from the court.

(e) The court, upon receipt of a notice pursuant to subdivision (d), shall consider appropriate orders or instructions to enable the receiver to correct the substandard conditions or to terminate or limit the period of receivership.[571]

568.3. Any tenant of real property that is subject to receivership, a tenant association or organization, or any federal, state, or local enforcement agency, may file a motion in a receivership action for the purpose of seeking further instructions or orders from the court, if either of the following is true:

(a) Substandard conditions exist, as defined by Section 17920.3 or 17920.10 of the Health and Safety Code.

(b) A dispute or controversy exists concerning the powers or duties of the receiver affecting a tenant or the public.[572]

568.5. A receiver may, pursuant to an order of the court, sell real or personal property in the receiver's possession upon the notice and in the manner prescribed by Article 6 (commencing with

Section 701.510) of Chapter 3 of Division 2 of Title 9. The sale is not final until confirmed by the court.[126]

568.6. A receiver appointed at the request of the Public Utilities Commission pursuant to Section 1825 of the Public Utilities Code shall control and operate Pacific Gas and Electric Company upon such terms and conditions as the court prescribes.[769]

569. Funds in the hands of a receiver may be deposited in one or more interest bearing accounts in the name and for the benefit of the receivership estate with one or more financial institutions, provided that all of the following conditions are satisfied:
(a) The deposits are fully guaranteed or insured under federal law.
(b) The financial institution in which the funds are deposited is not a party to the action in which the receiver was appointed.
(c) The receiver does not own 1 percent or more in value of the outstanding stock of the financial institution, is not an officer, director, or employee of the financial institution, and is not a sibling, whether by the whole or half-blood, spouse, aunt, uncle, nephew, niece, ancestor, or lineal descendant of an owner, officer, employee, or director.[401]

570. A receiver having any funds in his hands belonging to a person whose whereabouts are unknown to him, shall, before receiving his discharge as such receiver, publish a notice, in one or more newspapers published in the county, at least once a week for four consecutive weeks, setting forth the name of the owner of any unclaimed funds, the last known place of residence or post office address of such owner and the amount of such unclaimed funds. Any funds remaining in his hands unclaimed for 30 days after the date of the last publication of such notice, shall be reported to the court, and upon order of the court, all such funds must be paid into the State Treasury accompanied with a copy of the order, which must set forth the facts required in the notice herein provided. Such funds shall be deemed to have been received by the State under Chapter 7 (commencing with Section 1500) of Title 10 of Part 3 of this code and may be recovered in the manner prescribed therein.
All costs and expenses connected with such advertising shall be paid out of the funds the whereabouts of whose owners are unknown.[52]

Chapter 5A: Undertaking of Persons Handling Private Property or Funds

Chapter 5A added by Stats. 1963, Ch. 575.

571. If a referee or commissioner is appointed by a court and the duties of the referee or commissioner will, or are reasonably anticipated to, involve the custody of personal property or the receipt or disbursement of moneys, the order of appointment shall provide that before entering upon the duties, the referee or commissioner shall execute an undertaking to the State of California, to the effect that the referee or commissioner will faithfully discharge the duties of referee or commissioner, as the case may be, and obey the orders of the court therein. The order of appointment shall specify the amount of the undertaking, but a failure to so specify shall not invalidate the order.[132]

Chapter 6: Deposit in Court

Chapter 6 enacted 1872.

572. When it is admitted by the pleadings, or shown upon the examination of a party to the action, that he or she has in his or her possession, or under his or her control, any money or other thing capable of delivery, which, being the subject of litigation, is held by him or her as trustee for another party, or which belongs or which is due to another party or which should, under the circumstances of the case be held by the court pending final disposition of the action, the court may order the same, upon motion, to be deposited in court or delivered to such party, upon those conditions that may be just, subject to the further direction of the court.[242]

573. Whenever money is paid into or deposited in the court under this chapter, it shall be deposited with the court's treasury as provided in Section 68084 of the Government Code.[563]

574. Whenever, in the exercise of its authority, a court has ordered the deposit or delivery of money, or other thing, and the order is disobeyed, the court, beside punishing the disobedience, may make an order requiring the sheriff or marshal to take the money, or thing, and deposit or deliver it in conformity with the direction of the court.[370]

TITLE 7A: PRETRIAL CONFERENCES

Title 7a added by Stats. 1955, Ch. 632.

575. The Judicial Council may promulgate rules governing pretrial conferences, and the time, manner and nature thereof, in civil cases at issue, or in one or more classes thereof, in the superior courts.[506]

575.1. (a) The presiding judge of each superior court may prepare, with the assistance of appropriate committees of the court, proposed local rules designed to expedite and facilitate the business of the court. The rules need not be limited to those actions on the civil active list, but may provide for the supervision and judicial management of actions from the date they are filed. Rules prepared pursuant to this section shall be submitted for consideration to the judges of the court and, upon approval by a majority of the judges, the judges shall have the proposed rules published and submitted to the local bar and others, as specified by the Judicial Council, for consideration and recommendations.

(b) After a majority of the judges have officially adopted the rules, they shall be filed with the Judicial Council as required by Section 68071 of the Government Code and as specified in rules adopted by the Judicial Council. The Judicial Council shall prescribe rules to ensure that a complete current set of local rules and amendments, for each county in the state, is made available for public examination in each county. The local rules shall also be published for general distribution in accordance with rules adopted by the Judicial Council. Each court shall make its local rules available for inspection and copying in every location of the court that generally accepts filing of papers. The court may impose a reasonable charge for copying the rules and may impose a reasonable page limit on copying. The rules shall be accompanied by a notice indicating where a full set of the rules may be purchased.

(c) If a judge of a court adopts a rule that applies solely to cases in that judge's courtroom, or a particular branch or district of a court adopts a rule that applies solely to cases in that particular branch or district of a court, the court shall publish these rules as part of the general publication of rules required by the California Rules of Court. The court shall organize the rules so that rules on a common subject, whether individual, branch, district, or courtwide appear sequentially. Individual judges' rules and branch and district rules are local rules of court for purposes of this section and for purposes of the adoption, publication, comment, and filing requirements set forth in the Judicial Council rules applicable to local court rules.[532]

575.2. (a) Local rules promulgated pursuant to Section 575.1 may provide that if any counsel, a party represented by counsel, or a party if in pro se, fails to comply with any of the requirements thereof, the court on motion of a party or on its own motion may strike out all or any part of any pleading of that party, or, dismiss the action or proceeding or any part thereof, or enter a judgment by default against that party, or impose other penalties of a lesser nature as otherwise provided by law, and may order that party or his or her counsel to pay to the moving party the reasonable expenses in making the motion, including reasonable attorney fees. No penalty may be imposed under this section without prior notice to, and an opportunity to be heard by, the party against whom the penalty is sought to be imposed.
(b) It is the intent of the Legislature that if a failure to comply with these rules is the responsibility of counsel and not of the party, any penalty shall be imposed on counsel and shall not adversely affect the party's cause of action or defense thereto.[519]

576. Any judge, at any time before or after commencement of trial, in the furtherance of justice, and upon such terms as may be proper, may allow the amendment of any pleading or pretrial conference order.[48]

TITLE 8: OF THE TRIAL AND JUDGMENT IN CIVIL ACTIONS

Title 8 enacted 1872.

Chapter 1: Judgment in General

Chapter 1 enacted 1872.

577. A judgment is the final determination of the rights of the parties in an action or proceeding.[1]

577.5. In any judgment, or execution upon such judgment, the amount shall be computed and stated in dollars and cents, rejecting fractions.[28]

578. Judgment may be given for or against one or more of several plaintiffs, and for or against one or more of several defendants; and it may, when the justice of the case requires it, determine the ultimate rights of the parties on each side, as between themselves.[1]

579. In an action against several defendants, the Court may, in its discretion, render judgment against one or more of them, leaving the action to proceed against the others, whenever a several judgment is proper.[1]

580. (a) The relief granted to the plaintiff, if there is no answer, cannot exceed that demanded in the complaint, in the statement required by Section

425.11, or in the statement provided for by Section 425.115; but in any other case, the court may grant the plaintiff any relief consistent with the case made by the complaint and embraced within the issue. The court may impose liability, regardless of whether the theory upon which liability is sought to be imposed involves legal or equitable principles.

(b) Notwithstanding subdivision (a), the following types of relief may not be granted in a limited civil case:

(1) Relief exceeding the maximum amount in controversy for a limited civil case as provided in Section 85, exclusive of attorney's fees, interest, and costs.

(2) A permanent injunction, except as otherwise authorized by statute.

(3) A determination of title to real property.

(4) Declaratory relief, except as authorized by Section 86.[592]

580a. Whenever a money judgment is sought for the balance due upon an obligation for the payment of which a deed of trust or mortgage with power of sale upon real property or any interest therein was given as security, following the exercise of the power of sale in such deed of trust or mortgage, the plaintiff shall set forth in his or her complaint the entire amount of the indebtedness which was secured by the deed of trust or mortgage at the time of sale, the amount for which the real property or interest therein was sold and the fair market value thereof at the date of sale and the date of that sale. Upon the application of either party made at least 10 days before the time of trial the court shall, and upon its own motion the court at any time may, appoint one of the probate referees provided for by law to appraise the property or the interest therein sold as of the time of sale. The referee shall file his or her appraisal with the clerk and that appraisal shall be admissible in evidence. The referee shall take and subscribe an oath to be attached to the appraisal that he or she has truly, honestly and impartially appraised the property to the best of his or her knowledge and ability. Any referee so appointed may be called and examined as a witness by any party or by the court itself. The court must fix the compensation of the referee in an amount as determined by the court to be reasonable, but those fees shall not exceed similar fees for similar services in the community where the services are rendered, which may be taxed and allowed in like manner as other costs. Before rendering any judgment the court shall find the fair market value of the real property, or interest therein sold, at the time of sale. The court may render judgment for not more than the amount by which the entire amount of the indebtedness due at the time of sale exceeded the fair market value of the real property or interest therein sold at the time of sale with interest thereon from the date of the sale; provided, however, that in no event shall the amount of the judgment, exclusive of interest after the date of sale, exceed the difference between the amount for which the property was sold and the entire amount of the indebtedness secured by the deed of trust or mortgage. Any such action must be brought within three months of the time of sale under the deed of trust or mortgage. No judgment shall be rendered in any such action until the real property or interest therein has first been sold pursuant to the terms of the deed of trust or mortgage, unless the real property or interest therein has become valueless.[259]

580b. (a) Except as provided in subdivision (c), no deficiency shall be owed or collected, and no deficiency judgment shall lie, for any of the following:

(1) After a sale of real property or an estate for years therein for failure of the purchaser to complete his or her contract of sale.

(2) Under a deed of trust or mortgage given to the vendor to secure payment of the balance of the purchase price of that real property or estate for years therein.

(3) Under a deed of trust or mortgage on a dwelling for not more than four families given to a lender to secure repayment of a loan that was used to pay all or part of the purchase price of that dwelling, occupied entirely or in part by the purchaser. For purposes of subdivision (b), a loan described in this paragraph is a "purchase money loan."

(b) No deficiency shall be owed or collected, and no deficiency judgment shall lie, on a loan, refinance, or other credit transaction (collectively, a "credit transaction") that is used to refinance a purchase money loan, or subsequent refinances of a purchase money loan, except to the extent that in a credit transaction the lender or creditor advances new principal (hereafter "new advance") that is not applied to an obligation owed or to be owed under the purchase money loan, or to fees, costs, or related expenses of the credit transaction. A new credit transaction shall be deemed to be a purchase money loan except as to the principal amount of a new advance. For purposes of this section, any payment of principal shall be deemed to be applied first to the principal balance of the purchase money loan, and then to the principal balance of a new advance, and interest payments shall be applied to any interest due and owing. This subdivision applies only to credit transactions that are executed on or after January 1, 2013.

(c) The fact that no deficiency shall be owed or collected under the circumstances set forth in subdivisions (a) and (b) does not affect the liability that a guarantor, pledgor, or other surety might otherwise have with respect to the deficiency, or that might otherwise be satisfied in whole or in part from other collateral pledged to secure the obligation that is the subject of the deficiency.

(d) When both a chattel mortgage and a deed of trust or mortgage have been given to secure payment of the balance of the combined purchase price of both real and personal property, no deficiency judgment shall lie under any one thereof if no deficiency judgment would lie under the deed of trust or mortgage on the real property or estate for years therein.[695]

580c. In all cases where existing deeds of trust or mortgages are judicially foreclosed, unless a different amount is set up in the mortgage or deed of trust, and in all cases of mortgages and deeds of trust executed after this act takes effect, the mortgagor or trustor may be required to pay only such amount as trustee's or attorney's fees for processing the judicial foreclosure as the court may find reasonable and also the actual cost of publishing, recording, mailing and posting notices, litigation guarantee, and litigation cost of suit.[228]

580d. (a) Except as provided in subdivision (b), no deficiency shall be owed or collected, and no deficiency judgment shall be rendered for a deficiency on a note secured by a deed of trust or mortgage on real property or an estate for years therein executed in any case in which the real property or estate for years therein has been sold by the mortgagee or trustee under power of sale contained in the mortgage or deed of trust.

(b) The fact that no deficiency shall be owed or collected under the circumstances set forth in subdivision (a) does not affect the liability that a guarantor, pledgor, or other surety might otherwise have with respect to the deficiency, or that might otherwise be satisfied in whole or in part from other collateral pledged to secure the obligation that is the subject of the deficiency.

(c) This section does not apply to a deed of trust, mortgage, or other lien given to secure the payment of bonds or other evidences of indebtedness authorized or permitted to be issued by the Commissioner of Financial Protection and Innovation or which is made by a public utility subject to the Public Utilities Act (Part 1 (commencing with Section 201) of Division 1 of the Public Utilities Code).[801]

580e. (a) (1) No deficiency shall be owed or collected, and no deficiency judgment shall be requested or rendered for any deficiency upon a note secured solely by a deed of trust or mortgage for a dwelling of not more than four units, in any case in which the trustor or mortgagor sells the dwelling for a sale price less than the remaining amount of the indebtedness outstanding at the time of sale, in accordance with the written consent of the holder of the deed of trust or mortgage, provided that both of the following have occurred:

(A) Title has been voluntarily transferred to a buyer by grant deed or by other document of conveyance that has been recorded in the county where all or part of the real property is located.

(B) The proceeds of the sale have been tendered to the mortgagee, beneficiary, or the agent of the mortgagee or beneficiary, in accordance with the parties' agreement.

(2) In circumstances not described in paragraph (1), when a note is not secured solely by a deed of trust or mortgage for a dwelling of not more than four units, no judgment shall be rendered for any deficiency upon a note secured by a deed of trust or mortgage for a dwelling of not more than four units, if the trustor or mortgagor sells the dwelling for a sale price less than the remaining amount of the indebtedness outstanding at the time of sale, in accordance with the written consent of the holder of the deed of trust or mortgage. Following the sale, in accordance with the holder's written consent, the voluntary transfer of title to a buyer by grant deed or by other document of conveyance recorded in the county where all or part of the real property is located, and the tender to the mortgagee, beneficiary, or the agent of the mortgagee or beneficiary of the sale proceeds, as agreed, the rights, remedies, and obligations of any holder, beneficiary,

mortgagee, trustor, mortgagor, obligor, obligee, or guarantor of the note, deed of trust, or mortgage, and with respect to any other property that secures the note, shall be treated and determined as if the dwelling had been sold through foreclosure under a power of sale contained in the deed of trust or mortgage for a price equal to the sale proceeds received by the holder, in the manner contemplated by Section 580d.

(b) A holder of a note shall not require the trustor, mortgagor, or maker of the note to pay any additional compensation, aside from the proceeds of the sale, in exchange for the written consent to the sale.

(c) If the trustor or mortgagor commits either fraud with respect to the sale of, or waste with respect to, the real property that secures the deed of trust or mortgage, this section shall not limit the ability of the holder of the deed of trust or mortgage to seek damages and use existing rights and remedies against the trustor or mortgagor or any third party for fraud or waste.

(d) (1) This section shall not apply if the trustor or mortgagor is a corporation, limited liability company, limited partnership, or political subdivision of the state.

(2) This section shall not apply to any deed of trust, mortgage, or other lien given to secure the payment of bonds or other evidence of indebtedness authorized, or permitted to be issued, by the Commissioner of Financial Protection and Innovation, or that is made by a public utility subject to the Public Utilities Act (Part 1 (commencing with Section 201) of Division 1 of the Public Utilities Code).

(e) Any purported waiver of subdivision (a) or (b) shall be void and against public policy.[802]

580.5. (a) For purposes of this section:

(1) "Beneficiary" means a "beneficiary" as defined in paragraph (3) of subdivision (a) of Section 5102 of the Commercial Code.

(2) "Issuer" means an "issuer" as defined in paragraph (9) of subdivision (a) of Section 5102 of the Commercial Code.

(3) "Letter of credit" means a "letter of credit" as defined in paragraph (10) of subdivision (a) of Section 5102 of the Commercial Code whether or not the engagement is governed by Division 5 (commencing with Section 5101) of the Commercial Code.

(b) With respect to an obligation which is secured by a mortgage or a deed of trust upon real property or an estate for years therein and which is also supported by a letter of credit, neither the presentment, receipt of payment, or enforcement of a draft or demand for payment under the letter of credit by the beneficiary of the letter of credit nor the honor or payment of, or the demand for reimbursement, receipt of reimbursement or enforcement of any contractual, statutory or other reimbursement obligation relating to, the letter of credit by the issuer of the letter of credit shall, whether done before or after the judicial or nonjudicial foreclosure of the mortgage or deed of trust or conveyance in lieu thereof, constitute any of the following:

(1) An action within the meaning of subdivision (a) of Section 726, or a failure to comply with any other statutory or judicial requirement to proceed first against security.

(2) A money judgment for a deficiency or a deficiency judgment within the meaning of Section 580a, 580b, or 580d, or subdivision (b) of Section 726, or the functional equivalent of any such judgment.

(3) A violation of Section 580a, 580b, 580d, or 726.[357]

580.7. (a) For purposes of this section:

(1) "Beneficiary" means a "beneficiary" as defined in paragraph (3) of subdivision (a) of Section 5102 of the Commercial Code.

(2) "Customer" means an "applicant" as defined in paragraph (2) of subdivision (a) of Section 5102 of the Commercial Code.

(3) "Letter of credit" means a "letter of credit" as defined in paragraph (10) of subdivision (a) of Section 5102 of the Commercial Code whether or not the engagement is governed by Division 5 (commencing with Section 5101) of the Commercial Code.

(b) No letter of credit shall be enforceable by any party thereto in a loan transaction in which all of the following circumstances exist:

(1) The customer is a natural person.

(2) The letter of credit is issued to the beneficiary to avoid a default of the existing loan.

(3) The existing loan is secured by a purchase money deed of trust or purchase money mortgage on real property containing one to four residential units, at least one of which is owned and occupied, or was intended at the time the existing loan was made, to be occupied by the customer.

(4) The letter of credit is issued after the effective date of this section.[358]

581. (a) As used in this section:

(1) "Action" means any civil action or special proceeding.

(2) "Complaint" means a complaint and a cross-complaint.

(3) "Court" means the court in which the action is pending.

(4) "Defendant" includes a cross-defendant.

(5) "Plaintiff" includes a cross-complainant.

(6) "Trial." A trial shall be deemed to actually commence at the beginning of the opening statement or argument of any party or his or her counsel, or if there is no opening statement, then at the time of the administering of the oath or affirmation to the first witness, or the introduction of any evidence.

(b) An action may be dismissed in any of the following instances:

(1) With or without prejudice, upon written request of the plaintiff to the clerk, filed with papers in the case, or by oral or written request to the court at any time before the actual commencement of trial, upon payment of the costs, if any.

(2) With or without prejudice, by any party upon the written consent of all other parties.

(3) By the court, without prejudice, when no party appears for trial following 30 days' notice of time and place of trial.

(4) By the court, without prejudice, when dismissal is made pursuant to the applicable provisions of Chapter 1.5 (commencing with Section 583.110).

(5) By the court, without prejudice, when either party fails to appear on the trial and the other party appears and asks for dismissal.

(c) A plaintiff may dismiss his or her complaint, or any cause of action asserted in it, in its entirety, or as to any defendant or defendants, with or without prejudice prior to the actual commencement of trial.

(d) Except as otherwise provided in subdivision (e), the court shall dismiss the complaint, or any cause of action asserted in it, in its entirety or as to any defendant, with prejudice, when upon the trial and before the final submission of the case, the plaintiff abandons it.

(e) After the actual commencement of trial, the court shall dismiss the complaint, or any causes of action asserted in it, in its entirety or as to any defendants, with prejudice, if the plaintiff requests a dismissal, unless all affected parties to the trial consent to dismissal without prejudice or by order of the court dismissing the same without prejudice on a showing of good cause.

(f) The court may dismiss the complaint as to that defendant when:

(1) Except where Section 597 applies, after a demurrer to the complaint is sustained without leave to amend and either party moves for dismissal.

(2) Except where Section 597 applies, after a demurrer to the complaint is sustained with leave to amend, the plaintiff fails to amend it within the time allowed by the court and either party moves for dismissal.

(3) After a motion to strike the whole of a complaint is granted without leave to amend and either party moves for dismissal.

(4) After a motion to strike the whole of a complaint or portion thereof is granted with leave to amend the plaintiff fails to amend it within the time allowed by the court and either party moves for dismissal.

(g) The court may dismiss without prejudice the complaint in whole, or as to that defendant, when dismissal is made under the applicable provisions of Chapter 1.5 (commencing with Section 583.110).

(h) The court may dismiss without prejudice the complaint in whole, or as to that defendant, when dismissal is made pursuant to Section 418.10.

(i) No dismissal of an action may be made or entered, or both, under paragraph (1) of subdivision (b) where affirmative relief has been sought by the cross-complaint of a defendant or if there is a motion pending for an order transferring the action to another court under the provisions of Section 396b.

(j) No dismissal may be made or entered, or both, under paragraph (1) or (2) of subdivision (b) except upon the written consent of the attorney for the party or parties applying therefor, or if consent of the attorney is not obtained, upon order of dismissal by the court after notice to the attorney.

(k) No action may be dismissed which has been determined to be a class action under the provisions of this code unless and until notice that the court deems adequate has been given and the court orders the dismissal.

(l) The court may dismiss, without prejudice, the complaint in whole, or as to that defendant when either party fails to appear at the trial and the other party appears and asks for the dismissal.

(m) The provisions of this section shall not be deemed to be an exclusive enumeration of the court's power to dismiss an action or dismiss a complaint as to a defendant.[325]

581.5. In a case involving consumer

debt, as defined in Section 1788.2 of the Civil Code, and as regulated under Title 1.6C.5 (commencing with Section 1788.50) of Part 4 of Division 3 of the Civil Code, if the defendant debtor appears for trial on the scheduled trial date, and the plaintiff debt buyer either fails to appear or is not prepared to proceed to trial, and the court does not find a good cause for continuance, the court may, in its discretion, dismiss the action with or without prejudice. Notwithstanding any other law, in this instance, the court may award the defendant debtor's costs of preparing for trial, including, but not limited to, lost wages and transportation expenses.[683]

581c. (a) Only after, and not before, the plaintiff has completed his or her opening statement, or after the presentation of his or her evidence in a trial by jury, the defendant, without waiving his or her right to offer evidence in the event the motion is not granted, may move for a judgment of nonsuit.
(b) If it appears that the evidence presented, or to be presented, supports the granting of the motion as to some but not all of the issues involved in the action, the court shall grant the motion as to those issues and the action shall proceed as to the issues remaining. Despite the granting of the motion, no final judgment shall be entered prior to the termination of the action, but the final judgment in the action shall, in addition to any matters determined in the trial, award judgment as determined by the motion herein provided for.
(c) If the motion is granted, unless the court in its order for judgment otherwise specifies, the judgment of nonsuit operates as an adjudication upon the merits.
(d) In actions which arise out of an injury to the person or to property, when a motion for judgment of nonsuit was granted on the basis that the defendant was without fault, no other defendant during trial, over plaintiff's objection, may attempt to attribute fault to or comment on the absence or involvement of the defendant who was granted the motion.[385]

581d. A written dismissal of an action shall be entered in the clerk's register and is effective for all purposes when so entered.
All dismissals ordered by the court shall be in the form of a written order signed by the court and filed in the action and those orders when so filed shall constitute judgments and be effective for all purposes, and the clerk shall note those judgments in the register of actions in the case.[393]

582. In all other cases judgment shall be rendered on the merits.[27]

582.5. In a limited civil case in which the defendant has appeared, if the judgment or order is for the payment of money by the defendant, the defendant shall pay the judgment immediately or at any time and upon terms and conditions, including installment payments, that the court may prescribe. The court may amend the terms and conditions for payment of the judgment or order at any time to provide for installment payments for good cause upon motion by a party and notice to all affected parties, regardless of the nature of the underlying debt and regardless of whether the moving party appeared before entry of the judgment or order. In any determination regarding the imposition of terms and conditions upon the payment of the judgment, the court shall consider any factors that would be relevant to the determination of a claim for exemption pursuant to Chapter 4 (commencing with Section 703.010) of Division 2 of Title 9 of Part 2 or the examination of a debtor pursuant to Article 2 (commencing with Section 708.110) of Chapter 6 of Division 2 of Title 9.[394]

Chapter 1.5: Dismissal for Delay in Prosecution

Chapter 1.5 added by Stats. 1984, Ch. 1705, Sec. 5.

Article 1: Definitions and General Provisions

Article 1 added by Stats. 1984, Ch. 1705, Sec. 5.

583.110. As used in this chapter, unless the provision or context otherwise requires:
(a) "Action" includes an action commenced by cross-complaint or other pleading that asserts a cause of action or claim for relief.
(b) "Complaint" includes a cross-complaint or other initial pleading.
(c) "Court" means the court in which the action is pending.
(d) "Defendant" includes a cross-defendant or other person against whom an action is commenced.
(e) "Plaintiff" includes a cross-complainant or other person by whom an action is commenced.
(f) "Service" includes return of summons.[232]

583.120. (a) This chapter applies to a civil action and does not apply to a special proceeding except to the extent incorporated by reference in the special proceeding.
(b) Notwithstanding subdivision (a), the court may, by rule or otherwise under inherent authority of the court, apply this chapter to a special proceeding or part of a special proceeding except to the extent such application would be inconsistent with the character of the special proceeding or the statute governing the special proceeding.[232]

583.130. It is the policy of the state that a plaintiff shall proceed with reasonable diligence in the prosecution of an action but that all parties shall cooperate in bringing the action to trial or other disposition. Except as otherwise provided by statute or by rule of court adopted pursuant to statute, the policy favoring the right of parties to make stipulations in their own interests and the policy favoring trial or other disposition of an action on the merits are generally to be preferred over the policy that requires dismissal for failure to proceed with reasonable diligence in the prosecution of an action in construing the provisions of this chapter.[232]

583.140. Nothing in this chapter abrogates or otherwise affects the principles of waiver and estoppel.[232]

583.150. This chapter does not limit or affect the authority of a court to dismiss an action or impose other sanctions under a rule adopted by the court pursuant to Section 575.1 or by the Judicial Council pursuant to statute, or otherwise under inherent authority of the court.[232]

583.160. This chapter applies to a motion for dismissal made in an action commenced before, on, or after the effective date of this chapter, except that in the case of an action commenced before the effective date of this chapter:

(a) A motion for dismissal made pursuant to notice given before, on, or within one year after the effective date of this chapter is governed by the applicable law in effect immediately before the effective date and for this purpose the law in effect immediately before the effective date continues in effect.

(b) This chapter does not affect an order dismissing an action made before the effective date of this chapter.[232]

583.161. A petition filed pursuant to Section 299, 2250, 2330, or 7600 of the Family Code shall not be dismissed pursuant to this chapter if any of the following conditions exist:

(a) An order for child support or an order regarding child custody or visitation has been issued in connection with the proceeding and the order has not been (1) terminated by the court or (2) terminated by operation of law pursuant to Sections 3022, 3900, 3901, 4007, and 4013 of the Family Code.

(b) An order for spousal support has been issued in connection with the proceeding and the order has not been terminated by the court.

(c) A personal conduct restraining order has been issued pursuant to the Domestic Violence Prevention Act (Division 10 (commencing with Section 6200) of the Family Code) and the order has not been terminated by operation of law or by the court.

(d) An issue in the case has been bifurcated and one of the following has occurred:

(1) A separate trial has been conducted pursuant to Section 2337 of the Family Code.

(2) A separate trial has been conducted pursuant to the California Rules of Court.[682]

Article 2: Mandatory Time for Service of Summons

Article 2 added by Stats. 1984, Ch. 1705, Sec. 5.

583.210. (a) The summons and complaint shall be served upon a defendant within three years after the action is commenced against the defendant. For the purpose of this subdivision, an action is commenced at the time the complaint is filed.

(b) Proof of service of the summons shall be filed within 60 days after the time the summons and complaint must be served upon a defendant.[568]

583.220. The time within which service must be made pursuant to this article does not apply if the defendant enters into a stipulation in writing or does another act that constitutes a general appearance in the action. For the purpose of this section none of the following constitutes a general appearance in the action:

(a) A stipulation pursuant to Section 583.230 extending the time within which service must be made.

(b) A motion to dismiss made pursuant to this chapter, whether joined with a motion to quash service or a motion to set aside a default judgment, or otherwise.

(c) An extension of time to plead after a motion to dismiss made pursuant to this chapter.[232]

583.230. The parties may extend the time within which service must be made pursuant to this article by the following means:

(a) By written stipulation. The stipulation need not be filed but, if it is not filed, the stipulation shall be brought to the attention of the court if relevant to a motion for dismissal.

(b) By oral agreement made in open court, if entered in the minutes of the court or a transcript is made.[232]

583.240. In computing the time within which service must be made pursuant to this article, there shall be excluded the time during which any of the following conditions existed:

(a) The defendant was not amenable to the process of the court.

(b) The prosecution of the action or proceedings in the action was stayed and the stay affected service.

(c) The validity of service was the subject of litigation by the parties.

(d) Service, for any other reason, was impossible, impracticable, or futile due to causes beyond the plaintiff's control. Failure to discover relevant facts or evidence is not a cause beyond the plaintiff's control for the purpose of this subdivision.[232]

583.250. (a) If service is not made in an action within the time prescribed in this article:

(1) The action shall not be further prosecuted and no further proceedings shall be held in the action.

(2) The action shall be dismissed by the court on its own motion or on motion of any person interested in the action, whether named as a party or not, after notice to the parties.

(b) The requirements of this article are mandatory and are not subject to extension, excuse, or exception except as expressly provided by statute.[232]

Article 3: Mandatory Time for Bringing Action to Trial or New Trial

Article 3 added by Stats. 1984, Ch. 1705, Sec. 5.

583.310. An action shall be brought to trial within five years after the action is commenced against the defendant.[232]

583.320. (a) If a new trial is granted in the action the action shall again be brought to trial within the following times:

(1) If a trial is commenced but no judgment is entered because of a mistrial or because a jury is unable to reach a decision, within three years after the order of the court declaring the mistrial or the disagreement of the jury is entered.

(2) If after judgment a new trial is granted and no appeal is taken, within three years after the order granting the new trial is entered.

(3) If on appeal an order granting a new trial is affirmed or a judgment is reversed and the action remanded for a new trial, within three years after the remittitur is filed by the clerk of the trial court.

(b) Nothing in this section requires that an action again be brought to trial before expiration of the time prescribed in Section 583.310.[232]

583.330. The parties may extend the time within which an action must be brought to trial pursuant to this article by the following means:

(a) By written stipulation. The stipulation need not be filed but, if it is not filed, the stipulation shall be brought to the attention of the court if relevant to a motion for dismissal.

(b) By oral agreement made in open court, if entered in the minutes of the court or a transcript is made.[232]

583.340. In computing the time within which an action must be brought to trial pursuant to this article, there shall be excluded the time during which any of the following conditions existed:
(a) The jurisdiction of the court to try the action was suspended.
(b) Prosecution or trial of the action was stayed or enjoined.
(c) Bringing the action to trial, for any other reason, was impossible, impracticable, or futile.[232]

583.350. If the time within which an action must be brought to trial pursuant to this article is tolled or otherwise extended pursuant to statute with the result that at the end of the period of tolling or extension less than six months remains within which the action must be brought to trial, the action shall not be dismissed pursuant to this article if the action is brought to trial within six months after the end of the period of tolling or extension.[232]

583.360. (a) An action shall be dismissed by the court on its own motion or on motion of the defendant, after notice to the parties, if the action is not brought to trial within the time prescribed in this article.
(b) The requirements of this article are mandatory and are not subject to extension, excuse, or exception except as expressly provided by statute.[232]

Article 4: Discretionary Dismissal for Delay
Article 4 added by Stats. 1984, Ch. 1705, Sec. 5.

583.410. (a) The court may in its discretion dismiss an action for delay in prosecution pursuant to this article on its own motion or on motion of the defendant if to do so appears to the court appropriate under the circumstances of the case.
(b) Dismissal shall be pursuant to the procedure and in accordance with the criteria prescribed by rules adopted by the Judicial Council.[232]

583.420. (a) The court may not dismiss an action pursuant to this article for delay in prosecution except after one of the following conditions has occurred:
(1) Service is not made within two years after the action is commenced against the defendant.
(2) The action is not brought to trial within the following times:
(A) Three years after the action is commenced against the defendant unless otherwise prescribed by rule under subparagraph (B).
(B) Two years after the action is commenced against the defendant if the Judicial Council by rule adopted pursuant to Section 583.410 so prescribes for the court because of the condition of the court calendar or for other reasons affecting the conduct of litigation or the administration of justice.
(3) A new trial is granted and the action is not again brought to trial within the following times:
(A) If a trial is commenced but no judgment is entered because of a mistrial or because a jury is unable to reach a decision, within two years after the order of the court declaring the mistrial or the disagreement of the jury is entered.
(B) If after judgment a new trial is granted and no appeal is taken, within two years after the order

granting the new trial is entered.

(C) If on appeal an order granting a new trial is affirmed or a judgment is reversed and the action remanded for a new trial, within two years after the remittitur is filed by the clerk of the trial court.

(b) The times provided in subdivision (a) shall be computed in the manner provided for computation of the comparable times under Articles 2 (commencing with Section 583.210) and 3 (commencing with Section 583.310).[232]

583.430. (a) In a proceeding for dismissal of an action pursuant to this article for delay in prosecution the court in its discretion may require as a condition of granting or denial of dismissal that the parties comply with such terms as appear to the court proper to effectuate substantial justice.

(b) The court may make any order necessary to effectuate the authority provided in this section, including, but not limited to, provisional and conditional orders.[232]

Chapter 2: Judgment Upon Failure to Answer

Chapter 2 enacted 1872.

585. Judgment may be had, if the defendant fails to answer the complaint, as follows:

(a) In an action arising upon contract or judgment for the recovery of money or damages only, if the defendant has, or if more than one defendant, if any of the defendants have, been served, other than by publication, and no answer, demurrer, notice of motion to strike of the character specified in subdivision (f), notice of motion to transfer pursuant to Section 396b, notice of motion to dismiss pursuant to Article 2 (commencing with Section 583.210) of Chapter 1.5 of Title 8, notice of motion to quash service of summons or to stay or dismiss the action pursuant to Section 418.10, or notice of the filing of a petition for writ of mandate as provided in Section 418.10 has been filed with the clerk of the court within the time specified in the summons, or within further time as may be allowed, the clerk, upon written application of the plaintiff, and proof of the service of summons, shall enter the default of the defendant or defendants, so served, and immediately thereafter enter judgment for the principal amount demanded in the complaint, in the statement required by Section 425.11, or in the statement provided for in Section 425.115, or a lesser amount if credit has been acknowledged, together with interest allowed by law or in accordance with the terms of the contract, and the costs against the defendant, or defendants, or against one or more of the defendants. If, by rule of court, a schedule of attorneys' fees to be allowed has been adopted, the clerk may include in the judgment attorneys' fees in accordance with the schedule (1) if the contract provides that attorneys' fees shall be allowed in the event of an action thereon, or (2) if the action is one in which the plaintiff is entitled by statute to recover attorneys' fees in addition to money or damages. The plaintiff shall file a written request at the time of application for entry of the default of the defendant or defendants, to have attorneys' fees fixed by the court, whereupon, after the entry of the default, the court shall hear the application for determination of the attorneys' fees and shall render judgment for the attorneys' fees and for the other relief demanded in the complaint, in the statement required by Section 425.11, or in the statement provided for in Section 425.115, or a lesser amount if credit has been acknowledged, and the costs against the defendant, or defendants, or against one or more of the defendants.

(b) In other actions, if the defendant has been served, other than by publication, and no answer, demurrer, notice of motion to strike of the character specified in subdivision (f), notice of motion to transfer pursuant to Section 396b, notice of motion to dismiss pursuant to Article 2 (commencing with Section 583.210) of Chapter 1.5 of Title 8, notice of motion to quash service of summons or to stay or dismiss the action pursuant to Section 418.10 or notice of the filing of a petition for writ of mandate as provided in Section 418.10 has been filed with the clerk of the court within the time specified in the summons, or within further time as may be allowed, the clerk, upon written application of the plaintiff, shall enter the default of the defendant. The plaintiff thereafter may apply to the court for the relief demanded in the complaint. The court shall hear the evidence offered by the plaintiff, and shall render judgment in the plaintiff's favor for that relief, not exceeding the amount stated in the complaint, in the statement required by Section 425.11, or in the statement provided for by Section 425.115, as appears by the evidence to be just. If the taking of an account, or the proof of any fact, is necessary to enable the court to give judgment or to carry the judgment into effect, the court may take the account or hear the proof, or may, in its discretion, order a reference for that purpose. If the action is for the recovery of damages, in whole or in part, the court may order the damages to be assessed by a jury; or if, to determine the amount of damages, the examination of a long account is involved, by a reference as above provided.

(c) In all actions where the service of the summons was by publication, upon the expiration of the time for answering, and upon proof of the publication and that no answer, demurrer, notice of motion to strike of the character specified in subdivision (f), notice of motion to transfer pursuant to Section 396b, notice of motion to dismiss pursuant to Article 2 (commencing with Section 583.210) of Chapter 1.5 of Title 8, notice of motion to quash service of summons or to stay or dismiss the action pursuant to Section 418.10, or notice of the filing of a petition for writ of mandate as provided in Section 418.10 has been filed, the clerk, upon written application of the plaintiff, shall enter the default of the defendant. The plaintiff thereafter may apply to the court for the relief demanded in the complaint; and the court shall hear the evidence offered by the plaintiff, and shall render judgment in the plaintiff's favor for that relief, not exceeding the amount stated in the complaint, in the statement required by Section 425.11, or in the statement provided for in Section 425.115, as appears by the evidence to be just. If the defendant is not a resident of the state, the court shall require the plaintiff, or the plaintiff's agent, to be examined, on oath, respecting any payments that have been made to the plaintiff, or to anyone for the plaintiff's use, on account of any demand mentioned in the complaint, in the statement required by Section 425.11, or in the statement provided for in Section 425.115, and may render judgment for the amount that the plaintiff is entitled to recover. In all cases affecting the title to or possession of real property, where the service of the summons was by publication and the defendant has failed to answer, no judgment shall be rendered upon proof of mere occupancy, unless the occupancy has continued for the time and has been of the character necessary to confer title by prescription. In all cases where the plaintiff bases a claim upon a paper title, the court shall require evidence establishing the plaintiff's equitable right to judgment before rendering judgment. In actions involving only the possession of real property where the complaint is verified and shows by proper allegations that no party to the action claims title to the real property involved, either by prescription, accession, transfer, will, or succession, but only the possession thereof, the court may render judgment upon proof of occupancy by plaintiff and ouster by defendant.

(d) In the cases referred to in subdivisions (b) and (c), or upon an application to have attorneys' fees fixed by the court pursuant to subdivision (a), the court in its discretion may permit the use of affidavits, in lieu of personal testimony, as to all or any part of the evidence or proof required or permitted to be offered, received, or heard in those cases. The facts stated in the affidavit or affidavits shall be within the personal knowledge of the affiant and shall be set forth with particularity, and each affidavit shall show affirmatively that the affiant, if sworn as a witness, can testify competently thereto.

(e) If a defendant files a cross-complaint against another defendant or the plaintiff, a default may be entered against that party on that cross-complaint if the plaintiff or that cross-defendant has been served with that cross-complaint and has failed to file an answer, demurrer, notice of motion to strike of the character specified in subdivision (f), notice of motion to transfer pursuant to Section 396b, notice of motion to dismiss pursuant to Article 2 (commencing with Section 583.210) of Chapter 1.5 of Title 8, notice of motion to quash service of summons or to stay or dismiss the action pursuant to Section 418.10, or notice of the filing of a petition for a writ of mandate as provided in Section 418.10 within the time specified in the summons, or within another time period as may be allowed. However, no judgment may separately be entered on that cross-complaint unless a separate judgment may, in fact, be properly awarded on that cross-complaint and the court finds that a separate judgment on that cross-complaint would not substantially delay the final disposition of the action between the parties.

(f) A notice of motion to strike within the meaning of this section is a notice of motion to strike the whole or any part of a pleading filed within the time which the moving party is required otherwise to plead to that pleading. The notice of motion to strike shall specify a hearing date set in accordance with Section 1005. The filing of a notice of motion does not extend the time within which to demur.

(g) This section shall remain in effect only until January 1, 2027, and as of that date is repealed.[892]

585. Judgment may be had, if the defendant fails to answer the complaint, as follows:

(a) In an action arising upon contract or judgment for the recovery of money or damages only, if the defendant has, or if more than one defendant, if any of the defendants have, been served, other than by publication, and no answer, demurrer, notice of motion to strike of the character specified in subdivision (f), notice of motion to transfer pursuant to Section 396b, notice of motion to dismiss pursuant to Article 2 (commencing with Section 583.210) of Chapter 1.5 of Title 8, notice of motion to quash service of summons or to stay or dismiss the action pursuant to Section 418.10, or notice of the filing of a petition for writ of mandate as provided in Section 418.10 has been filed with the clerk of the court within the time specified in the summons, or within further time as may be allowed, the clerk, upon written application of the plaintiff, and proof of service of the summons, shall enter the default of the defendant or defendants, so served, and immediately thereafter enter judgment for the principal amount demanded in the complaint, in the statement required by Section 425.11, or in the statement provided for in Section 425.115, or a lesser amount if credit has been acknowledged, together with interest allowed by law or in accordance with the terms of the contract, and the costs against the defendant, or defendants, or against one or more of the defendants. If, by rule of court, a schedule of attorney's fees to be allowed has been adopted, the clerk may include in the judgment attorney's fees in accordance with the schedule (1) if the contract provides that attorney's fees shall be allowed in the event of an action thereon, or (2) if the action is one in which the plaintiff is entitled by statute to recover attorney's fees in addition to money or damages. The plaintiff shall file a written request at the time of application for entry of the default of the defendant or defendants, to have attorney's fees fixed by the court, whereupon, after the entry of the default, the court shall hear the application for determination of the attorney's fees and shall render judgment for the attorney's fees and for the other relief demanded in the complaint, in the statement required by Section 425.11, or in the statement provided for in Section 425.115, or a lesser amount if credit has been acknowledged, and the costs against the defendant, or defendants, or against one or more of the defendants.

(b) In other actions, if the defendant has been served, other than by publication, and no answer, demurrer, notice of motion to strike of the character specified in subdivision (f), notice of motion to transfer pursuant to Section 396b, notice of motion to dismiss pursuant to Article 2 (commencing with Section 583.210) of Chapter 1.5 of Title 8, notice of motion to quash service of summons or to stay or dismiss the action pursuant to Section 418.10 or notice of the filing of a petition for writ of mandate as provided in Section 418.10 has been filed with the clerk of the court within the time specified in the summons, or within further time as may be allowed, the clerk, upon written application of the plaintiff, and proof of service of the summons, shall enter the default of the defendant. The plaintiff thereafter may apply to the court for the relief demanded in the complaint. The court shall hear the evidence offered by the plaintiff, and shall render judgment in the plaintiff's favor for that relief, not exceeding the amount stated in the complaint, in the statement required by Section 425.11, or in the statement provided for by Section 425.115, as appears by the evidence to be just. If the taking of an account, or the proof of any fact, is necessary to enable the court to give judgment or to carry the judgment into effect, the court may take the account or hear the proof, or may, in its discretion, order a reference for that purpose. If the action is for the recovery of damages, in whole or in part, the court may order the damages to be assessed by a jury; or if, to determine the amount of damages, the examination of a long account is involved, by a reference as above provided.

(c) In all actions where the service of the summons was by publication, upon the expiration of the time for answering, and upon proof of the publication and that no answer, demurrer, notice of motion to strike of the character specified in subdivision (f), notice of motion to transfer pursuant to Section 396b, notice of motion to dismiss pursuant to Article 2 (commencing with Section 583.210) of Chapter 1.5 of Title 8, notice of motion to quash service of summons or to stay or dismiss the action pursuant to Section 418.10, or notice of the filing of a petition for writ of mandate as provided in Section 418.10 has been filed, the clerk, upon written application of the plaintiff, shall enter the default of the defendant. The plaintiff thereafter may apply to the court for the relief demanded in the complaint; and the court shall hear the evidence offered by the plaintiff, and shall render judgment in the plaintiff's favor for that relief, not exceeding the amount stated in the complaint, in the statement required by Section 425.11, or in the statement provided for in Section 425.115, as appears by the evidence to be just. If the defendant is not a resident of the state, the court shall require the plaintiff, or the plaintiff's agent, to be examined, on oath, respecting any payments that have been made to the plaintiff, or to anyone for the plaintiff's use, on account of any demand mentioned in the complaint, in the statement required by Section 425.11, or in the statement provided for in Section 425.115, and may render judgment for the amount that the plaintiff is entitled to recover. In all cases affecting the title to or possession of real property, where the service of the summons was by publication and the defendant has failed to answer, no judgment shall be rendered upon proof of mere occupancy, unless the occupancy has continued for the time and has been of the character necessary to confer title by prescription. In all cases where the plaintiff bases a claim upon a paper title, the court shall require evidence establishing the plaintiff's equitable right to judgment before rendering judgment. In actions involving only the possession of real property where the complaint is verified and shows by proper allegations that no party to the action claims title to the real property involved, either by prescription, accession, transfer, will, or succession, but only the possession thereof, the court may render judgment upon proof of occupancy by plaintiff and ouster by defendant.

(d) In the cases referred to in subdivisions (b) and (c), or upon an application to have attorney's fees fixed by the court pursuant to subdivision (a), the court in its discretion may permit the use of affidavits, in lieu of personal testimony, as to all or any part of the evidence or proof required or permitted to be offered, received, or heard in those cases. The facts stated in the affidavit or affidavits shall be within the personal knowledge of the affiant and shall be set forth with particularity, and each affidavit shall show affirmatively that the affiant, if sworn as a witness, can testify competently thereto.

(e) If a defendant files a cross-complaint against another defendant or the plaintiff, a default may be entered against that party on that cross-complaint if the plaintiff or that cross-defendant has been served with that cross-complaint and has failed to file an answer, demurrer, notice of motion to strike of the character specified in subdivision (f), notice of motion to transfer pursuant to Section 396b, notice of motion to dismiss pursuant to Article 2 (commencing with Section 583.210) of Chapter 1.5 of Title 8, notice of motion to quash service of summons or to stay or dismiss the action pursuant to Section 418.10, or notice of the filing of a petition for a writ of mandate as provided in Section 418.10 within the time specified in the summons, or within another time period as may be allowed. However, no judgment may separately be entered on that cross-complaint unless a separate judgment may, in fact, be properly awarded on that cross-complaint and the court finds that a separate judgment on that cross-complaint would not substantially delay the final disposition of the action between the parties.

(f) A notice of motion to strike within the meaning of this section is a notice of motion to strike the whole or any part of a pleading filed within the time which the moving party is required otherwise to plead to that pleading. The notice of motion to strike shall specify a hearing date set in accordance with Section 1005. The filing of a notice of motion does not extend the time within which to demur.

(g) This section shall become operative on January 1, 2027.[893]

585.5. (a) Every application to enter default under subdivision (a) of Section 585 shall include, or be accompanied by, an affidavit stating facts showing that the action is or is not subject to Section 1812.10 or 2984.4 of the Civil Code or subdivision (b) of Section 395.

(b) When a default or default judgment has been entered without full compliance with Section 1812.10 or 2984.4 of the Civil Code, or subdivision (b) of Section 395, the defendant may serve and file a notice of motion to set aside the default or default judgment and for leave to defend the action in the proper court. The notice of motion shall be served and filed within 60 days after the defendant first receives notice of levy under a writ of execution, or notice of any other procedure for enforcing, the default judgment.

(c) A notice of motion to set aside a default or default judgment and for leave to defend the action in the proper court shall designate as the time for making the motion a date prescribed by subdivision (b) of Section

1005, and it shall be accompanied by an affidavit showing under oath that the action was not commenced in the proper court according to Section 1812.10 or 2984.4 of the Civil Code or subdivision (b) of Section 395. The party shall serve and file with the notice a copy of the answer, motion, or other pleading proposed to be filed in the action.

(d) Upon a finding by the court that the motion was made within the period permitted by subdivision (b) and that the action was not commenced in the proper court, it shall set aside the default or default judgment on such terms as may be just and shall allow such a party to defend the action in the proper court.

(e) Unless the plaintiff can show that the plaintiff used reasonable diligence to avoid filing the action in the improper court, upon a finding that the action was commenced in the improper court the court shall award the defendant actual damages and costs, including reasonable attorney's fees.[292]

586. (a) In the following cases the same proceedings shall be had, and judgment shall be rendered in the same manner, as if the defendant had failed to answer:

(1) If the complaint has been amended, and the defendant fails to answer it, as amended, or demur thereto, or file a notice of motion to strike, of the character specified in Section 585, within 30 days after service thereof or within the time allowed by the court.

(2) If the demurrer to the complaint is overruled and a motion to strike, of the character specified in Section 585, is denied, or where only one thereof is filed, if the demurrer is overruled or the motion to strike is denied, and the defendant fails to answer the complaint within the time allowed by the court.

(3) If a motion to strike, of the character specified in Section 585, is granted in whole or in part, and the defendant fails to answer the unstricken portion of the complaint within the time allowed by the court, no demurrer having been sustained or being then pending.

(4) If a motion to quash service of summons or to stay or dismiss the action has been filed, or writ of mandate sought and notice thereof given, as provided in Section 418.10, and upon denial of the motion or writ, the defendant fails to respond to the complaint within the time provided in that section or as otherwise provided by law.

(5) If the demurrer to the answer is sustained and the defendant fails to amend the answer within the time allowed by the court.

(6) (A) If a motion to transfer pursuant to Section 396b is denied and the defendant fails to respond to the complaint within the time allowed by the court pursuant to subdivision (e) of Section 396b or within the time provided in subparagraph (C).

(B) If a motion to transfer pursuant to Section 396b is granted and the defendant fails to respond to the complaint within 30 days of the mailing of notice of the filing and case number by the clerk of the court to which the action or proceeding is transferred or within the time provided in subparagraph (C).

(C) If the order granting or denying a motion to transfer pursuant to Section 396a or 396b is the subject of an appeal pursuant to Section 904.2 in which a stay is granted or of a mandate proceeding pursuant to Section 400, the court having jurisdiction over the trial, upon application or on its own motion after the appeal or mandate proceeding becomes final or upon earlier termination of a stay, shall allow the defendant a reasonable time to respond to the complaint. Notice of the order allowing the defendant further time to respond to the complaint shall be promptly served by the party who obtained the order or by the clerk if the order is made on the court's own motion.

(7) If a motion to strike the answer in whole, of the character specified in Section 585, is granted without leave to amend, or if a motion to strike the answer in whole or in part, of the character specified in Section 585, is granted with leave to amend and the defendant fails to amend the answer within the time allowed by the court.

(8) If a motion to dismiss pursuant to Section 583.250 is denied and the defendant fails to respond within the time allowed by the court.

(b) For the purposes of this section, "respond" means to answer, to demur, or to move to strike.[593]

587. An application by a plaintiff for entry of default under subdivision (a), (b), or (c) of Section 585 or Section 586 shall include an affidavit stating that a copy of the application has been mailed to the defendant's attorney of record or, if none, to the defendant at his or her last known address and the date on which the copy was mailed. If no such address of the defendant is known to the plaintiff or plaintiff's attorney, the affidavit shall state that fact.

No default under subdivision (a), (b), or (c) of Section 585 or Section 586 shall be entered, unless the affidavit is filed. The nonreceipt of the notice shall not invalidate or constitute ground for setting aside any judgment.[355]

587.5. As used in this chapter, unless the context otherwise specifically requires, the following terms apply:

(a) "Complaint" includes a cross-complaint.

(b) "Defendant" includes a cross-defendant.

(c) "Plaintiff" includes a cross-complainant.[243]

Chapter 3: Issues-The Mode of Trial and Postponements

Chapter 3 enacted 1872.

588. Issues arise upon the pleadings when a fact or a conclusion of law is maintained by the one party and is controverted by the other. They are of two kinds:

1. Of law; and,
2. Of fact.[1]

589. An issue of law arises:

(a) Upon a demurrer to the complaint, cross-complaint, or answer, or to some part thereof.

(b) Upon a motion to strike made pursuant to Section 435, 436, or 473.[199]

590. An issue of fact arises:

1. Upon a material allegation in the complaint controverted by the answer; and,
2. Upon new matters in the answer, except an issue of law is joined thereon.[1]

591. An issue of law must be tried by the court, unless it is referred upon consent; provided, however, that failure on the part of any person filing any

demurrer to prosecute the same may be construed as a waiver of such demurrer, except as otherwise provided in Section 430.80 of this code.[134]

[592.] Section Five Hundred and Ninety-two. In actions for the recovery of specific, real, or personal property, with or without damages, or for money claimed as due upon contract, or as damages for breach of contract, or for injuries, an issue of fact must be tried by a jury, unless a jury trial is waived, or a reference is ordered, as provided in this Code. Where in these cases there are issues both of law and fact, the issue of law must be first disposed of. In other cases, issues of fact must be tried by the Court, subject to its power to order any such issue to be tried by a jury, or to be referred to a referee, as provided in this Code.[2]

594. (a) In superior courts either party may bring an issue to trial or to a hearing, and, in the absence of the adverse party, unless the court, for good cause, otherwise directs, may proceed with the case and take a dismissal of the action, or a verdict, or judgment, as the case may require; provided, however, if the issue to be tried is an issue of fact, proof shall first be made to the satisfaction of the court that the adverse party has had 15 days' notice of such trial or five days' notice of the trial in an unlawful detainer action as specified in subdivision (b). If the adverse party has served notice of trial upon the party seeking the dismissal, verdict, or judgment at least five days prior to the trial, the adverse party shall be deemed to have had notice.

(b) The notice to the adverse party required by subdivision (a) shall be served by mail on all the parties by the clerk of the court not less than 20 days prior to the date set for trial. In an unlawful detainer action where notice is served by mail that service shall be mailed not less than 10 days prior to the date set for trial. If notice is not served by the clerk as required by this subdivision, it may be served by mail by any party on the adverse party not less than 15 days prior to the date set for trial, and in an unlawful detainer action where notice is served by mail that service shall be mailed not less than 10 days prior to the date set for trial. The time provisions of Section 1013 shall not serve to extend the notice of trial requirements under this subdivision for unlawful detainer actions. If notice is served by the clerk, proof thereof may be made by introduction into evidence of the clerk's certificate pursuant to subdivision (3) of Section 1013a or other competent evidence. If notice is served by a party, proof may be made by introduction into evidence of an affidavit or certificate pursuant to subdivision (1) or (2) of Section 1013a or other competent evidence. The provisions of this subdivision are exclusive.[507]

594a. The court may, of its own motion, postpone the trial, if at the time fixed for the trial the court is engaged in the trial of another action; or if, as provided in section 473 of this code, an amendment of the pleadings, or the allowance of time to make such amendment, or to plead, renders a postponement necessary.[17]

595. The trial of any civil action, or proceeding in a court, or of any administrative proceeding before a state board or commission or officer, irrespective of the date of the filing

thereof or when it became at issue, or the hearing of any motion, demurrer, or other proceeding, shall be postponed to a date certain when it appears to the court, board, commission, or officer before which such action or proceeding is pending that either a party thereto, or any attorney of record therein (whether he became an attorney of record before or after the commencement of a legislative session or before or after his appointment to a legislative committee), or a principal witness, is a Member of the Legislature of this state and that the Legislature is in session or in recess (not exceeding a recess of forty (40) days) or that a legislative interim committee of which he is a duly appointed member is meeting, or is to meet within a period which the court finds does not exceed the time reasonably necessary to enable the member to reach the committee meeting by the ordinary mode of travel. When the Legislature is in session or in recess such action or proceeding shall not, without the consent of the attorney of record therein, be brought on for trial or hearing before the expiration of thirty (30) days next following final adjournment of the Legislature or the commencement of a recess of more than forty (40) days. If a date is available during recess, continuance shall be given if possible to such earlier date. When a legislative committee is meeting or is to meet within a period which the court finds does not exceed the time reasonably necessary to enable the member to reach the committee meeting by the ordinary mode of travel, such action or proceeding shall not, without the consent of the attorney of record therein, be brought on for trial or hearing before the expiration of such period necessary following the adjournment or recess of the committee meeting as the court finds is reasonably necessary to enable the member to reach the place of trial or hearing by the ordinary mode of travel from the place of the committee meeting, unless at the expiration of that period the Legislature is to be in session; and in that case the action or proceeding shall not, without such consent, be brought on for trial or hearing before the expiration of thirty (30) days next following final adjournment or the commencement of a recess of more than forty (40) days. If a date is available during the recess, continuance shall be given to such earlier date. However, any postponement granted under the provisions of this paragraph shall suspend for the same period of time as the postponement, the running of any period of time for any ruling or proceeding by a court, board, commission, or officer, or for the performance by any party of any act affected by said postponement.

Granting of a continuance pursuant to this section is mandatory unless the court determines that such continuance would defeat or abridge a right to relief pendente lite in a paternity action or a right to invoke a provisional remedy such as pendente lite support in a domestic relations controversy, attachment and sale of perishable goods, receivership of a failing business, and temporary restraining order or preliminary injunction, and that the continuance should not be granted.[69]

595.1. The term "proceeding in a court" as it is used in Section 595 shall include any discovery proceeding, pretrial conference, deposition, interrogatory, or any other proceeding arising out of a pending civil action.

The enactment of this section at the 1965 Regular Session of the Legislature does not constitute a change in, but is declaratory of, the preexisting law.[55]

595.2. In all cases, the court shall postpone a trial, or the hearing of any motion or demurrer, for a period not to exceed thirty (30) days, when all attorneys of record of parties who have appeared in the action agree in writing to such postponement.[56]

595.3. In actions involving the title to mining claims, or involving trespass for damage upon mining claims, if it be made to appear to the satisfaction of the court that, in order that justice may be done and the action fairly tried on its merits, it is necessary that further developments should be made, underground or upon the surface of the mining claims involved in such action, the court shall grant the postponement of the trial of the action, giving the party a reasonable time in which to prepare for trial and to do said development work.[56]

595.4. A motion to postpone a trial on the ground of the absence of evidence can only be made upon affidavit showing the materiality of the evidence expected to be obtained, and that due diligence has been used to procure it. The court may require the moving party, where application is made on account of the absence of a material witness, to state upon affidavit the evidence which he expects to obtain; and if the adverse party thereupon admits that such evidence would be given, and that it be considered as actually given on the trial, or offered and overruled as improper, the trial must not be postponed.[56]

596. The party obtaining a postponement of a trial, if required by the adverse party, must consent that the testimony of any witness of such adverse party, who is in attendance, be then taken by deposition before a judge or clerk of the court in which the case is pending, or before such notary public as the court may indicate, which must accordingly be done; and the testimony so taken may be read on the trial, with the same effect, and subject to the same objections, as if the witnesses were produced.[29]

597. When the answer pleads that the action is barred by the statute of limitations, or by a prior judgment, or that another action is pending upon the same cause of action, or sets up any other defense not involving the merits of the plaintiff's cause of action but constituting a bar or ground of abatement to the prosecution thereof, the court may, either upon its own motion or upon the motion of any party, proceed to the trial of the special defense or defenses before the trial of any other issue in the case, and if the decision of the court, or the verdict of the jury, upon any special defense so tried (other than the defense of another action pending) is in favor of the defendant pleading the same, judgment for the defendant shall thereupon be entered and no trial of other issues in the action shall be had unless that judgment shall be reversed on appeal or otherwise set aside or vacated; and where the defense of another action pending or a demurrer based upon subdivision (c) of Section 430.10 is

sustained (and no other special defense is sustained) an interlocutory judgment shall be entered in favor of the defendant pleading the same to the effect that no trial of other issues shall be had until the final determination of that other action, and the plaintiff may appeal from the interlocutory judgment in the same manner and within the same time as is now or may be hereafter provided by law for appeals from judgments. If the decision of the court, or the verdict of the jury, upon the special defense or defenses so tried is in favor of the plaintiff, trial of the other issues shall thereafter be had either upon the court's own motion or upon the motion of any party, and judgment shall be entered thereon in the same manner and with the same effect as if all the issues in the case had been tried at one time. In such an event any and all decisions or verdicts upon the special defense or defenses, and all rulings on the trial thereof shall be deemed excepted to and may be reviewed on motion for a new trial or upon appeal from the judgment.

This section also applies to the trial of special defenses pleaded in an answer to a cross-complaint or a demurrer based upon subdivision (c) of Section 430.10, and if the decision of the court or the verdict of the jury upon the special defense or defenses is in favor of the cross-defendant, no further trial shall be had upon the issues raised by the cross-complaint, but trial of the other issues in the action shall thereafter be had either upon the court's own motion or upon the motion of any party, and after the trial thereof the judgment shall be entered in the action as is justified by the decision or verdict on such other issues, considered in connection with the decision or verdict upon the trial of such an affirmative defense raised in the answer to the cross-complaint.[244]

597.5. In an action against a physician or surgeon, dentist, registered nurse, dispensing optician, optometrist, registered physical therapist, podiatrist, licensed psychologist, osteopathic physician and surgeon, chiropractor, clinical laboratory bioanalyst, clinical laboratory technologist, veterinarian, or a licensed hospital as the employer of any such person, based upon the person's alleged professional negligence, or for rendering professional services without consent, or for error or omission in the person's practice, if the answer pleads that the action is barred by the statute of limitations, and if any party so moves or the court upon its own motion requires, the issues raised thereby must be tried separately and before any other issues in the case are tried. If the issue raised by the statute of limitations is finally determined in favor of the plaintiff, the remaining issues shall then be tried.[322]

598. The court may, when the convenience of witnesses, the ends of justice, or the economy and efficiency of handling the litigation would be promoted thereby, on motion of a party, after notice and hearing, make an order, no later than the close of pretrial conference in cases in which such pretrial conference is to be held, or, in other cases, no later than 30 days before the trial date, that the trial of any issue or any part thereof shall precede the trial of any other issue or any part thereof in the case, except for special defenses which may be tried first pursuant to Sections 597 and 597.5. The court, on

its own motion, may make such an order at any time. Where trial of the issue of liability as to all causes of action precedes the trial of other issues or parts thereof, and the decision of the court, or the verdict of the jury upon such issue so tried is in favor of any party on whom liability is sought to be imposed, judgment in favor of such party shall thereupon be entered and no trial of other issues in the action as against such party shall be had unless such judgment shall be reversed upon appeal or otherwise set aside or vacated. If the decision of the court, or the verdict of the jury upon the issue of liability so tried shall be against any party on whom liability is sought to be imposed, or if the decision of the court or the verdict of the jury upon any other issue or part thereof so tried does not result in a judgment being entered pursuant to this chapter, then the trial of the other issues or parts thereof shall thereafter be had at such time, and if a jury trial, before the same or another jury, as ordered by the court either upon its own motion or upon the motion of any party, and judgment shall be entered in the same manner and with the same effect as if all the issues in the case had been tried at one time.[110]

599. (a) Notwithstanding any other law and unless ordered otherwise by a court or otherwise agreed to by the parties, a continuance or postponement of a trial or arbitration date extends any deadlines that have not already passed as of March 19, 2020, applicable to discovery, including the exchange of expert witness information, mandatory settlement conferences, and summary judgment motions in the same matter. The deadlines are extended for the same length of time as the continuance or postponement of the trial date.

(b) This section shall remain in effect only during the state of emergency proclaimed by the Governor on March 4, 2020, related to the COVID-19 pandemic and 180 days after the end, pursuant to Section 8629 of the Government Code, of that state of emergency and is repealed on that date.[791]

Chapter 4: Trial by Jury

Chapter 4 enacted 1872.

Article 2: Conduct of the Trial

Article 2 enacted 1872.

607. When the jury has been sworn, the trial must proceed in the following order, unless the court, for special reasons otherwise directs:

1. The plaintiff may state the issue and his case;
2. The defendant may then state his defense, if he so wishes, or wait until after plaintiff has produced his evidence;
3. The plaintiff must then produce the evidence on his part;
4. The defendant may then open his defense, if he has not done so previously;
5. The defendant may then produce the evidence on his part;
6. The parties may then respectively offer rebutting evidence only, unless the court, for good reason, in furtherance of justice, permit them to offer evidence upon their original case;
7. When the evidence is concluded, unless the case is submitted to the jury on either side or on both sides without argument, the plaintiff must commence and may conclude the argument;

8. If several defendants having separate defenses, appear by different counsel, the court must determine their relative order in the evidence and argument;

9. The court may then charge the jury.[54]

607a. In every case which is being tried before the court with a jury, it shall be the duty of counsel for the respective parties, before the first witness is sworn, to deliver to the judge presiding at the trial and serve upon opposing counsel, all proposed instructions to the jury covering the law as disclosed by the pleadings. Thereafter, and before the commencement of the argument, counsel may deliver to such judge, and serve upon opposing counsel, additional proposed instructions to the jury upon questions of law developed by the evidence and not disclosed by the pleadings. All proposed instructions shall be typewritten, each on a separate sheet of paper. Before the commencement of the argument, the court, on request of counsel, must: (1) decide whether to give, refuse, or modify the proposed instructions; (2) decide which instructions shall be given in addition to those proposed, if any; and (3) advise counsel of all instructions to be given. However, if, during the argument, issues are raised which have not been covered by instructions given or refused, the court may, on request of counsel, give additional instructions on the subject matter thereof.[41]

608. In charging the jury the Court may state to them all matters of law which it thinks necessary for their information in giving their verdict; and, if it state the testimony of the case, it must inform the jury that they are the exclusive judges of all questions of fact. The Court must furnish to either party, at the time, upon request, a statement in writing of the points of law contained in the charge, or sign, at the time, a statement of such points prepared and submitted by the counsel of either party.[1]

609. Where either party asks special instructions to be given to the jury, the Court must either give such instruction, as requested, or refuse to do so, or give the instruction with a modification, in such manner that it may distinctly appear what instructions were given in whole or in part.[1]

611. If the jury are permitted to separate, either during the trial or after the case is submitted to them, they shall be admonished by the court that it is their duty not to conduct research, disseminate information, or converse with, or permit themselves to be addressed by, any other person on any subject of the trial, and that it is their duty not to form or express an opinion thereon until the case is finally submitted to them. The court shall clearly explain, as part of the admonishment, that the prohibition on research, dissemination of information, and conversation applies to all forms of electronic and wireless communication.[653]

612. Upon retiring for deliberation the jury may take with them all papers which have been received as evidence in the cause, except depositions, or copies of such papers as ought not, in the opinion of the court, to be taken from the person having them in possession; and they may also take with them any exhibits which the court may deem proper, notes of the testimony

or other proceedings on the trial, taken by themselves or any of them, but none taken by any other person.[20]

612.5. Upon the jury retiring for deliberation, the court shall advise the jury of the availability of a written copy of the jury instructions. The court may, at its discretion, provide the jury with a copy of the written instructions given. However, if the jury requests the court to supply a copy of the written instructions, the court shall supply the jury with a copy.[251]

613. When the case is finally submitted to the jury, they may decide in court or retire for deliberation. If they retire, they must be kept together in some convenient place, under charge of an officer, until at least three-fourths of them agree upon a verdict or are discharged by the court. Unless by order of the court, the officer having them under his or her charge shall not permit any communication to be made to them, including any form of electronic or wireless communication, or make any himself or herself, except to ask them if they or three-fourths of them are agreed upon a verdict. The officer shall not, before their verdict is rendered, communicate to any person the state of their deliberations, or the verdict agreed upon.[654]

614. After the jury have retired for deliberation, if there be a disagreement between them as to any part of the testimony, or if they desire to be informed of any point of law arising in the cause, they may require the officer to conduct them into Court. Upon their being brought into Court, the information required must be given in the presence of, or after notice to, the parties or counsel.[1]

614.5. Except for good cause shown, the judge in his or her discretion need not be present in the court while testimony previously received in evidence is read to the jury.[253]

616. In all cases where the jury are discharged without having rendered a verdict, or are prevented from giving a verdict, by reason of accident or other cause, during the progress of the trial, or after the cause is submitted to them, except as provided in Section 630, the action may be again tried immediately, or at a future time, as the court may direct.[26]

617. While the jury are absent the Court may adjourn from time to time, in respect to other business; but it is nevertheless open for every purpose connected with the cause submitted to the jury, until a verdict is rendered or the jury discharged. The Court may direct the jury to bring in a sealed verdict, at the opening of the Court, in case of an agreement during a recess or adjournment for the day.[5]

618. When the jury, or three-fourths of them, have agreed upon a verdict, they must be conducted into court and the verdict rendered by their foreperson. The verdict must be in writing, signed by the foreperson, and must be read to the jury by the clerk, and the inquiry made whether it is their verdict. Either party may require the jury to be polled, which is done by the court or clerk, asking each juror if it is the juror's verdict. If upon inquiry or polling, more than one-fourth of the jurors disagree thereto, the jury must be sent out again, but if no disagreement is expressed, the verdict is complete and the jury discharged from the case.[601]

619. When the verdict is announced, if it is informal or insufficient, in not covering the issue submitted, it may be corrected by the jury under the advice of the Court, or the jury may be again sent out.[1]

Article 3: The Verdict
Article 3 enacted 1872.

624. The verdict of a jury is either general or special. A general verdict is that by which they pronounce generally upon all or any of the issues, either in favor of the plaintiff or defendant; a special verdict is that by which the jury find the facts only, leaving the judgment to the Court. The special verdict must present the conclusions of fact as established by the evidence, and not the evidence to prove them; and those conclusions of fact must be so presented as that nothing shall remain to the Court but to draw from them conclusions of law.[1]

625. In all cases the court may direct the jury to find a special verdict in writing, upon all, or any of the issues, and in all cases may instruct them, if they render a general verdict, to find upon particular questions of fact, to be stated in writing, and may direct a written finding thereon. In all cases in which the issue of punitive damages is presented to the jury the court shall direct the jury to find a special verdict in writing separating punitive damages from compensatory damages. The special verdict or finding must be filed with the clerk and entered upon the minutes. Where a special finding of facts is inconsistent with the general verdict, the former controls the latter, and the court must give judgment accordingly.[188]

626. When a verdict is found for the plaintiff in an action for the recovery of money, or for the cross-complainant when a cross-complaint for the recovery of money is established, the jury must also find the amount of the recovery.[74]

[627.] Section Six Hundred and Twenty-seven. In an action for the recovery of specific personal property, if the property has not been delivered to the plaintiff, or the defendant, by his answer, claim a return thereof, the jury, if their verdict be in favor of the plaintiff, or, if being in favor of defendant, they also find that he is entitled to a return thereof, must find the value of the property, and, if so instructed, the value of specific portions thereof, and may at the same time assess the damages, if any are claimed in the complaint or answer, which the prevailing party has sustained by reason of the taking or detention of such property.[2]

628. In superior courts upon receipt of a verdict, an entry must be made in the minutes of the court, specifying the time of trial, the names of the jurors and witnesses, and setting out the verdict at length; and where a special verdict is found, either the judgment rendered thereon, or if the case be reserved for argument or further consideration, the order thus reserving it.[508]

629. (a) The court, before the expiration of its power to rule on a motion for a new trial, either of its own motion, after five days' notice, or on motion of a party against whom a verdict has been rendered, shall render judgment in favor of the aggrieved party notwithstanding the verdict whenever a motion for a directed verdict for the aggrieved party should have been

granted had a previous motion been made.
(b) A motion for judgment notwithstanding the verdict shall be made within the period specified by Section 659 for the filing and service of a notice of intention to move for a new trial. The moving, opposing, and reply briefs and any accompanying documents shall be filed and served within the periods specified by Section 659a, and the hearing on the motion shall be set in the same manner as the hearing on a motion for new trial under Section 660. The making of a motion for judgment notwithstanding the verdict shall not extend the time within which a party may file and serve notice of intention to move for a new trial. The court shall not rule upon the motion for judgment notwithstanding the verdict until the expiration of the time within which a motion for a new trial must be served and filed, and if a motion for a new trial has been filed with the court by the aggrieved party, the court shall rule upon both motions at the same time. The power of the court to rule on a motion for judgment notwithstanding the verdict shall not extend beyond the last date upon which it has the power to rule on a motion for a new trial. If a motion for judgment notwithstanding the verdict is not determined before that date, the effect shall be a denial of that motion without further order of the court.
(c) If the motion for judgment notwithstanding the verdict is denied and if a new trial is denied, the appellate court shall, if it appears that the motion for judgment notwithstanding the verdict should have been granted, order judgment to be so entered on appeal from the judgment or from the order denying the motion for judgment notwithstanding the verdict.
(d) If a new trial is granted to the party moving for judgment notwithstanding the verdict, and the motion for judgment notwithstanding the verdict is denied, the order denying the motion for judgment notwithstanding the verdict shall nevertheless be reviewable on appeal from that order by the aggrieved party. If the court grants the motion for judgment notwithstanding the verdict or of its own motion directs the entry of judgment notwithstanding the verdict and likewise grants the motion for a new trial, the order granting the new trial shall be effective only if, on appeal, the judgment notwithstanding the verdict is reversed, and the order granting a new trial is not appealed from or, if appealed from, is affirmed.[708]

630. (a) Unless the court specified an earlier time for making a motion for directed verdict, after all parties have completed the presentation of all of their evidence in a trial by jury, any party may, without waiving his or her right to trial by jury in the event the motion is not granted, move for an order directing entry of a verdict in its favor.
(b) If it appears that the evidence presented supports the granting of the motion as to some, but not all, of the issues involved in the action, the court shall grant the motion as to those issues and the action shall proceed on any remaining issues. Despite the granting of such a motion, no final judgment shall be entered prior to the termination of the action, but the final judgment, in addition to any matter determined in the trial, shall reflect the

verdict ordered by the court as determined by the motion for directed verdict.

(c) If the motion is granted, unless the court in its order directing entry of the verdict specifies otherwise, it shall operate as an adjudication upon the merits.

(d) In actions which arise out of an injury to a person or property, when a motion for directed verdict was granted on the basis that a defendant was without fault, no other defendant during trial, over plaintiff's objection, shall attempt to attribute fault to or comment on the absence or involvement of the defendant who was granted the motion.

(e) The order of the court granting the motion for directed verdict is effective without any assent of the jury.

(f) When the jury for any reason has been discharged without having rendered a verdict, the court on its own motion or upon motion of a party, notice of which was given within 10 days after discharge of the jury, may order judgment to be entered in favor of a party whenever a motion for directed verdict for that party should have been granted had a previous motion been made. Except as otherwise provided in Section 12a, the power of the court to act under the provisions of this section shall expire 30 days after the day upon which the jury was discharged, and if judgment has not been ordered within that time the effect shall be the denial of any motion for judgment without further order of the court.[245]

Chapter 4.5: Voluntary Expedited Jury Trials

Heading of Chapter 4.5 amended by Stats. 2015, Ch. 330, Sec. 1.

630.01. For purposes of this chapter:

(a) "Expedited jury trial" means a consensual, binding jury trial before a reduced jury panel and a judicial officer.

(b) "High/low agreement" means a written agreement entered into by the parties that specifies a minimum amount of damages that a plaintiff is guaranteed to receive from the defendant, and a maximum amount of damages that the defendant will be liable for, regardless of the ultimate verdict returned by the jury. Neither the existence of, nor the amounts contained in, any high/low agreements may be disclosed to the jury.

(c) "Post-trial motions" does not include motions relating to costs and attorney's fees, motions to correct a judgment for a clerical error, and motions to enforce a judgment.[656]

630.02. The rules and procedures applicable to expedited jury trials are as follows:

(a) The procedures in this chapter and in the implementing rules of court shall apply to expedited jury trials, unless the parties agree otherwise, as permitted under subparagraph (E) of paragraph (1) of subdivision (e) of Section 630.03, and the court so orders.

(b) Any matters not expressly addressed in this chapter, in the implementing rules of court, or in a consent order authorized by this chapter and the implementing rules, are governed by applicable statutes and rules governing civil actions.[635]

630.03. (a) All parties agreeing to participate in an expedited jury trial and, if represented, their counsel, shall sign a proposed consent order granting an expedited jury trial.

(b) Except as provided in subdivision (d), the agreement to participate in the expedited jury trial process is binding upon the parties, unless either of the following occurs:

(1) All parties stipulate to end the agreement to participate.

(2) The court, on its own motion or at the request of a party by noticed motion, finds that good cause exists for the action not to proceed under the rules of this chapter.

(c) Any agreement to participate in an expedited jury trial under this chapter may be entered into only after a dispute has arisen and an action has been filed.

(d) The court shall approve the use of an expedited jury trial and any high/low agreements or other stipulations for an expedited jury trial involving either of the following:

(1) A self-represented litigant.

(2) A minor, an incompetent person, or a person for whom a conservator has been appointed.

(e) The proposed consent order submitted to the court shall include all of the following:

(1) A preliminary statement that each named party and any insurance carrier responsible for providing coverage or defense on behalf of that party, individually identified in the proposed consent order, have been informed of the rules and procedures for an expedited jury trial and provided with a Judicial Council information sheet regarding expedited jury trials, have agreed to take part in or, in the case of a responsible insurance carrier, not object to, the expedited jury trial process, and have agreed to all the specific provisions set forth in the consent order.

(2) The parties' agreement to all of the following:

(A) That all parties waive all rights to appeal and to move for directed verdict or make any post-trial motions, except as provided in Sections 630.08 and 630.09.

(B) That each side shall have up to five hours in which to complete voir dire and to present its case.

(C) That the jury shall be composed of eight or fewer jurors with no alternates.

(D) That each side shall be limited to three peremptory challenges, unless the court permits an additional challenge in cases with more than two sides as provided in Section 630.04.

(E) That the trial and pretrial matters will proceed under subparagraphs (A) to (D), inclusive, and, unless the parties expressly agree otherwise in the proposed consent order, under all other provisions in this chapter and in the implementing rules of court.

(f) The court shall issue the consent order as proposed by the parties, unless the court finds good cause why the action should not proceed through the expedited jury trial process, in which case the court shall deny the proposed consent order in its entirety.[709]

630.04. (a) Juries in expedited jury trial cases shall be composed of eight jurors, unless the parties have agreed to fewer. No alternates shall be selected.

(b) The court shall allow each side three peremptory challenges. If there are more than two parties in a case and more than two sides, as determined by the court under subdivision (c) of Section 231, the parties may request one additional peremptory challenge each, which is to be granted by the court as the interests of justice may require.[635]

630.05. Nothing in this chapter is intended to preclude a jury from deliberating as long as needed.[635]

630.06. (a) The rules of evidence apply in expedited jury trials, unless the parties stipulate otherwise.
(b) Any stipulation by the parties to use relaxed rules of evidence may not be construed to eliminate, or in any way affect, the right of a witness or party to invoke any applicable privilege or other law protecting confidentiality.
(c) The right to issue subpoenas and notices to appear to secure the attendance of witnesses or the production of documents at trial shall be in accordance with this code.[635]

630.07. (a) The verdict in an expedited jury trial case is binding, subject to any written high/low agreement or other stipulations concerning the amount of the award agreed upon by the parties.
(b) A vote of six of the eight jurors is required for a verdict, unless the parties stipulate otherwise.[635]

630.08. (a) By agreeing to participate in the expedited jury trial process, the parties agree to waive any motions for directed verdict, motions to set aside the verdict or any judgment rendered by the jury, or motions for a new trial on the basis of inadequate or excessive damages.
(b) The court shall not set aside any verdict or any judgment, shall not direct that judgment be entered in favor of a party entitled to judgment as a matter of law, and shall not order a new trial, except on the grounds stated in Section 630.09.[658]

630.09. (a) By agreeing to participate in the expedited jury trial process, the parties agree to waive the right to bring post-trial motions or to appeal from the determination of the matter, except as provided in this section. The only grounds on which a party may move for a new trial or appeal are any of the following:
(1) Judicial misconduct that materially affected the substantial rights of a party.
(2) Misconduct of the jury.
(3) Corruption, fraud, or other undue means employed in the proceedings of the court, jury, or adverse party that prevented a party from having a fair trial.
(b) Within 10 court days of the entry of a jury verdict, a party may file with the clerk and serve on each adverse party a notice of the intention to move for a new trial on any of the grounds specified in subdivision (a). The notice shall be deemed to be a motion for a new trial.
(c) Except as provided in subdivision (b), parties to an expedited jury trial shall not make any post-trial motions except for motions relating to costs and attorney's fees, motions to correct a judgment for clerical error, and motions to enforce a judgment.
(d) Before filing an appeal, a party shall make a motion for a new trial under subdivision (b). If the motion for a new trial is denied, the party may appeal the judgment to the appropriate court with appellate jurisdiction and seek a new trial on any of the grounds specified in subdivision (a). Parties to an expedited jury trial may not appeal on any other ground.[635]

630.10. All statutes and rules governing costs and attorney's fees shall apply in expedited jury trials, unless the parties agree otherwise in the consent order.[635]

630.11. The Judicial Council shall, on or before July 1, 2016, update rules and forms to establish uniform procedures implementing the provisions of this chapter, including, but not limited to, rules for all of the following:
(a) Additional content of proposed consent orders.
(b) Pretrial exchanges and submissions.
(c) Pretrial conferences.
(d) Presentation of evidence and testimony.
(e) Any other procedures necessary to implement the provisions of this chapter.[710]

Chapter 4.6: Mandatory Expedited Jury Trials in Limited Civil Cases

Chapter 4.6 added by Stats. 2015, Ch. 330, Sec. 5.

630.20. (a) Except as provided in subdivisions (b) and (c), an action or special proceeding treated as a limited civil case pursuant to Article 1 (commencing with Section 85) of Chapter 5.1 of Title 1 of Part 1, including an action or special proceeding initially filed as a limited civil case or remanded as one thereafter, shall be conducted as a mandatory expedited jury trial pursuant to this chapter.
(b) Either party may opt out of the mandatory expedited jury trial procedures if any of the following criteria is met:
(1) Punitive damages are sought.
(2) Damages in excess of insurance policy limits are sought.
(3) A party's insurer is providing a legal defense subject to a reservation of rights.
(4) The case involves a claim reportable to a governmental entity.
(5) The case involves a claim of moral turpitude that may affect an individual's professional licensing.
(6) The case involves claims of intentional conduct.
(7) The case has been reclassified as unlimited pursuant to Section 403.020.
(8) The complaint contains a demand for attorney's fees, unless those fees are sought pursuant to Section 1717 of the Civil Code.
(9) The judge finds good cause exists for the action not to proceed under the rules of this chapter. Good cause includes, but is not limited to, a showing that a party needs more than five hours to present or defend the action and that the parties have been unable to stipulate to additional time.
(c) This chapter does not apply to a proceeding in forcible entry or forcible or unlawful detainer.
(d) A judgment in a limited civil case conducted as a mandatory expedited jury trial may be appealed to the appellate division of the superior court in which the case was tried.[711]

630.21. For purposes of this chapter:
(a) "Mandatory expedited jury trial" means a jury trial before a reduced jury panel and a judge, conducted pursuant to this chapter.
(b) "High/low agreement" means a written agreement entered into by the parties that specifies a minimum amount of damages that a plaintiff is guaranteed to receive from the defendant, and a maximum amount of damages that the defendant will be liable

for, regardless of the ultimate verdict returned by the jury. Neither the existence of, nor the amounts contained in, any high/low agreements may be disclosed to the jury.[711]

630.22. (a) The procedures in this chapter and in the implementing rules of court shall apply to mandatory expedited jury trials conducted in limited civil cases, unless the parties agree otherwise, as permitted under subdivision (d) of Section 630.23, and the court so orders.
(b) Any matters not expressly addressed in this chapter, in the implementing rules of court, or in an agreement authorized by this chapter and the implementing rules, are governed by applicable statutes and rules governing civil actions.[711]

630.23. The following rules and procedures apply to mandatory expedited jury trials conducted pursuant to this chapter:
(a) Each side shall have up to five hours in which to complete voir dire and to present its case.
(b) The jury shall be composed of eight jurors and one alternate, unless the parties have agreed to fewer jurors.
(c) Each side shall be limited to four peremptory challenges, unless the court permits an additional challenge in cases with more than two sides. If there are more than two parties in a case and more than two sides, as determined by the court under subdivision (c) of Section 231, the parties may request one additional peremptory challenge each, which is to be granted by the court as the interests of justice may require.
(d) The parties may agree to modify the rules and procedures specified in this chapter and the implementing rules of court, subject to the court's approval.[711]

630.24. Nothing in this chapter is intended to preclude a jury from deliberating as long as needed.[711]

630.25. (a) The rules of evidence apply to mandatory expedited jury trials conducted in limited civil cases, unless the parties stipulate otherwise.
(b) Any stipulation by the parties to use relaxed rules of evidence shall not be construed to eliminate, or in any way affect, the right of a witness or party to invoke any applicable privilege or other law protecting confidentiality.
(c) The right to issue subpoenas and notices to appear to secure the attendance of witnesses or the production of documents at trial shall be in accordance with this code.[711]

630.26. (a) A vote of six of the eight jurors is required for a verdict, unless the parties stipulate otherwise.
(b) The verdict in a limited civil case following a mandatory expedited jury trial case shall be appealable under subdivision (d) of Section 630.20 and subject to any written high/low agreement or other stipulations concerning the amount of the award agreed upon by the parties.[711]

630.27. All statutes and rules governing costs and attorney's fees shall apply in limited civil cases that are conducted as mandatory expedited jury trials, unless the parties stipulate otherwise.[711]

630.28. The Judicial Council shall, on or before July 1, 2016, adopt rules and forms to establish uniform procedures implementing the provisions of this chapter, including, rules for the following:

(a) Pretrial exchanges and submissions.
(b) Pretrial conferences.
(c) Opt-out procedures pursuant to subdivision (b) of Section 630.20.
(d) Presentation of evidence and testimony.
(e) Any other procedures necessary to implement the provisions of this chapter.[711]

630.29. Sections 630.20 to 630.27, inclusive, shall become operative on July 1, 2016.[711]

Chapter 5: Trial by the Court

Chapter 5 enacted 1872.

631. (a) The right to a trial by jury as declared by Section 16 of Article I of the California Constitution shall be preserved to the parties inviolate. In civil cases, a jury may only be waived pursuant to subdivision (f).
(b) At least one party demanding a jury on each side of a civil case shall pay a nonrefundable fee of one hundred fifty dollars ($150), unless the fee has been paid by another party on the same side of the case. The fee shall offset the costs to the state of providing juries in civil cases. If there are more than two parties to the case, for purposes of this section only, all plaintiffs shall be considered one side of the case, and all other parties shall be considered the other side of the case. Payment of the fee by a party on one side of the case shall not relieve parties on the other side of the case from waiver pursuant to subdivision (f).
(c) The fee described in subdivision (b) shall be due on or before the date scheduled for the initial case management conference in the action, except as follows:
(1) In unlawful detainer actions, the fees shall be due at least five days before the date set for trial.
(2) If no case management conference is scheduled in a civil action, or the initial case management conference occurred before June 28, 2012, and the initial complaint was filed on or after July 1, 2011, the fee shall be due no later than 365 calendar days after the filing of the initial complaint.
(3) If the initial case management conference occurred before June 28, 2012, and the initial complaint in the case was filed before July 1, 2011, the fee shall be due at least 25 calendar days before the date initially set for trial.
(4) If the party requesting a jury has not appeared before the initial case management conference, or first appeared more than 365 calendar days after the filing of the initial complaint, the fee shall be due at least 25 calendar days before the date initially set for trial.
(d) If a party failed to timely pay the fee described in subdivision (b) that was due between June 27, 2012, and November 30, 2012, the party will be relieved of a jury waiver on that basis only if the party pays the fee on or before December 31, 2012, or 25 calendar days before the date initially set for trial, whichever is earlier.
(e) The parties demanding a jury trial shall deposit with the clerk or judge, at the beginning of the second and each succeeding day's session, a sum equal to that day's fees and mileage of the jury, including the fees and mileage for the trial jury panel if the trial jury has not yet been selected and sworn. If more than one party has demanded a jury, the respective amount to be paid daily by each party demanding a jury

shall be determined by stipulation of the parties or by order of the court.

(f) A party waives trial by jury in any of the following ways:

(1) By failing to appear at the trial.

(2) By written consent filed with the clerk or judge.

(3) By oral consent, in open court, entered in the minutes.

(4) By failing to announce that a jury is required, at the time the cause is first set for trial, if it is set upon notice or stipulation, or within five days after notice of setting if it is set without notice or stipulation.

(5) By failing to timely pay the fee described in subdivision (b), unless another party on the same side of the case has paid that fee.

(6) By failing to deposit with the clerk or judge, at the beginning of the second and each succeeding day's session, the sum provided in subdivision (e).

(g) The court may, in its discretion upon just terms, allow a trial by jury although there may have been a waiver of a trial by jury.

(h) The court shall transmit the fee described in subdivision (b) to the State Treasury for deposit in the Trial Court Trust Fund within 45 calendar days after the end of the month in which the fee is paid to the court.[664]

631.2. (a) Notwithstanding any other provision of law, the superior court may pay jury fees in civil cases from general funds of the court available therefor. Nothing in this section shall be construed to change the requirements for the deposit of jury fees in any civil case by the appropriate party to the litigation at the time and in the manner otherwise provided by law. Nothing in this section shall preclude the right of the superior court to be reimbursed by the party to the litigation liable therefor for any payment of jury fees pursuant to this section. Nothing in this section shall preclude the right of the county to be reimbursed by the party to the litigation liable therefor for any payment of jury fees pursuant to this section as it read in Section 4 of Chapter 10 of the Statutes of 1988, or pursuant to former Section 631.1 as it read in Section 1 of Chapter 144 of the Statutes of 1971.

(b) The party who has demanded trial by jury shall reimburse the superior court for the fees and mileage of all jurors appearing for voir dire examination, except those jurors who are excused and subsequently on the same day are called for voir dire examination in another case.[669]

631.3. (a) Notwithstanding any other law, when a party to the litigation has deposited jury fees with the judge or clerk and that party waives a jury or obtains a continuance of the trial, or the case is settled, none of the deposit shall be refunded if the court finds there has been insufficient time to notify the jurors that the trial would not proceed at the time set. If the jury fees so deposited are not refunded for any of these reasons, or if a refund of jury fees deposited with the judge or clerk has not been requested, in writing, by the depositing party within 20 business days from the date on which the jury is waived or the action is settled, dismissed, or a continuance thereof granted, the fees shall be transmitted to the Controller for deposit into the Trial Court Trust Fund.

(b) All jury fees and mileage fees that may accrue by reason of a juror serving on more than one case in the same day shall be transmitted to the Controller for deposit into the Trial Court Trust Fund. All jury fees that were deposited with the court in advance of trial pursuant to Section 631 prior to January 1, 1999, and that remain on deposit in cases that were settled, dismissed, or otherwise disposed of, and three years have passed since the date the case was settled, dismissed, or otherwise disposed of, shall be transmitted to the Controller for deposit into the Trial Court Trust Fund.

(c) The fee described in subdivision (b) of Section 631 shall be nonrefundable and is not subject to this section.[668]

631.5. In all cases of eminent domain the deposits of jury fees and mileage provided for in section 631 of this code shall be made by the party seeking condemnation regardless of which party shall have demanded a jury trial, and the trial shall not proceed until such deposits are made.[21]

631.7. Ordinarily, unless the court otherwise directs, the trial of a civil action tried by the court without a jury shall proceed in the order specified in Section 607.[53]

631.8. (a) After a party has completed his presentation of evidence in a trial by the court, the other party, without waiving his right to offer evidence in support of his defense or in rebuttal in the event the motion is not granted, may move for a judgment. The court as trier of the facts shall weigh the evidence and may render a judgment in favor of the moving party, in which case the court shall make a statement of decision as provided in Sections 632 and 634, or may decline to render any judgment until the close of all the evidence. The court may consider all evidence received, provided, however, that the party against whom the motion for judgment has been made shall have had an opportunity to present additional evidence to rebut evidence received during the presentation of evidence deemed by the presenting party to have been adverse to him, and to rehabilitate the testimony of a witness whose credibility has been attacked by the moving party. Such motion may also be made and granted as to any cross-complaint.

(b) If it appears that the evidence presented supports the granting of the motion as to some but not all the issues involved in the action, the court shall grant the motion as to those issues and the action shall proceed as to the issues remaining. Despite the granting of such a motion, no final judgment shall be entered prior to the termination of the action, but the final judgment in such action shall, in addition to any matters determined in the trial, award judgment as determined by the motion herein provided for.

(c) If the motion is granted, unless the court in its order for judgment otherwise specifies, such judgment operates as an adjudication upon the merits.[246]

632. (a) In superior courts, upon the trial of a question of fact by the court, written findings of fact and conclusions of law shall not be required. The court shall issue a statement of decision explaining the factual and legal basis for its decision as to each of the principal controverted issues at trial upon the request of any party appearing at the trial. The request must be made within 10 days after the court announces a tentative decision unless the trial is concluded within one calendar

day or in less than eight hours over more than one day in which event the request must be made prior to the submission of the matter for decision. The request for a statement of decision shall specify those controverted issues as to which the party is requesting a statement of decision. After a party has requested the statement, any party may make proposals as to the content of the statement of decision.

(b) The statement of decision shall be in writing, unless the parties appearing at trial agree otherwise; however, when the trial is concluded within one calendar day or in less than 8 hours over more than one day, the statement of decision may be made orally on the record in the presence of the parties.

(c) This section shall remain in effect only until January 1, 2027, and as of that date is repealed.[896]

632. (a) In superior courts, upon the trial of a question of fact by the court, written findings of fact and conclusions of law shall not be required. The court shall issue a statement of decision explaining the factual and legal basis for its decision as to each of the principal controverted issues at trial upon the request of any party appearing at the trial. The request must be made in writing, or orally if there is an official record of the proceeding being transcribed, prior to the submission of the matter for decision. The request for a statement of decision shall specify those controverted issues as to which the party is requesting a statement of decision.

(b) The statement of decision shall be in writing, unless the parties appearing at trial agree otherwise. The written statement of decision shall be served on all parties who appeared at trial. However, when the trial is concluded within one calendar day or in less than eight hours over more than one day, the statement of decision may be made orally on the record in the presence of the parties. The statement of decision need not summarize all evidence admitted at trial.

(c) If a statement of decision is not timely requested under subdivision (a), the court may announce its ruling on all relief sought without a statement of decision. Alternatively, the court may, in its sole discretion, issue a statement of decision even though one has not been requested.

(d) If a party has requested a statement of decision, the court may order a party or parties to prepare a draft statement of decision within a specified time period. The court shall thereafter issue its statement of decision.

(e) (1) Any party may, within 10 days after the statement of decision has been served by the court on the parties, serve and file objections to the statement of decision.

(2) If no objections are filed, the statement of decision becomes final upon the expiration of the time for filing objections.

(3) If objections are timely filed, the court may, but is not required to, set a hearing.

(4) If objections are ruled upon, with or without a hearing, the ruling shall be served on all parties who appeared at the trial. The statement of decision, including any amended statement of decision that the court may issue after sustaining any objection in whole or in part, shall become final upon issuance of the ruling, unless otherwise stated in the statement of decision.

(5) If any objections filed are not ruled

upon, unless the court orders otherwise, the objections are deemed overruled and the statement of decision becomes final on the later of the following dates:

(A) Thirty days after the time for objections has expired.

(B) If there was a hearing on objections, 30 days after the hearing.

(f) (1) The court may prepare and serve a proposed judgment or may order a party to prepare, lodge, and serve a proposed judgment, before or after the statement of decision is final.

(2) Any party may, within 10 days after service of the proposed judgment, serve and file objections thereto.

(g) (1) The court may, by written order, extend any of the times prescribed by this section. Further, at any time before the entry of judgment, the court may, for good cause shown and on such terms as may be just, excuse noncompliance with the time limits prescribed for doing any act required by this rule.

(2) In any action under the Family Code, the court may also, by written order and upon a finding of good cause, shorten any of the times prescribed by this section.

(h) (1) The Judicial Council shall adopt or amend all rules of court necessary to implement this section.

(2) The Judicial Council shall prepare forms that a party may use to request a statement of decision and that explain the requirements prescribed by this section on requesting a statement of decision.

(i) This section shall become operative on January 1, 2027.[897]

634. When a statement of decision does not resolve a controverted issue, or if the statement is ambiguous and the record shows that the omission or ambiguity was brought to the attention of the trial court either prior to entry of judgment or in conjunction with a motion under Section 657 or 663, it shall not be inferred on appeal or upon a motion under Section 657 or 663 that the trial court decided in favor of the prevailing party as to those facts or on that issue.[115]

635. In all cases where the decision of the court has been entered in its minutes, and when the judge who heard or tried the case is unavailable, the formal judgment or order conforming to the minutes may be signed by the presiding judge of the court or by a judge designated by the presiding judge.[320]

636. On a judgment for the plaintiff upon an issue of law, he may proceed in the manner prescribed by the first two subdivisions of Section 585, upon the failure of the defendant to answer. If judgment be for the defendant upon an issue of law, and the taking of an account, or the proof of any fact, be necessary to enable the Court to complete the judgment, a reference may be ordered, as in that section provided.[1]

Chapter 6: Of References and Trials by Referees

Chapter 6 enacted 1872.

638. A referee may be appointed upon the agreement of the parties filed with the clerk, or judge, or entered in the minutes, or upon the motion of a party to a written contract or lease that provides that any controversy arising therefrom shall be heard by a referee if the court finds a reference agreement exists between the parties:

(a) To hear and determine any or all of the issues in an action or proceeding, whether of fact or of law, and to report a statement of decision.

(b) To ascertain a fact necessary to enable the court to determine an action or proceeding.

(c) In any matter in which a referee is appointed pursuant to this section, a copy of the order shall be forwarded to the office of the presiding judge. The Judicial Council shall, by rule, collect information on the use of these referees. The Judicial Council shall also collect information on fees paid by the parties for the use of referees to the extent that information regarding those fees is reported to the court. The Judicial Council shall report thereon to the Legislature by July 1, 2003. This subdivision shall become inoperative on January 1, 2004.

(Amended by Stats. 2002, Ch. 1008, Sec. 4. Effective January 1, 2003.)

639. (a) When the parties do not consent, the court may, upon the written motion of any party, or of its own motion, appoint a referee in the following cases pursuant to the provisions of subdivision (b) of Section 640:

(1) When the trial of an issue of fact requires the examination of a long account on either side; in which case the referees may be directed to hear and decide the whole issue, or report upon any specific question of fact involved therein.

(2) When the taking of an account is necessary for the information of the court before judgment, or for carrying a judgment or order into effect.

(3) When a question of fact, other than upon the pleadings, arises upon motion or otherwise, in any stage of the action.

(4) When it is necessary for the information of the court in a special proceeding.

(5) When the court in any pending action determines that it is necessary for the court to appoint a referee to hear and determine any and all discovery motions and disputes relevant to discovery in the action and to report findings and make a recommendation thereon.

(b) In a discovery matter, a motion to disqualify an appointed referee pursuant to Section 170.6 shall be made to the court by a party either:

(A) Within 10 days after notice of the appointment, or if the party has not yet appeared in the action, a motion shall be made within 10 days after the appearance, if a discovery referee has been appointed for all discovery purposes.

(B) At least five days before the date set for hearing, if the referee assigned is known at least 10 days before the date set for hearing and the discovery referee has been assigned only for limited discovery purposes.

(c) When a referee is appointed pursuant to paragraph (5) of subdivision (a), the order shall indicate whether the referee is being appointed for all discovery purposes in the action.

(d) All appointments of referees pursuant to this section shall be by written order and shall include the following:

(1) When the referee is appointed pursuant to paragraph (1), (2), (3), or (4) of subdivision (a), a statement of the reason the referee is being appointed.

(2) When the referee is appointed pursuant to paragraph (5) of subdivision (a), the exceptional circumstances requiring the reference, which must be specific to the circumstances of the

particular case.

(3) The subject matter or matters included in the reference.

(4) The name, business address, and telephone number of the referee.

(5) The maximum hourly rate the referee may charge and, at the request of any party, the maximum number of hours for which the referee may charge. Upon the written application of any party or the referee, the court may, for good cause shown, modify the maximum number of hours subject to any findings as set forth in paragraph (6).

(6) (A) Either a finding that no party has established an economic inability to pay a pro rata share of the referee's fee or a finding that one or more parties has established an economic inability to pay a pro rata share of the referee's fees and that another party has agreed voluntarily to pay that additional share of the referee's fee. A court shall not appoint a referee at a cost to the parties if neither of these findings is made.

(B) In determining whether a party has established an inability to pay the referee's fees under subparagraph (A), the court shall consider only the ability of the party, not the party's counsel, to pay these fees. If a party is proceeding in forma pauperis, the party shall be deemed by the court to have an economic inability to pay the referee's fees. However, a determination of economic inability to pay the fees shall not be limited to parties that proceed in forma pauperis. For those parties who are not proceeding in forma pauperis, the court, in determining whether a party has established an inability to pay the fees, shall consider, among other things, the estimated cost of the referral and the impact of the proposed fees on the party's ability to proceed with the litigation.

(e) In any matter in which a referee is appointed pursuant to paragraph (5) of subdivision (a), a copy of the order appointing the referee shall be forwarded to the office of the presiding judge of the court. The Judicial Council shall, by rule, collect information on the use of these references and the reference fees charged to litigants, and shall report thereon to the Legislature by July 1, 2003. This subdivision shall become inoperative on January 1, 2004.[471]

640. (a) The court shall appoint as referee or referees the person or persons, not exceeding three, agreed upon by the parties.

(b) If the parties do not agree on the selection of the referee or referees, each party shall submit to the court up to three nominees for appointment as referee and the court shall appoint one or more referees, not exceeding three, from among the nominees against whom there is no legal objection. If no nominations are received from any of the parties, the court shall appoint one or more referees, not exceeding three, against whom there is no legal objection, or the court may appoint a court commissioner of the county where the cause is pending as a referee.

(c) Participation in the referee selection procedure pursuant to this section does not constitute a waiver of grounds for objection to the appointment of a referee under Section 641 or 641.2.[437]

640.5. It is the intent of the Legislature that the practice and cost of referring discovery disputes to outside referees be thoroughly reviewed. Therefore, in addition to the requirements of subdivision (e) of Section 639, the Judicial Council shall collect information from the trial courts on the use of referees in discovery matters pursuant to either Sections 638 and 639. The collected data shall include information on the number of referees, the cost to the parties, and the time spent by the discovery referee. The Judicial Council shall report thereon to the Legislature by July 1, 2003.[472]

641. A party may object to the appointment of any person as referee, on one or more of the following grounds:
(a) A want of any of the qualifications prescribed by statute to render a person competent as a juror, except a requirement of residence within a particular county in the state.
(b) Consanguinity or affinity, within the third degree, to either party, or to an officer of a corporation which is a party, or to any judge of the court in which the appointment shall be made.
(c) Standing in the relation of guardian and ward, conservator and conservatee, master and servant, employer and clerk, or principal and agent, to either party; or being a member of the family of either party; or a partner in business with either party; or security on any bond or obligation for either party.
(d) Having served as a juror or been a witness on any trial between the same parties.
(e) Interest on the part of the person in the event of the action, or in the main question involved in the action.
(f) Having formed or expressed an unqualified opinion or belief as to the merits of the action.
(g) The existence of a state of mind in the potential referee evincing enmity against or bias toward either party.[438]

641.2. In any action brought under Article 8 (commencing with Section 12600) of Chapter 6, Part 2, Division 3, Title 3 of the Government Code, a party may object to the appointment of any person as referee on the ground that the person is not technically qualified with respect to the particular subject matter of the proceeding.[439]

642. Objections, if any, to a reference or to the referee or referees appointed by the court shall be made in writing, and must be heard and disposed of by the court, not by the referee.[440]

643. (a) Unless otherwise directed by the court, the referees or commissioner must report their statement of decision in writing to the court within 20 days after the hearing, if any, has been concluded and the matter has been submitted.
(b) A referee appointed pursuant to Section 638 shall report as agreed by the parties and approved by the court.
(c) A referee appointed pursuant to Section 639 shall file with the court a report that includes a recommendation on the merits of any disputed issue, a statement of the total hours spent and the total fees charged by the referee, and the referee's recommended allocation of payment. The referee shall serve the report on all parties. Any party may file an objection to the referee's report or recommendations within 10 days after the referee serves and files the report, or within another time as the court may direct. The objection shall be served on the referee and all other parties. Responses to the objections shall be filed with the court

and served on the referee and all other parties within 10 days after the objection is served. The court shall review any objections to the report and any responses submitted to those objections and shall thereafter enter appropriate orders. Nothing in this section is intended to deprive the court of its power to change the terms of the referee's appointment or to modify or disregard the referee's recommendations, and this overriding power may be exercised at any time, either on the motion of any party for good cause shown or on the court's own motion.[441]

644. (a) In the case of a consensual general reference pursuant to Section 638, the decision of the referee or commissioner upon the whole issue must stand as the decision of the court, and upon filing of the statement of decision with the clerk of the court, judgment may be entered thereon in the same manner as if the action had been tried by the court.
(b) In the case of all other references, the decision of the referee or commissioner is only advisory. The court may adopt the referee's recommendations, in whole or in part, after independently considering the referee's findings and any objections and responses thereto filed with the court.[602]

645. The decision of the referee appointed pursuant to Section 638 or commissioner may be excepted to and reviewed in like manner as if made by the court. When the reference is to report the facts, the decision reported has the effect of a special verdict.[442]

645.1. (a) When a referee is appointed pursuant to Section 638, the referee's fees shall be paid as agreed by the parties. If the parties do not agree on the payment of fees and request the matter to be resolved by the court, the court may order the parties to pay the referee's fees as set forth in subdivision (b).
(b) When a referee is appointed pursuant to Section 639, at any time after a determination of ability to pay is made as specified in paragraph (6) of subdivision (d) of Section 639, the court may order the parties to pay the fees of referees who are not employees or officers of the court at the time of appointment, as fixed pursuant to Section 1023, in any manner determined by the court to be fair and reasonable, including an apportionment of the fees among the parties. For purposes of this section, the term "parties" does not include parties' counsel.[461]

645.2. The Judicial Council shall adopt all rules of court necessary to implement this chapter.[443]

Chapter 7: Provisions Relating to Trials in General

Chapter 7 enacted 1872.

Article 1: Exceptions

Article 1 enacted 1872.

646. An exception is an objection upon a matter of law to a decision made, either before or after judgment, by a Court, tribunal, Judge, or other judicial officer, in an action or proceeding. The exception must be taken at the time the decision is made, except as provided in section six hundred and forty-seven.[3]

647. All of the following are deemed excepted to: the verdict of the jury; the

final decision in an action or proceeding; an interlocutory order or decision, finally determining the rights of the parties, or some of them; an order or decision from which an appeal may be taken; an order sustaining or overruling a demurrer, allowing or refusing to allow an amendment to a pleading, striking out or refusing to strike out a pleading or a portion thereof, or refusing a continuance; an order made upon ex parte application, giving an instruction, refusing to give an instruction, or modifying an instruction requested; an order or decision made in the absence of the party or an order granting or denying a nonsuit or a motion to strike out evidence or testimony; a ruling sustaining or overruling an objection to evidence; and any statement or other action of the court in commenting upon or in summarizing the evidence. If the party, at the time when the order, ruling, action or decision is sought or made, or within a reasonable time thereafter, makes known his position thereon, by objection or otherwise, all other orders, rulings, actions or decisions are deemed to have been excepted to.[47]

Article 1.5: View by Trier of Fact
Article 1.5 added by Stats. 1975, Ch. 301.

651. (a) On its own motion or on the motion of a party, where the court finds that such a view would be proper and would aid the trier of fact in its determination of the case, the court may order a view of any of the following:

(1) The property which is the subject of litigation.

(2) The place where any relevant event occurred.

(3) Any object, demonstration, or experiment, a view of which is relevant and admissible in evidence in the case and which cannot with reasonable convenience be viewed in the courtroom.

(b) On such occasion, the entire court, including the judge, jury, if any, court reporter, if any, and any necessary officers, shall proceed to the place, property, object, demonstration, or experiment to be viewed. The court shall be in session throughout the view. At the view, the court may permit testimony of witnesses. The proceedings at the view shall be recorded to the same extent as the proceedings in the courtroom.[92]

Article 2: New Trials
Article 2 enacted 1872.

656. A new trial is a re-examination of an issue of fact in the same court after a trial and decision by a jury, court, or referee.[11]

657. The verdict may be vacated and any other decision may be modified or vacated, in whole or in part, and a new or further trial granted on all or part of the issues, on the application of the party aggrieved, for any of the following causes, materially affecting the substantial rights of such party:

1. Irregularity in the proceedings of the court, jury or adverse party, or any order of the court or abuse of discretion by which either party was prevented from having a fair trial.

2. Misconduct of the jury; and whenever any one or more of the jurors have been induced to assent to any general or special verdict, or to a finding on any question submitted to them by the court, by a resort to the determination of chance, such misconduct

may be proved by the affidavit of any one of the jurors.

3. Accident or surprise, which ordinary prudence could not have guarded against.

4. Newly discovered evidence, material for the party making the application, which he could not, with reasonable diligence, have discovered and produced at the trial.

5. Excessive or inadequate damages.

6. Insufficiency of the evidence to justify the verdict or other decision, or the verdict or other decision is against law.

7. Error in law, occurring at the trial and excepted to by the party making the application.

When a new trial is granted, on all or part of the issues, the court shall specify the ground or grounds upon which it is granted and the court's reason or reasons for granting the new trial upon each ground stated.

A new trial shall not be granted upon the ground of insufficiency of the evidence to justify the verdict or other decision, nor upon the ground of excessive or inadequate damages, unless after weighing the evidence the court is convinced from the entire record, including reasonable inferences therefrom, that the court or jury clearly should have reached a different verdict or decision.

The order passing upon and determining the motion must be made and entered as provided in Section 660 and if the motion is granted must state the ground or grounds relied upon by the court, and may contain the specification of reasons. If an order granting such motion does not contain such specification of reasons, the court must, within 10 days after filing such order, prepare, sign and file such specification of reasons in writing with the clerk. The court shall not direct the attorney for a party to prepare either or both said order and said specification of reasons.

On appeal from an order granting a new trial the order shall be affirmed if it should have been granted upon any ground stated in the motion, whether or not specified in the order or specification of reasons, except that (a) the order shall not be affirmed upon the ground of the insufficiency of the evidence to justify the verdict or other decision, or upon the ground of excessive or inadequate damages, unless such ground is stated in the order granting the motion and (b) on appeal from an order granting a new trial upon the ground of the insufficiency of the evidence to justify the verdict or other decision, or upon the ground of excessive or inadequate damages, it shall be conclusively presumed that said order as to such ground was made only for the reasons specified in said order or said specification of reasons, and such order shall be reversed as to such ground only if there is no substantial basis in the record for any of such reasons.[65]

657.1. A new trial may also be granted as provided in Section 914 of this code.[68]

658. When the application is made for a cause mentioned in the first, second, third and fourth subdivisions of Section 657, it must be made upon affidavits; otherwise it must be made on the minutes of the court.[200]

659. (a) The party intending to move for a new trial shall file with the clerk and serve upon each adverse party a

notice of their intention to move for a new trial, designating the grounds upon which the motion will be made and whether the same will be made upon affidavits or the minutes of the court, or both, either:

(1) After the decision is rendered and before the entry of judgment.

(2) Within 15 days of the date of serving notice of entry of judgment by the clerk of the court pursuant to Section 664.5, or service upon them by any party of written notice of entry of judgment, or within 180 days after the entry of judgment, whichever is earliest; provided, that upon the filing of the first notice of intention to move for a new trial by a party, each other party shall have 15 days after the service of that notice upon them to file and serve a notice of intention to move for a new trial.

(b) That notice of intention to move for a new trial shall be deemed to be a motion for a new trial on all the grounds stated in the notice. The times specified in paragraphs (1) and (2) of subdivision (a) shall not be extended by order or stipulation or by those provisions of Section 1013 that extend the time for exercising a right or doing an act where service is by mail.[866]

659a. Within 10 days of filing the notice, the moving party shall serve upon all other parties and file any brief and accompanying documents, including affidavits in support of the motion. The other parties shall have 10 days after that service within which to serve upon the moving party and file any opposing briefs and accompanying documents, including counter-affidavits. The moving party shall have five days after that service to file any reply brief and accompanying documents. These deadlines may, for good cause shown by affidavit or by written stipulation of the parties, be extended by any judge for an additional period not to exceed 10 days.[696]

660. (a) On the hearing of the motion, reference may be had in all cases to the pleadings and orders of the court on file, and when the motion is made on the minutes, reference may also be had to any depositions and documentary evidence offered at the trial and to the report of the proceedings on the trial taken by the phonographic reporter, or to any certified transcript of the report or if there be no such report or certified transcript, to proceedings occurring at the trial that are within the recollection of the judge; when the proceedings at the trial have been phonographically reported, but the reporter's notes have not been transcribed, the reporter shall, upon request of the court or either party, attend the hearing of the motion and read his or her notes, or such parts thereof as the court, or either party, may require.

(b) The hearing and determination of the motion for a new trial shall have precedence over all other matters except criminal cases, probate matters, and cases actually on trial, and it shall be the duty of the court to determine the motion at the earliest possible moment.

(c) Except as otherwise provided in Section 12a of this code, the power of the court to rule on a motion for a new trial shall expire 75 days after the mailing of notice of entry of judgment by the clerk of the court pursuant to Section 664.5 or 75 days after service on the moving party by any party of written notice of entry of judgment, whichever is earlier, or if that notice has not been given, 75 days after the filing of the first notice of intention to move for a new trial. If the motion is not determined within the 75-day period, or within that period as extended, the effect shall be a denial of the motion without further order of the court. A motion for a new trial is not determined within the meaning of this section until an order ruling on the motion is entered in the permanent minutes of the court or signed by the judge and filed with the clerk. The entry of a new trial order in the permanent minutes of the court shall constitute a determination of the motion even though that minute order, as entered, expressly directs that a written order be prepared, signed, and filed. The minute entry shall in all cases show the date on which the order is entered in the permanent minutes, but failure to comply with this direction shall not impair the validity or effectiveness of the order.[745]

661. The motion for a new trial shall be heard and determined by the judge who presided at the trial; provided, however, that in case of the inability of such judge or if at the time noticed for hearing thereon he is absent from the county where the trial was had, the same shall be heard and determined by any other judge of the same court. Upon the expiration of the time to file counter affidavits the clerk forthwith shall call the motion to the attention of the judge who presided at the trial, or the judge acting in his place, as the case may be, and such judge thereupon shall designate the time for oral argument, if any, to be had on said motion. Five (5) days' notice by mail shall be given of such oral argument, if any, by the clerk to the respective parties. Such motion, if heard by a judge other than the trial judge shall be argued orally or shall be submitted without oral argument, as the judge may direct, not later than ten (10) days before the expiration of the time within which the court has power to pass on the same.[18]

662. In ruling on such motion, in a cause tried without a jury, the court may, on such terms as may be just, change or add to the statement of decision, modify the judgment, in whole or in part, vacate the judgment, in whole or in part, and grant a new trial on all or part of the issues, or, in lieu of granting a new trial, may vacate and set aside the statement of decision and judgment and reopen the case for further proceedings and the introduction of additional evidence with the same effect as if the case had been reopened after the submission thereof and before a decision had been filed or judgment rendered. Any judgment thereafter entered shall be subject to the provisions of sections 657 and 659.[116]

662.5. (a) In any civil action where after trial by jury an order granting a new trial limited to the issue of damages would be proper, the trial court may in its discretion:

(1) If the ground for granting a new trial is inadequate damages, issue a conditional order granting the new trial unless the party against whom the verdict has been rendered consents to the addition of damages in an amount the court in its independent judgment determines from the evidence to be fair and reasonable.

(2) If the ground for granting a new trial is excessive damages, issue a conditional order granting the new trial unless the party in whose favor the

verdict has been rendered consents to the reduction of so much thereof as the court in its independent judgment determines from the evidence to be fair and reasonable.

(b) If a deadline for acceptance or rejection of the addition or reduction of damages is not set forth in the conditional order, the deadline is 30 days from the date the conditional order is served by the clerk of the court. Failure to respond to the order in accordance with this section shall be deemed a rejection of the addition or reduction of damages and a new trial limited to the issue of damages shall be granted automatically.

(c) A party filing and serving an acceptance of a conditionally ordered addition or reduction of damages shall concurrently serve and submit to the court a proposed amended judgment reflecting the modified judgment amount, as well as any other uncontested judgment awards.[661]

663. A judgment or decree, when based upon a decision by the court, or the special verdict of a jury, may, upon motion of the party aggrieved, be set aside and vacated by the same court, and another and different judgment entered, for either of the following causes, materially affecting the substantial rights of the party and entitling the party to a different judgment:

1. Incorrect or erroneous legal basis for the decision, not consistent with or not supported by the facts; and in such case when the judgment is set aside, the statement of decision shall be amended and corrected.

2. A judgment or decree not consistent with or not supported by the special verdict.[117]

663a. (a) A party intending to make a motion to set aside and vacate a judgment, as described in Section 663, shall file with the clerk and serve upon the adverse party a notice of his or her intention, designating the grounds upon which the motion will be made, and specifying the particulars in which the legal basis for the decision is not consistent with or supported by the facts, or in which the judgment or decree is not consistent with the special verdict, either:

(1) After the decision is rendered and before the entry of judgment.

(2) Within 15 days of the date of mailing of notice of entry of judgment by the clerk of the court pursuant to Section 664.5, or service upon him or her by any party of written notice of entry of judgment, or within 180 days after the entry of judgment, whichever is earliest.

(b) Except as otherwise provided in Section 12a, the power of the court to rule on a motion to set aside and vacate a judgment shall expire 75 days from the mailing of notice of entry of judgment by the clerk of the court pursuant to Section 664.5, or 75 days after service upon the moving party by any party of written notice of entry of the judgment, whichever is earlier, or if that notice has not been given, 75 days after the filing of the first notice of intention to move to set aside and vacate the judgment. If that motion is not determined within the 75-day period, or within that period as extended, the effect shall be a denial of the motion without further order of the court. A motion to set aside and vacate a judgment is not determined within the meaning of this section until an order ruling on the motion is entered in the

permanent minutes of the court, or signed by the judge and filed with the clerk. The entry of an order to set aside and vacate the judgment in the permanent minutes of the court shall constitute a determination of the motion even though that minute order, as entered, expressly directs that a written order be prepared, signed, and filed. The minute entry shall, in all cases, show the date on which the order is entered in the permanent minutes, but failure to comply with this direction shall not impair the validity or effectiveness of the order.
(c) The provisions of Section 1013 extending the time for exercising a right or doing an act where service is by mail shall not apply to extend the times specified in paragraphs (1) and (2) of subdivision (a).
(d) The moving, opposing, and reply briefs and any accompanying documents shall be filed and served within the periods specified by Section 659a and the hearing on the motion shall be set in the same manner as the hearing on a motion for new trial under Section 660.
(e) An order of the court granting a motion may be reviewed on appeal in the same manner as a special order made after final judgment.[747]

663.1. The court may grant a new trial of any action or proceeding when all of the following conditions exist:
(a) Any proposed bill of exceptions or statement of the case on motion for a new trial is lost or destroyed by reason of conflagration or other public calamity.
(b) No other record of the proceedings upon the trial thereof can be obtained.
(c) Such action or proceeding is subject to review by motion for new trial pending at the time of such loss or destruction.
(d) The court in which such action or proceeding is pending deems it impossible or impracticable to restore such proceedings and to settle a bill of exceptions or statement of the case containing such proceedings, so as to enable the court to review the judgment or order therein by motion for new trial.
(e) At the time of such loss or destruction a motion for new trial was pending.
In order to grant such new trial, it shall be unnecessary to have any bill of exceptions or statement of the case settled, but upon the facts recited in this section being shown to the satisfaction of the court by affidavit or otherwise, the court may grant such new trial.[30]

663.2. Pending the hearing of a motion pursuant to Section 663.1 to grant a new trial, the time within which a bill of exceptions may be prepared, served, or presented for settlement shall be extended and shall not commence to run until the decision upon the motion. The motion must be made within 30 days after the loss or destruction of the records.[30]

Chapter 8: The Manner of Giving and Entering Judgment

Chapter 8 enacted 1872.

664. (a) When trial by jury has been had, judgment must be entered by the clerk, in conformity to the verdict within 24 hours after the rendition of the verdict, whether or not a motion for judgment notwithstanding the verdict be pending, unless the court order the case to be reserved for argument or further consideration, or grant a stay of proceedings. If the trial has been had

by the court, judgment must be entered by the clerk, in conformity to the decision of the court, immediately upon the filing of such decision. In no case is a judgment effectual for any purpose until entered.
(b) This section shall remain in effect only until January 1, 2027, and as of that date is repealed.[898]

664. (a) When trial by jury has been had, judgment must be entered by the clerk, in conformity to the verdict within 24 hours after the rendition of the verdict, whether or not a motion for judgment notwithstanding the verdict is pending, unless the court orders the case to be reserved for argument or further consideration, or grants a stay of proceedings.
(b) If the trial has been had by the court, judgment must be entered by the clerk, in conformity to the decision of the court, by the following dates:
(1) If no statement of decision is requested, within 30 days after the filing of the court's decision.
(2) If a statement of decision is requested, within 30 days after the statement of decision becomes final.
(c) In no case is a judgment effectual for any purpose until entered.
(d) This section shall become operative on January 1, 2027.[899]

664.5. (a) In any contested action or special proceeding other than a small claims action or an action or proceeding in which a prevailing party is not represented by counsel, the party submitting an order or judgment for entry shall prepare and serve, a copy of the notice of entry of judgment to all parties who have appeared in the action or proceeding and shall file with the court the original notice of entry of judgment together with the proof of service. This subdivision does not apply in a proceeding for dissolution of marriage, for nullity of marriage, or for legal separation.
(b) Promptly upon entry of judgment in a contested action or special proceeding in which a prevailing party is not represented by counsel, the clerk of the court shall serve notice of entry of judgment to all parties who have appeared in the action or special proceeding and shall execute a certificate of service and place it in the court's file in the cause.
(c) For purposes of this section, "judgment" includes any judgment, decree, or signed order from which an appeal lies.
(d) Upon order of the court in any action or special proceeding, the clerk shall serve notice of entry of any judgment or ruling, whether or not appealable.
(e) The Judicial Council shall provide by rule of court that, upon entry of judgment in a contested action or special proceeding in which a state statute or regulation has been declared unconstitutional by the court, the Attorney General is promptly notified of the judgment and that a certificate of that service is placed in the court's file in the cause.[733]

664.6. (a) If parties to pending litigation stipulate, in a writing signed by the parties outside of the presence of the court or orally before the court, for settlement of the case, or part thereof, the court, upon motion, may enter judgment pursuant to the terms of the settlement. If the parties to the settlement agreement or their counsel stipulate in writing or orally before the court, the court may dismiss the case as to the settling parties without prejudice and retain jurisdiction over the parties to enforce the settlement until performance in full of the terms of the settlement.

(b) For purposes of this section, a writing is signed by a party if it is signed by any of the following:

(1) The party.

(2) An attorney who represents the party.

(3) If an insurer is defending and indemnifying a party to the action, an agent who is authorized in writing by the insurer to sign on the party's behalf. This paragraph does not apply if the party whom the insurer is defending would be liable under the terms of the settlement for any amount above the policy limits.

(c) Paragraphs (2) and (3) of subdivision (b) do not apply in a civil harassment action, an action brought pursuant to the Family Code, an action brought pursuant to the Probate Code, or a matter that is being adjudicated in a juvenile court or a dependency court.

(d) In addition to any available civil remedies, an attorney who signs a writing on behalf of a party pursuant to subdivision (b) without the party's express authorization shall, absent good cause, be subject to professional discipline.

(e) (1) If a plaintiff, cross-complainant, or other party seeking affirmative relief has filed a notice of conditional settlement, the court may, upon its own motion, without stipulation from the parties or their counsel, set an order to show cause as to why the court should not dismiss the entire action without prejudice and retain jurisdiction to enforce the settlement.

(2) This subdivision does not apply to actions brought pursuant to Chapter 5 of Title 3 of Part 2 of the Code of Civil Procedure (commencing with Section 378) and Part 13 of Division 2 of the Labor Code (commencing with Section 2698).

(f) If the Court enters judgment or dismisses the case without prejudice pursuant to this section, the following shall apply:

(1) A party may file a motion or other document pertaining to the settlement, including an application for determination of good faith settlement, a motion for the reduction or determination of a lien, a petition related to the compromise of the claim of a minor or person with a disability, or, if the terms of a settlement are not performed, a motion based upon such terms. Responsive filings and related documents may also be filed.

(2) The court shall exercise its retained jurisdiction if a party files a notice that a written settlement agreement required of all parties was not signed by all parties.

(3) A party who has paid a first appearance fee shall not be assessed a first appearance fee again for filing a motion, notice or other document pertaining to the settlement after entry of judgment or dismissal without prejudice.

(4) The clerk of the court shall accept any motion, notice, or other document properly filed by a party after entry of judgment or dismissal without prejudice.

(g) Nothing in this section shall preclude a party from filing a request for dismissal with prejudice after the court has dismissed the case without prejudice pursuant to this section.

(h) On or before January 1, 2025, the Judicial Council shall update or develop new forms or Rules of Court as necessary to implement this section.
(i) This section shall become operative on January 1, 2025.[823]

664.7. (a) Notwithstanding Section 664.6, if parties to a pending construction defect action stipulate personally or, where a party's contribution is paid on its behalf pursuant to a policy of insurance, the parties stipulate through their respective counsel, in a writing signed by the parties outside the presence of the court or orally before the court, for settlement of the case, or part thereof, the court, upon motion, may enter judgment pursuant to the terms of the settlement. If requested by the parties, the court may retain jurisdiction over the parties to enforce the settlement until performance in full of the terms of the settlement.
(b) It is the intent of the Legislature that this section modify the holding of Levy v. Superior Court (1995), 10 Cal. 4th 578, regarding the authority of counsel in a construction defect action to bind a party to a settlement.
(c) For purposes of this section, "construction defect action" shall mean any civil action that seeks monetary recovery against a developer, builder, design professional, general contractor, material supplier, or subcontractor of any residential dwelling based upon a claim for alleged defects in the design or construction of the residential dwelling unit.[388]

665. When the case is reserved for argument or further consideration, as mentioned in the last section, it may be brought by either party before the Court for argument.[1]

666. If a claim asserted in a cross-complaint is established at the trial and the amount so established exceeds the demand established by the party against whom the cross-complaint is asserted, judgment for the party asserting the cross-complaint must be given for the excess; or if it appears that the party asserting the cross-complaint is entitled to any other affirmative relief, judgment must be given accordingly.
When the amount found due to either party exceeds the sum for which the court is authorized to enter judgment, such party may remit the excess, and judgment may be rendered for the residue.[74]

667. In an action to recover the possession of personal property, judgment for the plaintiff may be for the possession or the value thereof, in case a delivery cannot be had, and damages for the detention. If the property has been delivered to the plaintiff, and the defendant claim a return thereof judgment for the defendant may be for a return of the property or the value thereof, in case a return cannot be had, and damages for taking and withholding the same.[124]

667.7. (a) In any action for injury or damages against a provider of health care services, a superior court shall, at the request of either party, enter a judgment ordering that money damages or its equivalent for future damages of the judgment creditor be paid in whole or in part by periodic payments rather than by a lump-sum payment if the award equals or exceeds two hundred fifty thousand dollars ($250,000) in future damages. In entering a judgment ordering the payment of future damages by periodic payments, the court shall make a specific finding as to the dollar amount of periodic payments which will compensate the judgment creditor for such future damages. As a condition to authorizing periodic payments of future damages, the court shall require the judgment debtor who is not adequately insured to post security adequate to assure full payment of such damages awarded by the judgment. Upon termination of periodic payments of future damages, the court shall order the return of this security, or so much as remains, to the judgment debtor.

(b) (1) The judgment ordering the payment of future damages by periodic payments shall specify the recipient or recipients of the payments, the dollar amount of the payments, the interval between payments, and the number of payments or the period of time over which payments shall be made. Such payments shall only be subject to modification in the event of the death of the judgment creditor.

(2) In the event that the court finds that the judgment debtor has exhibited a continuing pattern of failing to make the payments, as specified in paragraph (1), the court shall find the judgment debtor in contempt of court and, in addition to the required periodic payments, shall order the judgment debtor to pay the judgment creditor all damages caused by the failure to make such periodic payments, including court costs and attorney's fees.

(c) However, money damages awarded for loss of future earnings shall not be reduced or payments terminated by reason of the death of the judgment creditor, but shall be paid to persons to whom the judgment creditor owed a duty of support, as provided by law, immediately prior to their death. In such cases the court which rendered the original judgment, may, upon petition of any party in interest, modify the judgment to award and apportion the unpaid future damages in accordance with this subdivision.

(d) Following the occurrence or expiration of all obligations specified in the periodic payment judgment, any obligation of the judgment debtor to make further payments shall cease and any security given, pursuant to subdivision (a) shall revert to the judgment debtor.

(e) As used in this section:

(1) "Future damages" includes damages for future medical treatment, care or custody, loss of future earnings, loss of bodily function, or future pain and suffering of the judgment creditor.

(2) "Periodic payments" means the payment of money or delivery of other property to the judgment creditor at regular intervals.

(3) "Health care provider" means any person licensed or certified pursuant to Division 2 (commencing with Section 500) of the Business and Professions Code, or licensed pursuant to the Osteopathic Initiative Act, or the Chiropractic Initiative Act, or licensed pursuant to Chapter 2.5 (commencing with Section 1440) of Division 2 of the Health and Safety Code; and any clinic, health dispensary, or health facility, licensed pursuant to Division 2 (commencing with Section 1200) of the Health and Safety Code. "Health care provider" includes the legal representatives of a health care provider.

(4) "Professional negligence" means a negligent act or omission to act by a health care provider in the rendering

of professional services, which act or omission is the proximate cause of a personal injury or wrongful death, provided that such services are within the scope of services for which the provider is licensed and which are not within any restriction imposed by the licensing agency or licensed hospital.

(f) It is the intent of the Legislature in enacting this section to authorize the entry of judgments in malpractice actions against health care providers which provide for the payment of future damages through periodic payments rather than lump-sum payments. By authorizing periodic payment judgments, it is the further intent of the Legislature that the courts will utilize such judgments to provide compensation sufficient to meet the needs of an injured plaintiff and those persons who are dependent on the plaintiff for whatever period is necessary while eliminating the potential windfall from a lump-sum recovery which was intended to provide for the care of an injured plaintiff over an extended period who then dies shortly after the judgment is paid, leaving the balance of the judgment award to persons and purposes for which it was not intended. It is also the intent of the Legislature that all elements of the periodic payment program be specified with certainty in the judgment ordering such payments and that the judgment not be subject to modification at some future time which might alter the specifications of the original judgment.[795]

668. Except as provided in Section 668.5, the clerk of the superior court, must keep, with the records of the court, a book called the "judgment book," in which judgments must be entered.[509]

668.5. In those counties where the clerk of the court places individual judgments in the file of actions and either a microfilm copy of the individual judgment is made, or the judgment is entered in the register of actions, or into the court's electronic data-processing system, prior to placement of the judgment in the file of actions, the clerk shall not be required to enter judgments in a judgment book, and the date of filing the judgment with the clerk shall constitute the date of its entry.[193]

669. If a party dies after trial and submission of the case to a judge sitting without a jury for decision or after a verdict upon any issue of fact, and before judgment, the court may nevertheless render judgment thereon.[112]

670. In superior courts the following papers, without being attached together, shall constitute the judgment roll:

(a) In case the complaint is not answered by any defendant, the summons, with the affidavit or proof of service; the complaint; the request for entry of default with a memorandum indorsed thereon that the default of the defendant in not answering was entered, and a copy of the judgment; if defendant has appeared by demurrer, and the demurrer has been overruled, then notice of the overruling thereof served on defendant's attorney, together with proof of the service; and in case the service so made is by publication, the affidavit for publication of summons, and the order directing the publication of summons.

(b) In all other cases, the pleadings, all orders striking out any pleading in whole or in part, a copy of the verdict of the jury, the statement of decision of the court, or finding of the referee, and a copy of any order made on demurrer, or relating to a change of parties, and a copy of the judgment; if there are two or more defendants in the action, and any one of them has allowed judgment to pass against him or her by default, the summons, with proof of its service, on the defendant, and if the service on the defaulting defendant be by publication, then the affidavit for publication, and the order directing the publication of the summons.[510]

673. (a) An assignee of a right represented by a judgment may become an assignee of record by filing with the clerk of the court which entered the judgment an acknowledgment of assignment of judgment.

(b) An acknowledgment of assignment of judgment shall contain all of the following:

(1) The title of the court where the judgment is entered and the cause and number of the action.

(2) The date of entry of the judgment and of any renewals of the judgment and where entered in the records of the court.

(3) The name and address of the judgment creditor and name and last known address of the judgment debtor.

(4) A statement describing the right represented by the judgment that is assigned to the assignee.

(5) The name and address of the assignee.

(c) The acknowledgment of assignment of judgment shall be:

(1) Made in the manner of an acknowledgment of a conveyance of real property.

(2) Executed and acknowledged by the judgment creditor or by the prior assignee of record if there is one.

(d) (1) If an acknowledgment of assignment of judgment purports to be executed or acknowledged by an authorized agent of the judgment creditor or an authorized agent of a prior assignee of record, then documentation sufficient to evidence that authorization shall be filed together with the acknowledgment of assignment of judgment.

(2) Notwithstanding paragraph (1), an assignee of a right represented by a judgment may also become an assignee of record by filing with the clerk of the court that entered judgment a court order or other documentation that evidences assignment of judgment by operation of law.[762]

674. (a) Except as otherwise provided in Section 4506 of the Family Code, an abstract of a judgment or decree requiring the payment of money shall be certified by the clerk of the court where the judgment or decree was entered and shall contain all of the following:

(1) The title of the court where the judgment or decree is entered and cause and number of the action.

(2) The date of entry of the judgment or decree and of any renewals of the judgment or decree and where entered in the records of the court.

(3) The name and last known address of the judgment debtor and the address at which the summons was either personally served or mailed to the judgment debtor or the judgment debtor's attorney of record.

(4) The name and address of the judgment creditor.

(5) The amount of the judgment or

decree as entered or as last renewed.

(6) The last four digits of the social security number and driver's license number of the judgment debtor if they are known to the judgment creditor. If either or both of those sets of numbers are not known to the judgment creditor, that fact shall be indicated on the abstract of judgment.

(7) Whether a stay of enforcement has been ordered by the court and, if so, the date the stay ends.

(8) The date of issuance of the abstract.

(b) An abstract of judgment, recorded after January 1, 1979, that does not list the social security number and driver's license number of the judgment debtor, or either of them, as required by subdivision (a) or by Section 4506 of the Family Code, may be amended by the recording of a document entitled "Amendment to Abstract of Judgment." The Amendment to Abstract of Judgment shall contain all of the information required by this section or by Section 4506 of the Family Code, and shall set forth the date of recording and the book and page location in the records of the county recorder of the original abstract of judgment.

A recorded Amendment to Abstract of Judgment shall have priority as of the date of recordation of the original abstract of judgment, except as to any purchaser, encumbrancer, or lessee who obtained their interest after the recordation of the original abstract of judgment but prior to the recordation of the Amendment to Abstract of Judgment without actual notice of the original abstract of judgment. The purchaser, encumbrancer, or lessee without actual notice may assert as a defense against enforcement of the abstract of judgment the failure to comply with this section or Section 4506 of the Family Code regarding the contents of the original abstract of judgment notwithstanding the subsequent recordation of an Amendment to Abstract of Judgment. With respect to an abstract of judgment recorded between January 1, 1979, and July 10, 1985, the defense against enforcement for failure to comply with this section or Section 4506 of the Family Code may not be asserted by the holder of another abstract of judgment or involuntary lien, recorded without actual notice of the prior abstract, unless refusal to allow the defense would result in prejudice and substantial injury as used in Section 475. The recordation of an Amendment to Abstract of Judgment does not extend or otherwise alter the computation of time as provided in Section 697.310.

(c) (1) The abstract of judgment shall be certified in the name of the judgment debtor as listed on the judgment and may also include the additional name or names by which the judgment debtor is known as set forth in the affidavit of identity, as defined in Section 680.135, filed by the judgment creditor with the application for issuance of the abstract of judgment. Prior to the clerk of the court certifying an abstract of judgment containing any additional name or names by which the judgment debtor is known that are not listed on the judgment, the court shall approve the affidavit of identity. If the court determines, without a hearing or a notice, that the affidavit of identity states sufficient facts upon which the judgment creditor has identified the additional names of the judgment debtor, the court shall authorize the certification of the abstract of judgment with the additional name or names.

(2) The remedies provided in Section 697.410 apply to a recorded abstract of a money judgment based upon an affidavit of identity that appears to create a judgment lien on real property of a person who is not the judgment debtor.[596]

TITLE 8.5: UNIFORM FOREIGN-MONEY CLAIMS ACT

Title 8.5 added by Stats. 1991, Ch. 932, Sec. 1.

676. This title shall be known and may be cited as the Uniform Foreign-Money Claims Act.[290]

676.1. As used in this title:

(1) "Action" means a judicial proceeding or arbitration in which a payment in money may be awarded or enforced with respect to a foreign-money claim.

(2) "Bank-offered spot rate" means the spot rate of exchange at which a bank will sell foreign money at a spot rate.

(3) "Conversion date" means the banking day next preceding the date on which money, in accordance with this title, is (i) paid to a claimant in an action or distribution proceeding, (ii) paid to the official designated by law to enforce a judgment or award on behalf of a claimant, or (iii) used to recoup, setoff, or counterclaim in different moneys in an action or distribution proceeding.

(4) "Distribution proceeding" means a judicial or nonjudicial proceeding for the distribution of a fund in which one or more foreign-money claims is asserted and includes an accounting, an assignment for the benefit of creditors, a foreclosure, the liquidation or rehabilitation of a corporation or other entity, and the distribution of an estate, trust, or other fund.

(5) "Foreign money" means money other than money of the United States of America.

(6) "Foreign-money claim" means a claim upon an obligation to pay, or a claim for recovery of a loss, expressed in or measured by a foreign money.

(7) "Money" means a medium of exchange for the payment of obligations or a store of value authorized or adopted by a government or by intergovernmental agreement.

(8) "Money of the claim" means the money determined as proper pursuant to Section 676.4.

(9) "Person" means an individual, a corporation, government or governmental subdivision or agency, business trust, estate, trust, joint venture, partnership, association, two or more persons having a joint or common interest, or any other legal or commercial entity.

(10) "Rate of exchange" means the rate at which money of one country may be converted into money of another country in a free financial market convenient to or reasonably usable by a person obligated to pay or to state a rate of conversion. If separate rates of exchange apply to different kinds of transactions, the term means the rate applicable to the particular transaction giving rise to the foreign-money claim.

(11) "Spot rate" means the rate of exchange at which foreign money is sold by a bank or other dealer in foreign exchange for immediate or next day

availability or for settlement by immediate payment in cash or equivalent, by charge to an account, or by an agreed delayed settlement not exceeding two days.

(12) "State" means a State of the United States, the District of Columbia, the Commonwealth of Puerto Rico, or a territory or insular possession subject to the jurisdiction of the United States.[290]

676.2. (a) This title applies only to a foreign-money claim in an action or distribution proceeding.

(b) This title applies to foreign-money issues even if other law under the conflict-of-laws rules of this state applies to other issues in the action or distribution proceeding.[290]

676.3. (a) The effect of this title may be varied by agreement of the parties made before or after commencement of an action or distribution proceeding or the entry of judgment.

(b) Parties to a transaction may agree upon the money to be used in a transaction giving rise to a foreign-money claim and may agree to use different moneys for different aspects of the transaction. Stating the price in a foreign money for one aspect of a transaction does not alone require the use of that money for other aspects of the transaction.[290]

676.4. (a) The money in which the parties to a transaction have agreed that payment is to be made is the proper money of the claim for payment.

(b) If the parties to a transaction have not otherwise agreed, the proper money of the claim, as in each case may be appropriate, is one of the following:

(1) The money regularly used between the parties as a matter of usage or course of dealing.

(2) The money used at the time of a transaction in international trade, by trade usage or common practice, for valuing or settling transactions in the particular commodity or service involved.

(3) The money in which the loss was ultimately felt or will be incurred by the party claimant.[290]

676.5. (a) If an amount contracted to be paid in a foreign money is measured by a specified amount of a different money, the amount to be paid is determined on the conversion date.

(b) If an amount contracted to be paid in a foreign money is to be measured by a different money at the rate of exchange prevailing on a date before default, that rate of exchange applies only to payments made within a reasonable time after default, not exceeding 30 days. Thereafter, conversion is made at the bank-offered spot rate on the conversion date.

(c) A monetary claim is neither usurious nor unconscionable because the agreement on which it is based provides that the amount of the debtor's obligation to be paid in the debtor's money, when received by the creditor, shall equal a specified amount of the foreign money of the country of the creditor. If, because of unexcused delay in payment of a judgment or award, the amount received by the creditor does not equal the amount of the foreign money specified in the agreement, the court or arbitrator shall amend the judgment or award accordingly.[290]

676.6. (a) A person may assert a claim in a specified foreign money. If a foreign-money claim is not asserted, the

claimant makes the claim in United States dollars.
(b) An opposing party may allege and prove that a claim, in whole or in part, is in a different money than that asserted by the claimant.
(c) A person may assert a defense, setoff, recoupment, or counterclaim in any money without regard to the money of other claims.
(d) The determination of the proper money of the claim is a question of law.[290]

676.7. (a) Except as provided in subdivision (c), a judgment or award on a foreign-money claim shall be stated in an amount of the money of the claim.
(b) A judgment or award on a foreign-money claim is payable in that foreign money or, at the option of the debtor, in the amount of United States dollars which will purchase that foreign money on the conversion date at a bank-offered spot rate.
(c) Assessed costs shall be entered in United States dollars.
(d) Each payment in United States dollars shall be accepted and credited on a judgment or award on a foreign-money claim in the amount of the foreign money that could be purchased by the dollars at a bank-offered spot rate of exchange at or near the close of business on the conversion date for that payment.
(e) A judgment or award made in an action or distribution proceeding on both (1) a defense, setoff, recoupment, or counterclaim and (2) the adverse party's claim, shall be netted by converting the money of the smaller into the money of the larger, and by subtracting the smaller from the larger, and specify the rates of exchange used.
(f) A judgment substantially in the following form complies with subdivision (a):
"IT IS ADJUDGED AND ORDERED, that Defendant (insert name) pay to Plaintiff (insert name) the sum of (insert amount in the foreign money) plus interest on that sum at the rate of (insert rate--see Section 676.9) percent a year or, at the option of the judgment debtor, the number of United States dollars which will purchase the (insert name of foreign money) with interest due, at a bank-offered spot rate at or near the close of business on the banking day next before the day of payment, together with assessed costs of (insert amount) United States dollars.'
(g) If a contract claim is of the type covered by subdivision (a) or (b) of Section 676.5, the judgment or award shall be entered for the amount of money stated to measure the obligation to be paid in the money specified for payment or, at the option of the debtor, the number of United States dollars which will purchase the computed amount of the money of payment on the conversion date at a bank-offered spot rate.
(h) A judgment shall be entered in foreign money in the same manner, and has the same effect as a lien, as other judgments. It may be discharged by payment.[290]

676.8. The rate of exchange prevailing at or near the close of business on the day the distribution proceeding is initiated governs all exchanges of foreign money in a distribution proceeding. A foreign-money claimant in a distribution proceeding shall assert its claim in the named foreign money and show the amount of United States dollars resulting from a conversion as of the date the proceeding was initiated.[290]

676.9. (a) With respect to a foreign-money claim, recovery of prejudgment or pre-award interest and the rate of interest to be applied in the action or distribution proceeding, except as provided in subdivision (b), are matters of the substantive law governing the right to recovery under the conflict-of-laws rules of this state.
(b) The court or arbitrator shall increase or decrease the amount of prejudgment or pre-award interest otherwise payable in a judgment or award in foreign money to the extent required by the law of this state governing a failure to make or accept an offer of settlement or offer of judgment, or conduct by a party or its attorney causing undue delay or expense.
(c) A judgment or award on a foreign-money claim bears interest at the rate applicable to judgments of this state.[290]

676.10. (a) If an action is brought to enforce a judgment of another jurisdiction expressed in a foreign money and the judgment is recognized in this state as enforceable, the enforcing judgment shall be entered as provided in Section 676.7, whether or not the foreign judgment confers an option to pay in an equivalent amount of United States dollars.
(b) A foreign judgment may be enforced in accordance with Title 11 (commencing with Section 1710.10) of Part 3.
(c) A satisfaction or partial payment made upon the foreign judgment, on proof thereof, shall be credited against the amount of foreign money specified in the judgment, notwithstanding the entry of judgment in this state.
(d) A judgment entered on a foreign-money claim only in United States dollars in another state shall be enforced in this state in United States dollars only.[290]

676.11. (a) Computations under this section are for the limited purposes of the section and do not affect computation of the United States dollar equivalent of the money of the judgment for the purpose of payment.
(b) For the limited purpose of facilitating the enforcement of provisional remedies in an action, the value in United States dollars of assets to be seized or restrained pursuant to a writ of attachment, garnishment, execution, or other legal process, the amount of United States dollars at issue for assessing costs, or the amount of United States dollars involved for a surety bond or other court-required undertaking, shall be ascertained as provided in subdivisions (c) and (d).
(c) A party seeking process, costs, bond, or other undertaking under subdivision (b) shall compute in United States dollars the amount of the foreign money claimed from a bank-offered spot rate prevailing at or near the close of business on the banking day next preceding the filing of a request or application for the issuance of process or for the determination of costs, or an application for a bond or other court-required undertaking.
(d) A party seeking the process, costs, bond, or other undertaking under subdivision (b) shall file with each request or application an affidavit or certificate executed in good faith by its counsel or a bank officer, stating the market quotation used and how it was obtained,

and setting forth the calculation. Affected court officials incur no liability, after a filing of the affidavit or certificate, for acting as if the judgment were in the amount of United States dollars stated in the affidavit or certificate.[290]

676.12. (a) If, after an obligation is expressed or a loss is incurred in a foreign money, the country issuing or adopting that money substitutes a new money in place of that money, the obligation or the loss is treated as if expressed or incurred in the new money at the rate of conversion the issuing country establishes for the payment of like obligations or losses denominated in the former money.
(b) If substitution under subdivision (a) occurs after a judgment or award is entered on a foreign-money claim, the court or arbitrator shall amend the judgment or award by a like conversion of the former money.[290]

676.13. Unless displaced by particular provisions of this title, the principles of law and equity, including the law merchant, and the law relative to capacity to contract, principal and agent, estoppel, fraud, misrepresentation, duress, coercion, mistake, bankruptcy, or other validating or invalidating causes supplement its provisions.[290]

676.14. This title shall be applied and construed to effectuate its general purpose to make uniform the law with respect to the subject of this title among states enacting it.[290]

676.15. If any provision of this title or its application to any person or circumstance is held invalid, that invalidity does not affect other provisions or applications of this title which can be given effect without the invalid provision or application, and to this end the provisions of this title are severable.[290]

676.16. This title applies to actions and distribution proceedings commenced on or after January 1, 1992.[290]

TITLE 9: ENFORCEMENT OF JUDGMENTS

Title 9 repealed and added by Stats. 1982, Ch. 1364, Sec. 2.

DIVISION 1: DEFINITIONS AND GENERAL PROVISIONS

Division 1 added by Stats. 1982, Ch. 1364, Sec. 2.

Chapter 1: Short Title and Definitions

Chapter 1 added by Stats. 1982, Ch. 1364, Sec. 2.

680.010. This title shall be known and may be cited as the Enforcement of Judgments Law.[170]

680.110. Unless the provision or context otherwise requires, the definitions in this chapter govern the construction of this title.[170]

680.120. "Account debtor" means "account debtor" as defined in paragraph (3) of subdivision (a) of Section 9102 of the Commercial Code.[419]

680.130. "Account receivable" means "account" as defined in paragraph (2) of subdivision (a) of Section 9102 of the Commercial Code.[420]

680.135. "Affidavit of Identity" means an affidavit or declaration executed by a judgment creditor, under penalty of perjury, that is filed with the clerk of the court in which the judgment is entered at the time the judgment creditor files for a writ of execution or an abstract of judgment. The affidavit of identity shall set forth the case name and number, the name of the judgment debtor stated in the judgment, the additional name or names by which the judgment debtor is known, and the facts upon which the judgment creditor has relied in obtaining the judgment debtor's additional name or names. The affidavit of identity shall not include the name or names of persons, including any corporations, partnerships, or any legal entities not separately named in the judgment in which the judgment debtor is a partner, shareholder, or member, other than the judgment debtor.[435]

680.140. "Chattel paper" means "chattel paper" as defined in paragraph (11) of subdivision (a) of Section 9102 of the Commercial Code.[421]

680.145. "Child support" includes family support.[295]

680.150. "Costs" means costs and disbursements, including but not limited to statutory fees, charges, commissions, and expenses.[170]

680.160. "Court" means the court where the judgment sought to be enforced was entered.[170]

680.170. "Deposit account" means "deposit account" as defined in paragraph (29) of subdivision (a) of Section 9102 of the Commercial Code.[422]

680.180. "Document of title" means "document" as defined in paragraph (30) of subdivision (a) of Section 9102 of the Commercial Code. A document of title is negotiable if it is negotiable within the meaning of Section 7104 of the Commercial Code.[423]

680.190. "Equity" means the fair market value of the interest of the judgment debtor in property, or in the case of community property the fair market value of the interest of the judgment debtor and the spouse of the judgment debtor in the property, over and above all liens and encumbrances on the interest superior to the judgment creditor's lien.[170]

680.200. "Financial institution" means a state or national bank, state or federal savings and loan association or credit union, or like organization, and includes a corporation engaged in a safe deposit business.[170]

680.210. "General intangibles" means "general intangibles," as defined in paragraph (42) of subdivision (a) of Section 9102 of the Commercial Code, consisting of rights to payment.[424]

680.220. "Instrument" means "instrument", as defined in paragraph (47) of subdivision (a) of Section 9102 of the Commercial Code.[425]

680.230. "Judgment" means a judgment, order, or decree entered in a court of this state.[170]

680.240. "Judgment creditor" means the person in whose favor a judgment is rendered or, if there is an assignee of record, means the assignee of record. Unless the context otherwise requires, the term also includes the guardian or conservator of the estate, personal representative, or other successor in interest of the judgment creditor or assignee of record.[170]

680.250. "Judgment debtor" means the person against whom a judgment is rendered.[170]

680.260. "Levying officer" means the

sheriff or marshal.[371]

680.270. "Money judgment" means that part of a judgment that requires the payment of money.[170]

680.280. "Person" includes a natural person, a corporation, a partnership or other unincorporated association, a general partner of a partnership, a limited liability company, and a public entity.[338]

680.290. "Personal property" includes both tangible and intangible personal property.[170]

680.300. "Principal amount of the judgment" means the total amount of the judgment as entered or as last renewed, together with the costs thereafter added to the judgment pursuant to Section 685.090, reduced by any partial satisfactions of such amount and costs and by any amounts no longer enforceable.[170]

680.310. "Property" includes real and personal property and any interest therein.[170]

680.320. "Real property" includes any right in real property, including but not limited to a leasehold interest in real property.[170]

680.330. "Registered process server" means a person registered as a process server pursuant to Chapter 16 (commencing with Section 22350) of Division 8 of the Business and Professions Code.[170]

680.340. "Secured party" means "secured party" as defined in paragraph (73) of subdivision (a) of Section 9102 of the Commercial Code.[693]

680.345. "Security" means a "security" as defined in Section 8102 of the Commercial Code.[170]

680.350. "Security agreement" means "security agreement" as defined in paragraph (74) of subdivision (a) of Section 9102 of the Commercial Code.[694]

680.360. "Security interest" means "security interest" as defined in Section 1201 of the Commercial Code.[170]

680.365. "Spousal support" includes support for a former spouse.[170]

680.370. "Tangible personal property" includes chattel paper, documents of title, instruments, securities, and money.[170]

680.380. "Writ" includes a writ of execution, a writ of possession of personal property, a writ of possession of real property, and a writ of sale.[170]

Chapter 2: General Provisions

Chapter 2 added by Stats. 1982, Ch. 1364, Sec. 2.

681.010. Except as otherwise provided by statute:
(a) A money judgment is enforceable as provided in Division 2 (commencing with Section 695.010).
(b) A judgment for possession of personal property is enforceable as provided in Chapter 2 (commencing with Section 714.010) of Division 3.
(c) A judgment for possession of real property is enforceable as provided in Chapter 3 (commencing with Section 715.010) of Division 3.
(d) A judgment for sale of real or personal property is enforceable as provided in Chapter 4 (commencing with Section 716.010) of Division 3.
(e) A judgment requiring performance of an act not described in subdivisions

(a) to (d), inclusive, or requiring forbearance from performing an act, is enforceable as provided in Chapter 5 (commencing with Section 717.010) of Division 3.[170]

681.020. An assignee of a judgment is not entitled to enforce the judgment under this title unless an acknowledgment of assignment of judgment to that assignee has been filed or the assignee has otherwise become an assignee of record under Section 673.[772]

681.030. (a) The Judicial Council may provide by rule for the practice and procedure in proceedings under this title.
(b) The Judicial Council may prescribe the form of the applications, notices, orders, writs, and other papers to be used under this title. The Judicial Council may prescribe forms in languages other than English. The timely completion and return of a Judicial Council form prescribed in a language other than English has the same force and effect as the timely completion and return of an English language form.
(c) The Judicial Council shall prepare a form containing all of the following:
(1) A list of each of the federal and this state's exemptions from enforcement of a money judgment against a natural person.
(2) A citation to the relevant statute of the United States or this state which creates each of the exemptions.
(3) Information on how to obtain the list of exemption amounts published pursuant to subdivision (f) of Section 703.150.[815]

681.035. The California Law Revision Commission is authorized to maintain a continuing review of and submit recommendations to the Governor and the Legislature concerning enforcement of judgments.[680]

681.040. If a paper is required or permitted to be filed with a levying officer under this title, the paper is considered filed when it is actually received by the levying officer.[170]

681.050. If any provision or clause of this title or application thereof to any person or circumstances is held invalid, the invalidity does not affect other provisions or applications of this title which can be given effect without the invalid provision or application, and to this end the provisions of this title are severable.[170]

Chapter 3: Period for Enforcement and Renewal of Judgments

Chapter 3 added by Stats. 1982, Ch. 1364, Sec. 2.

Article 1: Period for Enforcement of Judgments

Article 1 added by Stats. 1982, Ch. 1364, Sec. 2.

683.010. Except as otherwise provided by statute or in the judgment, a judgment is enforceable under this title upon entry.[170]

683.020. Except as otherwise provided by statute, upon the expiration of 10 years after the date of entry of a money judgment or a judgment for possession or sale of property:
(a) The judgment may not be enforced.
(b) All enforcement procedures pursuant to the judgment or to a writ or order issued pursuant to the judgment shall cease.

(c) Any lien created by an enforcement procedure pursuant to the judgment is extinguished.[170]

683.030. If a money judgment is payable in installments, the 10-year period of enforceability prescribed by Section 683.020 runs as to each installment from the date the installment becomes due and runs as to costs from the date the costs are added to the judgment pursuant to Section 685.090.[170]

683.040. If the judgment creditor applies for a writ for the enforcement of a judgment and the application is made more than 10 years after the date the judgment was entered or renewed, the application shall be accompanied by an affidavit of a person having knowledge of the facts stating facts showing that the issuance of the writ sought in the application is not barred under this chapter. A copy of the affidavit shall be attached to the writ when issued.[170]

683.050. (a) Except as provided in subdivision (b), nothing in this chapter limits any right the judgment creditor may have to bring an action on a judgment, but any such action shall be commenced within the period prescribed by Section 337.5.
(b) Notwithstanding subdivision (a), no action on a judgment may be brought on a judgment identified in subdivision (c) of Section 683.110.[808]

Article 2: Renewal of Judgments
Article 2 added by Stats. 1982, Ch. 1364, Sec. 2.

683.110. (a) The period of enforceability of a money judgment or a judgment for possession or sale of property may be extended by renewal of the judgment as provided in this article.
(b) A judgment shall not be renewed under this article if the application for renewal is filed within five years from the time the judgment was previously renewed under this article.
(c) Notwithstanding subdivision (a), a judgment creditor may renew the period of enforceability of the following types of money judgments only once pursuant to subdivision (c) of Section 683.120:
(1) A judgment on a claim related to medical expenses if the principal amount of the money judgment remaining unsatisfied against a debtor is under two hundred thousand dollars ($200,000).
(2) A judgment on a claim related to personal debt if the principal amount of the money judgment remaining unsatisfied against a debtor is under fifty thousand dollars ($50,000).
(d) For purposes of this section, the following definitions apply:
(1) "Debtor" means a natural person from whom money is due or owing or alleged to be due or owing.
(2) "Due or owing" does not include debts incurred due to or obtained by tortious or fraudulent conduct or judgments for unpaid wages, damages, or penalties owed to an employee.
(3) "Personal debt" means money due or owing or alleged to be due or owing from a natural person arising out of a transaction in which the money, property, insurance, or services which are the subject of the transaction are primarily for the debtor's personal, family, or household purposes.[816]

683.120. (a) The judgment creditor may renew a judgment by filing an application for renewal of the judgment with the court in which the judgment was entered.

(b) Except as otherwise provided in this article, the filing of the application renews the judgment in the amount determined under Section 683.150 and extends the period of enforceability of the judgment as renewed for a period of 10 years from the date the application is filed.

(c) Notwithstanding subdivisions (a) and (b), for a judgment identified in subdivision (c) of Section 683.110, a judgment creditor may renew the judgment only once. The filing of the application under this subdivision renews the judgment in the amount determined under Section 683.150 and extends the period of enforceability of the judgment as renewed for a period of five years from the date the application is filed. No application may be filed if the judgment was renewed on or before December 31, 2022.

(d) In the case of a money judgment payable in installments, for the purposes of enforcement and of any later renewal, the amount of the judgment as renewed shall be treated as a lump-sum money judgment entered on the date the application is filed.[809]

683.130. (a) In the case of a lump-sum money judgment or a judgment for possession or sale of property, the application for renewal of the judgment may be filed at any time before the expiration of the 10-year period of enforceability provided by Section 683.020 or, if the judgment is a renewed judgment, at any time before the expiration of the 10-year period of enforceability of the renewed judgment provided by Section 683.120.

(b) In the case of a money judgment payable in installments, the application for renewal of the judgment may be filed:

(1) If the judgment has not previously been renewed, at any time as to past due amounts that at the time of filing are not barred by the expiration of the 10-year period of enforceability provided by Sections 683.020 and 683.030.

(2) If the judgment has previously been renewed, within the time specified by subdivision (a) as to the amount of the judgment as previously renewed and, as to any past due amounts that became due and payable after the previous renewal, at any time before the expiration of the 10-year period of enforceability provided by Sections 683.020 and 683.030.[781]

683.140. The application for renewal of the judgment shall be executed under oath and shall include all of the following:

(a) The title of the court where the judgment is entered and the cause and number of the action.

(b) The date of entry of the judgment and of any renewals of the judgment and where entered in the records of the court.

(c) The name and address of the judgment creditor and the name and last known address of the judgment debtor. However, the judgment creditor shall omit the name of a judgment debtor from the application for a writ of execution if the liability of that judgment debtor has ceased with regard to the judgment, including either of the following occurrences:

(1) The judgment debtor has obtained a discharge of the judgment pursuant to Title 11 of the United States Code and notice thereof has been filed with the court.

(2) The judgment creditor files an acknowledgment of satisfaction of judgment with regard to the judgment debtor pursuant to Chapter 1 (commencing with Section 724.010) of Division 5.

(d) In the case of a money judgment, the information necessary to compute the amount of the judgment as renewed. In the case of a judgment for possession or sale of property, a description of the performance remaining due.[689]

683.150. (a) Upon the filing of the application, the court clerk shall enter the renewal of the judgment in the court records.

(b) The fee for filing an application for renewal of judgment is as provided in subdivision (b) of Section 70626 of the Government Code.

(c) In the case of a money judgment, the entry of renewal shall show the amount of the judgment as renewed. Except as provided in subdivisions (d) and (e), this amount is the amount required to satisfy the judgment on the date of the filing of the application for renewal and includes the fee for the filing of the application for renewal.

(d) In the case of a money judgment payable in installments not previously renewed, the amount of the judgment as renewed is the total of the past due installments, the costs added to the judgment pursuant to Section 685.090, and the accrued interest, which remains unsatisfied and is enforceable on the date of the filing of the application for renewal and includes the fee for the filing of the application for renewal.

(e) In the case of a money judgment payable in installments previously renewed, the amount of the judgment as renewed under the latest renewal is the total of the following which remains unsatisfied and is enforceable on the date of the filing of the application for the latest renewal:

(1) The amount of the judgment as renewed under the previous renewal.

(2) The past due installments that became due and payable after the previous renewal.

(3) The costs that have been added to the judgment pursuant to Section 685.090 after the previous renewal.

(4) The interest that has accrued on the amounts described in paragraphs (1), (2), and (3) since the last renewal.

(5) The fee for filing the application for renewal.

(f) In the case of a judgment for possession or sale of property, the entry of renewal shall describe the performance remaining due.[564]

683.160. (a) The judgment creditor shall serve a notice of renewal of the judgment on the judgment debtor. Service shall be made personally or by first-class mail and proof of service shall be filed with the court clerk. The notice shall be in a form prescribed by the Judicial Council and shall inform the judgment debtor that the judgment debtor has 60 days within which to make a motion to vacate or modify the renewal.

(b) Until proof of service is filed pursuant to subdivision (a), no writ may be issued, nor may any enforcement proceedings be commenced to enforce the judgment, except to the extent that the judgment would be enforceable had it not been renewed.[810]

683.170. (a) The renewal of a judgment pursuant to this article may be vacated on any ground that would be a defense to an action on the judgment, including the ground that the amount of the renewed judgment as entered pursuant to this article is incorrect, and shall be vacated if the application for renewal was filed within five years from the time the judgment was previously renewed under this article.

(b) Not later than 60 days after service of the notice of renewal pursuant to Section 683.160, the judgment debtor may apply by noticed motion under this section for an order of the court vacating the renewal of the judgment. The notice of motion shall be served on the judgment creditor. Service shall be made personally or by mail.

(c) Upon the hearing of the motion, the renewal may be ordered vacated upon any ground provided in subdivision (a), and another and different renewal may be entered, including, but not limited to, the renewal of the judgment in a different amount if the decision of the court is that the judgment creditor is entitled to renewal in a different amount.[811]

683.180. (a) If a judgment lien on an interest in real property has been created pursuant to a money judgment and the judgment is renewed pursuant to this article, the duration of the judgment lien is extended until 10 years from the date of the filing of the application for renewal if, before the expiration of the judgment lien, a certified copy of the application for renewal is recorded with the county recorder of the county where the real property subject to the judgment lien is located.

(b) A judgment lien on an interest in real property that has been transferred subject to the lien is not extended pursuant to subdivision (a) if the transfer was recorded before the application for renewal was filed unless both of the following requirements are satisfied:

(1) A copy of the application for renewal is personally served on the transferee.

(2) Proof of such service is filed with the court clerk within 90 days after the filing of the application for renewal.[180]

683.190. If a lien (other than a judgment lien on an interest in real property or an execution lien) has been created by an enforcement procedure pursuant to a judgment and the judgment is renewed pursuant to this article, the duration of the lien is extended, subject to any other limitations on its duration under this title, until 10 years from the date of the filing of the application for renewal of the judgment if, before the expiration of the lien, a certified copy of the application for renewal is served on or filed with the same person and in the same manner as the notice or order that created the lien.[170]

683.200. If a judgment is renewed pursuant to this article, any enforcement proceeding previously commenced pursuant to the judgment or to a writ or order issued pursuant to the judgment that would have ceased pursuant to Section 683.020 had the judgment not been renewed may be continued, subject to any other limitations provided in this title, if, before the expiration of the prior 10-year period of enforceability, a certified copy of the application for renewal of the judgment is filed with the levying officer, receiver, or other officer acting pursuant to such writ or order or, in other cases, is filed in the enforcement proceeding.[170]

683.210. A judgment may be renewed

notwithstanding any stay of enforcement of the judgment, but the renewal of the judgment does not affect the stay of enforcement.[170]

683.220. If a judgment is renewed pursuant to this article, the date of the filing of the application for renewal shall be deemed to be the date that the period for commencing an action on the renewed judgment commences to run under Section 337.5.[170]

Article 3: Application of Chapter
Article 3 added by Stats. 1982, Ch. 1364, Sec. 2.

683.310. Except as otherwise provided in the Family Code, this chapter does not apply to a judgment or order made or entered pursuant to the Family Code.[445]

683.320. This chapter does not apply to a money judgment against a public entity that is subject to Section 965.5 or 970.1 of the Government Code.[170]

Chapter 4: Manner of Service of Writs, Notices, and Other Papers

Chapter 4 added by Stats. 1982, Ch. 1364, Sec. 2.

Article 1: Service on Attorney of Creditor or Debtor
Article 1 added by Stats. 1982, Ch. 1364, Sec. 2.

684.010. Subject to Chapter 1 (commencing with Section 283) of Title 5 of Part 1 of this code and Section 215 of the Family Code, when a notice, order, or other paper is required to be served under this title on the judgment creditor, it shall be served on the judgment creditor's attorney of record rather than on the judgment creditor if the judgment creditor has an attorney of record.[296]

684.020. (a) Except as provided in subdivision (b), when a writ, notice, order, or other paper is required to be served under this title on the judgment debtor, it shall be served on the judgment debtor instead of the attorney for the judgment debtor.
(b) The writ, notice, order, or other paper shall be served on the attorney specified by the judgment debtor rather than on the judgment debtor if all of the following requirements are satisfied:
(1) The judgment debtor has filed with the court and served on the judgment creditor a request that service on the judgment debtor under this title be made by serving the attorney specified in the request. Service on the judgment creditor of the request shall be made personally or by mail. The request shall include a consent, signed by the attorney, to receive service under this title on behalf of the judgment debtor.
(2) The request has not been revoked by the judgment debtor.
(3) The consent to receive service has not been revoked by the attorney.
(c) A request or consent under subdivision (b) may be revoked by filing with the court a notice revoking the request or consent. A copy of the notice revoking the request or consent shall be served on the judgment creditor. Service shall be made personally or by mail. The judgment creditor is not bound by the revocation until the judgment creditor has received a copy of the notice revoking the request or consent.[170]

684.030. Sections 684.010 and 684.020 do not apply to either of the following:
(a) A subpoena or other process to require the attendance of a party.
(b) A paper to bring a party into contempt.[170]

684.040. If service on an attorney is required under this article, service on the attorney shall be made in any of the following ways:
(a) By personal delivery to the attorney.
(b) By service in the manner provided in subdivision (1) of Section 1011.
(c) By mail in the manner provided in Section 684.120.[170]

684.050. Service on the attorney for the judgment creditor or the judgment debtor pursuant to the provisions of this article constitutes service on the judgment creditor or judgment debtor for the purposes of this title.[170]

Article 2: Manner of Service Generally
Article 2 added by Stats. 1982, Ch. 1364, Sec. 2.

684.110. (a) (1) Subject to subdivisions (b), (c), and (d), if legal process is required to be personally served under this title, service shall be made in the same manner as a summons is served under Chapter 4 (commencing with Section 413.10) of Title 5.
(2) For purposes of this title, the term "legal process" shall refer to each and all of the writs, notices, orders, or other papers required or permitted to be served pursuant to this title.
(b) If the legal process is required to be personally served under this title and service on an attorney is required under Article 1 (commencing with Section 684.010), service shall be made on the attorney in the manner provided in Section 684.040.
(c) If the legal process is required to be personally served on (1) a financial institution in connection with a deposit account or with property held for safekeeping, as collateral for an obligation owed to the financial institution or in a safe-deposit box, (2) a title insurer (as defined in Section 12340.4 of the Insurance Code) or underwritten title company (as defined in Section 12340.5 of the Insurance Code), or (3) an industrial loan company (as defined in Section 18003 of the Financial Code), service shall be made at the office or branch that has actual possession of the property levied upon or at which a deposit account levied upon is carried and shall be made upon the officer, manager, or other person in charge of the office or branch at the time of service. For purposes of this section, the office or branch at which a deposit account levied upon is carried shall mean the branch, office, or other location where the financial institution maintains the account.
(d) Notwithstanding subdivision (c), with respect to legal process served on a financial institution, if the financial institution has designated a central location for service of legal process pursuant to Section 684.115, unless the financial institution elects to treat legal process served at a branch or office as effective, that legal process so served on the branch or office will not reach those accounts or property and need not be reported on the financial institution's garnishee memorandum.
(e) Notwithstanding subdivision (c), a financial institution, title insurer, or industrial loan company, in its discretion and without violating any obligation to

its customer, may act upon service of legal process at any of its offices or branches, whether or not the office or branch is the location wherein accounts or property that may be reached by the process is or are maintained or located.[675]

684.115. (a) A financial institution may, and if it has more than nine branches or offices at which it conducts its business within this state shall, designate one or more central locations for service of legal process within this state. Each designated location shall be referred to as a "central location." A financial institution may designate a third-party agent as a central location for service of legal process. If a financial institution designates a third-party agent as a central location, the financial institution shall designate at least one additional central location that is not located in the same county as another designated central location. The financial institution may designate the same third-party agent as multiple central locations for service of legal process if the third-party agent maintains physical locations in multiple counties.

(b) If a financial institution elects or is required to designate a central location for service of legal process, pursuant to subdivision (a), the financial institution shall file a notice of its designation with the Department of Financial Protection and Innovation which filing shall be effective upon filing and shall contain all of the following:

(1) The physical address of the central location.

(2) The days and hours during which service will be accepted at the central location and, if the central location is a third-party agent, the name of the third party agent.

(3) If the central location will not accept service of legal process directed at deposit accounts maintained or property held at all of the financial institution's branches or offices within this state, or if the service accepted at the central location will not apply to safe-deposit boxes or other property of the judgment debtor held by or for the judgment debtor, the filing shall also contain sufficient information to permit a determination of the limitation or limitations, including, in the case of a limitation applicable to certain branches or offices, an identification of the branches or offices as to which service at the central location will not apply and the nature of the limitation applicable to those branches or offices. If the limitation will apply to all branches or offices of the financial institution within this state, the filing may indicate the nature of the limitation and that it applies to all branches or offices, in lieu of an identification of branches or offices as to which the limitation applies. To the extent that a financial institution's designation of a central location for service of legal process covers the process directed at deposit accounts, safe-deposit boxes, or other property of the judgment debtor held by or for the judgment debtor at a particular branch or office located within this state, the branch or office shall be a branch or office covered by central process.

(c) Should a financial institution required to designate a central location fail to do so, each branch of that institution located in this state shall be deemed to be a central location at which service of legal process may be made, and all of the institution's branches or offices located within this state shall be deemed to be a branch or office covered by central process.

(d) Subject to any limitation noted pursuant to paragraph (3) of subdivision (b), service of legal process at a central location of a financial institution shall be effective against all deposit accounts and all property held for safekeeping, as collateral for an obligation owed to the financial institution or in a safe-deposit box if the same is described in the legal process and held by the financial institution at any branch or office covered by central process and located within this state. However, while service of legal process at the central location will establish a lien on all property, if any property other than deposit accounts is physically held by the financial institution in a county other than that in which the designated central location is located, the financial institution shall include in its garnishee's memorandum the location or locations of the property, and the judgment creditor shall obtain a writ of execution covering the property and directed to the levying officer in that county to accomplish the turnover of the property and shall forward the writ and related required documentation to the levying officer in the county in which the property is held.

(e) A financial institution may modify or revoke any designation made pursuant to subdivision (a) by filing the modification or revocation with the Department of Financial Protection and Innovation. The modification or revocation shall be effective when the Department of Financial Protection and Innovation's records have been updated to reflect the modification or revocation, provided that the judgment creditor may rely upon the superseded designation during the 30-day period following the effective date of the revocation or modification.

(f) (1) The Department of Financial Protection and Innovation shall update its online records to reflect a filing by a financial institution pursuant to subdivisions (a) and (b) or a modification or revocation filed by a financial institution pursuant to subdivision (e) within 10 business days following the filing by the financial institution. The Department of Financial Protection and Innovation's internet website shall reflect the date its online records for each financial institution have most recently been updated.

(2) The Department of Financial Protection and Innovation shall provide any person requesting it with a copy of each current filing made by a financial institution pursuant to subdivisions (a) and (b). The Department of Financial Protection and Innovation may satisfy its obligation under this subdivision by posting all current designations of a financial institution, or the pertinent information therein, on an internet website available to the public without charge, and if that information is made available, the Department of Financial Protection and Innovation may impose a reasonable fee for furnishing that information in any other manner.

(g) As to deposit accounts maintained or property held for safekeeping, as collateral for an obligation owed to the financial institution or in a safe-deposit box at a branch or office covered by central process, service of legal process at a location other than a central location designated by the financial institution shall not be effective unless the financial institution, in its absolute discretion, elects to act upon the process at that location as if it were effective. In the absence of an election, the financial institution may respond to the legal process by mailing or delivery of the garnishee's memorandum to the levying officer within the time otherwise provided therefor, with a statement on the garnishee's memorandum that the legal process was not properly served at the financial institution's designated location for receiving legal process, and, therefore, was not processed, and the address at which the financial institution is to receive legal process.

(h) If any legal process is served at a central location of a financial institution pursuant to this section, all related papers to be served on the financial institution shall be served at that location, unless agreed to the contrary between the serving party and the financial institution.

(i) This subdivision shall apply whenever a financial institution operates within this state at least one branch or office in addition to its head office or main office, as applicable, or a financial institution headquartered in another state operates more than one branch or office within this state, and no central location has been designated or deemed to have been designated by the institution for service of legal process relating to deposit accounts maintained at the financial institution's head office or main office, as applicable, and branches located within this state. If a judgment creditor reasonably believes that, pursuant to Section 700.140 and, if applicable, Section 700.160, any act of enforcement would be effective against a specific deposit account maintained at a financial institution described in this subdivision, the judgment creditor may file with the financial institution a written request that the financial institution identify the branch or office within this state at which a specified account might be maintained by the financial institution. The written request shall contain the following statements or information:

(1) The name of the person reasonably believed by the judgment creditor to be a person in whose name the specified deposit account stands.

(2) If the name of the person reasonably believed by the judgment creditor to be a person in whose name the specified deposit account stands is not a judgment debtor identified in the writ of execution, a statement that a person reasonably believed by the judgment creditor to be a person in whose name the specified deposit account stands will be appropriately identified in the legal process to be served pursuant to Section 700.160, including any supplementary papers, such as a court order or affidavit if the same will be required by Section 700.160.

(3) The specific identifying number of the account reasonably believed to be maintained with the financial institution and standing in the name of the judgment debtor or other person.

(4) The address of the requesting party.

(5) An affidavit by the judgment creditor or the judgment creditor's counsel stating substantially the following: "I hereby declare that this deposit account location request complies with Section 684.115 of the Code of Civil

Procedure, that the account or accounts of the judgment debtor or other person or persons appropriately identified in the legal process and specified herein are subject to a valid writ of execution, or court order, that I have a reasonable belief, formed after an inquiry reasonable under the circumstances, that the financial institution receiving this deposit account location request has an account standing in the name of the judgment debtor or other person or persons appropriately identified in the legal process, and that information pertaining to the location of the account will assist the judgment creditor in enforcing the judgment."

(j) The affidavit contemplated by subdivision (i) shall be signed by the judgment creditor or the judgment creditor's counsel and filed at the financial institution's head office located within this state or, if the financial institution's head office is in another state, at one of its branches or offices within this state. Failure to comply with the requirements of subdivision (i) and this subdivision shall be sufficient basis for the financial institution to refuse to produce the information that would otherwise be required by subdivision (k).

(k) Within 10 banking days following receipt by a financial institution at the applicable location specified in subdivision (j) of a request contemplated by subdivision (i), as to each specific deposit account identified in the request contemplated by subdivision (i), the financial institution shall respond by mailing, by first-class mail with postage prepaid, to the requester's address as specified in the request a response indicating the branch or office location of the financial institution at which the specified deposit account might be maintained, or, if the specified deposit account, if it exists, would not be maintained at a specific location, at least one place within this state at which legal process relating to the deposit account should or may be served. The response to be furnished pursuant to this subdivision shall not require the financial institution to determine whether an account exists or, if an account does exist, whether it would be reached by the legal process, rather, the branch or office location shall be determined and reported by the financial institution based solely upon its determination that an account with the identifying number provided by the requester would be maintained at that branch if an account did exist, and the response shall not contain any information about the name in which the account stands or any other information concerning the account, if it exists. If more than one account number is specified in the request, the financial institution's responses as to some or all of those account numbers may be combined in a single writing.

(l) A response furnished in good faith by the financial institution pursuant to subdivision (k) shall not be deemed to violate the privacy of any person in whose name the specified deposit account stands nor the privacy of any other person, and shall not require the consent of the person in whose name the account stands nor that of any other person.

(m) A financial institution shall not notify the person in whose name the specified deposit account stands or any other person related to the specified account of the receipt of any request made pursuant to subdivision (i) and affecting that person's or persons' accounts at the financial institution, provided that the financial institution shall have no liability for its failure to comply with the provisions of this subdivision.

(n) For purposes of this section, "third-party agent" means a non-financial institution entity, such as a corporation, that is in the business of accepting service of legal process on behalf of financial institutions and other businesses. Third-party agent does not include a licensed attorney or law firm acting on behalf of a financial institution.[846]

684.120. (a) Except as otherwise provided in this title, if a writ, notice, order, or other paper is to be served by mail under this title, it shall be sent by first-class mail (unless some other type of mail is specifically required) and shall be deposited in a post office, mailbox, sub-post office, substation, mail chute, or other like facility regularly maintained by the United States Postal Service, in a sealed envelope, with postage paid, addressed as follows:

(1) If an attorney is being served in place of the judgment creditor or judgment debtor as provided in Section 684.010 or 684.020, to the attorney at the last address given by the attorney on any paper filed in the proceeding and served on the party making the service.

(2) If any other person is being served, to such person at the person's current mailing address if known or, if unknown, at the address last given by the person on any paper filed in the proceeding and served on the party making the service.

(3) If the mailing cannot be made as provided in paragraph (1) or (2), to the person at the person's last known address.

(b) Service by mail is complete at the time of deposit; but, unless the court prescribes a shorter period of time, any prescribed period of notice and any right or duty to do any act or make any response within any prescribed period or on a date certain after a paper is served by mail is extended:

(1) Five days if the place of address is within the State of California.

(2) Ten days if the place of address is outside the State of California but within the United States.

(3) Twenty days if the place of address is outside the United States.

(c) The writ, notice, order, or other paper served by mail under this section shall bear a notation of the date and place of mailing or be accompanied by an unsigned copy of the affidavit or certificate of mailing. This subdivision is directory only.[170]

684.130. (a) If the levying officer is required by any provision of this title to serve any writ, order, notice, or other paper on any person, the judgment creditor shall include in the instructions to the levying officer the correct name and address of the person. The judgment creditor shall use reasonable diligence to ascertain the correct name and address of the person.

(b) (1) Where the judgment upon which the writ is issued is for personal debt, as defined in subdivision (d) of Section 683.110, this subdivision shall apply.

(2) The judgment creditor shall also provide the levying officer with a declaration stating that the judgment creditor has verified using reasonable diligence within the past 12 months

that the judgment debtor's address is correct to the best of the declarant's knowledge, and describing the verification dates and the methods used, which may include, but are not limited to, the following methods:

(A) Receipt of correspondence from the judgment debtor, dated no more than 12 months before the execution of the declaration, that includes a return address or other comparable verification of the judgment debtor's address.

(B) Transmittal of a letter or legal pleading by certified mail, or other method of transmission through the United States Postal Service providing a return receipt, to the judgment debtor's address, with a return receipt dated no more than 12 months before the execution of the declaration that is signed by the judgment debtor.

(C) Verification of the judgment debtor's current address by a commercial address verification service, including skip-tracing, or, if reasonably available, a public record database, followed by dispatch of a letter or legal pleading, by first-class mail to the verified address, that was not returned to sender.

(3) The levying officer shall not accept or serve any writ, order, notice, or other paper on any person if the judgment creditor fails to provide a declaration as described in paragraph (2).

(4) Upon notice by the judgment debtor that the requirements of this section have not been met, the court shall stay the notice of levy or earnings withholding order until the requirements of this section have been satisfied.

(5) The judgment creditor's cost of verification of the judgment debtor's address is not recoverable.

(6) The judgment creditor shall file with the court the signed declaration within 10 business days after delivering the declaration to the levying officer.

(7) The declaration required by this section may be signed by any individual with adequate knowledge of the verification, including, but not limited to, a custodian of records. If the judgment creditor is represented by an attorney, the declaration may be signed by any employee of the attorney or the attorney's law firm with adequate knowledge of the verification, including, but not limited to, a custodian of records.

(c) Unless the levying officer has actual knowledge that the name or address included in the instructions is incorrect, the levying officer shall rely on the instructions in serving the writ, order, notice, or other paper on the person.[901]

684.140. If a provision of this title provides for service by the levying officer of an order, notice, or other paper that runs in favor of a particular person, personal service of the paper may be made by the person or the person's agent if the levying officer gives permission. The levying officer's permission may be evidenced by a certificate signed by the levying officer. This section does not authorize the levying officer to give permission to serve a writ or notice of levy. If service is made by a person or the person's agent pursuant to this section, the cost of the service is not a recoverable cost. Nothing in this section limits the authority of a registered process server provided in this title.[170]

Article 3: Proof of Service
Article 3 added by Stats. 1982, Ch. 1364, Sec. 2.

684.210. If service of notice of a court hearing is required under this title, proof of service of the notice shall be made at or before the hearing to the satisfaction of the court.[170]

684.220. Proof of service or of posting or publication under this title may be made by, but is not limited to, the following means:
(a) If service is made in the same manner as a summons is served under Chapter 4 (commencing with Section 413.10) of Title 5, proof of service may be made in the manner provided in Article 5 (commencing with Section 417.10) of that chapter.
(b) If service is made in the same manner as a summons is served under Section 415.10 or 415.20, proof of service may be made by affidavit of the person making the service showing the time, place, and manner of service and the facts showing that the service was made in accordance with the applicable statutory provisions. The affidavit shall recite or in other manner show the name of the person to whom the papers served were delivered and, if appropriate, the title of the person or the capacity in which the person was served.
(c) Proof of service by mail as provided in Section 684.120 may be made in the manner prescribed in Section 1013a.
(d) Proof of posting may be made by the affidavit of the person who posted the notice, showing the time and place of posting.
(e) Proof of publication may be made by the affidavit of the publisher or printer, or the foreman or principal clerk of the publisher or printer, showing the time and place of publication.
(f) Proof of service may be made by the written admission of the person served.
(g) Proof of service however made, or of posting or publication, may be made by testimonial evidence.[170]

Article 4: Application of Chapter
Article 4 added by Stats. 1982, Ch. 1364, Sec. 2.

684.310. Except for Sections 684.130 and 684.140, the provisions of Article 1 (commencing with Section 684.010) and Article 2 (commencing with Section 684.110) do not apply to service under Chapter 5 (commencing with Section 706.010) of Division 2 (wage garnishment).[170]

Chapter 5: Interest and Costs
Chapter 5 added by Stats. 1982, Ch. 1364, Sec. 2.

685.010. (a) (1) Except as provided in paragraph (2), interest accrues at the rate of 10 percent per annum on the principal amount of a money judgment remaining unsatisfied.
(2) (A) For judgments entered on or after January 1, 2023, or where an application for renewal of judgment is filed on or after January 1, 2023, interest accrues at the rate of 5 percent per annum on the principal amount of a money judgment remaining unsatisfied in the following cases:
(i) The principal amount of a money judgment of under two hundred thousand dollars ($200,000) remaining unsatisfied against a debtor for a claim related to medical expenses.
(ii) The principal amount of a money judgment of under fifty

thousand dollars ($50,000) remaining unsatisfied against a debtor for a claim related to personal debt.

(B) The claims specified in subparagraph (A) include, but are not limited to, a claim based on any of the following transactions:

(i) An agreement governing the use of a credit card as defined in subdivision (a) of Section 1747.02 of the Civil Code.

(ii) A conditional sale contract as defined in subdivision (a) of Section 2981 of the Civil Code.

(iii) A deferred deposit transaction as defined in subdivision (a) of Section 23001 of the Financial Code.

(C) For purposes of this paragraph, the following definitions apply:

(i) "Debtor" means a natural person from whom money is due or owing or alleged to be due or owing.

(ii) "Due or owing" does not include debts incurred due to or obtained by tortious or fraudulent conduct or judgments for unpaid wages, damages, or penalties owed to an employee.

(iii) "Personal debt" means money due or owing or alleged to be due or owing from a natural person arising out of a transaction in which the money, property, insurance, or services which are the subject of the transaction are primarily for the debtor's personal, family, or household purposes.

(b) The Legislature reserves the right to change the rate of interest provided in subdivision (a) at any time, regardless of the date of entry of the judgment or the date any obligation upon which the judgment is based was incurred. A change in the rate of interest may be made applicable only to the interest that accrues after the operative date of the statute that changes the rate.[817]

685.020. (a) Except as provided in subdivision (b), interest commences to accrue on a money judgment on the date of entry of the judgment.

(b) Unless the judgment otherwise provides, if a money judgment is payable in installments, interest commences to accrue as to each installment on the date the installment becomes due.[181]

685.030. (a) If a money judgment is satisfied in full pursuant to a writ under this title, interest ceases to accrue on the judgment:

(1) If the proceeds of collection are paid in a lump sum, on the date of levy.

(2) If the money judgment is satisfied pursuant to an earnings withholding order, on the date and in the manner provided in Section 706.024 or Section 706.028.

(3) In any other case, on the date the proceeds of sale or collection are actually received by the levying officer.

(b) If a money judgment is satisfied in full other than pursuant to a writ under this title, interest ceases to accrue on the date the judgment is satisfied in full.

(c) If a money judgment is partially satisfied pursuant to a writ under this title or is otherwise partially satisfied, interest ceases to accrue as to the part satisfied on the date the part is satisfied.

(d) For the purposes of subdivisions (b) and (c), the date a money judgment is satisfied in full or in part is the earliest of the following times:

(1) The date satisfaction is actually received by the judgment creditor.

(2) The date satisfaction is tendered to the judgment creditor or deposited in court for the judgment creditor.

(3) The date of any other performance that has the effect of satisfaction.

(e) The clerk of a court may enter in the Register of Actions a writ of execution on a money judgment as returned wholly satisfied when the judgment amount, as specified on the writ, is fully collected and only an interest deficit of no more than ten dollars ($10) exists, due to automation of the continual daily interest accrual calculation.[464]

685.040. The judgment creditor is entitled to the reasonable and necessary costs of enforcing a judgment. Attorney's fees incurred in enforcing a judgment are not included in costs collectible under this title unless otherwise provided by law. Attorney's fees incurred in enforcing a judgment are included as costs collectible under this title if the underlying judgment includes an award of attorney's fees to the judgment creditor pursuant to subparagraph (A) of paragraph (10) of subdivision (a) of Section 1033.5.[321]

685.050. (a) If a writ is issued pursuant to this title to enforce a judgment, the costs and interest to be satisfied in a levy under the writ are the following:

(1) The statutory fee for issuance of the writ.

(2) The amount of interest that has accrued from the date of entry or renewal of the judgment to the date of issuance of the writ, as adjusted for partial satisfactions, if the judgment creditor has filed an affidavit with the court clerk stating such amount.

(3) The amount of interest that accrues on the principal amount of the judgment remaining unsatisfied from the date of issuance of the writ until the date interest ceases to accrue.

(4) The levying officer's statutory costs for performing the duties under the writ.

(b) In a levy under the writ, the levying officer shall do all of the following:

(1) Collect the amount of costs and interest entered on the writ pursuant to paragraphs (1) and (2) of subdivision (a).

(2) Compute and collect the amount of additional interest required to be collected by paragraph (3) of subdivision (a) by reference to the daily interest entered on the writ. If amounts collected periodically do not fully satisfy the money judgment, the levying officer shall adjust the amount of daily interest to reflect the partial satisfactions, and make later collections by reference to the adjusted amount of daily interest.

(3) Determine and collect the amount of additional costs pursuant to paragraph (4) of subdivision (a).[625]

685.070. (a) The judgment creditor may claim under this section the following costs of enforcing a judgment, which shall not include costs exempted under this title:

(1) Statutory fees for preparing and issuing, and recording and indexing, an abstract of judgment or a certified copy of a judgment.

(2) Statutory fees for filing a notice of judgment lien on personal property.

(3) Statutory fees for issuing a writ for the enforcement of the judgment to the extent that the fees are not satisfied pursuant to Section 685.050.

(4) Statutory costs of the levying officer for performing the duties under a writ to the extent that the costs are not satisfied pursuant to Section 685.050 and the statutory fee of the levying officer for performing the duties under the Wage Garnishment Law to the extent that the fee has not been satisfied pursuant to the wage garnishment.

(5) Costs incurred in connection with any proceeding under Chapter 6 (commencing with Section 708.010) of Division 2 that have been approved as to amount, reasonableness, and necessity by the judge or referee conducting the proceeding.

(6) Attorney's fees, if allowed by Section 685.040.

(b) Before the judgment is fully satisfied but not later than two years after the costs have been incurred, the judgment creditor claiming costs under this section shall file a memorandum of costs with the court clerk and serve a copy on the judgment debtor. Service shall be made personally or by mail. The memorandum of costs shall be executed under oath by a person who has knowledge of the facts and shall state that to the person's best knowledge and belief the costs are correct, are reasonable and necessary, and have not been satisfied.

(c) Within 10 days after the memorandum of costs is served on the judgment debtor, the judgment debtor may apply to the court on noticed motion to have the costs taxed by the court. The notice of motion shall be served on the judgment creditor. Service shall be made personally or by mail. The court shall make an order allowing or disallowing the costs to the extent justified under the circumstances of the case.

(d) If no motion to tax costs is made within the time provided in subdivision (c), the costs claimed in the memorandum are allowed.

(e) If a memorandum of costs for the costs specified in subdivision (a) is filed at the same time as an application for a writ of execution, these statutory costs not already allowed by the court in an amount not to exceed one hundred dollars ($100) in the aggregate may be included in the amount specified in the writ of execution, subject to subsequent disallowance as ordered by the court pursuant to a motion to tax if filed by the debtor. The memorandum of costs shall contain the following statement: "The fees sought under this memorandum may be disallowed by a court upon a motion to tax filed by the debtor notwithstanding the fees having been included in the writ of execution." The inclusion of the above costs in the writ of execution or the pendency of the motion to tax on these costs shall not be cause for the clerk of the court to delay issuing the writ of execution or for the levying officer to delay enforcing the writ of execution.

(f) Section 1013, extending the time within which a right may be exercised or an act may be done, applies to this section.[852]

685.080. (a) The judgment creditor may claim costs authorized by Section 685.040 by noticed motion. The motion shall be made before the judgment is satisfied in full, but not later than two years after the costs have been incurred. The costs claimed under this section may include, but are not limited to, costs that may be claimed under Section 685.070 and costs incurred but not approved by the court or referee in a proceeding under Chapter 6 (commencing with Section 708.010) of Division 2.

(b) The notice of motion shall describe the costs claimed, shall state their amount, and shall be supported by an affidavit of a person who has knowledge of the facts stating that to the person's best knowledge and belief the costs are correct, are reasonable and necessary, and have not been satisfied. The notice of motion shall be served on the judgment debtor. Service shall be made personally or by mail.

(c) The court shall make an order allowing or disallowing the costs to the extent justified under the circumstances of the case.[170]

685.090. (a) Costs are added to and become a part of the judgment:

(1) Upon the filing of an order allowing the costs pursuant to this chapter.

(2) If a memorandum of costs is filed pursuant to Section 685.070 and no motion to tax is made, upon the expiration of the time for making the motion.

(3) As specified in Section 685.095.

(b) The costs added to the judgment pursuant to this section are included in the principal amount of the judgment remaining unsatisfied.

(c) If a writ or earnings withholding order is outstanding at the time the costs are added to the judgment pursuant to this section, the levying officer shall add the amount of those costs to the amount to be collected pursuant to the writ or earnings withholding order if the levying officer receives either of the following before the writ or earnings withholding order is returned:

(1) A certified copy of the court order allowing the costs.

(2) A certificate from the clerk of the court that the costs have been added to the judgment where the costs have been added to the judgment after a memorandum of costs has been filed pursuant to Section 685.070 and no motion to tax has been made within the time allowed for making the motion.

(d) The levying officer shall include the costs described in subdivision (c) in the amount of the sale or collection distributed to the judgment creditor only if the levying officer receives the certified copy of the court order or the clerk's certificate before the distribution is made.[346]

685.095. When a writ is served by a levying officer or registered process server, the costs for that service, as determined pursuant to Section 1033.5, shall be added to and become part of the judgment.[255]

685.100. (a) Except as otherwise provided by law:

(1) As a prerequisite to the performance by the levying officer of a duty under this title, the judgment creditor shall deposit a sum of money with the levying officer sufficient to pay the costs of performing the duty.

(2) As a prerequisite to the taking of property into custody by the levying officer, whether by keeper or otherwise, the judgment creditor shall deposit with the levying officer a sum of money sufficient to pay the costs of taking the property and keeping it safely for a period not to exceed 15 days. If continuation of the custody of

the property is required, the levying officer shall, from time to time, demand orally or in writing that the judgment creditor deposit additional amounts to cover estimated costs for periods not to exceed 30 days each. A written demand may be mailed or delivered to the judgment creditor. The judgment creditor has not less than three business days after receipt of the demand within which to comply with the demand. If the amount demanded is not paid within the time specified in the oral or written demand, the levying officer shall release the property.

(b) The levying officer is not liable for failure to take or hold property unless the judgment creditor has complied with the provisions of this section.[170]

685.110. Nothing in this chapter affects the law relating to prejudgment interest.[170]

Chapter 6: Enforcement After Death of Judgment Creditor or Judgment Debtor

Chapter 6 added by Stats. 1982, Ch. 1364, Sec. 2.

686.010. After the death of the judgment creditor, the judgment may be enforced as provided in this title by the judgment creditor's executor or administrator or successor in interest.[171]

686.020. After the death of the judgment debtor, enforcement of a judgment against property in the judgment debtor's estate is governed by the Probate Code, and not by this title.[266]

Chapter 7: Levying Officers

Chapter 7 added by Stats. 1982, Ch. 1364, Sec. 2.

687.010. (a) The judgment creditor shall give the levying officer instructions in writing. The instructions shall be signed by the judgment creditor's attorney of record or, if the judgment creditor does not have an attorney of record, by the judgment creditor. The instructions shall contain the information needed or requested by the levying officer to comply with this title, including, but not limited to, all of the following:

(1) An adequate description of any property to be levied upon.

(2) A statement whether the property is a dwelling.

(3) If the property is a dwelling, whether it is real or personal property.

(4) The name of the judgment debtor. If the judgment debtor is other than a natural person, the type of legal entity shall be stated.

(b) Subject to subdivision (c), the levying officer shall act in accordance with the written instructions to the extent the actions are taken in conformance with the provisions of this title.

(c) Except to the extent the levying officer has actual knowledge that the information is incorrect, the levying officer may rely on any information contained in the written instructions.

(d) The levying officer instructions may be transmitted electronically to the levying officer pursuant to Chapter 2 (commencing with Section 263) of Title 4 of Part 1.

(e) If the instructions directing the levying officer to perform a levy are accompanied by a writ of execution for money, possession, or sale of personal or real property issued by the court as an electronic record, as defined in subdivision (b) of Section 263.1, or a document printed from an electronic record issued by the court, the instructions shall also include all of the following information, as stated in the writ:

(1) The date of issuance of the writ.

(2) The name of each judgment creditor and judgment debtor.

(3) The amount of the total judgment for money, a description of the property subject to a judgment for possession or sale, or both the amount and the description.

(4) A statement indicating that the accompanying writ is either of the following:

(A) An original writ, or a copy of the original writ issued by the court as an electronic record, not already in the possession of the levying officer.

(B) A copy of the original writ already in possession of the levying officer.

(f) Except to the extent the levying officer has actual knowledge that the information in the electronic writ has been altered, the levying officer may proceed in the same manner as if in possession of a paper version of the original writ.[688]

687.020. (a) As used in this section, "instrument" means a check, draft, money order, or other order for the withdrawal of money from a financial institution, the United States, any state, or any public entity within any state.

(b) If an instrument is payable to the judgment debtor on demand and comes into the possession of a levying officer pursuant to this title, the levying officer shall promptly endorse and present the instrument for payment.

(c) The levying officer shall endorse the instrument by writing on the instrument (1) the name of the judgment debtor, (2) the name and official title of the levying officer, (3) the title of the court where the judgment is entered, and (4) the date of entry of the judgment and where entered in the records of the court. The endorsement is as valid as if the instrument were endorsed by the judgment debtor. No financial institution or public entity on which the instrument is drawn is liable to any person for payment of the instrument to the levying officer rather than to the judgment debtor by reason of the endorsement. No levying officer is liable by reason of endorsing, presenting, and obtaining payment of the instrument.

(d) If it appears from the face of the instrument that it has been tendered to the judgment debtor in satisfaction of a claim or demand and that endorsement of the instrument is considered a release and satisfaction by the judgment debtor of the claim or demand, the levying officer shall not endorse the instrument unless the judgment debtor has first endorsed it to the levying officer. If the judgment debtor does not endorse the instrument to the levying officer, the levying officer shall hold the instrument for 30 days and is not liable to the judgment debtor or to any other person for delay in presenting it for payment. At the end of the 30-day holding period, the levying officer shall return the instrument to the maker.[170]

687.030. Except as otherwise provided by statute, where the method of levy upon property requires that the property be taken into custody or where the levying officer is otherwise directed to take property into custody, the levying officer may do so by any of the following methods:

(a) Removing the property to a place of safekeeping.
(b) Installing a keeper.
(c) Otherwise obtaining possession or control of the property.[170]

687.040. (a) The levying officer or registered process server is not liable for actions taken in conformance with the provisions of this title, including actions taken in conformance with the provisions of this title in reliance on information contained in the written instructions of the judgment creditor, or in reliance on information provided to the levying officer by a registered process server pursuant to subdivision (d) of Section 699.080 or subdivision (e) of Section 706.101 or subdivision (b) of Section 715.040 or other provision, except to the extent the levying officer or registered process server has actual knowledge that the information is incorrect. Nothing in this subdivision limits any liability the judgment creditor may have if the levying officer or registered process server acts on the basis of incorrect information given in the written instructions.
(b) Unless the levying officer is negligent in the care or handling of the property, the levying officer is not liable to either the judgment debtor or the judgment creditor for loss by fire, theft, injury, or damage of any kind to personal property while (1) in the possession of the levying officer either in a warehouse or other storage place or in the custody of a keeper or (2) in transit to or from a warehouse or other storage place.[182]

687.050. The levying officer has a special lien, dependent upon possession, on personal property levied upon in the amount of the levying officer's costs for which an advance has not been made.[170]

Chapter 8: Enforcement of State Tax Liability

Chapter 8 added by Stats. 1982, Ch. 1364, Sec. 2.

Article 1: Enforcement Pursuant to Warrant or Notice of Levy

Article 1 added by Stats. 1982, Ch. 1364, Sec. 2.

688.010. A proceeding for the purpose of the remedies provided under this article is a limited civil case if (a) the amount of liability sought to be collected does not exceed the maximum amount in controversy for a limited civil case provided in Section 85, and (b) the legality of the liability being enforced is not contested by the person against whom enforcement is sought.[594]

688.020. (a) Except as otherwise provided by statute, if a warrant may properly be issued by the state, or by a department or agency of the state, pursuant to any provision of the Public Resources Code, Revenue and Taxation Code, or Unemployment Insurance Code, and the warrant may be levied with the same effect as a levy pursuant to a writ of execution, the state or the department or agency of the state authorized to issue the warrant may use any of the remedies available to a judgment creditor, including, but not limited to, those provided in Chapter 6 (commencing with Section 708.010) of Division 2.
(b) The proper court for the enforcement of those remedies is a court of any of the following counties:

(1) The county where the debtor resides.

(2) The county where the property against which enforcement is sought is located.

(3) If the debtor does not reside in this state, any county of this state.

(4) This section shall become operative on January 1, 2014.[612]

688.030. (a) If pursuant to any provision of the Public Resources Code, Revenue and Taxation Code (excluding Sections 3201 to 3204, inclusive), or Unemployment Insurance Code, property is levied upon pursuant to a warrant or notice of levy issued by the state or by a department or agency of the state for the collection of a liability:

(1) If the debtor is a natural person, the debtor is entitled to the same exemptions to which a judgment debtor is entitled. Except as provided in subdivisions (b) and (c), the claim of exemption shall be made, heard, and determined as provided in Chapter 4 (commencing with Section 703.010) of Division 2 in the same manner as if the property were levied upon under a writ of execution.

(2) A third person may claim ownership or the right to possession of the property or a security interest in or lien on the property. Except as provided in subdivisions (b) and (c) or as otherwise provided by statute, the third-party claim shall be made, heard, and determined as provided in Division 4 (commencing with Section 720.010) in the same manner as if the property were levied upon under a writ of execution.

(b) In the case of a levy pursuant to a notice of levy:

(1) The claim of exemption or the third-party claim shall be filed with the state department or agency that issued the notice of levy.

(2) The state department or agency that issued the notice of levy shall perform the duties of the levying officer, except that the state department or agency need not give itself the notices that the levying officer is required to serve on a judgment creditor or creditor or the notices that a judgment creditor or creditor is required to give to the levying officer. The state department or agency in performing the duties of the levying officer under this paragraph has no obligation to search public records or otherwise seek to determine whether any lien or encumbrance exists on property sold or collected.

(c) A claim of exemption or a third-party claim pursuant to this section shall be heard and determined in the superior court in the county where the property levied upon is located.

(d) This section shall become operative on January 1, 2014.[613]

688.040. For the purpose of this article, as used in this title:

(a) "Judgment creditor" or "creditor" means the state or the department or agency of the state seeking to collect the liability.

(b) "Judgment debtor" or "debtor" means the debtor from whom the liability is sought to be collected.[170]

688.050. For the purpose of applying Section 694.080, 703.050, or 703.100, the date of creation of a tax lien is the earliest of the following times:

(a) The time when a notice of state tax lien is recorded or filed pursuant to Chapter 14 (commencing with Section 7150) of Division 7 of Title 1 of the Government Code.

(b) The time when the property is levied upon pursuant to a warrant or notice of levy or notice to withhold issued by the state or by a department or agency of the state.

(c) The time when any other act is performed that creates or perfects a lien on specific property as distinguished from a lien on the debtor's property generally.[170]

Article 2: Enforcement of Judgment for Taxes

Article 2 added by Stats. 1982, Ch. 1364, Sec. 2.

688.110. Except as otherwise provided by statute, if a judgment is entered on a claim for taxes by a public entity, the judgment is enforceable pursuant to this title in the same manner as any other money judgment.[170]

Chapter 9: Enforcement of Support Judgments

Chapter 9 added by Stats. 1996, Ch. 957, Sec. 4.

689.010. For the purpose of the remedies provided under this chapter, jurisdiction is conferred upon the superior court.[373]

689.020. (a) Except as otherwise provided by statute, whenever a warrant may properly be issued by a local child support agency pursuant to Section 17522 of the Family Code, and the warrant may be levied with the same effect as a levy pursuant to a writ of execution, the local child support agency may use any of the remedies available to a judgment creditor, including, but not limited to, those provided in Chapter 6 (commencing with Section 708.010) of Division 2.

(b) The proper court for the enforcement of the remedies provided under this chapter is the superior court in the county where the local child support agency enforcing the support obligation is located.[446]

689.030. (a) Whenever the local child support agency, pursuant to Section 17522 of the Family Code, levies upon property pursuant to a warrant or notice of levy for the collection of a support obligation:

(1) If the debtor is a natural person, the debtor is entitled to the same exemptions to which a judgment debtor is entitled. Except as provided in subdivisions (b) and (c), the claim of exemption shall be made, heard, and determined as provided in Chapter 4 (commencing with Section 703.010) of Division 2 in the same manner as if the property were levied upon under a writ of execution.

(2) A third person may claim ownership or the right to possession of the property or a security interest in or lien on the property. Except as provided in subdivisions (b) and (c) or as otherwise provided by statute, the third-party claim shall be made, heard, and determined as provided in Division 4 (commencing with Section 720.010) in the same manner as if the property were levied upon under a writ of execution.

(b) In the case of a warrant or notice of levy issued pursuant to Section 17522 of the Family Code, the claim of exemption or the third-party claim shall be filed with the local child support agency that issued the warrant or notice of levy.

(c) A claim of exemption or a third-party claim pursuant to this section shall be heard and determined in the court specified in Section 689.010 in the county where the local child support agency enforcing the support obligation is located.[447]

689.040. (a) Notwithstanding any other provision of law, in the case of a writ of execution issued by a court of competent jurisdiction pursuant to Chapter 3 (commencing with Section 699.010) and Chapter 5 (commencing with Section 706.010) of Division 2, the local child support agency, when enforcing a support obligation pursuant to Division 17 (commencing with Section 17000) of the Family Code, may perform the duties of the levying officer, except that the local child support agency need not give itself the notices that the levying officer is required to serve on a judgment creditor or creditor or the notices that a judgment creditor or creditor is required to give to the levying officer.
(b) Notwithstanding subdivision (a) of Section 700.140, if the writ of execution is for a deposit or credits or personal property in the possession or under the control of a bank or savings and loan association, the local child support agency may deliver or mail the writ of execution to a centralized location designated by the bank or savings and loan association. If the writ of execution is received at the designated central location, it will apply to all deposits and credits and personal property held by the bank or savings and loan association regardless of the location of that property.[448]

689.050. For the purpose of this chapter:
(a) "Judgment creditor" or "creditor" means the local child support agency seeking to collect a child or spousal support obligation pursuant to a support order.
(b) "Judgment debtor" or "debtor" means the debtor from whom the support obligation is sought to be collected.[449]

Chapter 10: Enforcement of Judgments by Labor Commissioner

Chapter 10 added by Stats. 2015, Ch. 803, Sec. 1.

690.020. For the purpose of the remedies provided under this chapter, jurisdiction is conferred upon the superior court.[721]

690.030. (a) Except as otherwise provided by statute, whenever a warrant or notice of levy may properly be issued by the Labor Commissioner pursuant to Section 96.8 of the Labor Code, and the warrant may be levied with the same effect as a levy pursuant to a writ of execution, the Labor Commissioner may use any of the remedies available to a judgment creditor, including, but not limited to, those provided in Chapter 6 (commencing with Section 708.010) of Division 2.
(b) The proper court for the enforcement of the remedies provided under this chapter is the superior court of any of the following counties:
(1) The county where the employee resides.
(2) The county where the judgment debtor resides.
(3) The county where the person against whom the levy or warrant was issued resides.[721]

690.040. (a) Whenever the Labor Commissioner, pursuant to Section 96.8 of the Labor Code, levies upon property pursuant to a warrant or notice of levy for the collection of an unsatisfied judgment or award:

(1) If the debtor is a natural person, the debtor is entitled to the same exemptions to which a judgment debtor is entitled. Except as provided in subdivisions (b) and (c), the claim of exemption shall be made, heard, and determined as provided in Chapter 4 (commencing with Section 703.010) of Division 2 in the same manner as if the property were levied upon under a writ of execution.

(2) A third person may claim ownership or the right to possession of the property or a security interest in or lien on the property. Except as provided in subdivisions (b) and (c) or as otherwise provided by statute, the third-party claim shall be made, heard, and determined as provided in Division 4 (commencing with Section 720.010) in the same manner as if the property were levied upon under a writ of execution.

(b) In the case of a warrant or notice of levy issued pursuant to Section 96.8 of the Labor Code, the claim of exemption or the third-party claim shall be filed with the Labor Commissioner.

(c) A claim of exemption or a third-party claim pursuant to this section shall be heard and determined in a superior court specified in subdivision (b) of Section 690.030.[721]

690.050. (a) Notwithstanding any other law, in the case of a writ of execution issued by a court of competent jurisdiction pursuant to Chapter 3 (commencing with Section 699.010) and Chapter 5 (commencing with Section 706.010) of Division 2, the Labor Commissioner, when collecting an unsatisfied judgment or award pursuant to Section 96.8 of the Labor Code, may perform the duties of the levying officer, except that the Labor Commissioner need not give himself or herself the notices that the levying officer is required to serve on a judgment creditor or the notices that a judgment creditor is required to give to the levying officer.

(b) Notwithstanding subdivision (a) of Section 700.140 and Sections 700.150, 700.160, and 700.170, if the levy is for a deposit, credits, money, or property in the possession or under the control of a bank or savings and loan association or for an account receivable or other general intangible owed to the judgment debtor by an account debtor, the Labor Commissioner may deliver or mail a notice of levy to a centralized location designated by the bank or savings and loan association or, in the case of an account receivable or other general intangible, to the agent for service of process of the account debtor. If the notice of levy is received at the designated central location for the bank or savings and loan association, the notice of levy will apply to all deposits, credits, money, and personal property held by the bank or savings and loan association regardless of the location of that property. The notice of levy may be issued directly by the Labor Commissioner, whether or not a court has issued a writ of execution, and shall contain all of the information required to be included in a writ of execution under Section 699.520 and in a notice of levy under Section 699.540.[721]

Chapter 20: Transitional Provisions

Chapter 20 added by Stats. 1982, Ch. 1364, Sec. 2.

694.010. As used in this chapter:

(a) "Operative date" means July 1, 1983.
(b) "Prior law" means the applicable law in effect on June 30, 1983.[170]

694.020. Except as otherwise provided in this chapter, this title on and after its operative date applies to all proceedings commenced prior thereto unless in the opinion of the court application of a particular provision of this title would substantially interfere with the effective conduct of the proceedings or the rights of the parties or other interested persons, in which case the particular provision of this title does not apply and prior law applies.[170]

694.030. (a) Except for a judgment described in Section 683.310 or 683.320, the period for enforcement of a money judgment or a judgment for possession or sale of property entered prior to the operative date is governed on and after the operative date by Chapter 3 (commencing with Section 683.010).
(b) Notwithstanding subdivision (a), even though a judgment to which subdivision (a) applies is not renewable pursuant to Chapter 3 (commencing with Section 683.010) because the time for filing an application for renewal has expired, the judgment may be renewed under Chapter 3 (commencing with Section 683.010) if the court which entered the judgment determines, on noticed motion filed within two years after the operative date, that authority to enforce the judgment after the 10-year period provided in former Section 681 would have been granted if a motion had been made under former Section 685 and the court, in its discretion, makes an order authorizing the renewal of the judgment. The notice of motion shall be served personally or by mail on the judgment debtor.[170]

694.040. (a) Except as provided in subdivision (c), property levied upon or otherwise subjected to process for enforcement of a money judgment or a judgment for possession or sale of property prior to the operative date is subject to prior law relating to sale or delivery of possession.
(b) The duties to be performed in the execution of a writ or order for the enforcement of a money judgment or a judgment for possession or sale of property that is served prior to the operative date are governed by prior law.
(c) The manner of payment at a sale of property pursuant to a writ or order after the operative date is governed by Section 701.590.[170]

694.050. (a) Except as provided in subdivision (b), property levied upon, or property to be sold upon which foreclosure or other proceedings for sale have been commenced, prior to the operative date that would have been sold subject to the right of redemption under prior law shall be sold subject to the right of redemption and may be redeemed as provided by prior law.
(b) If the judgment creditor and judgment debtor agree in writing, property described in subdivision (a) may be sold as provided in this title rather than subject to the right of redemption.
(c) Property sold prior to the operative date subject to the right of redemption under prior law may be redeemed as provided by prior law.[170]

694.060. Notwithstanding Section 708.230, an action may be commenced pursuant to Section 708.210 within one year after the operative date if the action could have been commenced under prior law on the day before the operative date.[170]

694.070. (a) A third-party claim filed prior to the operative date is governed by prior law.
(b) A demand for a third-party claim served on a secured party prior to the operative date is governed by prior law.

694.080. The exemptions from enforcement of a money judgment provided by this title do not apply to property levied upon or otherwise subjected to a lien prior to the operative date. Whether such property is exempt is determined by the exemptions provided by law at the time the lien was created.[170]

694.090. On and after the operative date, a declaration of homestead made under prior law pursuant to Title 5 (commencing with Section 1237) of Part 4 of Division 2 of the Civil Code is effective only to the extent provided in Article 5 (commencing with Section 704.910) of Chapter 4 of Division 2.[170]

DIVISION 2: ENFORCEMENT OF MONEY JUDGMENTS

Division 2 added by Stats. 1982, Ch. 1364, Sec. 2.

Chapter 1: General Provisions

Chapter 1 added by Stats. 1982, Ch. 1364, Sec. 2.

Article 1: Property Subject to Enforcement of Money Judgment
Article 1 added by Stats. 1982, Ch. 1364, Sec. 2.

695.010. (a) Except as otherwise provided by law, all property of the judgment debtor is subject to enforcement of a money judgment.
(b) If property of the judgment debtor was attached in the action but was transferred before entry of the money judgment in favor of the judgment creditor, the property is subject to enforcement of the money judgment so long as the attachment lien remains effective.[215]

695.020. (a) Community property is subject to enforcement of a money judgment as provided in the Family Code.
(b) Unless the provision or context otherwise requires, if community property that is subject to enforcement of a money judgment is sought to be applied to the satisfaction of a money judgment:
(1) Any provision of this division that applies to the property of the judgment debtor or to obligations owed to the judgment debtor also applies to the community property interest of the spouse of the judgment debtor and to obligations owed to the other spouse that are community property.
(2) Any provision of this division that

applies to property in the possession or under the control of the judgment debtor also applies to community property in the possession or under the control of the spouse of the judgment debtor.[297]

695.030. (a) Except as otherwise provided by statute, property of the judgment debtor that is not assignable or transferable is not subject to enforcement of a money judgment.
(b) The following property is subject to enforcement of a money judgment:
(1) An interest in a trust, to the extent provided by law.
(2) A cause of action for money or property that is the subject of a pending action or special proceeding.[249]

695.035. (a) A lessee's interest in real property may be applied to the satisfaction of a money judgment in any of the following circumstances:
(1) If the lessee has the right voluntarily to sublet the property or assign the interest in the lease.
(2) If the lessee has the right voluntarily to sublet the property or assign the interest in the lease subject to standards or conditions and the purchaser at the execution sale or other assignee agrees to comply with the standards or conditions that would have had to be complied with had the lessee voluntarily sublet the property or assigned the interest in the lease.
(3) If the lessee has the right voluntarily to sublet the property or assign the interest in the lease with the consent of the lessor, in which case the obligation of the lessor to consent to the assignment is subject to the same standard that would apply had the lessee voluntarily sublet the property or assigned the interest in the lease.
(4) In any other case, if the lessor consents in writing.
(b) A provision in a lease for the termination or modification of the lease upon an involuntary transfer or assignment of the lessee's interest is ineffective to the extent that such provision would prevent the application of the lessee's interest to the satisfaction of the money judgment under subdivision (a).[170]

695.040. Property that is not subject to enforcement of a money judgment may not be levied upon or in any other manner applied to the satisfaction of a money judgment. If property that is not subject to enforcement of a money judgment has been levied upon, the property may be released pursuant to the claim of exemption procedure provided in Article 2 (commencing with Section 703.510) of Chapter 4.[170]

695.050. A money judgment against a public entity is not enforceable under this division if the money judgment is subject to Chapter 1 (commencing with Section 965) of, or Article 1 (commencing with Section 970) of Chapter 2 of, Part 5 of Division 3.6 of Title 1 of the Government Code.[170]

695.060. Except as provided in Section 708.630, a license issued by a public entity to engage in any business, profession, or activity is not subject to enforcement of a money judgment.[170]

695.070. (a) Notwithstanding the transfer or encumbrance of property subject to a lien created under this division, if the property remains subject to the lien after the transfer or encumbrance, the money judgment may be enforced against the property in the same manner and to the same extent as

if it had not been transferred or encumbered.
(b) If the judgment debtor dies after the transfer of property that remains subject to a lien created under this division, the money judgment may be enforced against the property as provided in subdivision (a).[267]

Article 2: Amount to Satisfy Money Judgment
Article 2 added by Stats. 1982, Ch. 1364, Sec. 2.

695.210. The amount required to satisfy a money judgment is the total amount of the judgment as entered or renewed with the following additions and subtractions:
(a) The addition of costs added to the judgment pursuant to Section 685.090.
(b) The addition of interest added to the judgment as it accrues pursuant to Sections 685.010 to 685.030, inclusive.
(c) The subtraction of the amount of any partial satisfactions of the judgment.
(d) The subtraction of the amount of any portion of the judgment that is no longer enforceable.[327]

695.211. (a) Every money judgment or order for child support shall provide notice that interest on arrearages accrues at the legal rate.
(b) The notice provisions required by this section shall be incorporated in the appropriate Judicial Council forms.
(c) Upon implementation of the California Child Support Automation System prescribed in Chapter 4 (commencing with Section 10080) of Part 1 of Division 9 of the Welfare and Institutions Code and certification of the California Child Support Automation System by the United States Department of Health and Human Services, whenever a statement of account is issued by the local child support agency in any child support action, the statement shall include a statement of an amount of current support, arrears, and interest due.[450]

695.215. Payment in satisfaction of a money judgment, including payment of a severable portion of the money judgment, interest thereon, and associated costs, does not constitute a waiver of the right to appeal, except to the extent that the payment is the product of compromise or is coupled with an agreement not to appeal. Payment in satisfaction of a severable portion of a money judgment, interest thereon, and associated costs, does not constitute a waiver of the right to appeal other portions of the money judgment.[753]

695.220. Money received in satisfaction of a money judgment, except a money judgment for support, is to be credited as follows:
(a) The money is first to be credited against the amounts described in subdivision (b) of Section 685.050 that are collected by the levying officer.
(b) Any remaining money is next to be credited against any fee due the court pursuant to Section 6103.5 or 68511.3 of the Government Code, which are to be remitted to the court by the levying officer.
(c) Any remaining money is next to be credited against the accrued interest that remains unsatisfied.
(d) Any remaining money is to be credited against the principal amount of the judgment remaining unsatisfied. If the judgment is payable in installments, the remaining money is to be credited

against the matured installments in the order in which they matured.[331]

695.221. Satisfaction of a money judgment for support shall be credited as follows:
(a) The money shall first be credited against the current month's support.
(b) Any remaining money shall next be credited against the principal amount of the judgment remaining unsatisfied. If the judgment is payable in installments, the remaining money shall be credited against the matured installments in the order in which they matured.
(c) Any remaining money shall be credited against the accrued interest that remains unsatisfied.
(d) In cases enforced pursuant to Part D (commencing with Section 651) of Subchapter 4 of Chapter 7 of Title 42 of the United States Code, if a lump-sum payment is collected from a support obligor who has money judgments for support owing to more than one family, effective September 1, 2006, all support collected shall be distributed pursuant to guidelines developed by the Department of Child Support Services.
(e) Support collections received between January 1, 2009, and April 30, 2020, inclusive, shall be distributed by the Department of Child Support Services as follows:
(1) Notwithstanding subdivisions (a), (b), and (c), a collection received as a result of a federal tax refund offset shall first be credited against the principal amount of past due support that has been assigned to the state pursuant to Section 11477 of the Welfare and Institutions Code and federal law and then any interest due on that past due support, prior to the principal amount of any other past due support remaining unsatisfied and then any interest due on that past due support.
(2) The following shall be the order of distribution of child support collections through September 30, 2000, except for federal tax refund offset collections, for child support received for families and children who are former recipients of Aid to Families with Dependent Children (AFDC) program benefits or former recipients of Temporary Assistance for Needy Families (TANF) program benefits:
(A) The money shall first be credited against the current month's support.
(B) Any remaining money shall next be credited against interest that accrued on arrearages owed to the family or children \since leaving the AFDC program or the TANF program and then the arrearages.
(C) Any remaining money shall next be credited against interest that accrued on arrearages owed during the time the family or children received benefits under the AFDC program or the TANF program and then the arrearages.
(D) Any remaining money shall next be credited against interest that accrued on arrearages owed to the family or children prior to receiving benefits from the AFDC program or the TANF program and then the arrearages.
(f) Support collections received on or after May 1, 2020, shall be distributed by the Department of Child Support Services in accordance with Section 657(a)(2)(B) of Title 42 of the United States Code, as amended by Section 7301(b)(1) of the federal Deficit Reduction Act of 2005, in such a manner as to distribute all support collections

to families first to the maximum extent permitted by federal law.[785]

Chapter 2: Liens

Chapter 2 added by Stats. 1982, Ch. 1364, Sec. 2.

Article 1: General Provisions

Article 1 added by Stats. 1982, Ch. 1364, Sec. 2.

697.010. Except as otherwise provided by statute, a lien created under this division or under Title 6.5 (commencing with Section 481.010) (attachment) is a lien for the amount required to satisfy the money judgment.[170]

697.020. (a) If a lien is created on property pursuant to Title 6.5 (commencing with Section 481.010) (attachment) and after judgment in the action a lien is created pursuant to this division on the same property under the same claim while the earlier lien is in effect, the priority of the later lien relates back to the date the earlier lien was created.
(b) If a lien is created on property pursuant to this division and a later lien of the same or a different type is created pursuant to this division on the same property under the same judgment while the earlier lien is in effect, the priority of the later lien relates back to the date the earlier lien was created.
(c) Nothing in this section affects priorities or rights of third persons established while the earlier lien was in effect under the law governing the earlier lien.[170]

697.030. Subject to Sections 683.180 to 683.200, inclusive, and to Section 697.040, except where a shorter period is provided by statute, a lien created pursuant to this title is effective during the period of enforceability of the judgment.[170]

697.040. (a) If enforcement of the judgment is stayed on appeal by the giving of a sufficient undertaking under Chapter 2 (commencing with Section 916) of Title 13:
(1) Existing liens created under this division are extinguished.
(2) New liens may not be created under this division during the period of the stay.
(b) Unless the court otherwise expressly orders, a stay of enforcement of the judgment under Section 918 does not extinguish or prevent the creation of a lien under Article 2 (commencing with Section 697.310) or Article 3 (commencing with Section 697.510); but, unless the court otherwise expressly orders, no other liens may be created or continued under this division during the period of the stay of enforcement.
(c) Unless the court expressly orders otherwise, if enforcement of the judgment is stayed pursuant to Section 1699 or 1710.50:
(1) Existing liens created under this division are extinguished.
(2) New liens may not be created under this division during the period of the stay.[170]

697.050. If a lien created pursuant to this division is extinguished, property held subject to the lien shall be released unless the property is to be held under another lien or the property is ordered by the court to be held pending resolution of a dispute concerning its proper disposition.[170]

697.060. (a) An abstract or certified copy of a money judgment of a court of the United States that is enforceable in this state may be recorded to create a judgment lien on real property pursuant to Article 2 (commencing with Section 697.310).

(b) A notice of judgment lien based on a money judgment of a court of the United States that is enforceable in this state may be filed to create a judgment lien on personal property pursuant to Article 3 (commencing with Section 697.510).[170]

Article 2: Judgment Lien on Real Property
Article 2 added by Stats. 1982, Ch. 1364, Sec. 2.

697.310. (a) Except as otherwise provided by statute, a judgment lien on real property is created under this section by recording an abstract of a money judgment with the county recorder.

(b) Unless the money judgment is satisfied or the judgment lien is released, subject to Section 683.180 (renewal of judgment), a judgment lien created under this section continues until 10 years from the date of entry of the judgment.

(c) The creation and duration of a judgment lien under a money judgment entered pursuant to Section 117 or 582.5 of this code or Section 16380 of the Vehicle Code or under a similar judgment is governed by this section, notwithstanding that the judgment may be payable in installments.[395]

697.320. (a) A judgment lien on real property is created under this section by recording an abstract, a notice of support judgment, an interstate lien form promulgated by the federal Secretary of Health and Human Services pursuant to Section 652(a)(11) of Title 42 of the United States Code, or a certified copy of either of the following money judgments with the county recorder:

(1) A judgment for child, family, or spousal support payable in installments.

(2) A judgment entered pursuant to Section 667.7 (judgment against health care provider requiring periodic payments).

(b) Unless the money judgment is satisfied or the judgment lien is released, a judgment lien created under paragraph (1) of subdivision (a) or by recording an interstate lien form, as described in subdivision (a), continues during the period the judgment remains enforceable. Unless the money judgment is satisfied or the judgment lien is released, a judgment lien created under paragraph (2) of subdivision (a) continues for a period of 10 years from the date of its creation. The duration of a judgment lien created under paragraph (2) of subdivision (a) may be extended any number of times by recording, during the time the judgment lien is in existence, a certified copy of the judgment in the manner provided in this section for the initial recording; this rerecording has the effect of extending the duration of the judgment lien created under paragraph (2) of subdivision (a) until 10 years from the date of the rerecording.[521]

697.330. (a) In the case of a money judgment entered on an order, decision, or award made under Division 4 (commencing with Section 3200) of the Labor Code (workers' compensation):

(1) If the judgment is for a lump sum, a judgment lien on real property is created by recording an abstract of

the judgment as provided in Section 697.310 and, except as otherwise provided in Division 4 (commencing with Section 3200) of the Labor Code, the judgment lien is governed by the provisions applicable to a judgment lien created under Section 697.310.

(2) If the judgment is for the payment of money in installments, a judgment lien on real property is created by recording a certified copy of the judgment as provided in Section 697.320 and, except as otherwise provided in Division 4 (commencing with Section 3200) of the Labor Code, the lien is governed by the provisions applicable to a judgment lien created under Section 697.320.

(b) Nothing in this section limits or affects any provision of Division 4 (commencing with Section 3200) of the Labor Code.[170]

697.340. Except as provided in Section 704.950:

(a) A judgment lien on real property attaches to all interests in real property in the county where the lien is created (whether present or future, vested or contingent, legal or equitable) that are subject to enforcement of the money judgment against the judgment debtor pursuant to Article 1 (commencing with Section 695.010) of Chapter 1 at the time the lien was created, but does not reach rental payments, a leasehold estate with an unexpired term of less than two years, the interest of a beneficiary under a trust, or real property that is subject to an attachment lien in favor of the creditor and was transferred before judgment.

(b) If any interest in real property in the county on which a judgment lien could be created under subdivision (a) is acquired after the judgment lien was created, the judgment lien attaches to such interest at the time it is acquired.[216]

697.350. (a) Except as otherwise provided by statute, a judgment lien on real property is a lien for the amount required to satisfy the money judgment.

(b) A judgment lien on real property created under a money judgment payable in installments pursuant to Section 116.620 or 582.5 of this code or Section 16380 of the Vehicle Code or under a similar judgment is in the full amount required to satisfy the judgment, but the judgment lien may not be enforced for the amount of unmatured installments unless the court so orders.

(c) A judgment lien created pursuant to Section 697.320 is a lien for the amount of the installments as they mature under the terms of the judgment, plus accrued interest and the costs as they are added to the judgment pursuant to Chapter 5 (commencing with Section 685.010) of Division 1, and less the amount of any partial satisfactions, but does not become a lien for any installment until it becomes due and payable under the terms of the judgment.[617]

697.360. (a) If a judgment lien on real property has been created under a money judgment that is thereafter modified as to its amount, an abstract of the modified judgment or a certified copy of the order modifying the judgment may be recorded in the same manner as an abstract of judgment or a certified copy of the judgment is recorded to create a judgment lien.

(b) If a judgment lien on real property has been created under a money judgment that is thereafter modified to reduce its amount, the judgment lien continues under the terms of the judgment as modified, whether or not the modification is recorded as provided in subdivision (a).

(c) If a judgment lien on real property has been created under a money judgment that is thereafter modified to increase its amount, the judgment lien continues under the terms of the original judgment until such time as the modification is recorded as provided in subdivision (a). Upon such recording, the judgment lien extends to the judgment as modified, but the priority for the additional amount under the judgment as modified dates from the time the modification is recorded.

(d) Notwithstanding subdivision (c), if a judgment lien on real property has been created under a money judgment, by recording of an abstract of support judgment under paragraph (1) of subdivision (a) of Section 697.320, and the support order is thereafter modified to increase its amount, the judgment lien extends to the judgment as modified without the need for recording of another abstract of support judgment, but the priority for the additional amount under the judgment dates from the time the modification is effective.

(e) A support obligee shall respond in a timely manner to (1) a title or escrow company request for a demand statement needed to close an escrow relating to a support judgment lien, or (2) a support obligor who claims an error exists in the amount of alleged arrears.

(f) A support obligor who complies with the procedure specified in Division 5 (commencing with Section 724.010) shall be entitled to the remedies specified therein.[348]

697.370. (a) The judgment creditor may do either of the following:

(1) Release from the judgment lien all or a part of the real property subject to the lien.

(2) Subordinate to another lien or encumbrance the judgment lien on all or a part of the real property subject to the judgment lien.

(b) A release or subordination is sufficient if it is executed by the judgment creditor in the same manner as an acknowledgment of satisfaction of judgment and contains all of the following:

(1) A description of the real property being released or on which the lien is being subordinated. If the judgment debtor does not have an interest of record in the real property, the release or subordination shall show the name of the record owner. If all of the real property of the judgment debtor in a county in which the lien is recorded is being released from the judgment lien, or if the judgment debtor has no known interest in any real property in that county, the release shall, in lieu of containing a description of the property being released, contain a statement substantially as follows: "This is a release from the judgment lien described herein of all of the interests in real property in ____ County presently owned or hereafter acquired of the herein named judgment debtor subject to the lien."

(2) The date the judgment lien was created and where in the records of the county the abstract of judgment or certified copy of the judgment was

recorded to create the lien.

(3) The title of the court where the judgment is entered and the cause and number of the action.

(4) The date of entry of the judgment and of any subsequent renewals and where entered in the records of the court.

(5) The name and address of the judgment creditor, the judgment creditor's assignee, if any, and the judgment debtor whose interest in real property is released from the judgment lien or with respect to whom the judgment lien is subordinated.

(c) A release or subordination substantially complying with the requirements of this section is effective even though it contains minor errors that are not seriously misleading.

(d) The execution of a release or subordination of a judgment lien pursuant to this section does not release or subordinate the judgment lien as to judgment debtors not named in the release pursuant to paragraph (5) of subdivision (b).[254]

697.380. (a) As used in this section:

(1) "Installment judgment lien" means a judgment lien created under Section 697.320.

(2) "Lump-sum judgment lien" means a judgment lien created under Section 697. 310.

(b) Except as otherwise provided by law, the rules stated in this section govern the priorities of judgment liens on real property.

(c) A lump-sum judgment lien has priority over any other lump-sum judgment lien thereafter created.

(d) A lump-sum judgment lien has priority over an installment judgment lien as to all of the following:

(1) Installments that mature on the installment judgment after the lump-sum judgment lien is created.

(2) Interest that accrues on the installment judgment after the lump-sum judgment lien is created.

(3) Costs that are added to the installment judgment after the lump-sum judgment lien is created.

(e) An installment judgment lien has priority over a lump-sum judgment lien as to all of the following:

(1) Installments that have matured on the installment judgment before the lump-sum judgment lien is created.

(2) Interest that has accrued on the installment judgment before the lump-sum judgment lien is created.

(3) Costs that have been added to the installment judgment before the lump-sum judgment lien is created.

(f) If an installment judgment lien has been created and another installment judgment lien is thereafter created, the first installment judgment lien has priority over the second installment judgment lien as to the installments that have matured on the judgment at the time the second installment judgment lien is created, the interest that has accrued prior to that time on the judgment, and the costs that have been added prior to that time to the judgment pursuant to Chapter 5 (commencing with Section 685.010) of Division 1. Thereafter, priorities are determined by the time at which each installment matures on a judgment, the time the interest accrues on a judgment, and the time costs are added to a judgment pursuant to Chapter 5 (commencing with Section 685.010) of Division 1.

(g) For the purposes of this section, if two judgment liens attach to the same property at the same time under subdivision (b) of Section 697.340 (after-acquired property), the judgment lien that was first created has priority as to all amounts that are due and payable on that judgment at the time the property is acquired.[170]

697.390. If an interest in real property that is subject to a judgment lien is transferred or encumbered without satisfying or extinguishing the judgment lien:
(a) The interest transferred or encumbered remains subject to a judgment lien created pursuant to Section 697.310 in the same amount as if the interest had not been transferred or encumbered.
(b) The interest transferred or encumbered remains subject to a judgment lien created pursuant to Section 697.320 in the amount of the lien at the time of transfer or encumbrance plus interest thereafter accruing on such amount.[217]

697.400. (a) The judgment creditor, judgment debtor, or owner of real property subject to a judgment lien on real property created under Section 697.310, may record in the office of the county recorder an acknowledgment of satisfaction of judgment executed as provided in Section 724.060 or a court clerk's certificate of satisfaction of judgment issued pursuant to Section 724.100. Upon such recording, the judgment lien created under the judgment that has been satisfied is extinguished as a matter of record.
(b) The judgment creditor, judgment debtor, or owner of real property subject to a judgment lien on real property created under Section 697.320, may record in the office of the county recorder an acknowledgment of satisfaction of matured installments under an installment judgment if the acknowledgment is executed as provided in Section 724.250. Upon such recording, the judgment lien is extinguished as a matter of record to the extent of the satisfied installments described in the acknowledgment of satisfaction.
(c) The judgment creditor, the judgment debtor, or the owner of real property subject to a judgment lien, including a property owner described in Section 697.410, may record in the office of the county recorder a release or subordination of a judgment lien on real property if the release or subordination is executed as provided in Section 697.370.[170]

697.410. (a) If a recorded abstract of a money judgment or certified copy of a money judgment appears to create a judgment lien on real property of a person who is not the judgment debtor because the name of the property owner is the same as or similar to that of the judgment debtor, the erroneously identified property owner may deliver to the judgment creditor a written demand for a recordable document releasing the lien. The demand shall be accompanied by proof to the satisfaction of the judgment creditor that the property owner is not the judgment debtor and that the property is not subject to enforcement of the judgment against the judgment debtor.
(b) Within 15 days after receipt of the property owner's demand and proof satisfactory to the judgment creditor that the property owner is not the judgment debtor and that the property is not subject to enforcement of the judgment, the judgment creditor shall

deliver to the property owner a recordable document releasing the lien on the property of such owner. If the judgment creditor improperly fails to deliver a recordable document releasing the lien within the time allowed, the judgment creditor is liable to the property owner for all damages sustained by reason of such failure and shall also forfeit one hundred dollars ($100) to the property owner.

(c) If the judgment creditor does not deliver a recordable document pursuant to subdivision (b), the property owner may apply to the court on noticed motion for an order releasing the judgment lien on the property of such owner. Notice of motion shall be served on the judgment creditor. Service shall be made personally or by mail. Upon presentation of evidence to the satisfaction of the court that the property owner is not the judgment debtor and that the property is not subject to enforcement of the judgment, the court shall order the judgment creditor to prepare and deliver a recordable document releasing the lien or shall itself order the release of the judgment lien on the property of such owner. The court order may be recorded in the office of the county recorder with the same effect as the recordable document demanded by the property owner.

(d) The court shall award reasonable attorney's fees to the prevailing party in any proceeding maintained pursuant to this section.

(e) The damages provided by this section are not in derogation of any other damages or penalties to which an aggrieved person may be entitled by law.[170]

697.420. (a) A judgment creditor may apply to the court for an order reinstating a judgment lien on real property with the same priority it held immediately before it was released. Subject to subdivisions (b) and (c), the court shall grant the application. Upon entry of the order the clerk shall do the following:

(1) Note in the court's records that the judgment is no longer satisfied to the extent of the returned funds or property.

(2) Issue to the judgment creditor a certificate and notice of reinstatement of judgment lien. The certificate of reinstatement of judgment lien shall identify the judgment and parties, the unsatisfied judgment amount, and the relevant recording or filing information from the original abstract of judgment.

(b) (1) The application for reinstatement of a lien under subdivision (a) shall be filed with a declaration by the judgment creditor that includes and certifies all of the following:

(A) The title of the court, the case name and number, and the date and amount of the original judgment and any renewals thereof.

(B) A statement that the judgment creditor released a lien or liens in the reasonable belief that the money judgment was satisfied. This statement shall include:

(i) Information sufficient to identify the liens that were released, including the county or counties in which an abstract of judgment was recorded, and the recording dates and numbers of those recordings.

(ii) The details of any acknowledgment of full or partial satisfaction of judgment that was filed or entered as a result of the prior application of funds, including the date, county, and recording number of any acknowledgment of full or partial satisfaction of judgment recorded by the judgment creditor.

(C) A statement that after a lien was released, the judgment creditor was ordered pursuant to paragraph (2) or (3) of subdivision (d) of Section 703.580 to return to the judgment debtor property levied or wages garnished in satisfaction of the money judgment. A copy of the order shall be attached as an exhibit to the declaration.

(D) A statement that the judgment creditor returned, and the judgment debtor received, all property and wages ordered returned.

(E) A statement that but for the court's order pursuant to paragraph (2) or (3) of subdivision (d) of Section 703.580, the money judgment would have been fully satisfied or that the property returned to the judgment creditor was identified in a recorded acknowledgment of full or partial satisfaction of judgment.

(F) A statement that the judgment creditor is not appealing the order to return funds pursuant to subdivision (d) of Section 703.580.

(2) Knowingly certifying the accuracy of false information under paragraph (1) shall be subject to a civil penalty of not more than one thousand five hundred dollars ($1,500).

(c) (1) The judgment creditor shall serve upon the judgment debtor by first-class mail to the address verified pursuant to paragraph (2) of subdivision (b) of Section 684.130 a copy of the application for an order reinstating a released lien.

(2) The judgment debtor may, within 15 days of service of the application, file a declaration stating that the funds or property identified by the judgment debtor pursuant to subparagraph (D) of paragraph (1) of subdivision (b) have not been returned.

(3) If a declaration under paragraph (2) is filed, the court shall deny the application and the judgment creditor shall file a noticed motion to be heard by the court in order to reinstate a lien and its priority.

(4) If no objection is filed under this subdivision, the clerk's reinstatement of the lien and its priority shall be automatically effective.

(d) An application under this section shall be filed in the action in which the judgment creditor was ordered, pursuant to paragraph (2) or (3) of subdivision (d) of Section 703.580, to return to the judgment debtor property levied or wages garnished in satisfaction of the money judgment.

(e) Attorney's fees are not recoverable under this section.

(f) The judgment creditor may record the certificate in the same manner as an abstract of judgment, and that recordation shall have the effect of restoring the lien's priority as if the prior release or satisfaction had not occurred.

(g) This section shall become operative on July 1, 2026.[902]

Article 3: Judgment Lien on Personal Property

Article 3 added by Stats. 1982, Ch. 1364, Sec. 2.

697.510. (a) A judgment lien on personal property described in Section 697.530 is created by filing a notice of judgment lien in the office of the Secretary of State pursuant to this article.

A judgment lien may be created under this article only if the judgment is a money judgment that was first entered in this state after June 30, 1983. Except as provided in subdivision (b) of Section 697.540, a judgment lien may not be created under this article if the money judgment is payable in installments unless all of the installments under the judgment have become due and payable at the time the notice of judgment lien is filed.

(b) Except as otherwise provided in subdivision (c), (e), or (g), the judgment lien continues for five years from the date of filing.

(c) The effectiveness of a filed judgment lien lapses on the expiration of the period described in subdivision (b) unless, before the lapse, a continuation statement is filed pursuant to subdivision (d). Upon lapse, the judgment lien created by the filing of a notice pursuant to subdivision (a) ceases to be effective.

(d) A continuation statement may be filed only within the six-month period prior to the expiration of the five-year period specified in subdivision (b).

(e) A continuation statement that is not filed within the six-month period prescribed by subdivision (d) is ineffective. Upon timely filing of a continuation statement, the effectiveness of the initial notice of judgment lien continues for a period of five years commencing on the day on which the notice of judgment lien would have become ineffective in the absence of the filing. Upon the expiration of the five-year period, the notice of judgment lien lapses in the same manner as provided in subdivision (c), unless, before the lapse, another continuation statement is filed pursuant to subdivision (d). Succeeding continuation statements may be filed in the same manner to continue the effectiveness of the initial notice of judgment lien.

(f) For purposes of this section, "continuation statement" means an amendment of a notice of judgment lien that does both of the following:

(1) Identifies, by its file number, the initial notice of judgment lien to which it relates.

(2) Indicates that it is a continuation statement for, or that it is filed to continue the effectiveness of, the identified notice of judgment lien.

(g) (1) Notwithstanding any other provision of this section, the lien created by this section is extinguished at the earliest to occur of the following:

(A) The money judgment is satisfied.

(B) The period of enforceability of the judgment, including any extension thereof pursuant to Article 2 (commencing with Section 683.110) of Chapter 3 of Division 1, terminates.

(C) The judgment lien is terminated or released.

(2) If the lien created by this section is extinguished, the judgment creditor shall file a statement of release within 20 days after the judgment creditor receives an authenticated demand from the judgment debtor. For the purposes of this subdivision, "authenticated demand" means either a signed written demand or an executed or otherwise encrypted demand delivered electronically that identifies the judgment debtor and the demand for a statement of release.

(h) If a judgment creditor does not file a statement of release pursuant to subdivision (g), the person who made the demand may apply to the court on noticed motion for an order releasing the judgment lien. Notice of the motion shall be filed in the county where the judgment was rendered and notice of the motion shall be served on the judgment creditor. Service shall be made personally or by mail. Upon presentation of evidence to the satisfaction of the court that the judgment lien has been extinguished pursuant to subdivision (g), the court shall order the judgment creditor to prepare and file the statement of release or shall itself order the release of the judgment lien. The court order may be filed in the office of the Secretary of State and shall have the same effect as the statement of release demanded under subdivision (g).

(i) The court shall award reasonable attorney's fees to the prevailing party in any action or proceeding maintained pursuant to this section.

(j) Nothing in this section is in derogation of any other relief to which an aggrieved person may be entitled by law.

(k) The fees for filing and indexing a record under this section, or for responding to a request for information from the filing office, are as set forth in Section 9525 of the Commercial Code.

(l) The provisions of Sections 9522 and 9523 of the Commercial Code shall apply to a notice of judgment lien to the same extent as to a filed financing statement.

(m) Terms for which definitions are not set forth in Division 1 (commencing with Section 680.010) have the definitions set forth in the Commercial Code.[622]

697.520. A judgment lien on personal property may be created pursuant to this article as an alternative or in addition to a lien created by levy under a writ of execution pursuant to Chapter 3 (commencing with Section 699.010) or by use of an enforcement procedure provided by Chapter 6 (commencing with Section 708.010).[170]

697.530. (a) A judgment lien on personal property is a lien on all interests in the following personal property that are subject to enforcement of the money judgment against the judgment debtor pursuant to Article 1 (commencing with Section 695.010) of Chapter 1 at the time when the lien is created if the personal property is, at that time, any of the following:

(1) Accounts receivable, and the judgment debtor is located in this state.

(2) Chattel paper, as defined in paragraph (11) of subdivision (a) of Section 9102 of the Commercial Code, and the judgment debtor is located in this state.

(3) Equipment, located within this state.

(4) Farm products, located within this state.

(5) Inventory, located within this state.

(6) Negotiable documents of title, located within this state.

(b) If any interest in personal property on which a judgment lien could be created under subdivision (a) is acquired after the judgment lien was created, the judgment lien attaches to the interest at the time it is acquired.

(c) To the extent provided by Section 697.620, a judgment lien on personal property continues on the proceeds received upon the sale, collection, or other disposition of the property subject to the judgment lien.

(d) Notwithstanding any other provision of this section, the judgment lien does not attach to:

(1) A vehicle or vessel required to be registered with the Department of Motor Vehicles or a mobilehome or commercial coach required to be registered pursuant to the Health and Safety Code.

(2) As-extracted collateral, as defined in paragraph (6) of subdivision (a) of Section 9102 of the Commercial Code, and timber to be cut.

(3) The inventory of a retail merchant held for sale except to the extent that the inventory of the retail merchant consists of durable goods having a unit retail value of at least five hundred dollars ($500). For the purposes of this paragraph, "retail merchant" does not include either of the following:

(A) A person whose sales for resale exceeded 75 percent in dollar volume of the person's total sales of all goods during the 12 months preceding the filing of the notice of judgment lien on personal property.

(B) A cooperative association organized pursuant to Chapter 1 (commencing with Section 54001) of Division 20 of the Food and Agricultural Code (agricultural cooperative associations) or Part 3 (commencing with Section 13200) of Division 3 of Title 1 of the Corporations Code (Fish Marketing Act).

(e) If property subject to a lien under this article becomes a fixture, as defined in paragraph (41) of subdivision (a) of Section 9102 of the Commercial Code, the judgment lien on that property is extinguished.

(f) Notwithstanding the filing of a notice of judgment lien, subject to the provisions of Chapter 6 (commencing with Section 708.010), a person obligated on an account receivable or chattel paper is authorized to pay or compromise the amount without notice to or consent of the judgment creditor unless and until there is a levy pursuant to Chapter 3 (commencing with Section 699.010).

(g) For purposes of this section, whether a person is located in this state is determined in accordance with Section 9307 of the Commercial Code, except that the location of a registered organization, as defined in paragraph (71) of subdivision (a) of Section 9102 of the Commercial Code, that is organized under the law of another state is determined without regard to subdivision (e) of Section 9307 of the Commercial Code.[875]

697.540. (a) Except as otherwise provided by statute, a judgment lien on personal property is a lien for the amount required to satisfy the money judgment.

(b) A judgment lien on personal property created under a money judgment payable in installments pursuant to Section 117 or 582.5 of this code or pursuant to Section 16380 of the Vehicle Code is in the full amount required to satisfy the judgment, but the judgment lien may not be enforced for the amount of unmatured installments unless the court so orders.[396]

697.550. The notice of judgment lien on personal property shall be executed under oath by the judgment creditor's attorney if the judgment creditor has an attorney of record or, if the judgment creditor does not have an attorney of record, by the judgment creditor and shall contain the following information:

(a) The name and mailing address of the judgment creditor.

(b) The name and last known mailing address of the judgment debtor.

(c) A statement that: "All property subject to enforcement of a money judgment against the judgment debtor to which a judgment lien on personal property may attach under Section 697.530 of the Code of Civil Procedure is subject to this judgment lien."

(d) The title of the court where the judgment is entered and the cause and number of the action.

(e) The date of entry of the judgment and of any subsequent renewals and where entered in the records of the court.

(f) The amount required to satisfy the judgment at the date of the notice.

(g) The date of the notice.[170]

697.560. At the time of filing the notice of judgment lien on personal property or promptly thereafter, the judgment creditor shall serve a copy of the notice of judgment lien on the judgment debtor. Service shall be made personally or by mail. The failure to comply with this requirement does not affect the validity of the judgment lien.[170]

697.570. Upon presentation of a notice of judgment lien on personal property for filing and tender of the filing fee to the office of the Secretary of State, the notice of judgment lien shall be filed, marked, and indexed in the same manner as a financing statement. The fee for filing in the office of the Secretary of State is the same as the fee for filing a financing statement in the standard form. A notice shall not be filed if it is presented for filing more than 10 days after the date of the notice.[170]

697.580. (a) Upon the request of any person, the Secretary of State shall issue a certificate showing whether there is on file in that office on the date and hour stated therein any notice of judgment lien on personal property filed against the property of a particular person named in the request. If a notice of judgment lien is on file, the certificate shall state the date and hour of filing of each such notice and any notice affecting any such notice of judgment lien and the name and address of the judgment creditor.

(b) Upon request, the Secretary of State shall furnish a copy of any notice of judgment lien or notice affecting a notice of judgment lien. The certificate shall be issued as part of a combined certificate pursuant to Section 9528 of the Commercial Code, and the fee for the certificate and copies shall be in accordance with that section.[426]

697.590. (a) As used in this section:

(1) "Filing" means:

(A) With respect to a judgment lien on personal property, the filing of a notice of judgment lien in the office of the Secretary of State to create a judgment lien on personal property under this article.

(B) With respect to a security interest or agricultural lien, as defined in paragraph (5) of subdivision (a) of Section 9102 of the Commercial Code, the filing of a financing statement pursuant to Division 9 (commencing with Section 9101) of the Commercial Code.

(2) "Perfection" means perfection of a security interest or agricultural lien

pursuant to Division 9 (commencing with Section 9101) of the Commercial Code.

(3) "Personal property" means:

(A) With respect to a judgment lien on personal property, the property to which a judgment lien has attached pursuant to this article.

(B) With respect to a security interest, the collateral subject to a security interest pursuant to Division 9 (commencing with Section 9101) of the Commercial Code.

(C) With respect to an agricultural lien, the farm products subject to an agricultural lien pursuant to Division 9 (commencing with Section 9101) of the Commercial Code.

(4) "Purchase money security interest" has the same meaning as used in Section 9103 of the Commercial Code.

(b) Except as provided in subdivisions (d), (e), (g), and (h), priority between a judgment lien on personal property and a conflicting security interest or agricultural lien in the same personal property shall be determined according to this subdivision. Conflicting interests rank according to priority in time of filing or perfection. In the case of a judgment lien, priority dates from the time filing is first made covering the personal property. In the case of a security interest or agricultural lien, priority dates from the earlier of the time a filing is first made covering the personal property or the time the security interest or agricultural lien is first perfected, if there is no period thereafter when there is neither filing nor perfection.

(c) For the purposes of subdivision (b), a date of filing or perfection as to personal property is also a date of filing or perfection as to proceeds.

(d) A purchase money security interest has priority over a conflicting judgment lien on the same personal property or its proceeds if the purchase money security interest is perfected at the time the judgment debtor, as a debtor under the security agreement, receives possession of the personal property or within 20 days thereafter.

(e) If a purchase money security interest in inventory has priority over a judgment lien pursuant to subdivision (d) and a conflicting security interest has priority over the purchase money security interest in the same inventory pursuant to Section 9324 of the Commercial Code, the conflicting security interest also has priority over the judgment lien on the inventory subject to the purchase money security interest, notwithstanding that the conflicting security interest would not otherwise have priority over the judgment lien.

(f) A judgment lien that has attached to personal property, and that is also subordinate under subdivision (b) to a security interest in the same personal property, is subordinate to the security interest only to the extent that the security interest secures advances made before the judgment lien attached or within 45 days thereafter or made without knowledge of the judgment lien or pursuant to a commitment entered into without knowledge of the judgment lien. For the purpose of this subdivision, a secured party shall be deemed not to have knowledge of a judgment lien on personal property until (1) the judgment creditor serves a copy of the notice of judgment lien on the secured party personally or by mail and (2) the secured party has knowledge of the judgment lien on personal property, as "knowledge" is defined in Section 1201 of the Commercial Code. If service on the secured party is by mail, it shall be sent to the secured party at the address shown in the financing statement or security agreement.

(g) A perfected agricultural lien on personal property has priority over a judgment lien on the same personal property if the statute creating the agricultural lien so provides.

(h) A security interest in personal property perfected by the filing of a financing statement under the law of a jurisdiction other than this state, or perfected by another method pursuant to the law of a jurisdiction other than this state, has priority over a judgment lien in the same personal property.[618]

697.600. (a) A judgment lien on personal property has priority over any other judgment lien thereafter created on the property.

(b) For the purpose of this section, if two or more judgment liens attach to after-acquired property at the same time under subdivision (b) of Section 697.530, the judgment lien first filed has priority.[170]

697.610. Except as provided in Sections 9617 and 9622 of the Commercial Code, a judgment lien on personal property continues notwithstanding the sale, exchange, or other disposition of the property, unless the person receiving the property is one of the following:

(a) A buyer in ordinary course of business (as defined in Section 1201 of the Commercial Code) who, under Section 9320 of the Commercial Code, would take free of a security interest created by the seller.

(b) A lessee in ordinary course of business (as defined in paragraph (15) of subdivision (a) of Section 10103 of the Commercial Code) who, under Section 9321 of the Commercial Code, would take free of a security interest created by the lessor.

(c) A holder to whom a negotiable document of title has been duly negotiated within the meaning of Section 7501 of the Commercial Code.

(d) A purchaser of chattel paper who, under Section 9330 of the Commercial Code, would have priority over another security interest in the chattel paper.[427]

697.620. (a) As used in this section:

(1) "Cash proceeds" means money, checks, deposit accounts, and the like.

(2) "Proceeds" means identifiable cash proceeds received upon the sale, exchange, collection, or other disposition of property subject to a judgment lien on personal property.

(b) Except as provided in subdivision (c), the judgment lien on personal property continues in the proceeds with the same priority.

(c) In the event of insolvency proceedings (as defined in Section 1201 of the Commercial Code) instituted by or against the judgment debtor, the judgment lien continues under subdivision (b) only in the following proceeds:

(1) Proceeds in a separate deposit account containing only proceeds.

(2) Proceeds in the form of money which are neither commingled with other money nor deposited in a deposit account prior to the insolvency proceedings.

(3) Proceeds in the form of checks and the like which are not deposited

in a deposit account prior to the insolvency proceedings.[170]

697.640. (a) The judgment creditor, judgment debtor, owner of property subject to a judgment lien on personal property created under the judgment, or a person having a security interest in or a lien on the property subject to the judgment lien, may file in the office of the Secretary of State an acknowledgment of satisfaction of judgment executed as provided in Section 724.060 or a court clerk's certificate of satisfaction of judgment issued pursuant to Section 724.100, together with a statement containing the name of the judgment creditor, the name and address of the judgment debtor, and the file number of the notice of judgment lien. Upon such filing, the judgment lien created under the judgment that has been satisfied is extinguished as a matter of record. The fee for filing the acknowledgment or certificate is the same as the fee for filing a termination statement under Section 9404 of the Commercial Code.

(b) The filing officer shall treat an acknowledgment of satisfaction of judgment, or court clerk's certificate of satisfaction of judgment, and statement filed pursuant to this section in the same manner as a termination statement filed pursuant to Section 9525 of the Commercial Code.[428]

697.650. (a) The judgment creditor may by a writing do any of the following:

(1) Release the judgment lien on all the personal property subject to the lien of a sole judgment debtor or of all the judgment debtors.

(2) If the notice of judgment lien names more than one judgment debtor, release the judgment lien on all the personal property subject to the lien of one or more but of less than all the judgment debtors.

(3) Release the judgment lien on all or a part of the personal property subject to the lien.

(4) Subordinate to a security interest or other lien or encumbrance the judgment lien on all or a part of the personal property subject to the judgment lien.

(b) A statement of release or subordination is sufficient if it is signed by the judgment creditor and contains the name and address of the judgment debtor, the file number of the notice of judgment lien, and wording appropriate to bring the statement within one of the paragraphs of subdivision (a). In the case of a release under paragraph (3) of subdivision (a), the statement of release shall also describe the property being released. In the case of a subordination under paragraph (4) of subdivision (a), the statement of subordination shall also describe the property on which the judgment lien is being subordinated and describe the security interest or other lien or encumbrance to which the judgment lien is being subordinated.

(c) The filing officer shall treat the filing of a statement of release pursuant to paragraph (1) of subdivision (a) of this section in the same manner as a termination statement filed pursuant to Sections 9513 and 9519 of the Commercial Code. The filing officer shall treat the filing of a statement of release pursuant to paragraph (2) of subdivision (a) of this section in the same manner as a comparable amendment filed pursuant to Sections 9512 and

9519 of the Commercial Code. The filing officer shall treat the filing of a statement of release pursuant to paragraph (3) of subdivision (a) of this section and the filing of a statement of subordination filed pursuant to paragraph (4) of subdivision (a) of this section in the same manner as a statement of release filed pursuant to Sections 9512 and 9519 of the Commercial Code.
(d) The fee for filing the statement is the same as that provided in Section 9525 of the Commercial Code.[429]

697.660. (a)If a notice of judgment lien on personal property filed in the office of the Secretary of State appears to create a judgment lien on personal property of a person who is not the judgment debtor because the name of the property owner is the same as or similar to that of the judgment debtor, the erroneously identified property owner or a person having a security interest in or a lien on the property may deliver to the judgment creditor a written demand that the judgment creditor file in the office of the Secretary of State a statement releasing the lien as to the property of such owner. The demand shall be accompanied by proof to the satisfaction of the judgment creditor that the property owner is not the judgment debtor and that the property is not subject to enforcement of the judgment against the judgment debtor.
(b) Within 15 days after receipt of the demand and proof satisfactory to the judgment creditor that the property owner is not the judgment debtor and that the property is not subject to enforcement of the judgment, the judgment creditor shall file in the office of the Secretary of State a statement releasing the lien on the property of such owner. If the judgment creditor improperly fails to file the statement of release within the time allowed, the judgment creditor is liable to the person who made the demand for all damages sustained by reason of such failure and shall also forfeit one hundred dollars ($100) to such person.
(c) If the judgment creditor does not file a statement of release pursuant to subdivision (b), the person who made the demand may apply to the court on noticed motion for an order releasing the judgment lien on the property of such owner. Notice of motion shall be served on the judgment creditor. Service shall be made personally or by mail. Upon presentation of evidence to the satisfaction of the court that the property owner is not the judgment debtor and that the property is not subject to enforcement of the judgment, the court shall order the judgment creditor to prepare and file the statement of release or shall itself order the release of the judgment lien on the property of such owner. The court order may be filed in the office of the Secretary of State with the same effect as the statement of release demanded under subdivision (a).
(d) The court shall award reasonable attorney's fees to the prevailing party in any action or proceeding maintained pursuant to this section.
(e) The damages provided by this section are not in derogation of any other damages or penalties to which an aggrieved person may be entitled by law.
(f) The fee for filing a statement of release or court order under this section is the same as that provided in Section 9525 of the Commercial Code.[430]

697.670. (a) The Secretary of State may prescribe, provided that a cost-savings would be achieved thereby:

(1) The forms for the notice of judgment lien on personal property and the statement of continuation, release, or subordination provided for in this article.

(2) The form for the statement provided for in Section 697.640 and the situations when that form is required or is not required.

(b) A form prescribed by the Secretary of State for a notice or statement pursuant to subdivision (a) is deemed to comply with this article and supersedes any requirements specified in this article for the notice or statement.[623]

697.680. (a) A judgment creditor may apply to the court for an order reinstating a released lien on personal property and its priority at the time of cancellation. Subject to subdivisions (b) and (c), the court shall order the reinstatement of a lien with the same priority that it held at the time of cancellation. Upon entry of the order the clerk shall do the following:

(1) Note in the court's records that the judgment is no longer satisfied to the extent of the returned funds or property.

(2) Issue to the judgment creditor a certificate and notice of reinstatement of judgment lien. The certificate of reinstatement of judgment lien shall identify the judgment and parties, the unsatisfied judgment amount, and the filing number and date of the original notice of judgment lien filed with the Secretary of State.

(b) (1) The application for reinstatement of a lien under subdivision (a) shall be filed with a declaration by the judgment creditor that includes and certifies all of the following:

(A) The title of the court, the case name and number, and the date and amount of the original judgment and any renewals thereof.

(B) A statement that the judgment creditor released a lien or liens in the reasonable belief that the money judgment was satisfied. This statement shall include:

(i) Information sufficient to identify the liens that were released, including the county or counties in which an abstract of judgment was recorded, the recording dates and numbers of those recordings and, if applicable, the filing date and number of any notice of judgment lien on personal property that was filed with the Secretary of State.

(ii) The details of any acknowledgment of full or partial satisfaction of judgment that was filed or entered as a result of the prior application of funds, including the date, county, and recording number of any acknowledgment of full or partial satisfaction of judgment recorded by the judgment creditor.

(C) A statement that after a lien was released, the judgment creditor was ordered pursuant to paragraph (2) or (3) of subdivision (d) of Section 703.580 to return to the judgment debtor property levied or wages garnished in satisfaction of the money judgment. A copy of the order shall be attached as an exhibit to the declaration.

(D) A statement that the judgment creditor returned, and the judgment debtor received, all property and wages ordered returned.

(E) A statement that but for the

court's order pursuant to paragraph (2) or (3) of subdivision (d) of Section 703.580, the money judgment would have been fully satisfied or that the property returned to the judgment creditor was identified in a recorded acknowledgment of full or partial satisfaction of judgment.

(F) A statement that the judgment creditor is not appealing the order to return funds pursuant to subdivision (d) of Section 703.580.

(2) knowingly providing false information shall be subject to a civil penalty in an amount up to $1,500

(c) (1) The judgment creditor shall serve upon the judgment debtor by first-class mail to the address verified pursuant to paragraph (2) of subdivision (b) of Section 684.130 a copy of the application for an order reinstating a released lien.

(2) The judgment debtor may, within 15 days of service of the application, file a declaration stating that the funds or property identified by the judgment debtor pursuant to subparagraph (D) of paragraph (1) of subdivision (b) have not been returned.

(3) If a declaration under paragraph (2) is filed, the court shall deny the application and the judgment creditor shall file a noticed motion to be heard by the court in order to reinstate a lien and its priority.

(4) If no objection is filed, the clerk's reinstatement of the lien and its priority shall be automatically effective.

(d) An application under this section shall be filed in the action in which the judgment creditor was ordered, pursuant to paragraph (2) or (3) of subdivision (d) of Section 703.580, to return to the judgment debtor property levied or wages garnished in satisfaction of the money judgment.

(e) Attorney's fees are not recoverable under this section.

(f) The judgment creditor may record the certificate in the same manner as an abstract of judgment, and that recordation shall have the effect of restoring the lien's priority as if the prior release or satisfaction had not occurred.

(g) This section shall become operative on July 1, 2026.[903]

Article 4: Execution Lien

Article 4 added by Stats. 1982, Ch. 1364, Sec. 2.

697.710. A levy on property under a writ of execution creates an execution lien on the property from the time of levy until the expiration of two years after the date of issuance of the writ unless the judgment is sooner satisfied.[170]

697.720. Subject to Section 701.630, if an interest in real property subject to an execution lien is transferred or encumbered, the interest transferred or encumbered remains subject to the lien after the transfer or encumbrance.[170]

697.730. (a) Subject to Section 701.630 and except as provided in subdivision (b), if tangible personal property subject to an execution lien is in the custody of a levying officer and is transferred or encumbered, the property remains subject to the lien after the transfer or encumbrance.

(b) If a levy upon tangible personal property of a going business is made by the levying officer placing a keeper in charge of the business, a purchaser or lessee of property subject to the execution lien takes the property free of the execution lien if the purchaser or lessee is one of the following:

(1) A buyer in ordinary course of business (as defined in Section 1201 of the Commercial Code) who, under Section 9320 of the Commercial Code, would take free of a security interest created by his or her seller.

(2) A lessee in ordinary course of business (as defined in paragraph (15) of subdivision (a) of Section 10103 of the Commercial Code) who, under Section 9321 of the Commercial Code, would take free of a security interest created by the lessor.[431]

697.740. Except as provided in Sections 9617 and 9622 of the Commercial Code and in Section 701.630, if personal property subject to an execution lien is not in the custody of a levying officer and the property is transferred or encumbered, the property remains subject to the lien after the transfer or encumbrance except where the transfer or encumbrance is made to one of the following persons:

(a) A person who acquires an interest in the property under the law of this state for reasonably equivalent value without knowledge of the lien. For purposes of this subdivision, value is given for a transfer or encumbrance if, in exchange for the transfer or encumbrance, property is transferred or an antecedent debt is secured or satisfied.

(b) A buyer in ordinary course of business (as defined in Section 1201 of the Commercial Code) who, under Section 9320 of the Commercial Code, would take free of a security interest created by the seller or encumbrancer.

(c) A lessee in ordinary course of business (as defined in paragraph (15) of subdivision (a) of Section 10103 of the Commercial Code) or a licensee in the ordinary course of business (as defined in subdivision (a) of Section 9321 of the Commercial Code) who, under Section 9321 of the Commercial Code, would take free of a security interest created by the lessor or the licensor.

(d) A holder in due course (as defined in Section 3302 of the Commercial Code) of a negotiable instrument within the meaning of Section 3104 of the Commercial Code.

(e) A holder to whom a negotiable document of title has been duly negotiated within the meaning of Section 7501 of the Commercial Code.

(f) A protected purchaser (as defined in Section 8303 of the Commercial Code) of a security or a person entitled to the benefits of Section 8502 or 8510 of the Commercial Code.

(g) A purchaser of chattel paper who gives new value and takes possession of the chattel paper in good faith and in the ordinary course of the purchaser's business or a purchaser of an instrument who gives value and takes possession of the instrument in good faith.

(h) A holder of a purchase money security interest (as defined in Section 9103 of the Commercial Code).

(i) A collecting bank holding a security interest in items being collected, accompanying documents and proceeds, pursuant to Section 4210 of the Commercial Code.

(j) A person who acquires any right or interest in letters of credit, advices of credit, or money.

(k) A person who acquires any right or interest in property subject to a certificate of title statute of another jurisdiction under the law of which indication of a security interest on the certificate of title is required as a condition of perfection of the security interest.[432]

697.750. Notwithstanding Section 697.740, except as provided in Section 9617 of the Commercial Code and in Section 701.630, if (1) growing crops, (2) timber to be cut, or (3) minerals or the like (including oil or gas) to be extracted or accounts receivable resulting from the sale thereof at wellhead or minehead are subject to an execution lien and are transferred or encumbered, the property remains subject to the execution lien after the transfer or encumbrance.[433]

Article 5: Other Liens Created by Enforcement Process
Article 5 added by Stats. 1982, Ch. 1364, Sec. 2.

697.910. This article applies to liens created by any of the following:
(a) An examination proceeding as provided in Section 708.110, 708.120, or 708.205.
(b) A creditor's suit as provided in Section 708.250.
(c) A charging order as provided in Section 708.320.[170]

697.920. Except as provided in Section 9617 of the Commercial Code and in Section 701.630, a lien described in Section 697.910 continues on property subject to the lien, notwithstanding the transfer or encumbrance of the property subject to the lien, unless the transfer or encumbrance is made to a person listed in Section 697.740.[434]

Chapter 3: Execution

Chapter 3 added by Stats. 1982, Ch. 1364, Sec. 2.

Article 1: General Provisions
Article 1 added by Stats. 1982, Ch. 1364, Sec. 2.

699.010. Except as otherwise provided by statute, this chapter governs enforcement of a money judgment by a writ of execution.[170]

699.020. At any time after delivery of a writ of execution to a levying officer and before its return, a person indebted to the judgment debtor may pay to the levying officer the amount of the debt or so much thereof as is necessary to satisfy the money judgment. The levying officer shall give a receipt for the amount paid and such receipt is a discharge for the amount paid.[170]

699.030. If personal property sought to be levied upon is located in a private place of the judgment debtor:
(a) The levying officer making the levy shall demand delivery of the property by the judgment debtor and shall advise the judgment debtor that the judgment debtor may be liable for costs and attorney's fees incurred in any further proceedings to obtain delivery of the property. If the judgment debtor does not deliver the property, the levying officer shall make no further effort to obtain custody of the property and shall promptly notify the judgment creditor of the failure to obtain custody of the property.
(b) The judgment creditor may apply to the court ex parte, or on noticed motion if the court so directs or a court rule so requires, for an order directing the levying officer to seize the

property in the private place. The application may be made whether or not a writ has been issued and whether or not demand has been made pursuant to subdivision (a). The application for the order shall describe with particularity both the property sought to be levied upon, and the place where it is to be found, according to the best knowledge, information, and belief of the judgment creditor. The court may not issue the order unless the judgment creditor establishes that there is probable cause to believe that property sought to be levied upon is located in the place described. The levying officer making the levy, at the time delivery of the property pursuant to the order is demanded, shall announce his or her identity, purpose, and authority. If the property is not voluntarily delivered, the levying officer may cause the building or enclosure where the property is believed to be located to be broken open in such manner as the levying officer reasonably believes will cause the least damage, but if the levying officer reasonably believes that entry and seizure of the property will involve a substantial risk of death or serious bodily harm to any person, the levying officer shall refrain from entering and shall promptly make a return to the court setting forth the reasons for believing that the risk exists. In such a case, the court shall make such orders as may be appropriate.[170]

699.040. (a)If a writ of execution is issued, the judgment creditor may apply to the court ex parte, or on noticed motion if the court so directs or a court rule so requires, for an order directing the judgment debtor to transfer to the levying officer either or both of the following:

(1) Possession of the property sought to be levied upon if the property is sought to be levied upon by taking it into custody.

(2) Possession of documentary evidence of title to property of or a debt owed to the judgment debtor that is sought to be levied upon. An order pursuant to this paragraph may be served when the property or debt is levied upon or thereafter.

(b) The court may issue an order pursuant to this section upon a showing of need for the order.

(c) The order shall be personally served on the judgment debtor and shall contain a notice to the judgment debtor that failure to comply with the order may subject the judgment debtor to arrest and punishment for contempt of court.[170]

699.060. (a) The levying officer shall release property levied upon when the levying officer receives a written direction to release the property from the judgment creditor's attorney of record or, if the judgment creditor does not have an attorney of record, from the judgment creditor, or when the levying officer receives a certified copy of a court order for release, or when otherwise required to release the property. The release shall include the signature and name of the attorney or judgment creditor issuing the release. The release extinguishes any execution lien or attachment lien in favor of the judgment creditor on the property released.

(b) If the property to be released has been taken into custody under the levy, it shall be released to the person from whom it was taken unless otherwise ordered by the court. If the person does not claim the property to be released, the levying officer shall retain custody of the property and shall serve on the person a notice of where possession of the property may be obtained. Service shall be made personally or by mail. If the person does not claim the property within 30 days after the notice is served, the levying officer shall sell the property in the manner provided by Article 6 (commencing with Section 701.510), other than cash, which does not have a value exceeding its face value. The levying officer shall deposit the proceeds of sale and cash, after first deducting the levying officer's costs, with the county treasurer of the county where the property is located, payable to the order of the person. If the amount deposited is not claimed by the person, or the legal representative of the person, within five years after the deposit is made by making application to the treasurer or other official designated by the county, it shall be paid into the general fund of the county.

(c) If the property to be released has not been taken into custody under the levy, the levying officer shall release the property by issuing a written notice of release and serving it on the person who was served with a copy of the writ and a notice of levy to create the lien. Service shall be made personally or by mail.

(d) If the property to be released was levied upon by recording or filing a copy of the writ and a notice of levy, the levying officer shall record or file a written notice of release in the same office.

(e) The levying officer is not liable for releasing property in accordance with this section nor is any other person liable for acting in conformity with the release.

(f) The written direction to release property specified in subdivision (a) may be transmitted electronically to the levying officer pursuant to Chapter 2 (commencing with Section 263) of Title 4 of Part 1.[641]

699.070. (a) The court may appoint a receiver or order the levying officer to take any action the court orders that is necessary to preserve the value of property levied upon, including but not limited to selling the property, if the court determines that the property is perishable or will greatly deteriorate or greatly depreciate in value or that for some other reason the interests of the parties will be best served by the order. An order may be made under this subdivision upon application of the judgment creditor, the judgment debtor, or a person who has filed a third-party claim pursuant to Division 4 (commencing with Section 720.010). The application shall be made on noticed motion if the court so directs or a court rule so requires. Otherwise, the application may be made ex parte.

(b) If the levying officer determines that property levied upon is extremely perishable or will greatly deteriorate or greatly depreciate in value before a court order pursuant to subdivision (a) could be obtained, the levying officer may take any action necessary to preserve the value of the property or may sell the property. The levying officer is not liable for a determination made in good faith under this subdivision.

(c) Except as otherwise provided by order of the court, a sale of property pursuant to this section shall be made in the manner provided by Article 6 (commencing with Section 701.510) and the proceeds shall be applied to the satisfaction of the money judgment in the manner provided by Article 7 (commencing with Section 701.810). Notwithstanding subdivisions (b) and (d) of Section 701.530, notice of sale shall be posted and served at a reasonable time before the sale, considering the character and condition of the property.

(d) If a receiver is appointed, the court shall fix the daily fee of the receiver and may order the judgment creditor to pay the fees and expenses of the receiver in advance or may direct that the whole or any part of the fees and expenses be paid from the proceeds of any sale of the property. Except as otherwise provided in this section, the provisions of Chapter 5 (commencing with Section 564) and Chapter 5a (commencing with Section 571) of Title 7 govern the appointment, qualifications, powers, rights, and duties of a receiver appointed under this section.[170]

699.080. (a) A registered process server may levy under a writ of execution on the following types of property:

(1) Real property, pursuant to Section 700.015.

(2) Growing crops, timber to be cut, or minerals or the like including oil and gas, to be extracted or accounts receivable resulting from the sale thereof at the wellhead or minehead, pursuant to Section 700.020.

(3) Personal property in the custody of a levying officer, pursuant to Section 700.050.

(4) Personal property used as a dwelling, pursuant to subdivision (a) of Section 700.080.

(5) Deposit accounts, pursuant to Section 700.140.

(6) Property in a safe-deposit box, pursuant to Section 700.150.

(7) Accounts receivable or general intangibles, pursuant to Section 700.170.

(8) Final money judgments, pursuant to Section 700.190.

(9) Interest of a judgment debtor in personal property in the estate of a decedent, pursuant to Section 700.200.

(b) Before levying under the writ of execution, the registered process server shall cause to be deposited with the levying officer a copy of the writ and the fee, as provided by Section 26721 of the Government Code.

(c) If a registered process server levies on property pursuant to subdivision (a), the registered process server shall do both of the following:

(1) Comply with the applicable levy, posting, and service provisions of Article 4 (commencing with Section 700.010).

(2) Request any third person served to give a garnishee's memorandum to the levying officer in compliance with Section 701.030 on a form provided by the registered process server.

(d) Within five court days after levy under this section, all of the following shall be filed with the levying officer:

(1) The writ of execution.

(2) A proof of service by the registered process server stating the manner of levy performed.

(3) Proof of service of the copy of the writ and notice of levy on other persons, as required by Article 4 (commencing with Section 700.010).

(4) Instructions in writing, as required by the provisions of Section 687.010.

(e) If the fee provided by Section 26721 of the Government Code has been paid, the levying officer shall perform all other duties under the writ as if the levying officer had levied under the writ and shall return the writ to the court. If the registered process server does not comply with subdivisions (b) and (d), the levy is ineffective and the levying officer shall not be required to perform any duties under the writ, and may issue a release for any property sought to be levied upon.

(f) The fee for services of a registered process server under this section is a recoverable cost pursuant to Section 1033.5.

(g) A registered process server may levy more than once under the same writ of execution, provided that the writ is still valid.[727]

699.090. If property that is required by law to be registered or recorded in the name of the owner is levied upon under a writ of execution and it appears at the time of the levy that the judgment debtor was the registered or record owner of the property and the judgment creditor caused the levy to be made and the lien maintained in good faith and in reliance upon such registered or recorded ownership, neither the judgment creditor, the levying officer, nor the sureties on an undertaking given by the judgment creditor pursuant to Chapter 2 (commencing with Section 720.110) or Chapter 3 (commencing with Section 720.210) of Division 4 is liable to a third person for the levy itself.[170]

Article 2: Writ of Execution and Notice of Levy

Article 2 added by Stats. 1982, Ch. 1364, Sec. 2.

699.510. (a) Subject to subdivision (b), after entry of a money judgment, a writ of execution shall be issued by the clerk of the court, upon application of the judgment creditor, and shall be directed to the levying officer in the county where the levy is to be made and to any registered process server. The clerk of the court shall give priority to the application for, and issuance of, writs of execution on orders or judgments for child support and spousal support. A separate writ shall be issued for each county where a levy is to be made. Writs may be issued successively until the money judgment is satisfied, except that a new writ may not be issued for a county until the expiration of 180 days after the issuance of a prior writ for that county unless the prior writ is first returned.

(b) If the judgment creditor seeks a writ of execution to enforce a judgment made, entered, or enforceable pursuant to the Family Code, in addition to the requirements of this article, the judgment creditor shall satisfy the requirements of any applicable provisions of the Family Code.

(c) (1) The writ of execution shall be issued in the name of the judgment debtor as listed on the judgment, except that the judgment creditor shall omit the name of a judgment debtor from the application for a writ of execution if the liability of that judgment debtor has ceased with regard to the judgment, including either of the following occurrences:

(A) The judgment debtor has obtained a discharge of the judgment pursuant to Title 11 of the United States Code and notice thereof has been filed with the court.

(B) The judgment creditor files an acknowledgment of satisfaction of judgment with regard to the judgment debtor pursuant to Chapter 1 (commencing with Section 724.010) of Division 5.

(2) The writ of execution shall include the additional name or names, and the type of legal entity, by which the judgment debtor is known, as set forth in the affidavit of identity, as defined in Section 680.135, filed by the judgment creditor with the application for issuance of the writ of execution. Prior to the clerk of the court issuing a writ of execution containing any additional name or names by which the judgment debtor is known that are not listed on the judgment, the court shall approve the affidavit of identity. If the court determines, without a hearing or a notice, that the affidavit of identity states sufficient facts upon which the judgment creditor has identified the additional names of the judgment debtor, the court shall authorize the issuance of the writ of execution with the additional name or names.

(d) In any case where the writ of execution lists any name other than that listed on the judgment, the person in possession or control of the levied property, if other than the judgment debtor, shall not pay to the levying officer the amount or deliver the property being levied upon until being notified to do so by the levying officer. The levying officer may not require the person, if other than the judgment debtor, in possession or control of the levied property to pay the amount or deliver the property levied upon until the expiration of 15 days after service of notice of levy.

(e) If a person who is not the judgment debtor has property erroneously subject to an enforcement of judgment proceeding based upon an affidavit of identity, the person shall be entitled to the recovery of reasonable attorney's fees and costs from the judgment creditor incurred in releasing the person's property from a writ of execution, in addition to any other damages or penalties to which an aggrieved person may be entitled to by law, including Division 4 (commencing with Section 720.010).[690]

699.520. The writ of execution shall require the levying officer to whom it is directed to enforce the money judgment and shall include the following information:

(a) The date of issuance of the writ.

(b) The title of the court in which the judgment is entered and the cause and number of the action.

(c) Whether the judgment is for wages owed, child support, or spousal support. This subdivision shall become operative on September 1, 2020.

(d) The name and address of the judgment creditor and the name and last known address of the judgment debtor. If the judgment debtor is other than a natural person, the type of legal entity shall be stated.

(e) The date of the entry of the judgment and of any subsequent renewals and where entered in the records of the court.

(f) The total amount of the money judgment as entered or renewed, together with costs thereafter added to the judgment pursuant to Section 685.090 and the accrued interest on the judgment from the date of entry or renewal of the judgment to the date of issuance of the writ, reduced by any

partial satisfactions and by any amounts no longer enforceable.
(g) The amount required to satisfy the money judgment on the date the writ is issued.
(h) The amount of interest accruing daily on the principal amount of the judgment from the date the writ is issued.
(i) Whether any person has requested notice of sale under the judgment and, if so, the name and mailing address of that person.
(j) The sum of the fees and costs added to the judgment pursuant to Section 6103.5 or Article 6 (commencing with Section 68630) of Chapter 2 of Title 8 of the Government Code, and which is in addition to the amount owing to the judgment creditor on the judgment.
(k) Whether the writ of execution includes any additional names of the judgment debtor pursuant to an affidavit of identity, as defined in Section 680.135.
(l) A statement indicating whether the case is limited or unlimited.[780]

699.530. (a) Upon delivery of the writ of execution to the levying officer to whom the writ is directed, together with the written instructions of the judgment creditor, the levying officer shall execute the writ in the manner prescribed by law.
(b) The levying officer may not levy upon any property under the writ after the expiration of 180 days from the date the writ was issued.[170]

699.540. The notice of levy required by Article 4 (commencing with Section 700.010) shall inform the person notified of all of the following:
(a) The capacity in which the person is notified.
(b) The property that is levied upon.
(c) The person's rights under the levy, including all of the following:
(1) The right to claim an exemption pursuant to Chapter 4 (commencing with Section 703.010).
(2) The right to make a third-party claim pursuant to Division 4 (commencing with Section 720.010).
(3) The right to, and the limitations of, the automatic exemption pursuant to Section 704.220. This paragraph shall become operative on September 1, 2020.
(d) The person's duties under the levy.
(e) All names listed in the writ of execution pursuant to an affidavit of identity, as defined in Section 680.135, if any.[755]

699.545. A copy of the original notice of levy which has been served upon a third party holding the property sought to be levied upon and the affidavit of identity, as defined in Section 680.135, if any, if served upon the judgment debtor or any other party, shall suffice as the notice of levy to that person.[436]

699.550. In any case where property has been levied upon and, pursuant to a levy, a copy of the writ of execution and a notice of levy are required by statute to be posted or to be served on or mailed to the judgment debtor or other person, failure to post, serve, or mail the copy of the writ and the notice does not affect the execution lien created by the levy. Failure to serve on or mail to the judgment debtor a list of exemptions does not affect the execution lien created by the levy.[170]

699.560. (a) Except as provided in

subdivisions (b) and (c), the writ expires and the levying officer to whom the writ of execution is delivered shall return the writ to the court, or store the writ as provided in Section 263.6, and file a return with the court reporting the levying officer's actions and an accounting of amounts collected, and costs incurred, at the earliest of the following times:

(1) Two years from the date of issuance of the writ, unless paragraph (1) of subdivision (a) of Section 706.022 is applicable.

(2) Promptly after all of the duties under the writ are performed.

(3) When return is requested in writing by the judgment creditor.

(4) If no levy takes place under the writ within 180 days after its issuance, promptly after the expiration of the 180-day period.

(5) Upon expiration of the time for enforcement of the money judgment.

(b) If a levy has been made under Section 700.200 upon an interest in personal property in the estate of a decedent, the writ shall be returned within the time prescribed in Section 700.200.

(c) If a levy has been made under Section 5103 of the Family Code on the judgment debtor's right to the payment of benefits from an employee pension benefit plan, the writ shall be returned within the time prescribed in that section.

(d) If a levy has been made under the Wage Garnishment Law (Chapter 5 (commencing with Section 706.010)), and the earnings withholding order remains in effect, the writ of execution shall be returned as provided in subdivision (a) and a supplemental return shall be made as provided in Section 706.033.

(e) Subject to the limitations in subdivision (c) of Section 263, a levying officer may electronically file with the court the return, containing the information required by subdivision (a), pursuant to Chapter 2 (commencing with Section 263) of Title 4 of Part 1.[642]

Article 3: Property Subject to Execution
Article 3 added by Stats. 1982, Ch. 1364, Sec. 2.

699.710. Except as otherwise provided by law, all property that is subject to enforcement of a money judgment pursuant to Article 1 (commencing with Section 695.010) of Chapter 1 is subject to levy under a writ of execution to satisfy a money judgment.[170]

699.720. (a) The following types of property are not subject to execution:

(1) An alcoholic beverage license that is transferable under Article 5 (commencing with Section 24070) of Chapter 6 of Division 9 of the Business and Professions Code.

(2) The interest of a partner in a partnership or member in a limited liability company if the partnership or the limited liability company is not a judgment debtor.

(3) A cause of action that is the subject of a pending action or special proceeding.

(4) A judgment in favor of the judgment debtor prior to the expiration of the time for appeal from the judgment or, if an appeal is filed, prior to the final determination of the appeal.

(5) A debt (other than earnings) owing and unpaid by a public entity.

(6) The loan value of an unmatured life insurance, endowment, or annuity policy.

(7) A franchise granted by a public entity and all the rights and privileges of the franchise.
(8) The interest of a trust beneficiary.
(9) A contingent remainder, executory interest, or other interest in property that is not vested.
(10) Property in a guardianship or conservatorship estate.
(b) Nothing in subdivision (a) affects or limits the right of the judgment creditor to apply property to the satisfaction of a money judgment pursuant to any applicable procedure other than execution.[356]

699.730. (a) Notwithstanding any other law, the principal place of residence of a judgment debtor is not subject to sale under execution of a judgment lien based on a consumer debt unless the debt was secured by the debtor's principal place of residence at the time it was incurred. As used in this subdivision, "consumer debt" means debt incurred by an individual primarily for personal, family, or household purposes.
(b) Subdivision (a) does not apply to any of the following types of unpaid debts:
(1) Wages or employment benefits.
(2) Taxes.
(3) Child support.
(4) Spousal support.
(5) Fines and fees owed to governmental units.
(6) Tort judgments.
(7) (A) Debts, other than student loan debt, owed to a financial institution at the time of execution on the judgment lien, if both of the following requirements are met:
(i) The amount of the original judgment on which the lien is based, when entered, was greater than seventy-five thousand dollars($75,000), as adjusted pursuant to Section 703.150.
(ii) The amount owed on the outstanding judgment at the time of execution on the judgment lien is greater than seventy-five thousand dollars ($75,000), as adjusted pursuant to Section 703.150.
(B) As used in this paragraph, the following terms have the following meanings:
(i) "Financial institution" means a financial institution, as defined in Section 680.200.
(ii) "Student loan debt" means debt based on any loan made to finance postsecondary education expenses, including tuition, fees, books, supplies, room and board, transportation, and personal expenses. Student loan debt includes debt based on a loan made to refinance a student loan, but does not include debt secured by the debtor's principal place of residence at the time it was incurred.[775]

Article 4: Methods of Levy
Article 4 added by Stats. 1982, Ch. 1364, Sec. 2.

700.010. (a) At the time of levy pursuant to this article or promptly thereafter, the levying officer shall serve a copy of the following on the judgment debtor:
(1) The writ of execution.
(2) A notice of levy.
(3) If the judgment debtor is a natural person, a copy of the form listing exemptions prepared by the Judicial Council pursuant to subdivision (c) of Section 681.030, the list of exemption

amounts published pursuant to subdivision (e) of Section 703.150, a copy of the form that the judgment debtor may use to make a claim of exemption pursuant to Section 703.520, and a copy of the form the judgment debtor may use to provide a financial statement pursuant to Section 703.530.

(4) Any affidavit of identity, as defined in Section 680.135, for names of the debtor listed on the writ of execution.

(b) Service under this section shall be made personally or by mail.[684]

700.015. (a) To levy upon real property, the levying officer shall record with the recorder of the county where the real property is located a copy of the writ of execution and a notice of levy that describes the property levied upon and states that the judgment debtor's interest in the described property has been levied upon. If the judgment debtor's interest in the real property stands upon the records of the county in the name of a person other than the judgment debtor, the notice of levy shall identify the third person and the recorder shall index the copy of the writ and notice of levy in the names of both the judgment debtor and the third person.

(b) At the time of levy or promptly thereafter, the levying officer shall serve a copy of the writ and a notice of levy on any third person in whose name the judgment debtor's interest in the real property stands upon the records of the county. Service shall be made personally or by mail. If service on the third person is by mail, it shall be sent to the person at the address for such person, if any, shown by the records of the office of the tax assessor of the county where the real property is located or, if no address is so shown, to the person at the address used by the county recorder for the return of the instrument creating the interest of the third person in the property.

(c) At the time of levy or promptly thereafter, the levying officer shall serve a copy of the writ and a notice of levy on one occupant of the real property. Service on the occupant shall be made by leaving the copy of the writ and a notice of levy with the occupant personally or, in the occupant's absence, with a person of suitable age and discretion found upon the real property when service is attempted who is either an employee or agent of the occupant or a member of the occupant's household. If unable to serve such an occupant at the time service is attempted, the levying officer shall post the copy of the writ and the notice of levy in a conspicuous place on the real property. If the real property described in the notice of levy consists of more than one distinct lot, parcel, or governmental subdivision and any of the lots, parcels, or governmental subdivisions lies with relation to any of the others so as to form one or more continuous, unbroken tracts, only one service or posting need be made under this subdivision as to each continuous, unbroken tract.[170]

700.020. (a) To levy upon (1) growing crops, (2) timber to be cut, or (3) minerals or the like (including oil and gas) to be extracted or accounts receivable resulting from the sale thereof at the wellhead or minehead, the levying officer shall record with the recorder of the county where those crops, timber, or minerals or the like are located a copy of the writ of execution and a notice of levy that describes the property levied upon and states that the judgment debtor's interest in the described property has been levied upon and describes the real property where the crops, timber, or minerals or the like are located. If the judgment debtor's interest in the crops, timber, minerals or the like, or if the real property where the crops, timber, or minerals or the like are located, stands upon the records of the county in the name of a person other than the judgment debtor, the notice of levy shall identify the third person and the recorder shall index the copy of the writ and notice of levy in the names of both the judgment debtor and the third person.

(b) At the time of levy or promptly thereafter, the levying officer shall serve a copy of the writ and a notice of levy personally or by mail on the following persons:

(1) Any third person in whose name the judgment debtor's interest in the crops, timber, minerals or the like stands upon the records of the county and any third person in whose name the real property stands upon the records of the county. If service on the third person is by mail, it shall be sent to the person at the address for the person, if any, shown by the records of the office of the assessor of the county where the real property is located or, if no address is so shown, to the person at the address used by the county recorder for the return of the instrument creating the interest of the third person in the property.

(2) Any secured party who has filed a financing statement with respect to the crops, timber, or minerals or the like or the accounts receivable, prior to the date of levy on the property.

(c) At the time of levy or promptly thereafter, the levying officer shall serve a copy of the writ and a notice of levy on one occupant of the real property where the crops, timber, or minerals or the like are located. Service on the occupant shall be made by leaving the copy of the writ and a notice of levy with the occupant personally or, in the occupant's absence, with a person of suitable age and discretion found upon the real property when service is attempted who is either an employee or agent of the occupant or a member of the occupant's household. If he or she is unable to serve an occupant or suitable person at the time service is attempted, the levying officer shall post the copy of the writ and the notice of levy in a conspicuous place on the real property. However, the posting requirement of the preceding sentence shall not apply where the levy is made upon minerals or the like (but not including oil or gas) and no dwelling is located on the real property. If the real property described in the notice of levy consists of more than one distinct lot, parcel, or governmental subdivision and any of the lots, parcels, or governmental subdivisions lies with relation to any of the others so as to form one or more continuous, unbroken tracts, only one service or posting need be made under this subdivision as to each continuous, unbroken tract.[329]

700.030. Unless another method of levy is provided by this article, to levy upon tangible personal property in the possession or under the control of the judgment debtor, the levying officer shall take the property into custody.[170]

700.040. (a) Unless another method of

levy is provided by this article, to levy upon tangible personal property in the possession or under the control of a third person, the levying officer shall personally serve a copy of the writ of execution and a notice of levy on the third person.

(b) If goods are in the possession of a bailee who has issued a negotiable document of title therefor, the goods may not be levied upon but the negotiable document of title may be levied upon in the manner provided by Section 700.120. If goods are in the possession of a bailee other than one who has issued a negotiable document of title therefor, the goods may be levied upon in the manner provided by Section 700.060. As used in this subdivision, "bailee" means "bailee" as defined in Section 7102 of the Commercial Code.[170]

700.050. (a) To levy upon personal property in the custody of a levying officer:

(1) If the writ of execution is directed to the levying officer having custody of the property, the judgment creditor shall deliver the writ to the levying officer.

(2) If the writ of execution is directed to a levying officer other than the levying officer having custody of the property, the levying officer to whom the writ is directed shall serve a copy of the writ and a notice of levy on the levying officer having custody. Service shall be made personally or by mail.

(b) The levying officer having custody of the property shall comply with the writs in the order they are received and is not subject to the provisions of Article 5 (commencing with Section 701.010) (duties and liabilities of third persons after levy).[170]

700.060. (a) To levy upon goods in the possession of a bailee (as defined in Section 7102 of the Commercial Code) other than one who has issued a negotiable document of title therefor, the levying officer shall personally serve a copy of the writ of execution and a notice of levy on the bailee.

(b) If the goods described in subdivision (a) are subject to a security interest, the levying officer shall, if so instructed by the judgment creditor, serve a copy of the writ of execution and a notice of levy on the secured party. Service shall be made personally or by mail.[170]

700.070. To levy upon tangible personal property of a going business in the possession or under the control of the judgment debtor, the levying officer shall comply with Section 700.030, except to the extent that the judgment creditor instructs that levy be made in the following manner:

(a) The levying officer shall place a keeper in charge of the business for the period requested by the judgment creditor. During the period, the business may continue to operate in the ordinary course of business provided that all sales are final and are for cash or its equivalent. For the purpose of this subdivision, a check is the equivalent of cash. The levying officer is not liable for accepting payment in the form of a cash equivalent. The keeper shall take custody of the proceeds from all sales unless otherwise directed by the judgment creditor.

(b) The levying officer shall take the tangible personal property into exclusive custody at the earliest of the following times:

(1) At any time the judgment debtor objects to placement of a keeper in charge of the business.

(2) At any time when requested by the judgment creditor.

(3) At the end of 10 days from the time the keeper is placed in charge of the business.

(c) Where a keeper is placed in a business for the purpose of taking into custody tangible personal property consisting solely of money or equivalent proceeds of sales, the provisions of subdivision (b) shall not apply, and the levying officer shall take such property into exclusive custody at the end of each daily keeper period.[375]

700.080. (a) To levy upon personal property used as a dwelling, the levying officer shall serve a copy of the writ of execution and a notice of levy on one occupant of the property. Service on the occupant shall be made by leaving the copy of the writ and the notice of levy with the occupant personally or, in the occupant's absence, with a person of suitable age and discretion found at the property when service is attempted who is a member of the occupant's family or household. If unable to serve the occupant at the time service is attempted, the levying officer shall make the levy by posting the copy of the writ and the notice of levy in a conspicuous place on the property.

(b) If the judgment creditor so instructs, the levying officer shall place a keeper in charge of the property for a period requested by the judgment creditor.

(c) The judgment creditor may apply to the court on noticed motion for an order directing the levying officer to remove the occupants. The notice of motion shall be served on any legal owner and any junior lienholder who was served pursuant to Section 700.090, on the occupant, and, if the judgment debtor is not the occupant, on the judgment debtor. Service shall be made personally or by mail. At the hearing on the motion the court shall determine the occupant's right to possession and shall make an order including terms and conditions that are appropriate under the circumstances of the case.

(d) Personal property used as a dwelling shall include a mobilehome, whether the mobilehome is occupied or unoccupied at the time of the levy.[345]

700.090. If a vehicle or vessel is levied upon and a certificate of ownership has been issued by the Department of Motor Vehicles for such vehicle or vessel and the certificate of ownership is still in effect, or if a manufactured home, mobilehome, or commercial coach is levied upon and a permanent title record has been established by the Department of Housing and Community Development for such manufactured home, mobilehome, or commercial coach the levying officer shall determine from the appropriate department the name and address of the legal owner and each junior lienholder of the property levied upon. If the legal owner or junior lienholder is not the judgment debtor and is not in possession of the vehicle, vessel, manufactured home, mobilehome, or commercial coach, the levying officer shall at the time of levy or promptly thereafter serve a copy of the writ of execution and a notice of levy on the legal owner or junior lienholder. Service shall be made personally or by mail.[196]

700.100. (a) To levy upon chattel paper, the levying officer shall:
(1) If the chattel paper is in the possession of the judgment debtor, take the chattel paper into custody.
(2) If the chattel paper is in the possession of a third person, personally serve a copy of the writ of execution and a notice of levy on the third person.
(b) If the levying officer obtains custody of the chattel paper or if pursuant to a security agreement the judgment debtor has liberty to collect or compromise the chattel paper or to accept the return of goods or make repossessions, the levying officer shall, if so instructed by the judgment creditor, serve a copy of the writ of execution and a notice of levy on the account debtor. Service shall be made personally or by mail.
(c) In addition to any other rights created by a levy on chattel paper, the levy creates a lien on the judgment debtor's rights in specific goods subject to the chattel paper.[170]

700.110. (a) To levy upon an instrument, the levying officer shall:
(1) If the instrument is in the possession of the judgment debtor, take the instrument into custody.
(2) If the instrument is in the possession of a third person, personally serve a copy of the writ of execution and a notice of levy on the third person.
(b) If the levying officer obtains custody of the instrument, the levying officer shall, if the judgment creditor so instructs, serve a copy of the writ of execution and a notice of levy on the obligor. Service shall be made personally or by mail.[170]

700.120. To levy upon a negotiable document of title, the levying officer shall:
(a) If the negotiable document of title is in the possession of the judgment debtor, take the negotiable document of title into custody.
(b) If the negotiable document of title is in the possession of a third person, personally serve a copy of the writ of execution and a notice of levy on the third person.[170]

700.130. To levy upon a security, the levying officer shall comply with Section 8112 of the Commercial Code. The legal process referred to in Section 8112 of the Commercial Code means the legal process required by the state in which te chief executive office of the issuer of the security is located and, where that state is California, means personal service by the levying officer of a copy of the writ of execution and notice of levy on the person who is to be served.[360]

700.140. (a) Subject to Sections 684.115 and 700.160, to levy upon a deposit account, the levying officer shall personally serve a copy of the writ of execution and a notice of levy on the financial institution with which the deposit account is maintained.
(b) The execution lien that arises upon service of a writ of execution and notice of levy reaches only amounts in a deposit account at the time of service on the financial institution, including the amount of any deposit not yet fi-

nally collected unless the deposit is returned unpaid to the financial institution.

(c) The levying officer shall serve a copy of the writ of execution and a notice of levy on any third person in whose name any deposit account described therein stands. Service shall be made personally or by mail as follows:

(1) At the time of levy or promptly thereafter, if the party seeking the levy informs the levying officer of the person and his, her, or its residence or business address.

(2) Promptly following the levying officer's receipt of a garnishee's memorandum if service was not accomplished pursuant to paragraph (1) if the garnishee's memorandum identifies the person and his, her, or its residence or business address.

(d) The financial institution shall not honor a withdrawal request or a check or other order for the payment of money from the deposit account if presentment of the withdrawal request or item to the financial institution occurs during the time the execution lien is in effect unless, following the withdrawal or payment, sufficient funds are available to cover the levy. For these purposes, a withdrawal from the deposit account to cover the financial institution's standard fee or charge for processing the levy shall not be considered a payment of money from the account in violation of this subdivision.

(e) During the time the execution lien is in effect, the financial institution is not liable to any person for any of the following:

(1) Performance of the duties of a garnishee under the levy.

(2) Nonpayment of a check or other order for the payment or transfer of money drawn or presented against the deposit account if the nonpayment is pursuant to the requirements of subdivision (d).

(3) Refusal to pay a withdrawal from the deposit account if the refusal is pursuant to the requirements of subdivision (d).

(f) When the amount levied upon pursuant to this section is paid to the levying officer, the execution lien on the deposit account levied upon terminates.

(g) For the purposes of this section, none of the following is a third person in whose name the deposit account stands:

(1) A person who is only a person named as the beneficiary of a Totten trust account.

(2) A person who is only a payee designated in a pay-on-death provision in an account pursuant to Section 18318.5 of the Financial Code or Section 5140 of the Probate Code, or other similar provision.

(3) A person who is only acting in a representative or custodial capacity with respect to benefits paid or payable by the United States government. Rather, accounts maintained by the representative or custodian shall be deemed to stand in the beneficiary's name, and the amounts therein shall be covered by a levy against the beneficiary.

(h) For purposes of this section, final payment of a deposit shall be deemed to have occurred in accordance with Section 4215 or 11210 of the Commercial Code or with automated clearinghouse or Federal Reserve System rule, regulation, operating circular, or similar governing document, as applicable to the deposit. If, for any reason, a deposit is returned by the financial institution upon which it is drawn, the deposit shall not be deemed finally collected for purposes of this subdivision regardless of any later payment by the financial institution upon which the deposit is drawn.[676]

700.150. (a) Subject to Section 700.160, to levy upon property in a safe-deposit box, the levying officer shall personally serve a copy of the writ of execution and a notice of levy on the financial institution with which the safe-deposit box is maintained.

(b) At the time of the levy or promptly thereafter, the levying officer shall serve a copy of the writ of execution and a notice of levy on any third person in whose name the safe-deposit box stands. Service shall be made personally or by mail.

(c) During the time the execution lien is in effect, the financial institution may not permit the removal of any of the contents of the safe-deposit box except as directed by the levying officer.

(d) Upon receipt of a garnishee's memorandum from the financial institution indicating a safe-deposit box is under levy, the levying officer shall promptly mail a written notice to the judgment creditor demanding an additional fee as required by Section 26723 of the Government Code, plus the costs to open the safe-deposit box and seize and store the contents. The levying officer shall release the levy on the safe-deposit box if the judgment creditor does not pay the required fee, plus costs, within three business days plus the extended time period specified in subdivision (a) of Section 1013 for service by mail by the levying officer.

(e) The levying officer may first give the person in whose name the safe-deposit box stands an opportunity to open the safe-deposit box to permit the removal pursuant to the levy of the property levied upon. The financial institution may refuse to permit the forcible opening of the safe-deposit box to permit the removal of the property levied upon unless the levying officer or the judgment creditor pays in advance the cost of forcibly opening the safe-deposit box and of repairing any damage caused thereby.

(f) The levying officer shall give the judgment creditor at least three court days' advance notice of the date and time the levying officer will open the safe-deposit box and seize the contents thereof, and the judgment creditor shall be entitled to be present at that time.

(g) During the time the execution lien is in effect, the financial institution is not liable to any person for any of the following:

(1) Performance of the duties of a garnishee under the levy.

(2) Refusal to permit access to the safe-deposit box by the person in whose name it stands.

(3) Removal of any of the contents of the safe-deposit box pursuant to the levy.

(h) If the levying officer removes any property from the safe-deposit box to satisfy the levy, but allows other property to remain in the safe-deposit box, the execution lien is released automatically with respect to any property that remains in the safe-deposit box.[677]

700.160. (a) Except as provided in subdivision (b), a deposit account or safe-deposit box standing in the name of a person other than the judgment debtor, either alone or together with third persons, is not subject to levy under Section 700.140 or 700.150 unless the legal process served on the third party includes a court order authorizing the levy.

(b) A court order is not required to levy on a deposit account or safe-deposit box standing in the name of any of the following:

(1) The judgment debtor, whether alone or together with third persons.

(2) The judgment debtor's spouse or registered domestic partner, whether alone or together with other persons, provided an affidavit is delivered to the financial institution at the time of levy showing that person is the judgment debtor's spouse or registered domestic partner.

(3) A fictitious business name, provided a copy of an unexpired statement certified in accordance with Section 17926 of the Business and Professions Code is delivered to the financial institution at the time of levy, the fictitious business name statement does not list any person other than the judgment debtor, the judgment debtor's spouse or the judgment debtor's registered domestic partner as the person or persons doing business under the fictitious business name, and, if a person other than the judgment debtor is listed in the statement, an affidavit stating that the other person is the judgment debtor's spouse or registered domestic partner is delivered to the financial institution at the time of the levy.

(4) The additional name of a judgment debtor listed on the legal process pursuant to an affidavit of identity as provided by Section 680.135, whether alone or together with third persons.

(c) In any case where a deposit account in the name of a person other than the judgment debtor, whether alone or together with the judgment debtor, is levied upon, the financial institution shall not pay to the levying officer the amount levied upon until being notified to do so by the levying officer. The levying officer may not require the financial institution to pay the amount levied upon until the expiration of 15 days after service of notice of levy on the third person.[678]

700.170. (a) Unless another method of levy is provided by this article, to levy upon an account receivable or general intangible, the levying officer shall personally serve a copy of the writ of execution and a notice of levy on the account debtor.

(b) If a levy is made under subdivision (a) and payments on the account receivable or general intangible are made to a person other than the judgment debtor (whether pursuant to a security agreement, assignment for collection, or otherwise), the levying officer shall, if so instructed by the judgment creditor, personally serve a copy of the writ of execution and a notice of levy on such third person. Service of the copy of the writ and notice of levy on such third person is a levy on any amounts owed to the judgment debtor by such third person.[170]

700.180. (a) The following property may be levied upon pursuant to this article notwithstanding that the property levied upon is the subject of a pending action or special proceeding:

(1) Real property.

(2) Growing crops, timber to be cut, or minerals or the like (including oil

(2) ... and gas) to be extracted or accounts receivable resulting from the sale thereof at the wellhead or minehead.

(3) Tangible personal property in the possession or under the control of the judgment debtor or in the custody of a levying officer.

(4) The interest of a judgment debtor in personal property in the estate of a decedent, whether the interest arises by testate or intestate succession.

(b) Except as provided in subdivision (a), a levy upon property that is the subject of an action or special proceeding pending at the time of the levy is not effective.

(c) If a levy is attempted but is ineffective under subdivision (b) and the levying officer has requested a garnishee's memorandum under Section 701.030 in connection with the ineffective levy, the garnishee's memorandum shall include the following information in addition to that required by Section 701.030:

(1) A statement that the levy on the property is not effective because the property is the subject of a pending action or special proceeding.

(2) The title of the court, cause, and number of the pending action or proceeding.

(d) For the purpose of this section, an action or proceeding is pending from the time the action or proceeding is commenced until judgment has been entered and the time for appeal has expired or, if an appeal is filed, until the appeal has been finally determined.

(e) Nothing in this section affects or limits the right of the judgment creditor to obtain a lien pursuant to Article 5 (commencing with Section 708.410) of Chapter 6.[170]

700.190. (a) As used in this section, "final money judgment" means a money judgment after the time for appeal from the judgment has expired or, if an appeal is filed, after the appeal has been finally determined.

(b) To levy upon a final money judgment, the levying officer shall file a copy of the writ of execution and a notice of levy with the clerk of the court that entered the final money judgment. The court clerk shall endorse upon the judgment a statement of the existence of the execution lien and the time it was created. If an abstract of the judgment is issued, it shall include a statement of the execution lien in favor of the judgment creditor.

(c) At the time of levy or promptly thereafter, the levying officer shall serve a copy of the writ of execution and a notice of levy on the judgment debtor obligated to pay the final money judgment levied upon. Service shall be made personally or by mail.[218]

700.200. (a) To levy upon the interest of the judgment debtor in personal property in the estate of a decedent, whether the interest arises by testate or intestate succession, the levying officer shall personally serve a copy of the writ and a notice of levy on the personal representative of the decedent. The levy does not impair the powers of the representative over the property for the purposes of administration.

(b) The personal representative shall report the levy to the court in which the estate is being administered when any petition for distribution is filed. If a decree orders distribution to the judgment debtor, the court making the decree shall order the property levied upon to be delivered to the levying officer. The property may not be deliv-

ered to the levying officer until the decree distributing the property has become final. To the extent the property delivered to the levying officer is not necessary to satisfy the money judgment, it shall be released to the judgment debtor.
(c) Promptly after the property is delivered to the levying officer pursuant to subdivision (b), the levying officer shall serve a notice describing the property on the judgment debtor. Service shall be made personally or by mail. Notwithstanding Section 703.520, a claim of exemption for the property described in the notice may be made within 10 days after the notice was served on the judgment debtor.
(d) Notwithstanding Section 697.710, an execution lien created by a levy pursuant to this section continues for a period of one year after the decree distributing the interest has become final unless the judgment is sooner satisfied.
(e) A writ under which a levy is made pursuant to this section shall be returned not later than one year after the date the decree distributing the interest has become final.[170]

Article 5: Duties and Liabilities of Third Persons After Levy
Article 5 added by Stats. 1982, Ch. 1364, Sec. 2.

701.010. (a) Except as otherwise provided by statute, when a levy is made by service of a copy of the writ of execution and a notice of levy on a third person, the third person at the time of levy or promptly thereafter shall comply with this section.
(b) Unless the third person has good cause for failure or refusal to do so:
(1) The third person shall deliver to the levying officer any of the property levied upon that is in the possession or under the control of the third person at the time of levy unless the third person claims the right to possession of the property.
(2) To the extent that the third person does not deny an obligation levied upon, or claim a priority over the judgment creditor's lien, the third person shall pay to the levying officer both of the following:
(A) The amount of the obligation levied upon that is due and payable to the judgment debtor at the time of levy.
(B) Amounts that become due and payable to the judgment debtor on the obligation levied upon during the period of the execution lien.
(3) If the third person makes a delivery or payment to the levying officer pursuant to this section, the third person shall execute and deliver any documents necessary to effect the transfer of the property.
(c) For the purposes of this section, "good cause" includes, but is not limited to, a showing that the third person did not know or have reason to know of the levy from all the facts and circumstances known to the third person.[170]

701.020. (a) If a third person is required by this article to deliver property to the levying officer or to make payments to the levying officer and the third person fails or refuses without good cause to do so, the third person is liable to the judgment creditor for whichever of the following is the lesser amount:
(1) The value of the judgment debtor's interest in the property or the amount of the payments required to be made.

(2) The amount required to satisfy the judgment pursuant to which the levy is made.

(b) The third person's liability continues until the earliest of the following times:

(1) The time when the property levied upon is delivered to the levying officer or the payments are made to the levying officer.

(2) The time when the property levied upon is released pursuant to Section 699. 060.

(3) The time when the judgment is satisfied or discharged.

(c) If the third person's liability is established, the court that determines the liability may, in its discretion, require the third person to pay the costs and reasonable attorney's fees incurred by the judgment creditor in establishing the liability.[170]

701.030. (a) At the time of service of a copy of the legal process on a third person, the levying officer shall request the third person to give the levying officer a garnishee's memorandum containing the information required by this section. Within 10 days after the legal process is served, the third person shall mail or deliver the garnishee's memorandum to the levying officer whether or not the levy is effective.

(b) The garnishee's memorandum shall be executed under oath and shall contain the following information, as applicable:

(1) A description of any property of the judgment debtor sought to be levied upon that is not delivered to the levying officer and the reason for not delivering the property.

(2) A description of any property of the judgment debtor not sought to be levied upon that is in the possession or under the control of the third person at the time of levy.

(3) A statement of the amount and terms of any obligation to the judgment debtor sought to be levied upon that is due and payable and is not paid to the levying officer, and the reason for not paying the obligation.

(4) A statement of the amount and terms of any obligation to the judgment debtor sought to be levied upon that is not due and payable at the time of levy.

(5) A statement of the amount and terms of any obligation to the judgment debtor at the time of levy not sought to be levied upon.

(6) A description of claims and rights of other persons to the property or obligation levied upon that are known to the third person and the names and addresses of those other persons.

(7) A statement that the garnishee holds neither any property nor any obligations in favor of the judgment debtor.

(c) If a garnishee's memorandum is received from the third person, the levying officer shall retain a copy and promptly mail or deliver a copy of the memorandum to the judgment creditor.

(d) Except as provided in subdivisions (e) and (f), if a third person does not give the levying officer a garnishee's memorandum within the time provided in subdivision (a), or does not provide complete information, the third person may, in the court's discretion, be required to pay the costs and reasonable attorney's fees incurred in any proceedings to obtain the information required in the garnishee's memorandum.

(e) Notwithstanding subdivision (a), when the levy is made upon a deposit account or upon property in a safe-deposit box, the financial institution need not give a garnishee's memorandum to the levying officer if the financial institution fully complies with the levy and, if a garnishee's memorandum is required, the garnishee's memorandum needs to provide information with respect only to property that is carried on the records available at the office or branch where the levy is made provided that if a levy has been served at a central location designated by a financial institution in accordance with Section 684.115, the garnishee's memorandum shall apply to all offices and branches of the financial institution except to the extent acceptance of the levy at those central locations is limited pursuant to paragraph (3) of subdivision (b) of Section 684.115.

(f) Notwithstanding subdivision (a), the third person need not give a garnishee's memorandum to the levying officer if both of the following conditions are satisfied:

(1) The third person has delivered to the levying officer all of the property sought to be levied upon.

(2) The third person has paid to the levying officer the amount due at the time of levy on any obligation to the judgment debtor that was levied upon, and there is no additional amount that thereafter will become payable on the obligation levied upon.

(g) The garnishee may electronically transmit the garnishee's memorandum to the levying officer pursuant to Chapter 2 (commencing with Section 263) of Title 4 of Part 1.[847]

701.035. A third person who gives a garnishee's memorandum pursuant to this title is not liable to any person for the disclosure in the garnishee's memorandum of any information contained in the garnishee's memorandum.[183]

701.040. (a) Except as otherwise ordered by the court upon a determination that the judgment creditor's lien has priority over the security interest, if property levied upon is subject to a security interest that attached prior to levy, the property or obligation is subject to enforcement of the security interest without regard to the levy unless the property is in the custody of the levying officer; but, if the execution lien has priority over the security interest, the secured party is liable to the judgment creditor for any proceeds received by the secured party from the property to the extent of the execution lien.

(b) After the security interest is satisfied, the secured party shall deliver any excess property, and pay any excess payments or proceeds of property, remaining in the possession of the secured party to the levying officer for the purposes of the levy, as provided in Section 9615 of the Commercial Code, unless otherwise ordered by the court or directed by the levying officer.[270]

701.050. After service of a copy of the writ of execution and a notice of levy on an account debtor obligated on an account receivable, chattel paper, or general intangible:

(a) If the account debtor has been making payments or is required to make payments to the judgment debtor, the account debtor shall make payments to the levying officer as they become due unless otherwise directed by court order or by the levying officer. Payments made to the judgment debtor after the account debtor has received notice of the levy do not discharge the obligation of the account debtor to make payments as required by this subdivision.

(b) If the account debtor has been making payments to a third person or is required to make payments to a third person (whether pursuant to a security agreement, assignment for collection, or otherwise), the account debtor shall continue to make such payments to the third person notwithstanding the levy until the account debtor receives notice that the obligation to the third person is satisfied or is otherwise directed by court order or by the third person. After the account debtor receives notice that the obligation to the third person is satisfied, the account debtor shall make payments to the levying officer as they become due unless otherwise directed by court order or by the levying officer.

(c) If pursuant to a security agreement the judgment debtor has liberty to accept the return of goods or make repossessions under the account receivable or chattel paper, the account debtor shall deliver to the levying officer property returnable to the judgment debtor unless otherwise directed by court order or by the levying officer.[170]

701.060. If the levying officer obtains custody of an instrument levied upon and serves the obligor under the instrument pursuant to the levy, the obligor shall make payments to the levying officer as they become due. Payments made to a person other than the levying officer do not discharge the obligation of the obligor to make payments as required by this section if the payments are made after the obligor has received notice of the levy.[170]

701.070. If a final money judgment has been levied upon and the levying officer has served the judgment debtor under the final money judgment levied upon, the judgment debtor shall make any payments due under the judgment to the levying officer. Payments made to a person other than the levying officer do not discharge the obligation of the judgment debtor under the final money judgment levied upon if the payments are made after the judgment debtor has received notice of the levy.[219]

Article 6: Sale and Collection
Article 6 added by Stats. 1982, Ch. 1364, Sec. 2.

701.510. Subject to Sections 687.020 and 701.520, the levying officer shall sell all property that has been levied upon except:

(a) Tangible personal property may not be sold until the levying officer obtains custody of the property.

(b) Cash may not be sold unless it has a value exceeding its face value.[170]

701.520. (a) Except as provided in this section, any of the following property that has been levied upon shall be collected rather than sold:

(1) Accounts receivable.
(2) Chattel paper.
(3) General intangibles.
(4) Final money judgments.
(5) Instruments that are not customarily transferred in an established market.
(6) Instruments that represent an obligation arising out of the sale or lease

of property, a license to use property, the furnishing of services, or the loan of money where the property sold or leased or licensed for use, the services furnished, or the money loaned was used by an individual primarily for personal, family, or household purposes.

(b) At the time of levy on property described in subdivision (a) or thereafter, the judgment creditor may serve a notice of intended sale of the property on the judgment debtor. Service shall be made personally or by mail. A copy of the notice of intended sale and proof of service on the judgment debtor shall be filed with the court and with the levying officer. The notice of intended sale shall describe the property and state that it will be sold at an execution sale unless, within the time allowed after service of the notice of intended sale, the judgment debtor applies to the court on noticed motion for an order that the property be collected rather than sold.

(c) Within 10 days after service of the notice of intended sale, the judgment debtor may apply to the court on noticed motion for an order that the property be collected rather than sold. A judgment debtor who so applies shall, within the time allowed for the application, serve a copy of the notice of motion on the judgment creditor and file a copy of the notice of motion with the levying officer. Service of the copy of the notice of motion on the judgment creditor shall be made personally or by mail. If the copy of the notice of motion is not filed with the levying officer within the time allowed, the levying officer shall proceed to sell the property. If a copy of the notice of motion is filed with the levying officer within the time allowed, the levying officer shall continue to collect the property until otherwise ordered by the court.

(d) At the hearing on the motion, the court may in its discretion order that the property be sold or be collected depending on the equities and circumstances of the particular case. If the court orders that the property be sold, the order may specify terms and conditions of sale. If the court orders that the property be collected, the court may condition its order on an assignment of the property by the judgment debtor to the judgment creditor pursuant to Article 6 (commencing with Section 708.510) of Chapter 6.[170]

701.530. (a) Notice of sale of personal property shall be in writing, shall state the date, time, and place of sale, and shall describe the property to be sold.

(b) Not less than 10 days before a sale of personal property, notice of sale shall be posted and served on the judgment debtor by the levying officer. Service shall be made personally or by mail.

(c) Posting under this section shall be in three public places in:

(1) The city in which the property is to be sold if it is to be sold in a city.

(2) The county in which the property is to be sold if it is not to be sold in a city.

(d) A sale of personal property of an individual may not take place until the expiration of the time during which the judgment debtor may make a claim of exemption under subdivision (a) of Section 703.520.[511]

701.540. (a) Notice of sale of an interest in real property shall be in writing, shall state the date, time, and place of sale, shall describe the interest to be sold, and shall give a legal description of the real property and its street address or other common designation, if any. If the real property has no street address or other common designation, the notice of sale shall include a statement that directions to its location may be obtained from the levying officer upon oral or written request or, in the discretion of the levying officer, the notice of sale may contain directions to its location. Directions are sufficient if information as to the location of the real property is given by reference to the direction and approximate distance from the nearest crossroads, frontage road, or access road. If an accurate legal description of the real property is given, the validity of the notice and sale is not affected by the fact that the street address or other common designation, or directions to its location, are erroneous or omitted.

(b) Not less than 20 days before the date of sale, notice of sale of an interest in real property shall be served, mailed, and posted by the levying officer as provided in subdivisions (c), (d), (e), and (f).

(c) Notice of sale shall be served on the judgment debtor. Service shall be made personally or by mail.

(d) Notice of sale shall be posted in the following places:

(1) One public place in the city in which the interest in the real property is to be sold if it is to be sold in a city or, if not to be sold in a city, one public place in the county in which the interest in the real property is to be sold.

(2) A conspicuous place on the real property.

(e) At the time notice is posted pursuant to paragraph (2) of subdivision (d), notice of sale shall be served or service shall be attempted on one occupant of the real property. Service on the occupant shall be made by leaving the notice with the occupant personally or, in the occupant's absence, with any person of suitable age and discretion found upon the real property at the time service is attempted who is either an employee or agent of the occupant or a member of the occupant's household. If the levying officer is unable to serve an occupant, as specified, at the time service is attempted, the levying officer is not required to make any further attempts to serve an occupant.

(f) If the property described in the notice of sale consists of more than one distinct lot, parcel, or governmental subdivision and any of the lots, parcels, or governmental subdivisions lies with relation to any of the others so as to form one or more continuous, unbroken tracts, only one service pursuant to subdivision (e) and posting pursuant to paragraph (2) of subdivision (d) need be made as to each continuous, unbroken tract.

(g) Notice of sale shall be published pursuant to Section 6063 of the Government Code, with the first publication at least 20 days prior to the time of sale, in a newspaper of general circulation published in the city in which the real property or a part thereof is situated if any part thereof is situated in a city or, if not, in a newspaper of general circulation published in the public notice district in which the real property or a part thereof is situated. If no newspaper of general circulation is published in the city or public notice district, notice of sale shall be published in a newspaper of general circulation in the county in which the real property or a part thereof is situated.

(h) Not earlier than 30 days after the date of levy, the judgment creditor shall determine the names of all persons having liens on the real property on the date of levy that are of record in the office of the county recorder and shall instruct the levying officer to mail notice of sale to each lienholder at the address used by the county recorder for the return of the instrument creating the lien after recording. The levying officer shall mail notice to each lienholder, at the address given in the instructions, not less than 20 days before the date of sale.

(i) For the purposes of this section, publication of notice in a public notice district is governed by Chapter 1.1 (commencing with Section 6080) of Division 7 of Title 1 of the Government Code.[729]

701.545. Notice of sale of an interest in real property, other than a leasehold estate with an unexpired term of less than two years at the time of levy, may not be given pursuant to Section 701.540 until the expiration of 120 days after the date notice of levy on the interest in real property was served on the judgment debtor.[170]

701.547. A notice of sale shall contain the substance of the following statement: "Prospective bidders should refer to Sections 701.510 to 701.680, inclusive, of the Code of Civil Procedure for provisions governing the terms, conditions, and effect of the sale and the liability of defaulting bidders."[170]

701.550. (a) In addition to the notice of sale required by this article, the levying officer shall, at the time notice of sale is posted pursuant to Section 701.530 or 701.540, mail notice of sale to any person who has requested notice of the sale pursuant to this section.

(b) A request for notice of sale under this section made prior to the issuance of the writ shall be in writing and shall be filed with the clerk of the court where the judgment is entered. The request shall specify the title of the court, the cause and number of the action in which the judgment was entered, and the date of entry thereof, and shall state the address to which the notice of sale is to be mailed. The name and address of the person requesting notice of sale under this subdivision shall be noted on the writ.

(c) A person who desires notice of sale of particular property that has been levied upon may file a request for notice of sale with the levying officer who will conduct the sale. The request shall contain the information specified by the levying officer as needed in order to comply with the request.[170]

701.555. In addition to the notice of sale required by this article, the judgment creditor may advertise the sale in the classified or other advertising section of a newspaper of general circulation or other publication and may recover reasonable costs of such advertising. The judgment debtor may also advertise the sale at the judgment debtor's own expense.[170]

701.560. (a) Failure to give notice of sale as required by this article does not invalidate the sale.

(b) A levying officer who sells property without giving the required notice is liable to the judgment creditor and the judgment debtor for actual damages caused by failure to give notice.[170]

701.570. (a) A sale of property shall be held at the date, time, and place specified in the notice of sale, which shall be in the county where the property or a part thereof is situated and between the hours of nine in the morning and five in the afternoon. Subject to subdivision (d), real property consisting of one parcel, or of two or more contiguous parcels, situated in two or more counties may be sold in one county as instructed by the judgment creditor.
(b) The sale shall be made at auction to the highest bidder.
(c) If personal property capable of manual delivery is to be sold, it shall be within the view of those who attend the sale unless, upon application of the judgment creditor or the judgment debtor, the court orders otherwise.
(d) Property shall be sold separately or in such groups or lots as are likely to bring the highest price. The judgment debtor may request that the property be sold separately or together and may request that the property be sold in a particular order. If the judgment debtor is not present at the sale, the request may be made in writing and delivered to the levying officer prior to the sale. The levying officer shall honor the request if, in the opinion of the levying officer, the requested manner of sale is likely to yield an amount at least equal to any other manner of sale or the amount required to satisfy the money judgment. The levying officer is not liable for a decision made in good faith under this subdivision.
(e) After sufficient property has been sold to yield the amount required to satisfy the money judgment, no more shall be sold.[170]

701.580. The judgment debtor and judgment creditor together may request in writing that a sale be postponed to an agreed day and hour. The request shall be delivered to the levying officer conducting the sale, and the levying officer shall, by public declaration at the time and place originally fixed for the sale, postpone the sale to the day and hour fixed in the request. Notice of any additional postponements shall be given by public declaration by the levying officer at the time and place last appointed for the sale. No other notice of postponed sale need be given. A postponed sale shall be held at the place originally fixed for the sale.[170]

701.590. (a) Except as otherwise provided in this section, the purchaser at a sale shall pay in cash or by certified check or cashier's check.
(b) The judgment creditor may bid by giving the levying officer a written receipt crediting all or part of the amount required to satisfy the judgment, except that the levying officer's costs remaining unsatisfied and the amount of preferred labor claims, exempt proceeds, and any other claim that is required by statute to be satisfied, shall be paid in cash or by certified check or cashier's check.
(c) If the highest bid for an interest in real property sold exceeds five thousand dollars ($5,000), the highest bidder may elect to treat the sale as a credit transaction. A person who makes the election shall deposit at least five thousand dollars ($5,000) or 10 percent of the amount bid, whichever is greater, and within 10 days after the date of the sale shall pay the balance due plus costs accruing with regard to the property sold and interest accruing at the rate on money judgments on the

balance of the amount bid from the date of sale until the date of payment.

(d) If the highest bid for an item, group, or lot of personal property sold exceeds two thousand five hundred dollars ($2,500), the highest bidder may elect to treat the sale as a credit transaction. A person who makes the election shall deposit at least two thousand five hundred dollars ($2,500) or 10 percent of the amount bid, whichever is greater, and within 10 days after the date of the sale shall pay the balance due plus costs accruing with regard to the property sold and interest accruing at the rate on money judgments on the balance of the amount bid from the date of sale until the date of payment.

(e) A person who makes the election under subdivision (c) or (d) is not entitled to possession of the property sold until the amount bid, plus accruing costs and interest, have been paid.[170]

701.600. If the highest bidder does not pay the amount bid as prescribed by Section 701.590:

(a) The levying officer shall sell the property:

(1) If the default occurs at the sale, either to the next highest bidder at the amount of the next highest bid if such bidder agrees or to the highest bidder at a new sale held immediately.

(2) If the default occurs after the sale to a credit bidder pursuant to subdivision (c) of Section 701.590, to the highest bidder at a new sale.

(b) The levying officer shall apply the amount of any deposit made pursuant to subdivision (c) of Section 701.590 in the following order:

(1) To the satisfaction of costs accruing with regard to the property sold from the date of the sale until the date the property is resold, including costs of resale.

(2) To the satisfaction of interest at the rate on money judgments on the amount bid from the date of the sale until the date the property is resold.

(3) To the amount required to satisfy the money judgment in the order of distribution prescribed by Section 701.810 or Section 704.850, whichever is applicable.

(c) If there is a sale to the next highest bidder or to the highest bidder at a new sale, the defaulting bidder is liable for the following amounts in an action by the judgment creditor or judgment debtor:

(1) The amount bid, less the amount obtained from the resale of the property and the amount of any deposit applied pursuant to subdivision (b). The amount recovered pursuant to this paragraph shall be distributed in the manner prescribed by Section 701.810 or Section 704.850, whichever is applicable.

(2) Any costs accruing with regard to the property sold from the date of sale until the date the property is resold, including costs of resale.

(3) Interest at the rate on money judgments on the amount bid from the date of the sale until the date the property is resold.

(4) Costs and attorney's fees incurred in the action under this subdivision.

(d) The levying officer may, in the levying officer's discretion, reject any subsequent bid of the defaulting bidder.[170]

701.610. The levying officer may not be a purchaser or have an interest in any purchase at a sale.[170]

701.620. (a) Property may not be sold

unless the amount bid exceeds the total of the following amounts:

(1) The amount of all preferred labor claims that are required by Section 1206 to be satisfied from the proceeds.

(2) The amount of any state tax lien (as defined in Section 7162 of the Government Code) that is superior to the judgment creditor's lien.

(3) If the purchaser is not the judgment creditor, the amount of any deposit made pursuant to Section 720.260 with interest thereon at the rate on money judgments from the date of the deposit to the date of the sale.

(b) Property for which a proceeds exemption is provided by Section 704.010 (motor vehicle), 704.020 (household furnishings and other personal effects), or 704.060 (tools of trade), may not be sold unless the amount bid exceeds the sum of any amount under subdivision (a) and the amount of the proceeds exemption.

(c) If a minimum bid required for the sale of property pursuant to this section is not received, the levying officer shall promptly release the property.[170]

701.630. If property is sold pursuant to this article, the lien under which it is sold, any liens subordinate thereto, and any state tax lien (as defined in Section 7162 of the Government Code) on the property sold are extinguished.[170]

701.640. The purchaser of property at an execution sale acquires any interest of the judgment debtor in the property sold (1) that is held on the effective date of the lien under which the property was sold or (2) that is acquired between such effective date and the date of sale.[170]

701.650. (a) When the purchaser of personal property pays the amount due:

(1) If the property is capable of manual delivery, the levying officer shall deliver the property to the purchaser and, if the purchaser so requests, shall execute and deliver a certificate of sale to the purchaser.

(2) If the property is not tangible personal property or if it is otherwise not capable of manual delivery, the levying officer shall execute and deliver a certificate of sale to the purchaser.

(b) If property or a certificate is delivered pursuant to subdivision (a), the levying officer shall sign or endorse any document or instrument in the levying officer's possession relating to the title to or the right to possession of the property and deliver it to the purchaser.[170]

701.660. When the purchaser of an interest in real property pays the amount due to the levying officer, including any amount required to be paid as a documentary transfer tax pursuant to Section 11911 of the Revenue and Taxation Code, the levying officer conducting the sale shall execute and deliver a deed of sale to the purchaser, record a duplicate of the deed of sale in the office of the county recorder, and forward to the county or city and county any documentary transfer tax paid by the purchaser.[643]

701.670. The certificate of sale or deed of sale shall contain all of the following:

(a) The title of the court where the judgment was entered under which the sale was made and the cause and number of the action.

(b) The date of entry of the judgment and of any subsequent renewals and where entered in the records of the court.
(c) The name and address of the judgment creditor and the name and last known address of the judgment debtor.
(d) A description of the property sold.
(e) The date of sale.[170]

701.680. (a) Except as provided in paragraph (1) of subdivision (c), a sale of property pursuant to this article is absolute and shall not be set aside for any reason.
(b) If the judgment is reversed, vacated, or otherwise set aside, the judgment debtor may recover from the judgment creditor the proceeds of a sale pursuant to the judgment with interest at the rate on money judgments to the extent the proceeds were applied to the satisfaction of the judgment.
(c) If the sale was improper because of irregularities in the proceedings, because the property sold was not subject to execution, or for any other reason:
(1) The judgment debtor, or the judgment debtor's successor in interest, may commence an action within 90 days after the date of sale to set aside the sale if the purchaser at the sale is the judgment creditor. Subject to paragraph (2), if the sale is set aside, the judgment of the judgment creditor is revived to reflect the amount that was satisfied from the proceeds of the sale and the judgment creditor is entitled to interest on the amount of the judgment as so revived as if the sale had not been made. Any liens extinguished by the sale of the property are revived and reattach to the property with the same priority and effect as if the sale had not been made.
(2) The judgment debtor, or the judgment debtor's successor in interest, may recover damages caused by the impropriety. If damages are recovered against the judgment creditor, they shall be offset against the judgment to the extent the judgment is not satisfied. If damages are recovered against the levying officer, they shall be applied to the judgment to the extent the judgment is not satisfied.
(d) For the purposes of subdivision (c), the purchaser of the property at the sale is not a successor in interest.
(e) This section does not affect, limit, or eliminate a judgment debtor's equitable right of redemption.[700]

Article 7: Distribution of Proceeds of Sale or Collection
Article 7 added by Stats. 1982, Ch. 1364, Sec. 2.

701.810. Except as otherwise provided by statute, the levying officer shall distribute the proceeds of sale or collection in the following order:
(a) To persons having preferred labor claims that are required by Section 1206 to be satisfied from the proceeds, in the amounts required by Section 1206 to be satisfied.
(b) To the state department or agency having a state tax lien (as defined in Section 7162 of the Government Code) that is superior to the judgment creditor's lien, in the amount of the lien.
(c) If a deposit has been made pursuant to Section 720.260 and the purchaser at the sale is not the judgment creditor, to the judgment creditor in the amount required to repay the deposit with interest thereon at the rate

on money judgments from the date of the deposit.

(d) To the judgment debtor in the amount of any applicable exemption of proceeds pursuant to Section 704.010 (motor vehicle), 704.020 (household furnishings and other personal effects), or 704.060 (tools of trade), except that such proceeds shall be used to satisfy all of the following in the order of their respective priorities:

(1) Any consensual liens and encumbrances, and any liens for labor or materials, that are subordinate to the judgment creditor's lien.

(2) Subject to Section 688.030, any state tax lien (as defined in Section 7162 of the Government Code) on the property sold if the notice of state tax lien on the property has been recorded or filed pursuant to Section 7171 of the Government Code prior to the time the levying officer received the proceeds of the sale or collection.

(e) To the levying officer for the reimbursement of the levying officer's costs for which an advance has not been made.

(f) To the judgment creditor to satisfy the following, in the following order:

(1) First, any costs and interest accruing on the judgment after issuance of the writ pursuant to which the sale or collection is conducted.

(2) Second, the principal amount due on the judgment with costs and interest, as entered on the writ.

(g) To any other judgment creditors who have delivered writs to the levying officer, accompanied by instructions to levy upon the judgment debtor's property or the proceeds of its sale or collection, or any other persons actually known by the levying officer to have a claim, lien, or other interest subordinate to the judgment creditor's lien that is extinguished by the sale and that is not otherwise satisfied pursuant to this section, in the amounts to which they are entitled in order of their respective priorities.

(h) To the judgment debtor in the amount remaining.[626]

701.820. (a) Promptly after a sale or collection under this title, the levying officer shall distribute the proceeds to the persons entitled thereto or, in cases covered by Section 701.830, deposit the proceeds with the court.

(b) Except as otherwise provided by statute, the proceeds shall be paid to the persons entitled thereto within 30 days after the proceeds are received by the levying officer.

(c) If the proceeds are not received by the levying officer in one payment, the levying officer may accumulate proceeds received during a 30-day period and the accumulated proceeds shall be paid to the persons entitled thereto not later than 10 days after the expiration of the 30-day period.

(d) When proceeds are received by the levying officer in the form of a check or other form of noncash payment that is to be honored upon presentation by the levying officer for payment, the proceeds are not received for the purposes of this section until the check or other form of noncash payment has actually been honored upon presentation for payment.

(e) The provisions of Section 26680 of the Government Code apply to the levying officer only if all of the following conditions are satisfied:

(1) The levying officer has failed to

pay the proceeds or deposit them with the court as provided in this article within the time provided in this section.

(2) Upon such failure, a person entitled to any of the proceeds has filed, in person or by certified mail, with the levying officer a written demand for the payment of the proceeds to the persons entitled thereto.

(3) The levying officer has failed within 10 days after the demand is filed to pay to the person filing the demand the proceeds to which that person is entitled.

(f) If all proceeds have not been received within 10 days after the filing of the demand specified by paragraph (3) of subdivision (e), a judgment creditor may file an ex parte application for an order directing the levying officer to show cause why relief should not be granted pursuant to Section 26680 of the Government Code. The order shall name a date and time for the levying officer to appear not less than 20 and not more than 30 days after filing of the application. If the levying officer pays all proceeds as provided in subdivision (e) of Section 701.810 to the judgment creditor no later than 10 days prior to the hearing, the judgment creditor shall notify the court of full payment no later than three days prior to the hearing and the court shall withdraw the order and vacate the hearing.

(g) An ex parte application filed pursuant to subdivision (f) shall state the date and manner of all of the following:

(1) Delivery of the writ of execution to the levying officer.

(2) Remittance of the proceeds to the levying officer.

(3) Filing of the 10-day demand pursuant to subdivision (e).

(h) If the court finds that the facts alleged in the ex parte application filed pursuant to subdivision (f) to be knowingly false, or made in bad faith, the court may award costs and reasonable attorney fees to the levying officer.[627]

701.830. (a) If there are conflicting claims to all or a portion of the proceeds of sale or collection known to the levying officer before the proceeds are distributed, the levying officer may deposit with the court the proceeds that are the subject of the conflicting claims instead of distributing such proceeds under Section 701.810. Any interested person may apply on noticed motion for an order for the distribution of the proceeds deposited with the court. A copy of the notice of motion shall be served on such persons as the court shall by order determine in such manner as the court prescribes. Any interested person may request time for filing a response to the motion for an order for the distribution of the proceeds, for discovery proceedings in connection with the motion, or for other preparation for the hearing on the motion, and the court shall grant a continuance for a reasonable time for any of these purposes.

(b) Except as provided in subdivision (c), at the hearing on the motion the court shall determine the issues presented by the motion and make an order for the distribution of the proceeds deposited with the court.

(c) The court shall not determine the issues presented by the motion and instead shall abate the hearing until the issues presented by the motion can be determined in a civil action in the following cases if:

(1) The court is not the proper court under any other provision of law for the trial of a civil action with respect to the subject matter of the motion and any interested person at or prior to the hearing objects to the determination of the issues presented by the motion by the court.

(2) A civil action is pending with respect to the subject matter of the motion and jurisdiction has been obtained in the court in which the civil action is pending.

(3) The court determines that the matter should be determined in a civil action.[170]

Chapter 4: Exemptions

Chapter 4 added by Stats. 1982, Ch. 1364, Sec. 2.

Article 1: General Provisions

Article 1 added by Stats. 1982, Ch. 1364, Sec. 2.

703.010. Except as otherwise provided by statute:

(a) The exemptions provided by this chapter or by any other statute apply to all procedures for enforcement of a money judgment.

(b) The exemptions provided by this chapter or by any other statute do not apply if the judgment to be enforced is for the foreclosure of a mortgage, deed of trust, or other lien or encumbrance on the property other than a lien created pursuant to this division or pursuant to Title 6.5 (commencing with Section 481.010) (attachment).[170]

703.020. (a) The exemptions provided by this chapter apply only to property of a natural person.

(b) The exemptions provided in this chapter may be claimed by any of the following persons:

(1) In all cases, by the judgment debtor or a person acting on behalf of the judgment debtor.

(2) In the case of community property, by the spouse of the judgment debtor, whether or not the spouse is also a judgment debtor under the judgment.

(3) In the case of community property, by the domestic partner of the judgment debtor, as defined in Section 297 of the Family Code, whether or not the domestic partner is also a judgment debtor under the judgment.[701]

703.030. (a) An exemption for property that is described in this chapter or in any other statute as exempt may be claimed within the time and in the manner prescribed in the applicable enforcement procedure. If the exemption is not so claimed, the exemption is waived and the property is subject to enforcement of a money judgment.

(b) Except as otherwise specifically provided by statute, property that is described in this chapter or in any other statute as exempt without making a claim is not subject to any procedure for enforcement of a money judgment.

(c) Nothing in this section limits the authority of the court pursuant to Section 473 to relieve a person upon such terms as may be just from failure to claim an exemption within the time and in the manner prescribed in the applicable enforcement procedure.[170]

703.040. A purported contractual or other prior waiver of the exemptions provided by this chapter or by any other statute, other than a waiver by failure to claim an exemption required to be claimed or otherwise made at the time enforcement is sought, is against public policy and void.[170]

703.050. (a) The determination whether property is exempt or the amount of an exemption shall be made by application of the exemption statutes in effect (1) at the time the judgment creditor's lien on the property was created or (2) if the judgment creditor's lien on the property is the latest in a series of overlapping liens created when an earlier lien on the property in favor of the judgment creditor was in effect, at the time the earliest lien in the series of overlapping liens was created.
(b) This section applies to all judgments, whether based upon tort, contract, or other legal theory or cause of action that arose before or after the operative date of this section, and whether the judgment was entered before or after the operative date of this section.
(c) Notwithstanding subdivision (a), in the case of a levy of execution, the procedures to be followed in levying upon, selling, or releasing property, claiming, processing, opposing, and determining exemptions, and paying exemption proceeds, shall be governed by the law in effect at the time the levy of execution is made on the property.[170]

703.060. (a) The Legislature finds and declares that generally persons who enter into contracts do not do so in reliance on an assumption that the exemptions in effect at the time of the contract will govern enforcement of any judgment based on the contract, that liens imposed on property are imposed not as a matter of right but as a matter of privilege granted by statute for purposes of priority, that no vested rights with respect to exemptions are created by the making of a contract or imposition of a lien, that application of exemptions and exemption procedures in effect at the time of enforcement of a judgment is essential to the proper balance between the rights of judgment debtors and judgment creditors and has a minimal effect on the economic stability essential for the maintenance of private and public faith in commercial matters, and that it is the policy of the state to treat all judgment debtors equally with respect to exemptions and exemption procedures in effect at the time of enforcement of a money judgment. To this end, the Legislature reserves the right to repeal, alter, or add to the exemptions and the procedures therefor at any time and intends, unless otherwise provided by statute, that any repeals, alterations, or additions apply upon their operative date to enforcement of all money judgments, whether based upon tort, contract, or other legal theory or cause of action that arose before or after the operative date of the repeals, alterations, or additions, whether the judgment was entered before or after the operative date of the repeals, alterations, or additions.
(b) All contracts shall be deemed to have been made and all liens on property shall be deemed to have been created in recognition of the power of the state to repeal, alter, and add to statutes providing for liens and exemptions from the enforcement of money judgments.[170]

703.070. Except as otherwise provided by statute:
(a) The exemptions provided by this chapter or by any other statute apply to a judgment for child, family, or spousal support.
(b) If property is exempt without making a claim, the property is not subject to being applied to the satisfaction of a judgment for child, family, or spousal support.
(c) Except as provided in subdivision (b), if property sought to be applied to the satisfaction of a judgment for child, family, or spousal support is shown to be exempt under subdivision (a) in appropriate proceedings, the court shall, upon noticed motion of the judgment creditor, determine the extent to which the exempt property nevertheless shall be applied to the satisfaction of the judgment. In making this determination, the court shall take into account the needs of the judgment creditor, the needs of the judgment debtor and all the persons the judgment debtor is required to support, and all other relevant circumstances. The court shall effectuate its determination by an order specifying the extent to which the otherwise exempt property is to be applied to the satisfaction of the judgment.[298]

703.080. (a) Subject to any limitation provided in the particular exemption, a fund that is exempt remains exempt to the extent that it can be traced into deposit accounts or in the form of cash or its equivalent.
(b) The exemption claimant has the burden of tracing an exempt fund.
(c) The tracing of exempt funds in a deposit account shall be by application of the lowest intermediate balance principle unless the exemption claimant or the judgment creditor shows that some other method of tracing would better serve the interests of justice and equity under the circumstances of the case.[170]

703.090. If a judgment creditor has failed to oppose a claim of exemption within the time allowed by Section 703.550 or if property has been determined by a court to be exempt, and the judgment creditor thereafter levies upon or otherwise seeks to apply the property toward the satisfaction of the same money judgment, the judgment creditor is not entitled to recover the subsequent costs of collection unless the property is applied to satisfaction of the judgment.[170]

703.100. (a) Subject to subdivision (b), the determination whether property is exempt shall be made under the circumstances existing at the earliest of the following times:
(1) The time of levy on the property.
(2) The time of the commencement of court proceedings for the application of the property to the satisfaction of the money judgment.
(3) The time a lien is created under Title 6.5 (commencing with Section 481.010) (attachment) or under this title.
(b) The court, in its discretion, may take into consideration any of the following changes that have occurred between the time of levy or commencement of enforcement proceedings or creation of the lien and the time of the hearing:
(1) A change in the use of the property if the exemption is based upon the use of property and if the property was used for the exempt purpose at

the time of the levy or the commencement of enforcement proceedings or the creation of the lien but is used for a nonexempt purpose at the time of the hearing.

(2) A change in the value of the property if the exemption is based upon the value of property.

(3) A change in the financial circumstances of the judgment debtor and spouse and dependents of the judgment debtor if the exemption is based upon their needs.[170]

703.110. If the judgment debtor is married:

(a) The exemptions provided by this chapter or by any other statute apply to all property that is subject to enforcement of a money judgment, including the interest of the spouse of the judgment debtor in community property. The fact that one or both spouses are judgment debtors under the judgment or that property sought to be applied to the satisfaction of the judgment is separate or community does not increase or reduce the number or amount of the exemptions. Where the property exempt under a particular exemption is limited to a specified maximum dollar amount, unless the exemption provision specifically provides otherwise, the two spouses together are entitled to one exemption limited to the specified maximum dollar amount, whether one or both of the spouses are judgment debtors under the judgment and whether the property sought to be applied to the satisfaction of the judgment is separate or community.

(b) If an exemption is required by statute to be applied first to property not before the court and then to property before the court, the application of the exemption to property not before the court shall be made to the community property and separate property of both spouses, whether or not such property is subject to enforcement of the money judgment.

(c) If the same exemption is claimed by the judgment debtor and the spouse of the judgment debtor for different property, and the property claimed by one spouse, but not both, is exempt, the exemption shall be applied as the spouses agree. If the spouses are unable to agree, the exemption shall be applied as directed by the court in its discretion.[184]

703.115. In determining an exemption based upon the needs of the judgment debtor and the spouse and dependents of the judgment debtor or an exemption based upon the needs of the judgment debtor and the family of the judgment debtor, the court shall take into account all property of the judgment debtor and, to the extent the judgment debtor has a spouse and dependents or family, all property of such spouse and dependents or family, including community property and separate property of the spouse, whether or not such property is subject to enforcement of the money judgment.[185]

703.130. Pursuant to the authority of paragraph (2) of subsection (b) of Section 522 of Title 11 of the United States Code, the exemptions set forth in subsection (d) of Section 522 of Title 11 of the United States Code (Bankruptcy) are not authorized in this state.[624]

703.140. (a) In a case under Title 11 of the United States Code, all of the exemptions provided by this chapter, including the homestead exemption, other than the provisions of subdivision (b) are applicable regardless of whether there is a money judgment against the debtor or whether a money judgment is being enforced by execution sale or any other procedure, but the exemptions provided by subdivision (b) may be elected in lieu of all other exemptions provided by this chapter, as follows:

(1) If spouses are joined in the petition, they jointly may elect to utilize the applicable exemption provisions of this chapter other than the provisions of subdivision (b), or to utilize the applicable exemptions set forth in subdivision (b), but not both.

(2) (A) If the petition is filed individually, and not jointly, for a spouse, the exemptions provided by this chapter other than the provisions of subdivision (b) are applicable, except that, if both of the spouses effectively waive in writing the right to claim, during the period the case commenced by filing the petition is pending, the exemptions provided by the applicable exemption provisions of this chapter, other than subdivision (b), in any case commenced by filing a petition for either of them under Title 11 of the United States Code, then they may elect to instead utilize the applicable exemptions set forth in subdivision (b).

(B) Notwithstanding subparagraph (A), a waiver is not required from a debtor who is living separate and apart from their spouse as of the date the petition commencing the case under Title 11 of the United States Code is filed, unless, on the petition date, the debtor and the debtor's spouse shared an ownership interest in property that could be exempted as a homestead under Article 4 of this chapter.

(3) If the petition is filed for an unmarried person, that person may elect to utilize the applicable exemption provisions of this chapter other than subdivision (b), or to utilize the applicable exemptions set forth in subdivision (b), but not both.

(b) The following exemptions may be elected as provided in subdivision (a):

(1) The debtor's aggregate interest, not to exceed twenty-nine thousand two hundred seventy-five dollars ($29,275) in value, in real property or personal property that the debtor or a dependent of the debtor uses as a residence, in a cooperative that owns property that the debtor or a dependent of the debtor uses as a residence.

(2) The debtor's interest, not to exceed seven thousand five hundred dollars ($7,500) in value, in one or more motor vehicles.

(3) The debtor's interest, not to exceed seven hundred twenty-five dollars ($725) in value in any particular item, in household furnishings, household goods, wearing apparel, appliances, books, animals, crops, or musical instruments, that are held primarily for the personal, family, or household use of the debtor or a dependent of the debtor.

(4) The debtor's aggregate interest, not to exceed one thousand seven hundred fifty dollars ($1,750) in value, in jewelry held primarily for the personal, family, or household use of the debtor or a dependent of the debtor.

(5) The debtor's aggregate interest, not to exceed one thousand five hundred fifty dollars ($1,550) in value,

plus any unused amount of the exemption provided under paragraph (1), in any property.

(6) The debtor's aggregate interest, not to exceed eight thousand seven hundred twenty-five dollars ($8,725) in value, in any implements, professional books, or tools of the trade of the debtor or the trade of a dependent of the debtor.

(7) Any unmatured life insurance contract owned by the debtor, other than a credit life insurance contract.

(8) The debtor's aggregate interest, not to exceed fifteen thousand six hundred fifty dollars ($15,650) in value, in any accrued dividend or interest under, or loan value of, any unmatured life insurance contract owned by the debtor under which the insured is the debtor or an individual of whom the debtor is a dependent.

(9) Professionally prescribed health aids for the debtor, the debtor's spouse, or a dependent of the debtor, including vehicles converted for use by the debtor, the debtor's spouse, or a dependent of the debtor, who has a disability. Conversion of a vehicle for use by a person who has a disability includes altering the interior, installing steering, a wheelchair lift, or motorized steps, or modifying the operation of the vehicle.

(10) The debtor's right to receive any of the following:

(A) A social security benefit, unemployment compensation, or a local public assistance benefit.

(B) A veterans' benefit.

(C) A disability, illness, or unemployment benefit.

(D) Alimony, support, or separate maintenance, to the extent reasonably necessary for the support of the debtor and any dependent of the debtor.

(E) A payment under a stock bonus, pension, profit-sharing, annuity, or similar plan or contract on account of illness, disability, death, age, or length of service, to the extent reasonably necessary for the support of the debtor and any dependent of the debtor, unless all of the following apply:

(i) That plan or contract was established by or under the auspices of an insider that employed the debtor at the time the debtor's rights under the plan or contract arose.

(ii) The payment is on account of age or length of service.

(iii) That plan or contract does not qualify under Section 401(a), 403(a), 403(b), 408, or 408A of the Internal Revenue Code of 1986.

(F) The aggregate interest, not to exceed seven thousand five hundred dollars ($7,500), in vacation credits or accrued, or unused, vacation pay, sick leave, family leave, or wages, as defined in Section 200 of the Labor Code.

(11) The debtor's right to receive, or property that is traceable to, any of the following:

(A) An award under a crime victim's reparation law.

(B) A payment under a settlement agreement arising out of or regarding the debtor's employment, to the extent reasonably necessary for the support of the debtor, the debtor's spouse, or a dependent of the debtor.

(C) A payment on account of the wrongful death of an individual of whom the debtor was a dependent, to the extent reasonably necessary for the support of the debtor and any dependent of the debtor.

(D) A payment under a life insurance contract that insured the life of an individual of whom the debtor was a spouse or dependent on the date of that individual's death, to the extent reasonably necessary for the support of the debtor and any dependent of the debtor.

(E) A payment, not to exceed twenty-nine thousand two hundred seventy-five dollars ($29,275) on account of personal bodily injury of the debtor, the debtor's spouse, or an individual of whom the debtor is a dependent.

(F) A payment in compensation of loss of future earnings of the debtor or an individual of whom the debtor is or was a spouse or dependent, to the extent reasonably necessary for the support of the debtor and the debtor's spouse or a dependent of the debtor.

(12) Money held in an account owned by the judgment debtor and established pursuant to the Golden State Scholarshare Trust Act (Article 19 (commencing with Section 69980) of Chapter 2 of Part 42 of Division 5 of Title 3 of the Education Code), subject to the following limits:

(A) The amount exempted for contributions to an account during the 365-day period prior to the date of filing of the debtor's petition for bankruptcy, in the aggregate during this period, shall not exceed the amount of the annual gift tax exclusion under Section 2503(b) of the Internal Revenue Code of 1986, as amended, in effect at the time of the filing of the debtor's petition for bankruptcy.

(B) The amount exempted for contributions to an account during the period commencing 730 days prior to and ending 366 days prior to the date of filing of the debtor's petition for bankruptcy, in the aggregate during this period, shall not exceed the amount of the annual gift tax exclusion under Section 2503(b) of the Internal Revenue Code of 1986, as amended, in effect at the time of the filing of the debtor's petition for bankruptcy

(C) For the purposes of this paragraph, "account" includes all accounts having the same beneficiary.

(D) This paragraph is not subject to the requirements of Section 703.150.

(c) In a case under Title 11 of the United States Code, the value of the property claimed as exempt and the debtor's exemptions provided by this chapter with respect to such property shall be determined as of the date the bankruptcy petition is filed. In a case where the debtor's equity in a residence is less than or equal to the amount of the debtor's allowed homestead exemption as of the date the bankruptcy petition is filed, any appreciation in the value of the debtor's interest in the property during the pendency of the case is exempt.[803]

703.150. (a) On April 1, 2004, and at each three-year interval ending on April 1 thereafter, the dollar amounts of exemptions provided in subdivision (b) of Section 703.140 in effect immediately before that date shall be adjusted as provided in subdivision (d).

(b) On April 1, 2007, and at each three-year interval ending on April 1 thereafter, the dollar amounts of exemptions provided in Article 3 (commencing

with Section 704.010) in effect immediately before that date shall be adjusted as provided in subdivision (d).
(c) On April 1, 2022, and at each three-year interval ending on April 1 thereafter, the dollar amount set forth in paragraph (7) of subdivision (b) of Section 699.730 in effect immediately before that date shall be adjusted as provided in subdivision (d).
(d) The Judicial Council shall determine the amount of the adjustment based on the change in the annual California Consumer Price Index for All Urban Consumers, published by the Department of Industrial Relations, for the most recent three-year period ending on December 31 preceding the adjustment, with each adjusted amount rounded to the nearest twenty-five dollars ($25).
(e) Beginning April 1, 2004, the Judicial Council shall publish a list of the current dollar amounts of exemptions provided in subdivision (b) of Section 703.140 and in Article 3 (commencing with Section 704.010), and the dollar amount set forth in paragraph (7) of subdivision (b) of Section 699.730, together with the date of the next scheduled adjustment.
(f) Adjustments made under subdivision (a) do not apply with respect to cases commenced before the date of the adjustment, subject to any contrary rule applicable under the federal Bankruptcy Code. The applicability of adjustments made under subdivisions (b), (c), and (d) is governed by Section 703.050.[840]

Article 2: Procedure for Claiming Exemptions After Levy
Article 2 added by Stats. 1982, Ch. 1364, Sec. 2.

703.510. (a) Except as otherwise provided by statute, property that has been levied upon may be claimed to be exempt as provided in this article.
(b) If property in a deposit account that is exempt without making a claim, as described in subdivision (b) of Section 704.080 or subdivision (a) of Section 704.220, is levied upon, the property shall be released by the financial institution holding the judgment debtor's deposit account within five business days of the financial institution receiving written notice from the judgment debtor setting forth the facts supporting the exemption without the necessity of making a claim under this title. The judgment debtor's written notice to the financial institution shall be served via first-class mail on the judgment creditor or judgment creditor's attorney of record within five business days of notice being sent by the judgment debtor to the financial institution. The written notice shall be addressed to the financial institution identified pursuant to subdivision (c) or (d) of Section 684.110.
(c) If property that is exempt without making a claim is levied upon, other than the property in a deposit account described in subdivision (b), the property may be released pursuant to the exemption procedure provided in this article.[853]

703.520. (a) The claimant may make a claim of exemption by filing with the levying officer, either in person or by mail, a claim of exemption together with a copy of the claim. If the claimant is personally served, the claim shall be made within 15 days after the date the notice of levy on the property claimed to be exempt is served on the judgment debtor. If the claimant is served by mail, the claim shall be made within 20 days after the date the notice of levy on the property claimed to be exempt is served on the judgment debtor. If the claim is filed by mail and assigned a tracking number by the United States Postal Service or another common carrier, the filing shall be deemed complete on the date the claim is postmarked. If the claim is filed by mail and not assigned a tracking number, the filing shall be deemed complete on the date the claim is received by the levying officer.

(b) The claim of exemption shall be executed under oath and shall include all of the following:

(1) The name of the claimant and the mailing address where service of a notice of opposition to the claim may be made upon the claimant.

(2) The name and last known address of the judgment debtor if the claimant is not the judgment debtor.

(3) A description of the property claimed to be exempt. If an exemption is claimed pursuant to Section 704.010 or 704.060, the claimant shall describe all other property of the same type, including exempt proceeds of the property of the same type, owned by the judgment debtor alone or in combination with others on the date of levy and identify the property, whether or not levied upon, to which the exemption is to be applied. If an exemption is claimed pursuant to subdivision (b) of Section 704.100, the claimant shall state the nature and amount of all other property of the same type owned by the judgment debtor or the spouse of the judgment debtor alone or in combination with others on the date of levy.

(4) A financial statement if required by Section 703.530.

(5) A citation of the provision of this chapter or other statute upon which the claim is based.

(6) A statement of the facts necessary to support the claim.

(c) Notwithstanding subdivision (a), for a personal debt as defined in subdivision (d) of Section 683.110, a claimant may file a claim of exemption more than 20 days after the date the notice of levy is served on the judgment debtor pursuant to Sections 703.580 and 706.105. The levying officer may, nonetheless, release the funds to the judgment creditor at any time after the expiration of the 20-day period.[904]

703.530. (a) If property is claimed as exempt pursuant to a provision exempting property to the extent necessary for the support of the judgment debtor and the spouse and dependents of the judgment debtor, the claim of exemption shall include a financial statement.

(b) The financial statement shall include all of the following information:

(1) The name of the spouse of the judgment debtor.

(2) The name, age, and relationship of all persons dependent upon the judgment debtor or the spouse of the judgment debtor for support.

(3) All sources and the amounts of earnings and other income of the judgment debtor and the spouse and dependents of the judgment debtor.

(4) A list of the assets of the judgment

debtor and the spouse and dependents of the judgment debtor and the value of such assets.

(5) All outstanding obligations of the judgment debtor and the spouse and dependents of the judgment debtor.

(c) The financial statement shall be executed under oath by the judgment debtor and, unless the spouses are living separate and apart, by the spouse of the judgment debtor.[170]

703.540. Promptly after the filing of the claim of exemption, the levying officer shall serve both of the following on the judgment creditor personally or by mail:

(a) A copy of the claim of exemption.

(b) A notice of claim of exemption stating that the claim of exemption has been made and that the levying officer will release the property unless, within the time allowed as specified in the notice, both of the following are filed with the levying officer:

(1) A copy of the notice of opposition to the claim of exemption.

(2) A copy of the notice of motion for an order determining the claim of exemption.[170]

703.550. (a) Within 15 days after service of the notice of claim of exemption, a judgment creditor who opposes the claim of exemption shall file with the court a notice of opposition to the claim of exemption and a notice of motion for an order determining the claim of exemption and shall file with the levying officer a copy of the notice of opposition and a copy of the notice of motion. Upon the filing of the copies of the notice of opposition and notice of motion, the levying officer shall promptly file the claim of exemption with the court. If copies of the notice of opposition and notice of motion are not filed with the levying officer within the time allowed, the levying officer shall immediately release the property to the extent it is claimed to be exempt.

(b) This section shall become operative on September 1, 2020.[756]

703.560. The notice of opposition to the claim of exemption shall be executed under oath and shall include both of the following:

(a) An allegation either (1) that the property is not exempt under the provision of this chapter or other statute relied upon or (2) that the equity in the property claimed to be exempt is in excess of the amount provided in the applicable exemption.

(b) A statement of the facts necessary to support the allegation.[170]

703.570. (a) (1) The hearing on the motion shall be held not later than 30 days from the date the notice of motion was filed with the court unless continued by the court for good cause. Where the judgment upon which the writ is issued is for personal debt, as defined in subdivision (d) of Section 683.110, if the hearing is delayed by the court and cannot be set within 30 days of notice of the motion, a party may seek by ex parte application, and the court shall issue, an order staying any levy or garnishment with respect to the property subject to the claim of exemption until the hearing occurs.

(2) The filing of an ex parte application under this section is not a general appearance and shall not constitute a waiver of the right to bring a motion under Section 418.10.

(b) Not less than 10 days prior to the hearing, the judgment creditor shall serve a notice of the hearing and a copy of the notice of opposition to the claim of exemption on the claimant and on the judgment debtor, if other than the claimant. Service shall be made personally or by mail.[905]

703.580. (a) The claim of exemption and notice of opposition to the claim of exemption do not constitute an appearance pursuant to Section 1014. The power of the court over the exemption claimant is limited to determining the claim of exemption.
(b) At a hearing under this section, the exemption claimant has the burden of proof.
(c) The claim of exemption is deemed controverted by the notice of opposition to the claim of exemption and both shall be received in evidence. If no other evidence is offered, the court, if satisfied that sufficient facts are shown by the claim of exemption (including the financial statement if one is required) and the notice of opposition, may make its determination thereon. If a claim of exemption asserts that money in a judgment debtor's deposit account is or was necessary for the support of the judgment debtor and the spouse and dependents of the judgment debtor as provided in Section 704.225, the court shall review the judgment debtor's financial statement and make findings thereon. If not satisfied, the court may order the hearing continued for the production of other evidence, oral or documentary.
(d) At the conclusion of the hearing, the court shall determine by order whether or not the property is exempt in whole or in part.
(1) Subject to Section 703.600, the order is determinative of the right of the judgment creditor to apply the property to the satisfaction of the judgment.
(2) Where the judgment upon which the writ is issued is for personal debt, as defined in subdivision (d) of Section 683.110, the court shall order the return of any property that was exempt without the need for a claim and that was levied upon within the 12 months preceding the date of the order on the claim of exemption. This paragraph does not limit a judge's authority to order, for good cause, the return of any exempt property taken more than 12 months preceding the date of the order on the claim of exemption.
(3) Where the judgment upon which the writ is issued is for personal debt, as defined in subdivision (d) of Section 683.110, the court shall order the return of any property that the debtor has demonstrated would have been exempt by claim of exemption and that was levied upon within the six months preceding the date of the order on the claim of exemption. This paragraph does not limit a judge's authority to order, for good cause, the return of any exempt property taken more than six months preceding the date of the order on the claim of exemption.
(4) If property is exempt without the need for a claim under this title or as a result of a claim of exemption, the court shall order the return of the exempt property from the levying officer, judgment creditor, or other person who is in possession of the property, to the judgment debtor. A levying officer shall return the exempt property within 20 business days of receipt of notice of the order. A judgment creditor shall return the exempt

property within 10 business days of entry of the order.

(e) The court clerk shall promptly transmit a certified copy of the order to the levying officer. Subject to Section 703.610, the levying officer shall, in compliance with the order, release the property or apply the property to the satisfaction of the money judgment.

(f) Unless otherwise ordered by the court, if an exemption is not determined within the time provided by Section 703.570, the property claimed to be exempt shall be released.[854]

703.590. If the court extends the time allowed for an act to be done under this article, written notice of the extension shall be filed with the levying officer and, unless notice is waived, shall be served promptly on the opposing party. Service shall be made personally or by mail.[170]

703.600. An appeal lies from any order made under this article.[397]

703.610. (a) Except as otherwise provided by statute or ordered by the court, the levying officer shall not release, sell, or otherwise dispose of the property for which an exemption is claimed until an appeal is waived, the time to file an appeal has expired, or the exemption is finally determined.

(b) At any time while the exemption proceedings are pending, upon motion of the judgment creditor or a claimant, or upon its own motion, the court may make any orders for disposition of the property that may be proper under the circumstances of the case, except that such order may not require the release to the judgment creditor of property that would be exempt without a claim of exemption. The order may be modified or vacated by the court at any time during the pendency of the exemption proceedings upon any terms that are just, except that such order may not require the release to the judgment creditor of property that would be exempt without a claim of exemption.

(c) If an appeal of the determination of a claim of exemption is taken, notice of the appeal shall be given to the levying officer and the levying officer shall hold, release, or dispose of the property in accordance with the provisions governing enforcement and stay of enforcement of money judgments pending appeal. Where the judgment upon which the writ is issued is for personal debt, as defined in subdivision (d) of Section 683.110, if an earnings withholding order has been served upon the judgment debtor's employer, notice of the appeal shall also be given to the judgment debtor's employer who shall, upon receipt of the notice, immediately suspend any further garnishment of the judgment debtor's wages for the pendency of the appeal and until ordered by the court to resume garnishment.[855]

Article 3: Exempt Property
Article 3 added by Stats. 1982, Ch. 1364, Sec. 2.

704.010. (a) Any combination of the following is exempt in the amount of seven thousand five hundred dollars ($7,500):

(1) The aggregate equity in motor vehicles.

(2) The proceeds of an execution sale of a motor vehicle.

(3) The proceeds of insurance or other indemnification for the loss,

damage, or destruction of a motor vehicle.

(b) Proceeds exempt under subdivision (a) are exempt for a period of 90 days after the time the proceeds are actually received by the judgment debtor.

(c) For the purpose of determining the equity, the fair market value of a motor vehicle shall be determined by reference to used car price guides customarily used by California automobile dealers unless the motor vehicle is not listed in such price guides.

(d) If the judgment debtor has only one motor vehicle and it is sold at an execution sale, the proceeds of the execution sale are exempt in the amount of seven thousand five hundred dollars ($7,500) without making a claim. The levying officer shall consult and may rely upon the records of the Department of Motor Vehicles in determining whether the judgment debtor has only one motor vehicle. In the case covered by this subdivision, the exemption provided by subdivision (a) is not available.[804]

704.020. (a) Household furnishings, appliances, provisions, wearing apparel, and other personal effects are exempt in the following cases:

(1) If ordinarily and reasonably necessary to, and personally used or procured for use by, the judgment debtor and members of the judgment debtor's family at the judgment debtor's principal place of residence.

(2) Where the judgment debtor and the judgment debtor's spouse live separate and apart, if ordinarily and reasonably necessary to, and personally used or procured for use by, the spouse and members of the spouse's family at the spouse's principal place of residence.

(b) In determining whether an item of property is "ordinarily and reasonably necessary" under subdivision (a), the court shall take into account both of the following:

(1) The extent to which the particular type of item is ordinarily found in a household.

(2) Whether the particular item has extraordinary value as compared to the value of items of the same type found in other households.

(c) If an item of property for which an exemption is claimed pursuant to this section is an item of the type ordinarily found in a household but is determined not to be exempt because the item has extraordinary value as compared to the value of items of the same type found in other households, the proceeds obtained at an execution sale of the item are exempt in the amount determined by the court to be a reasonable amount sufficient to purchase a replacement of ordinary value if the court determines that a replacement is reasonably necessary. Proceeds exempt under this subdivision are exempt for a period of 90 days after the proceeds are actually received by the judgment debtor.[170]

704.030. Material that in good faith is about to be applied to the repair or improvement of a residence is exempt if the equity in the material does not exceed three thousand five hundred dollars ($3,500) in the following cases:

(a) If purchased in good faith for use in the repair or improvement of the judgment debtor's principal place of residence.

(b) Where the judgment debtor and the judgment debtor's spouse live separate and apart, if purchased in good faith for use in the repair or improvement of the spouse's principal place of residence.[773]

704.040. Jewelry, heirlooms, and works of art are exempt to the extent that the aggregate equity therein does not exceed eight thousand seven hundred twenty-five dollars ($8,725).[774]

704.050. (a) Health aids reasonably necessary to enable the judgment debtor or the spouse or a dependent of the judgment debtor to work or sustain health, and prosthetic and orthopedic appliances, are exempt.

(b) Health aids described in subdivision (a) include vehicles converted for use by the debtor, the debtor's spouse, or a dependent of the debtor, who has a disability. Conversion of a vehicle for use by a person who has a disability includes altering the interior, installing steering, a wheelchair lift, or motorized steps, or modifying the operation of the vehicle.[805]

704.060. (a) Tools, implements, instruments, materials, uniforms, furnishings, books, equipment, one commercial motor vehicle, one vessel, and other personal property are exempt to the extent that the aggregate equity therein does not exceed:

(1) Eight thousand seven hundred twenty-five dollars ($8,725), if reasonably necessary to and actually used by the judgment debtor in the exercise of the trade, business, or profession by which the judgment debtor earns a livelihood.

(2) Eight thousand seven hundred twenty-five dollars ($8,725), if reasonably necessary to and actually used by the spouse of the judgment debtor in the exercise of the trade, business, or profession by which the spouse earns a livelihood.

(3) Twice the amount of the exemption provided in paragraph (1), if reasonably necessary to and actually used by the judgment debtor and by the spouse of the judgment debtor in the exercise of the same trade, business, or profession by which both earn a livelihood. In the case covered by this paragraph, the exemptions provided in paragraphs (1) and (2) are not available.

(b) If property described in subdivision (a) is sold at an execution sale, or if it has been lost, damaged, or destroyed, the proceeds of the execution sale or of insurance or other indemnification are exempt for a period of 90 days after the proceeds are actually received by the judgment debtor or the judgment debtor's spouse. The amount exempt under this subdivision is the amount specified in subdivision (a) that applies to the particular case less the aggregate equity of any other property to which the exemption provided by subdivision (a) for the particular case has been applied.

(c) Notwithstanding subdivision (a), a motor vehicle is not exempt under subdivision (a) if there is a motor vehicle exempt under Section 704.010 which is reasonably adequate for use in the trade, business, or profession for which the exemption is claimed under this section.

(d) Notwithstanding subdivisions (a) and (b):

(1) The amount of the exemption for a commercial motor vehicle under paragraph (1) or (2) of subdivision (a) is limited to four thousand eight hundred fifty dollars ($4,850).

(2) The amount of the exemption for a commercial motor vehicle under paragraph (3) of subdivision (a) is limited to twice the amount of the exemption provided in paragraph (1) of this subdivision.[790]

704.070. (a) As used in this section:

(1) "Earnings withholding order" means an earnings withholding order under Chapter 5 (commencing with Section 706.010) (Wage Garnishment Law).

(2) "Paid earnings" means earnings as defined in Section 706.011 that were paid to the employee during the 30-day period ending on the date of the levy. For the purposes of this paragraph, where earnings that have been paid to the employee are sought to be subjected to the enforcement of a money judgment other than by a levy, the date of levy is deemed to be the date the earnings were otherwise subjected to the enforcement of the judgment.

(3) "Earnings assignment order for support" means an earnings assignment order for support as defined in Section 706.011.

(b) Paid earnings that can be traced into deposit accounts or in the form of cash or its equivalent as provided in Section 703.080 are exempt in the following amounts:

(1) All of the paid earnings are exempt if prior to payment to the employee they were subject to an earnings withholding order or an earnings assignment order for support.

(2) Disposable earnings that would otherwise not be subject to levy under Section 706.050 that are levied upon or otherwise sought to be subjected to the enforcement of a money judgment are exempt if prior to payment to the employee they were not subject to an earnings withholding order or an earnings assignment order for support.[757]

704.080. (a) For the purposes of this section:

(1) "Deposit account" means a deposit account in which payments of public benefits or social security benefits are directly deposited by the government or its agent.

(2) "Social security benefits" means payments authorized by the Social Security Administration for regular retirement and survivors' benefits, supplemental security income benefits, coal miners' health benefits, and disability insurance benefits. "Public benefits" means aid payments authorized pursuant to subdivision (a) of Section 11450 of the Welfare and Institutions Code, payments for supportive services as described in Section 11323.2 of the Welfare and Institutions Code, and general assistance payments made pursuant to Section 17000.5 of the Welfare and Institutions Code.

(b) A deposit account is exempt without making a claim in the following amount:

(1) One thousand seven hundred fifty dollars ($1,750) where one depositor is the designated payee of the directly deposited public benefits payments.

(2) Three thousand five hundred dollars ($3,500) where one depositor is the designated payee of directly deposited social security payments.

(3) Two thousand six hundred dollars ($2,600) where two or more depositors are the designated payees of the directly deposited public benefits payments, unless those depositors are joint payees of directly deposited payments that represent a benefit to only

one of the depositors, in which case the exemption under paragraph (1) applies.

(4) Five thousand two hundred fifty dollars ($5,250) where two or more depositors are the designated payees of directly deposited social security payments, unless those depositors are joint payees of directly deposited payments that represent a benefit to only one of the depositors, in which case the exemption under paragraph (2) applies.

(c) The amount of a deposit account that exceeds the exemption provided in subdivision (b) is exempt to the extent that it consists of payments of public benefits or social security benefits.

(d) Notwithstanding Article 5 (commencing with Section 701.010) of Chapter 3, when a deposit account is levied upon or otherwise sought to be subjected to the enforcement of a money judgment, the financial institution that holds the deposit account shall either place the amount that exceeds the exemption provided in subdivision (b) in a suspense account or otherwise prohibit withdrawal of that amount pending notification of the failure of the judgment creditor to file the affidavit required by this section or the judicial determination of the exempt status of the amount. Within 10 business days after the levy, the financial institution shall provide the levying officer with a written notice stating (1) that the deposit account is one in which payments of public benefits or social security benefits are directly deposited by the government or its agent and (2) the balance of the deposit account that exceeds the exemption provided by subdivision (b). Promptly upon receipt of the notice, the levying officer shall serve the notice on the judgment creditor. Service shall be made personally or by mail.

(e) Notwithstanding the procedure prescribed in Article 2 (commencing with Section 703.510), whether there is an amount exempt under subdivision (c) shall be determined as follows:

(1) Within five days after the levying officer serves the notice on the judgment creditor under subdivision (d), a judgment creditor who desires to claim that the amount is not exempt shall file with the court an affidavit alleging that the amount is not exempt and file a copy with the levying officer. The affidavit shall be in the form of the notice of opposition provided by Section 703.560, and a hearing shall be set and held, and notice given, as provided by Sections 703.570 and 703.580. For the purpose of this subdivision, the "notice of opposition to the claim of exemption" in Sections 703.570 and 703.580 means the affidavit under this subdivision.

(2) If the judgment creditor does not file the affidavit with the levying officer and give notice of hearing pursuant to Section 703.570 within the time provided in paragraph (1), the levying officer shall release the deposit account and shall notify the financial institution.

(3) The affidavit constitutes the pleading of the judgment creditor, subject to the power of the court to permit amendments in the interest of justice. The affidavit is deemed controverted and no counteraffidavit is required.

(4) At a hearing under this subdivision, the judgment debtor has the burden of proving that the excess amount is exempt.

(5) At the conclusion of the hearing, the court by order shall determine whether or not the amount of the deposit account is exempt pursuant to subdivision (c) in whole or in part and shall make an appropriate order for its prompt disposition. No findings are required in a proceeding under this subdivision.

(6) Upon determining the exemption claim for the deposit account under subdivision (c), the court shall immediately transmit a certified copy of the order of the court to the financial institution and to the levying officer. If the order determines that all or part of the excess is exempt under subdivision (c), with respect to the amount of the excess which is exempt, the financial institution shall transfer the exempt excess from the suspense account or otherwise release any restrictions on its withdrawal by the judgment debtor. The transfer or release shall be effected within three business days of the receipt of the certified copy of the court order by the financial institution.

(f) If the judgment debtor claims that a portion of the amount is exempt other than pursuant to subdivision (c), the claim of exemption shall be made pursuant to Article 2 (commencing with Section 703.510). If the judgment debtor also opposes the judgment creditor's affidavit regarding an amount exempt pursuant to subdivision (c), both exemptions shall be determined at the same hearing, provided the judgment debtor has complied with Article 2 (commencing with Section 703.510).[764]

704.090. (a) The funds of a judgment debtor confined in a prison or facility under the jurisdiction of the Department of Corrections or the Department of the Youth Authority or confined in any county or city jail, road camp, industrial farm, or other local correctional facility, held in trust for or to the credit of the judgment debtor, in an inmate's trust account or similar account by the state, county, or city, or any agency thereof, are exempt without making a claim in the amount of one thousand seven hundred fifty dollars ($1,750). If the judgment debtor is married, each spouse is entitled to a separate exemption under this section or the spouses may combine their exemptions.

(b) Notwithstanding subdivision (a), if the judgment is for a restitution fine or order imposed pursuant to subdivision (a) of Section 13967 of the Government Code, as operative on or before September 28, 1994, or Section 1203.04 of the Penal Code, as operative on or before August 2, 1995, or Section 1202.4 of the Penal Code, the funds held in trust for, or to the credit of, a judgment debtor described in subdivision (a) are exempt in the amount of three hundred twenty-five dollars ($325) without making a claim. The exemption provided in this subdivision is not subject to adjustment under Section 703.150.[765]

704.100. (a) Unmatured life insurance policies (including endowment and annuity policies), but not the loan value of such policies, are exempt without making a claim.

(b) The aggregate loan value of unmatured life insurance policies (including endowment and annuity policies) is subject to the enforcement of a money judgment but is exempt in the amount of thirteen thousand nine hundred

seventy-five dollars ($13,975). If the judgment debtor is married, each spouse is entitled to a separate exemption under this subdivision, and the exemptions of the spouses may be combined, regardless of whether the policies belong to either or both spouses and regardless of whether the spouse of the judgment debtor is also a judgment debtor under the judgment. The exemption provided by this subdivision shall be first applied to policies other than the policy before the court and then, if the exemption is not exhausted, to the policy before the court.
(c) Benefits from matured life insurance policies (including endowment and annuity policies) are exempt to the extent reasonably necessary for the support of the judgment debtor and the spouse and dependents of the judgment debtor.[766]

704.105. Money held in an account owned by the judgment debtor and established pursuant to the Golden State Scholarshare Trust Act (Article 19 (commencing with Section 69980) of Chapter 2 of Part 42 of Division 5 of Title 3 of the Education Code) is exempt without making a claim, subject to the following limitations:
(a) The amount exempted for contributions to an account during the 365-day period prior to the date of entry of a money judgment, in the aggregate during this period, shall not exceed the amount of the annual gift tax exclusion under Section 2503(b) of the Internal Revenue Code of 1986, as amended, in effect at the time of entry of the money judgment.
(b) The amount exempted for contributions to an account during the period commencing 730 days prior to and ending 366 days prior to the date of entry of a money judgment, in the aggregate during this period, shall not exceed the amount of the annual gift tax exclusion under Section 2503(b) of the Internal Revenue Code of 1986, as amended, in effect at the time of entry of the money judgment.
(c) For the purposes of this section, "account" includes all accounts having the same beneficiary.
(d) This section is not subject to the requirements of Section 703.150.[796]

704.110. (a) As used in this section:
(1) "Public entity" means the state, or a city, city and county, county, or other political subdivision of the state, or a public trust, public corporation, or public board, or the governing body of any of them, but does not include the United States except where expressly so provided.
(2) "Public retirement benefit" means a pension or an annuity, or a retirement, disability, death, or other benefit, paid or payable by a public retirement system.
(3) "Public retirement system" means a system established pursuant to statute by a public entity for retirement, annuity, or pension purposes or payment of disability or death benefits.
(b) All amounts held, controlled, or in process of distribution by a public entity derived from contributions by the public entity or by an officer or employee of the public entity for public retirement benefit purposes, and all rights and benefits accrued or accruing to any person under a public retirement system, are exempt without making a claim.
(c) Notwithstanding subdivision (b), where an amount described in subdivision (b) becomes payable to a person

and is sought to be applied to the satisfaction of a judgment for child, family, or spousal support against that person:

(1) Except as provided in paragraphs (2) and (3), the amount is exempt only to the extent that the court determines under subdivision (c) of Section 703.070.

(2) If the amount sought to be applied to the satisfaction of the judgment is payable periodically, the amount payable is subject to an earnings assignment order for support as defined in Section 706.011, or any other applicable enforcement procedure, but the amount to be withheld pursuant to the assignment order or other procedure shall not exceed the amount permitted to be withheld on an earnings withholding order for support under Section 706.052. The paying entity may deduct from the payment being made to the judgment debtor, for each payment made pursuant to an earnings assignment order under this paragraph, an amount reflecting the actual cost of administration caused by the assignment order of up to two dollars ($2) for each payment.

(3) If the intercept procedure provided for in Section 11357 of the Welfare and Institutions Code is used for benefits that are payable periodically, the amount to be withheld shall not exceed the amount permitted to be withheld on an earnings withholding order for support under Section 706.052.

(4) If the amount sought to be applied to the satisfaction of the judgment is payable as a lump-sum distribution, the amount payable is subject to the intercept procedure provided in Section 11357 of the Welfare and Institutions Code or any other applicable enforcement procedure.

(d) All amounts received by any person, a resident of the state, as a public retirement benefit or as a return of contributions and interest thereon from the United States or a public entity or from a public retirement system are exempt.[372]

704.111. Alimony, support, and separate maintenance, to the extent reasonably necessary for the support of the debtor and any dependent of the debtor, are exempt.[512]

704.113. (a) As used in this chapter, "vacation credits" means vacation credits accumulated by a state employee pursuant to Section 19858.1 of the Government Code or by any other public employee pursuant to any law for the accumulation of vacation credits applicable to the employee.

(b) The aggregate interest, not to exceed seven thousand five hundred dollars ($7,500), in vacation credits or accrued, or unused, vacation pay, sick leave, or family leave is exempt.

(c) Amounts paid periodically or as a lump sum representing vacation credits are subject to any earnings withholding order served under Chapter 5 (commencing with Section 706.010) or any earnings assignment order for support as defined in Section 706.011 and are exempt to the same extent as earnings of a judgment debtor.[513]

704.114. (a) Notwithstanding any other provision of law, service of an earnings assignment order for support, or an order or notice to withhold income for child support on any public entity described in Section 704.110, other than the United States government, creates a lien on all employee contributions in the amount necessary to satisfy a support judgment as determined under Section 695.210 to the extent that the judgment remains enforceable.

(b) The public entity shall comply with any request for a return of employee contributions by an employee named in the order or notice to withhold by delivering the contributions to the clerk of the court in which the support order was awarded or last registered, unless the entity has received a certified copy of an order or administrative notice terminating the earnings assignment order for support.

(c) Upon receipt of moneys pursuant to this section, the clerk of the court, within 10 days, shall send written notice of the receipt of the deposit to the parties and to the local child support agency enforcing any order pursuant to Section 17400 of the Family Code.

(d) Moneys received pursuant to this section are subject to any procedure available to enforce an order for support, but if no enforcement procedure is commenced after 30 days have elapsed from the date the notice of receipt is sent, the clerk shall, upon request, return the moneys to the public entity that delivered the moneys to the court unless the public entity has informed the court in writing that the moneys shall be released to the employee.

(e) A court shall not directly or indirectly condition the issuance, modification, or termination of, or condition the terms or conditions of, any order for support upon the making of a request for the return of employee contributions by an employee.[451]

704.115. (a) As used in this section, "retirement plan" means:

(1) Private retirement plans, including, but not limited to, union retirement plans.

(2) Profit-sharing plans designed and used for retirement purposes.

(3) Self-employed retirement plans and individual retirement annuities or accounts provided for in the Internal Revenue Code of 1986, as amended, including individual retirement accounts qualified under Section 408 or 408A of that code, to the extent the amounts held in the plans, annuities, or accounts do not exceed the maximum amounts exempt from federal income taxation under that code.

(4) Retirement funds to the extent that those funds are in a fund or account that is exempt from taxation under Sections 403, 414, or 457 of the Internal Revenue Code of 1986, as amended, to the extent the amounts held in the plans, annuities, or accounts do not exceed the maximum amounts exempt from federal income taxation under that code and are not otherwise exempt under federal law.

(b) All amounts held, controlled, or in process of distribution by a retirement plan, for the payment of benefits as an annuity, pension, retirement allowance, disability payment, or death benefit from a retirement plan are exempt.

(c) Notwithstanding subdivision (b), where an amount described in subdivision (b) becomes payable to a person and is sought to be applied to the satisfaction of a judgment for child, family, or spousal support against that person:

(1) Except as provided in paragraph (2), the amount is exempt only to the

extent that the court determines under subdivision (c) of Section 703.070.

(2) If the amount sought to be applied to the satisfaction of the judgment is payable periodically, the amount payable is subject to an earnings assignment order for support as defined in Section 706.011 or any other applicable enforcement procedure, but the amount to be withheld pursuant to the assignment order or other procedure shall not exceed the amount permitted to be withheld on an earnings withholding order for support under Section 706.052.

(d) After payment, the amounts described in subdivision (b) and all contributions and interest thereon returned to any member of a retirement plan are exempt.

(e) (1) Notwithstanding subdivisions (b) and (d), except as provided in subdivision (f), the amounts described in paragraphs (3) and (4) of subdivision (a) are exempt only to the extent necessary to provide for the support of the judgment debtor when the judgment debtor retires and for the support of the spouse and dependents of the judgment debtor, taking into account all resources that are likely to be available for the support of the judgment debtor when the judgment debtor retires.

(2) For personal debt, as defined in subdivision (d) of Section 683.110, the amount necessary to provide for the support of the judgment debtor cannot be, unless otherwise provided by federal law, less than the amount listed in subsection (n) of Section 522 of Title 11 of the United States Code, as adjusted in accordance with subsection (b) of Section 104 of Title 11 of the United States Code. The exempt amount may be aggregated across all retirement plans in the judgment debtor's name. The exempt amount may be reduced to the extent that such value is attributable to any portion of any property the debtor disposed of with the intent to hinder, delay, or defraud a creditor, and that the debtor could not have exempted at the time the debtor so disposed of the property.

(3) In determining the amount to be exempt under this subdivision, the court shall allow the judgment debtor such additional amount as is necessary to pay any federal and state income taxes owed as a result of the application of funds in a retirement plan to the satisfaction of the money judgment.

(f) Where the amounts described in paragraphs (3) and (4) of subdivision (a) are payable periodically, the amount of the periodic payment that may be applied to the satisfaction of a money judgment is the amount that may be withheld from a like amount of earnings under Chapter 5 (commencing with Section 706.010) (Wage Garnishment Law). To the extent a lump-sum distribution from an individual retirement account is treated differently from a periodic distribution under this subdivision, any lump-sum distribution from an account qualified under Section 408A of the Internal Revenue Code shall be treated the same as a lump-sum distribution from an account qualified under Section 408 of the Internal Revenue Code for purposes of determining whether any of that payment may be applied to the satisfaction of a money judgment.[856]

704.120. (a) Contributions by workers

payable to the Unemployment Compensation Disability Fund and by employers payable to the Unemployment Fund are exempt without making a claim.

(b) Before payment, amounts held for payment of the following benefits are exempt without making a claim:

(1) Benefits payable under Division 1 (commencing with Section 100) of the Unemployment Insurance Code.

(2) Incentives payable under Division 2 (commencing with Section 5000) of the Unemployment Insurance Code.

(3) Benefits payable under an employer's plan or system to supplement unemployment compensation benefits of the employees generally or for a class or group of employees.

(4) Unemployment benefits payable by a fraternal organization to its bona fide members.

(5) Benefits payable by a union due to a labor dispute.

(c) After payment, the benefits described in subdivision (b) are exempt.

(d) During the payment of benefits described in paragraph (1) of subdivision (b) to a judgment debtor under a support judgment, the judgment creditor may, through the appropriate local child support agency, seek to apply the benefit payment to satisfy the judgment as provided by Section 17518 of the Family Code.

(e) During the payment of benefits described in paragraphs (2) to (5), inclusive, of subdivision (b) to a judgment debtor under a support judgment, the judgment creditor may, directly or through the appropriate local child support agency, seek to apply the benefit payments to satisfy the judgment by an earnings assignment order for support as defined in Section 706.011 or any other applicable enforcement procedure. If the benefit is payable periodically, the amount to be withheld pursuant to the assignment order or other procedure shall be 25 percent of the amount of each periodic payment or any lower amount specified in writing by the judgment creditor or court order, rounded down to the nearest whole dollar. Otherwise, the amount to be withheld shall be the amount the court determines under subdivision (c) of Section 703.070. The paying entity may deduct from each payment made pursuant to an assignment order under this subdivision an amount reflecting the actual cost of administration caused by the assignment order up to two dollars ($2) for each payment.[452]

704.130. (a) Before payment, benefits from a disability or health insurance policy or program are exempt without making a claim. After payment, the benefits are exempt.

(b) Subdivision (a) does not apply to benefits that are paid or payable to cover the cost of health care if the judgment creditor is a provider of health care whose claim is the basis on which the benefits are paid or payable.

(c) During the payment of disability benefits described in subdivision (a) to a judgment debtor under a support judgment, the judgment creditor or local child support agency may seek to apply the benefit payments to satisfy the judgment by an earnings assignment order for support, as defined in Section 706.011, or any other applicable enforcement procedure, but the amount to be withheld pursuant to the earnings assignment order or other procedure shall not exceed the amount permitted to be withheld on an earnings assignment order for support under Section 706.052.[453]

704.140. (a) Except as provided in Article 5 (commencing with Section 708.410) of Chapter 6, a cause of action for personal injury is exempt without making a claim.
(b) Except as provided in subdivisions (c) and (d), an award of damages or a settlement arising out of personal injury is exempt to the extent necessary for the support of the judgment debtor and the spouse and dependents of the judgment debtor.
(c) Subdivision (b) does not apply if the judgment creditor is a provider of health care whose claim is based on the providing of health care for the personal injury for which the award or settlement was made.
(d) Where an award of damages or a settlement arising out of personal injury is payable periodically, the amount of such periodic payment that may be applied to the satisfaction of a money judgment is the amount that may be withheld from a like amount of earnings under Chapter 5 (commencing with Section 706.010) (Wage Garnishment Law).[170]

704.150. (a) Except as provided in Article 5 (commencing with Section 708.410) of Chapter 6, a cause of action for wrongful death is exempt without making a claim.
(b) Except as provided in subdivision (c), an award of damages or a settlement arising out of the wrongful death of the judgment debtor's spouse or a person on whom the judgment debtor or the judgment debtor's spouse was dependent is exempt to the extent reasonably necessary for support of the judgment debtor and the spouse and dependents of the judgment debtor.
(c) Where an award of damages or a settlement arising out of the wrongful death of the judgment debtor's spouse or a person on whom the judgment debtor or the judgment debtor's spouse was dependent is payable periodically, the amount of such a periodic payment that may be applied to the satisfaction of a money judgment is the amount that may be withheld from a like amount of earnings under Chapter 5 (commencing with Section 706.010) (Wage Garnishment Law).[170]

704.160. (a) Except as provided by Chapter 1 (commencing with Section 4900) of Part 3 of Division 4 of the Labor Code, before payment, a claim for workers' compensation or workers' compensation awarded or adjudged is exempt without making a claim. Except as specified in subdivision (b), after payment, the award is exempt.
(b) Notwithstanding any other provision of law, during the payment of workers' compensation temporary disability benefits described in subdivision (a) to a support judgment debtor, the support judgment creditor may, through the appropriate local child support agency, seek to apply the workers' compensation temporary disability benefit payment to satisfy the support judgment as provided by Section 17404 of the Family Code.
(c) Notwithstanding any other provision of law, during the payment of workers' compensation temporary disability benefits described in subdivision (a) to a support judgment debtor under a support judgment, including a judgment for reimbursement of public assistance, the judgment creditor may,

directly or through the appropriate local child support agency, seek to apply the temporary disability benefit payments to satisfy the support judgment by an earnings assignment order for support, as defined in Section 5208 of the Family Code, or any other applicable enforcement procedure. The amount to be withheld pursuant to the earnings assignment order for support or other enforcement procedure shall be 25 percent of the amount of each periodic payment or any lower amount specified in writing by the judgment creditor or court order, rounded down to the nearest dollar. Otherwise, the amount to be withheld shall be the amount the court determines under subdivision (c) of Section 703.070. The paying entity may deduct from each payment made pursuant to an order assigning earnings under this subdivision an amount reflecting the actual cost of administration of this assignment, up to two dollars ($2) for each payment.

(d) Unless the provision or context otherwise requires, the following definitions govern the construction of this section.

(1) "Judgment debtor" or "support judgment debtor" means a person who is owing a duty of support.

(2) "Judgment creditor" or "support judgment creditor" means the person to whom support has been ordered to be paid.

(3) "Support" refers to an obligation owing on behalf of a child, spouse, or family; or an amount owing pursuant to Section 17402 of the Family Code. It also includes past due support or arrearage when it exists.[454]

704.170. Before payment, aid provided pursuant to Division 9 (commencing with Section 10000) of the Welfare and Institutions Code or similar aid provided by a charitable organization or a fraternal benefit society as defined in Section 10990 of the Insurance Code, is exempt without making a claim. After payment, the aid is exempt.[170]

704.180. Before payment, relocation benefits for displacement from a dwelling which are to be paid pursuant to Chapter 16 (commencing with Section 7260) of Division 7 of Title 1 of the Government Code or the federal "Uniform Relocation Assistance and Real Property Acquisition Policies Act of 1970" (42 U.S.C. Sec. 4601 et seq.), as amended, are exempt without making a claim. After payment, the benefits are exempt.[170]

704.190. (a) As used in this section, "institution of higher education" means "institution of higher education" as defined in Section 1141(a) of Title 20 of the United States Code, as amended.

(b) Before payment, financial aid for expenses while attending school provided to a student by an institution of higher education is exempt without making a claim. After payment, the aid is exempt.[170]

704.200. (a) As used in this section:

(1) "Cemetery" has the meaning provided by Section 7003 of the Health and Safety Code.

(2) "Family plot" is a plot that satisfies the requirements of Section 8650 of the Health and Safety Code.

(3) "Plot" has the meaning provided by Section 7022 of the Health and Safety Code.

(b) A family plot is exempt without making a claim.

(c) Except as provided in subdivision (d), a cemetery plot for the judgment

debtor and the spouse of the judgment debtor is exempt.
(d) Land held for the purpose of sale or disposition as cemetery plots or otherwise is not exempt.[170]

704.210. Property that is not subject to enforcement of a money judgment is exempt without making a claim.[170]

704.220. (a) Money in the judgment debtor's deposit account in an amount equal to or less than the minimum basic standard of adequate care for a family of four for Region 1, established by Section 11452 of the Welfare and Institutions Code and as annually adjusted by the State Department of Social Services pursuant to Section 11453 of the Welfare and Institutions Code, is exempt without making a claim.
(b) (1) Subdivision (a) does not preclude or reduce a judgment debtor's right to any other exemption provided by state or federal law.
(2) If the financial institution holding the judgment debtor's deposit account has actual knowledge that the judgment debtor is entitled to one or more exemptions that the financial institution is required to apply pursuant to federal law or state law other than that set forth in subdivision (a), the following shall apply:
(A) If the sum of the amount of money in the deposit account that would be exempt from levy under the additional exemptions is less than or equal to the amount set forth in subdivision (a), the additional exemptions described in this paragraph shall be considered encompassed within the exemption set forth in subdivision (a) and subdivision (a) shall apply.
(B) If the sum of the amount of money in the deposit account that would be exempt from levy under the additional exemptions is greater than the amount set forth in subdivision (a), subdivision (a) shall not apply and instead money in the deposit account equal to or less than the sum of the additional exemptions is exempt without making a claim.
(c) Subdivision (a) does not apply to money levied upon to satisfy any of the following:
(1) A levy to satisfy a judgment for wages owed, child support, or spousal support. For purposes of this paragraph, "wages owed" includes damages and penalties.
(2) A provision of the Public Resources Code, Revenue and Taxation Code, or Unemployment Insurance Code.
(3) A warrant or notice of levy issued by the state, or any department or agency thereof, for the collection of a liability.
(d) A levy against a judgment debtor's deposit account shall include a written description of the requirements of this section.
(e) (1) The exemption applies per debtor, not per account.
(2) If a judgment debtor holds an interest in multiple accounts at a single financial institution, the judgment creditor or judgment debtor may file an ex parte application in the superior court in which the judgment was entered for a hearing to establish how and to which account the exemption should be applied. Subject to a service of an order issued in that hearing, if any, the financial institution may determine how and to which account the exemption should be applied. This paragraph does not create a cause of action against a judgment

creditor who executes a levy or against a financial institution that complies with a levy pursuant to the court's determination.

(3) If a judgment debtor holds an interest in multiple accounts at two or more financial institutions, the judgment creditor shall, and the judgment debtor may, file an ex parte application in the superior court in which the judgment was entered for a hearing to establish how and to which account the exemption should be applied. Subject to a service of an order issued in that hearing, if any, the financial institutions shall comply with the levy subject to the exemption. This paragraph does not create a cause of action against a judgment creditor who executes a levy or against a financial institution which complies with a levy pursuant to the court's determination.

(4) Notwithstanding paragraph (2), if a judgment debtor holds multiple accounts at a single financial institution, and those accounts cumulatively contain an amount less than or equal to the amount specified in subdivision (a), the financial institution shall protect the full amount in those accounts.

(5) Notwithstanding paragraph (2), if a judgment debtor holds multiple accounts at a single financial institution, and each of those accounts contains an amount less than the amount specified in subdivision (a) but the accounts cumulatively contain an amount greater than the amount specified in subdivision (a), the financial institution shall protect an aggregate amount equal to the amount specified in subdivision (a).

(f) Subdivision (e) of Section 700.140 applies to a financial institution acting under this section.

(g) The Judicial Council shall amend or adopt all forms necessary to implement this section. The forms shall clearly delineate the amount of funds exempt from levy by a financial institution, including funds exempted by this section.

(h) This section shall become operative on September 1, 2020.[857]

704.225. Money in a judgment debtor's deposit account that is not otherwise exempt under this chapter is exempt to the extent necessary for the support of the judgment debtor and the spouse and dependents of the judgment debtor.[758]

704.230. Money provided to the judgment debtor by the Federal Emergency Management Agency (FEMA) is exempt without making a claim.[759]

704.235. (a) A one-time lump-sum payment made from a HOPE trust account, as defined in subdivision (a) of Section 18997.51 of the Welfare and Institutions Code, shall be exempt without making a claim, except as provided in subdivision (b).

(b) A one-time lump-sum payment described in subdivision (a) is not exempt from a levy in connection with child support, spousal support, family support, or a criminal restitution.

(c) A financial institution that receives a payment described in subdivision (a) directly from the state shall treat the payment as exempt from levy if it is designated "HOPE trust account payment" or if the payment is otherwise sufficiently identified to inform the financial institution that the payment is a HOPE trust account payment.[871]

Article 4: Homestead Exemption
Article 4 added by Stats. 1982, Ch. 1364, Sec. 2.

704.710. As used in this article:
(a) "Dwelling" means a place where a person resides and may include but is not limited to the following:
(1) A house together with the outbuildings and the land upon which they are situated.
(2) A mobilehome together with the outbuildings and the land upon which they are situated.
(3) A boat or other waterborne vessel.
(4) A condominium, as defined in Section 783 of the Civil Code.
(5) A planned development, as defined in Section 11003 of the Business and Professions Code.
(6) A stock cooperative, as defined in Section 11003.2 of the Business and Professions Code.
(7) A community apartment project, as defined in Section 11004 of the Business and Professions Code.
(b) "Family unit" means any of the following:
(1) The judgment debtor and the judgment debtor's spouse if the spouses reside together in the homestead.
(2) The judgment debtor and at least one of the following persons who the judgment debtor cares for or maintains in the homestead:
(A) The minor child or minor grandchild of the judgment debtor or the judgment debtor's spouse or the minor child or grandchild of a deceased spouse or former spouse.
(B) The minor brother or sister of the judgment debtor or judgment debtor's spouse or the minor child of a deceased brother or sister of either spouse.
(C) The father, mother, grandfather, or grandmother of the judgment debtor or the judgment debtor's spouse or the father, mother, grandfather, or grandmother of a deceased spouse.
(D) An unmarried relative described in this paragraph who has attained the age of majority and is unable to take care of or support himself or herself.
(3) The judgment debtor's spouse and at least one of the persons listed in paragraph (2) who the judgment debtor's spouse cares for or maintains in the homestead.
(c) "Homestead" means the principal dwelling (1) in which the judgment debtor or the judgment debtor's spouse resided on the date the judgment creditor's lien attached to the dwelling, and (2) in which the judgment debtor or the judgment debtor's spouse resided continuously thereafter until the date of the court determination that the dwelling is a homestead. Where exempt proceeds from the sale or damage or destruction of a homestead are used toward the acquisition of a dwelling within the six-month period provided by Section 704.720, "homestead" also means the dwelling so acquired if it is the principal dwelling in which the judgment debtor or the judgment debtor's spouse resided continuously from the date of acquisition until the date of the court determination that the dwelling is a homestead, whether or not an abstract or certified copy of a judgment was recorded to create a judgment lien before the dwelling was acquired.
(d) "Spouse" does not include a married person following entry of a judgment decreeing legal separation of the

parties, unless such married persons reside together in the same dwelling.[201]

704.720. (a) A homestead is exempt from sale under this division to the extent provided in Section 704.800.
(b) If a homestead is sold under this division or is damaged or destroyed or is acquired for public use, the proceeds of sale or of insurance or other indemnification for damage or destruction of the homestead or the proceeds received as compensation for a homestead acquired for public use are exempt in the amount of the homestead exemption provided in Section 704.730. The proceeds are exempt for a period of six months after the time the proceeds are actually received by the judgment debtor, except that, if a homestead exemption is applied to other property of the judgment debtor or the judgment debtor's spouse during that period, the proceeds thereafter are not exempt.
(c) If the judgment debtor and spouse of the judgment debtor reside in separate homesteads, only the homestead of one of the spouses is exempt and only the proceeds of the exempt homestead are exempt.
(d) If a judgment debtor is not currently residing in the homestead, but his or her separated or former spouse continues to reside in or exercise control over possession of the homestead, that judgment debtor continues to be entitled to an exemption under this article until entry of judgment or other legally enforceable agreement dividing the community property between the judgment debtor and the separated or former spouse, or until a later time period as specified by court order. Nothing in this subdivision shall entitle the judgment debtor to more than one exempt homestead. Notwithstanding subdivision (d) of Section 704.710, for purposes of this article, "spouse" may include a separated or former spouse consistent with this subdivision.[595]

704.730. (a) The amount of the homestead exemption is the greater of the following:
(1) The countywide median sale price for a single-family home in the calendar year prior to the calendar year in which the judgment debtor claims the exemption, not to exceed six hundred thousand dollars ($600,000).
(2) Three hundred thousand dollars ($300,000).
(b) The amounts specified in this section shall adjust annually for inflation, beginning on January 1, 2022, based on the change in the annual California Consumer Price Index for All Urban Consumers, published by the Department of Industrial Relations, for the most recent one-year period ending on December 31 preceding the adjustment, with each adjusted amount rounded to the nearest twenty-five dollars ($25).[841]

704.740. (a) Except as provided in subdivision (b), the interest of a natural person in a dwelling may not be sold under this division to enforce a money judgment except pursuant to a court order for sale obtained under this article and the dwelling exemption shall be determined under this article.
(b) If the dwelling is personal property or is real property in which the judgment debtor has a leasehold estate with an unexpired term of less than two years at the time of levy:
(1) A court order for sale is not required and the procedures provided

in this article relating to the court order for sale do not apply.

(2) An exemption claim shall be made and determined as provided in Article 2 (commencing with Section 703.510).[220]

704.750. (a) Promptly after a dwelling is levied upon (other than a dwelling described in subdivision (b) of Section 704.740), the levying officer shall serve notice on the judgment creditor that the levy has been made and that the property will be released unless the judgment creditor complies with the requirements of this section. Service shall be made personally or by mail. Within 20 days after service of the notice, the judgment creditor shall apply to the court for an order for sale of the dwelling and shall file a copy of the application with the levying officer. If the judgment creditor does not file the copy of the application for an order for sale of the dwelling within the allowed time, the levying officer shall release the dwelling.

(b) If the dwelling is located in a county other than the county where the judgment was entered:

(1) The judgment creditor shall apply to the superior court of the county where the dwelling is located.

(2) The judgment creditor shall file with the application an abstract of judgment in the form prescribed by Section 674 or, in the case of a judgment described in Section 697.320, a certified copy of the judgment.

(3) The judgment creditor shall pay the filing fee for a motion as provided in subdivision (a) of Section 70617 of the Government Code.[873]

704.760. The judgment creditor's application shall be made under oath, shall describe the dwelling, and shall contain all of the following:

(a) A statement whether or not the records of the county tax assessor indicate that there is a current homeowner's exemption or disabled veteran's exemption for the dwelling and the person or persons who claimed any such exemption.

(b) A statement, which may be based on information and belief, whether the dwelling is a homestead and the amount of the homestead exemption, if any, and a statement whether or not the records of the county recorder indicate that a homestead declaration under Article 5 (commencing with Section 704.910) that describes the dwelling has been recorded by the judgment debtor or the spouse of the judgment debtor.

(c) A statement of the amount of any liens or encumbrances on the dwelling, the name of each person having a lien or encumbrance on the dwelling, and the address of such person used by the county recorder for the return of the instrument creating such person's lien or encumbrance after recording.

(d) A statement that the judgment is based on a consumer debt, as defined in subdivision (a) of Section 699.730, or that the judgment is not based on a consumer debt, and if the judgment is based on a consumer debt, whether the judgment is based on a consumer debt that was secured by the debtor's principal place of residence at the time it was incurred or a statement indicating which of the exemptions listed in subdivision (b) of Section 699.730 are applicable. If the statement indicates that paragraph (7) of subdivision (b) is applicable, the statement shall also provide the dollar amount of the original judgment on which the lien is based. If there is more than one basis, the statement shall indicate all bases that are applicable.[776]

704.770. (a) Upon the filing of the application by the judgment creditor, the court shall set a time and place for hearing and order the judgment debtor to show cause why an order for sale should not be made in accordance with the application. The time set for hearing shall be not later than 45 days after the application is filed or such later time as the court orders upon a showing of good cause.

(b) Not later than 30 days before the time set for hearing, the judgment creditor shall do both of the following:

(1) Serve on the judgment debtor a copy of the order to show cause, a copy of the application of the judgment creditor, and a copy of the notice of the hearing in the form prescribed by the Judicial Council. Service shall be made personally or by mail.

(2) Personally serve a copy of each document listed in paragraph (1) on an occupant of the dwelling or, if there is no occupant present at the time service is attempted, post a copy of each document in a conspicuous place at the dwelling.[234]

704.780. (a) The burden of proof at the hearing is determined in the following manner:

(1) If the records of the county tax assessor indicate that there is a current homeowner's exemption or disabled veteran's exemption for the dwelling claimed by the judgment debtor or the judgment debtor's spouse, the judgment creditor has the burden of proof that the dwelling is not a homestead. If the records of the county tax assessor indicate that there is not a current homeowner's exemption or disabled veteran's exemption for the dwelling claimed by the judgment debtor or the judgment debtor's spouse, the burden of proof that the dwelling is a homestead is on the person who claims that the dwelling is a homestead.

(2) If the application states the amount of the homestead exemption, the person claiming the homestead exemption has the burden of proof that the amount of the exemption is other than the amount stated in the application.

(b) The court shall determine whether the dwelling is exempt. If the court determines that the dwelling is exempt, the court shall determine the amount of the homestead exemption and the fair market value of the dwelling. The court shall make an order for sale of the dwelling subject to the homestead exemption, unless the court determines that the sale of the dwelling would not be likely to produce a bid sufficient to satisfy any part of the amount due on the judgment pursuant to Section 704.800. The order for sale of the dwelling subject to the homestead exemption shall specify the amount of the proceeds of the sale that is to be distributed to each person having a lien or encumbrance on the dwelling and shall include the name and address of each such person. Subject to the provisions of this article, the sale is governed by Article 6 (commencing with Section 701.510) of Chapter 3. If the court determines that the dwelling is not exempt, the court shall make an order for sale of the

property in the manner provided in Article 6 (commencing with Section 701.510) of Chapter 3.
(c) The court clerk shall transmit a certified copy of the court order (1) to the levying officer and (2) if the court making the order is not the court in which the judgment was entered, to the clerk of the court in which the judgment was entered.
(d) The court may appoint a qualified appraiser to assist the court in determining the fair market value of the dwelling. If the court appoints an appraiser, the court shall fix the compensation of the appraiser in an amount determined by the court to be reasonable, not to exceed similar fees for similar services in the community where the dwelling is located.[342]

704.790. (a) This section applies in any case where the court makes an order for sale of the dwelling upon a hearing at which none of the following appeared:
(1) The judgment debtor.
(2) The judgment debtor's spouse.
(3) The attorney for the judgment debtor.
(4) The attorney for the judgment debtors spouse.
(b) Not later than 10 days after the date of the order for sale, the judgment creditor shall serve a copy of the order and a notice of the order in the form prescribed by the Judicial Council:
(1) Personally or by mail on the judgment debtor and the judgment debtor's spouse.
(2) Personally on an occupant of the dwelling or, if there is no occupant present at the time service is attempted, post a copy of the order and notice in a conspicuous place at the dwelling.
(c) Proof of service and of any posting shall be filed with the court and with the levying officer. If the judgment creditor fails to comply with this subdivision and with subdivision (b) in any case where this section applies, the dwelling may not be sold under the order for sale.
(d) If, within 10 days after service of notice of the order, the judgment debtor or the judgment debtor's spouse files with the levying officer a declaration that the absence of the judgment debtor and the judgment debtor's spouse or the attorney for the judgment debtor or the judgment debtor's spouse from the hearing was due to mistake, inadvertence, surprise, or excusable neglect and that the judgment debtor or spouse of the judgment debtor wishes to assert the homestead exemption, the levying officer shall transmit the declaration forthwith to the court. Upon receipt of the declaration, the court shall set a time and place for hearing to determine whether the determinations of the court should be modified. The time set for hearing shall be not later than 20 days after receipt of the declaration. The court clerk shall cause notice of the hearing promptly to be given to the parties.[235]

704.800. (a) If no bid is received at a sale of a homestead pursuant to a court order for sale that exceeds the amount of the homestead exemption plus any additional amount necessary to satisfy all liens and encumbrances on the property, including but not limited to any attachment or judgment lien, the homestead shall not be sold and shall be released and is not thereafter subject to a court order for sale upon subsequent application by the same judgment creditor for a period of one year.

(b) If no bid is received at the sale of a homestead pursuant to a court order for sale that is 90 percent or more of the fair market value determined pursuant to Section 704.780, the homestead shall not be sold unless the court, upon motion of the judgment creditor, does one of the following:

(1) Grants permission to accept the highest bid that exceeds the amount of the minimum bid required by subdivision (a).

(2) Makes a new order for sale of the homestead.[170]

704.810. Levy on a homestead that is subject to a lien or encumbrance is not by itself grounds for acceleration of the obligation secured by the lien or encumbrance, notwithstanding any provision of the obligation, lien, or encumbrance and if the homestead is sold pursuant to court order under this article the amount payable to satisfy a lien or encumbrance shall not include any penalty for prepayment.[170]

704.820. If the dwelling is owned by the judgment debtor as a joint tenant or tenant in common or if the interest of the judgment debtor in the dwelling is a leasehold or other interest less than a fee interest:

(a) At an execution sale of a dwelling, the interest of the judgment debtor in the dwelling and not the dwelling shall be sold. If there is more than one judgment debtor of the judgment creditor, the interests of the judgment debtors in the dwelling shall be sold together and each of the judgment debtors entitled to a homestead exemption is entitled to apply his or her exemption to his or her own interest.

(b) For the purposes of this section, all references in this article to the "dwelling" or "homestead" are deemed to be references to the interest of the judgment debtor in the dwelling or homestead.[170]

704.830. The provisions of Sections 703.590 and 703.600 apply to proceedings under this article.[170]

704.840. (a) Except as provided in subdivision (b), the judgment creditor is entitled to recover reasonable costs incurred in a proceeding under this article.

(b) If no bid is received at a sale of a homestead pursuant to a court order for sale that exceeds the amount of the homestead exemption plus any additional amount necessary to satisfy all liens and encumbrances on the property, the judgment creditor is not entitled to recover costs incurred in a proceeding under this article or costs of sale.[170]

704.850. (a) The levying officer shall distribute the proceeds of sale of a homestead in the following order:

(1) To the discharge of all liens and encumbrances, if any, on the property.

(2) To the judgment debtor in the amount of any applicable exemption of proceeds pursuant to Section 704.720.

(3) To the levying officer for the reimbursement of the levying officer's costs for which an advance has not been made.

(4) To the judgment creditor to satisfy the following:

(A) First, costs and interest accruing after issuance of the writ pursuant to which the sale is conducted.

(B) Second, the amount due on the

judgment with costs and interest, as entered on the writ.

(5) To the judgment debtor in the amount remaining.

(b) Sections 701.820 and 701.830 apply to distribution of proceeds under this section.[170]

Article 5: Declared Homesteads

Article 5 added by Stats. 1982, Ch. 1364, Sec. 2.

704.910. As used in this article:

(a) "Declared homestead" means the dwelling described in a homestead declaration.

(b) "Declared homestead owner" includes both of the following:

(1) The owner of an interest in the declared homestead who is named as a declared homestead owner in a homestead declaration recorded pursuant to this article.

(2) The declarant named in a declaration of homestead recorded prior to July 1, 1983, pursuant to former Title 5 (commencing with Section 1237) of Part 4 of Division 2 of the Civil Code and the spouse of such declarant.

(c) "Dwelling" means any interest in real property (whether present or future, vested or contingent, legal or equitable) that is a "dwelling" as defined in Section 704.710, but does not include a leasehold estate with an unexpired term of less than two years or the interest of the beneficiary of a trust.

(d) "Homestead declaration" includes both of the following:

(1) A homestead declaration recorded pursuant to this article.

(2) A declaration of homestead recorded prior to July 1, 1983, pursuant to former Title 5 (commencing with former Section 1237) of Part 4 of Division 2 of the Civil Code.

(e) "Spouse" means a "spouse" as defined in Section 704.710.[170]

704.920. A dwelling in which an owner or spouse of an owner resides may be selected as a declared homestead pursuant to this article by recording a homestead declaration in the office of the county recorder of the county where the dwelling is located. From and after the time of recording, the dwelling is a declared homestead for the purposes of this article.[170]

704.930. (a) A homestead declaration recorded pursuant to this article shall contain all of the following:

(1) The name of the declared homestead owner. Spouses both may be named as declared homestead owners in the same homestead declaration if each owns an interest in the dwelling selected as the declared homestead.

(2) A description of the declared homestead.

(3) A statement that the declared homestead is the principal dwelling of the declared homestead owner or such person's spouse, and that the declared homestead owner or such person's spouse resides in the declared homestead on the date the homestead declaration is recorded.

(b) The homestead declaration shall be executed and acknowledged in the manner of an acknowledgment of a conveyance of real property by at least one of the following persons:

(1) The declared homestead owner.

(2) The spouse of the declared homestead owner.

(3) The guardian or conservator of the person or estate of either of the persons listed in paragraph (1) or (2). The guardian or conservator may execute, acknowledge, and record a homestead

declaration without the need to obtain court authorization.

(4) A person acting under a power of attorney or otherwise authorized to act on behalf of a person listed in paragraph (1) or (2).

(c) The homestead declaration shall include a statement that the facts stated in the homestead declaration are known to be true as of the personal knowledge of the person executing and acknowledging the homestead declaration. If the homestead declaration is executed and acknowledged by a person listed in paragraph (3) or (4) of subdivision (b), it shall also contain a statement that the person has authority to so act on behalf of the declared homestead owner or the spouse of the declared homestead owner and the source of the person's authority.[725]

704.940. A homestead declaration does not restrict or limit any right to convey or encumber the declared homestead. A homestead declaration, when properly recorded, is prima facie evidence of the facts therein stated, and conclusive evidence thereof in favor of a purchaser or encumbrancer in good faith and for a valuable consideration.[170]

704.950. (a) Except as provided in subdivisions (b) and (c), a judgment lien on real property created pursuant to Article 2 (commencing with Section 697.310) of Chapter 2 does not attach to a declared homestead if both of the following requirements are satisfied:

(1) A homestead declaration describing the declared homestead was recorded prior to the time the abstract or certified copy of the judgment was recorded to create the judgment lien.

(2) The homestead declaration names the judgment debtor or the spouse of the judgment debtor as a declared homestead owner.

(b) This section does not apply to a judgment lien created under Section 697.320 by recording a certified copy of a judgment for child, family, or spousal support.

(c) A judgment lien attaches to a declared homestead in the amount of any surplus over the total of the following:

(1) All liens and encumbrances on the declared homestead at the time the abstract of judgment or certified copy of the judgment is recorded to create the judgment lien.

(2) The homestead exemption set forth in Section 704.730.[299]

704.960. (a) If a declared homestead is voluntarily sold, the proceeds of sale are exempt in the amount provided by Section 704.730 for a period of six months after the date of sale.

(b) If the proceeds of a declared homestead are invested in a new dwelling within six months after the date of a voluntary sale or within six months after proceeds of an execution sale or of insurance or other indemnification for damage or destruction are received, the new dwelling may be selected as a declared homestead by recording a homestead declaration within the applicable six-month period. In such case, the homestead declaration has the same effect as if it had been recorded at the time the prior homestead declaration was recorded.[170]

704.965. If a homestead declaration is recorded prior to the operative date of an amendment to Section 704.730 which increases the amount of the homestead exemption, the amount of the exemption for the purposes of subdivision (c) of Section 704.950 and Section 704.960 is the increased amount, except that, if the judgment creditor obtained a lien on the declared homestead prior to the operative date of the amendment to Section 704.730, the exemption for the purposes of subdivision (c) of Section 704.950 and Section 704.960 shall be determined as if that amendment to Section 704.730 had not been enacted.[203]

704.970. Whether or not a homestead declaration has been recorded:
(a) Nothing in this article affects the right of levy pursuant to a writ of execution.
(b) Any levy pursuant to a writ of execution on a dwelling (as defined in Section 704.710) and the sale pursuant thereto shall be made in compliance with Article 4 (commencing with Section 704.710) and the judgment debtor and the judgment creditor shall have all the rights and benefits provided by that article.[170]

704.980. (a) A declared homestead may be abandoned by a declaration of abandonment under this section, whether the homestead declaration was recorded pursuant to this article or pursuant to former Title 5 (commencing with former Section 1237) of Part 4 of Division 2 of the Civil Code.
(b) A declaration of abandonment shall be executed and acknowledged in the manner of an acknowledgment of a conveyance of real property. It shall be executed and acknowledged by a declared homestead owner or by a person authorized to act on behalf of a declared homestead owner. If it is executed and acknowledged by a person authorized to act on behalf of a declared homestead owner, the declaration shall contain a statement that the person has authority to act on behalf of the declared homestead owner and the source of the person's authority.
(c) The declaration of abandonment does not affect the declared homestead of any person other than the declared homestead owner named in the declaration of abandonment.[170]

704.990. (a) A declared homestead is abandoned by operation of law as to a declared homestead owner if the declared homestead owner or a person authorized to act on behalf of the declared homestead owner executes, acknowledges, and records a new homestead declaration for the declared homestead owner on different property. An abandonment under this subdivision does not affect the declared homestead of any person other than the declared homestead owner named in the new homestead declaration.
(b) Notwithstanding subdivision (a), if a homestead declaration is recorded which includes property described in a previously recorded homestead declaration, to the extent that the prior homestead declaration is still valid, the new homestead declaration shall not be considered an abandonment of the prior declared homestead.[170]

704.995. (a) The protection of the declared homestead from any creditor having an attachment lien, execution lien, or judgment lien on the dwelling continues after the death of the declared homestead owner if, at the time of the death, the dwelling was the principal dwelling of one or more of the following persons to whom all or part of the interest of the deceased declared homestead owner passes:

(1) The surviving spouse of the decedent.
(2) A member of the family of the decedent.
(b) The protection of the declared homestead provided by subdivision (a) continues regardless of whether the decedent was the sole owner of the declared homestead or owned the declared homestead with the surviving spouse or a member of the decedent's family and regardless of whether the surviving spouse or the member of the decedent's family was a declared homestead owner at the time of the decedent's death.
(c) The amount of the homestead exemption is determined pursuant to Section 704.730 depending on the circumstances of the case at the time the amount is required to be determined.[221]

Chapter 5: Wage Garnishment

Chapter 5 added by Stats. 1982, Ch. 1364, Sec. 2.

Article 1: Short Title; Definitions

Article 1 added by Stats. 1982, Ch. 1364, Sec. 2.

706.010. This chapter shall be known and may be cited as the "Wage Garnishment Law."[170]

706.011. As used in this chapter:
(a) "Disposable earnings" means the portion of an individual's earnings that remains after deducting all amounts required to be withheld by law.
(b) "Earnings" means compensation payable by an employer to an employee for personal services performed by such employee, whether denominated as wages, salary, commission, bonus, or otherwise.
(c) "Earnings withholding order for elder or dependent adult financial abuse" means an earnings withholding order, made pursuant to Article 5 (commencing with Section 706.100) and based on a money judgment in an action for elder or adult dependent financial abuse under Section 15657.5 of the Welfare and Institutions Code.
(d) "Earnings assignment order for support" means an order, made pursuant to Chapter 8 (commencing with Section 5200) of Part 5 of Division 9 of the Family Code or Section 3088 of the Probate Code, which requires an employer to withhold earnings for support.
(e) "Employee" means a public officer and any individual who performs services subject to the right of the employer to control both what shall be done and how it shall be done.
(f) "Employer" means a person for whom an individual performs services as an employee.
(g) "Judgment creditor," as applied to the state, means the specific state agency seeking to collect a judgment or tax liability.
(h) "Judgment debtor" includes a person from whom the state is seeking to collect a tax liability under Article 4 (commencing with Section 706.070), whether or not a judgment has been obtained on such tax liability.
(i) "Person" includes an individual, a corporation, a partnership or other unincorporated association, a limited liability company, and a public entity.[670]

Article 2: General Provisions

Article 2 added by Stats. 1982, Ch. 1364, Sec. 2.

706.020. Except for an earning assignment order for support, the earnings of an employee shall not be required to be withheld by an employer for payment of a debt by means of any judicial procedure other than pursuant to this chapter.[300]

706.021. Notwithstanding any other provision of this title, a levy of execution upon the earnings of an employee shall be made by service of an earnings withholding order upon the judgment debtor's employer in accordance with this chapter.[906]

706.022. (a) A judgment creditor shall not enforce an earnings withholding order beyond the period of enforceability as defined in Section 683.020 or, if renewed, as provided for in subdivision (c) of Section 683.120. As used in this section, "withholding period" means the period which commences on the 30th day after service of an earnings withholding order upon the judgment debtor's employer. If a claim of exemption is filed with the levying officer, and the employer is given actual notice before the close of business on the 29th day after the service of the earnings withholding order on the judgment debtor's employer, the withholding period commences on the 45th day after service of the earnings withholding order on the judgment debtor's employer. The withholding period shall continue until the earliest of the following dates:

(1) The date the employer has withheld the full amount required to satisfy the order.

(2) The date of termination specified in a court order served on the employer.

(3) The date of termination specified in a notice of termination served on the employer by the levying officer.

(4) The date of termination of a dormant or suspended earnings withholding order as determined pursuant to Section 706.032.

(b) Except as otherwise provided by statute, an employer shall withhold the amounts required by an earnings withholding order from all earnings of the employee payable for any pay period of the employee which ends during the withholding period.

(c) An employer is not liable for any amounts withheld and paid over to the levying officer pursuant to an earnings withholding order prior to service upon the employer pursuant to paragraph (2) or (3) of subdivision (a).[907]

706.023. Except as otherwise provided in this chapter:

(a) An employer shall comply with the first earnings withholding order served upon the employer.

(b) If the employer is served with two or more earnings withholding orders on the same day, the employer shall comply with the order issued pursuant to the judgment first entered. If two or more orders served on the same day are based on judgments entered upon the same day, the employer shall comply with whichever one of the orders the employer selects.

(c) If an earnings withholding order is served while an employer is required to comply with another earnings withholding order with respect to the earnings of the same employee, the subsequent order is ineffective and the employer shall not withhold earnings pursuant to the subsequent order, except as provided in subdivision (d).

(d) Notwithstanding any other provisions of this section, a withholding order for elder or dependent adult financial abuse has priority over any other earning withholding order except for a withholding order for support under Section 706.030 and a withholding order for taxes under Section 706.072.

(1) An employer upon whom a withholding order for elder or dependent adult financial abuse is served shall withhold and pay over earnings of the employee pursuant to that order notwithstanding the requirements of another earnings withholding order except as provided in paragraph (2).

(2) An employer shall not withhold earnings of an employee pursuant to an earnings withholding order for elder or dependent adult financial abuse if a withholding order for support or for taxes is in effect or if a prior withholding order for elder or dependent adult financial abuse is in effect. In that case, the subsequent withholding order for elder or dependent financial abuse is ineffective.

(3) When an employer is required to cease withholding earnings pursuant to a prior earnings withholding order, the employer shall notify the levying officer who served the prior earnings withholding order that a supervening earnings withholding order for elder or dependent financial abuse is in effect.[629]

706.024. (a) The amount required to satisfy an earnings withholding order is the total amount required to satisfy the writ of execution on the date the order is issued, with the following additions and subtractions:

(1) The addition of the statutory fee for service of the order and any other statutory fees for performing duties under the order.

(2) The addition of costs added to the order pursuant to Section 685.090.

(3) The subtraction of the amount of any partial satisfactions.

(4) The addition of daily interest accruing after issuance of the order, as adjusted for partial satisfactions.

(b) From time to time the levying officer, in the levying officer's discretion, may give written notice to the employer of the amount required to satisfy the earnings withholding order and the employer shall determine the total amount to withhold based upon the levying officer's notice, notwithstanding a different amount stated in the order originally served on the employer.

(c) If the full amount required to satisfy the earnings withholding order as stated in the order or in the levying officer's notice under subdivision (b) is withheld from the judgment debtor's earnings, interest ceases to accrue on that amount.[314]

706.025. (a) Except as provided in subdivision (b), the amount required to be withheld pursuant to an earnings withholding order shall be paid monthly to the levying officer not later than the 15th day of each month. The initial monthly payment shall include all amounts required to be withheld from the earnings of the employee during the preceding calendar month up to the close of the employee's pay period ending closest to the last day of that month, and thereafter each monthly payment shall include amounts withheld from the employee's earnings for services rendered in the interim up to the close of the employee's pay period ending closest to the last day of the preceding calendar month.

(b) The employer may elect to pay the amounts withheld to the levying officer more frequently than monthly. If the employer so elects, payment of the amount withheld from the employee's earnings for each pay period shall be made not later than 10 days after the close of the pay period.[170]

706.026. (a) The levying officer shall receive and account for all amounts paid by the employer pursuant to Section 706.025 and shall pay the amounts so received over to the person entitled thereto at least once every 30 days.
(b) At least once every two years, the levying officer shall file an accounting with the court, as provided by Section 699.560, for all amounts collected under the earnings withholding order, including costs and interest added to the amount due. Subject to the limitations in subdivision (c) of Section 263, the levying officer may electronically file the accounting with the court, pursuant to Chapter 2 (commencing with Section 263) of Title 4 of Part 1.[644]

706.027. If the judgment pursuant to which the earnings withholding order is issued is satisfied before the order otherwise terminates pursuant to Section 706.022, the judgment creditor shall promptly notify the levying officer who shall promptly terminate the order by serving a notice of termination on the employer.[170]

706.028. (a) "Final earnings withholding order for costs and interest" means an earnings withholding order for the collection only of unsatisfied costs and interest, which is issued after an earlier earnings withholding order has been returned satisfied.
(b) After the amount stated as owing in a prior earnings withholding order is paid, the judgment creditor may obtain a final earnings withholding order for costs and interest to collect amounts of costs and interest that were not collected under the prior earnings withholding order.
(c) A final earnings withholding order for costs and interest shall be enforced in the same manner as other earnings withholding orders.
(d) Satisfaction of the amount stated as owing in a final earnings withholding order for costs and interest is equivalent to satisfaction of the money judgment. For this purpose, interest ceases to accrue on the date of issuance of the final earnings withholding order and no additional costs may be added after that date, except for the statutory fee for service of the order and any other statutory fees for performing duties under the order.[315]

706.029. Service of an earnings withholding order creates a lien upon the earnings of the judgment debtor that are required to be withheld pursuant to the order and upon all property of the employer subject to the enforcement of a money judgment in the amount required to be withheld pursuant to such order. The lien continues for a period of one year from the date the earnings of the judgment debtor become payable unless the amount required to be withheld pursuant to the order is paid as required by law.[170]

706.030. (a) A "withholding order for support" is an earnings withholding order issued on a writ of execution to collect delinquent amounts payable under a judgment for the support of a child, or spouse or former spouse, of the judgment debtor. A withholding order for support shall be denoted as such on its face.
(b) The local child support agency may issue a withholding order for support

on a notice of levy pursuant to Section 17522 of the Family Code to collect a support obligation.

(1) When the local child support agency issues a withholding order for support, a reference in this chapter to a levying officer is deemed to mean the local child support agency who issues the withholding order for support.

(2) Service of a withholding order for support issued by the local child support agency may be made by first-class mail or in any other manner described in Section 706.101. Service of a withholding order for support issued by the local child support agency is complete when it is received by the employer or a person described in paragraph (1) or (2) of subdivision (a) of Section 706.101, or if service is by first-class mail, service is complete as specified in Section 1013.

(3) The local child support agency shall serve upon the employer the withholding order for support, a copy of the order, and a notice informing the support obligor of the effect of the order and of his or her right to hearings and remedies provided in this chapter and in the Family Code. The notice shall be accompanied by the forms necessary to obtain an administrative review and a judicial hearing and instructions on how to file the forms. Within 10 days from the date of service, the employer shall deliver to the support obligor a copy of the withholding order for support, the forms to obtain an administrative review and judicial hearing, and the notice. If the support obligor is no longer employed by the employer and the employer does not owe the support obligor any earnings, the employer shall inform the local child support agency that the support obligor is no longer employed by the employer.

(4) An employer who fails to comply with paragraph (3) shall be subject to a civil penalty of five hundred dollars ($500) for each occurrence.

(5) The local child support agency shall provide for an administrative review to reconsider or modify the amount to be withheld for arrearages pursuant to the withholding order for support, if the support obligor requests a review at any time after service of the withholding order. The local child support agency shall provide the review in the same manner and timeframes provided for resolution of a complaint pursuant to Section 17800 of the Family Code. The local child support agency shall notify the employer if the review results in any modifications to the withholding order for support. If the local child support agency cannot complete the administrative review within 30 calendar days of receipt of the complaint, the local child support agency shall notify the employer to suspend withholding any disputed amount pending the completion of the review and the determination by the local child support agency.

(6) Nothing in this section prohibits the support obligor from seeking a judicial determination of arrearages pursuant to subdivision (c) of Section 17256 of the Family Code or from filing a motion for equitable division of earnings pursuant to Section 706.052 either prior to or after the administrative review provided by this section.

Within five business days after receiving notice of the obligor having filed for judicial relief pursuant to this section, the local child support agency shall notify the employer to suspend withholding any disputed amount pending a determination by the court. The employer shall then adjust the withholding within not more than nine days of receiving the notice from the local child support agency.

(c) Notwithstanding any other provision of this chapter:

(1) An employer shall continue to withhold pursuant to a withholding order for support until the earliest of the dates specified in paragraph (1), (2), or (3) of subdivision (a) of Section 706.022, except that a withholding order for support shall automatically terminate one year after the employment of the employee by the employer terminates.

(2) A withholding order for support has priority over any other earnings withholding order. An employer upon whom a withholding order for support is served shall withhold and pay over earnings of the employee pursuant to that order notwithstanding the requirements of another earnings withholding order.

(3) Subject to paragraph (2) and to Article 3 (commencing with Section 706.050), an employer shall withhold earnings pursuant to both a withholding order for support and another earnings withholding order simultaneously.

(4) An employer who willfully fails to withhold and forward support pursuant to a valid earnings withholding order for support issued and served upon the employer pursuant to this chapter is liable to the support obligee, as defined in Section 5214 of the Family Code, for the amount of support not withheld, forwarded, or otherwise paid to the support obligee.

(5) Notwithstanding any other provision of law, an employer shall send all earnings withheld pursuant to a withholding order for support to the levying officer or the State Disbursement Unit as described in Section 17309 of the Family Code within the time period specified by federal law.

(6) Once the State Disbursement Unit as described in Section 17309 of the Family Code is operational, all support payments made pursuant to an earnings withholding order shall be made to that unit.

(7) Earnings withheld pursuant to an earnings withholding order for support shall be credited toward satisfaction of a support judgment as specified in Section 695.221.[534]

706.031. (a) Nothing in this chapter affects an earnings assignment order for support.

(b) An earnings assignment order for support shall be given priority over any earnings withholding order. An employer upon whom an earnings assignment order for support is served shall withhold and pay over the earnings of the employee pursuant to the assignment order notwithstanding the requirements of any earnings withholding order. When an employer is required to cease withholding earnings pursuant to an earnings withholding order, the employer shall notify the levying officer who served the earnings withholding order that a supervening earnings assignment order for support is in effect.

(c) Subject to subdivisions (b), (d), and (e), an employer shall withhold earnings of an employee pursuant to both an earnings assignment order for support and an earnings withholding order.

(d) The employer shall withhold pursuant to an earnings withholding order only to the extent that the sum of the amount withheld pursuant to any earnings assignment order for support and the amount withheld pursuant to the earnings withholding order does not exceed the amount that may be withheld under Article 3 (commencing with Section 706.050).

(e) The employer shall withhold pursuant to an earnings withholding order for taxes only to the extent that the sum of the amount withheld pursuant to any earnings assignment order for support and the amount withheld pursuant to the earnings withholding order for taxes does not exceed the amount that may be withheld under Article 4 (commencing with Section 706.070).[301]

706.032. (a) Except as otherwise provided by statute:

(1) If withholding under an earnings withholding order ceases because the judgment debtor's employment has terminated, the earnings withholding order terminates at the conclusion of a continuous 180-day period during which no amounts are withheld under the order.

(2) If withholding under an earnings withholding order ceases because the judgment debtor's earnings are subject to an order or assignment with higher priority, the earnings withholding order terminates at the conclusion of a continuous two-year period during which no amounts are withheld under the order.

(b) If an earnings withholding order has terminated pursuant to subdivision (a), the employer shall return the order to the levying officer along with a statement of the reasons for returning the order.[316]

706.033. If the writ is returned before the earnings withholding order terminates, on termination of the earnings withholding order the levying officer shall make a supplemental return on the writ. The supplemental return shall contain the same information as an original return pursuant to Section 699.560.[317]

706.034. The employer may deduct from the earnings of the employee the sum of one dollar and fifty cents ($1.50) for each payment made in accordance with an earnings withholding order issued pursuant to this chapter.[553]

Article 3: Restrictions on Earnings Withholding

Article 3 added by Stats. 1982, Ch. 1364, Sec. 2.

706.050. (a) Except as otherwise provided in this chapter, the maximum amount of disposable earnings of an individual judgment debtor for any workweek that is subject to levy under an earnings withholding order shall not exceed the lesser of the following:

(1) Twenty percent of the individual's disposable earnings for that week.

(2) Forty percent of the amount by which the individual's disposable earnings for that week exceed 48 times the state minimum hourly wage in effect at the time the earnings are payable. If a judgment debtor works in a location where the local minimum hourly wage

is greater than the state minimum hourly wage, the local minimum hourly wage in effect at the time the earnings are payable shall be used for the calculation made pursuant to this paragraph.

(b) For any pay period other than weekly, the following multipliers shall be used to determine the maximum amount of disposable earnings subject to levy under an earnings withholding order that is proportional in effect to the calculation described in paragraph (2) of subdivision (a), except as specified in paragraph (1):

(1) For a daily pay period, the amounts shall be identical to the amounts described in subdivision (a).

(2) For a biweekly pay period, multiply the applicable hourly minimum wage by 96 work hours.

(3) For a semimonthly pay period, multiply the applicable hourly minimum wage by 104 work hours.

(4) For a monthly pay period, multiply the applicable hourly minimum wage by 208 work hours.

(c) This section shall become operative on September 1, 2023.[807]

706.051. (a) For the purposes of this section, "family of the judgment debtor" includes the spouse or former spouse of the judgment debtor.

(b) Except as provided in subdivision (c), the portion of the judgment debtor's earnings that the judgment debtor proves is necessary for the support of the judgment debtor or the judgment debtor's family supported in whole or in part by the judgment debtor is exempt from levy under this chapter.

(c) The exemption provided in subdivision (b) is not available if any of the following exceptions applies:

(1) The debt was incurred pursuant to an order or award for the payment of attorney's fees under Section 2030, 3121, or 3557 of the Family Code.

(2) The debt was incurred for personal services rendered by an employee or former employee of the judgment debtor.

(3) The order is a withholding order for support under Section 706.030.

(4) The order is one governed by Article 4 (commencing with Section 706.070) (state tax order).[662]

706.052. (a) Except as provided in subdivision (b), one-half of the disposable earnings (as defined by Section 1672 of Title 15 of the United States Code) of the judgment debtor, plus any amount withheld from the judgment debtor's earnings pursuant to any earnings assignment order for support, is exempt from levy under this chapter where the earnings withholding order is a withholding order for support under Section 706.030.

(b) Except as provided in subdivision (c), upon motion of any interested party, the court shall make an equitable division of the judgment debtor's earnings that takes into account the needs of all the persons the judgment debtor is required to support and shall effectuate such division by an order determining the amount to be withheld from the judgment debtor's earnings pursuant to the withholding order for support.

(c) An order made under subdivision (b) may not authorize the withholding of an amount in excess of the amount that may be withheld for support under federal law under Section 1673 of Title 15 of the United States Code.[302]

Article 4: Earnings Withholding Order for Taxes

Article 4 added by Stats. 1982, Ch. 1364, Sec. 2.

706.070. As used in this article:
(a) "State" means the State of California and includes any officer, department, board, or agency thereof.
(b) "State tax liability" means an amount for which the state has a state tax lien as defined in Section 7162 of the Government Code excluding a state tax lien created pursuant to the Fish and Game Code.
(c) For purposes of an earnings withholding order for taxes issued by the Franchise Tax Board, "state tax liability" also includes any liability under Part 10 (commencing with Section 17001), Part 10.2 (commencing with Section 18401), or Part 11 (commencing with Section 23001) of Division 2 of the Revenue and Taxation Code that is due and payable within the meaning of subdivision (b) of Section 19221 of the Revenue and Taxation Code, and unpaid. The amendments to this section by the act adding this subdivision shall apply to any amount that is unpaid on or after the effective date of that act, or any amount that first becomes due and payable, and unpaid, after the effective date of that act.[663]

706.071. This chapter does not limit the state's right to collect a state tax liability except that (a) no levy upon earnings of an employee held by an employer is effective unless such levy is made in accordance with the provisions of this chapter and (b) other methods of collection may not be used to require an employer to withhold earnings of an employee in payment of a state tax liability.[170]

706.072. (a) A "withholding order for taxes" is an earnings withholding order issued pursuant to this article to collect a state tax liability and shall be denoted as a withholding order for taxes on its face.
(b) A withholding order for taxes may only be issued under one of the following circumstances:
(1) The existence of the state tax liability appears on the face of the taxpayer's return, including a case where such tax liability is disclosed from the taxpayer's return after errors in mathematical computations in the return have been corrected.
(2) The state tax liability has been assessed or determined as provided by statute and the taxpayer had notice of the proposed assessment or determination and had available an opportunity to have the proposed assessment or determination reviewed by appropriate administrative procedures. If the taxpayer makes a timely request for review of the assessment or determination, the state shall not issue a withholding order for taxes until the administrative review procedure is completed. If the taxpayer is given notice of the proposed assessment or determination but does not make a timely request for review, the state may issue a withholding order for taxes.
(c) In any case where a state tax liability has been assessed or determined prior to July 1, 1983, and the state determines that the requirement of subdivision (b) may not have been satisfied, the state may send a "Notice of Proposed Issuance of Withholding Order for Taxes" to the taxpayer at the taxpayer's last known address by first-class mail, postage prepaid. The notice

shall advise the taxpayer that the taxpayer may have the assessment or determination reviewed by appropriate administrative procedures and state how such a review may be obtained. If the taxpayer is sent such a notice and requests such a review within 30 days from the date the notice was mailed to the taxpayer, the state shall provide appropriate administrative procedures for review of the assessment or determination and shall not issue the withholding order for taxes until the administrative review procedure is completed. If the taxpayer is sent such a notice and does not request such a review within 30 days from the date the notice was mailed to the taxpayer, the state may issue the withholding order for taxes.

(d) A withholding order for taxes may be issued whether or not the state tax liability has been reduced to judgment.[170]

706.073. Except as otherwise provided in this article, the provisions of this chapter govern the procedures and proceedings concerning a withholding order for taxes. For the purposes of this article, a reference in this chapter to a "levying officer" shall be deemed to mean the specific state agency seeking to collect a state tax liability under this article.[170]

706.074. (a) The state may itself issue a withholding order for taxes under this section to collect a state tax liability. The order shall specify the total amount required to be withheld pursuant to the order (unpaid tax liability including any penalties, accrued interest, and costs).

(b) Unless a lesser amount is specified in the order, the amount to be withheld by the employer each pay period pursuant to an order issued under this section is the amount required to be withheld under Section 1673(a) of Title 15 of the United States Code, and is not subject to the exception provided in Section 1673(b) of Title 15 of the United States Code.[170]

706.075. (a) This section applies to any withholding order for taxes issued under this article.

(b) Together with the withholding order for taxes, the state shall serve upon the employer an additional copy of the order and a notice informing the taxpayer of the effect of the order and of his right to hearings and remedies provided in this chapter. Within 10 days from the date of service, the employer shall deliver to the taxpayer a copy of the order and the notice, except that immediate delivery shall be made where a jeopardy withholding order for taxes has been served. If the taxpayer is no longer employed by the employer and the employer does not owe the taxpayer any earnings, the employer is not required to make such delivery.

(c) The state shall provide for an administrative hearing to reconsider or modify the amount to be withheld pursuant to the withholding order for taxes, and the taxpayer may request such a hearing at any time after service of the order. If the taxpayer requests a hearing, the hearing shall be provided, and the matter shall be determined, within 15 days after the request is received by the state. The determination of the amount to be withheld is subject to the standard provided in subdivision (b) of Section 706.051. Judicial review of the determination made pursuant to this subdivision by the state may be had only if a petition for a writ of mandate pursuant to Section 1094.5 is filed within 90 days from the date that written notice of the state's determination was delivered or mailed to the taxpayer.

(d) The employer is not subject to any civil liability for failure to comply with subdivision (b). Nothing in this subdivision limits the power of a court to hold the employer in contempt of court for failure to comply with subdivision (b).[170]

706.076. (a) A withholding order for taxes may be issued pursuant to this section requiring the employer of the taxpayer to withhold an amount in excess of the amount that may be required to be withheld pursuant to an order issued under Section 706.074.

(b) The state may, at any time, apply to a court of record in the county where the taxpayer was last known to reside for the issuance of a withholding order for taxes under this section to collect a state tax liability.

(c) The application for the order shall include a statement under oath that the state has served upon the taxpayer both of the following:

(1) A copy of the application.

(2) A notice informing the taxpayer of the purpose of the application and the right of the taxpayer to appear at the court hearing on the application.

(d) Upon the filing of the application, the court shall immediately set the matter for hearing and the court clerk shall send a notice of the time and place of the hearing by first-class mail, postage prepaid, to the state and the taxpayer. The notice shall be deposited in the mail at least 10 days before the day set for the hearing.

(e) After hearing, the court shall issue a withholding order for taxes which shall require the taxpayer's employer to withhold and pay over all earnings of the taxpayer other than that amount which the taxpayer proves is exempt under subdivision (b) of Section 706.051, but in no event shall the amount to be withheld be less than that permitted to be withheld under Section 706.050.

(f) The state may issue a temporary earnings holding order, which shall be denoted as such on its face, in any case where the state intends to apply for a withholding order for taxes under this section and has determined that the collection of the state tax liability will be jeopardized in whole or in part if the temporary earnings holding order is not issued. The temporary earnings holding order shall be directed to the taxpayer's employer and shall require the employer to retain in the employer's possession or under the employer's control all or such portion of the earnings of the taxpayer then or thereafter due as is specified in the order. Together with the temporary earnings holding order, the state shall serve upon the employer an additional copy of the order and a notice informing the taxpayer of the effect of the order and of the right to the remedies provided in this chapter. Upon receipt of the order, the employer shall deliver to the taxpayer a copy of the order and notice. If the taxpayer is no longer employed by the employer and the employer does not owe the taxpayer any earnings, the employer is not required to make such delivery. The temporary earnings holding order expires 15 days from the date it is served on the employer unless it is extended by the court on ex parte application for good cause shown. If a temporary earnings holding order is served on an employer, the state may not thereafter, for a period of six months, serve on the same employer another temporary earnings holding order for the same employee unless the court for good cause shown otherwise orders. Sections 706.153 and 706.154 apply to temporary earnings holding orders issued under this section.[170]

706.077. (a) Subject to subdivision (b), an employer upon whom a withholding order for taxes is served shall withhold and pay over earnings of the employee pursuant to such order and shall cease to withhold earnings pursuant to any prior earnings withholding order except that a withholding order for support shall be given priority as provided in Section 706.030. When an employer is required to cease withholding earnings pursuant to an earlier earnings withholding order, the employer shall notify the levying officer who served the earlier earnings withholding order that a supervening withholding order for taxes is in effect.
(b) An employer shall not withhold earnings of an employee pursuant to a withholding order for taxes if a prior withholding order for taxes is in effect, and, in such case, the subsequent withholding order for taxes is ineffective.[170]

706.078. (a) Except as provided in subdivision (b), the employer shall not withhold pursuant to a withholding order for taxes from earnings of the employee payable for any pay period of such employee that ends prior to the 10th day after service of the order.
(b) A "jeopardy withholding order for taxes," which shall be denoted as such on its face, is a withholding order for taxes that requires that the employer withhold pursuant to the order from earnings due to the employee at the time of service of the order on the employer and from earnings thereafter due. A jeopardy withholding order for taxes may be issued only where the state has determined that the collection of a state tax liability will be jeopardized in whole or in part by delaying the time when withholding from earnings commences.
(c) An employer shall continue to withhold pursuant to a withholding order for taxes until the amount specified in the order has been paid in full or the order is withdrawn, except that the order automatically terminates one year after the employment of the employee by the employer terminates. The state shall promptly serve on the employer a notice terminating the withholding order for taxes if the state tax liability for which the withholding order for taxes was issued is satisfied before the employer has withheld the full amount specified in the order, and the employer shall discontinue withholding in compliance with such notice.[170]

706.080. Service of a withholding order for taxes or of any other notice or document required under this chapter in connection with a withholding order for taxes may be made by the state by first-class mail, postage prepaid, or by any authorized state employee. Service of a withholding order for taxes is complete when it is received by the employer or a person described in paragraph (1) or (2) of subdivision (a) of Section 706.101. Service of, or the providing of, any other notice or document required to be served or provided under this chapter in connection with a withholding order for taxes is complete when the notice or document is deposited in the mail addressed to the last known address of the person on whom it is served or to whom it is to be provided.[170]

706.081. Except for the forms referred to in Section 706.076, the state shall prescribe the form of any order, notice, or other document required by this chapter in connection with a withholding order for taxes notwithstanding Sections 706.100 and 706.120, and any form so prescribed is deemed to comply with this chapter.[170]

706.082. No review of the taxpayer's tax liability shall be permitted in any court proceedings under this chapter.[170]

706.084. Where a warrant, notice of levy, or notice or order to withhold is served on the employer to enforce a state tax liability of a person who is an employee of that employer, it shall be deemed to be a withholding order for taxes as to any earnings that are subject to the provisions of this chapter if both of the following requirements are satisfied:
(a) The form provides notice on its face that it is to be treated as a withholding order for taxes as to any earnings that are subject to the provisions of this chapter.
(b) The form provides all the information provided in a withholding order for taxes.[170]

Article 5: Procedure for Earnings Withholding Orders and Exemption Claims
Article 5 added by Stats. 1982, Ch. 1364, Sec. 2.

706.100. Notwithstanding any other provision of law, the Judicial Council may provide by rule for the practice and procedure in proceedings under this chapter except for the state's administrative hearings provided by Article 4 (commencing with Section 706.070).[170]

706.101. (a) An earnings withholding order shall be served by the levying officer upon the employer by delivery of the order to any of the following:
(1) The managing agent or person in charge, at the time of service, of the branch or office where the employee works or the office from which the employee is paid. In the case of a state employee, the office from which the employee is paid does not include the Controller's office unless the employee works directly for the Controller's office.
(2) Any person to whom a copy of the summons and of the complaint may be delivered to make service on the employer under Article 4 (commencing with Section 416.10) of Chapter 4 of Title 5.
(b) Service of an earnings withholding order shall be made by personal delivery as provided in Section 415.10 or 415.20 or by delivery by first-class mail, postage prepaid. When service is made by first-class mail, service is complete at the time of receipt of the earnings withholding order, as indicated in the employer's return, or the date of mailing if the date of receipt is not indicated on the employer's return. If the levying officer attempts service

by first-class mail under this subdivision and does not receive the employer's return within 15 days from the date of mailing, the levying officer shall make service as provided in Article 3 (commencing with Section 415.10) of Chapter 4 of Title 5. For purposes of this section, "employer's return" refers to the Judicial Council-issued form specified by Section 706.126.

(c) The state may issue an earnings withholding order directly, without the use of a levying officer, for purposes of collecting overpayments of unemployment compensation or disability benefits pursuant to Article 4 (commencing with Section 1375) of Chapter 5 of Part 1 of, and Article 5 (commencing with Section 2735) of Chapter 2 of Part 2 of, Division 1 of the Unemployment Insurance Code. The earnings withholding order shall be served by registered or certified mail, postage prepaid, with return receipt requested. Service is deemed complete at the time the return receipt is executed by, or on behalf of, the recipient. If the state does not receive a return receipt within 15 days from the date of deposit in the mail of the withholding order, the state shall refer the earnings withholding order to a levying officer for service in accordance with subdivision (b).

(d) Except as provided in subdivision (b) or (c), service of any notice or document under this chapter may be made by first-class mail, postage prepaid. If service is made on the employer after the employer's return has been received by the levying officer, the service shall be made by first-class mail, postage prepaid, on the person designated in the employer's return to receive notices and at the address indicated in the employer's return, whether or not that address is within the county. This subdivision does not preclude service by personal delivery (1) on the employer before the employer's return has been received by the levying officer or (2) on the person designated in the employer's return after its receipt.

(e) Notwithstanding subdivision (b), if the judgment creditor so requests, the levying officer shall make service of the earnings withholding order by personal delivery as provided in Section 415.10 or 415.20.[645]

706.102. (a) If a writ of execution has been issued to the county where the judgment debtor's employer is to be served and the time specified in subdivision (b) of Section 699.530 for levy on property under the writ has not expired, a judgment creditor may apply for the issuance of an earnings withholding order by filing an application with a levying officer in such county who shall promptly issue an earnings withholding order.

(b) This section does not apply where the earnings withholding order is a withholding order for taxes.[170]

706.103. (a) The levying officer shall serve upon the designated employer all of the following:

(1) The original and one copy of the earnings withholding order.

(2) The form for the employer's return.

(3) The notice to the employee of the earnings withholding order.

(4) A copy of the form that the judgment debtor may use to make a claim of exemption.

(5) A copy of the form the judgment

debtor may use to provide a financial statement.

(b) At the time the levying officer makes service pursuant to subdivision (a), the levying officer shall provide the employer with a copy of the employer's instructions referred to in Section 706.127. The Judicial Council may adopt rules prescribing the circumstances when compliance with this subdivision is not required.

(c) No earnings withholding order shall be served upon the employer after the time specified in subdivision (b) of Section 699.530.[858]

706.104. Any employer who is served with an earnings withholding order shall:

(a) Deliver to the judgment debtor a copy of the earnings withholding order, the notice to employee of earnings withholding, a copy of the form that the judgment debtor may use to make a claim of exemption, and a copy of the form the judgment debtor may use to provide a financial statement within 10 days from the date of service. If the judgment debtor is no longer employed by the employer and the employer does not owe the employee any earnings, the employer is not required to make such delivery. The employer is not subject to any civil liability for failure to comply with this subdivision. Nothing in this subdivision limits the power of a court to hold the employer in contempt of court for failure to comply with this subdivision.

(b) Complete the employer's return on the form provided by the levying officer and mail it by first-class mail, postage prepaid, to the levying officer within 15 days from the date of service. If the earnings withholding order is ineffective, the employer shall state in the employer's return that the order will not be complied with for this reason and shall return the order to the levying officer with the employer's return.[685]

706.105. (a) A judgment debtor may claim an exemption under Section 706.051 under either of the following circumstances:

(1) No prior hearing has been held with respect to the earnings withholding order.

(2) There has been a material change in circumstances since the time of the last prior hearing on the earnings withholding order.

(b) A claim of exemption shall be made by filing with the levying officer an original and one copy of (1) the judgment debtor's claim of exemption and (2) the judgment debtor's financial statement.

(c) Upon filing of the claim of exemption, the levying officer shall promptly send to the judgment creditor, at the address stated in the application for the earnings withholding order, by first-class mail, postage prepaid, all of the following:

(1) A copy of the claim of exemption.

(2) A copy of the financial statement.

(3) A notice of claim of exemption. The notice shall state that the claim of exemption has been filed and that the earnings withholding order will be terminated, or modified to reflect the amount of earnings claimed to be exempt in the claim of exemption, unless a notice of opposition to the claim of exemption is filed with the levying officer by the judgment creditor within 10 days after the date of the mailing of the notice of claim of exemption.

(d) A judgment creditor who desires to contest a claim of exemption shall, within 10 days after the date of the mailing of the notice of claim of exemption, file with the levying officer a notice of opposition to the claim of exemption.

(e) (1) If a notice of opposition to the claim of exemption is filed with the levying officer within the 10-day period, the judgment creditor is entitled to a hearing on the claim of exemption. If the judgment creditor desires a hearing on the claim of exemption, the judgment creditor shall file a notice of motion for an order determining the claim of exemption with the court within 10 days after the date the levying officer mailed the notice of claim of exemption. If the notice of motion is so filed, the hearing on the motion shall be held not later than 30 days from the date the notice of motion was filed unless continued by the court for good cause. Where the judgment upon which the writ is issued is for personal debt, as defined in subdivision (d) of Section 683.110, if the hearing is delayed by the court and cannot be set within 30 days of notice of the motion, a party may seek by ex parte application, and the court shall issue, an order staying any levy or garnishment with respect to the property subject to the claim of exemption until the hearing occurs. At the time prescribed by subdivision (b) of Section 1005, the judgment creditor shall give written notice of the hearing to the levying officer and shall serve a notice of the hearing and a copy of the notice of opposition to the claim of exemption on the judgment debtor and, if the claim of exemption so requested, on the attorney for the judgment debtor. Service is deemed made when the notice of the hearing and a copy of the notice of opposition to the claim of exemption are deposited in the mail, postage prepaid, addressed to the judgment debtor at the address stated in the claim of exemption and, if service on the attorney for the judgment debtor was requested in the claim of exemption, to the attorney at the address stated in the claim of exemption. The judgment creditor shall file proof of the service with the court. After receiving the notice of the hearing and before the date set for the hearing, the levying officer shall file the claim of exemption and the notice of opposition to the claim of exemption with the court.

(2) The filing of an ex parte application under this section is not a general appearance and shall not constitute a waiver of the right to bring a motion under Section 418.10.

(f) If the levying officer does not receive a notice of opposition to the claim of exemption within the 10-day period after the date of mailing of the notice of claim of exemption and a notice of the hearing not later than 10 days after the filing of the notice of opposition to the claim of exemption, the levying officer shall serve on the employer one of the following:

(1) A notice that the earnings withholding order has been terminated if all of the judgment debtor's earnings were claimed to be exempt.

(2) A modified earnings withholding order that reflects the amount of earnings claimed to be exempt in the claim of exemption if only a portion of the judgment debtor's earnings was claimed to be exempt.

(g) If, after hearing, the court orders that the earnings withholding order be modified or terminated, the clerk shall promptly transmit a certified copy of the order to the levying officer who shall promptly serve on the employer of the judgment debtor (1) a copy of the modified earnings withholding order or (2) a notice that the earnings withholding order has been terminated.

(1) Where the judgment debtor's wages are exempt without making a claim, the court shall terminate or modify the earnings withholding order, and shall order the return by a date certain of all of the judgment debtor's exempt wages. Where the judgment upon which the writ is issued is for personal debt, as defined in subdivision (d) of Section 683.110, the court shall order the return by a date certain of any wages that were exempt without the need for a claim and that were garnished for up to 12 months preceding the date of the order on the claim of exemption. This paragraph does not limit a judge's authority to order, for good cause, the return of any exempt property taken more than 12 months preceding the date of the order on the claim of exemption.

(2) Where the judgment debtor's wages are exempt as the result of a claim of exemption, the court shall terminate or modify the earnings withholding order, and shall order the return by a date certain of all of the judgment debtor's exempt wages. Where the judgment upon which the writ is issued is for personal debt, as defined in subdivision (d) of Section 683.110, the court shall order the return by a date certain any wages that the debtor has demonstrated would have been exempt by claim of exemption and that were garnished for up to six months preceding the date of the order on the claim of exemption. This paragraph does not limit a judge's authority to order, for good cause, the return of any exempt property taken more than six months preceding the date of the order on the claim of exemption

(3) If the court determines that any amount withheld pursuant to the earnings withholding order should be paid to the judgment debtor, the court shall order the levying officer, judgment creditor, or other person, who is in possession of the property, to return the exempt property to the judgment debtor. A levying officer shall return the exempt property within 20 business days of receipt of notice of the order. A judgment creditor shall return the exempt property within 10 business days of entry of the order.

(h) If the earnings withholding order is terminated by the court, unless the court otherwise orders or unless there is a material change of circumstances since the time of the last prior hearing on the earnings withholding order, the judgment creditor may not apply for another earnings withholding order directed to the same employer with respect to the same judgment debtor for a period of 100 days following the date of service of the earnings withholding order or 60 days after the date of the termination of the order, whichever is later. Where the judgment upon which the writ is issued is for personal debt, as defined in subdivision (d) of Section 683.110, the judgment creditor may not apply for another earnings withholding order directed to the same employer with respect to the same judgment debtor for a period of 100 days following the date of service of the earnings withholding order or 60 days after the date of the termination of the order, whichever is later.

(i) If an employer has withheld and paid over amounts pursuant to an earnings withholding order after the date of termination of the order but prior to the receipt of notice of its termination, the judgment debtor may recover those amounts only from the levying officer if the levying officer still holds those amounts or, if those amounts have been paid over to the judgment creditor, from the judgment creditor. If the employer has withheld amounts pursuant to an earnings withholding order after termination of the order but has not paid over those amounts to the levying officer, the employer shall pay those amounts to the judgment debtor within five business days of the end of the next pay period.

(j) An appeal lies from any court order under this section denying a claim of exemption or modifying or terminating an earnings withholding order. An appeal by the judgment creditor from an order modifying or terminating the earnings withholding order does not stay the order from which the appeal is taken. Notwithstanding the appeal, until the order modifying or terminating the earnings withholding order is set aside or modified, the order allowing the claim of exemption in whole or in part shall be given the same effect as if the appeal had not been taken.

(k) This section does not apply to a withholding order for support or a withholding order for taxes.[908]

706.106. No findings are required in court proceedings under this chapter.[170]

706.108. (a) If a writ of execution has been issued to the county where the judgment debtor's employer is to be served and the time specified in subdivision (b) of Section 699.530 for levy on property under the writ has not expired, a judgment creditor may deliver an application for issuance of an earnings withholding order to a registered process server who may then issue an earnings withholding order.

(b) If the registered process server has issued the earnings withholding order, the registered process server, before serving the earnings withholding order, shall cause to be deposited with the levying officer a copy of the writ of execution, the application for issuance of an earnings withholding order, a copy of the earnings withholding order, and the fee, as provided by Section 26750 of the Government Code.

(c) A registered process server may serve an earnings withholding order on an employer whether the earnings withholding order was issued by a levying officer or by a registered process server, but no earnings withholding order may be served after the time specified in subdivision (b) of Section 699.530. In performing this function, the registered process server shall serve upon the designated employer all of the following:

(1) The original and one copy of the earnings withholding order.

(2) The form for the employer's return.

(3) The notice to the employee of the earnings withholding order.

(4) A copy of the form that the judgment debtor may use to make a claim of exemption.

(5) A copy of the form the judgment debtor may use to provide a financial statement.

(6) A copy of the employer's instructions referred to in Section 706.127, except as otherwise prescribed in rules adopted by the Judicial Council.

(d) Within five court days after service under this section, all of the following shall be filed with the levying officer:

(1) The writ of execution, if it is not already in the hands of the levying officer.

(2) Proof of service on the employer of the papers listed in subdivision (c).

(3) Instructions in writing, as required by the provisions of Section 687.010.

(e) If the fee provided by Section 26750 of the Government Code has been paid, the levying officer shall perform all other duties required by this chapter as if the levying officer had served the earnings withholding order. If the registered process server does not comply with subdivisions (b), where applicable, and (d), the service of the earnings withholding order is ineffective and the levying officer shall not be required to perform any duties under the order, and may terminate the order and release any withheld earnings to the judgment debtor.

(f) The fee for services of a registered process server under this section is a recoverable cost pursuant to Section 1033.5.[728]

706.109. An earnings withholding order may not be issued against the earnings of the spouse of the judgment debtor except by court order upon noticed motion.[231]

Article 6: Forms; Employer's Instructions

Article 6 added by Stats. 1982, Ch. 1364, Sec. 2.

706.120. Except as provided in Section 706.081, the Judicial Council shall prescribe the form of the applications, notices, claims of exemption, orders, and other documents required by this chapter as provided in Section 681.030, and only such forms may be used to implement this chapter.[170]

706.121. The "application for issuance of earnings withholding order" shall be executed under oath and shall include all of the following:

(a) The name, the last known address, and, if known, the social security number of the judgment debtor.

(b) The name and address of the judgment creditor.

(c) The court where the judgment was entered and the date the judgment was entered.

(d) Whether the judgment is based in whole or in part on a claim for elder or dependent adult financial abuse and, if in part, how much of the judgment arises from that claim.

(e) The date of issuance of a writ of execution to the county where the earnings withholding order is sought.

(f) The total amount required to satisfy the order on the date of issuance (which may not exceed the amount required to satisfy the writ of execution on the date of issuance of the order plus the levying officer's statutory fee for service of the order).

(g) The name and address of the employer to whom the order will be directed.

(h) The name and address of the person to whom the withheld money is to be paid by the levying officer.[630]

706.122. The "notice to employee of earnings withholding order" shall contain a statement that informs the employee in simple terms of the nature of a wage garnishment, the right to an exemption, the procedure for claiming an exemption, and any other information the Judicial Council determines would be useful to the employee and appropriate for inclusion in the notice, including all of the following:
(a) The named employer has been ordered to withhold from the earnings of the judgment debtor the amounts required to be withheld under Section 706.050, or such other amounts as are specified in the earnings withholding order, and to pay these amounts over to the levying officer for transmittal to the person specified in the order in payment of the judgment described in the order.
(b) The manner of computing the amounts required to be withheld pursuant to Section 706.050.
(c) The judgment debtor may be able to keep more or all of the judgment debtor's earnings if the judgment debtor proves that the additional earnings are necessary for the support of the judgment debtor or the judgment debtor's family supported in whole or in part by the judgment debtor.
(d) If the judgment debtor wishes a court hearing to prove that amounts should not be withheld from the judgment debtor's earnings because they are necessary for the support of the judgment debtor or the judgment debtor's family supported in whole or in part by the judgment debtor, the judgment debtor shall file with the levying officer an original and one copy of the "judgment debtor's claim of exemption" and an original and one copy of the "judgment debtor's financial statement."[686]

706.123. The "judgment debtor's claim of exemption" shall be executed under oath. The claim of exemption shall indicate how much the judgment debtor believes should be withheld from the judgment debtor's earnings each pay period by the employer pursuant to the earnings withholding order and shall state the judgment debtor's present mailing address.[170]

706.124. The "judgment debtor's financial statement" shall be executed as provided in Section 703.530 and contain all of the information required by that section and the following additional information:
(a) Whether any earnings withholding orders are in effect with respect to the earnings of the judgment debtor or the spouse or dependents of the judgment debtor.
(b) Whether any earnings assignment orders for support are in effect with respect to the earnings of the judgment debtor or the spouse or dependents of the judgment debtor.[303]

706.125. The "earnings withholding order" shall include all of the following:
(a) The name, address, and, if known, the social security number of the judgment debtor.
(b) The name and address of the employer to whom the order is directed.
(c) The court where the judgment was entered, the date the judgment was entered, and the name of the judgment creditor.
(d) Whether the judgment is based in whole or in part on a claim for elder or dependent adult financial abuse and, if

in part, how much of the judgment arises from the claim.

(e) The date of issuance of the writ of execution to the county where the earnings withholding order is sought.

(f) The total amount required to satisfy the order on the date of issuance (which may not exceed the amount required to satisfy the writ of execution on the date of issuance of the order plus the levying officer's statutory fee for service of the order).

(g) A description of the withholding period and an order to the employer to withhold from the earnings of the judgment debtor for each pay period the amount required to be withheld under Section 706.050 or the amount specified in the order subject to Section 706.024, as the case may be, for the pay periods ending during the withholding period.

(h) An order to the employer to pay over to the levying officer at a specified address the amount required to be withheld and paid over pursuant to the order in the manner and within the times provided by law.

(i) An order that the employer fill out the "employer's return" and return it by first-class mail, postage prepaid, to the levying officer at a specified address within 15 days after service of the earnings withholding order.

(j) An order that the employer deliver to the judgment debtor a copy of the earnings withholding order and the "notice to employee of earnings withholding order" within 10 days after service of the earnings withholding order; but, if the judgment debtor is no longer employed by the employer and the employer does not owe the employee any earnings, the employer is not required to make the delivery.

(k) The name and address of the levying officer.[631]

706.126. (a) The "employer's return" shall be executed under oath. The form for the return provided to the employer shall state all of the following information:

(1) The name and address of the levying officer to whom the form is to be returned.

(2) A direction that the form be mailed to the levying officer by first-class mail, postage prepaid, no later than 15 days after the date of service of the earnings withholding order.

(3) The name, the address, and, if known, the social security number of the judgment debtor.

(b) In addition, the employer's return form shall require the employer to supply all of the following information:

(1) The date the earnings withholding order was served on the employer.

(2) Whether the judgment debtor is employed by the employer or whether the employer otherwise owes earnings to the employee.

(3) If the judgment debtor is employed by the employer or the employer otherwise owes earnings to the employee, the amount of the employee's earnings for the last pay period and the length of this pay period.

(4) Whether the employer was required on the date of service to comply with an earlier earnings withholding order and, if so, the name of the judgment creditor who secured the earlier order, the levying officer who served such order, the date it was issued, the date it was served, the expiration date of such order, and which of the earnings withholding orders the employer is required to comply with under the applicable statutory

rules concerning the priority of such orders.
(5) Whether the employer was required on the date of service to comply with an earnings assignment order for support and, if so, the court which issued such assignment order and the date it was issued and any other information the Judicial Council determines is needed to identify the order.
(6) The name and address of the person to whom notices to the employer are to be sent.
(7) The date on which the employer provided the employee a copy of the earnings withholding order and the notice of earnings withholding order, the name and title of the person who provided the order and notice, and a short description of the manner in which the order and notice were provided.[909]

706.127. (a) The Judicial Council shall prepare "employer's instructions" for employers and revise or supplement these instructions to reflect changes in the law or rules regulating the withholding of earnings.
(b) Except to the extent that they are included in the forms required to be provided by the employer to the levying officer, the Judicial Council shall publish and provide to the levying officers copies of the employer's instructions.[170]

706.128. The "judgment creditor's notice of opposition to the claim of exemption" shall be executed under oath and shall include all of the following:
(a) The name, last known address, and, if known, the social security number of the judgment debtor.
(b) The name and address of the judgment creditor.
(c) The date of mailing of the notice of claim of exemption.
(d) The amount of the judgment debtor's claim of exemption which the judgment creditor claims is not exempt.
(e) The factual and legal grounds for the judgment creditor's opposition to the claim of exemption.[170]

706.129. The levying officer shall have copies of the forms for the "judgment debtor's claim of exemption" and "judgment debtor's financial statement" available at the levying officer's office for distribution without charge to a person who desires to make a claim of exemption under Section 706.051.[170]

Article 7: Administration and Enforcement
Article 7 added by Stats. 1982, Ch. 1364, Sec. 2.

706.151. The Judicial Council may perform all acts required by the Administrator of the Wage and Hour Division of the United States Department of Labor as conditions to exemption of this state from the earnings garnishment provisions of the Consumer Credit Protection Act of 1968 (15 U.S.C. Secs. 1671–1677), including, but not limited to:
(a) Representing and acting on behalf of the state in relation to the Administrator of the Wage and Hour Division and the administrator's representatives with regard to any matter relating to, or arising out of, the application, interpretation, and enforcement of the laws of this state regulating withholding of earnings.
(b) Submitting to the Administrator of the Wage and Hour Division in duplicate and on a current basis, a certified

copy of every statute of this state affecting earnings withholding, and a certified copy of any decision in any case involving any of those statutes, made by the Supreme Court of this state.

(c) Submitting to the Administrator of the Wage and Hour Division any information relating to the enforcement of earnings withholding laws of this state which the administrator may request.[170]

706.152. If an employer withholds earnings pursuant to this chapter and, with the intent to defraud either the judgment creditor or the judgment debtor, fails to pay such withheld earnings over to the levying officer, the employer is guilty of a misdemeanor.[170]

706.153. (a) No employer shall defer or accelerate any payment of earnings to an employee with the intent to defeat or diminish the judgment creditor's rights under an earnings withholding order issued pursuant to the procedures provided by this chapter.

(b) If an employer violates this section, the judgment creditor may bring a civil action against the employer to recover the amount that would have been withheld and paid over pursuant to this chapter had the employer not violated this section. The remedy provided by this subdivision is not exclusive.[170]

706.154. (a) If an employer fails to withhold or to pay over the amount the employer is required to withhold and pay over pursuant to this chapter, the judgment creditor may bring a civil action against the employer to recover such amount. The remedy provided by this subdivision is not exclusive.

(b) Notwithstanding subdivision (a), an employer who complies with any written order or written notice which purports to be given or served in accordance with the provisions of this chapter is not subject to any civil or criminal liability for such compliance unless the employer has actively participated in a fraud.[170]

Chapter 6: Miscellaneous Creditors' Remedies

Chapter 6 added by Stats. 1982, Ch. 1364, Sec. 2.

Article 1: Written Interrogatories to Judgment Debtor

Article 1 added by Stats. 1982, Ch. 1364, Sec. 2.

708.010. (a) Except as provided in this section and in subdivision (b) of Section 708.020, the procedure in this article may be used at any time a money judgment is enforceable.

(b) If enforcement of the judgment is stayed on appeal by the giving of a sufficient undertaking under Chapter 2 (commencing with Section 916) of Title 13, all proceedings under this article are stayed. In any other case where the enforcement of the judgment is stayed, all proceedings under this article are stayed unless the court otherwise expressly orders.[170]

708.020. (a) The judgment creditor may propound written interrogatories to the judgment debtor, in the manner provided in Chapter 13 (commencing with Section 2030.010) of Title 4 of Part 4, requesting information to aid in enforcement of the money judgment. The judgment debtor shall answer the interrogatories in the manner and within the time provided by Chapter

13 (commencing with Section 2030.010) of Title 4 of Part 4.

(b) The judgment creditor may not serve interrogatories pursuant to this section within 120 days after the judgment debtor has responded to interrogatories previously served pursuant to this section or within 120 days after the judgment debtor has been examined pursuant to Article 2 (commencing with Section 708.110), and the judgment debtor is not required to respond to any interrogatories so served.

(c) Interrogatories served pursuant to this section may be enforced, to the extent practicable, in the same manner as interrogatories in a civil action.

(d) The limitation provided by Chapter 13 (commencing with Section 2030.010) of Title 4 of Part 4 on the number of interrogatories that may be propounded applies to each set of interrogatories propounded from time to time pursuant to this section, but does not apply cumulatively to interrogatories propounded by the judgment creditor to the judgment debtor.[549]

708.030. (a) The judgment creditor may demand that any judgment debtor produce and permit the party making the demand, or someone acting on that party's behalf, to inspect and to copy a document that is in the possession, custody, or control of the party on whom the demand is made in the manner provided in Chapter 14 (commencing with Section 2031.010) of Title 4 of Part 4, if the demand requests information to aid in enforcement of the money judgment. The judgment debtor shall respond and comply with the demand in the manner and within the time provided by Chapter 14 (commencing with Section 2031.010) of Title 4 of Part 4.

(b) The judgment creditor may not serve interrogatories or inspection demands pursuant to this section or Section 708.020 within 120 days after the judgment debtor has responded to the interrogatories or demands previously served pursuant to this section or Section 708.020, or within 120 days after the judgment debtor has been examined pursuant to Article 2 (commencing with Section 708.110), and the judgment debtor is not required to respond to any discovery so served.

(c) Inspection demands served pursuant to this section may be enforced to the extent practicable, in the same manner as inspection demands in a civil action.[550]

Article 2: Examination Proceedings
Article 2 added by Stats. 1982, Ch. 1364, Sec. 2.

708.110. (a) The judgment creditor may apply to the proper court for an order requiring the judgment debtor to appear before the court, or before a referee appointed by the court, at a time and place specified in the order, to furnish information to aid in enforcement of the money judgment.

(b) If the judgment creditor has not caused the judgment debtor to be examined under this section during the preceding 120 days, the court shall make the order upon ex parte application of the judgment creditor.

(c) If the judgment creditor has caused the judgment debtor to be examined under this section during the preceding 120 days, the court shall make the order if the judgment creditor by affidavit or otherwise shows good cause for the order. The application shall be made on noticed motion if the court so directs or a court rule so requires. Otherwise, it may be made ex parte.

(d) The judgment creditor shall personally serve a copy of the order on the judgment debtor not less than 30 days before the date set for the examination. Service shall be made in the manner specified in Section 415.10. Service of the order creates a lien on the personal property of the judgment debtor for a period of one year from the date of the order unless extended or sooner terminated by the court.

(e) Except as provided in section 708.111, the order shall contain the following statement in 14-point boldface type if printed or in capital letters if typed: "NOTICE TO JUDGMENT DEBTOR. If you fail to appear at the time and place specified in this order, you may be subject to arrest and punishment for contempt of court and the court may make an order requiring you to pay the reasonable attorney's fees incurred by the judgment creditor in this proceeding."[824]

708.111. (a) This section applies to an application pursuant to Section 708.110 by a judgment creditor with a judgment concerning a consumer debt awarded on or after January 1, 2025.

(b) "Consumer debt" as used in this Section means any obligation or alleged obligation of a consumer to pay money arising out of a transaction in which the money, property, insurance, or services which are the subject of the transaction are primarily for personal, family, or household purposes. Consumer debt does not include debts incurred due to, or obtained by tortious or fraudulent conduct or judgments for unpaid wages, damages, or penalties owed to an employee. Consumer debt does not include rental debt, which means unpaid rent or other unpaid financial obligation of a tenant under the tenancy that has come due.

(c) Notwithstanding subdivision (e) of Section 708.110, if the order issued pursuant to section 708.110 requires a judgment debtor to appear in a case concerning consumer debt, as indicated by the judgment creditor in the application and order for appearance and examination, the order shall be accompanied by the Judicial Council form containing the list of exemptions from the enforcement judgments adopted pursuant to Section 681.030 and the notice of financial affidavit and financial affidavit forms adopted by the Judicial Council pursuant to subdivision (h). The order shall contain the following statement in 14-point boldface type if printed or in capital letters if typed: "NOTICE TO JUDGMENT DEBTOR. If you fail to appear at the time and place specified in this order, the court may make an order requiring you to pay the reasonable attorney's fees and costs incurred by the judgment creditor in this proceeding. Instead of appearing at the examination, you may file a notice of judgment debtor's financial affidavit in a form prescribed by the court and signed under penalty of perjury and serve copies of all filed documents and the financial affidavit on the judgment creditor no later than 15 days prior to the date set for the examination."

(d) If the judgment debtor in a case concerning consumer debt states in a financial affidavit, signed under penalty of perjury, that all of their income and assets are exempt, and files with the court a notice of financial affidavit with a proof of service, the court shall cancel the examination and provide notice of cancellation to the parties. If copies of the financial affidavit are not timely served or the notice and proof of service are not timely filed with the court, the court shall not cancel the examination.

(1) Within 15 days after the filing of the notice and proof of service of the financial affidavit, a judgment creditor who objects to the affidavit shall file with the court a notice of motion for an order determining the need for the debtor to appear for a debtor's examination. If the notice of motion is not timely filed with the court, the debtor's examination shall remain canceled.

(2) The notice of motion for an order determining the need for a debtor to appear for a debtor's examination shall include a declaration executed under oath and include a statement of facts showing good cause why a debtor's examination is necessary notwithstanding the debtor's financial affidavit. In an action in which the consumer debt is secured by real property or personal property, a showing of good cause is established when the plaintiff demonstrates that the debtor has not provided the plaintiff with accurate information regarding the location or condition of the security, the status of insurance on the security, or the status of the taxes due on the security.

(3) The judgment creditor shall file and serve the motion described in paragraph (1) pursuant to Section 1005 and the hearing shall be held pursuant to the same section.

(4) The financial affidavit and motion for an order determining the need for a debtor to appear for a debtor's examination, as well as any pleading filed in support of the motion and any reply by the judgment debtor, shall constitute the pleadings, subject to the power of the court to permit amendments in the interest of justice.

(5) If no other evidence is offered, the court, if satisfied that sufficient facts are shown by the financial affidavit and the notice of motion, may make its determination thereon. If not satisfied, the court shall order the hearing continued for the production of other oral or documentary evidence.

(6) At the conclusion of the hearing, the court shall determine by order whether the judgment debtor shall appear for a debtor's examination. If the judgment debtor is ordered to appear, the judgment creditor shall schedule the time and place of the examination with the court. There shall be no filing fee for the judgment creditor to refile the application and order for appearance and examination for the rescheduled exam. The judgment creditor is not required to serve the application and order by personal service, but may serve them by mail or electronic service at least 30 days before the date set for examination, pursuant to Sections 1013 and 1010.6.

(7) If the examination is canceled because the judgment creditor does not object or for another reason, the judgment creditor shall not file another application and order for appearance and examination until one year from the date of the prior filed application and order for appearance and examination.

(e) The financial affidavit shall include the following information:

(1) The number of people relying on

the judgment debtor for support, including spouse, dependents, and other household members.

(2) Gross monthly income from employment, including withholdings and take home pay.

(3) Total monthly income from all sources other than employment.

(4) Property owned, including cash, bank accounts, real estate equity, vehicles (e.g., cars, motorcycles, and boats), jewelry, securities, certificates of deposit, entity ownership, life insurance policies, and tax refunds.

(5) Itemized monthly expenses.

(6) Any outstanding debts, including balance owed and to whom.

(7) Any other facts which support the claim of exemption.

(f) In a case concerning consumer debt in which the judgment debtor claims property is exempt pursuant to law exempting property to the extent necessary for the support of the judgment debtor and the spouse and dependents of the judgment debtor, the financial affidavit shall also include the following information. The financial affidavit shall also be signed under penalty of perjury by the spouse of the judgment debtor, unless the spouses are living separate and apart.

(1) The name of the spouse of the judgment debtor.

(2) The age and relationship of all persons dependent upon the judgment debtor or the spouse of the judgment debtor for support.

(3) All sources and the amounts of earnings and other income of the spouse and dependents of the judgment debtor.

(4) A list of the assets of the spouse and dependents of the judgment debtor and the value of such assets.

(5) All outstanding debts of the spouse and dependents of the judgment debtor

(g) A judgment debtor in a case concerning consumer debt who elects to file a financial affidavit in lieu of appearing before the court for an examination shall serve a copy of all filed documents on the judgment creditor no later than 15 days prior to the date set for the examination.

(h) The Judicial Council shall adopt a notice of financial affidavit form and a financial affidavit form and revise any existing forms as necessary to implement the requirements of this section.

(i) Notwithstanding Section 708.170, 1209, or 1993, or any other applicable law or court rule, for a case involving consumer debt:

(1) No warrant for arrest or to appear shall be issued for a judgment debtor in a case concerning consumer debt who fails to appear for an examination under this section or to file and serve the judgment debtor's financial affidavit. In such cases, the court shall issue an order to show cause to determine whether to issue a warrant to compel the attendance of the judgment debtor.

(2) The court shall provide a judgment debtor who is ordered to appear pursuant to an order to show cause described in paragraph (1) with a reasonable opportunity to complete and file a judgment debtor's financial affidavit described in subdivision (e). The warrant to compel the attendance of the judgment debtor shall be satisfied by the judgment debtor's appearance or the filing of a notice of financial affidavit and proof of service pursuant to subdivision (d) certifying that the notice and financial affidavit was

served on the judgment creditor.[825]

708.120. (a) Upon ex parte application by a judgment creditor who has a money judgment and proof by the judgment creditor by affidavit or otherwise to the satisfaction of the proper court that a third person has possession or control of property in which the judgment debtor has an interest or is indebted to the judgment debtor in an amount exceeding two hundred fifty dollars ($250), the court shall make an order directing the third person to appear before the court, or before a referee appointed by the court, at a time and place specified in the order, to answer concerning such property or debt. The affidavit in support of the judgment creditor's application may be based on the affiant's information and belief.

(b) Not less than 10 days prior to the date set for the examination, a copy of the order shall be:

(1) Served personally on the third person.

(2) Served personally or by mail on the judgment debtor.

(c) If the property in the third person's possession or control in which the judgment debtor has an interest or the debt owed by the third person to the judgment debtor is described in the affidavit or application for an order under subdivision (a) in a manner reasonably adequate to permit it to be identified, service of the order on the third person creates a lien on the judgment debtor's interest in the property or on the debt for a period of one year from the date of the order unless extended or sooner terminated by the court.

(d) The judgment debtor may claim that all or any portion of the property or debt is exempt from enforcement of a money judgment by application to the court on noticed motion, filed with the court and personally served on the judgment creditor not later than three days before the date set for the examination. The judgment debtor shall execute an affidavit in support of the application that includes all of the matters set forth in subdivision (b) of Section 703.520. If a claim of exemption is made pursuant to this section, a notice of opposition to the claim of exemption is not required. The court shall determine any claim of exemption made pursuant to this section. Failure of the judgment debtor to make a claim of exemption does not preclude the judgment debtor from later claiming the exemption unless the property or debt is described in the order in a manner reasonably adequate to permit it to be identified and the judgment debtor receives notice of the examination proceeding at least 10 days before the date set for the examination.

(e) An order made pursuant to subdivision (a) shall contain the following statements in 14-point boldface type if printed or in capital letters if typed:

(1) "NOTICE TO PERSON SERVED. If you fail to appear at the time and place specified in this order, you may be subject to arrest and punishment for contempt of court and the court may make an order requiring you to pay the reasonable attorney's fees incurred by the judgment creditor in this proceeding."

(2) "NOTICE TO JUDGMENT DEBTOR. The person in whose favor the judgment was entered in this action claims that the person to be examined pursuant to this order has possession or control of property

which is yours or owes you a debt. This property or debt is as follows: (Description of property or debt).

If you claim that all or any portion of this property or debt is exempt from enforcement of the money judgment, you must file your exemption claim in writing with the court and personally serve a copy on the judgment creditor not later than three days before the date set for the examination. You must appear at the time and place set for this examination to establish your claim of exemption or your exemption may be waived."

(f) An order made pursuant to subdivision (a) is not effective unless, at the time it is served on the third person, the person serving the order tenders to the third person fees for the mileage necessary to be traveled from the third person's residence to the place of examination. The mileage fees shall be in the same amount generally provided for witnesses when legally required to attend civil proceedings in the court where the examination proceeding is to be conducted.[347]

708.130. (a) Witnesses may be required to appear and testify before the court or referee in an examination proceeding under this article in the same manner as upon the trial of an issue.

(b) The privilege prescribed by Article 4 (commencing with Section 970) of Chapter 4 of Division 8 of the Evidence Code does not apply in an examination proceeding under this article.[170]

708.140. (a) The examination proceedings authorized by this article may be conducted by a referee appointed by the court. The referee may issue, modify, or vacate an order authorized by Section 708.205, may make a protective order authorized by Section 708.200, and may issue a warrant authorized by Section 708.170, and has the same power as the court to grant adjournments, to preserve order, and to subpoena witnesses to attend the examination, but only the court that ordered the reference has power to do the following:

(1) Punish for contempt for disobeying an order of the referee.

(2) Make an award of attorney's fees pursuant to Section 708.170.

(3) Determine a contested claim of exemption or determine a third-party claim under Section 708.180.

(b) Only a member of the State Bar of California is eligible for appointment as a referee pursuant to this article. A person who was duly appointed as a referee prior to July 1, 1983, pursuant to the law in operation at the time of appointment, and who is available to perform the duties of a referee on July 1, 1983, shall be exempt from the requirements of this subdivision.

(c) Nothing in subdivision (a) limits the power of a court to appoint a temporary judge pursuant to Section 21 of Article VI of the California Constitution.[186]

708.150. (a) (1) If a corporation, partnership, association, trust, limited liability company, or other organization is served with an order to appear for an examination, it shall designate to appear and be examined one or more officers, directors, managing agents, or other persons who are familiar with its property and debts.

(2) If a corporation, partnership, association, trust, limited liability company, or other organization served

with an order to appear for an examination fails to designate a person to appear pursuant to paragraph (1), the order to appear for an examination shall be deemed to have been made to and served upon the individuals designated in the manner described in paragraph (2) of subdivision (c).

(b) If the order to appear for an examination requires the appearance of a specified individual, the specified individual shall appear for the examination and may be accompanied by one or more officers, directors, managing agents, or other persons familiar with the property and debts of the corporation, partnership, association, trust, limited liability company, or other organization.

(c) If the order to appear for the examination does not require the appearance of a specified individual, the order shall advise the corporation, partnership, association, trust, limited liability company, or other organization of all of the following:

(1) The organization's duty to make a designation under paragraph (1) of subdivision (a).

(2) That the organization's failure to make a designation under paragraph (1) of subdivision (a) shall result in the order to appear for the examination to be deemed to have been made to, and require the appearance of, the following:

(A) If the organization is a corporation registered with the Secretary of State, a natural person named as the chief financial officer in the corporation's most recent filing with the Secretary of State. If no one is so named, a natural person named as the chief executive officer in the corporation's most recent filing with the Secretary of State. If no one is so named, a natural person named as the secretary in the corporation's most recent filing with the Secretary of State.

(B) If the organization is a limited liability company registered with the Secretary of State, the first natural person named as a manager or member in the limited liability company's most recent filing with the Secretary of State.

(C) If the organization is a limited partnership registered with the Secretary of State, the first natural person named as a general partner in the limited partnership's most recent filing with the Secretary of State.

(D) If the organization is not registered with the Secretary of State or the organization's filings with the Secretary of State do not identify a natural person as described in subparagraph (A), (B), or (C), a natural person identified by the judgment creditor as being familiar with the property and debts of the organization, together with an affidavit or declaration signed by the judgment creditor that sets forth the factual basis for the identification of the individual. The affidavit or declaration shall be served on the organization together with the order.

(3) That service of an order to appear for an examination upon an organization by any method permitted under this code or the Corporations Code, including service on the agent of the organization for service of process, shall be deemed effective service of the order to appear upon the individuals identified under subparagraphs (A), (B), (C), and (D) of paragraph (2).

(d) A corporation, partnership, association, trust, limited liability company, or other organization, whether or not a party, may appear at an examination through any authorized officer, director, or employee, whether or not the person is an attorney.

(e) The powers of the court under Section 708.170 extend to natural persons ordered to appear and served pursuant to this section.

(f) This section shall be strictly construed and its requirements may not be varied by local rule or otherwise.[784]

708.160. (a) Except as otherwise provided in this section, the proper court for examination of a person under this article is the court in which the money judgment is entered.

(b) A person sought to be examined may not be required to attend an examination before a court located outside the county in which the person resides or has a place of business unless the distance from the person's place of residence or place of business to the place of examination is less than 150 miles.

(c) If a person sought to be examined does not reside or have a place of business in the county where the judgment is entered, the superior court in the county where the person resides or has a place of business is a proper court for examination of the person.

(d) If the judgment creditor seeks an examination of a person before a court other than the court in which the judgment is entered, the judgment creditor shall file an application that shall include all of the following:

(1) An abstract of judgment in the form prescribed by Section 674.

(2) An affidavit in support of the application stating the place of residence or place of business of the person sought to be examined.

(3) Any necessary affidavit or showing for the examination as required by Section 708.110 or 708.120.

(4) The filing fee for a motion as provided in subdivision (a) of Section 70617 of the Government Code.[565]

708.170. (a) If an order requiring a person to appear for an examination under subdivision (e) of Section 708.110 was served by a sheriff, marshal, a person specially appointed by the court in the order, or a registered process server, and the person fails to appear:

(1) The court may do either of the following:

(A) Pursuant to a warrant, have the person brought before the court to answer for the failure to appear and may punish the person for contempt.

(B) Issue a warrant for the arrest of the person who failed to appear as required by the court order, pursuant to Section 1993.

(2) If the person's failure to appear is without good cause, the judgment creditor shall be awarded reasonable attorney's fees incurred in the examination proceeding. Attorney's fees awarded against the judgment debtor shall be added to and become part of the principal amount of the judgment.

(b) A person who willfully makes an improper service of an order for an examination which subsequently results in the arrest pursuant to subdivision (a) of the person who fails to appear is guilty of a misdemeanor.[826]

708.180. (a) Subject to subdivision (b), if a third person examined pursuant to Section 708.120 claims an interest in the property adverse to the judgment debtor or denies the debt, the court may, if the judgment creditor so requests, determine the interests in the property or the existence of the debt. The determination is conclusive as to the parties to the proceeding and the third person, but an appeal may be taken from the determination. The court may grant a continuance for a reasonable time for discovery proceedings, the production of evidence, or other preparation for the hearing.

(b) The court may not make the determination provided in subdivision (a) if the third person's claim is made in good faith and any of the following conditions is satisfied:

(1) The court would not be a proper court for the trial of an independent civil action (including a creditor's suit) for the determination of the interests in the property or the existence of the debt, and the third person objects to the determination of the matter under subdivision (a).

(2) At the time an order for examination pursuant to Section 708.120 is served on the third person a civil action (including a creditor's suit) is pending with respect to the interests in the property or the existence of the debt.

(3) The court determines that the interests in the property or the existence of the debt should be determined in a creditor's suit.

(c) Upon application of the judgment creditor made ex parte, the court may make an order forbidding transfer of the property to the judgment debtor or payment of the debt to the judgment debtor until the interests in the property or the existence of the debt is determined pursuant to subdivision (a) or until a creditor's suit may be commenced and an order obtained pursuant to Section 708.240. An undertaking may be required in the discretion of the court. The court may modify or vacate the order at any time with or without a hearing on such terms as are just.

(d) Upon application of the judgment creditor upon noticed motion, the court may, if it determines that the judgment debtor probably owns an interest in the property or that the debt probably is owed to the judgment debtor, make an order forbidding the transfer or other disposition of the property to any person or forbidding payment of the debt until the interests in the property or the existence of the debt is determined pursuant to subdivision (a) or until a creditor's suit may be commenced and an order obtained pursuant to Section 708.240. The court shall require the judgment creditor to furnish an undertaking as provided in Section 529. The court may modify or vacate the order at any time after notice and hearing on such terms as are just.[398]

708.190. The court may permit a person claiming an interest in the property or debt sought to be applied in an examination proceeding to intervene in the proceeding and may determine the person's rights in the property or debt pursuant to Section 708.180.[170]

708.200. In any proceeding under this article, the court may, on motion of the person to be examined or on its own motion, make such protective orders as justice may require.[170]

708.205. (a) Except as provided in subdivision (b), at the conclusion of a proceeding pursuant to this article, the court may order the judgment debtor's

interest in the property in the possession or under the control of the judgment debtor or the third person or a debt owed by the third person to the judgment debtor to be applied toward the satisfaction of the money judgment if the property is not exempt from enforcement of a money judgment. Such an order creates a lien on the property or debt.
(b) If a third person examined pursuant to Section 708.120 claims an interest in the property adverse to the judgment debtor or denies the debt and the court does not determine the matter as provided in subdivision (a) of Section 708.180, the court may not order the property or debt to be applied toward the satisfaction of the money judgment but may make an order pursuant to subdivision (c) or (d) of Section 708.180 forbidding transfer or payment to the extent authorized by that section.[170]

Article 3: Creditor's Suit
Article 3 added by Stats. 1982, Ch. 1364, Sec. 2.

708.210. If a third person has possession or control of property in which the judgment debtor has an interest or is indebted to the judgment debtor, the judgment creditor may bring an action against the third person to have the interest or debt applied to the satisfaction of the money judgment.[170]

708.220. The judgment debtor shall be joined in an action brought pursuant to this article but is not an indispensable party. The residence of the judgment debtor may not be considered in the determination of proper venue unless otherwise provided by contract between the judgment debtor and the third person.[170]

708.230. (a)Except as provided in subdivision (b), an action shall be commenced pursuant to this article before the expiration of the later of the following times:
(1) The time when the judgment debtor may bring an action against the third person concerning the property or debt.
(2) One year after creation of a lien on the property or debt pursuant to this title if the lien is created at the time when the judgment debtor may bring an action against the third person concerning the property or debt.
(b) An action may not be commenced pursuant to this article after the period for enforcement of the money judgment has expired.
(c) Notwithstanding Section 683.020, if an action is commenced pursuant to this article within the time permitted in this section, the action may be prosecuted to judgment.[170]

708.240. The judgment creditor may apply to the court in which an action under this article is pending for either or both of the following:
(a) An order restraining the third person from transferring to the judgment debtor the property in which the judgment debtor is claimed to have an interest or from paying to the judgment debtor the alleged debt. The order shall be made on noticed motion if the court so directs or a court rule so requires. Otherwise, the order may be made on ex parte application. The order shall remain in effect until judgment is entered in the action or until such earlier time as the court may provide in the order. An undertaking may be required in the discretion of the

court. The court may modify or vacate the order at any time with or without a hearing on such terms as are just.

(b) A temporary restraining order or a preliminary injunction or both, restraining the third person from transferring to any person or otherwise disposing of the property in which the judgment debtor is claimed to have an interest, pursuant to Chapter 3 (commencing with Section 525) of Title 7, and the court may make, dissolve, and modify such orders as provided therein.[170]

708.250. Service of summons on the third person creates a lien on the interest of the judgment debtor in the property or on the debt owed to the judgment debtor that is the subject of an action under this article.[170]

708.260. (a)In an action brought pursuant to this article, the judgment debtor may claim that all or any portion of the property or debt is exempt from enforcement of a money judgment. The claim shall be made by application to the court on noticed motion, filed with the court and served on the judgment creditor not later than 30 days before the date set for trial. Service shall be made personally or by mail. The judgment debtor shall execute an affidavit in support of the application that includes all of the matters set forth in subdivision (b) of Section 703.520. No notice of opposition to the claim of exemption is required. If the judgment debtor has not been named as a party to the action, the judgment debtor may obtain an order under Section 389 that the judgment debtor be made a party. Except as provided in subdivision (b), failure of the judgment debtor to make a claim of exemption is a waiver of the exemption.

(b) Failure of the judgment debtor to make a claim of exemption in an action brought pursuant to this article is not a waiver of the exemption if both of the following conditions are satisfied:

(1) The judgment debtor has not been served with process in the action that contains a description of the property or debt reasonably adequate to permit it to be identified.

(2) The judgment debtor does not have actual notice of the pendency of the action and the identity of the property or the nature of the debt in issue.[170]

708.270. There is no right to a jury trial in an action under this article.[170]

708.280. (a)The court shall determine any exemption claim made in the action. If the judgment debtor establishes to the satisfaction of the court that the property or debt is exempt from enforcement of a money judgment, the court shall so adjudge and may not make the orders referred to in subdivisions (b), (c), and (d).

(b) If the judgment creditor establishes that the third person has property in which the judgment debtor has an interest or is indebted to the judgment debtor, the court shall render judgment accordingly. The property or debt may be applied to the satisfaction of the judgment creditor's judgment against the judgment debtor as ordered by the court.

(c) If the court determines that the third person has property in which the judgment debtor has an interest, the court may order the third person not to transfer the property until it can be levied upon or otherwise applied to the satisfaction of the judgment.

(d) If the court determines that the third person has transferred property that was subject to a lien in favor of the judgment creditor or, contrary to court order of which the third person has notice, has paid the debt to the judgment debtor or has transferred the property, the court shall render judgment against the third person in an amount equal to the lesser of the following:

(1) The value of the judgment debtor's interest in the property or the amount of the debt.

(2) The amount of the judgment creditor's judgment against the judgment debtor remaining unsatisfied.[170]

708.290. Costs incurred by or taxed against the judgment creditor in an action under this article may not be recovered from the judgment debtor as a cost of enforcing the judgment.[170]

Article 4: Charging Orders

Article 4 added by Stats. 1982, Ch. 1364, Sec. 2.

708.310. If a money judgment is rendered against a partner or member but not against the partnership or limited liability company, the judgment debtor's interest in the partnership or limited liability company may be applied toward the satisfaction of the judgment by an order charging the judgment debtor's interest pursuant to Section 15907.03, 16504, or 17705.03 of the Corporations Code.[788]

708.320. (a) A lien on a judgment debtor's interest in a partnership or limited liability company is created by service of a notice of motion for a charging order on the judgment debtor and on either of the following:

(1) All partners or the partnership.

(2) All members or the limited liability company.

(b) If a charging order is issued, the lien created pursuant to subdivision (a) continues under the terms of the order. If issuance of the charging order is denied, the lien is extinguished.[484]

Article 5: Lien in Pending Action or Proceeding

Article 5 added by Stats. 1982, Ch. 1364, Sec. 2.

708.410. (a)A judgment creditor who has a money judgment against a judgment debtor who is a party to a pending action or special proceeding may obtain a lien under this article, to the extent required to satisfy the judgment creditor's money judgment, on both of the following:

(1) Any cause of action of such judgment debtor for money or property that is the subject of the action or proceeding.

(2) The rights of such judgment debtor to money or property under any judgment subsequently procured in the action or proceeding.

(b) To obtain a lien under this article, the judgment creditor shall file a notice of lien and an abstract or certified copy of the judgment creditor's money judgment in the pending action or special proceeding.

(c) At the time of the filing under subdivision (b) or promptly thereafter, the judgment creditor shall serve on all parties who, prior thereto, have made an appearance in the action or special proceeding a copy of the notice of lien and a statement of the date when the notice of lien was filed in the action or special proceeding. Service shall be made personally or by mail. Failure to serve all parties as required by this subdivision does not affect the lien created by the filing under subdivision (b), but the rights of a party are not affected by the lien until the party has notice of the lien.

(d) For the purpose of this article, an action or special proceeding is pending until the time for appeal from the judgment has expired or, if an appeal is filed, until the appeal has been finally determined.[170]

708.420. The notice of lien under Section 708.410 shall contain all of the following:

(a) A statement that a lien has been created under this article and the title of the court and the cause and number of the pending action or proceeding in which the notice of lien is filed.

(b) The name and last known address of the judgment debtor.

(c) The name and address of the judgment creditor.

(d) The title of the court where the judgment creditor's money judgment is entered and the cause and number of the action, the date of entry of the judgment, and the date of any subsequent renewals, and where entered in the records of the court.

(e) The amount required to satisfy the judgment creditor's money judgment at the time the notice of lien is filed in the action or proceeding.

(f) A statement that the lien attaches to any cause of action of the judgment debtor that is the subject of the action or proceeding and to the judgment debtor's rights to money or property under any judgment subsequently procured in the action or proceeding.

(g) A statement that no compromise, dismissal, settlement, or satisfaction of the pending action or proceeding or any of the judgment debtor's rights to money or property under any judgment procured therein may be entered into by or on behalf of the judgment debtor, and that the judgment debtor may not enforce the judgment debtor's rights to money or property under any judgment procured in the action or proceeding by a writ or otherwise, unless one of the following requirements is satisfied:

(1) The prior approval by order of the court in which the action or proceeding is pending has been obtained.

(2) The written consent of the judgment creditor has been obtained or the judgment creditor has released the lien.

(3) The money judgment of the judgment creditor has been satisfied.

(h) A statement that the judgment debtor may claim an exemption for all or any portion of the money or property within 30 days after the judgment debtor has notice of the creation of the lien and a statement that, if the exemption is not claimed within the time allowed, the exemption is waived.[170]

708.430. (a)The court in which the action or special proceeding is pending may permit a judgment creditor who has obtained a lien under this article to intervene in the action or proceeding pursuant to Section 387.

(b) For the purposes of Sections 708.450 and 708.470, a judgment creditor shall be deemed to be a party to the action or special proceeding even though the judgment creditor has not become a party to the action or proceeding under subdivision (a).[170]

708.440. (a)Except as provided in subdivision (c) of Section 708.410, unless the judgment creditor's money judgment is first satisfied or the lien is released, the judgment recovered in the action or special proceeding in favor of the judgment debtor may not be enforced by a writ or otherwise, and no compromise, dismissal, settlement, or satisfaction of the pending action or special proceeding or the judgment procured therein may be entered into by or on behalf of the judgment debtor, without the written consent of the judgment creditor or authorization by order of the court obtained under subdivision (b).

(b) Upon application by the judgment debtor, the court in which the action or special proceeding is pending or the judgment procured therein is entered may, in its discretion, after a hearing, make an order described in subdivision (a) that may include such terms and conditions as the court deems necessary. The application for an order under this subdivision shall be made on noticed motion. The notice of motion shall be served on the judgment creditor. Service shall be made personally or by mail.[170]

708.450. (a) If a lien is created under this article, the judgment debtor may claim that all or any portion of the money or property that the judgment debtor may recover in the action or special proceeding is exempt from enforcement of a money judgment. The claim shall be made by application on noticed motion to the court in which the action or special proceeding is pending, filed and served on the judgment creditor not later than 30 days after the judgment debtor has notice of the creation of the lien. Service shall be made personally or by mail. The judgment debtor shall execute an affidavit in support of the application that includes all the matters set forth in subdivision (b) of Section 703.520. No notice of opposition to the claim of exemption is required. The failure of the judgment debtor to make a claim of exemption under this section constitutes a waiver of the exemption.

(b) The court may determine the exemption claim at any time prior to the entry of judgment in the action or special proceeding or may consolidate the exemption hearing with the hearing on a motion pursuant to Section 708.470.

(c) If the judgment debtor establishes to the satisfaction of the court that the right of the judgment debtor to money or property under the judgment in the action or special proceeding is all or partially exempt from enforcement of a money judgment, the court shall order the termination of the lien created under this article on the exempt portion of the money or property.[222]

708.460. (a) If a lien is created pursuant to this article, the court clerk shall endorse upon the judgment recovered in the action or special proceeding a statement of the existence of the lien and the time it was created.

(b) Any abstract issued upon the judgment shall include a statement of the lien in favor of the judgment creditor.[170]

708.470. (a) If the judgment debtor is entitled to money or property under the judgment in the action or special proceeding and a lien created under this article exists, upon application of any party to the action or special proceeding, the court may order that the judgment debtor's rights to money or property under the judgment be applied to the satisfaction of the lien created under this article as ordered by the court. Application for an order under this section shall be on noticed motion. The notice of motion shall be served on all other parties. Service shall be made personally or by mail.

(b) If the judgment determines that the judgment debtor has an interest in property, the court may order the party having custody or control of the property not to transfer the property until it can be levied upon or otherwise applied to the satisfaction of the lien created under this article.

(c) If the court determines that a party (other than the judgment debtor) having notice of the lien created under this article has transferred property that was subject to the lien or has paid an amount to the judgment debtor that was subject to the lien, the court shall render judgment against the party in an amount equal to the lesser of the following:

(1) The value of the judgment debtor's interest in the property or the amount paid the judgment debtor.

(2) The amount of the judgment creditor's lien created under this article.[170]

708.480. A lien created under this article may be enforced by any applicable procedure:

(a) After the judgment subject to the lien is entered and the time for appeal from the judgment has expired.

(b) If an appeal is filed from the judgment subject to the lien, after the appeal is finally determined.[170]

Article 6: Assignment Order

Article 6 added by Stats. 1982, Ch. 1364, Sec. 2.

708.510. (a)Except as otherwise provided by law, upon application of the judgment creditor on noticed motion, the court may order the judgment debtor to assign to the judgment creditor or to a receiver appointed pursuant to Article 7 (commencing with Section 708.610) all or part of a right to payment due or to become due, whether or not the right is conditioned on future developments, including but not limited to the following types of payments:

(1) Wages due from the federal government that are not subject to withholding under an earnings withholding order.

(2) Rents.

(3) Commissions.

(4) Royalties.

(5) Payments due from a patent or copyright.

(6) Insurance policy loan value.

(b) The notice of the motion shall be served on the judgment debtor. Service shall be made personally or by mail.

(c) Subject to subdivisions (d), (e), and (f), in determining whether to order an assignment or the amount of an assignment pursuant to subdivision (a), the court may take into consideration all relevant factors, including the following:

(1) The reasonable requirements of a judgment debtor who is a natural person and of persons supported in whole or in part by the judgment debtor.

(2) Payments the judgment debtor is required to make or that are deducted in satisfaction of other judgments and

wage assignments, including earnings assignment orders for support.

(3) The amount remaining due on the money judgment.

(4) The amount being or to be received in satisfaction of the right to payment that may be assigned.

(d) A right to payment may be assigned pursuant to this article only to the extent necessary to satisfy the money judgment.

(e) When earnings or periodic payments pursuant to a pension or retirement plan are assigned pursuant to subdivision (a), the amount of the earnings or the periodic payments assigned shall not exceed the amount that may be withheld from a like amount of earnings under Chapter 5 (commencing with Section 706.010) (Wage Garnishment Law).

(f) Where a specific amount of the payment or payments to be assigned is exempt by another statutory provision, the amount of the payment or payments to be assigned pursuant to subdivision (a) shall not exceed the amount by which the payment or payments exceed the exempt amount.[304]

708.520. (a)When an application is made pursuant to Section 708.510 or thereafter, the judgment creditor may apply to the court for an order restraining the judgment debtor from assigning or otherwise disposing of the right to payment that is sought to be assigned. The application shall be made on noticed motion if the court so directs or a court rule so requires. Otherwise, it may be made ex parte.

(b) The court may issue an order pursuant to this section upon a showing of need for the order. The court, in its discretion, may require the judgment creditor to provide an undertaking.

(c) The court may modify or vacate the order at any time with or without a hearing on such terms as are just.

(d) The order shall be personally served upon the judgment debtor and shall contain a notice to the judgment debtor that failure to comply with the order may subject the judgment debtor to being held in contempt of court.[170]

708.530. (a) Except as provided in subdivision (b), the effect and priority of an assignment ordered pursuant to this article is governed by Section 955.1 of the Civil Code. For the purpose of priority, an assignee of a right to payment pursuant to this article shall be deemed to be a bona fide assignee for value under the terms of Section 955.1 of the Civil Code.

(b) An assignment of the right to future rent ordered under this article is recordable as an instrument affecting real property and the priority of such an assignment is governed by Section 1214 of the Civil Code.[223]

708.540. The rights of an obligor are not affected by an order assigning the right to payment until notice of the order is received by the obligor. For the purpose of this section, “obligor” means the person who is obligated to make payments to the judgment debtor or who may become obligated to make payments to the judgment debtor depending upon future developments.[170]

708.550. (a) The judgment debtor may claim that all or a portion of the right to payment is exempt from enforcement of a money judgment by application to the court on noticed motion filed not later than three days before the date set for the hearing on the judgment creditor’s application for an

assignment order. The judgment debtor shall execute an affidavit in support of the application that includes all of the matters set forth in subdivision (b) of Section 703.520. Failure of the judgment debtor to make a claim of exemption is a waiver of the exemption.
(b) The notice of the motion shall be personally served on the judgment creditor not later than three days before the date set for the hearing.
(c) The court shall determine any claim of exemption made pursuant to this section at the hearing on issuance of the assignment order.[170]

708.560. (a) Either the judgment creditor or the judgment debtor may apply to the court on noticed motion for an order to modify or set aside the assignment order. The notice of motion shall be served on the other party. Service shall be made personally or by mail.
(b) The court shall make an order modifying or setting aside the assignment order upon a showing that there has been a material change in circumstances since the time of the previous hearing on the assignment order. The court may order a reassignment of the right to payments as necessary. The order shall state whether and to what extent it applies to payments already made.[170]

Article 7: Receiver to Enforce Judgment
Article 7 added by Stats. 1982, Ch. 1364, Sec. 2.

708.610. The provisions of Chapter 5 (commencing with Section 564) and Chapter 5a (commencing with Section 571) of Title 7 govern the appointment, qualifications, powers, rights, and duties of a receiver appointed under this article.[170]

708.620. The court may appoint a receiver to enforce the judgment where the judgment creditor shows that, considering the interests of both the judgment creditor and the judgment debtor, the appointment of a receiver is a reasonable method to obtain the fair and orderly satisfaction of the judgment.[170]

708.630. (a) The judgment debtor's interest in an alcoholic beverage license may be applied to the satisfaction of a money judgment only as provided in this section.
(b) The court may appoint a receiver for the purpose of transferring the judgment debtor's interest in an alcoholic beverage license that is transferable under Article 5 (commencing with Section 24070) of Chapter 6 of Division 9 of the Business and Professions Code, unless the judgment debtor shows in the proceeding to appoint a receiver that the amount of delinquent taxes described in Section 24049 of the Business and Professions Code and claims of creditors with priority over the judgment creditor pursuant to Section 24074 of the Business and Professions Code exceed the probable sale price of the license.
(c) The receiver may exercise the powers of the licensee as necessary and in exercising such powers shall comply with the applicable provisions of Division 9 (commencing with Section 23000) of the Business and Professions Code and applicable regulations of the Department of Alcoholic Beverage Control. An application shall be filed to transfer the license to the receiver and a temporary retail permit

shall be obtained during the pendency of the transfer.[170]

Article 8: Collection of Judgment Where Judgment Debtor Is Creditor of Public Entity

Article 8 added by Stats. 1982, Ch. 1364, Sec. 2.

708.710. As used in this article:
(a) "Local public entity" means any public entity other than the state.
(b) "Public entity" means the state, a county, city, district, public authority, public agency, and any other political subdivision in the state.
(c) "State" means the State of California.
(d) "State agency" means a state office, officer, department, division, bureau, board, commission or agency claims against which are paid by warrants drawn by the Controller.[170]

708.720. (a) If a public entity owes money to the judgment debtor, the obligation of the public entity may be applied to the satisfaction of the money judgment against the judgment debtor only in the manner provided by (1) this article, (2) Chapter 5 (commencing with Section 706.010) (wage garnishment), or (3) Article 5 (commencing with Section 708.410) (lien in pending action or proceeding).
(b) The earnings of a public officer or employee shall not be withheld pursuant to this article. Except as expressly provided by law, the earnings of a public officer or employee may be withheld for the payment of a money judgment only pursuant to Chapter 5 (commencing with Section 706.010).
(c) If the obligation of a public entity to pay money to the judgment debtor is the subject of a pending action or special proceeding, the procedure in this article does not apply. The payment of the obligation that is the subject of the pending action or special proceeding may be applied to the satisfaction of the money judgment against the judgment debtor only in the manner provided in Article 5 (commencing with Section 708.410).[170]

708.730. (a) If money is owing and unpaid to the judgment debtor by a public entity, the judgment creditor may file, in the manner provided in this article, an abstract of the money judgment or a certified copy of the money judgment, together with an affidavit that states that the judgment creditor desires the relief provided by this article and states the exact amount then required to satisfy the judgment. The judgment creditor may state in the affidavit any fact tending to establish the identity of the judgment debtor.
(b) Promptly after filing the abstract or certified copy of the judgment and the affidavit with the public entity, the judgment creditor shall serve notice of the filing on the judgment debtor. Service shall be made personally or by mail.
(c) If the judgment is for support and related costs and money is owing and unpaid to the judgment debtor by a state agency, including, but not limited to, money owing and unpaid to the judgment debtor by a state agency on a claim for refund from the Franchise Tax Board under the Personal Income Tax Law, Part 10 (commencing with Section 17001) of Division 2 of the Revenue and Taxation Code, or the Bank and Corporation Tax Law, Part 11 (commencing with Section 23001) of Division 2 of the Revenue and Tax-

ation Code or as a result of the judgment debtor's winnings in the California State Lottery, and the local child support agency is enforcing the support obligation pursuant to Section 17400 of the Family Code, the claim may be submitted as follows: The local child support agency may file the affidavit referred to in subdivision (a) without filing an abstract or certified copy of the judgment. In lieu thereof, the affidavit shall also state that an abstract of the judgment could be obtained. Where there is more than one judgment debtor, the local child support agency may include all the judgment debtors in a single affidavit. Separate affidavits need not be submitted for each judgment debtor. The affidavit need not on its face separately identify each judgment debtor or the exact amount required to satisfy the judgment, so long as it incorporates by reference forms or other automated data transmittals, as required by the Department of Child Support Services, which contain this information. Affidavits submitted pursuant to this subdivision by the local child support agency shall meet the standards and procedures prescribed by the state agency to which the affidavit is submitted, except that those affidavits submitted with respect to moneys owed and unpaid to the judgment debtor as a result of a claim for refund from the Franchise Tax Board under the Personal Income Tax Law, Part 10 (commencing with Section 17001) of Division 2 of the Revenue and Taxation Code, or the Bank and Corporation Tax Law, Part 11 (commencing with Section 23001) of Division 2 of the Revenue and Taxation Code, shall meet the standards and procedures prescribed by the Franchise Tax Board.

In serving the notice required by subdivision (b), the Director of the Department of Child Support Services or his or her designee may act in lieu of the judgment creditor as to judgments enforced under this division.

(d) If the judgment is for child, spousal, or family support and related costs and money is owing and unpaid to the judgment debtor by a state agency on a claim for refund from the Franchise Tax Board under the Personal Income Tax Law, Part 10 (commencing with Section 17001) of Division 2 of the Revenue and Taxation Code, or the Bank and Corporation Tax Law, Part 11 (commencing with Section 23001) of Division 2 of the Revenue and Taxation Code, or as a result of the judgment debtor's winnings in the California State Lottery, the judgment creditor may file with the court an abstract or a certified copy of the judgment ordering the payment of child, spousal, or family support, together with a request that the court issue a Notice of Support Arrearage, as provided in Section 708.780, to which any personal income tax refunds and lottery winnings owed the judgment debtor by the State of California will be subject. The request shall be accompanied by an affidavit, signed under penalty of perjury, which shall state that the judgment creditor desires the relief provided by this subdivision and shall state the exact amount then required to satisfy the judgment. In addition, the affidavit shall specify the beginning and ending dates of all periods during which the arrearage for support occurred, specify the arrearage for each month, and state that the support is at least 90 days overdue or is overdue in an amount equal to 90 days of support. It shall also certify that the child or children are not recipients, and during the period for which payment is requested, were not recipients, of Aid to Families with Dependent Children and there was no assignment to a state or county agency of support and shall certify on information and belief that there is not current or past action by a district attorney pending for support or support enforcement on the judgment creditor's behalf.

The request shall have attached a proof of service showing that copies of the request, the affidavit, and the abstract or certified copy of the judgment ordering the payment of support have been served on the judgment debtor and the district attorney of the county in which the support judgment is entered. Service shall be by certified mail, postage prepaid, return receipt requested, to the last known address of the party to be served, or by personal service.

This subdivision does not apply in any instance in which a district attorney initiated or participated as counsel in the action for support or if support is required to be paid through a district attorney's office.

The Department of Child Support Services shall, upon request, inform the Legislature of the use and effect of this subdivision on or before December 31, 2000.

This subdivision shall become operative on January 1, 1996, and shall become inoperative on December 31, 2000.

(e) For purposes of this section, "support" means an obligation owing on behalf of a child, spouse, or family, or combination thereof.[455]

708.740. (a) Except as provided in subdivision (e), if money is owing and unpaid to the judgment debtor by a state agency, the judgment creditor shall file the abstract or certified copy of the judgment and the affidavit with the state agency owing the money to the judgment debtor prior to the time the state agency presents the claim of the judgment debtor to the Controller. Where the affidavit is prepared under subdivision (c) of Section 708.730, the affidavit shall be filed with the Department of Child Support Services, and no abstract need be filed. Filing of the affidavit with the department shall be sufficient to require the Controller to transfer the funds claimed by the judgment debtor, notwithstanding that the claim of the judgment debtor has been filed with another state agency.

(b) When presenting the claim of the judgment debtor to the Controller, the state agency shall do all of the following:

(1) Note the fact of the filing of the abstract or certified copy of the judgment and the affidavit.

(2) State the amount required to satisfy the judgment as shown by the affidavit.

(3) State any amounts advanced to the judgment debtor by the state, or owed by the judgment debtor to the state, for expenses or for any other purpose.

(c) Except as provided in subdivisions (d) and (e), to discharge the claim of the judgment debtor, the Controller shall (1) deposit with the court, by a warrant or check payable to the court, the amount due the judgment debtor (after deducting an amount sufficient to reimburse the state for any amounts advanced to the judgment debtor or owed by the judgment debtor to the state) required to satisfy the money judgment as shown by the affidavit in full or to the greatest extent and (2) pay the balance thereof, if any, to the judgment debtor.

(d) Where an affidavit stating the existence of a judgment for support has been submitted to the Department of Child Support Services, pursuant to subdivision (c) of Section 708.730, to discharge the claim of a judgment debtor, the Controller shall direct payment to the county agency designated by the local child support agency in his or her affidavit.

(e) Where the judgment is for support and the money owed is for lottery winnings or a refund of overpayment of tax, penalty, interest, or interest allowable with respect to an overpayment under Part 10 (commencing with Section 17001) of Division 2 of the Revenue and Taxation Code, and the support obligation is not being enforced pursuant to Section 17400 of the Family Code, the judgment creditor may file the abstract or certified copy of the judgment with the local child support agency of the county in which the support judgment is entered or registered. The local child support agency shall then file the claim of the judgment creditor pursuant to subdivision (c) of Section 708.730. When funds are received by the local child support agency, it shall discharge any claim of the judgment debtor by forwarding those sums to the clerk of the court pursuant to subdivision (c) of this section. Any and all notices otherwise required of a judgment creditor or the clerk of the court, and any litigation to enforce rights under this subdivision shall be the responsibility of the judgment creditor, the same as if service had been directly on the Controller without the intervention of the local child support agency.

(f) Where the claim of the judgment debtor is less than ten dollars ($10) and the claim of the judgment creditor arises under an affidavit filed pursuant to subdivision (c) of Section 708.730, the Controller may disregard the claim of the judgment creditor and forward any and all sums due to the judgment debtor. In the event that there is more than one claimant for a refund, the Franchise Tax Board shall have discretion in allocating the overpayment among claimants.

(g) Should two or more local child support agencies submit claims on behalf of a judgment creditor, the Controller in his or her discretion may select which claim or claims he or she shall honor.

(h) Any claims which are honored in behalf of a judgment creditor shall be considered as refunds of tax overpayments to the judgment debtor.

(i) For purposes of this section, "support" means an obligation owing on behalf of a child, spouse, or family, or combination thereof.[456]

708.750. If money is owing and unpaid to the judgment debtor by a public entity other than a state agency, the judgment creditor shall file the abstract or certified copy of the judgment and the affidavit with the auditor of the public entity or, if there is no auditor, with the official whose duty corresponds to that of auditor. To discharge the claim of the judgment debtor, the auditor or other official shall (1) deposit with the court by a warrant or check payable to the court, the amount due the judgment debtor (after deducting an amount sufficient to reimburse the public entity for any amounts advanced to the judgment debtor or owed by the judgment debtor to the public entity) required to satisfy the money judgment as shown by the affidavit in full or to the greatest extent and (2) pay the balance thereof, if any, to the judgment debtor.[170]

708.755. (a) Upon compliance with this section, the lien of a judgment creditor pursuant to this article is created against a lottery prize to be paid in annual installments and shall continue in force and effect until the judgment is paid or expires, whichever occurs first. For the lien to continue in effect, the judgment creditor shall do all of the following:

(1) Commencing with the second installment against which the judgment lien creditor asserts its lien, annually file with the lottery an affidavit stating that the judgment has not been satisfied and the amount of the remaining unsatisfied judgment, including interest and costs, if any. This affidavit shall be filed with the lottery not less than 45 days, nor more than 90 days, before the annual payment due date on the prize that is the subject of the judgment lien.

(2) If the judgment lien is renewed, file with the lottery a certified copy of the renewal application, as authorized in this code not less than 45 days, nor more than 90 days, before the annual payment due date on the prize that is the subject of the judgment lien, in order for the judgment lien to be effective in continuing the existing judgment lien against the annual lottery prize payments.

(b) If the judgment lien creditor fails to file the annual statement, renewal of judgment, or renewal of abstract, the lien shall expire. Expiration of a[647] lien for failure to comply with this section shall not preclude the judgment creditor from commencing a new procedure under this article to enforce the judgment, to the extent that the judgment otherwise continues to be enforceable under applicable law.[343]

708.760. (a) If the judgment debtor named in the abstract or certified copy of the judgment filed pursuant to this article is a contractor upon a public work, the cost of which is to be paid out of public moneys voted, appropriated, or otherwise set apart for such purpose, only so much of the contract price shall be deemed owing and unpaid within the meaning of Section 708.740 or 708.750 as may remain payable under the terms of the contractor's contract, upon the completion thereof, after deducting sums due and to become due to persons described in Section 9100 of the Civil Code. In ascertaining the sums due or to become due to such persons, only claims which are filed against the moneys due or to become due to the judgment debtor in accordance with Chapter 4 (commencing with Section 9350) of Title 3 of Part 6 of Division 4 of the Civil Code shall be considered.

(b) The Controller, auditor, or other public disbursing officer whose duty it is to make payments under the provisions of the contract may not deposit an amount with the court pursuant to this article until the contract is completed, but may deposit an amount with the court to satisfy the claim of the judgment debtor before the payments specified in subdivision (a) are made so long as a sufficient amount is retained for the satisfaction of the claims of persons described in Section 9100 of the Civil Code.

708.770. (a) Except as provided in subdivision (g), promptly after deposit with the court by the public entity, the court clerk shall cause a notice of deposit to be served on the judgment debtor. Service shall be made personally or by mail.

(b) Within 10 days after service of the notice of deposit pursuant to subdivision (a), the judgment debtor who claims an exemption shall do both of the following:

(1) File with the court a claim of exemption and a notice of motion for an order determining the claim of exemption. The claim of exemption shall include all of the matters set forth in subdivision (b) of Section 703.520.

(2) Serve on the judgment creditor a copy of the notice of motion, a copy of the claim of exemption, and a notice of hearing on the motion. Service shall be made personally or by mail.

(c) The hearing on the motion shall be held not later than 30 days from the date the notice of motion was filed with the court unless continued by the court for good cause.

(d) Within 10 days after the judgment creditor is served under subdivision (b), the judgment creditor who opposes the motion shall do both of the following:

(1) File with the court a notice of opposition to the claim of exemption. The notice of opposition to the claim of exemption shall be executed under oath and shall include all of the matters set forth in Section 703.560.

(2) Serve on the judgment debtor a copy of the notice of opposition to the claim of exemption. Service shall be made personally or by mail.

(e) Subdivisions (a) to (d), inclusive, of Section 703.580 and Sections 703.590 and 703.600 apply to a claim of exemption made pursuant to this section.

(f) The failure of the judgment debtor to make a claim of exemption under this section constitutes a waiver of the exemption.

(g) In lieu of service of the notice of deposit described herein, where a state agency has been served with an affidavit pursuant to subdivision (c) of Section 708.730 and has presented the claim of the judgment creditor to the Controller pursuant to subdivision (a) of Section 708.740, the state agency shall cause a notice of deposit to be sent to the judgment debtor instructing the judgment debtor to file any and all requests for relief with the district attorney who filed the affidavit, or the court clerk if the seizure arises under subdivision (e) of Section 708.740. Except in those cases arising under subdivision (e) of Section 708.740, the judgment debtor shall file the request for relief with the district attorney within 15 days after service of notice from the public agency, or the judgment debtor shall be deemed to have waived any claim he or she might otherwise have. If the matter cannot be resolved with the district attorney, the district attorney shall so advise the judgment debtor and the judgment debtor shall then be authorized to commence proceedings under this section or any other appropriate provision of law. The notice from the district attorney shall for any limitation have the same effect as a notice of deposit un-

der subdivision (a). Service of any notice or request under this subdivision shall be made personally or by mail.
Claims arising from the filing of an abstract or certified copy of a judgment, under subdivision (e) of Section 708.740 shall be governed by the procedure and limitations set forth in subdivisions (a) through (f).[195]

708.775. After the expiration of the period allowed for claiming an exemption under Section 708.770 if no exemption has been claimed, or after the determination of the claim of exemption if an exemption is claimed within the period allowed for claiming the exemption under Section 708.770, the court shall pay the nonexempt portion of the money deposited to which the judgment creditor is entitled to the judgment creditor and the balance thereof, if any, to the judgment debtor, unless some other disposition is required by law.[170]

708.780. (a) Filing of the abstract or certified copy of the judgment and the affidavit pursuant to this article creates a lien on the money owing and unpaid to the judgment debtor by the public entity in an amount equal to that which may properly be applied to the satisfaction of the money judgment under this article.
(b) When an affidavit is filed pursuant to subdivision (c) of Section 708.730, it shall apply to all claims for refund from the Franchise Tax Board under the Personal Income Tax Law, Part 10 (commencing with Section 17001) of Division 2 of the Revenue and Taxation Code, or the Bank and Corporation Tax Law, Part 11 (commencing with Section 23001) of Division 2 of the Revenue and Taxation Code, which the judgment debtor subsequently claims during a period one year after filing of the affidavit, or October 1 of the year following the filing of the affidavit, whichever occurs later, the same as if claims for these overpayments were filed by the judgment debtor with the appropriate state agency on the date the affidavit was filed.
(c) When a request is filed pursuant to subdivision (d) of Section 708.730 with the court, the clerk of the court shall issue a Notice of Support Arrearage. The clerk of the court shall issue the notice 30 days after the request was filed pursuant to subdivision (d) of Section 708.730 without a hearing if no objection has been raised by the judgment debtor pursuant to this subdivision. If an objection has been raised, the notice shall not be ordered until after a hearing. The notice shall contain the name of the person ordered to pay support and his or her social security number; the amount of the arrearage determined by the court; whether the arrearage is for child, spousal, or family support and the specific combination thereof; a statement of how the recipient may challenge the statement of arrearage; and the name, address, and social security number of the person to whom the arrearage is owed. Upon the clerk of the court issuing the Notice of Support Arrearage, a copy of the request, the affidavit, and the notice shall be served by the party who requested the court to issue the Notice of Support Arrearage upon the person ordered to pay support and the Controller. Service may be personal, in accordance with Section 1011, or by mail, in accordance with Section 1013. Service

upon the Controller shall be at the Controller's office in Sacramento.

The judgment debtor may object to the request or affidavit upon any of the following grounds: (1) there is an error in the amount of the arrearage stated in the affidavit; (2) the alleged judgment debtor is not the judgment debtor from whom the support is due; (3) the amount to be intercepted exceeds that allowable under federal law; (4) a default in payment of the support for 30 days has not occurred; or (5) other necessary factual allegations contained in the affidavit are erroneous.

Upon receipt of the Notice of Support Arrearage, the Controller shall take reasonable measures to deduct from any personal income tax refunds and lottery winnings owed and processed for payment to the judgment debtor and deposit with the court a warrant, subject to Sections 708.770 and 708.775, with service of a copy of the warrant upon the local child support agency of the county in which the support judgment is entered, payable to the court, the amount due the judgment creditor (after deducting an amount sufficient to reimburse the state for any amounts advanced to the judgment debtor or owed by the judgment debtor to the state) required to satisfy the money judgment as shown by the affidavit in full or to the greatest extent, and pay the balance thereof, if any, to the judgment debtor. At any hearing pursuant to Section 708.770, the judgment debtor may challenge the distribution of these funds on exemption or other grounds, including, but not limited to, an allegation that the judgment has been satisfied or that service was improper. The notice shall not apply to any money which is exempt by law from execution. The Controller shall determine the cost of enforcing the notice and may establish a notice filing fee not to exceed five dollars ($5).

Service of the Notice of Support Arrearage and of the request and affidavit pursuant to this subdivision creates a lien on the money owing and unpaid to the judgment debtor which shall become effective 30 days following service upon the Controller. This notice shall remain in effect for four years from the date of its issuance or until the arrearage for which the notice was issued is satisfied, whichever occurs first.

Any person who files a request with the court to issue a Notice of Support Arrearage pursuant to subdivision (d) of Section 708.730 shall notify the court and the Controller of any satisfaction of the arrearage after the Notice of Support Arrearage has been issued by the clerk of the court. The notice to the court and the Controller shall be filed with the court and the Controller and served upon the local child support agency of the county in which the support judgment is entered within 30 days of the satisfaction or discharge and shall show a partial or full satisfaction of the arrearage or any other resolution of the arrearage.

Upon filing and service, the Notice of Support Arrearage shall be of no force and effect.

The State Department of Social Services shall, upon request, inform the Legislature of the use and effect of this subdivision on or before December 31, 2001.

This subdivision shall become operative on January 1, 1996, and shall become inoperative on December 31, 2001.
(d) For purposes of this section, "support" means an obligation owing on behalf of a child, spouse, or family, or combination thereof.[409]

708.785. (a) The judgment creditor upon filing the abstract or certified copy of the judgment and the affidavit shall pay a fee of six dollars ($6) to the public entity with which it is filed.
(b) Fees received by the state under this section shall be deposited to the credit of the fund from which payments were, or would be, made on account of collection under this article.[170]

708.790. No public officer or employee is liable for failure to perform a duty imposed by this article unless sufficient information is furnished by the abstract or certified copy of the judgment together with the affidavit to enable the officer or employee in the exercise of reasonable diligence to ascertain the identity of the judgment debtor therefrom and from the papers and records on file in the office in which the officer or employee works. The word "office" as used in this section does not include any branch or subordinate office located in a different city.[170]

708.795. Except as to sums due and unpaid under a judgment for support, nothing in this article authorizes the filing against an overpayment of tax, penalty, or interest, or interest allowable with respect to an overpayment, under Part 10 (commencing with Section 17001), or Part 11 (commencing with Section 23001) of Division 2 of the Revenue and Taxation Code or under Division 6 (commencing with Section 13000) of the Unemployment Insurance Code.[226]

Article 9: Enforcement Against Franchise
Article 9 added by Stats. 1982, Ch. 1364, Sec. 2.

708.910. As used in this article, "franchise" means a franchise granted by a public entity and all the rights and privileges thereof, other than the franchise of being a corporation.[170]

708.920. (a) The court may, in its discretion, order a franchise applied to the satisfaction of a money judgment upon application by the judgment creditor made on noticed motion. The notice of motion shall be served on the judgment debtor and the public entity that granted the franchise. Service shall be made personally or by mail. In exercising its discretion, the court shall determine whether application of the franchise to the satisfaction of the judgment is proper taking into account all the circumstances of the case, including but not limited to the nature of the franchise, whether the franchise is by its terms transferable, and the likelihood that application of the franchise to the satisfaction of the judgment will yield a substantial amount.
(b) If the court orders application of the franchise to the satisfaction of the judgment, application shall be by such means as appears proper to the court, including but not limited to sale of the franchise, assignment of the franchise or proceeds of the franchise, or appointment of a receiver. The court may include in its order, or make additional orders containing, provisions to effectuate the application of the franchise

to the satisfaction of the judgment, including but not limited to provisions relating to the place of sale of the franchise, possession of the property of the judgment debtor necessary for the exercise of the franchise, receipt of proceeds of the franchise, recovery of penalties imposed by law and recoverable for injury to the franchise or for damages or other cause, and the judgment debtor's powers, duties, and liability for penalties and forfeitures.[170]

708.930. Notwithstanding any other provision of this article, an order for application of a franchise to the satisfaction of a money judgment is subject to all applicable laws governing sale, transfer, or other actions concerning the franchise, including but not limited to any necessary approvals by the Public Utilities Commission or local public entities and compliance with statutory or administrative regulations.[170]

Article 10: Other Enforcement Procedures
Article 10 added by Stats. 1982, Ch. 1364, Sec. 2.

709.010. (a) As used in this section, "trust" has the meaning provided in Section 82 of the Probate Code.
(b) The judgment debtor's interest as a beneficiary of a trust is subject to enforcement of a money judgment only upon petition under this section by a judgment creditor to a court having jurisdiction over administration of the trust as prescribed in Part 5 (commencing with Section 17000) of Division 9 of the Probate Code. The judgment debtor's interest in the trust may be applied to the satisfaction of the money judgment by such means as the court, in its discretion, determines are proper, including but not limited to imposition of a lien on or sale of the judgment debtor's interest, collection of trust income, and liquidation and transfer of trust property by the trustee.
(c) Nothing in this section affects the limitations on the enforcement of a money judgment against the judgment debtor's interest in a trust under Chapter 2 (commencing with Section 15300) of Part 2 of Division 9 of the Probate Code, and the provisions of this section are subject to the limitations of that chapter.[250]

709.020. The judgment creditor may apply to the court on noticed motion for an order applying to the satisfaction of a money judgment a contingent remainder, executory interest, or other interest of the judgment debtor in property that is not vested in the judgment debtor. The interest of the judgment debtor may be applied to the satisfaction of the money judgment by such means as the court, in its discretion, determines are proper to protect the interests of both the judgment debtor and judgment creditor, including but not limited to the imposition of a lien on or the sale of the judgment debtor's interest.[170]

709.030. Property in a guardianship or conservatorship estate is not subject to enforcement of a money judgment by a procedure provided in this division, but the judgment creditor may apply to the court in which the guardianship or conservatorship proceeding is pending under Division 4 (commencing with Section 1400) of the Probate Code for an order requiring payment of the judgment.[170]

ENDNOTES

[1]Enacted 1872.

[2]Amended by Code Amendments 1873-74, Ch. 383.

[3]Amended by Code Amendments 1875-76, Ch. 517.

[4]Amended by Code Amendments 1880, Ch. 15.

[5]Amended by Code Amendments 1880, Ch. 21.

[6]Repealed and added by Code Amendments 1880, Ch. 35.

[7]Amended by Stats. 1897, Ch. 21.

[8]Amended by Stats. 1897, Ch. 47.

[9]Amended by Stats. 1907, Ch. 272.

[10]Amended by Stats. 1907, Ch. 372.

[11]Amended by Stats. 1907, Ch. 380.

[12]Amended by Stats. 1911, Ch. 733.

[13]Amended by Stats. 1917, Ch. 217.

[14]Added by Stats. 1921, Ch. 384.

[15]Amended by Stats. 1933, Ch. 742.

[16]Amended by Stats. 1933, Ch. 743.

[17]Added by Stats. 1933, Ch. 744.

[18]Amended by Stats. 1933, Ch. 744

[19]Amended by Stats. 1939, Ch. 63.

[20]Amended by Stats. 1939, Ch. 753.

[21]Added by Stats. 1939, Ch. 806.

[22]Amended by Stats. 1943, Ch. 151.

[23]Amended by Stats. 1943, Ch. 405.

[24]Added by Stats. 1945, Ch. 360.

[25]Added by Stats. 1947, Ch. 306.

[26]Amended by Stats. 1947, Ch. 984.

[27]Amended by Stats. 1947, Ch. 990.

[28]Added by Stats. 1951, Ch. 655.

[29]Amended by Stats. 1951, Ch. 1737.

[30]Added by Stats. 1953, Ch. 52.

[31]Added by Stats. 1953, Ch. 328.

[32]Amended by Stats. 1953, Ch. 655.

[33]Added by Stats. 1955, Ch. 59.

[34]Amended by Stats. 1955, Ch. 208.

[35]Amended by Stats. 1955, Ch. 417.

[36]Amended by Stats. 1955, Ch. 886.

[37]Amended by Stats. 1957, Ch. 719.

[38]Added by Stats. 1957, Ch. 1345.

[39]Amended by Stats. 1957, Ch. 1365.

[40]Added by Stats. 1957, Ch. 1498.

[41]Amended by Stats. 1957, Ch. 1698.

[42]Added by Stats. 1959, Ch. 426.

[43]Amended by Stats. 1959, Ch. 594.

[44]Amended by Stats. 1961, Ch. 435.

[45]Added by Stats. 1961, Ch. 727.

[46]Added by Stats. 1961, Ch. 1370.

[47]Amended by Stats. 1963, Ch. 99.

[48]Added by Stats. 1963, Ch. 882.

[49]Added by Stats. 1963, Ch. 1471.

[50]Amended by Stats. 1963, Ch. 1715.

[51]Added by Stats. 1963, Ch. 1715.

[52]Amended by Stats. 1963, Ch. 1762.

[53]Added by Stats. 1965, Ch. 299.

[54]Amended by Stats. 1965, Ch. 841.

[55]Added by Stats. 1965, Ch. 1890.

[56]Added by Stats. 1965, Ch. 1989.

[57]Amended by Stats. 1965, Ch. 299.

[58]Amended by Stats. 1965, Ch. 894.

[59]Amended by Stats. 1965, Ch. 2044.

[60]Added by Stats. 1967, Ch. 17.

[61]Amended by Stats. 1967, Ch. 17.

[62]Added by renumbering Section 48 by Stats. 1967, Ch. 17.

[63]Added by renumbering Section 53 by Stats. 1967, Ch. 17.

[64]Added by renumbering Section 61.4 by Stats. 1967, Ch. 17.

[65]Amended by Stats. 1967, Ch. 72.

[66]Amended by Stats. 1967, Ch. 161.

[67]Added by Stats. 1967, Ch. 1326.

[68]Added by Stats. 1968, Ch. 387.

[69]Amended by Stats. 1968, Ch. 698.

[70]Amended by Stats. 1969, Ch. 1608.

[71]Added by Stats. 1969, Ch. 1610.

[72]Added by Stats. 1970, Ch. 89.

[73]Added by Stats. 1971, Ch. 244.

[74]Amended by Stats. 1971, Ch. 244.

[75]Added by Stats. 1971, Ch. 1661.

[76]Repealed and added by Stats. 1972, Ch. 73.

[77]Added by Stats. 1972, Ch. 118.

[78]Amended by Stats. 1972, Ch. 579.

[79]Added by Stats. 1972, Ch. 594.

[80]Amended by Stats. 1972, Ch. 594.

[81]Amended by Stats. 1972, Ch. 601.

[82]Added by Stats. 1972, Ch. 1162.

[83]Amended by Stats. 1972, Ch. 719.

[84]Added by Stats. 1972, Ch. 1057.

[85]Added by Stats. 1973, Ch. 526.

[86]Amended by Stats. 1974, Ch. 429.

[87]Amended by Stats. 1974, Ch. 273.

[88]Added by Stats. 1974, Ch. 332.

[89]Added by Stats. 1974, Ch. 1516.

[90]Added by Stats. 1975, 2nd Ex. Sess., Ch. 1.

[91]Amended by Stats. 1975, 2nd Ex. Sess., Ch. 2.

[92]Added by Stats. 1975, Ch. 301.

[93]Amended by Stats. 1975, Ch. 670.

[94]Added by Stats. 1975, Ch. 1156.

[95]Added by Stats. 1975, Ch. 1240.

[96]Amended by Stats. 1975, Ch. 1240.

[97]Amended by Stats. 1975, Ch. 1241.

[98]Amended by Stats. 1976, Ch. 145.

[99]Added by Stats. 1976, Ch. 282.

[100]Added by Stats. 1976, Ch. 437.

[101]Amended by Stats. 1976, Ch. 437.

[102]Amended by Stats. 1976, Ch. 789.

[103]Added by Stats. 1977, Ch. 7.

[104]Amended by Stats. 1977, Ch. 93.

[105]Amended by Stats. 1977, Ch. 235.

[106]Added by Stats. 1977, Ch. 499.

[107]Amended by Stats. 1978, Ch. 1305.

[108]Amended by Stats. 1979, Ch. 173.

[109]Amended by Stats. 1979, Ch. 177.

[110]Amended by Stats. 1979, Ch. 349.

[111]Added by Stats. 1979, Ch. 513.

[112]Amended by Stats. 1980, Ch. 124, Sec. 2.

[113]Amended by Stats. 1981, Ch. 88, Sec. 1.

[114]Amended by Stats. 1981, Ch. 714, Sec. 68.

[115]Amended by Stats. 1981, Ch. 900, Sec. 2.

[116]Amended by Stats. 1981, Ch. 900, Sec. 4.

[117]Amended by Stats. 1981, Ch. 900, Sec. 5.

[118]Added by Stats. 1982, Ch. 106, Sec. 1.

[119]Amended by Stats. 1982, Ch. 517, Sec. 118.

[120]Amended by Stats. 1982, Ch. 517, Sec. 125.

[121]Amended by Stats. 1982, Ch. 249, Sec. 1.

[122]Amended by Stats. 1982, Ch. 497, Sec. 32. Operative July 1, 1983, by Sec. 185 of Ch. 497.

[123]Amended by Stats. 1982, Ch. 497, Sec. 33. Operative July 1, 1983, by Sec. 185 of Ch. 497.

[124]Amended by Stats. 1982, Ch. 497, Sec. 37. Operative July 1, 1983, by Sec. 185 of Ch. 497.

[125]Amended by Stats. 1982, Ch. 517, Sec. 107.

[126]Amended by Stats. 1982, Ch. 497, Sec. 35. Operative July 1, 1983, by Sec. 185 of Ch. 497.

[127]Amended by Stats. 1982, Ch. 517, Sec. 114.

[128]Amended by Stats. 1982, Ch. 517, Sec. 115.

[129]Amended by Stats. 1982, Ch. 517, Sec. 119.

[130]Amended by Stats. 1982, Ch. 517, Sec. 127.

[131]Amended by Stats. 1982, Ch. 517, Sec. 128.

[132]Amended by Stats. 1982, Ch. 517, Sec. 129.

[133]Added by Stats. 1982, Ch. 704, Sec. 4.

[134]Amended by Stats. 1982, Ch. 704, Sec. 9.

[135]Added by Stats. 1982, Ch. 1198, Sec. 5. Operative July 1, 1983, by Sec. 70 of Ch. 1198.

[136]Amended by Stats. 1982, Ch. 1198, Sec. 8. Operative July 1, 1983, by Sec. 70 of Ch. 1198.

[137]Added by Stats. 1982, Ch. 1198, Sec. 9. Operative July 1, 1983, by Sec. 70 of Ch. 1198.

[138]Added by Stats. 1982, Ch. 1198, Sec. 15. Operative July 1, 1983, by Sec. 70 of Ch. 1198.

[139]Added by Stats. 1982, Ch. 1198, Sec. 16. Operative July 1, 1983, by Sec. 70 of Ch. 1198.

[140]Added by Stats. 1982, Ch. 1198, Sec. 17. Operative July 1, 1983, by Sec. 70 of Ch. 1198.

[141]Added by Stats. 1982, Ch. 1198, Sec. 18. Operative July 1, 1983, by Sec. 70 of Ch. 1198.

[142]Added by Stats. 1982, Ch. 1198, Sec. 20. Operative July 1, 1983, by Sec. 70 of Ch. 1198.

[143]Added by Stats. 1982, Ch. 1198, Sec. 21. Operative July 1, 1983, by Sec. 70 of Ch. 1198.

[144]Amended by Stats. 1982, Ch. 1198, Sec. 23. Operative July 1, 1983, by Sec. 70 of Ch. 1198.

[145]Amended by Stats. 1982, Ch. 1198, Sec. 25. Operative July 1, 1983, by Sec. 70 of Ch. 1198.

[146]Amended by Stats. 1982, Ch. 1198, Sec. 26. Operative July 1, 1983, by Sec. 70 of Ch. 1198.

[147]Amended by Stats. 1982, Ch. 1198, Sec. 30. Operative July 1, 1983, by Sec. 70 of Ch. 1198.

[148]Amended by Stats. 1982, Ch. 1198, Sec. 34. Operative July 1, 1983, by Sec. 70 of Ch. 1198.

[149]Amended by Stats. 1982, Ch. 1198, Sec. 35. Operative July 1, 1983, by Sec. 70 of Ch. 1198.

[150]Amended by Stats. 1982, Ch. 1198, Sec. 36. Operative July 1, 1983, by Sec. 70 of Ch. 1198.

[151]Amended by Stats. 1982, Ch. 1198, Sec. 37. Operative July 1, 1983, by Sec. 70 of Ch. 1198.

[152]Amended by Stats. 1982, Ch. 1198, Sec. 39. Operative July 1, 1983, by Sec. 70 of Ch. 1198.

[153]Amended by Stats. 1982, Ch. 1198, Sec. 41. Operative July 1, 1983, by Sec. 70 of Ch. 1198.

[154]Amended by Stats. 1982, Ch. 1198, Sec. 42.5. Operative July 1, 1983, by Sec. 70 of Ch. 1198.

[155]Amended by Stats. 1982, Ch. 1198, Sec. 43. Operative July 1, 1983, by Sec. 70 of Ch. 1198.

[156]Amended by Stats. 1982, Ch. 1198, Sec. 44. Operative July 1, 1983, by Sec. 70 of Ch. 1198.

[157]Amended by Stats. 1982, Ch. 1198, Sec. 46. Operative July 1, 1983, by Sec. 70 of Ch. 1198.

[158]Added by Stats. 1982, Ch. 1198, Sec. 48. Operative July 1, 1983, by Sec. 70 of Ch. 1198.

[159]Added by Stats. 1982, Ch. 1198, Sec. 50. Operative July 1, 1983, by Sec. 70 of Ch. 1198.

[160]Repealed and added by Stats. 1982, Ch. 1198, Sec. 50. Operative July 1, 1983, by Sec. 70 of Ch. 1198.

[161]Amended by Stats. 1982, Ch. 1198, Sec. 52. Operative July 1, 1983, by Sec. 70 of Ch. 1198.

[162]Amended by Stats. 1982, Ch. 1198, Sec. 53. Operative July 1, 1983, by Sec. 70 of Ch. 1198.

[163]Amended by Stats. 1982, Ch. 1198, Sec. 60. Operative July 1, 1983, by Sec. 70 of Ch. 1198.

[164]Added by Stats. 1982, Ch. 1518, Sec. 1.

[165]Amended by Stats. 1982, Ch. 1198, Sec. 54. Operative July 1, 1983, by Sec. 70 of Ch. 1198.

[166]Added by Stats. 1982, Ch. 1198, Sec. 57. Operative July 1, 1983, by Sec. 70 of Ch. 1198.

[167]Amended by Stats. 1982, Ch. 1198, Sec. 59. Operative July 1, 1983, by Sec. 70 of Ch. 1198.

[168]Amended by Stats. 1982, Ch. 1198, Sec. 61. Operative July 1, 1983, by Sec. 70 of Ch. 1198.

[169]Amended by Stats. 1982, Ch. 1198, Sec. 62.5. Operative July 1, 1983, by Sec. 70 of Ch. 1198.

[170]Added by Stats. 1982, Ch. 1364, Sec. 2. Operative July 1, 1983, by Sec. 3 of Ch. 1364

[171]Repealed and added by Stats. 1982, Ch. 1364, Sec. 2. Operative July 1, 1983, by Sec. 3 of Ch. 1364.

[172]Added by Stats. 1982, Ch. 1581, Sec. 1

[173]Added by Stats. 1982, Ch. 1624, Sec. 1.

[174]Amended by Stats. 1982, Ch. 1642, Sec. 1. Operative June 6, 1984, pursuant to Sec. 3 of Ch. 1642.

[175]Amended by Stats. 1983, Ch. 102, Sec. 2. Effective June 16, 1983.

[176]Amended by Stats. 1983, Ch. 102, Sec. 3. Effective June 16, 1983.

[177]Amended by Stats. 1983, Ch. 155, Sec. 4. Effective June 30, 1983. Operative July 1, 1983, by Sec. 32 of Ch. 155.

[178]Amended by Stats. 1983, Ch. 155, Sec. 5.5. Effective June 30, 1983. Operative July 1, 1983, by Sec. 32 of Ch. 155.

[179]Added by Stats. 1983, Ch. 155, Sec. 8.3. Effective June 30, 1983. Operative July 1, 1983, by Sec. 32 of Ch. 155.

[180]Amended by Stats. 1983, Ch. 155, Sec. 9.5. Effective June 30, 1983. Operative July 1, 1983, by Sec. 32 of Ch. 155.

[181]Amended by Stats. 1983, Ch. 155, Sec. 10. Effective June 30, 1983. Operative July 1, 1983, by Sec. 32 of Ch. 155.

[182]Amended by Stats. 1983, Ch. 155, Sec. 11. Effective June 30, 1983. Operative July 1, 1983, by Sec. 32 of Ch. 155.

[183]Added by Stats. 1983, Ch. 155, Sec. 14.6. Effective June 30, 1983. Operative July 1, 1983, by Sec. 32 of Ch. 155.

[184]Amended by Stats. 1983, Ch. 155, Sec. 14.7. Effective June 30, 1983. Operative July 1, 1983, by Sec. 32 of Ch. 155.

[185]Added by Stats. 1983, Ch. 155, Sec. 15. Effective June 30, 1983. Operative July 1, 1983, by Sec. 32 of Ch. 155.

[186]Amended by Stats. 1983, Ch. 155, Sec. 19. Effective June 30, 1983. Operative July 1, 1983, by Sec. 32 of Ch. 155.

[187]Amended by Stats. 1983, Ch. 176, Sec. 1.

[188]Amended by Stats. 1983, Ch. 176, Sec. 2.

[189]Added by Stats. 1983, Ch. 254, Sec. 3.

[190]Added by Stats. 1983, Ch. 279, Sec. 1.

[191]Added by Stats. 1983, Ch. 279, Sec. 2.

[192]Added by Stats. 1983, Ch. 279, Sec. 3.

[193]Amended by Stats. 1983, Ch. 464, Sec. 1.

[194]Amended by Stats. 1983, Ch. 938, Sec. 1. Effective September 20, 1983.

[195]Amended by Stats. 1983, Ch. 1010, Sec. 3.

[196]Amended by Stats. 1983, Ch. 1124, Sec. 10.

[197]Amended by Stats. 1983, Ch. 1167, Sec. 2.

[198] Amended by Stats. 1983, Ch. 1167, Sec. 4.

[199]Amended by Stats. 1983, Ch. 1167, Sec. 8.

[200]Amended by Stats. 1983, Ch. 1167, Sec. 9.

[201]Amended by Stats. 1983, Ch. 1159, Sec. 11. Operative July 1, 1984, by Sec. 17 of Ch. 1159.

[202]Amended by Stats. 1984, Ch. 191, Sec. 1.

[203]Added by Stats. 1984, Ch. 454, Sec. 2.

[204]Amended by Stats. 1984, Ch. 538, Sec. 2.

[205]Amended by Stats. 1984, Ch. 538, Sec. 2.5.

[206]Amended by Stats. 1984, Ch. 538, Sec. 6.5.

[207]Repealed and added by Stats. 1984, Ch. 538, Sec. 6.3.

[208]Amended by Stats. 1984, Ch. 538, Sec. 7.

[209]Amended by Stats. 1984, Ch. 538, Sec. 7.5.

[210]Amended by Stats. 1984, Ch. 538, Sec. 8.

[211]Added by Stats. 1984, Ch. 538, Sec. 9.

[212]Amended by Stats. 1984, Ch. 538, Sec. 10.

[213]Added by Stats. 1984, Ch. 538, Sec. 11.

[214]Amended by Stats. 1984, Ch. 538, Sec. 14.

[215]Amended by Stats. 1984, Ch. 538, Sec. 17.

[216]Amended by Stats. 1984, Ch. 538, Sec. 18.

[217]Amended by Stats. 1984, Ch. 538, Sec. 19.

[218]Amended by Stats. 1984, Ch. 538, Sec. 25.3.

[219]Added by Stats. 1984, Ch. 538, Sec. 25.5.

[220]Amended by Stats. 1984, Ch. 538, Sec. 26.

[221]Added by Stats. 1984, Ch. 538, Sec. 27.

[222]Amended by Stats. 1984, Ch. 538, Sec. 31.

[223]Amended by Stats. 1984, Ch. 538, Sec. 32.

[224]Added by Stats. 1984, Ch. 759, Sec. 1.

[225]Amended by Stats. 1984, Ch. 797, Sec. 1.

[226]Amended by Stats. 1984, Ch. 1007, Sec. 3.

[227]Repealed and added by Stats. 1984, Ch. 1555, Sec. 2.

[228]Amended by Stats. 1984, Ch. 1730, Sec. 6.

[229]Added by Stats. 1984, Ch. 1555, Sec. 6.

[230]Added by Stats. 1984, Ch. 1555, Sec. 8.

[231]Added by Stats. 1984, Ch. 1671, Sec. 20.

[232]Added by Stats. 1984, Ch. 1705, Sec. 5.

[233]Added by Stats. 1985, Ch. 41, Sec. 2.

[234]Amended by Stats. 1985, Ch. 41, Sec. 7.

[235]Amended by Stats. 1985, Ch. 41, Sec. 8.

[236]Added by Stats. 1985, Ch. 1450, Sec. 2. Operative January 1, 1989, by Sec. 6 of Ch. 1450.

[237]Repealed and added by Stats. 1985, Ch. 1450, Sec. 2. Operative January 1, 1989, by Sec. 6 of Ch. 1450.

[238]Amended by Stats. 1986, Ch. 383, Sec. 7.

[239]Amended by Stats. 1986, Ch. 540, Sec. 2.

[240]Amended by Stats. 1986, Ch. 540, Sec. 4.

[241]Amended by Stats. 1986, Ch. 540, Sec. 5.

[242]Amended by Stats. 1986, Ch. 540, Sec. 6.

[243]Added by Stats. 1986, Ch. 540, Sec. 10.

[244]Amended by Stats. 1986, Ch. 540, Sec. 11.

[245]Amended by Stats. 1986, Ch. 540, Sec. 12.

[246]Amended by Stats. 1986, Ch. 540, Sec. 13.

[247]Amended by Stats. 1986, Ch. 953, Sec. 3.

[248]Amended by Stats. 1986, Ch. 820, Sec. 16. Operative July 1, 1987, by Sec. 43 of Ch. 820.

[249]Amended by Stats. 1986, Ch. 820, Sec. 17. Operative July 1, 1987, by Sec. 43 of Ch. 820.

[250]Amended by Stats. 1986, Ch. 820, Sec. 18. Operative July 1, 1987, by Sec. 43 of Ch. 820.

[251]Amended by Stats. 1986, Ch. 1045, Sec. 1.

[252]Added by Stats. 1987, Ch. 62, Sec. 1.

[253]Added by Stats. 1987, Ch. 88, Sec. 1. Effective July 2, 1987.

[254]Amended by Stats. 1987, Ch. 254, Sec. 1.

[255]Amended by Stats. 1987, Ch. 1080, Sec. 4.

[256]Amended by Stats. 1988, Ch. 727, Sec. 1.

[257]Amended by Stats. 1988, Ch. 1205, Sec. 1.

[258]Amended by Stats. 1988, Ch. 1199, Sec. 2. Operative July 1, 1989, by Sec. 119 of Ch. 1199.

[259]Amended by Stats. 1988, Ch. 1199, Sec. 6. Operative July 1, 1989, by Sec. 119 of Ch. 1199.

[260]Added by Stats. 1988, Ch. 1245, Sec. 2.

[261]Repealed and added by Stats. 1988, Ch. 1245, Sec. 2.

[262]Added by Stats. 1988, Ch. 1410, Sec. 1.

[263]Amended by Stats. 1989, Ch. 445, Sec. 1.

[264]Amended by Stats. 1989, Ch. 693, Sec. 2.

[265]Amended by Stats. 1989, Ch. 1416, Sec. 13.

[266]Amended by Stats. 1989, Ch. 1416, Sec. 21.

[267]Amended by Stats. 1989, Ch. 1416, Sec. 22.

[268]Amended by Stats. 1989, Ch. 1417, Sec. 1.

[269]Amended by Stats. 1989, Ch. 1417, Sec. 2.

[270]Amended (as added by Stats. 1990, Ch. 1125, Sec. 1.5) by Stats. 1999, Ch. 991, Sec. 24.5. Effective January 1, 2000. Amending action operative July 1, 2001, by Sec. 75 of Ch. 991. Section initially operative (in amended form) January 1, 2002, pursuant to Stats.

1990, Ch. 1125, Sec. 5, as amended by Stats. 1998, Ch. 932.

[271]Added by Stats. 1990, Ch. 1232, Sec. 1.

[272]Added by Stats. 1990, Ch. 1305, Sec. 3. Note: Prior to 1991, this subject matter was in Chapter 5A, comprising Sections 116 to 117.24.

[273]Added by Stats. 1990, Ch. 1305, Sec. 3.

[274]Amended (as added by Stats. 1990, Ch. 1305) by Stats. 1990, Ch. 1683, Sec. 6.

[275]Amended by Stats. 1990, Ch. 1491, Sec. 6.

[276]Added by Stats. 1990, Ch. 1683, Sec. 5.

[277]Added by Stats. 1991, Ch. 915, Sec. 2.

[278]Amended by Stats. 1991, Ch. 915, Sec. 12.

[279]Amended by Stats. 1991, Ch. 915, Sec. 13.

[280]Added by Stats. 1991, Ch. 915, Sec. 17.

[281]Amended by Stats. 1991, Ch. 915, Sec. 20.

[282]Amended by Stats. 1991, Ch. 915, Sec. 21.

[283]Amended by Stats. 1991, Ch. 915, Sec. 22.

[284]Amended by Stats. 1991, Ch. 915, Sec. 23.

[285]Amended by Stats. 1991, Ch. 915, Sec. 27.

[286]Amended by Stats. 1991, Ch. 915, Sec. 28.

[287]Amended by Stats. 1991, Ch. 915, Sec. 30.

[288]Amended by Stats. 1991, Ch. 915, Sec. 31.

[289]Amended by Stats. 1991, Ch. 915, Sec. 35.

[290]Added by Stats. 1991, Ch. 932, Sec. 1.

[291]Amended by Stats. 1991, Ch. 1090, Sec. 2.

[292]Amended by Stats. 1991, Ch. 1090, Sec. 3.

[293]Added by Stats. 1992, Ch. 163, Sec. 16. Effective January 1, 1993. Operative January 1, 1994, by Sec. 161 of Ch. 163.

[294]Amended by Stats. 1992, Ch. 163, Sec. 19. Effective January 1, 1993. Operative January 1, 1994, by Sec. 161 of Ch. 163.

[295]Added by Stats. 1992, Ch. 163, Sec. 29. Effective January 1, 1993. Operative January 1, 1994, by Sec. 161 of Ch. 163.

[296]Amended by Stats. 1992, Ch. 163, Sec. 32. Effective January 1, 1993. Operative January 1, 1994, by Sec. 161 of Ch. 163.

[297]Amended by Stats. 1992, Ch. 163, Sec. 33. Effective January 1, 1993. Operative January 1, 1994, by Sec. 161 of Ch. 163.

[298]Amended by Stats. 1992, Ch. 163, Sec. 37. Effective January 1, 1993. Operative January 1, 1994, by Sec. 161 of Ch. 163.

[299]Amended by Stats. 1992, Ch. 163, Sec. 44. Effective January 1, 1993. Operative January 1, 1994, by Sec. 161 of Ch. 163.

[300]Amended by Stats. 1992, Ch. 163, Sec. 46. Effective January 1, 1993. Operative January 1, 1994, by Sec. 161 of Ch. 163.

[301]Amended by Stats. 1992, Ch. 163, Sec. 47. Effective January 1, 1993. Operative January 1, 1994, by Sec. 161 of Ch. 163.

[302]Amended by Stats. 1992, Ch. 163, Sec. 48. Effective January 1, 1993. Operative January 1, 1994, by Sec. 161 of Ch. 163.

[303]Amended by Stats. 1992, Ch. 163, Sec. 49. Effective January 1, 1993. Operative January 1, 1994, by Sec. 161 of Ch. 163.

[304]Amended by Stats. 1992, Ch. 163, Sec. 51. Effective January 1, 1993. Operative January 1, 1994, by Sec. 161 of Ch. 163.

[305]Amended by Stats. 1992, Ch. 178, Sec. 7. Effective January 1, 1993.

[306]Added by Stats. 1992, Ch. 178, Sec. 8. Effective January 1, 1993.

[307]Amended by Stats. 1992, Ch. 178, Sec. 10. Effective January 1, 1993.

[308]Added by Stats. 1992, Ch. 178, Sec. 11. Effective January 1, 1993.

[309]Amended by Stats. 1992, Ch. 178, Sec. 12. Effective January 1, 1993.

[310]Added by Stats. 1992, Ch. 178, Sec. 13. Effective January 1, 1993.

[311]Added by Stats. 1992, Ch. 178, Sec. 17. Effective January 1, 1993.

[312]Amended by Stats. 1992, Ch. 178, Sec. 18. Effective January 1, 1993.

[313]Added by Stats. 1992, Ch. 178, Sec. 20. Effective January 1, 1993.

[314]Added by Stats. 1992, Ch. 283, Sec. 6. Effective July 21, 1992.

[315]Repealed and added by Stats. 1992, Ch. 283, Sec. 9. Effective July 21, 1992.

[316]Added by Stats. 1992, Ch. 283, Sec. 11. Effective July 21, 1992.

[317]Added by Stats. 1992, Ch. 283, Sec. 12. Effective July 21, 1992.

[318]Added by Stats. 1992, Ch. 615, Sec. 5. Effective January 1, 1993.

[319]Added by Stats. 1992, Ch. 883, Sec. 2. Effective January 1, 1993.

[320]Amended by Stats. 1992, Ch. 876, Sec. 5. Effective January 1, 1993.

[321]Amended by Stats. 1992, Ch. 1348, Sec. 3. Effective January 1, 1993.

[322]Amended by Stats. 1993, Ch. 226, Sec. 5. Effective January 1, 1994.

[323]Amended by Stats. 1993, Ch. 456, Sec. 3.5. Effective January 1, 1994.

[324]Amended by Stats. 1993, Ch. 456, Sec. 7. Effective January 1, 1994.

[325]Amended by Stats. 1993, Ch. 456, Sec. 9. Effective January 1, 1994.

[326]Amended by Stats. 1993, Ch. 589, Sec. 25. Effective January 1, 1994.

[327]Amended by Stats. 1993, Ch. 876, Sec. 9. Effective October 6, 1993.

[328]Amended by Stats. 1993, Ch. 836, Sec. 2. Effective January 1, 1994.

[329]Amended by Stats. 1993, Ch. 1187, Sec. 1.5. Effective January 1, 1994.

[330]Repealed and added by Stats. 1992, Ch. 178, Sec. 26. Effective January 1, 1993.

[331]Amended by Stats. 1994, Ch. 75, Sec. 1. Effective May 20, 1994.

[332]Amended by Stats. 1994, Ch. 146, Sec. 20. Effective January 1, 1995.

[333]Amended by Stats. 1994, Ch. 156, Sec. 1. Effective July 11, 1994.

[334]Amended by Stats. 1994, Ch. 231, Sec. 1. Effective January 1, 1995.

[335]Amended by Stats. 1994, Ch. 493, Sec. 2. Effective September 12, 1994.

[336]Amended by Stats. 1994, Ch. 1010, Sec. 58. Effective January 1, 1995.

[337]Amended by Stats. 1994, Ch. 1010, Sec. 59. Effective January 1, 1995.

[338]Amended by Stats. 1994, Ch. 1010, Sec. 60. Effective January 1, 1995.

[339]Added by Stats. 1994, Ch. 1083, Sec. 3. Effective January 1, 1995.

[340]Added by Stats. 1994, Ch. 1083, Sec. 5. Effective January 1, 1995.

[341]Amended by Stats. 1994, Ch. 1269, Sec. 2.8. Effective January 1, 1995.

[342]Amended by Stats. 1995, Ch. 196, Sec. 8. Effective July 31, 1995.

[343]Added by renumbering Section 708.750 (as added by Stats. 1995, Ch.

363) by Stats. 1996, Ch. 124, Sec. 14. Effective January 1, 1997.

[344]Added by Stats. 1995, Ch. 366, Sec. 2. Effective January 1, 1996.

[345]Amended by Stats. 1995, Ch. 446, Sec. 2. Effective January 1, 1996.

[346]Amended by Stats. 1995, Ch. 576, Sec. 3. Effective January 1, 1996.

[347]Amended by Stats. 1995, Ch. 576, Sec. 3.6. Effective January 1, 1996.

[348]Amended by Stats. 1995, Ch. 583, Sec. 1. Effective January 1, 1996.

[349]Amended (as amended by Stats. 1995, Ch. 591, Sec. 1) by Stats. 1997, Ch. 222, Sec. 1. Effective January 1, 1998.

[350]Amended (as amended by Stats. 1995, Ch. 591, Sec. 3) by Stats. 1997, Ch. 222, Sec. 4. Effective January 1, 1998.

[351]Amended by Stats. 1995, Ch. 796, Sec. 4. Effective January 1, 1996.

[352]Added by Stats. 1995, Ch. 796, Sec. 5. Effective January 1, 1996.

[353]Repealed and added by Stats. 1995, Ch. 796, Sec. 8. Effective January 1, 1996.

[354]Repealed (in Sec. 4) and added by Stats. 1994, Ch. 1062, Sec. 5. Effective January 1, 1995. Section operative January 1, 1999, by its own provisions.

[355]Amended by Stats. 1995, Ch. 796, Sec. 12. Effective January 1, 1996.

[356]Amended by Stats. 1996, Ch. 57, Sec. 1. Effective June 6, 1996.

[357]Amended by Stats. 1996, Ch. 176, Sec. 2. Effective January 1, 1997.

[358]Amended by Stats. 1996, Ch. 176, Sec. 3. Effective January 1, 1997.

[359]Amended by Stats. 1996, Ch. 497, Sec. 1.5. Effective January 1, 1997.

[360]Amended by Stats. 1996, Ch. 497, Sec. 3. Effective January 1, 1997.

[361]Amended by Stats. 1996, Ch. 713, Sec. 4. Effective September 23, 1996.

[362]Amended by Stats. 1996, Ch. 713, Sec. 6. Effective September 23, 1996.

[363]Amended by Stats. 1996, Ch. 713, Sec. 7. Effective September 23, 1996.

[364]Amended by Stats. 1996, Ch. 636, Sec. 2. Effective September 19, 1996.

[365]Amended by Stats. 1996, Ch. 872, Sec. 6. Effective January 1, 1997.

[366]Amended by Stats. 1996, Ch. 872, Sec. 7. Effective January 1, 1997.

[367]Amended by Stats. 1996, Ch. 872, Sec. 11. Effective January 1, 1997.

[368]Amended by Stats. 1996, Ch. 872, Sec. 12. Effective January 1, 1997.

[369]Amended by Stats. 1996, Ch. 872, Sec. 14. Effective January 1, 1997.

[370]Amended by Stats. 1996, Ch. 872, Sec. 15. Effective January 1, 1997.

[371]Amended by Stats. 1996, Ch. 872, Sec. 16. Effective January 1, 1997.

[372]Amended by Stats. 1996, Ch. 927, Sec. 1.5. Effective January 1, 1997.

[373]Added by Stats. 1996, Ch. 957, Sec. 4. Effective January 1, 1997.

[374]Amended by Stats. 1996, Ch. 1159, Sec. 10. Effective January 1, 1997.

[375]Amended by Stats. 1996, Ch. 1159, Sec. 11. Effective January 1, 1997.

[376]Added by Stats. 1997, Ch. 222, Sec. 3. Effective January 1, 1998.

[377]Amended by Stats. 1997, Ch. 222, Sec. 6. Effective January 1, 1998.

[378]Amended by Stats. 1997, Ch. 222, Sec. 7. Effective January 1, 1998.

[379]Amended by Stats. 1997, Ch. 222, Sec. 8. Effective January 1, 1998.

[380]Amended by Stats. 1997, Ch. 222, Sec. 9. Effective January 1, 1998.

[381]Amended by Stats. 1997, Ch. 222, Sec. 10. Effective January 1, 1998.

[382]Amended by Stats. 1997, Ch. 510, Sec. 1. Effective January 1, 1998.

[383]Amended by Stats. 1998, Ch. 14, Sec. 3. Effective January 1, 1999.

[384]Amended by Stats. 1998, Ch. 123, Sec. 1. Effective January 1, 1999.

[385]Amended by Stats. 1998, Ch. 200, Sec. 1. Effective January 1, 1999.

[386]Added by Stats. 1998, Ch. 706, Sec. 2. Effective September 22, 1998.

[387]Added by Stats. 1998, Ch. 706, Sec. 3. Effective September 22, 1998.

[388]Added by Stats. 1998, Ch. 856, Sec. 1. Effective January 1, 1999.

[389]Amended by Stats. 1998, Ch. 931, Sec. 36. Effective September 28, 1998.

[390]Amended by Stats. 1998, Ch. 931, Sec. 37. Effective September 28, 1998.

[391]Amended by Stats. 1998, Ch. 931, Sec. 39. Effective September 28, 1998.

[392]Amended by Stats. 1998, Ch. 931, Sec. 48. Effective September 28, 1998.

[393]Amended by Stats. 1998, Ch. 931, Sec. 79. Effective September 28, 1998.

[394]Added by Stats. 1998, Ch. 931, Sec. 80. Effective September 28, 1998.

[395]Amended by Stats. 1998, Ch. 931, Sec. 90. Effective September 28, 1998.

[396]Amended by Stats. 1998, Ch. 931, Sec. 92. Effective September 28, 1998.

[397]Amended by Stats. 1998, Ch. 931, Sec. 93. Effective September 28, 1998.

[398]Amended by Stats. 1998, Ch. 931, Sec. 95. Effective September 28, 1998.

[399]Amended by Stats. 1998, Ch. 932, Sec. 14. Effective January 1, 1999.

[400]Amended by Stats. 1998, Ch. 932, Sec. 15. Effective January 1, 1999.

[401]Amended by Stats. 1998, Ch. 932, Sec. 16. Effective January 1, 1999.

[402]Amended by Stats. 1999, Ch. 176, Sec. 1. Effective January 1, 2000.

[403]Added by Stats. 1999, Ch. 216, Sec. 4. Effective July 28, 1999.

[404]Added by Stats. 1999, Ch. 344, Sec. 11. Effective September 7, 1999.

[405]Added by Stats. 1999, Ch. 344, Sec. 3. Effective September 7, 1999.

[406]Added by Stats. 1999, Ch. 344, Sec. 4. Effective September 7, 1999.

[407]Amended by Stats. 1999, Ch. 344, Sec. 10. Effective September 7, 1999.

[408]Amended by Stats. 1999, Ch. 662, Sec. 1. Effective January 1, 2000.

[409]Amended by Stats. 1999, Ch. 652, Sec. 2. Effective January 1, 2000.

[410]Amended by Stats. 1999, Ch. 827, Sec. 1. Effective October 10, 1999.

[411]Amended by Stats. 1999, Ch. 991, Sec. 11.5. Effective January 1, 2000. Operative July 1, 2001, by Sec. 75 of Ch. 991.

[412]Amended by Stats. 1999, Ch. 991, Sec. 12. Effective January 1, 2000. Operative July 1, 2001, by Sec. 75 of Ch. 991.

[413]Amended by Stats. 1999, Ch. 991, Sec. 12.1. Effective January 1, 2000. Operative July 1, 2001, by Sec. 75 of Ch. 991.

[414]Amended by Stats. 1999, Ch. 991, Sec. 12.2. Effective January 1, 2000. Operative July 1, 2001, by Sec. 75 of Ch. 991.

[415]Amended by Stats. 1999, Ch. 991, Sec. 12.3. Effective January 1, 2000. Operative July 1, 2001, by Sec. 75 of Ch. 991.

[416]Amended by Stats. 1999, Ch. 991, Sec. 13. Effective January 1, 2000. Operative July 1, 2001, by Sec. 75 of Ch. 991.

[417]Amended by Stats. 1999, Ch. 991, Sec. 13.1. Effective January 1, 2000. Operative July 1, 2001, by Sec. 75 of Ch. 991.

[418]Amended by Stats. 1999, Ch. 991, Sec. 15. Effective January 1, 2000. Operative July 1, 2001, by Sec. 75 of Ch. 991.

[419]Amended by Stats. 1999, Ch. 991, Sec. 15.5. Effective January 1, 2000. Operative July 1, 2001, by Sec. 75 of Ch. 991.

[420]Amended by Stats. 1999, Ch. 991, Sec. 16. Effective January 1, 2000. Operative July 1, 2001, by Sec. 75 of Ch. 991.

[421]Amended by Stats. 1999, Ch. 991, Sec. 16.1. Effective January 1, 2000. Operative July 1, 2001, by Sec. 75 of Ch. 991.

[422]Amended by Stats. 1999, Ch. 991, Sec. 16.2. Effective January 1, 2000. Operative July 1, 2001, by Sec. 75 of Ch. 991.

[423]Amended by Stats. 1999, Ch. 991, Sec. 16.3. Effective January 1, 2000. Operative July 1, 2001, by Sec. 75 of Ch. 991.

[424]Amended by Stats. 1999, Ch. 991, Sec. 17. Effective January 1, 2000. Operative July 1, 2001, by Sec. 75 of Ch. 991.

[425]Amended by Stats. 1999, Ch. 991, Sec. 17.1. Effective January 1, 2000. Operative July 1, 2001, by Sec. 75 of Ch. 991.

[426]Amended by Stats. 1999, Ch. 991, Sec. 17.5. Effective January 1, 2000. Operative July 1, 2001, by Sec. 75 of Ch. 991.

[427]Amended by Stats. 1999, Ch. 991, Sec. 19. Effective January 1, 2000. Operative July 1, 2001, by Sec. 75 of Ch. 991.

[428]Amended by Stats. 1999, Ch. 991, Sec. 20. Effective January 1, 2000. Operative July 1, 2001, by Sec. 75 of Ch. 991.

[429]Amended by Stats. 1999, Ch. 991, Sec. 21. Effective January 1, 2000. Operative July 1, 2001, by Sec. 75 of Ch. 991.

[430]Amended by Stats. 1999, Ch. 991, Sec. 21.5. Effective January 1, 2000. Operative July 1, 2001, by Sec. 75 of Ch. 991.

[431]Amended by Stats. 1999, Ch. 991, Sec. 22. Effective January 1, 2000. Operative July 1, 2001, by Sec. 75 of Ch. 991.

[432]Amended by Stats. 1999, Ch. 991, Sec. 23. Effective January 1, 2000. Operative July 1, 2001, by Sec. 75 of Ch. 991.

[433]Amended by Stats. 1999, Ch. 991, Sec. 23.1. Effective January 1, 2000. Operative July 1, 2001, by Sec. 75 of Ch. 991.

[434]Amended by Stats. 1999, Ch. 991, Sec. 23.2. Effective January 1, 2000. Operative July 1, 2001, by Sec. 75 of Ch. 991.

[435]Added by Stats. 2000, Ch. 639, Sec. 2. Effective January 1, 2001.

[436]Amended by Stats. 2000, Ch. 639, Sec. 6. Effective January 1, 2001.

[437]Amended by Stats. 2000, Ch. 644, Sec. 3. Effective January 1, 2001.

[438]Amended by Stats. 2000, Ch. 644, Sec. 4. Effective January 1, 2001

[439]Amended by Stats. 2000, Ch. 644, Sec. 5. Effective January 1, 2001.

[440]Repealed and added by Stats. 2000, Ch. 644, Sec. 7. Effective January 1, 2001.

[441]Amended by Stats. 2000, Ch. 644, Sec. 8. Effective January 1, 2001.

[442]Amended by Stats. 2000, Ch. 644, Sec. 10. Effective January 1, 2001.

[443]Added by Stats. 2000, Ch. 644, Sec. 12. Effective January 1, 2001.

[444]Amended by Stats. 2000, Ch. 688, Sec. 4. Effective January 1, 2001.

[445]Amended by Stats. 2000, Ch. 808, Sec. 5. Effective September 28, 2000.

[446]Amended by Stats. 2000, Ch. 808, Sec. 6. Effective September 28, 2000.

[447]Amended by Stats. 2000, Ch. 808, Sec. 7. Effective September 28, 2000.

[448]Amended by Stats. 2000, Ch. 808, Sec. 8. Effective September 28, 2000.

[449]Amended by Stats. 2000, Ch. 808, Sec. 9. Effective September 28, 2000.

[450]Amended by Stats. 2000, Ch. 808, Sec. 10. Effective September 28, 2000.

[451]Amended by Stats. 2000, Ch. 808, Sec. 13. Effective September 28, 2000.

[452] Amended by Stats. 2000, Ch. 808, Sec. 14. Effective September 28, 2000.

[453]Amended by Stats. 2000, Ch. 808, Sec. 15. Effective September 28, 2000.

[454]Amended by Stats. 2000, Ch. 808, Sec. 16. Effective September 28, 2000.

[455]Amended by Stats. 2000, Ch. 808, Sec. 18. Effective September 28, 2000.

[456]Amended by Stats. 2000, Ch. 808, Sec. 19. Effective September 28, 2000.

[457]Added by Stats. 2000, Ch. 1090, Sec. 1. Effective January 1, 2001.

[458]Added by Stats. 2001, Ch. 44, Sec. 2. Effective January 1, 2002.

[459]Amended by Stats. 2001, Ch. 44, Sec. 3. Effective January 1, 2002.

[460]Amended by Stats. 2001, Ch. 55, Sec. 1. Effective January 1, 2002.

[461]Amended by Stats. 2001, Ch. 159, Sec. 38.5. Effective January 1, 2002.

[462]Amended by Stats. 2001, Ch. 542, Sec. 1. Effective January 1, 2002.

[463]Amended by Stats. 2001, Ch. 812, Sec. 3. Effective January 1, 2002.

[464]Amended by Stats. 2001, Ch. 812, Sec. 4. Effective January 1, 2002.

[465]Amended by Stats. 2001, Ch. 824, Sec. 2. Effective January 1, 2002.

[466]Amended by Stats. 2001, Ch. 824, Sec. 3. Effective January 1, 2002.

[467]Amended by Stats. 2001, Ch. 824, Sec. 4. Effective January 1, 2002.

[468]Repealed and added by Stats. 2001, Ch. 824, Sec. 6. Effective January 1, 2002.

[469]Amended by Stats. 2000, Ch. 242, Sec. 1. Effective January 1, 2001.

[470]Added by Stats. 2000, Ch. 266, Sec. 2. Effective January 1, 2001.

[471]Amended by Stats. 2001, Ch. 362, Sec. 1. Effective January 1, 2002.

[472]Added by Stats. 2001, Ch. 362, Sec. 2. Effective January 1, 2002.

[473]Amended by Stats. 2002, Ch. 68, Sec. 1. Effective January 1, 2003.

[474]Amended by Stats. 2002, Ch. 68, Sec. 2. Effective January 1, 2003.

[475]Amended by Stats. 2002, Ch. 68, Sec. 3. Effective January 1, 2003.

[476]Amended by Stats. 2002, Ch. 68, Sec. 4. Effective January 1, 2003.

[477]Amended by Stats. 2002, Ch. 69, Sec. 1. Effective January 1, 2003.

[478]Amended by Stats. 2002, Ch. 71, Sec. 1. Effective January 1, 2003.

[479]Added by Stats. 2002, Ch. 247, Sec. 1. Effective January 1, 2003.

[480]Added by Stats. 2002, Ch. 332, Sec. 2. Effective January 1, 2003.

[481]Added by Stats. 2002, Ch. 448, Sec. 2. Effective January 1, 2003.

[482]Amended by Stats. 2002, Ch. 448, Sec. 3. Effective January 1, 2003.

[483]Added by Stats. 2002, Ch. 448, Sec. 4. Effective January 1, 2003.

[484]Amended by Stats. 2002, Ch. 451, Sec. 2. Effective January 1, 2003.

[485]Added by Stats. 2002, Ch. 708, Sec. 1. Effective January 1, 2003.

[486]Amended by Stats. 2022, Ch. 620, Sec. 3. (SB 1311) Effective January 1, 2023.

[487]Amended by Stats. 2002, Ch. 784, Sec. 22. Effective January 1, 2003.

[488]Amended by Stats. 2002, Ch. 784, Sec. 24. Effective January 1, 2003.

[489]Amended by Stats. 2002, Ch. 784, Sec. 25. Effective January 1, 2003.

[490]Amended by Stats. 2002, Ch. 784, Sec. 30. Effective January 1, 2003.

[491]Amended by Stats. 2002, Ch. 784, Sec. 32. Effective January 1, 2003. Implementation is subject to condition in subd. (a).

[492]Amended by Stats. 2002, Ch. 784, Sec. 33. Effective January 1, 2003.

[493]Amended by Stats. 2002, Ch. 784, Sec. 34. Effective January 1, 2003.

[494]Amended by Stats. 2002, Ch. 784, Sec. 35. Effective January 1, 2003.

[495]Amended by Stats. 2002, Ch. 784, Sec. 39. Effective January 1, 2003.

[496]Amended by Stats. 2002, Ch. 784, Sec. 40. Effective January 1, 2003.

[497]Amended by Stats. 2002, Ch. 784, Sec. 47. Effective January 1, 2003.

[498]Amended by Stats. 2002, Ch. 784, Sec. 49. Effective January 1, 2003.

[499]Amended by Stats. 2002, Ch. 784, Sec. 51. Effective January 1, 2003.

[500]Amended by Stats. 2002, Ch. 784, Sec. 55. Effective January 1, 2003.

[501]Amended by Stats. 2002, Ch. 784, Sec. 57. Effective January 1, 2003.

[502]Amended by Stats. 2002, Ch. 784, Sec. 58. Effective January 1, 2003.

[503]Amended by Stats. 2002, Ch. 784, Sec. 59. Effective January 1, 2003.

[504]Amended by Stats. 2002, Ch. 784, Sec. 60. Effective January 1, 2003.

[505]Amended (as amended by Stats. 2002, Ch. 784) by Stats. 2003, Ch. 449, Sec. 6. Effective January 1, 2004.

[506]Amended by Stats. 2002, Ch. 784, Sec. 61. Effective January 1, 2003.

[507]Amended by Stats. 2002, Ch. 784, Sec. 62. Effective January 1, 2003.

[508]Amended by Stats. 2002, Ch. 784, Sec. 63. Effective January 1, 2003.

[509]Amended by Stats. 2002, Ch. 784, Sec. 66. Effective January 1, 2003.

[510]Amended by Stats. 2002, Ch. 784, Sec. 67. Effective January 1, 2003.

[511]Amended by Stats. 2002, Ch. 784, Sec. 68. Effective January 1, 2003.

[512]Added by Stats. 2022, Ch. 716, Sec. 5. (SB 1099) Effective January 1, 2023.

[513]Amended by Stats. 2022, Ch. 716, Sec. 6. (SB 1099) Effective January 1, 2023.

[514]Amended by Stats. 2002, Ch. 806, Sec. 4. Effective January 1, 2003.

[515]Amended by Stats. 2002, Ch. 806, Sec. 5. Effective January 1, 2003.

[516]Amended by Stats. 2002, Ch. 806, Sec. 7. Effective January 1, 2003.

[517]Amended by Stats. 2002, Ch. 806, Sec. 8. Effective January 1, 2003.

[518]Repealed and added by Stats. 2002, Ch. 806, Sec. 12. Effective January 1, 2003.

[519]Amended by Stats. 2002, Ch. 806, Sec. 14. Effective January 1, 2003.

[520]Amended by Stats. 2002, Ch. 927, Sec. 1. Effective January 1, 2003.

[521]Amended by Stats. 2002, Ch. 927, Sec. 1.5. Effective January 1, 2003.

[522]Amended by Stats. 2002, Ch. 1008, Sec. 1. Effective January 1, 2003.

[523]Added by Stats. 2002, Ch. 1070, Sec. 2. Effective September 29, 2002.

[524]Amended by Stats. 2003, Ch. 62, Sec. 23. Effective January 1, 2004.

[525]Added by Stats. 2003, Ch. 128, Sec. 2. Effective January 1, 2004.

[526]Amended by Stats. 2003, Ch. 149, Sec. 1. Effective January 1, 2004.

[527]Amended by Stats. 2003, Ch. 149, Sec. 3. Effective January 1, 2004.

[528]Amended by Stats. 2003, Ch. 149, Sec. 4. Effective January 1, 2004.

[529]Amended by Stats. 2003, Ch. 149, Sec. 6. Effective January 1, 2004.

[530]Amended by Stats. 2003, Ch. 149, Sec. 7. Effective January 1, 2004

[531]Amended by Stats. 2003, Ch. 149, Sec. 8. Effective January 1, 2004.

[532]Amended by Stats. 2003, Ch. 149, Sec. 9. Effective January 1, 2004.

[533]Added by Stats. 2003, Ch. 353, Sec. 1. Effective January 1, 2004.

[534]Amended by Stats. 2003, Ch. 387, Sec. 1. Effective January 1, 2004.

[535]Amended by Stats. 2003, Ch. 449, Sec. 4. Effective January 1, 2004.

[536]Amended by Stats. 2003, Ch. 449, Sec. 5. Effective January 1, 2004.

[537]Amended by Stats. 2003, Ch. 449, Sec. 7. Effective January 1, 2004.

[538]Amended by Stats. 2003, Ch. 449, Sec. 8. Effective January 1, 2004.

[539]Amended by Stats. 2003, Ch. 719, Sec. 1. Effective January 1, 2004.

[540]Added by Stats. 2003, Ch. 873, Sec. 1. Effective January 1, 2004.

[541]Amended by Stats. 2004, Ch. 49, Sec. 1. Effective January 1, 2005.

[542]Amended by Stats. 2004, Ch. 171, Sec. 1. Effective January 1, 2005.

[543]Amended by Stats. 2004, Ch. 178, Sec. 2. Effective January 1, 2005.

[544]Amended by Stats. 2004, Ch. 178, Sec. 3. Effective January 1, 2005.

[545]Amended by Stats. 2004, Ch. 182, Sec. 5. Effective January 1, 2005. Operative July 1, 2005, by Sec. 64 of Ch. 182.

[546]Amended by Stats. 2004, Ch. 182, Sec. 8. Effective January 1, 2005. Operative July 1, 2005, by Sec. 64 of Ch. 182.

[547]Amended by Stats. 2004, Ch. 182, Sec. 7. Effective January 1, 2005. Operative July 1, 2005, by Sec. 64 of Ch. 182.

[548]Amended by Stats. 2004, Ch. 182, Sec. 10. Effective January 1, 2005. Operative July 1, 2005, by Sec. 64 of Ch. 182.

[549]Amended by Stats. 2004, Ch. 182, Sec. 11. Effective January 1, 2005. Operative July 1, 2005, by Sec. 64 of Ch. 182.

[550]Amended by Stats. 2004, Ch. 182, Sec. 12. Effective January 1, 2005. Operative July 1, 2005, by Sec. 64 of Ch. 182.

[551]Amended by Stats. 2004, Ch. 227, Sec. 10. Effective August 16, 2004.

[552]Amended by Stats. 2004, Ch. 227, Sec. 11. Effective August 16, 2004.

[553]Amended by Stats. 2004, Ch. 520, Sec. 1. Effective January 1, 2005.

[554]Added by Stats. 2004, Ch. 741, Sec. 1. Effective January 1, 2005.

[555]Amended by Stats. 2005, Ch. 75, Sec. 22. Effective July 19, 2005. Operative January 1, 2006, by Sec. 156 of Ch. 75.

[556]Amended by Stats. 2005, Ch. 75, Sec. 23. Effective July 19, 2005. Operative January 1, 2006, by Sec. 156 of Ch. 75.

[557]Amended by Stats. 2005, Ch. 75, Sec. 25. Effective July 19, 2005. Operative January 1, 2006, by Sec. 156 of Ch. 75.

[558]Amended by Stats. 2005, Ch. 75, Sec. 27. Effective July 19, 2005. Operative January 1, 2006, by Sec. 156 of Ch. 75.

[559]Amended by Stats. 2005, Ch. 75, Sec. 29. Effective July 19, 2005. Operative January 1, 2006, by Sec. 156 of Ch. 75.

[560]Amended by Stats. 2005, Ch. 75, Sec. 30. Effective July 19, 2005. Operative January 1, 2006, by Sec. 156 of Ch. 75.

[561]Amended by Stats. 2005, Ch. 75, Sec. 32. Effective July 19, 2005. Operative January 1, 2006, by Sec. 156 of Ch. 75.

[562]Amended by Stats. 2005, Ch. 75, Sec. 33. Effective July 19, 2005. Operative January 1, 2006, by Sec. 156 of Ch. 75.

[563]Repealed and added by Stats. 2005, Ch. 75, Sec. 35. Effective July 19, 2005. Operative January 1, 2006, by Sec. 156 of Ch. 75.

[564]Amended by Stats. 2005, Ch. 75, Sec. 36. Effective July 19, 2005. Operative January 1, 2006, by Sec. 156 of Ch. 75.

[565]Amended by Stats. 2005, Ch. 75, Sec. 38. Effective July 19, 2005. Operative January 1, 2006, by Sec. 156 of Ch. 75.

[566]Amended by Stats. 2005, Ch. 75, Sec. 39. Effective July 19, 2005. Operative January 1, 2006, by Sec. 156 of Ch. 75.

[567]Amended by Stats. 2005, Ch. 300, Sec. 2. Effective January 1, 2006.

[568]Amended by Stats. 2005, Ch. 300, Sec. 4. Effective January 1, 2006.

[569]Amended by Stats. 2025, Ch. 344, Sec. 1. (AB 863) Effective January 1, 2026.

[570]Added by Stats. 2005, Ch. 535, Sec. 2. Effective October 5, 2005.

[571]Amended by Stats. 2005, Ch. 595, Sec. 3. Effective January 1, 2006.

[572]Amended by Stats. 2005, Ch. 595, Sec. 4. Effective January 1, 2006.

[573]Added by Stats. 2005, Ch. 618, Sec. 3. Effective January 1, 2006.

[574]Amended by Stats. 2005, Ch. 618, Sec. 4. Effective January 1, 2006.

[575]Amended by Stats. 2005, Ch. 706, Sec. 4. Effective January 1, 2006.

[576]Amended by Stats. 2005, Ch. 706, Sec. 5. Effective January 1, 2006.

[577]Amended by Stats. 2005, Ch. 706, Sec. 9. Effective January 1, 2006.

[578]Amended by Stats. 2005, Ch. 706, Sec. 10. Effective January 1, 2006.

[579]Amended by Stats. 2005, Ch. 706, Sec. 12. Effective January 1, 2006.

[580]Repealed and added by Stats. 2005, Ch. 706, Sec. 7. Effective January 1, 2006.

[581]Amended by Stats. 2006, Ch. 167, Sec. 4. Effective January 1, 2007.

[582]Amended by Stats. 2006, Ch. 167, Sec. 7. Effective January 1, 2007.

[583]Amended by Stats. 2006, Ch. 167, Sec. 5. Effective January 1, 2007.

[584]Amended by Stats. 2006, Ch. 277, Sec. 1. Effective January 1, 2007.

[585]Added by Stats. 2006, Ch. 443, Sec. 2. Effective January 1, 2007.

[586]Amended by Stats. 2006, Ch. 538, Sec. 61. Effective January 1, 2007.

[587]Amended by Stats. 2006, Ch. 538, Sec. 63.5. Effective January 1, 2007.

[588]Amended by Stats. 2006, Ch. 538, Sec. 64. Effective January 1, 2007.

[589]Amended by Stats. 2006, Ch. 567, Sec. 4. Effective January 1, 2007.

[590]Amended (as amended by Stats. 2006, Ch. 567, Sec. 5) by Stats. 2009, Ch. 44, Sec. 1. (SB 319) Effective January 1, 2010.

[591]Amended by Stats. 2007, Ch. 15, Sec. 2. Effective January 1, 2008.

[592]Amended by Stats. 2007, Ch. 43, Sec. 5. Effective January 1, 2008.

[593]Amended by Stats. 2007, Ch. 43, Sec. 6. Effective January 1, 2008.

[594]Amended by Stats. 2007, Ch. 43, Sec. 7. Effective January 1, 2008.

[595]Amended by Stats. 2007, Ch. 153, Sec. 1. Effective January 1, 2008.

[596]Amended by Stats. 2007, Ch. 189, Sec. 1. Effective January 1, 2008.

[597]Amended by Stats. 2006, Ch. 567, Sec. 7. Effective January 1, 2007.

[598]Amended by Stats. 2007, Ch. 263, Sec. 3. Effective January 1, 2008.

[599]Amended by Stats. 2007, Ch. 263, Sec. 4. Effective January 1, 2008.

[600]Amended by Stats. 2007, Ch. 263, Sec. 5. Effective January 1, 2008.

[601]Amended by Stats. 2007, Ch. 263, Sec. 7. Effective January 1, 2008.

[602]Amended by Stats. 2007, Ch. 263, Sec. 8. Effective January 1, 2008.

[603]Amended by Stats. 2007, Ch. 568, Sec. 15. Effective January 1, 2008.

[604]Amended by Stats. 2007, Ch. 568, Sec. 16. Effective January 1, 2008.

[605]Amended by Stats. 2007, Ch. 738, Sec. 3. Effective January 1, 2008.

[606]Amended by Stats. 2007, Ch. 738, Sec. 4. Effective January 1, 2008.

[607]Amended by Stats. 2007, Ch. 738, Sec. 5. Effective January 1, 2008.

[608]Repealed and added by Stats. 2008, Ch. 56, Sec. 2. Effective January 1, 2009.

[609]Amended by Stats. 2008, Ch. 179, Sec. 34. Effective January 1, 2009.

[610]Amended by Stats. 2008, Ch. 179, Sec. 35. Effective January 1, 2009.

[611]Amended by Stats. 2008, Ch. 218, Sec. 1. Effective January 1, 2009.

[612]Repealed (in Sec. 1) and added by Stats. 2008, Ch. 552, Sec. 2. Effective January 1, 2009. Section operative January 1, 2014, by its own provisions.

[613]Repealed (in Sec. 3) and added by Stats. 2008, Ch. 552, Sec. 4. Effective January 1, 2009. Section operative January 1, 2014, by its own provisions.

[614]Amended (as added by Stats. 2009, Ch. 87, Sec. 2) by Stats. 2016, Ch. 703, Sec. 7. (AB 2881) Effective January 1, 2017. Section operative January 1, 2022, by its own provisions.

[615]Added by Stats. 2010, Ch. 41, Sec. 1. (AB 2119) Effective January 1, 2011.

[616]Amended by Stats. 2009, Ch. 140, Sec. 38. (AB 1164) Effective January 1, 2010.

[617]Amended by Stats. 2009, Ch. 140, Sec. 39. (AB 1164) Effective January 1, 2010.

[618]Amended by Stats. 2009, Ch. 153, Sec. 2. (AB 1549) Effective January 1, 2010.

[619]Added by Stats. 2009, Ch. 162, Sec. 2. (SB 285) Effective January 1, 2010.

[620]Amended by Stats. 2009, Ch. 348, Sec. 2. (SB 308) Effective January 1, 2010.

[621]Amended by Stats. 2009, Ch. 348, Sec. 3. (SB 308) Effective January 1, 2010.

[622]Amended by Stats. 2009, Ch. 410, Sec. 1. (AB 121) Effective January 1, 2010.

[623]Amended by Stats. 2009, Ch. 410, Sec. 2. (AB 121) Effective January 1, 2010.

[624]Amended by Stats. 2009, Ch. 500, Sec. 14. (AB 1059) Effective January 1, 2010.

[625]Amended by Stats. 2010, Ch. 4, Sec. 1. (AB 680) Effective January 1, 2011.

[626]Amended by Stats. 2010, Ch. 4, Sec. 2. (AB 680) Effective January 1, 2011.

[627]Amended by Stats. 2010, Ch. 4, Sec. 3. (AB 680) Effective January 1, 2011.

[628]Amended by Stats. 2010, Ch. 55, Sec. 1. (AB 1684) Effective January 1, 2011.

[629]Amended by Stats. 2010, Ch. 64, Sec. 2. (AB 2619) Effective January 1, 2011. Operative January 1, 2012, by Sec. 6 of Ch. 64.

[630]Amended by Stats. 2010, Ch. 64, Sec. 3. (AB 2619) Effective January 1, 2011. Operative January 1, 2012, by Sec. 6 of Ch. 64.

[631]Amended by Stats. 2010, Ch. 64, Sec. 4. (AB 2619) Effective January 1, 2011. Operative January 1, 2012, by Sec. 6 of Ch. 64.

[632]Amended by Stats. 2010, Ch. 328, Sec. 33. (SB 1330) Effective January 1, 2011.

[633]Amended by Stats. 2010, Ch. 131, Sec. 1. (AB 1894) Effective January 1, 2011.

[634]Amended by Stats. 2010, Ch. 572, Sec. 3. (AB 1596) Effective January 1, 2011. Operative January 1, 2012, by Sec. 28 of Ch. 572.

[635]Added by Stats. 2010, Ch. 674, Sec. 2. (AB 2284) Effective January 1, 2011.

[636]Amended by Stats. 2010, Ch. 686, Sec. 1. (AB 2487) Effective January 1, 2011.

[637]Amended by Stats. 2010, Ch. 680, Sec. 1. (AB 2394) Effective January 1, 2011.

[638]Amended by Stats. 2010, Ch. 680, Sec. 2. (AB 2394) Effective January 1, 2011.

[639]Amended by Stats. 2010, Ch. 680, Sec. 3. (AB 2394) Effective January 1, 2011.

[640]Added by Stats. 2010, Ch. 680, Sec. 4. (AB 2394) Effective January 1, 2011.

[641]Amended by Stats. 2010, Ch. 680, Sec. 6. (AB 2394) Effective January 1, 2011.

[642]Amended by Stats. 2010, Ch. 680, Sec. 9. (AB 2394) Effective January 1, 2011.

[643]Amended by Stats. 2010, Ch. 680, Sec. 11. (AB 2394) Effective January 1, 2011.

[644]Amended by Stats. 2010, Ch. 680, Sec. 12. (AB 2394) Effective January 1, 2011.

[645]Amended by Stats. 2010, Ch. 680, Sec. 13. (AB 2394) Effective January 1, 2011.

[646]Amended by Stats. 2010, Ch. 697, Sec. 22. (SB 189) Effective January 1, 2011. Operative July 1, 2012, by Sec. 105 of Ch. 697.

[647]Amended by Stats. 2010, Ch. 697, Sec. 23. (SB 189) Effective January 1, 2011. Operative July 1, 2012, by Sec. 105 of Ch. 697.

[648]Amended by Stats. 2010, Ch. 719, Sec. 7. (SB 856) Effective October 19, 2010.

[649]Added by Stats. 2010, Ch. 719, Sec. 8. (SB 856) Effective October 19, 2010.

[650]Amended by Stats. 2011, Ch. 49, Sec. 1. (SB 731) Effective January 1, 2012.

[651]Added by Stats. 2011, Ch. 49, Sec. 2. (SB 731) Effective January 1, 2012.

[652]Amended by Stats. 2011, Ch. 70, Sec. 1. (AB 173) Effective July 8, 2011.

[653]Amended by Stats. 2011, Ch. 181, Sec. 1. (AB 141) Effective January 1, 2012.

654Amended by Stats. 2011, Ch. 181, Sec. 2. (AB 141) Effective January 1, 2012.

655Amended by Stats. 2011, Ch. 296, Sec. 36. (AB 1023) Effective January 1, 2012.

656Amended by Stats. 2011, Ch. 296, Sec. 37. (AB 1023) Effective January 1, 2012.

657Amended by Stats. 2011, Ch. 296, Sec. 36.5. (AB 1023) Effective January 1, 2012.

658Amended by Stats. 2011, Ch. 296, Sec. 38. (AB 1023) Effective January 1, 2012.

659Amended by Stats. 2011, Ch. 308, Sec. 1. (SB 647) Effective January 1, 2012.

660Amended by Stats. 2011, Ch. 308, Sec. 2. (SB 647) Effective January 1, 2012.

661Amended by Stats. 2011, Ch. 409, Sec. 2. (AB 1403) Effective January 1, 2012.

662Amended by Stats. 2011, Ch. 694, Sec. 1. (AB 1388) Effective January 1, 2012.

663Amended by Stats. 2012, Ch. 37, Sec. 1. (SB 1015) Effective June 27, 2012.

664Amended by Stats. 2012, Ch. 342, Sec. 1. (AB 1481) Effective September 17, 2012.

665Amended by Stats. 2012, Ch. 417, Sec. 2. (AB 2274) Effective January 1, 2013.

666Amended by Stats. 2012, Ch. 417, Sec. 3. (AB 2274) Effective January 1, 2013.

667Amended by Stats. 2012, Ch. 417, Sec. 4. (AB 2274) Effective January 1, 2013.

668Amended by Stats. 2012, Ch. 342, Sec. 2. (AB 1481) Effective September 17, 2012.

669Amended by Stats. 2012, Ch. 470, Sec. 6. (AB 1529) Effective January 1, 2013.

670Amended by Stats. 2012, Ch. 474, Sec. 1. (AB 1775) Effective January 1, 2013. Operative July 1, 2013, by Sec. 3 of Ch. 474.

671Amended by Stats. 2012, Ch. 484, Sec. 1. (AB 2364) Effective January 1, 2013.

672Amended by Stats. 2012, Ch. 484, Sec. 2. (AB 2364) Effective January 1, 2013.

673Amended by Stats. 2012, Ch. 484, Sec. 3. (AB 2364) Effective January 1, 2013.

674Amended by Stats. 2012, Ch. 484, Sec. 4. (AB 2364) Effective January 1, 2013.

675Amended by Stats. 2012, Ch. 484, Sec. 6. (AB 2364) Effective January 1, 2013.

676Amended by Stats. 2012, Ch. 484, Sec. 8. (AB 2364) Effective January 1, 2013.

677Amended by Stats. 2012, Ch. 484, Sec. 9. (AB 2364) Effective January 1, 2013.

678Amended by Stats. 2012, Ch. 484, Sec. 10. (AB 2364) Effective January 1, 2013.

679Added by Stats. 2012, Ch. 470, Sec. 3. (AB 1529) Effective January 1, 2013.

680Added by Stats. 2013, Ch. 15, Sec. 1. (AB 567) Effective January 1, 2014.

681Amended by Stats. 2013, Ch. 31, Sec. 1. (SB 75) Effective June 27, 2013.

682Amended by Stats. 2013, Ch. 40, Sec. 1. (AB 522) Effective January 1, 2014.

683Added by Stats. 2013, Ch. 64, Sec. 3. (SB 233) Effective January 1, 2014.

[684]Amended by Stats. 2013, Ch. 64, Sec. 4. (SB 233) Effective January 1, 2014.

[685]Amended by Stats. 2013, Ch. 64, Sec. 6. (SB 233) Effective January 1, 2014.

[686]Amended by Stats. 2013, Ch. 64, Sec. 8. (SB 233) Effective January 1, 2014.

[687]Amended by Stats. 2013, Ch. 76, Sec. 21. (AB 383) Effective January 1, 2014.

[688]Amended by Stats. 2013, Ch. 156, Sec. 1. (AB 1167) Effective January 1, 2014.

[689]Amended by Stats. 2013, Ch. 176, Sec. 1. (SB 551) Effective January 1, 2014.

[690]Amended by Stats. 2013, Ch. 176, Sec. 2. (SB 551) Effective January 1, 2014.

[691]Amended by Stats. 2013, Ch. 531, Sec. 2. (AB 502) Effective January 1, 2014. Operative July 1, 2014, by Sec. 28 of Ch. 531.

[692]Amended by Stats. 2013, Ch. 531, Sec. 3. (AB 502) Effective January 1, 2014. Operative July 1, 2014, by Sec. 28 of Ch. 531.

[693]Amended by Stats. 2013, Ch. 531, Sec. 4. (AB 502) Effective January 1, 2014. Operative July 1, 2014, by Sec. 28 of Ch. 531.

[694]Amended by Stats. 2013, Ch. 531, Sec. 5. (AB 502) Effective January 1, 2014. Operative July 1, 2014, by Sec. 28 of Ch. 531.

[695]Amended by Stats. 2014, Ch. 71, Sec. 18. (SB 1304) Effective January 1, 2015.

[696]Amended by Stats. 2014, Ch. 93, Sec. 2. (AB 1659) Effective January 1, 2015.

[697]Amended by Stats. 2014, Ch. 144, Sec. 3. (AB 1847) Effective January 1, 2015.

[698]Amended by Stats. 2014, Ch. 144, Sec. 4. (AB 1847) Effective January 1, 2015.

[699]Amended by Stats. 2014, Ch. 144, Sec. 6. (AB 1847) Effective January 1, 2015.

[700]Amended by Stats. 2014, Ch. 183, Sec. 1. (AB 2317) Effective January 1, 2015.

[701]Amended by Stats. 2014, Ch. 415, Sec. 1. (AB 1945) Effective January 1, 2015.

[702]Amended by Stats. 2014, Ch. 913, Sec. 7. (AB 2747) Effective January 1, 2015.

[703]Amended by Stats. 2014, Ch. 470, Sec. 1. (AB 2256) Effective January 1, 2015.

[704]Amended (as amended by Stats. 2014, Ch. 425, Sec. 1) by Stats. 2017, Ch. 169, Sec. 1. (AB 984) Effective August 7, 2017.

[705]Added by Stats. 2015, Ch. 32, Sec. 2. (AB 432) Effective January 1, 2016.

[706]Amended by Stats. 2015, Ch. 115, Sec. 1. (AB 87) Effective January 1, 2016.

[707]Amended by Stats. 2015, Ch. 303, Sec. 39. (AB 731) Effective January 1, 2016.

[708]Amended by Stats. 2015, Ch. 303, Sec. 40. (AB 731) Effective January 1, 2016.

[709]Amended by Stats. 2015, Ch. 330, Sec. 2. (AB 555) Effective January 1, 2016.

[710]Amended by Stats. 2015, Ch. 330, Sec. 3. (AB 555) Effective January 1, 2016.

[711]Added by Stats. 2015, Ch. 330, Sec. 5. (AB 555) Effective January 1, 2016. Section operative July 1, 2016, pursuant to Section 630.29.

[712]Repealed (in Sec. 1) and added by Stats. 2015, Ch. 451, Sec. 2. (SB 491) Effective January 1, 2016. Section operative January 1, 2017, by its own provisions.

[713]Repealed (in Sec. 3) and added by Stats. 2015, Ch. 451, Sec. 4. (SB 491) Effective January 1, 2016. Section operative January 1, 2017, by its own provisions.

[714]Amended by Stats. 2015, Ch. 465, Sec. 1. (AB 538) Effective January 1, 2016.

[715]Added by Stats. 2015, Ch. 474, Sec. 2. (AB 15) Effective January 1, 2016.

[716]Amended (as amended by Stats. 2015, Ch. 418, Sec. 4) by Stats. 2020, Ch. 36, Sec. 20. (AB 3364) Effective January 1, 2021.

[717]Added by Stats. 2015, Ch. 676, Sec. 1. (SB 226) Effective January 1, 2016.

[718]Amended by Stats. 2015, Ch. 755, Sec. 5. (AB 1521) Effective October 10, 2015.

[719]Added by Stats. 2015, Ch. 755, Sec. 6. (AB 1521) Effective October 10, 2015.

[720]Repealed (in Sec. 2) and added by Stats. 2016, Ch. 33, Sec. 3. (SB 843) Effective June 27, 2016. Section operative January 1, 2021, by its own provisions.

[721]Added by Stats. 2015, Ch. 803, Sec. 1. (SB 588) Effective January 1, 2016.

[722]Amended by Stats. 2016, Ch. 50, Sec. 15. (SB 1005) Effective January 1, 2017.

[723]Amended by Stats. 2016, Ch. 94, Sec. 3. (AB 1709) Effective January 1, 2017.

[724]Amended by Stats. 2016, Ch. 50, Sec. 13. (SB 1005) Effective January 1, 2017.

[725]Amended by Stats. 2016, Ch. 50, Sec. 17. (SB 1005) Effective January 1, 2017.

[726]Amended by Stats. 2016, Ch. 102, Sec. 1. (AB 2211) Effective January 1, 2017.

[727]Amended by Stats. 2016, Ch. 102, Sec. 2. (AB 2211) Effective January 1, 2017.

[728]Amended by Stats. 2016, Ch. 102, Sec. 3. (AB 2211) Effective January 1, 2017.

[729]Amended by Stats. 2016, Ch. 703, Sec. 9. (AB 2881) Effective January 1, 2017.

[730]Amended by Stats. 2017, Ch. 131, Sec. 1. (AB 1693) Effective January 1, 2018.

[731]Amended (as amended by Stats. 2017, Ch. 273, Sec. 3) by Stats. 2020, Ch. 36, Sec. 19. (AB 3364) Effective January 1, 2021.

[732]Repealed and added by Stats. 2017, Ch. 302, Sec. 2. (AB 1541) Effective January 1, 2018.

[733]Amended by Stats. 2017, Ch. 319, Sec. 1. (AB 976) Effective January 1, 2018.

[734]Amended by Stats. 2017, Ch. 337, Sec. 1. (SB 658) Effective January 1, 2018.

[735]Repealed and added by Stats. 2017, Ch. 532, Sec. 2. (AB 1450) Effective January 1, 2018.

[736]Amended by Stats. 2017, Ch. 561, Sec. 20. (AB 1516) Effective January 1, 2018.

[737]Amended by Stats. 2017, Ch. 561, Sec. 21. (AB 1516) Effective January 1, 2018.

[738]Amended by Stats. 2017, Ch. 561, Sec. 22. (AB 1516) Effective January 1, 2018.

[739]Added by Stats. 2018, Ch. 45, Sec. 1. (SB 847) Effective June 27, 2018.

[740]Added by Stats. 2018, Ch. 45, Sec. 3. (SB 847) Effective June 27, 2018.

[741]Amended by Stats. 2018, Ch. 92, Sec. 39. (SB 1289) Effective January 1, 2019.

[742]Amended by Stats. 2018, Ch. 92, Sec. 40. (SB 1289) Effective January 1, 2019.

[743]Amended by Stats. 2018, Ch. 247, Sec. 2. (AB 1526) Effective January 1, 2019.

[744]Added by Stats. 2018, Ch. 248, Sec. 1. (AB 1531) Effective January 1, 2019.

[745]Amended by Stats. 2018, Ch. 317, Sec. 1. (AB 2230) Effective January 1, 2019.

[746]Amended by Stats. 2018, Ch. 319, Sec. 1. (AB 2376) Effective January 1, 2019.

[747]Amended by Stats. 2018, Ch. 317, Sec. 2. (AB 2230) Effective January 1, 2019.

[748]Amended by Stats. 2018, Ch. 423, Sec. 7. (SB 1494) Effective January 1, 2019.

[749]Amended by Stats. 2018, Ch. 776, Sec. 6. (AB 3250) Effective January 1, 2019.

[750]Added by Stats. 2018, Ch. 817, Sec. 1. (AB 2185) Effective January 1, 2019.

[751]Amended by Stats. 2019, Ch. 12, Sec. 1. (AB 622) Effective January 1, 2020.

[752]Amended by Stats. 2019, Ch. 13, Sec. 2. (AB 692) Effective January 1, 2020.

[753]Added by Stats. 2019, Ch. 48, Sec. 1. (AB 1361) Effective January 1, 2020.

[754]Added by Stats. 2019, Ch. 439, Sec. 1. (AB 800) Effective January 1, 2020.

[755]Amended by Stats. 2019, Ch. 552, Sec. 2. (SB 616) Effective January 1, 2020.

[756]Repealed (in Sec. 5) and added by Stats. 2019, Ch. 552, Sec. 6. (SB 616) Effective January 1, 2020. Section operative September 1, 2020, by its own provisions.

[757]Amended by Stats. 2019, Ch. 552, Sec. 7. (SB 616) Effective January 1, 2020.

[758]Added by Stats. 2019, Ch. 552, Sec. 9. (SB 616) Effective January 1, 2020.

[759]Added by Stats. 2019, Ch. 552, Sec. 10. (SB 616) Effective January 1, 2020.

[760]Amended by Stats. 2019, Ch. 591, Sec. 1. (SB 310) Effective January 1, 2020.

[761]Amended by Stats. 2019, Ch. 787, Sec. 3. (AB 668) Effective January 1, 2020.

[762]Amended by Stats. 2020, Ch. 36, Sec. 22. (AB 3364) Effective January 1, 2021.

[763]Amended by Stats. 2020, Ch. 51, Sec. 1. (AB 2445) Effective September 9, 2020.

[764]Amended by Stats. 2020, Ch. 81, Sec. 6. (SB 898) Effective January 1, 2021.

[765]Amended by Stats. 2020, Ch. 81, Sec. 7. (SB 898) Effective January 1, 2021.

[766]Amended by Stats. 2020, Ch. 81, Sec. 8. (SB 898) Effective January 1, 2021.

[767]Amended by Stats. 2020, Ch. 210, Sec. 1. (AB 1984) Effective January 1, 2021.

[768]Amended by Stats. 2020, Ch. 27, Sec. 1. (SB 350) Effective January 1, 2021.

[769]Added by Stats. 2020, Ch. 27, Sec. 2. (SB 350) Effective January 1, 2021.

[770]Added by renumbering Section 349¾ by Stats. 2020, Ch. 370, Sec. 34. (SB 1371) Effective January 1, 2021.

[771]Amended (as amended by Stats. 2015, Ch. 418, Sec. 4) by Stats. 2020,

Ch. 36, Sec. 20. (AB 3364) Effective January 1, 2021.

772Amended by Stats. 2020, Ch. 36, Sec. 23. (AB 3364) Effective January 1, 2021.

773Amended by Stats. 2020, Ch. 81, Sec. 3. (SB 898) Effective January 1, 2021.

774Amended by Stats. 2020, Ch. 81, Sec. 4. (SB 898) Effective January 1, 2021.

775Added by Stats. 2020, Ch. 218, Sec. 1. (AB 2463) Effective January 1, 2021.

776Amended by Stats. 2020, Ch. 218, Sec. 3. (AB 2463) Effective January 1, 2021.

777Amended by Stats. 2020, Ch. 230, Sec. 1. (SB 592) Effective January 1, 2021.

778Amended (as added by Stats. 2020, Ch. 318, Sec. 2) by Stats. 2025, Ch. 656, Sec. 1. (SB 645) Effective January 1, 2026.

779Amended by Stats. 2020, Ch. 370, Sec. 35. (SB 1371) Effective January 1, 2021.

780Amended by Stats. 2020, Ch. 370, Sec. 36. (SB 1371) Effective January 1, 2021.

781Amended by Stats. 2000, Ch. 808, Sec. 4. Effective September 28, 2000.

782Amended by Stats. 2021, Ch. 27, Sec. 8. (AB 832) Effective June 28, 2021. Repealed as of October 1, 2027, pursuant to Section 871.12.

783Amended by Stats. 2021, Ch. 27, Sec. 10. (AB 832) Effective June 28, 2021. Repealed as of October 1, 2027, by its own provisions. Note: Repeal affects Ch. 11, commencing with Section 871.10.

784Amended by Stats. 2021, Ch. 30, Sec. 1. (AB 1580) Effective January 1, 2022.

785Amended by Stats. 2021, Ch. 85, Sec. 1. (AB 135) Effective July 16, 2021.

786Amended by Stats. 2021, Ch. 124, Sec. 7. (AB 938) Effective January 1, 2022.

787Amended by Stats. 2021, Ch. 124, Sec. 8. (AB 938) Effective January 1, 2022.

788Amended by Stats. 2021, Ch. 124, Sec. 12. (AB 938) Effective January 1, 2022.

789Amended by Stats. 2021, Ch. 124, Sec. 9. (AB 938) Effective January 1, 2022.

790Amended by Stats. 2021, Ch. 124, Sec. 11. (AB 938) Effective January 1, 2022.

791Amended by Stats. 2021, Ch. 214, Sec. 6. (SB 241) Effective January 1, 2022. Conditionally repealed by its own provisions.

792Amended by Stats. 2021, Ch. 526, Sec. 3. (AB 716) Effective January 1, 2022.

793Amended by Stats. 2021, Ch. 615, Sec. 55. (AB 474) Effective January 1, 2022. Operative January 1, 2023, pursuant to Sec. 463 of Stats. 2021, Ch. 615.

794Amended (as amended by Stats. 2022, Ch. 258, Sec. 7) by Stats. 2023, Ch. 337, Sec. 1. (AB 631) Effective January 1, 2024.

795Amended by Stats. 2022, Ch. 17, Sec. 4. (AB 35) Effective January 1, 2023.

796Amended by Stats. 2022, Ch. 25, Sec. 2. (SB 956) Effective January 1, 2023.

797Amended by Stats. 2022, Ch. 84, Sec. 1. (AB 2391) Effective January 1, 2023.

[798]Amended by Stats. 2022, Ch. 84, Sec. 2. (AB 2391) Effective January 1, 2023.

[799]Amended by Stats. 2022, Ch. 326, Sec. 2. (AB 1981) Effective January 1, 2023.

[800]Amended by Stats. 2022, Ch. 452, Sec. 37. (SB 1498) Effective January 1, 2023.

[801]Amended by Stats. 2022, Ch. 452, Sec. 38. (SB 1498) Effective January 1, 2023.

[802]Amended by Stats. 2022, Ch. 452, Sec. 39. (SB 1498) Effective January 1, 2023.

[803]Amended by Stats. 2022, Ch. 716, Sec. 2.5. (SB 1099) Effective January 1, 2023.

[804]Amended by Stats. 2022, Ch. 716, Sec. 3. (SB 1099) Effective January 1, 2023.

[805]Amended by Stats. 2022, Ch. 716, Sec. 4. (SB 1099) Effective January 1, 2023.

[806]Amended by Stats. 2022, Ch. 843, Sec. 1. (SB 1279) Effective January 1, 2023.

[807]Repealed (in Sec. 1) and added by Stats. 2022, Ch. 849, Sec. 2. (SB 1477) Effective January 1, 2023. Operative September 1, 2023, by its own provisions.

[808]Amended by Stats. 2022, Ch. 883, Sec. 1. (SB 1200) Effective January 1, 2023.

[809]Amended by Stats. 2022, Ch. 883, Sec. 3. (SB 1200) Effective January 1, 2023.

[810]Amended by Stats. 2022, Ch. 883, Sec. 4. (SB 1200) Effective January 1, 2023.

[811]Amended by Stats. 2022, Ch. 883, Sec. 5. (SB 1200) Effective January 1, 2023.

[812]Added by Stats. 2023, Ch. 34, Sec. 6. (SB 133) Effective June 30, 2023.

[813]Amended by Stats. 2023, Ch. 131, Sec. 17. (AB 1754) Effective January 1, 2024.

[814]Amended by Stats. 2023, Ch. 131, Sec. 18. (AB 1754) Effective January 1, 2024.

[815]Amended by Stats. 2023, Ch. 131, Sec. 19. (AB 1754) Effective January 1, 2024.

[816]Amended by Stats. 2023, Ch. 131, Sec. 20. (AB 1754) Effective January 1, 2024.

[817]Amended by Stats. 2023, Ch. 131, Sec. 21. (AB 1754) Effective January 1, 2024.

[818]Amended (as amended by Stats. 2023, Ch. 343, Sec. 1) by Stats. 2024, Ch. 262, Sec. 1.5. (AB 2839) Effective September 17, 2024. Operative January 1, 2025, pursuant to Sec. 4 of Stats. 2024, Ch. 262. Repealed as of January 1, 2027, by its own provisions. See later operative version, as amended by Sec. 2.5 of Stats. 2024, Ch. 262.

[819]Amended (as amended by Stats. 2023, Ch. 343, Sec. 2) by Stats. 2024, Ch. 262, Sec. 2.5. (AB 2839) Effective September 17, 2024. Amending action operative January 1, 2025, pursuant to Sec. 5 of Stats. 2024, Ch. 262. Amended section operative January 1, 2027, by its own provisions.

[820]Amended by Stats. 2023, Ch. 478, Sec. 9. (AB 1756) Effective January 1, 2024.

[821]Amended by Stats. 2023, Ch. 478, Sec. 10. (AB 1756) Effective January 1, 2024.

[822]Amended by Stats. 2023, Ch. 478, Sec. 11. (AB 1756) Effective January 1, 2024.

[823]Repealed (in Sec. 12) and added by Stats. 2023, Ch. 478, Sec. 13. (AB 1756) Effective January 1, 2024. Operative January 1, 2025, by its own provisions.

[824]Amended by Stats. 2023, Ch. 562, Sec. 1. (AB 1119) Effective January 1, 2024.

[825]Added by Stats. 2023, Ch. 562, Sec. 2. (AB 1119) Effective January 1, 2024.

[826]Amended by Stats. 2023, Ch. 562, Sec. 3. (AB 1119) Effective January 1, 2024.

[827]Amended by Stats. 2023, Ch. 655, Sec. 1. (AB 452) Effective January 1, 2024.

[828]Amended (as added by Stats. 2023, Ch. 851, Sec. 2) by Stats. 2024, Ch. 955, Sec. 1. (AB 2224) Effective January 1, 2025.

[829]Amended by Stats. 2023, Ch. 688, Sec. 1. (AB 1414) Effective January 1, 2024.

[830]Added by Stats. 2023, Ch. 688, Sec. 2. (AB 1414) Effective January 1, 2024.

[831]Added by Stats. 2023, Ch. 779, Sec. 1. (SB 439) Effective January 1, 2024.

[832]Amended by Stats. 2023, Ch. 861, Sec. 2. (SB 71) Effective January 1, 2024.

[833]Amended by Stats. 2023, Ch. 861, Sec. 3. (SB 71) Effective January 1, 2024.

[834]Amended by Stats. 2023, Ch. 861, Sec. 4. (SB 71) Effective January 1, 2024.

[835]Amended by Stats. 2023, Ch. 861, Sec. 5. (SB 71) Effective January 1, 2024.

[836]Amended by Stats. 2023, Ch. 861, Sec. 6. (SB 71) Effective January 1, 2024.

[837]Added by Stats. 2023, Ch. 877, Sec. 1. (SB 558) Effective January 1, 2024.

[838]Amended by Stats. 2024, Ch. 51, Sec. 3. (AB 170) Effective July 2, 2024. Repealed as of January 1, 2027, by its own provisions.

[839]Amended by Stats. 2024, Ch. 51, Sec. 4. (AB 170) Effective July 2, 2024. Repealed as of January 1, 2027, by its own provisions.

[840]Amended by Stats. 2024, Ch. 80, Sec. 23. (SB 1525) Effective January 1, 2025.

[841]Amended by Stats. 2024, Ch. 80, Sec. 24. (SB 1525) Effective January 1, 2025.

[842]Amended by Stats. 2024, Ch. 99, Sec. 1. (AB 2049) Effective January 1, 2025.

[843]Amended by Stats. 2004, Ch. 193, Sec. 11. Effective January 1, 2005.

[844]Added by Stats. 2024, Ch. 204, Sec. 1. (AB 2985) Effective January 1, 2025.

[845]Amended by Stats. 2024, Ch. 222, Sec. 1. (AB 2067) Effective January 1, 2025.

[846]Amended by Stats. 2024, Ch. 222, Sec. 2. (AB 2067) Effective January 1, 2025.

[847]Amended by Stats. 2024, Ch. 222, Sec. 3. (AB 2067) Effective January 1, 2025.

[848]Amended by Stats. 2024, Ch. 257, Sec. 2. (AB 2867) Effective September 16, 2024.

[849]Added by Stats. 2024, Ch. 257, Sec. 3. (AB 2867) Effective September 16, 2024.

[850]Amended by Stats. 2024, Ch. 285, Sec. 1. (SB 393) Effective January 1, 2025.

[851]Amended by Stats. 2024, Ch. 444, Sec. 1. (SB 577) Effective January 1, 2025.

[852]Amended by Stats. 2024, Ch. 514, Sec. 2. (AB 2837) Effective January 1, 2025.

[853]Amended by Stats. 2024, Ch. 514, Sec. 3. (AB 2837) Effective January 1, 2025.

[854]Amended by Stats. 2024, Ch. 514, Sec. 5.5. (AB 2837) Effective January 1, 2025.

[855]Amended by Stats. 2024, Ch. 514, Sec. 6. (AB 2837) Effective January 1, 2025.

[856]Amended by Stats. 2024, Ch. 514, Sec. 7. (AB 2837) Effective January 1, 2025.

[857]Amended by Stats. 2024, Ch. 514, Sec. 8. (AB 2837) Effective January 1, 2025.

[858]Amended by Stats. 2024, Ch. 514, Sec. 11. (AB 2837) Effective January 1, 2025.

[859]Repealed (in Sec. 2) and added by Stats. 2024, Ch. 544, Sec. 3. (SB 899) Effective January 1, 2025. Operative January 1, 2026, by its own provisions.

[860]Added by Stats. 2024, Ch. 544, Sec. 4. (SB 899) Effective January 1, 2025. Operative January 1, 2026, by its own provisions.

[861]Added by Stats. 2024, Ch. 544, Sec. 5. (SB 899) Effective January 1, 2025. Operative January 1, 2026, by its own provisions.

[862]Amended by Stats. 2024, Ch. 557, Sec. 3. (AB 1979) Effective January 1, 2025.

[863]Amended by Stats. 2024, Ch. 654, Sec. 2. (SB 989) Effective January 1, 2025.

[864]Amended by Stats. 2024, Ch. 853, Sec. 18. (AB 3281) Effective January 1, 2025.

[865]Amended by Stats. 2024, Ch. 853, Sec. 19. (AB 3281) Effective January 1, 2025.

[866]Amended by Stats. 2024, Ch. 853, Sec. 20. (AB 3281) Effective January 1, 2025.

[867]Repealed (in Sec. 1) and added by Stats. 2024, Ch. 947, Sec. 2. (AB 2096) Effective January 1, 2025. Operative January 1, 2026, by its own provisions.

[868]Amended by Stats. 2024, Ch. 965, Sec. 1. (AB 2484) Effective January 1, 2025. Repealed as of January 1, 2027, by its own provisions.

[869]Amended by Stats. 2024, Ch. 967, Sec. 1. (AB 2499) Effective January 1, 2025.

[870]Repealed (in Sec. 11) and added by Stats. 2024, Ch. 812, Sec. 12. (AB 1899) Effective January 1, 2025. Operative January 1, 2026, by its own provisions.

[871]Added by Stats. 2024, Ch. 1010, Sec. 2. (SB 242) Effective January 1, 2025.

[872]Amended by Stats. 2025, Ch. 29, Sec. 1. (AB 223) Effective January 1, 2026.

[873]Amended by Stats. 2005, Ch. 75, Sec. 37. Effective July 19, 2005. Operative January 1, 2006, by Sec. 156 of Ch. 75.

[874]Amended by Stats. 2025, Ch. 147, Sec. 1. (AB 394) Effective January 1, 2026.

[875]Amended by Stats. 2025, Ch. 200, Sec. 9. (AB 1521) Effective January 1, 2026.

[876]Amended by Stats. 2025, Ch. 267, Sec. 1. (AB 561) Effective January 1, 2026.

[877]Amended by Stats. 2005, Ch. 300, Sec. 3. Effective January 1, 2006.

[878]Amended by Stats. 2025, Ch. 358, Sec. 2. (AB 268) Effective January 1, 2026.

[879]Amended by Stats. 2025, Ch. 403, Sec. 1. (SB 85) Effective January 1, 2026.

[880]Added by Stats. 2025, Ch. 527, Sec. 1. (SB 808) Effective January 1, 2026.

[881]Amended by Stats. 2025, Ch. 563, Sec. 4. (AB 747) Effective January 1, 2026. Repealed as of January 1, 2027,

by its own provisions. See later operative version added by Sec. 5 of Stats. 2025, Ch. 563.

[882]Repealed (in Sec. 4) and added by Stats. 2025, Ch. 563, Sec. 5. (AB 747) Effective January 1, 2026. Operative January 1, 2027, by its own provisions.

[883]Amended by Stats. 2025, Ch. 563, Sec. 6. (AB 747) Effective January 1, 2026. Repealed as of January 1, 2027, by its own provisions. See later operative version added by Sec. 7 of Stats. 2025, Ch. 563.

[884]Repealed (in Sec. 6) and added by Stats. 2025, Ch. 563, Sec. 7. (AB 747) Effective January 1, 2026. Operative January 1, 2027, by its own provisions.

[885]Amended by Stats. 2025, Ch. 563, Sec. 8. (AB 747) Effective January 1, 2026. Repealed as of January 1, 2027, by its own provisions. See later operative version added by Sec. 9 of Stats. 2025, Ch. 563.

[886]Repealed (in Sec. 8) and added by Stats. 2025, Ch. 563, Sec. 9. (AB 747) Effective January 1, 2026. Operative January 1, 2027, by its own provisions.

[887]Amended by Stats. 2025, Ch. 563, Sec. 10. (AB 747) Effective January 1, 2026. Repealed as of January 1, 2027, by its own provisions. See later operative version added by Sec. 11 of Stats. 2025, Ch. 563.

[888]Amended by Stats. 2025, Ch. 563, Sec. 12. (AB 747) Effective January 1, 2026. Repealed as of January 1, 2027, by its own provisions. See later operative version added by Sec. 13 of Stats. 2025, Ch. 563.

[889]Added by Stats. 2025, Ch. 563, Sec. 14. (AB 747) Effective January 1, 2026. Operative January 1, 2027, by its own provisions.

[890]Amended by Stats. 2025, Ch. 563, Sec. 15. (AB 747) Effective January 1, 2026. Repealed as of January 1, 2027, by its own provisions. See later operative version added by Sec. 16 of Stats. 2025, Ch. 563.

[891]Repealed (in Sec. 15) and added by Stats. 2025, Ch. 563, Sec. 16. (AB 747) Effective January 1, 2026. Operative January 1, 2027, by its own provisions.

[892]Amended by Stats. 2025, Ch. 563, Sec. 17. (AB 747) Effective January 1, 2026. Repealed as of January 1, 2027, by its own provisions. See later operative version added by Sec. 18 of Stats. 2025, Ch. 563.

[893]Repealed (in Sec. 17) and added by Stats. 2025, Ch. 563, Sec. 18. (AB 747) Effective January 1, 2026. Operative January 1, 2027, by its own provisions.

[894]Repealed (in Sec. 12) and added by Stats. 2025, Ch. 563, Sec. 13. (AB 747) Effective January 1, 2026. Operative January 1, 2027, by its own provisions.

[895]Repealed (in Sec. 10) and added by Stats. 2025, Ch. 563, Sec. 11. (AB 747) Effective January 1, 2026. Operative January 1, 2027, by its own provisions.

[896]Amended by Stats. 2025, Ch. 559, Sec. 1. (AB 515) Effective January 1, 2026. Repealed as of January 1, 2027, by its own provisions. See later operative version added by Sec. 2 of Stats. 2025, Ch. 559.

[897]Repealed (in Sec. 1) and added by Stats. 2025, Ch. 559, Sec. 2. (AB 515) Effective January 1, 2026. Operative January 1, 2027, by its own provisions.

[898]Amended by Stats. 2025, Ch. 559, Sec. 3. (AB 515) Effective January 1, 2026. Repealed as of January 1, 2027,

by its own provisions. See later operative version added by Sec. 4 of Stats. 2025, Ch. 559.

[899]Repealed (in Sec. 3) and added by Stats. 2025, Ch. 559, Sec. 4. (AB 515) Effective January 1, 2026. Operative January 1, 2027, by its own provisions.

[900]Amended by Stats. 2025, Ch. 682, Sec. 1. (AB 250) Effective January 1, 2026.

[901]Amended by Stats. 2025, Ch. 708, Sec. 1. (AB 774) Effective January 1, 2026.

[902]Added by Stats. 2025, Ch. 708, Sec. 2. (AB 774) Effective January 1, 2026. Operative July 1, 2026, by its own provisions.

[903]Added by Stats. 2025, Ch. 708, Sec. 3. (AB 774) Effective January 1, 2026. Operative July 1, 2026, by its own provisions.

[904]Amended by Stats. 2025, Ch. 708, Sec. 4. (AB 774) Effective January 1, 2026.

[905]Amended by Stats. 2025, Ch. 708, Sec. 5. (AB 774) Effective January 1, 2026.

[906]Amended by Stats. 2025, Ch. 708, Sec. 6. (AB 774) Effective January 1, 2026.

[907]Amended by Stats. 2025, Ch. 708, Sec. 7. (AB 774) Effective January 1, 2026.

[908]Amended by Stats. 2025, Ch. 708, Sec. 8. (AB 774) Effective January 1, 2026.

[909]Amended by Stats. 2025, Ch. 708, Sec. 9. (AB 774) Effective January 1, 2026.

www.ingramcontent.com/pod-product-compliance
Lightning Source LLC
LaVergne TN
LVHW021002300926
849160LV00007B/225

9798901135624